WORLD
THE DEFINITIVE VISUAL HISTORY
WAR II

WORLD WAR II

THE DEFINITIVE VISUAL HISTORY

FROM BLITZKRIEG TO THE ATOM BOMB

DK

**LONDON, NEW YORK, MELBOURNE,
MUNICH, AND DELHI**

DORLING KINDERSLEY

Senior Art Editor
Gadi Farfour

Senior Editor
Alison Sturgeon

Designers
Amy Orsborne, Priya Kukadia,
Elizabeth O'Neill, Dean Morris

Project Editors
Ferdie McDonald, Sam Atkinson,
Tarda Davison-Aitkins

Managing Art Editor
Karen Self

Managing Editor
Debra Wolter

Cartographers
Encompass Graphics Ltd, Brighton, UK;
Iorwerth Watkins; David Roberts

Picture Researcher
Sarah Smithies

Production Controller
Louise Daly

Production Editor
Maria Elia

Art Director
Bryn Walls

Reference Publisher
Jonathan Metcalf

Associate Publisher
Liz Wheeler

TOUCAN BOOKS LTD

Senior Designer
Thomas Keenes

Managing Editor
Ellen Dupont

Designers
Nick Avery, Phil Fitzgerald,
Leah Germann, Mark Scribbens

Senior Editor
Alice Peebles

Additional Text
Donald Sommerville

Editors
Natasha Kahn, Anna Southgate

Editorial Assistants
Abigail Keen, Tom Pocklington

First American Edition, 2009

Published in the United States by
DK Publishing
375 Hudson Street
New York, New York 10014

A Penguin Company

Copyright © 2009 Dorling Kindersley Limited

08 09 10 11   10 9 8 7 6 5 4 3 2 1

Published in Great Britain by Dorling Kindersley Limited.

A catalogue record for this book is available
from the Library of Congress.

ISBN: 978-0-7566-4278-5

DK books are available at special discounts when purchased in bulk for sales promotions,
premiums, fund-raising, or educational use. For details, contact: DK Publishing Special Markets,
375 Hudson Street, New York, New York 10014 or SpecialSales@dk.com.

Printed and bound by Star Standard in Singapore

See our complete catalogue at
www.dk.com

CONTENTS

1

THE SEEDS OF WAR
1914–1938

2

EUROPE GOES TO WAR
1939

5

THE SHIFTING BALANCE
1942

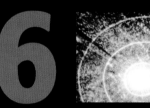

7

OVERWHELMING FORCE
1944

6

THE ALLIES TURN THE TIDE
1943

8

ENDGAME
1945

9

AFTERMATH
1946–1950 328

Foreword

World War II was the largest and most destructive war in history. It shaped the world my generation grew up in, and only now are its long shadows receding. Like any hugely complex historical event, World War II is hard to describe in print. Some brilliant scholars have managed, using impressionistic strokes, to sketch out its major features in relatively few pages, although, perhaps inevitably, their purposeful lines obscure its finer detail. Others have concentrated on specific aspects: shelves groan beneath books on, say, Normandy or the fighting in North Africa.

Many Western authors, writing in the chill of the Cold War, failed to recognize the pivotal importance of the Eastern Front, just as Russian historians, preoccupied with their own "Great Patriotic War," did not do justice to the Western Allies' efforts. In short, although there is now almost no aspect of the war that is not explored, it remains difficult to find an over-arching history of the conflict, unconstrained by national horizon or the rigid limitations of size and space, aimed at the general reader and properly supported, as such a history must be, by maps and illustrations.

I warmly commend this book because it provides exactly that accessible survey that has long been missing. It recognizes that this war flared up out of the embers of the previous one, and does not simply pay proper attention to the dangerous legacy of World War I in Europe, but assesses the effect of Japan's dissatisfaction with the fruits of its own participation. For instance events in China, too often neglected, are properly considered here. Both the war's causes, at one end, and its consequences, at the other, are viewed in the round, embedding the conflict in its broader context.

The events of the war were inter-related by long and complex threads, and it is misleading to consider any single episode, no matter how significant, in isolation. One of the many virtues of this book is that it tells, on the one hand, the stories of specific battles and campaigns but, on the other, its layout enables the reader to see how these relate to previous and subsequent events. It recognizes the role played by the machinery of war, but at the same time allows many participants to speak at length about their own experiences. The book's coverage is global. It encompasses events on land, at sea, and in the air, and includes not simply the actions of great men but also the achievements and endurance of the countless thousands of men and women who participated, in a myriad of ways, in this most titanic of all struggles.

RICHARD HOLMES, 2009

THE SEEDS OF WAR
1914–1938

1

The treaties that ended World War I left many countries bitter and resentful and failed to establish a lasting peace. In the political and economic uncertainties of the time, right-wing Nationalist parties had a strong appeal, most ominously Hitler's Nazis in Germany.

THE SEEDS OF WAR

Adolf Hitler's rise to power gained momentum as popular support for the Nazi Party grew in the early 1930s. Here Hitler addresses brown-shirted paramilitary supporters at a rally in 1933, the year he took office as chancellor of Germany.

Germany's annexation of Austria in 1938 was an indication of Hitler's territorial ambitions, but was achieved without force and welcomed by most Austrians.

The revolution of 1917 threw the old Russian empire into chaos, but under Lenin's leadership the Bolsheviks managed to establish a new empire in its place: the USSR, the world's first communist state.

The Spanish Civil War (1936–39) was a grim struggle between Right and Left. Germany and Italy lent greater support to Franco's Nationalists than the USSR provided for the Republicans.

Benito Mussolini, founder of the Italian Fascist movement, forced his way to power in 1922. His style of dictatorship revolved around a strong personality cult and dreams of reviving the glory of the Roman Empire.

Italy's conquest of Abyssinia in 1935–36 pitted modern European weaponry against a traditional African state. Here, Emperor Haile Selassie inspects Italian unexploded bombs.

EUROPE

The peace treaties that formally brought World War I to an end contained many of the seeds of the wider conflict of 1939–45. Germany lost its empire, had East Prussia cut off by the Polish Corridor, and was forced to pay the Allies huge financial reparations. The old Austro-Hungarian and Ottoman empires were broken up into smaller states. Among the Allies, Italy was disappointed not to have received greater territorial rewards, while Japan felt that its emergence as a world power had not been properly recognized. Finally, there was Russia. The 1917 Bolshevik revolution led to its leaving the war, but it was then wracked by civil war. After a brief attempt to spread communism into Europe, the USSR largely turned in on itself.

Weak governments and economic instability began to polarize political opinion to the Left and Right in a number of countries. It was the Right that won out in Italy, Germany, and Japan. By the early

1914—1938

Japan's conquests began in 1931. Taking advantage of the Chinese Civil War, its troops overran the northern province of Manchuria, where they established the puppet state of Manchukuo.

China suffered a second onslaught by the Japanese in 1937. Here Chinese troops take up positions along the Great Wall in a vain attempt to hold back the invaders.

The Wall Street Crash, which began in October 1929, wiped $30 billion off the value of the New York stock market in one week, causing unprecedented panic in the financial world.

The Chinese Civil War lasted from the 1920s to 1949. In 1935–36 the eventual victors, the Communists, undertook the "Long March" to escape the danger of encirclement by their enemies, the Kuomintang.

The Great Depression began in the US in the wake of the Wall Street Crash. As banks and businesses failed, more than 13 million men became unemployed. The economic slowdown soon affected all the world's capitalist economies and lasted until World War II.

THE WORLD 1918–1938
—— Frontiers 1925

Map labels:
CANADA, NEWFOUNDLAND, UNITED STATES OF AMERICA, Great Lakes, MEXICO, BRITISH HONDURAS, CUBA, HAITI, DOMINICAN REPUBLIC, VIRGIN ISLANDS, LEEWARD ISLANDS, GUATEMALA, EL SALVADOR, HONDURAS, NICARAGUA, COSTA RICA, PANAMA, CANAL ZONE, WINDWARD ISLANDS, BARBADOS, TRINIDAD AND TOBAGO, BRITISH GUIANA, DUTCH GUIANA, FRENCH GUIANA, VENEZUELA, COLOMBIA, ECUADOR, PERU, BRAZIL, BOLIVIA, PARAGUAY, CHILE, URUGUAY, ARGENTINA, FALKLAND ISLANDS, ATLANTIC OCEAN, PACIFIC OCEAN, Hawaiian Islands, Christmas Island, French Polynesia, GOLIA, INA, JAPANESE EMPIRE, FRENCH INDOCHINA, PHILIPPINE ISLANDS, GUAM, Mariana Islands (Japanese mandate), Marshall Islands (Japanese mandate), Caroline Islands (Japanese mandate), Gilbert Islands, BRITISH BORNEO, BRUNEI, SARAWAK, MALAYA, DUTCH EAST INDIES, PORTUGUESE TIMOR, TERRITORY OF NEW GUINEA, PAPUA, Nauru, Solomon Islands, Ellice Islands, Cook Islands, WESTERN SAMOA, AMERICAN SAMOA, New Hebrides, Fiji, Tonga, New Caledonia, AUSTRALIA

1930s Mussolini, Hitler, and the Japanese military were bent on territorial expansion. Japan seized Manchuria and went on to invade China. Italy overran Abyssinia and, after bringing Austria into the German fold, Hitler set about dismembering Czechoslovakia.

The Western democracies pinned their hopes for peace on the League of Nations and disarmament. The former proved to be deeply flawed. The United States did not join it and it lacked the means to enforce peace, as its failure to halt Japanese and Italian aggression showed. Economic depression precipitated by the 1929 Wall Street Crash also played its part in the failure. Mutual suspicion eventually proved the stumbling block to disarmament. Britain and France were forced to rearm, but they still hoped that appeasing the dictators might avert major war, especially since the Spanish Civil War revealed the horrors of modern warfare only too graphically

TIMELINE 1914–1938

Treaty of Versailles ▪ **League of Nations** ▪ Mussolini takes power ▪ Wall Street Crash ▪ Great Depression ▪ Japanese invade Manchuria ▪ **Rise of Hitler** ▪ Spanish Civil War ▪ Anschluss ▪ **Sino–Japanese War** ▪ Italians invade Abyssinia ▪ **Munich Crisis**

1914 – 1916	1917 – 1918	1919 – 1920	1921 – 1922	1923 – 1924	1925 – 1926

JANUARY 1919
Communist uprising in Berlin, led by the Spartacists.

FEBRUARY 1919
Start of Polish-Soviet War. Poles retain their independence.

OCTOBER 1925
Treaties of Locarno. France, Germany, and Belgium recognize as permanent the borders agreed at Versailles. Germany promises not to send troops into the Rhineland.

AUGUST 1914
Outbreak of World War I; Germany invades France.

1915
Stalemate in the trenches on the Western Front.

≪ Trench Warfare

APRIL 1917
US declares war on Germany.

JUNE 28 1919
Treaty of Versailles signed. Germany accepts guilt for the war, loses all its colonies as well as territories in Europe, and agrees to pay crippling war reparations.

OCTOBER 1922
Mussolini and about 30,000 supporters take part in the March on Rome. Mussolini forms Fascist government.

≪ German Maxim 08/15 machine-gun

FEBRUARY 1916
Germans launch attack on Verdun that develops into six-month bloodbath.

JULY 1916
Battle of the Somme. Attempt to break through German lines is a costly failure. 19,240 British soldiers killed on first day.

JULY 1917
Beginning of Third Battle of Ypres.

NOVEMBER 1917
Second Russian revolution. Bolsheviks seize power.

≫ The March on Rome

1923
Hyperinflation in Germany reaches its peak.

JANUARY 1923
French and Belgian troops occupy the Ruhr to force Germany to keep up reparation payments.

MARCH 1926
Death of Chinese leader Sun Yat-Sen. He is succeeded as leader of the Kuomintang by Chiang Kai-shek.

MAY 1926
General strike in Britain in support of coal miners called off after nine days.

≫ The Treaty of Versailles

OCTOBER 1922
Red Army takes Vladivostok, the last major action in the Russian Civil War.

DECEMBER 1922
Creation of the Union of Soviet Socialist Republics.

MARCH 1918
Russia and Germany sign Treaty of Brest-Litovsk.

NOVEMBER 11, 1918
War ends with signing of the Armistice in a railway car at Compiègne, France.

≪ Signing of the Armistice

1920
Germany begins to suffer from spiraling inflation.

NOVEMBER 8, 1923
Munich *Putsch*. Hitler leads failed attempt to overthrow Bavarian government.

1924
Hitler spends eight months in prison, where he writes *Mein Kampf*.

≫ The Munich *Putsch*

JULY 1926
Kuomintang begins a campaign in northern China in an attempt to reunify the country.

Hessische Landesbank
5000000 Notgeldschein über 5000000
Fünf Millionen Mark
739922

≪ Five million mark note

> "Do we wish to **restore Germany to freedom and power**? ... Men must not sleep; they ought to know that **a thunderstorm is coming up**."
>
> ADOLF HITLER AT A SPEECH IN MUNICH, APRIL 20, 1933

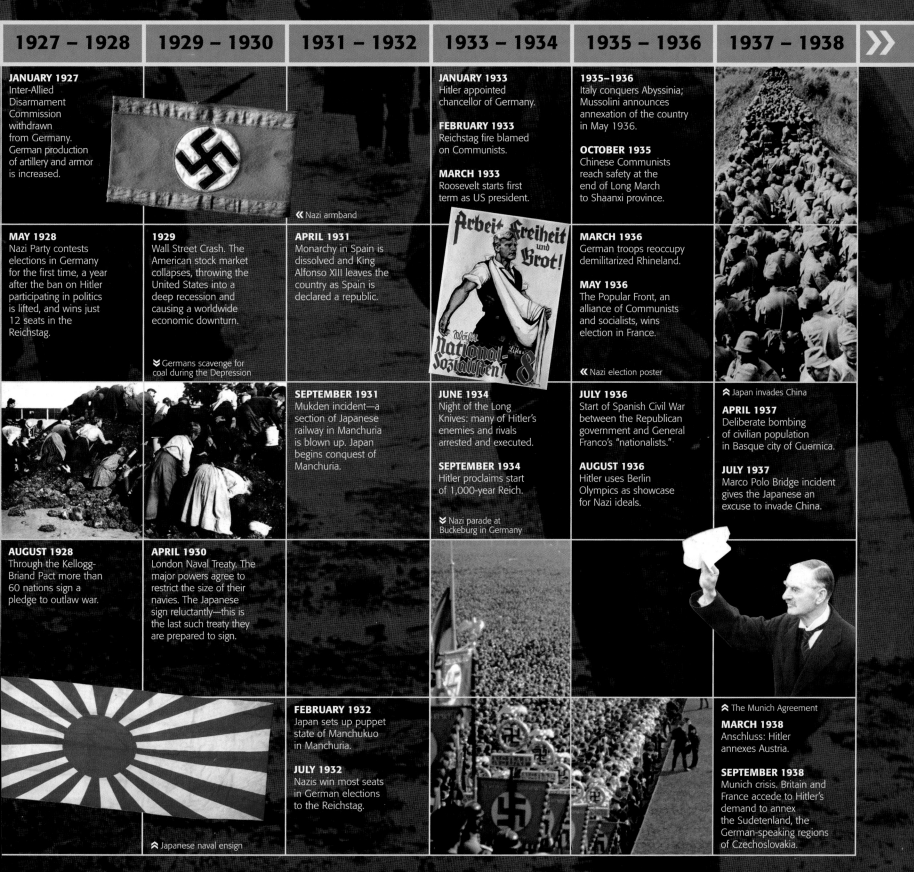

1927 – 1928	1929 – 1930	1931 – 1932	1933 – 1934	1935 – 1936	1937 – 1938

JANUARY 1927
Inter-Allied Disarmament Commission withdrawn from Germany. German production of artillery and armor is increased.

JANUARY 1933
Hitler appointed chancellor of Germany.

FEBRUARY 1933
Reichstag fire blamed on Communists.

MARCH 1933
Roosevelt starts first term as US president.

1935–1936
Italy conquers Abyssinia; Mussolini announces annexation of the country in May 1936.

OCTOBER 1935
Chinese Communists reach safety at the end of Long March to Shaanxi province.

« Nazi armband

MAY 1928
Nazi Party contests elections in Germany for the first time, a year after the ban on Hitler participating in politics is lifted, and wins just 12 seats in the Reichstag.

1929
Wall Street Crash. The American stock market collapses, throwing the United States into a deep recession and causing a worldwide economic downturn.

APRIL 1931
Monarchy in Spain is dissolved and King Alfonso XIII leaves the country as Spain is declared a republic.

MARCH 1936
German troops reoccupy demilitarized Rhineland.

MAY 1936
The Popular Front, an alliance of Communists and socialists, wins election in France.

⌄ Germans scavenge for coal during the Depression

« Nazi election poster

SEPTEMBER 1931
Mukden incident—a section of Japanese railway in Manchuria is blown up. Japan begins conquest of Manchuria.

JUNE 1934
Night of the Long Knives: many of Hitler's enemies and rivals arrested and executed.

SEPTEMBER 1934
Hitler proclaims start of 1,000-year Reich.

JULY 1936
Start of Spanish Civil War between the Republican government and General Franco's "nationalists."

AUGUST 1936
Hitler uses Berlin Olympics as showcase for Nazi ideals.

⌃ Japan invades China

APRIL 1937
Deliberate bombing of civilian population in Basque city of Guernica.

JULY 1937
Marco Polo Bridge incident gives the Japanese an excuse to invade China.

⌄ Nazi parade at Buckeburg in Germany

AUGUST 1928
Through the Kellogg-Briand Pact more than 60 nations sign a pledge to outlaw war.

APRIL 1930
London Naval Treaty. The major powers agree to restrict the size of their navies. The Japanese sign reluctantly—this is the last such treaty they are prepared to sign.

FEBRUARY 1932
Japan sets up puppet state of Manchukuo in Manchuria.

JULY 1932
Nazis win most seats in German elections to the Reichstag.

⌃ The Munich Agreement

MARCH 1938
Anschluss: Hitler annexes Austria.

SEPTEMBER 1938
Munich crisis. Britain and France accede to Hitler's demand to annex the Sudetenland, the German-speaking regions of Czechoslovakia.

⌃ Japanese naval ensign

« BEFORE

During the late 19th and early 20th centuries Europe was dominated by two alliances, the Triple Alliance of Germany, Austria-Hungary, and Italy, and the Triple Entente of France, Russia, and Britain.

SETTLING OLD SCORES

France wanted to reclaim its former eastern provinces of **Alsace and Lorraine**, which had been taken by Germany after the 1870–71 Franco-Prussian War. Germany was casting envious eyes over the British Empire and saw creating a navy as powerful as the Royal Navy as key to enlarging its own overseas possessions, while **Italy** was in dispute with Austria-Hungary over territory in the Alps. In the Balkans there was opposition from Serbia to Austria-Hungary's annexation of Bosnia and Hercegovina, which contained large Serbian minorities. Russia, keen to encourage fellow Slavs, supported Serbia.

THE CATALYST TO WAR

It was the Balkans that provided the spark that led to war. The Serbian nationalist Gavrilo Princip murdered the **Archduke Franz Ferdinand**, heir to the Austro-Hungarian throne, and his wife, when he was visiting Bosnia in late June 1914. The Austrians mobilized against Serbia, the Russians gave support to the Serbs, the Germans came in on the side of their Austrian ally, and the French then mobilized against Germany.

NEW WEAPONS OF WORLD WAR I

New technology—in particular, quick-firing machine-guns, allied to increasingly powerful heavy artillery—led to the unprecedented slaughter on both sides.

GERMAN MG08/15 MACHINE-GUN

Vladimir Ilyich Lenin
Having inspired the October Revolution in 1917, Lenin was elected head of state in November of that year. This poster shows Lenin encouraging the workers to take control of the factories, and to seize and redistribute wealth.

The War to End War

The war of 1914–18 was the culmination of growing tension in Europe, but it spread to many parts of the globe. It was marked by slaughter and the increasing application of technology on the main fronts, and by the end of the conflict empires had been lost, and the map of Europe was about to be redrawn.

It was widely believed by both sides that the war would be over by Christmas, but the opposing war plans did not work as expected.

By the end of that year the war on the Western Front had become virtually static, with rapid-fire weapons causing defense to become stronger than attack. Meanwhile, other theatres of war had opened outside of Europe. There were campaigns in Africa to seize German colonies; Turkey, which had been under German influence, joined the war on its side in October 1914; and troops from India landed at Basra and opened a front against the Turks in Mesopotamia (present-day Iraq). Likewise, the Caucasus, in soourthern Russia, became a battleground between the Russians and Turks. During 1915 Italy sided with France and Britain and became involved in a prolonged fight against the Austrians along their common border.

On the Western Front the years 1915–17 were marked by bloody deadlock. Allied offensives during 1915 failed to drive the Germans back. The Germans attempted to drain the French Army of resources and morale at Verdun during 1916, while both sides lost heavily during the primarily British offensive on the Somme that summer. Spring 1917 saw further Anglo-French attacks result in little gain and also mutinies in the French Army, which forced it onto the defensive. This left the British to carry out the main summer offensive, which took place in the Ypres sector and eventually became literally bogged down in the mud.

The war at sea

At sea, the Royal Navy had imposed a blockade of Germany and had only skirmished with elements of the German High Seas Fleet in the North Sea during the early part of the war. But in May 1916 they clashed at Jutland, off the coast of Denmark, after which the German High Seas Fleet withdrew back to port, not to

One major development of the war was in airpower. At the outset aircraft were used merely for reconnaissance, but soon came the fighter and the bomber.

venture out again. Instead the Germans concentrated on trying to throttle Britain's maritime supply lines with their submarines. This angered the United States, although President Woodrow Wilson was determined to stay outside the conflict, but

> **"Please to God** it may **soon be over** and that He will protect dear Bertie's life."
>
> GEORGE V DECLARING WAR ON GERMANY (BERTIE, HIS SON, BECAME GEORGE VI)

Under the terms of the Armistice, German forces in the West withdrew across the Rhine. Allied troops followed them and occupied the east bank of the river.

END OF EMPIRE

The war itself had resulted in the breakup of the Ottoman and Austro-Hungarian empires. Three of Europe's principal monarchies came to an end, with the former tsar of Russia being murdered. Indeed, Russia itself was now gripped by civil war, as the so-called Whites, aided by contingents from the wartime Allies, struggled to overthrow the Bolsheviks. Austria-Hungary and **Germany suffered the threat of revolution 18 ❯❯** in the aftermath of the fighting.

BATTLE FATIGUE

Many of the Allies were also exhausted. France had suffered massive losses and much of its northern regions were ravaged by war. Italy, too, was drained, while Britain was economically weak and was faced with having to police former Turkish territory in the Middle East.

NEW WORLD ORDER

The victorious Allies now gathered to work out peace terms designed to ensure that Europe would never again suffer as it had done during 1914–18. At the same time they established the **League of Nations 18 ❯❯**, a global structure designed to prevent future war.

French troops attack at Verdun, 1916
The battle lasted from February until December and cost the French 540,000 and the Germans 435,000 casualties. It was the longest battle of the war.

intelligence that the Germans were proposing an alliance with Mexico led the president to ask for a declaration of war in April 1917.

The war in the East

On the Russian front it was the Central Powers (Germany and Austria-Hungary) who enjoyed victory. In spite of an initially successful offensive in 1916, not just the Russian war machine, but the state as a whole was beginning to disintegrate. In March 1917 the tsar was deposed, although the country remained in the war. More sinister forces were at work, however. Left-wing elements were stirring up discontent within the army and there were increasing incidents of units refusing to fight. Then the Germans allowed Vladimir Ilyich Lenin, the exiled Bolshevik leader, to travel by train from Switzerland to

24 MILLION people died in the influenza pandemic that swept through Europe and many other parts of the world during 1918 and 1919.

Sweden from where he reached Russia and in October fomented a revolution that overthrew the government and took Russia out of the war.

With US troops beginning to arrive in France in ever-increasing numbers, the Germans realized that they would soon face overwhelming superiority on the Western Front. Consequently, during spring and early summer 1918 they launched a series of offensives against

the British and the French to snatch victory before the Americans arrived in strength. They failed to break through the Allied lines and were forced onto the defensive. In August the Allies launched a series of successful attacks, and began to drive the Germans steadily back.

By fall, the Allied naval blockade, pressure on the Western Front, and rising political unrest at home, forced Germany to seek an armistice at the beginning of November.

Signing the Armistice

The German delegation arrives in the early hours of November 11, 1918, to sign the Armistice, which brought the fighting to an end on the Western Front.

KEY
- ■ Troops mobilized
- ■ Military deaths
- ■ Troops mobilized
- ■ Military deaths

Mobilization and casualty figures

The human cost to both sides was horrific. These figures do not take account of the estimated 20 million wounded.

Troops in millions

Allied Powers: Russia, France, British Empire, Italy, USA, Others

Central Powers: Germany, Austria-Hungary, Turkey, Bulgaria

The Flawed Peace

The end of the war in November 1918 brought turmoil to many of the defeated nations as various groups struggled for power. The wartime Allies gathered to draw up peace treaties to ensure that never again would Europe experience the horrors that it had just lived through.

In January 1918 President Woodrow Wilson had published his so-called Fourteen Points that were to form the basis of peace in Europe. He called for the return of all territory that had been seized by the Central Powers (Germany, Austria-Hungary, the Ottoman Empire, and Bulgaria) in the war, and for ethnic groupings within the Austro-Hungarian Empire, together with Poland, to be allowed self-determination. Wilson advocated the establishment of a "general association of nations" throughout the world to ensure future peace. There was also general agreement that the armed forces of the defeated nations should be restricted in size so that they could not pose a threat. In addition, France and Britain wanted Germany and its allies to make financial reparation for the physical damage they had caused.

Negotiating the peace

It took a number of months to sort out the details and in the meantime there had been some major developments in Germany. Just before the Paris Peace Conference, a communist attempt to seize power in Berlin was put down with great severity by the so-called Freikorps—organized groups of anti-communists. A general election brought a socialist government into power, but fearing for its safety, it established itself at Weimar, 150 miles (240 km) southwest of Berlin, and was known as the Weimar government. In May 1919 the unforgiving Allies presented Germany with the terms on which they were prepared to make peace. The Germans were aghast at their severity and tried to get them watered down. The Allies were adamant and on June 28 Germany reluctantly signed the Treaty of Versailles. The country lost all its colonies and, through the granting of independence to Poland, East Prussia was isolated geographically from the rest of Germany by the so-called Polish

> **"Six million men** lie in graves, and four old men sit in Paris **partitioning the earth."**
> "NEW YORK NATION", JUNE 1919

◄◄ BEFORE

The German forces retreated across the Rhine in good order after the Armistice had been signed. They returned to a Germany seething with unrest.

THE END OF MONARCHY

Kaiser Wilhelm had been persuaded to abdicate on November 8 and the new Social Democrat government found itself facing a **communist-inspired insurrection**, with Bavaria declaring itself an independent socialist state. The Austro-Hungarian monarchy had also ended and the disparate parts that had made up its empire began to go their separate ways. The **Bolshevik government in Russia**, which was doing much to foment this unrest, was now deeply embroiled in civil war with anti-communist elements attempting to depose it. Contingents from the **Allies were supporting the Whites**, as the latter were called, in the extreme north of the country, the south, and in the extreme east. But the Whites lacked a central command and the ideological fire of the Reds.

A NEW HOPE

It was in this climate that the peacemakers gathered in Paris in January 1919 to deliberate over treaties with the vanquished states that would formally bring **World War I to an end** ◄◄ **16** and ensure that there would be no major war in the future.

Victorious leaders
French prime minister, Georges Clemenceau (*left*), and British prime minister, David Lloyd George, arrive for a session of the Paris Peace Conference.

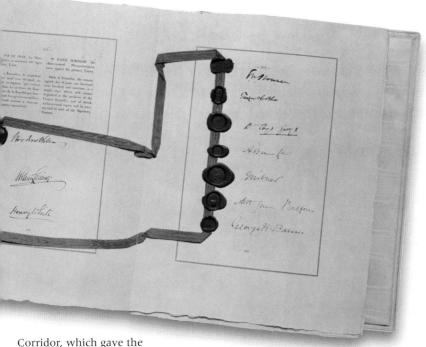

The Versailles Treaty
This page of the treaty bears the seals and signatures of the major delegates to the peace conference, including President Wilson and Lloyd George.

WOODROW WILSON

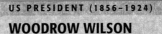

An academic and a lawyer, Woodrow Wilson did not seriously take up politics until 1910, when he was elected Governor of New Jersey as a Democrat. Two years later he became US President and was successful in keeping the United States out of the European war during his first term; he was re-elected in 1916 largely on this policy. When his country entered the conflict Wilson concerned himself more with shaping the postwar world than with the conduct of the war itself. His Fourteen Points were to be the blueprint for this and he was the first president to travel abroad while in office, when he attended the Paris Peace Conference in 1919. Prone to ill health, his efforts to establish the League of Nations resulted in him suffering a stroke, while the refusal of Congress to ratify the Treaty of Versailles also affected his health.

Corridor, which gave the Poles access to the Baltic through the port of Danzig (present-day Gdansk). The Rhineland was demilitarized, with Allied troops remaining in occupation, and France attaining control of the coal-rich Saarland. Germany was to be allowed no arms industry or offensive weapons like tanks and aircraft. The German army was to be reduced to a 100,000-man service force and the navy also drastically restricted. Further, Germany was also required to pay the

144

countries were represented at the first session of the League of Nations Assembly held in Geneva, Switzerland, in November 1920.

Allies $33 billion (some $400 billion today) within two years, an impossibility given the state of the country.

The other Axis powers also suffered. Hungary was given independence and the new states of Czechoslovakia and Yugoslavia formed, leaving an Austria much reduced in size and forbidden to form any sort of union with Germany. Turkey lost all its territories in the Middle East. These became mandates of Britain and France, while the Greeks were allowed to occupy land on both sides of the Bosphorus.

Apart from the peace treaties, the Paris Peace Conference also produced the League of Nations. It was to be a free association of states, rather than a military alliance, whose purpose would be to maintain peace throughout the world through disarmament and to provide the machinery to resolve disputes peacefully. It was to be based in Geneva, Switzerland.

The toothless enforcer

The League suffered from flaws at the outset. Most serious was that the United States, whose president had been its architect, declined to become a member. The US Senate refused to ratify it,

Germany's private armies
The badge of the Marine Brigade Ehrhardt, which fought the Communists for the government.

reflecting the fact that the majority of Americans no longer wanted to be embroiled in European affairs and desired a return to traditional isolationism. In addition, none of the defeated nations, nor Russia, were invited to join, and the League had no authority to enforce peace.

Even before the League of Nations Assembly had met for its first session, war broke out in Europe. Newly independent Poland was dissatisfied with its border with Russia and had during 1919 swallowed up much of western Ukraine. In April 1920 the Poles made a further advance, but were flung back by the Bolsheviks, who had all but been victorious in the civil war. A subsequent peace treaty left Poland with most of what it had gained in 1919. All this had taken place without any League of Nations involvement.

AFTER

The reparations that Germany had been forced to pay under the Treaty of Versailles soon brought about galloping inflation. A weak central government was unable to improve economic conditions, and German political opinion became polarized between the extreme Left and the extreme Right.

5 MILLION MARK NOTE

VERSAILLES REVERSED

Turkey, too, was dissatisfied by the **Treaty of Sèvres**, which brought it peace. In 1922 Turkish troops drove the Greeks from mainland Turkey and forced the **British to evacuate** their garrison at Chanak. Subsequently the Allies dropped all claims to territory on the Asian side of the Bosphorus.

FUTURE PROBLEMS

Yet two of the victors were also dissatisfied. Italy had gained territory from Austria, including the port of Trieste, but was disappointed not to be given any of Germany's African colonies. A series of weak governments served to increase discontent and political instability in Italy. This would result in **Mussolini seizing power 20 »**. Japan had gained German concessions in China and some minor Pacific islands, but did not feel that it was being treated as a major world power. Rapid population growth and a lack of natural resources would result in **Japan's invasion of Manchuria 32 »**.

Revolution in Berlin

Soldiers loyal to the socialist Weimar government engaging communist insurgents (known as Spartacists) on the streets of Berlin, January 1919.

‹‹ BEFORE

Fascism and Nazism were characterized by extreme nationalism and militarism, as well as rabid anti-Communism.

UNREST IN ITALY

Economically weak before the war, 1914–18 merely served to weaken Italy further. The Russian Revolution inspired a wave of industrial strikes, as well as **land seizures by peasants**, which the Italian government was powerless to prevent. There was also much **disappointment at the outcome of the peace treaties ‹‹ 18**. This first manifested itself in September 1919, when a group of nationalists seized the former Austrian **port of Fiume**, which was now part of the new state of Yugoslavia, and held it for 15 months before being evicted. By this time another, much larger, nationalist movement had materialized in northern Italy.

GERMANY FRUSTRATED

Two major factors served to fan the flames of **right wing extremism in Germany**. The first was disgust in some quarters that the Weimar government had accepted the **harsh Allied peace terms** without more of a fight. There was also a body of opinion that argued that the German Army had not been defeated in the field and that the politicians had stabbed it in the back by signing the **November 1918 Armistice agreement ‹‹ 16**. A new political group was about to be created that would reflect these views and more.

KEY MOMENT

THE MARCH ON ROME

On 27 October 1922 Fascist-instigated riots broke out in several Italian towns and its leadership called on the Italian prime minister to resign. Next morning four columns of Blackshirts set out from the north of the country for Rome. The government wanted to declare martial law, but King Victor Emmanuel refused, and while Mussolini was in Milan the king summoned him to Rome to form a government. The following day he accepted the King's offer in person. His men were still some way from Rome, and the king agreed that they could come by special train to the capital and parade. Mussolini's government featured Social Democrats, Catholics, Liberals, and only four Fascists. This would change.

Fascism and Nazism

The rise of Communism in Europe, encouraged by the October 1917 Russian Revolution, helped to trigger the creation of extreme right wing movements—Fascism in Italy and Nazism in Germany. Weak central government and general domestic discontent also encouraged this polariziation.

Benito Mussolini was a teacher turned journalist, who had fought in World War I. Disillusioned with the Italian Socialist government, in March 1919 he and a small group of men with mixed political persuasions formed the *Fascio di Combattimento* (literally, Fighting Band) in Milan. While the group was essentially nationalist, its policies were incoherent and as a result, it gained few votes in the October 1919 elections. Shortly after this Mussolini was arrested for plotting to overthrow the government by force, but he was released without charge, as the Fascist movement was not considered to be a threat.

Successive ineffectual governments attempted to placate both the Left and the Right in Italy, but without success, and as 1920 wore on political unrest increased. Mussolini seized on the instability of the time to change his essentially Socialist platform for a virulently anti-Communist one.

Fascist badge
The *Fasces* is an ancient Roman symbol of authority. The bundle of reeds indicates collective strength and the ax, power.

Fascist law and order

Mussolini's supporters wore black shirts, giving them their nickname, and frequently clashed with the Communists. They also worked to remove Communist-dominated town councils in northern Italy. Soon an increasing number of Italians began to view the Fascists as a bulwark of order in an otherwise fractured society. In May 1921 Mussolini and 34 of his followers were elected to seats in the Italian parliament. He advocated an alliance with the Socialists in order to broaden his political base, but his followers objected.

Finally, in August 1922 a general strike was called, at which point Mussolini declared that if the government failed to prevent it, the Fascists would. To reinforce the point they burned Socialist buildings in several cities in the north. Two months later Mussolini decided that the moment had come to march on the seat of government in Rome and seize power for himself (see left).

The great dictator

Once appointed prime minister, Mussolini obtained full powers for a year from parliament to carry out essential reforms. He also personally took over the key ministries, even though his Fascists were merely a minority in what was a coalition government. During the next three

Fighting the Communists
Blackshirts manning a barricade outside the Fascist HQ in Milan just prior to the March on Rome. Their main aim was to oust the Communists from town councils.

years Mussolini gradually assumed dictatorial powers. This culminated in a law, passed on Christmas Eve 1925, which made him no longer accountable to parliament. By now he had become known as "Il Duce" (The Leader) and three years later all political parties, other than the Fascists, were banned.

In the case of Germany the path to power for the Nazis proved to be a much longer one. Like Mussolini, Adolf

The Beer Hall Putsch
Hitler makes a speech in 1940 during the annual commemoration of the "Beer Hall *Putsch*." The coup attempt was launched during a rally in the same hall.

> " Either the Government will be given to us or **we shall seize it** by **marching on Rome**."
>
> **MUSSOLINI, TO HIS FOLLOWERS,** OCTOBER 1922

Hitler had been a combat soldier, but he was not the founder of what became the National Socialist German Workers' Party, or Nazi Party. This had been formed in Munich as the German Workers' Party by a small group of nationalists in the immediate aftermath

"There is no such thing as **treason against the traitors** of 1918."

HITLER, AT HIS TRIAL AFTER THE FAILED MUNICH PUTSCH, APRIL 1924

of the 1919 civil war in Bavaria. Hitler was still in the army and was sent to Bavaria to investigate nationalist groups and promptly joined this party. Within two years he had become chairman and had changed its name.

The Nazi philosophy

Hitler was determined to break the shackles of the treaty of Versailles and to make Germany a great nation again. Race issues were also at the forefront of his political manifesto. Hitler believed the Aryan race to be superior to all others, and that the Jews were as great an evil to the world as communism. Like Mussolini, he believed in strong-arm tactics to maintain order and

created the Sturmabteilungen (SA) as his storm troops and the Schutzstaffel (SS) as his personal bodyguards.

By 1923 Germany was in a desperate economic situation. It was unable to meet the reparations payments, so French troops occupied the industrial Ruhr region. Hitler believed the Weimar government was near to collapse and

staged a coup in Munich. It misfired and he was imprisoned for nine months, during which time he wrote his political testimony, *Mein Kampf* (*My Struggle*). Hitler was thereafter banned from speaking in public. In 1924 the Allies relaxed their demands on reparations payments and Germany's economic situation began to improve.

Nazi armband
The swastika is an ancient symbol from South Asia that was often regarded as a good luck charm. The Nazis saw it as representing the ancient Aryan race. This red cotton armband with an oak leaf border would have been worn by a high-ranking Nazi Party official.

Hitler's attack on Munich
Nazi storm troopers are trucked into Munich for Hitler's unsuccessful 1923 coup. The uprising in November also had the support of Erich von Ludendorff, the wartime chief of staff of the German Army.

AFTER

Extreme nationalism had taken hold of Italy, but in Germany Hitler had completely misjudged the mood of the country. The economy had strengthened, and people were optimistic about their future.

IL DUCE
The Italy that **Mussolini** created was certainly more efficient and stable than that which had gone before it. Much of the rest of Europe, as well as the US, was impressed by what he had been able to achieve; as it was said, Mussolini **"made the trains run on time."** But behind it all, Mussolini had another agenda with two principal aims: the Mediterranean was to be an Italian sea and he was determined to **expand Italy's African empire 34 ≫**.

FREEDOM TO SPEAK
The ban on Hitler's political activity was lifted in 1927. By this time, thanks to the relaxation of the conditions on the reparations payments, life for the average German had improved considerably, with **Berlin** having taken over from Paris as the most **vibrant capital** in Europe. Germany had also been admitted to the **League of Nations** and was regaining its self-respect. With support for the Nazis waning, Hitler now decided that the only way to gain power was to **take control of the country through its parliament 24 ≫**.

ITALIAN DICTATOR Born 1883 Died 1945

Benito Mussolini

> "I want to make **Italy great**, **respected**, and **feared**."
>
> BENITO MUSSOLINI, 1925

Eleven years before Adolf Hitler came to power as the leader of Nazi Germany, Mussolini was already turning Italy into Europe's first centralized fascist state. The first fascist dictator in Europe, he coined the term "Fascism" and developed its associated ideology. He went on to rule Italy as a dictator for the next 20 years; it was his disastrous involvement in World War II that ultimately led to his downfall.

Rise to power

Mussolini began his political life as a socialist but, always prone to dramatic changes of mind, he abandoned the tenets of socialism in favor of an extreme form of nationalism that he dubbed "Fascism." In 1919 he launched the *Fasci di Combattimento*, local-based fascist groups mainly attracting young patriotic war veterans. In 1921 these groups were brought together at a congress to found the Fascist Party, which had a strong right-wing nationalist, anti-liberal, and anti-socialist program.

Postwar Italy was in economic, social, and political turmoil, and Mussolini, a vain and egotistical man, presented himself to his nation as the only individual capable of restoring order. His emphasis on nationalism and the need to rid Italy of socialists won increasing support, particularly from the lower middle classes, industrialists, and wealthy agriculturalists.

In 1921 Mussolini was elected to the Chamber of Deputies, and his Fascist Party gained 35 seats in the Italian parliament. In 1922, as Italy's political crisis worsened, King Victor Emmanuel III was forced to invite Mussolini to form a government. The

The Battle for Grain
In 1925 Mussolini launched a "Battle for Grain," in which thousands of new farms were built on land reclaimed by draining the Pontine Marshes in central Italy. Grain output was increased, but at the expense of other crops.

"Il Duce"
In reality a short man, Mussolini required photos and other depictions of himself to project the sense of a powerful and commanding physical presence.

following year the Fascist Party gained more than 60 percent of the vote and Mussolini's hold on power was assured.

Over the next few years, using a skilfull mix of propaganda and force, Mussolini centralized control into his own hands. He suppressed political opposition, took over the press, and dismantled the parliamentary process. By 1928 he had turned Italy into a totalitarian state.

Dictatorial powers

As dictator, Mussolini personally headed the Fascist Party and militia and controlled many government ministries. At one point he was personally responsible for eight key ministries, ranging from public works through to foreign policy. He spent much of his time promoting himself as supreme leader and indoctrinating the population with the ideology of Fascism, which he described as the essential doctrine of the 20th century.

He also increasingly brought industry and agriculture under state control. Free trade unions were banned and a

Addressing his followers
An emotional orator and skilled propagandist, Mussolini addressed mass crowds in his drive to promote a cult of personality around himself. The Italian public were constantly told that Mussolini was always right.

Roman emperor
Mussolini made much of his "Roman" features; in this propaganda painting he is even superimposed over an image of Rome.

Yet Mussolini invaded Abyssinia (present-day Ethiopia) that same year, bringing condemnation from the League of Nations, and from 1936 he provided massive military support to General

Italy's war aims and victory, his nation was not ready for war. He sent troops into Greece, but they were ill-prepared and German troops had to be sent to help. In 1941 Mussolini followed Hitler's lead by declaring war on the United States. His obvious dependence on Hitler, and the introduction of anti-Jewish laws in Italy, lost him much support. So, too, did the constant military defeats. By 1943 Italy had lost prized possessions in Africa and suffered defeat on all fronts.

Mussolini's colleagues turned against him, and he was removed from office and imprisoned. Rescued by German paratroopers, he was taken to northern Italy, where under Hitler's instructions he set up a puppet government. In 1945, as Allied troops advanced through Italy, Mussolini was captured trying to escape to Switzerland, and was executed by Italian partisans.

"The **alliance** between Italy and Germany is not only between **two states** or **two armies** … but between **two peoples**."

BENITO MUSSOLINI, SPEECH DELIVERED IN ROME, FEBRUARY 23, 1941

"corporative state" developed, dividing the economy into different sectors and organizing employers and workers into party-controlled groups. In practice, Mussolini's new state was unwieldy, corrupt, and inefficient. Only party bureaucrats and the wealthier classes received much benefit from his policies.

Imperial dreams and defeat

Mussolini dreamed of establishing Italy as a significant European power, and saw himself as a great statesman. He wished to expand Italian influence in the Mediterranean and Africa, and sought to achieve this by diplomatic manoeuvring. He signed the Locarno Pact guaranteeing the borders of Belgium, France, and Germany, and by 1929 he was seen by Winston Churchill as a "Roman genius." From the mid-1930s, however, he took a more aggressive attitude. He was opposed to German designs on Austria, and in 1935 joined with Britain and France to form an anti-Hitler front.

Franco in the Spanish Civil War. Both actions alienated France and Britain and moved Italy closer to Nazi Germany. In 1938 Mussolini posed as a mediator at the Munich Conference but went on to sign a Pact of Steel with Germany, committing both their countries to mutual support in the event of war.

When war began, Mussolini initially kept Italy neutral, waiting to see how events progressed. After Germany's successful invasion of France, Mussolini eventually sided with Germany and declared war on France and Britain. Despite Mussolini's talk of

An ignominious death

The bodies of Mussolini and his mistress, Clara Petacci, were displayed at a gas station in Milan. Passers-by mutilated the bodies in a humiliating end for Il Duce.

« BEFORE

During the mid-1920s Germany began to recover economically and support for the political extremes was reduced.

1928 ELECTIONS
The failure of Hitler's **Munich putsch « 20–21** caused him to change his strategy. He would now pursue power through the ballot box. His first opportunity came with the elections to the Reichstag, the German parliament, in May 1928. He himself could not run since he was still technically an Austrian citizen. The elections proved a disappointment, with the Nazis gaining a mere 12 seats out of 491. A further boost to the German economy came the following year when the wartime Allies eased the **reparations payments « 18–19** still further, extending them until 1988.

WALL STREET CRASH
In October 1929 the **US stock market collapsed**. Economies all round the world suffered, especially that of Germany, which was still more fragile than most. This led to increasing unrest and presented Hitler with a new opportunity.

The bad old days
Under Nazi rule, scenes like this one showing men, women, and children scavenging for coal in the 1920s would become a thing of the past.

Hitler Takes Power

Unlike Mussolini, Hitler gained power through democratic means. It was only after he became chancellor of Germany that he showed his true colors, and in the space of a few weeks established an authoritarian regime that would brook no political opposition.

In March 1930 Germany's coalition government, led by the Social Democrats, resigned, unable to agree a coherent policy for dealing with the country's worsening economic situation. The president, the venerable wartime hero, Field Marshal Paul von Hindenburg, appointed the conservative financial expert, Heinrich Brüning, as chancellor. This was in response to political lobbying by the army. Brüning's government did not enjoy a majority in the Reichstag and could not get a bill to reform the national finances passed. Brüning therefore had it enacted as an emergency decree, which was allowed by the Constitution, but the Reichstag still blocked it and Brüning felt forced to go to the country.

"We have become once more true Germans …"
ADOLF HITLER, MARCH 1933

Changed political climate
The situation in Germany was now very different from what it had been in 1928. Both Communists and Nazis were vociferous in their efforts to drum up popular support and there were

Nazi election poster
The party's slogan for the May 1928 elections was aimed clearly at the unemployed, promising "Work, freedom, and bread."

frequent street fights between the two. The upshot was that the two extremist parties radically increased their share of the votes, with the Communists gaining 77 seats and the Nazis 107. This meant that the more moderate parties were no longer able to form a parliamentary majority and Brüning increasingly had to rule by decree. His severe financial measures, which included drastically cutting public expenditure, made him increasingly unpopular. True, in 1932 at the Lausanne Conference, he did manage to negotiate an end to the reparations payments and also tried to establish an economic union with Austria—although the International Court at The

Hague ruled that this was against the Versailles Treaty—but it was all too late to raise his popularity.

In the spring of 1932 Hindenburg's term as president came to an end. Brüning saw the Field Marshal as his best protection against the Nazis and other extremists and wanted him to remain in office. The Nazis and other nationalists objected and so Hindenburg had to stand for re-election. This time Hitler—who had

> **Nazi headquarters from 1931 to 1933 was the Brown House, a palatial former private residence on Briennerstrasse, Munich.**

finally gained German citizenship—and the Communist leader, Ernst Thälmann, stood against him. After a re-run Hindenburg was re-elected, winning 53 percent of the vote, with Hitler runner-up after gaining over one third. His star was clearly rising.

Jockeying for power

Hindenburg wanted Brüning to form a more right-wing cabinet to reflect the changing political face of Germany, but the latter refused and resigned. He was succeeded by Franz von Papen, who was rejected by all shades of

The new chancellor and the old president
In 1933, the first year of his chancellorship, Hitler sits next to Hindenburg at the annual commemoration of the German defeat of the Russians at Tannenberg in August 1914. On the right is Hermann Goering.

political opinion. And so, in July 1932 another general election was called. Street brawls were even more widespread than in 1930. The Nazis, with 209 seats, became the largest party in the Reichstag, but Hitler refused to join in any coalition and so another election was held that November. The Nazis won slightly fewer seats, partly because Papen had been taking a tough stand at the International Disarmament Conference and also because the economic situation had improved. This was not enough to save Papen, however. The army refused to support him, so to counter this Hindenburg made its spokesman, General Kurt von Schleicher, chancellor.

This was not what Hitler wanted at all. He moved to isolate Schleicher by allying himself to Papen, thus preventing the general from forming a government. Accepting the inevitable, on January 30, 1933, Hindenburg appointed Hitler chancellor, with Papen as vice-chancellor. With only two other Nazis in the cabinet, Papen believed that Hitler could be controlled, but he was soon proved wrong.

Hitler's first step was to call another general election for March 5. Then, on February 27 there was a fire at the Reichstag (see left). In the election that followed the Nazis gained only 44 percent of the vote, but it was enough. Building on the restrictions he had persuaded Hindenburg to put in place

> **17,277,180** **Germans voted for** the Nazi Party in the democratic elections of March 1933, the last to be held in the country until after 1945.

after the Reichstag fire, Hitler succeeded in getting his Enabling Act into the statute book on March 23. This gave him the right to rule by decree and effectively banned all political parties other than the Nazis. Within

weeks overt opposition to Hitler had been crushed. Germany was now a dictatorship in all but name.

The final end to democratic Germany came with Hindenburg's death on August 2, 1934. Hitler was now head of state and free to realize his dreams of a new Greater Germany.

> "The star of **Germany will rise** and **yours will sink** … I do not want your vote. Germany will be free, but **not through you**!"
>
> HITLER, TO THE SOCIAL DEMOCRATS IN THE ENABLING ACT DEBATE, MARCH 23, 1933

AFTER »

The new Germany soon found itself subject to unprecedented levels of state control. The Nazis instilled a sense of discipline in the German people that would contribute to their early successes in World War II.

NAZISM'S APPARENT SUCCESS
The **German economy quickly recovered 26–27 »** largely due to measures conceived under the Weimar republic, and accelerated rearmament. There were dramatic technological developments, some again already in existence as concepts, but implemented by the Nazis, ranging from aircraft to the highways. The organizational ability of the Nazi regime was demonstrated at the **1936 Olympic Games 28–29 »** and annual **Nuremberg rallies**. Many outside observers were impressed and approved of the new order.

THE DARK SIDE
As well as banning political dissent, Hitler could now concentrate on creating **a racially pure country 26–27 »**. At the same time he was intent on breaking the shackles of Versailles, even to the extent of **redrawing the map of Europe 34–35 »**. The Western democracies had their own problems and were slow to realize that Hitler's policies were a **threat to peace 36–37 »** and that he needed to be confronted.

KEY MOMENT

THE REICHSTAG FIRE

On the evening of February 27, 1933, a fire suddenly broke out in the Reichstag, the German parliament building in Berlin. Hermann Goering, Hitler's Minister of the Interior, was quickly on the scene. A feeble-minded Dutchman, Marinus van der Lubbe, was arrested on the spot and publicly accused by Goering of being a communist agent. The next day Hitler informed Hindenburg of the existence of a communist plot to subvert the state and persuaded him to sign an Emergency Decree for the Defense of People and State. This not only provided the government with emergency powers, it suspended basic civil liberties such as freedom of the press and freedom of assembly.

Some 4,000 people were arrested in connection with the fire, but only five, including the leader of the Communist Party

in parliament, appeared in court at Leipzig that September. Van der Lubbe alone was found guilty and executed. Whether he was actually responsible for the fire or whether it was started by the Nazis themselves has never been sufficiently proved either way.

BEFORE

Even before Hitler came to power in March 1933, he had the backing of his own powerful paramilitary forces, established in the early years of the Nazi Party.

THE SA, SS, AND HITLER YOUTH
The **SA (Sturmabteilungen)** took its name from the small units of storm troops used in German offensives toward the end of **World War I ≪ 16–17**. Established in 1920 to protect Nazi Party meetings against attacks from left-wing opponents, the SA were known as the Brown Shirts to distinguish them from the black-shirted members of the **SS (Schutzstaffel) ≪ 20–21**. The latter was a more sinister force, personally loyal to Hitler and steeped in his anti-Semitic ideology. The **Hitlerjugend (Hitler Youth)** was established in 1926 to train future members of these forces. Following the failure of the **1923 Putsch ≪ 20–21** the SA and the SS were disbanded, but were reestablished by 1926.

HITLER YOUTH DAGGER

NIGHT OF THE LONG KNIVES
The SA were half a million strong when Hitler came to power. Ernst Röhm, their leader, argued that they were the true national defense force and should take over this role from the army, the Heir. Hitler saw Röhm as a potential rival and in June 1934 ordered the whole of the SA on a month's leave. On the night of June 30 Hitler sent in his SS, and murdered many leading SA members, including Röhm. A number of other people whom Hitler thought of as a threat also lost their lives in the "Night of the Long Knives."

The Nazi State

Hitler's Germany was designed to prove that National Socialism could deliver the country from the misery of the postwar years. At the same time Nazism was a brutal ideology and a threat to peace.

To reinforce his place at the head of the German nation, Hitler was known as the *Führer*, or Leader. His aim was to reshape the German people through the elimination of divisions of class, religion, and ideology, and by purifying the race. Hence the introduction of concentration camps to remove "undesirables."

The Nazis began to establish special camps in March 1933, almost as soon as they had come to power. The first inmates were Communists, rounded up in the aftermath of the Reichstag Fire (see p.25). The camps came to be run by the SS and soon contained a wide variety of prisoners. These ranged from

Reichsarbeitsdienst (RAD) badge
The RAD (State Labor Service) was formed in July 1934 as a means of reducing unemployment. Its members worked on various construction projects.

liberal politicians and trades unionists to freemasons, homosexuals, and gypsies. It was, however, the Jews, whom Hitler hated above all else, who came to predominate.

Anti-Jewish legislation
Hitler's first action against the Jews was to proclaim a boycott of Jewish shops in April 1933. By the end of the year Jews were banned from holding public office, from teaching and farming, and from the arts. Then, in September 1935 came the Nuremberg Laws. Through these the Jews lost their citizenship and were prohibited from marrying Aryans. Later they were outlawed from the legal and medical professions.

Unsurprisingly, large numbers of Jews left the country—over half the 600,000 Jews in Germany in 1933 emigrated over the next six years. Among those who fled the Nazi regime were physicist Albert Einstein and novelist Thomas Mann—not Jewish himself, but his wife was Jewish—who both went to the US, as did many other prominent figures in the arts and sciences.

Propaganda and prosperity
There was little overt objection by the German people as a whole to this persecution and for a number of reasons. In the first place the Nazi propaganda machine under Josef

Nazis on parade
The choreography of Nazi rallies presented a picture of a highly motivated and disciplined mass, aided by stirring music and immaculate drill, as demonstrated here at the Harvest Thanksgiving festival at Buckeberg in 1937.

Goebbels was highly effective. Its primary aim was restore German pride and ranged from the Nazi banners that bedecked public buildings in every town and city to the massive parades at the annual Nuremberg Rally and the electrifying speeches by Hitler and his lieutenants. The success of the 1936 Berlin Olympics (see p.28) was also a great boost to national morale, besides impressing the rest of the world.

Education was another key Nazi weapon. Pupils were taught according to National Socialist principles. Textbooks were hastily rewritten and all teachers had to take an oath of loyalty to Hitler himself. Much emphasis was placed on physical fitness and boys were expected to join the Hitler Youth.

Hitler also brought full employment by revitalizing industry and encouraging new technology, especially in the field of armaments. There were also massive public works programs directed by the State Labour Service, the RAD. German males aged 19–25 were conscripted for six months' service in agriculture or public works, such as constructing Germany's impressive new network of *Autobahnen* (highways). As a means of raising the standard of living Hitler encouraged the development of the Volkswagen ("People's Car") to provide

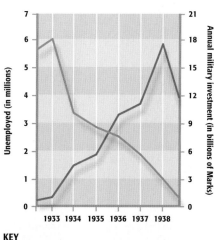

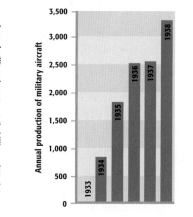

KEY
■ German unemployment
■ German military investment

German economic recovery
The tables demonstrate how rapidly Hitler reduced unemployment and increased military spending. The Luftwaffe quickly became the largest air force in Europe.

cheap motoring in much the same way as Henry Ford had done in the US with his Model T.

Hitler as ruler

When it came to running the country Hitler showed little interest in the routine work of government. He was content merely to spell out the overall policy to be followed and delegate the details to his subordinates. If any of his lieutenants became overly ambitious, there was always the memory of the

Night of the Long Knives (see BEFORE) to keep them in check. He brought the armed forces firmly under control by making them swear an oath of personal loyalty to him in return for confirming their position as defenders of the state.

After the February 1933 fire the Reichstag moved to the Kroll Opera House in Berlin. Hitler made many of his most famous speeches there, but the parliament itself became a mere rubber stamp to endorse Hitler's policies.

In parallel with his domestic overhaul, Hitler planned to restore Germany's prewar borders in order to give his people more *Lebensraum* (living space).

THE ARMED FORCES

Because they were banned from building tanks and aircraft, **German officers secretly went to Russia** to experiment with forbidden weapons in exchange for training the Russian armed forces. This meant that the groundwork for expanding and modernizing the German armed forces was already in place when Hitler came to power. One of his first acts was to put this into effect, including **creating an air force from scratch**. He understood that without powerful armed forces he could not realize his territorial ambitions.

GREATER GERMANY

Hitler's short-term aims were to **reoccupy the demilitarized Rhineland and then to reclaim the Saarland 34–35 ❯❯**. Beyond this he looked to form a union with Austria, removing the hated Polish Corridor, and dismantling what he saw as the artificial state of Czechoslovakia. All these plans ran counter to the Treaty of Versailles, and it was to be largely dependent on **the reactions of Britain and France 34–37 ❯❯** as to whether Hitler could reverse what had been agreed in 1919.

GERMAN POLITICIAN (1897–1945)

JOSEF GOEBBELS

Goebbels came from a Rhineland working-class Catholic family and received a university education. Unfit for military service in World War I, he developed nationalist and racist views and joined the Nazi Party in 1922. His intelligence and opportunist flair soon impressed, but not until 1926 did he ally himself with Hitler, who made him his propaganda chief three years later. Goebbels proved highly skilled in this role and remained close to Hitler until the end, dying with him in the Berlin Bunker.

The Berlin Olympics

For Adolf Hitler the 1936 Berlin Olympics was to be a showcase for Nazi achievement. The Games, which opened on August 1, 1936, was a spectacular event and Germany won 33 gold medals, more than any other country. But Hitler's dreams of demonstrating Aryan athletic supremacy were smashed by the achievements of black American Jesse Owens, who won four gold medals.

"The opening ceremony of the eleventh Olympic Games took place here this afternoon in the Stadium at the Reich Sports Field ... It was probably the longest ritual that has ever heralded the opening of these Games ... On top of the towers which flank the Marathon gate, a steel-helmeted military band was posted, the gestures of the conductor clear and tiny against the western sky and it was a sudden burst of music from them which announced the arrival of Herr Hitler. Amid a continuous thunder of cheering he appeared through the Marathon gate, followed by members of the International Olympic Committee in frock coats and chains of office. They slowly descended the steps and walked along the track to their places in the stand, after which the whole great audience joined in singing 'Deutschland über Alles' and the 'Horst Wesel' song with a tremendous-voiced fervour ... then a sudden 'Achtung' from the announcer, followed by the command 'Raise colours' ... The flags of the competing nations were hoisted ... the Olympic bell was tolled ... The Games were open."

THE "MANCHESTER GUARDIAN" CORRESPONDENT, E.A. MONTAGUE, DESCRIBING THE OPENING OF THE GAMES

"In Berlin we Greeks were especially honored coming from the mother country of the Olympics, but this did not make us blind to the fascist regime and the many showy majestic festivities which tried to show the world Germany's strength! I will never forget the athletic parade in the Berlin Stadium where the Greek team—as always—entered first and was saluted with great enthusiasm, and the coming into the stadium of the last torch-bearer with the Olympic flame. I will never forget my emotion and pride at that moment, but I wished that it was not Hitler and his regime that had the inspiration of the Olympic torch relay!"

GREEK ATHLETE DOMNITSA LANITIS DESCRIBING THE OPENING CEREMONY

Running the last leg
The opening ceremony of the 1936 Olympic Games saw the introduction of the torch relay, and the lighted torch was carried through seven countries—Greece, Bulgaria, Yugoslavia, Hungary, Czechoslovakia, Austria, and Germany. Fritz Schilgen of Germany was the final touch bearer.

The cost of change
The impact of the civil wars on the ordinary Chinese people was often dire, with homelessness and starvation becoming common.

Civil Wars in China

« BEFORE

At the turn of the 20th century China was under the feudal rule of the emperors and was being economically exploited by Western powers.

SUN YAT-SEN

Among those who wanted to right injustices and modernize China was **Sun Yat-sen**, who had been partially educated in Hawaii and had qualified as a doctor. Labeled a revolutionary, he spent many years in exile in Europe and the United States, and was very impressed by the American system of government. In 1911, while Sun Yat-sen was still in exile, there was a successful military uprising by the **Kuomintang (Nationalist Party)** in Wuchang, 400 miles (644 km) west of Shanghai. Its leaders immediately summoned Sun Yat-sen and proclaimed him **head of state**.

THE NEW REPUBLIC

Sun Yat-sen created a national assembly and the Republic of China came into being on **New Year's Day 1912**. But only the southern half of the country recognized him as their leader.

China became a republic in 1912, ending 2,000 years of Imperial rule, but much of the country did not recognize the new regime. The result was civil strife as the government tussled with the warlords and then with the Communists for control of the country. The situation was not resolved until 1949.

Having become head of state, Sun Yat-sen's first priority was to win over the commander of the army in northern China, Yuan Shikai. He promised Yuan the presidency of the new republic in return for his support of the revolution. Yuan obliged, but after the emperor abdicated Yuan became drunk with power, proclaiming

50,000 The number of troops massed for Chiang Kai-shek's fifth and final drive against the Communists in southern China.

himself emperor, and when Sun Yat-sen mounted an unsuccessful revolt against him Sun was exiled again. After Yuan's death in 1916 northern China became dominated by warlords.
  In 1917 Sun Yat-sen returned to China where he established a government in Guangzhou province. He prepared to take on the northern warlords by establishing the Whampoa

Promoting unity
A Kuomintang poster proclaims the Northern Expedition will unify the country and remove the foreign trade settlements.

Military Academy, placing his protégé, Chiang Kai-shek, in charge. He then levied heavy taxes in order to pay for the war that was to come, but this made him unpopular with the people. He also allied his Kuomintang party with the Communists in Russia and obtained a large amount of military aid and money from Moscow.

Attack on Shanghai

Sun Yat-sen died in 1925 so it was left to Chiang Kai-shek to mount the Northern Expedition. Its aims were to

crush the power of the warlords and to remove the foreign trade settlements. He set out for Shanghai, China's principal treaty port, which contained the main foreign settlements, in 1926. Defeating a number of warlords en route, he made rapid progress. The

Mountains in the south. Beginning in 1930, Chiang mounted a series of offensives, known as drives, to dislodge them. During the third drive he forced the Communists to withdraw further south, but they were not defeated.

100 THOUSAND men and women originally set out on Mao Zedong's Long March.

5 THOUSAND of those who marched survived, having covered 6,000km (3,700 miles).

Finally, in November 1933, and now with a German general as his principal adviser, Chiang Kai-shek launched his fifth drive. Using aircraft and a considerable amount of artillery, he isolated the Communists from the local communities that had been sustaining them. Hemmed in by rings of blockhouses, which the Nationalists had built to prevent their escape, the Communists faced total destruction.

The beginning of the March
Surrender was out of the question and so the Communists decided to break out. In June 1934 the first group moved out. This was a diversion and it was largely destroyed. Four months later the main body began its break out. It suffered heavy casualties, but the survivors pressed on westward. It was at this time that Mao Zedong took over the military leadership.

Having been constantly harassed by Nationalist forces, as well as by hostile locals, the Communist army reached the Tibetan border before turning north. Eventually, after crossing numerous mountain ranges and rivers, and having suffered great losses along the way, Zedong's army reached the

Western powers sent troops to reinforce their garrisons in Shanghai, but on the outskirts of the city Chiang halted.

Rifts had been growing between his Kuomintang and the Communists, who wanted to remove not just the foreigners, but China's landlord class as well. Chiang, however, realized that to unify the country he needed funding and that this could only come from the landlords and foreign trade. As a result, in April 1927 he turned against the Communists, arresting some of their leaders and expelling his Soviet advisers.

This marked the beginning of a new civil war in China. The Communists in the cities were quickly routed out,

"Internal pacification, then external resistance."
SLOGAN USED BY CHIANG KAI-SHEK

including in Beijing, which Chiang secured in 1928. The remainder withdrew to the hinterland, the main group taking refuge in the Jing Gang

Marching to salvation
Mao Zedong's soldiers on the Long March in October 1934. It was his leadership and their discipline and self-belief that drove them on. It helped ensure that the Communists were eventually triumphant.

CHINESE GENERAL AND POLITICIAN (1887–1975)

CHIANG KAI-SHEK

Born in 1887 of middle-class parents Chiang attended a military academy in China before furthering his military education in Japan. While there, he became imbued with republican ideas and, after service with the Japanese Army, returned to China when the Wuchang Uprising took place in 1911. On becoming leader of the Kuomintang in 1925, he made great efforts to modernize China, attempting to enthuse the people with Confucian moral values and self-discipline, but was constantly diverted by waging war. His conflicts with the Communists intensified after 1945, leading to a final defeat in 1949. He and his followers then withdrew to Formosa (present-day Taiwan), where he remained as head of state until his death.

"The Long March … has announced to 200 million people that the road of the Red Army is their only road to liberation."
MAO ZEDONG, 1935

relative safety of Shaanxi province in the extreme northwest of the country. Here they joined up with the remnants of two other Communist armies.

The Long March was a feat of epic endurance. While the military strength of the Communists had been severely reduced, the experience provided Mao Zedong with a framework on which he and his party could build a strategy to remove the Kuomintang from power.

AFTER

By the end of the Long March it appeared that Chiang Kai-shek had China under total control. But he would continually struggle to enforce his rule.

THE COMMUNISTS
Shaanxi province provided the Communists with a relatively safe haven. **They attracted local inhabitants to their ranks,** largely because of Mao

A STAMP HONOURING THE LONG MARCH

Zedong's insistence on fostering good relations with them. **Mao Zedong was thus able to rebuild his forces** and develop his strategy of revolutionary warfare. This was built around **cadres of Communists** who would go out into the countryside, **establish bases**, and recruit, train, and indoctrinate the local people. Eventually the Communists would be strong enough, and have enough popular support, to force the collapse of the Nationalist government and take control of the entire country.

THE JAPANESE THREAT
The Japanese, **desperate for more living space**, had been casting covetous eyes on China. They had already made their first move by **invading Manchuria << 32–33** in 1931.

Japan on the March

While it had all the trappings of a modern power, Japan in 1919 still operated under a feudal system. Forced to import raw materials, because of its lack of natural resources, and suffering a population explosion, which was causing severe unemployment, the country had become a powder keg.

Japan's empire
The map above shows the Japanese empire as it was in 1933. Manchuria was an important source of raw materials for Japan and was hotly disputed with Russia.

KEY
- Japanese empire 1930
- Japanese sphere of influence 1930
- Japanese conquests 1931–33

« **BEFORE**

After its dazzling victory over the Russians in 1905 Japan was determined to become a world power and take its place at the top table of nations.

WORLD WAR I
Through a treaty it had made with Britain, **Japan joined the Allies in 1914**, capturing German concessions in China and occupying islands owned by the Germans in the Pacific. Otherwise it contributed little, apart from sending a small naval force to help counter the submarine threat in the Mediterranean. **The Japanese were rewarded with some Pacific islands** and former German concessions in China.

NAVAL DISARMAMENT
To reduce the threat to its interests, the US held a **naval disarmament conference during 1921–22**. Restrictions on the size of ships were agreed and Japan was committed to maintaining a navy that was only 60 percent the size of those of Britain and the US. **Japan also agreed to uphold Chinese territorial integrity**. All this angered younger and more nationalist Japanese.

The agreements reached at the naval disarmament talks in Washington DC (see BEFORE) served to increase agitation in Japan for a form of government that would be better respected by the outside world. This was realized in 1924 when universal suffrage was introduced, but the transformation was far too quick. Corruption and a long history of insubordination by junior military officers were too deeply embedded to be eradicated overnight and the result was a series of political scandals. This drove many younger Japanese towards extreme nationalism.

Natural resources
Japan's difficult strategic position had also been driven home by a major earthquake, which struck Tokyo and the Kanto region on September 1, 1923. The principal naval base at Yokosuku also suffered, as significant oil supplies—enough for two years' operations—were lost. If the country had been at war when the earthquake had struck, the navy would have been crippled. It highlighted Japan's severe shortage of indigenous natural resources.

Nationalism ran strongest in Japan's armed forces and both the army and navy, and many officers became

"Daily we submit to **hypocrisy** and lies; While **national honor** lingering **dies**."
JAPANESE NATIONALIST ARMY OFFICERS' SONG

Taking control of Manchuria
Japanese troops begin the occupation of Manchuria in 1931–32, which was the prelude to the second Sino-Japanese War. The disunited Chinese forces in the region were unable to repel the invading army.

convinced that the only way to secure a reliable supply of raw materials and to gain respect on the world stage was through territorial expansion. Manchuria was the obvious target. As a result of the 1904–05 Russo-Japanese War Japan had been granted rights over the southern part of the territory. Some Japanese were settled there and were protected by the Japanese Kwantung Army. Manchuria was, however, still nominally part of China, but this did not prevent the Japanese from investing large sums of money in exploiting its resources. They had hesitated, however, from overrunning the whole of Manchuria for fear of falling out with Europe and the United States. As it was, the

Control of the skies
A Japanese aircraft crew in action during their virtually unopposed invasion of Manchuria in 1931. Rather than creating a single air force, Japan remained wedded to the idea of separate army and navy air forces.

Sign of the navy
The Japanese Navy ensign was inspired by its defeat of the Russian fleet at the Battle of the Tsushima Straits in May 1905.

Japan cemented its hold over Manchuria by renaming it Manchukuo and, to add insult to injury, it installed the last in the line of the Manchu dynasty, Henry Pu Yi (right), as its puppet monarch.

HENRY PU YI

WAR ON CHINA

The Chinese, wracked by **civil war between the government and the Communists ‹‹ 30–31**, were in no position to reclaim their lost Manchurian territory. Aware of this and encouraged by the weakness of the League of Nations, the **Japanese now prepared to take on China itself 40–41 ›**.

EUROPEAN FRIENDS

The Japanese also began to look for allies and it was inevitable that they should turn to the Fascist states in Europe, since both Italy and Germany were also demonstrating that they cared little for the **League of Nations 34–35 ›**. In addition, Germany would prove a valuable counterweight to the Soviet Union, which Japan also saw as a potential enemy and a threat to its hold on newly renamed Manchukuo.

WIDER AMBITIONS

The dream of creating a Japanese empire in oil-rich Southeast Asia began to take hold in some quarters of the government.

region was dominated by a Chinese warlord, Marshal Zhang, whom the Japanese had on more than one occasion tried to assassinate. In June 1928 they were eventually successful: two Kwantung Army staff officers organized the dynamiting of his personal train.

Japan invades Manchuria

The civilian government in Tokyo had not sanctioned Zhang's murder and tried to keep the Kwantung Army in

12 THOUSAND soldiers were in the Kwantung Army in 1906

700 THOUSAND soldiers were in the Kwantung Army in 1941

check, but it increasingly began to ignore their orders. Finally, in September 1931 an explosion took place on the South Manchurian Railway, close to a Chinese barracks. On this pretext Japanese troops occupied Mukden (present-day Shenyang) and steadily overran the rest of Manchuria.

China made a protest to the League of Nations over this naked aggression. The League demanded that the Japanese halt their hostile activities, but their

protestations were ignored, not least because Tokyo had effectively lost control over the Kwantung Army. The League lacked the wherewithal to take military action and its members were unwilling to impose sanctions on Japan, since they did not want their trade with the country affected at a time of general economic slump. Eventually the League sent out a commission to investigate

the situation. While recommending that Japan withdraw from Manchuria, it also concluded that the territory should be a semi-independent state and that Chinese forces should not be allowed back into the region.

In the meantime a group of officers had begun a series of assassinations of corrupt politicians and financiers. It culminated in the murder of the prime

minister, Inukai Tsuyoshi, at his home in May 1932. Thereafter it was the military who held the strings of power in Japan, and it was able to manipulate governments as it wished. The League of Nations' recommendations on the future of Manchuria was not to the taste of the military leadership, so in March 1933 Japan, one of the five permanent members, left the League.

TECHNOLOGY

AIRCRAFT CARRIERS

It was the British who first developed the aircraft carrier. During 1914–18 they quickly appreciated the value that aviation could have in reconnaissance for the fleet. The Royal Navy converted vessels into seaplane carriers and also installed facilities on their larger warships that would enable them to launch aircraft. The first true aircraft carrier,

with a flat-top configuration, was HMS *Furious*, a converted cruiser. It was built at Newcastle-upon-Tyne, England, and entered service in March 1918. While aircraft takeoffs were reasonably straightforward, safe landings were much more difficult. The introduction of arrester wires did, however, make them more viable. In the early 1920s the leading navies of

the world, including the Japanese, began to convert ships too large to conform to the Washington Naval Treaty (see BEFORE) into aircraft carriers. By 1939 the Americans, British, and Japanese had a number of aircraft carriers in their fleets, which would soon prove themselves superior to battleships as naval weapons.

JAPANESE CARRIER "AKAGI"

Rise of the Axis

In the course of the 1930s Nazi Germany and Fascist Italy became increasingly belligerent in their foreign policies—Germany within Europe and Italy in Africa. As it had over Japan and Manchuria, the League of Nations showed itself incapable of preventing their acts of aggression.

The aim of the Geneva disarmament conference of 1932–34 was to persuade all European nations to reduce their armed forces to the size of those of Germany. France, however, viewed the move as weakening its security. Germany, on the other hand, sought to increase its military strength to that of its neighbors. When this was refused, in October 1933 Hitler withdrew not only from the talks but also from the League of Nations.

The following year Hitler turned his attention to Austria, where Chancellor Engelbert Dollfuss, under threat from both Left and Right, had ruled without a parliament for two years. Hitler encouraged a Nazi coup and in July 1934 Dollfuss was murdered; but government troops regained control and Mussolini made clear his opposition to a Nazi takeover by massing troops on the border with Austria. Hitler was forced to back off.

700,000 The number of well-armed Italian troops, along with 150 aircraft, who faced 550,000 ill-equipped Abyssinians.

Hitler was to enjoy better fortune in 1935. A referendum in the state of Saarland resulted in an overwhelming vote for a return to Germany, and this duly occurred in March. In the same month, Hitler announced to the world the creation of a German air force, the Luftwaffe, and that he was dramatically increasing the size of his army. This was in flagrant breach of the Versailles treaty, but there were only muted protests from Britain and France.

Conquest of Abyssinia

Mussolini, meanwhile, was also flexing his muscles. He had initally hoped to use peaceful means to expand Italy's African empire by securing Abyssinia. He had signed a treaty of friendship with Emperor Haile Selassie in 1928, but the latter wanted to open his country to all nations and not just to Italy. Mussolini became increasingly irritated over this. In December 1934 Italian and Abyssinian forces clashed inside Abyssinia. Abyssinia appealed to the League of Nations, but it was more concerned about German rearmament. Indeed, in April 1935 Britain and France, whose main objective was to ensure that Mussolini did not ally himself to Hitler, met the Italians to discuss this problem, but did not raise the subject of Abyssinia.

Sensing the weakness of the Western European democracies, Mussolini's forces invaded Abyssinia in October 1935. By May 1936 the country had been overrun and Mussolini declared

Proclaiming the Axis

This 1938 German postage stamp celebrates the ever closer relationship between Hitler and Mussolini that developed after 1936. The slogan on the top reads: "Two peoples and one struggle.".

> **"A Rome-Berlin axis** around which all European states that desire **peace** can revolve.**"**
>
> MUSSOLINI ON THE OCTOBER 1936 TREATY WITH GERMANY

it to be Italian territory, the emperor having gone into exile in Britain. The League's response had been to impose limited economic sanctions, but these did not include coal and oil. Not being League members, neither Germany nor the US were bound by these sanctions.

The Rhineland

In March 1936 Hitler took advantage of the fact that much of the world was wringing its hands over Abyssinia to send his troops into the Rhineland. It was a calculated gamble, since Hitler's army was by no means ready for war and a firm response by Britian and France would probably have forced a climb-down. But they were in no position to fight another European war.

Leaving his empire

Emperor Haile Selassie rides out of Abyssinia during the closing stages of the Italian invasion. He escaped to Europe, where in June 1936 he delivered a moving, but fruitless, appeal to the League of Nations in Geneva.

A new partnership

Another consequence of the Abyssinian crisis was that Mussolini turned his back on Britain and France because of their part in imposing sanctions on his country. In October 1936 Germany and Italy signed a treaty of friendship, agreeing to recognize each other's interests: Germany's north of the Alps and Italy's to the south. It was at the signing of the treaty that Mussolini first spoke of a Rome-Berlin axis.

« **BEFORE**

Hitler's principal aim was not only to restore Germany's 1914 borders, but to expand them, while Mussolini was bent on enlarging Italy's African empire.

GERMAN TERRITORIAL AMBITIONS
When Hitler came to power in 1933 Germany was still severely restricted by the Treaty of Versailles « **18–19**. The Allies had withdrawn the last of their troops from the occupied Rhineland in 1930, but under Versailles the region was to remain demilitarized. There was also the industrially rich Saarland, which had been placed under League of Nations control and delegated to France. In the east there was the Polish Corridor, which separated East Prussia from the remainder of Germany and included part of resource-rich Silesia.

ITALIAN AFRICA
Italy's colonies comprised Eritrea and Italian Somaliland in the Horn of Africa, established in 1890 and 1905 respectively, and Libya, wrested from the Ottoman Empire in 1912. In the 1890s Italy had failed to conquer Abyssinia (present-day Ethiopia), and it was to that country that Mussolini's imperialist ambitions now turned.

AFTER »

Abyssinia proved to be almost the last nail in the coffin of the League of Nations. Its feeble response and the muted protests from Britain and France served merely to encourage Hitler and Mussolini.

THE AXIS GATHERS STRENGTH
The Anglo-French efforts to keep the two dictators apart had failed. Italy and Germany intervened together in the **Spanish Civil War 38–39** » and the bond between Hitler and Mussolini would be reinforced by the **Pact of Steel 50–51** » signed in 1939. Japan, too, would become allied to the Axis, signing the **Anti-Comintern Pact 40–41** » with Germany in November 1936. This alliance to counter the threat of Communism was joined by Italy in the following year.

Although he was still opposed to the idea of the annexation of Austria by Germany, Mussolini could no longer oppose his close ally's territorial ambitions. When, in 1938, Hitler managed to achieve *Anschluss* **with Austria 42–43** » without a single drop of blood being spilled, there was scarcely any protest from Fascist Italy.

Reoccupation of the Rhineland
German troops re-enter the Rhineland on March 1, 1936. The operation was very much a symbolic gesture, with just three infantry battalions crossing the Rhine. Had the French attacked, the Germans would have had to withdraw.

‹‹ BEFORE

The democracies sought to achieve global disarmament through conferences sponsored by the League of Nations and through treaties designed to prevent war.

In 1925, at the **Treaty of Locarno,** Italy and Britain agreed to be the guarantors of existing international borders in Europe. Then, in 1928, came the **Kellogg-Briand Pact,** when more than 60 nations pledged to outlaw war altogether. But hopes for disarmament and peace unraveled when **Hitler withdrew from the League of Nations in 1933** during the **Geneva Disarmament Conference ‹‹ 34–35**.

THREATS TO DEMOCRACY
Europe's democracies came under threat from both Left and Right. Violent confrontations

BRITISH FASCISTS
between the two political extremes had helped the **Fascists to take power in Italy ‹‹ 20** and **Hitler's Nazis to do the same in Germany ‹‹ 24–25**. In the 1920s and 30s France lived in fear of a Communist revolution, and Britain, even though its unions were weaker, was hit by a **General Strike in 1926**. Britain also had to face the threat of **Oswald Mosley's** home-grown Fascists.

Weakness of the Democracies

The Western democracies had, apart from the US, been exhausted by World War I. They were convinced that Europe could never afford another such conflict and pinned their hopes on the League of Nations and disarmament. They also had to weather severe economic depression.

Following the signing of the Treaty of Versailles in 1919, the principal aim of the Western democracies was to switch from a wartime to a peacetime economy. This meant demobilizing most of their now swollen armed forces and converting their munitions industries to the production of non-military goods.

For the US this was easier than for Britain and France, since its late entry into the conflict meant that its munitions industry had hardly been established on a wartime footing. At the same time, especially through loans to its European allies, its economy had been made stronger by the war. The United States also had few overseas possessions, so could reduce its armed forces to the bare minimum. While it encouraged international disarmament, it otherwise adopted an isolationist

foreign policy, refusing to join the League of Nations and turning in on itself. The US became gripped by a "get rich quick" mentality. Set against the freneticism of the Jazz Age, Americans in increasing numbers began to gamble on the stock market, whose rapid growth reflected an ever expanding economy.

Political instability
For Britain and France the transition from war to peace proved much more difficult. Both economies had been drained by over four years of war. France's manpower, in particular, had been

National Hunger March badge
On this march to Washington DC in December 1932, delegates of unemployed associations met government representatives to explain the desperate plight of the country's jobless.

gradually diminished, and a significant portion of the country, especially the industrial north, had been devastated. But like other European countries, France was bedeviled by a series of weak governments, usually coalitions of Left or Right. Some trades unions were vehemently Communist and took their line from Moscow. Strikes were a frequent occurence and the economy remained fragile. When the Popular Front, a left-wing coalition led by the socialist Léon Blum, was elected in 1936, the immediate response of the more combative industrial workers was to occupy their own factories.

The coalition government had to award them all pay raises in order to persuade them to go back to work.

Foreign policy and the Maginot Line
In terms of foreign and defense policy, French governments of all shades were determined that never again should Germany be allowed to invade, as it had done twice within the past century. One strategy was to encircle Germany with alliances. Thus the French supported Poland from the outset, but left-wing governments also reestablished a rapport with Russia. Alliances were also made with states in southeast Europe. As for Germany itself, successive French governments alternated between insisting on the terms of the Versailles Treaty being followed to the letter to a more conciliatory attitude over reparations.

A YOUNG MAN'S OPPORTUNITY

CCC

FOR WORK PLAY STUDY & HEALTH

APPLICATIONS TAKEN BY
ILLINOIS EMERGENCY RELIEF COMMISSION
ILLINOIS SELECTING AGENCY

Reviving the US economy
The Civilian Conservation Corps was a public works program introduced by President Roosevelt as part of his New Deal to lift the United States out of depression.

AFTER »

By the mid-1930s the Western economies had slowly begun to recover and the British and French were starting to take their first hesitant steps toward rearming.

Britain began to strengthen its air force in 1935 after Hitler had revealed **the existence of the Luftwaffe ‹‹ 34–35**. France followed a year later, but was more limited in what it could do because of the money being spent on the **Maginot Line** and a slower economic recovery.

PACIFISM AND APPEASEMENT
The 1930s also saw the emergence of a powerful pacifist movement, especially in Britain. This was vocal in its demand that the horrors of 1914–18 must not be repeated. In 1933 the **Oxford University Union** debated the motion: " This House **under no circumstances** will **fight for King and Country**." When the motion was passed by 275 votes to 173, the story was given extensive coverage in the press. The right-wing popular newspapers expressed horror and alarm that pacifism was so prevalent among the students of England's oldest university. Nevertheless, there were men in powerful positions who had **lived through World War I** and agreed with the students. Some British and French politicians began to believe that **if they gave Hitler much of what he wanted 42–43 »** a new European conflict would be avoided.

become not just a physical barrier, but a pyschological shield behind which the French people felt safe and secure.

Disillusion in Britain
Britain had not suffered France's physical devastation but was equally exhausted by the end of the war. The government's dream was to create a "land fit for heroes" and for a short time there was an economic boom, but it did not last. Traditional British industries fell into decline, with overseas customers having developed their own during the war. Coal had been a major export, but with oil now taking over from it there were no longer the markets for coal that there had been before 1914. High interest rates deterred new business start-ups and the result was a massive increase in unemployment. Spending on postwar reconstruction also had to be drastically cut and, as in France, industrial relations worsened, with strike action becoming commonplace as workers struggled to protect their jobs and wages.

The British defense budget suffered along with all other areas of public spending. The government introduced a rule that defense planning was to be done on the premise that there would be no war in Europe for ten years at least. The Ten Year Rule, as it was called, was renewed annually throughout the 1920s, after which it was reduced to five years. Priority was given to the defense of the empire, in particular India, and policing the former Turkish possessions of Iraq, Transjordan, and Palestine. Consequently there was little left to spend on the armed forces for British home defense.

The Great Depression
In October 1929 came the Wall Street Crash, when the US stock market bubble finally burst. Tens of thousands of Americans were made bankrupt overnight, banks collapsed, and the country went into deep recession. The shock waves of this quickly spread around the world and the struggling European economies were badly affected. It was little wonder that the Western democracies were in no position to counter German, Italian, and Japanese aggression.

Franklin D. Roosevelt, elected to his first term as US president in 1933, introduced his New Deal, based on public work schemes and relief for the poor, in the following year. But the US economy did not recover fully until, like the economies of Western Europe, it was once more on a war footing.

30 BILLION dollars was lost on the US stock market in a single week in October 1929, more than the US had spent on the whole of World War I.

Marching for work
In Britain the 1936 Jarrow Crusade was designed to draw public attention to the drastic economic situation in the north of England, even though by this time the overall economy was slowly improving.

As a physical deterrent to any future German invasion, the French came up with a plan to construct a line of modern fortifications along their eastern frontier. This was to be called the Maginot Line, after defense minister, André Maginot, who had been badly wounded during World War I. By 1930 work had started on it. It was to consume a massive portion of the French defence budget and would

Union strength in France
Workers leave the Renault works in Paris after successfully striking for more pay. Inflationary awards slowed France's recovery from the Depression.

"the false and demoralizing notion … that once we have fortifications the inviolability of our country is assured …"

FRENCH GENERAL, ADOLPHE GUILLAUMAT, 1922

BEFORE

Like other European countries, Spain suffered political turbulence after World War I, even though it had remained neutral throughout its duration.

KING ALFONSO XIII

DICTATORSHIP
A constitutional monarchy under Alfonso XIII, Spain briefly became a dictatorship when General Primo de Rivera seized power in 1925. For a while the country was stable, but de Rivera was unable to cope with the **effects of the Depression ≪ 36–37** and in early 1930 he was forced to resign.

FURTHER INSTABILITY
Democracy returned to Spain with left-wing parties in the ascendancy. They abolished the monarchy in 1931, declared the country a republic, and **sent King Alfonso XIII into exile**. Right- and left-wing governments followed amid increasing political unrest. Matters came to a head in 1936 when an alliance of left-wing parties called **the Popular Front**, defeated a coalition composed of Conservative Catholics and the more extreme **right-wing Falange Party**. The new government immediately banned the Falange, provoking a new wave of violence.

KEY MOMENT

GUERNICA

Guernica is a town in the Basque country on the north Spanish coast. In spring 1937 it had some 5,000 inhabitants, its numbers being swollen by Republican refugees. On April 26, in support of Nationalist operations designed to secure the city of Bilbao, aircraft of the German Condor Legion, with a few Italian planes, attacked the town. It was market day and besides destroying much of the town the bombing raid caused over 2,500, largely civilian, casualties. It brought home the nature and horrors of modern warfare to the outside world and inspired Spanish artist Pablo Picasso to paint one of his most famous paintings—*Guernica*.

DESTRUCTION OF GUERNICA

The Spanish Civil War

The bitter conflict between the Left and Right in Spain drew in both the Axis powers and Soviet Russia between 1936 and 1939. The Western democracies stood helplessly by, apparently powerless, but in fact unwilling, to intervene and end the involvement of external forces in the war.

The war at home
Republican troops attacking rebel army elements during the early days of the civil war. They were often merciless to those they captured, as were the Nationalists. Controlling Spain's cities was key to Franco's success.

The street fighting that broke out in 1936 as a result of the banning of the Falange was accompanied by Left-inspired land seizures and a wave of strikes. The Nationalists, as the right wing was collectively labeled, feared a Communist takeover and decided to take action.

In July 1936 General Francisco Franco, commanding the troops in Spanish Morocco, rebelled against the government. Similar military revolts took place in cities on the mainland, although those in Madrid and Barcelona were quickly crushed. Russia agreed to send equipment and volunteers to help the government, while Germany provided the aircraft to transport Franco and his men across to the mainland.

International support

Britain and France now stepped in, or rather didn't. Both declared that they would not intervene, although volunteers did flock to Spain, most to join the International Brigades on the Republican side, but a few to fight with the Nationalists. While Germany and Italy agreed, in principle at least, to Anglo-French proposals on non-intervention, they began to send troops and supplies to Franco, as did the Russians to the Republicans.

In November 1936 the Germans and Italians recognized Franco as the Spanish head of state, after he had forced the Republican government to leave Madrid and then besieged the capital. The Republicans also suffered increasing splits among their various

> **375,000** The number of soldiers and civilians killed during the Spanish civil war. A further 135,000 were executed or died in concentration camps in its aftermath.

factions, with Russian agents playing a sinister game among them in an attempt to establish a government that was subservient to Moscow.

The Western democracies continued to try to defuse the situation. In April 1937 new non-intervention measures were agreed upon by all the powers involved. To prevent further soldiers and weapons being sent to Spain, the British and French governments established a joint naval blockade

The International Brigades
This poster praises the International Brigades for their support of the Popular Front in its struggle against the Nationalists.

Early Nationalist gains
General Francisco Franco (fifth from the left) with some of his senior generals in Burgos, just after it had been won by the Nationalists in August 1936.

of the Spanish Atlantic coast; Italy and Germany did the same in the Mediterranean, but stressed that they would not withdraw their forces until Franco's victory was assured. A further drawback was that the agreement did not cover aircraft, a weakness that was forcibly brought home at Guernica (see p.38) at the end of that month.

Taking control
Franco's better-equipped forces continued to remorselessly drive back the Republicans

Condor Legion Crest
The Condor Legion was the cover name for the Luftwaffe in Spain. Some of Germany's leading pilots of World War II honed their skills in Spain fighting the Nationalists cause.

to the extent that by the end of 1937 the whole of the western half of the country and most of the north was in his hands. At the beginning of 1938 he formed his first proper government and six months later the last of the foreign volunteers had left the country. It was now only a matter of time before Franco gained total control and

increasing numbers of refugees began to cross the Pyrenees to camps that had been set up by the French. The Republican government itself fled in February 1939 and Britain and France were forced to recognize the Franco regime. Madrid fell to the Nationalists at the end of March in the same year and the war came to an end.

AFTER »

The Spanish Civil War did not in itself hasten the onset of World War II. But it did showcase modern German and Russian weaponry, and provide an insight into how the war would be fought.

WEAPONS LABORATORY
The Axis powers and Russia used the civil war to test new weapons and tactics, besides giving troops and airmen combat experience. **Germany reaped the most benefit**. It was in Spain that the Luftwaffe perfected the technique of divebombing, especially using the **Junkers Ju87 Stuka**, which became one of the weapons most feared by Allied ground troops during the early years of World War II. They were also able to improve the design of their tanks.

WRONG LESSONS
The Russians, however, came away with the **wrong lessons in terms of armored warfare**. They had developed the concept of using large formations of tanks as a decisive weapon, but their officers in Spain concluded that tanks were best suited to operating with infantry rather than on their own. Stalin, who was in the midst of purging his senior officer corps, accepted this flawed view, but would later regret it. Many Western observers also concluded that the **anti-tank gun was now more powerful than the tank**, forgetting that much of Spain consists of mountainous terrain, which favored defensive tactics.

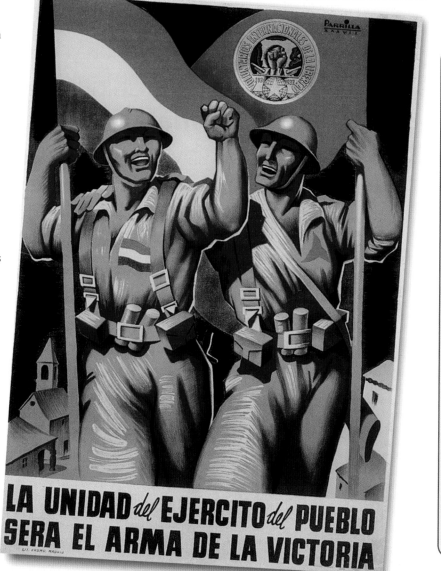

LA UNIDAD del EJERCITO del PUEBLO SERA EL ARMA DE LA VICTORIA

Japan Invades China

When Japan manufactured an excuse to invade China in 1937 it sparked a conflict that would last until the Japanese surrender in 1945. The invasion can be said to mark the start of World War II in the East.

In 1934 the Japanese government issued a highly provocative policy statement declaring that from now on it would be the guardian of peace in East Asia and that it would brook no interference in China's affairs by any other foreign state. At the end of the same year it declared that after two years it would be no longer bound by the 1922 Washington Naval Treaty on restricting the size of navies. The West was startled, but felt powerless to do anything about it, especially since Japan was no longer a member of the League of Nations.

Threats to the truce

Japan also began to nibble away further at Chinese territory, claiming that the Chinese had violated the Tanggu Truce by failing to crush anti-Japanese sentiment. It began to demand the removal of Chinese

BEFORE

Encouraged by its success in securing Manchuria, and driven by the fanatical nationalism in its armed forces, Japan had turned its attention to northern China.

THE LIMIT OF JAPANESE CONQUESTS

Before the end of the **conflict in Manchuria ❮❮ 32–33,** the Japanese overran the extreme northern Chinese province of Rehe and drove the Kuomintang forces south of the Great Wall of China. The Japanese emperor had given specific orders for his troops not to penetrate south of the Great Wall and so they halted.

THE TANGGU TRUCE

Hostilities were brought to an end by the Tanggu Truce of May 1933. The Japanese demanded a demilitarized zone extending 60 miles (100 km) south of the Great Wall and extending from Peking (present-day Beijing) to Tientsin, with Japanese patrols ensuring that it remained so. **Chiang Kai-shek,** engrossed as he was with trying to **crush the Communists ❮❮ 30–31,** acquiesced in this and also formally recognized the **Japanese puppet state of Manchukuo,** as Manchuria had now become.

While the truce did bring relative peace to northern China for a while, its people considered its terms humiliating. Furthermore, it did not diminish the Japanese military's desire to gain control of more of northern China.

officials hostile to the Japanese in some northern provinces. The Kuomintang generally agreed, preferring to maintain a veneer of sovereignty over these provinces rather than risk losing more territory through force. The Japanese then attempted to split the five northernmost provinces from China. This brought about a popular outcry, with demonstrations against the Japanese in many Chinese cities.

Significantly, Mao Zedong and the Communists also proclaimed their resistance to Japanese expansion. This was not just because Moscow had declared a united front against Fascism, which included Japan, but also because if China took up arms against Japan it would relieve the Kuomintang pressure on the Communists. Although he talked about military resistance, Chiang Kai-shek was afraid of Japan and continued with his campaign against the Communists.

Pretext for war

Matters eventually came to a head in July 1937. The Japanese, like the other countries with foreign legations in Peking, maintained a small garrison there. These soldiers left the city for maneuvers, but on July 7 they exchanged fire with Chinese troops in the area of the Marco Polo Bridge, 12 miles (19 km) southeast of the city. Japanese troops began to pass through the Great Wall into the demilitarized zone and demanded the withdrawal of Chinese troops from northern China. Chiang Kai-shek finally came off the fence and refused to comply with the Japanese. The result was all-out war.

The Japanese quickly secured Peking and Tientsin and then advanced rapidly southward. They placed Shanghai under siege. Chiang ordered the defenders to hold the city and they

Japan's conquests in China by 1939
The Japanese rapidly conquered large areas of northern and central China, and in 1938–39 turned their attention to coastal regions and ports, successfully cutting off most of China's trade links with the rest of the world.

KEY
- Japanese empire 1930
- Japanese conquests 1931–33
- Japanese conquests 1937–39

> "The Chinese soldier is **excellent material**, wasted and betrayed by **stupid leadership**."
>
> COLONEL JOSEPH STILWELL, US MILITARY ATTACHÉ IN CHINA, 1938

The West's view of Japan
This cartoon, published in Germany in 1935, shows Japan as a predatory octopus extending its tentacles to all parts of the world.

succeeded for three months before the Japanese broke in. By now China had gained the sympathy of the Western world, but nothing more than that. The Soviet Union, meanwhile, concerned over Japanese expansionism, signed a non-aggression pact with China, and Mao Zedong and his Communists also began to fight the Japanese.

As the Japanese swept southward their next target was Nanking, the seat of the Kuomintang government. On December 12, 1937, however, Japanese shore batteries and aircraft attacked

British and US naval and merchant vessels on the Yangtze River, just upstream from the city. President Roosevelt proposed that the British and Americans should impose a joint naval blockade on Japan to cut it off from its imports of raw materials. The British, fearing this would lead to war, declined. The Japanese then apologized.

Nanking fell to the Japanese on December 14, 1937. Over the next six weeks the occupying soldiers carried out

42,000 The number of Chinese civilians murdered in the Rape of Nanking according to the International Relief Committee of 1938, but the true number was much higher.

the most appalling atrocities, torching buildings, looting, torturing and killing civilians, and raping young women. The rest of the world was shocked, but did nothing. The Chinese estimate that some 300,000 people were murdered.

Chiang Kai-shek and his government had meanwhile withdrawn to Hankow, 400 miles (650 km) up the Yangtze River from Nanking. He was convinced that, however great its losses in terms of people and territory, China would outlast Japan. He therefore began to trade space for time. The Chinese troops, both Kuomintang and Communists, the latter now called the Eighth Route Army, did enjoy local victories, but these were never decisive enough to halt the Japanese invaders for long.

In the early summer of 1938 the Japanese began to advance on Hankow. Chiang Kai-shek's troops were unable to hold them and in August he and his government were forced to withdraw to Chungking, which would be their base for the next eight years. Between October and December the Japanese overran the southern province of Canton and virtually isolated the British colony of Hong Kong.

> **Chiang Kai-shek was much helped by his wife, Soong May-Ling, sister-in-law of Sun Yat-sen. Beautiful and highly intelligent, she had been educated in the US.**

Japanese troop train

A large detachment of the Kwantung Army is transported south through Manchukuo by rail to reinforce the troops fighting in northern China.

Foreign aid to China

The Soviet Union had been supplying Mao Zedong with weaponry and air support, but it was not until the end of 1938 that Chiang Kai-shek received any material aid from the West. Amid increasing clamor from the US media to provide help for China, President Roosevelt agreed to make a $25 million loan to the Kuomintang so that it could purchase weapons. Although the Chinese were a divided force and poorly organized and badly armed compared to the Japanese, they still enjoyed the advantage of fighting on home soil. But whether they could outlast the Japanese remained to be seen.

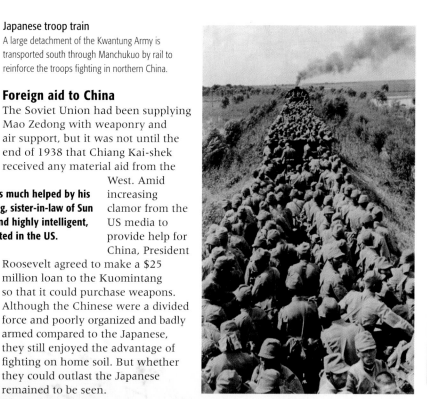

Japanese territorial ambitions were not limited to China; they also had their eyes on Soviet territory and Outer Mongolia.

SOVIET-JAPANESE CLASHES

Moscow's support for China resulted in **tension on the border with Manchukuo**. In 1937 there were clashes along the Amur River, and the following year the Soviets repulsed a more serious incursion in the east, near Lake Khasan.

In 1939 the Japanese in Manchukuo turned west to Outer Mongolia, with which the Russians had a non-aggression pact. The Japanese attempted to annex territory and in August the Soviets mounted a major attack, decisively **defeating them at Nomonhan (Khalkhyn Gol)** and driving them back into Manchukuo.

A ceasefire agreement was signed on 15 September. Thereafter the Japanese turned their attention toward **Southeast Asia 146–47, 158–59 »**, and not until the very end of World War II would there be any **further Russo-Japanese conflict 320–21 »**.

Relentless progress

A Japanese artillery column advances in southern China. The war demonstrated the hardiness of the Japanese soldier, which would be a decisive factor in the conquest of the European colonies in Southeast Asia in 1941–42.

BEFORE

Hitler's aim was to unite all the German peoples living in the various countries of Central and Eastern Europe. The largest number of these were the Austrians.

AUSTRO-GERMAN RAPPROCHEMENT
Having been thwarted in his **attempt to unite Austria with Germany ‹‹ 34** in 1934, Hitler now planned to annex Austria by peaceful means.

> From June 1933 any German who visited Austria had to pay 1,000 marks for the privilege. This penalty, which remained in force until 1936, ruined the Austrian tourist industry, encouraging Germans to visit Bavaria instead.

The first breakthrough came in July 1936 with the signing of the **Austro-German Agreement**. This ostensibly recognized Austria's sovereignty, but secret clauses within the agreement were very much in Germany's favor. The Austrians agreed to release political prisoners, including Nazis, and to allow the political opposition a say in government. While Austrian chancellor, Kurt Schuschnigg, believed this agreement put Austro-German relations on a firm footing, Hitler saw it as a lever to undermine Austrian independence. His **pact with Mussolini ‹‹ 34** later in 1936 also helped to isolate Austria.

PREPARING FOR WAR
In 1936 Hitler launched his Four-Year Plan, designed to put the German economy on a war footing. He appointed Goering to implement the plan, giving him extraordinary powers over private industry as well as government agencies. If he was to pursue his territorial demands, Hitler now felt that war in Europe was inevitable.

Appeasing Hitler

As the 1930s wore on and Nazi Germany grew ever stronger, Britain and France continued to rearm, but they were still loath to threaten force against Hitler. This encouraged Hitler to become increasingly aggressive in the territorial demands he made from Germany's neighbors.

Throughout 1937 the Germans fomented trouble in Austria through their Nazi cells. Matters came to a head in January 1938. Hearing of an assassination plot against him, Chancellor Schuschnigg ordered his police to raid a house used by a Nazi cell. They found plans for a Nazi revolt, which would provide the excuse for German forces to enter Austria to prevent German fighting German.

Outrageous demands
Horrified by this, Schuschnigg went to Germany to complain in person to Hitler. He was forced to listen to a lecture on the treatment of the Austrian Nazis. Hitler then demanded that all Austrian Nazis be released from jail and that the head of the Austrian Nazis be made interior minister and another Nazi sympathizer defense minister. Furthermore Austria's economy was to be absorbed by that of Germany. The Austrian chancellor refused to give in to these demands and organized a referendum of the Austrian people over whether they wanted to maintain their independence or accept *Anschluss* (union) with Germany.

Fearful that the vote would go the wrong way, Hitler ordered his troops into Austria on March 12, the eve of

the referendum. The Austrian Nazis had done their work well. The German soldiers were greeted by cheering crowds and there was no attempt to oppose them. The following day Schuschnigg resigned, was arrested, and spent until the end of the war in concentration camps. *Anschluss* had been achieved, with Austria now little more than a province of Greater Germany.

Britain and France made diplomatic protests over the annexation of Austria, but that was all. Neither was prepared for war and, in any event, there appeared to be little protest by the Austrian people themselves.

The Sudeten Germans
The British and French soon had to face another crisis provoked by Hitler. During 1937 Hitler had also set his sights on Czechoslovakia, a new state created by the Treaty of Versailles, and had drawn up plans for a surprise attack on it. The annexation of Austria meant that the Czechs were now surrounded on three sides by Germany.

Hitler made his first move almost as soon as Austria had been secured. The Sudetenland, the westernmost part of Czechoslovakia, had a sizeable German

Cheering the invaders
German troops occupying Austria in March 1939 are given an enthusiastic welcome by the people of Salzburg—complete with Nazi salutes and swastikas.

population, and Hitler instructed its leader, Konrad Henlein, to campaign for greater autonomy. He also began to threaten Czechoslovakia, which mobilized its armed forces and called on its ally, France, for support.

The French turned to the British and prime minister Neville Chamberlain went to Prague to try to persuade Czechoslovakia's president, Eduard Benes, to agree to Henlein's demands. The Germans, meanwhile, concentrated troops on the Czech border. Hitler told his generals that he would take military action if the matter had not been resolved by October 1938.

KEY MOMENT

KRISTALLNACHT

On November 7, 1938, a young German Jewish refugee shot and fatally wounded a German diplomat in Paris. Two nights later there was a wave of violent demonstrations throughout Germany. These had been carefully orchestrated by Goebbels and Reinhard Heydrich, head of the security services. The target was Jewish property—shops, private houses, and synagogues. The destruction was widespread—the name *Kristallnacht* (Crystal Night) comes from the vast quantities of broken glass that littered the streets—and almost 100 Jews were murdered. One outrageous consequence was that decrees were issued fining the Jewish population for the damage. Many countries protested and the US recalled its ambassador, but Hitler declared that this was of no concern to outsiders, accusing Britain of harboring a world Jewish conspiracy.

BROKEN SHOP WINDOWS AFTER KRISTALLNACHT

> " ... a quarrel in a **faraway country** between people of whom **we know nothing!**"
>
> NEVILLE CHAMBERLAIN IN A RADIO BROADCAST, SEPTEMBER 27, 1938

Chamberlain's triumphant return

Neville Chamberlain arrives back at Heston Aerodrome, after signing the Munich Agreement with Hitler. He declared that he had brought "peace with honour," which he believed was "peace for our time."

The brink of war

Hitler continued his saber-rattling and this resulted in an uprising by the Germans in Sudetenland in mid-September, which the Czech Army quickly crushed. Fearful that Hitler would now invade, the British prime minister, with French support, decided that he should meet Hitler in person to defuse the situation. In the meantime both Britain and France carried out a partial mobilization.

Chamberlain felt strongly that Sudetenland was not worth the horrors of another European war. Through the Munich Agreement of September 29,

> **Sudetenland had a population of two million ethnic Germans and 800,000 Czechs when it passed into German hands.**

the German parts of Sudetenland were exchanged for a declaration by Hitler that he had no further territorial

ambitions. The agreement was signed by Britain, France, Italy, and Germany, but the Czechs had no say in the matter. On October 1 German troops marched into Sudetenland, while Chamberlain returned in triumph to Britain, declaring that he had secured

peace. The British and French expressed wholesale relief that war had been averted, but Hitler was frustrated that he had been denied the opportunity to deal with the Czechoslovakian problem.

While Hitler planned his next moves on the European stage, attention in Germany and outside it turned to a dramatic new phase in the

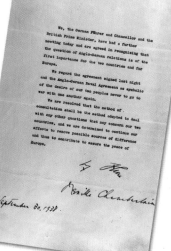

The infamous piece of paper

Hitler and Chamberlain met privately and produced a short version of the Munich Agreement, which they both signed. This was the piece of paper that Chamberlain waved to the crowd on his return to Britain.

persecution of the Jews. The night of November 9/10, 1938, which became known as *Kristallnacht* (see far left), saw the most widespread and concerted outbreak of violence yet directed against Germany's Jews.

Wir sind frei!

Deutschsprachiges Gebiet.

The Polish Corridor, which divided East Prussia from the rest of Germany, was Hitler's next territorial target.

The postmark includes a swastika and the triumphant slogan *"Wir sind frei!"* ("We are free!").

Slovakia would be persuaded by Hitler to declare independence in 1939, putting an end to the Czechoslovak state.

Austria is shown as fully incorporated into the new Greater Germany, although *Anschluss* had only taken place eight months before.

All the German-speaking regions in Czechoslovakia are indicated by red stripes. Sudetenland, which lay along the border with Germany, was occupied by German troops on October 1, 1938.

Proud Nazi postcard

This German postcard of 8 October 1938 celebrates the annexation of Sudetenland, the main German-speaking region of Czechoslovakia, just seven days before.

AFTER

Hitler soon made it clear that he had no intention of honoring his side of the Munich Agreement with regard to making no more territorial demands.

FURTHER DESIGNS ON CZECHOSLOVAKIA

Adopting the same strategy he had employed in Sudetenland, Hitler set out to encourage **internal unrest** in other parts of Czechoslovakia. He turned to the provinces of **Slovakia and Ruthenia,** which enjoyed a fair degree of autonomy, and encouraged them to demand even greater independence. This eventually sealed Czechoslovakia's fate and allowed German troops to **march into Prague 50 ≫** in March 1939.

OCCUPATION OF PRAGUE

DEMANDS FROM POLAND

On October 28, 1938, four weeks after the Munich Agreement, Hitler called on the Poles to hand over the **port of Danzig** and allow the Germans to construct **road and rail links** across **the Polish Corridor** to East Prussia. The Poles refused to agree to these demands, but on this occasion Hitler backed down. Less than a year later he would start World War II with a full-scale **invasion of Poland 58–59 ≫**.

2

EUROPE GOES
TO WAR

1939

The German and Soviet invasions of Poland,
followed by a Soviet invasion of Finland,
made it clear that a major European war
could no longer be averted. Britain and
France declared war against Germany
but were powerless to save Poland.

EUROPE GOES TO WAR

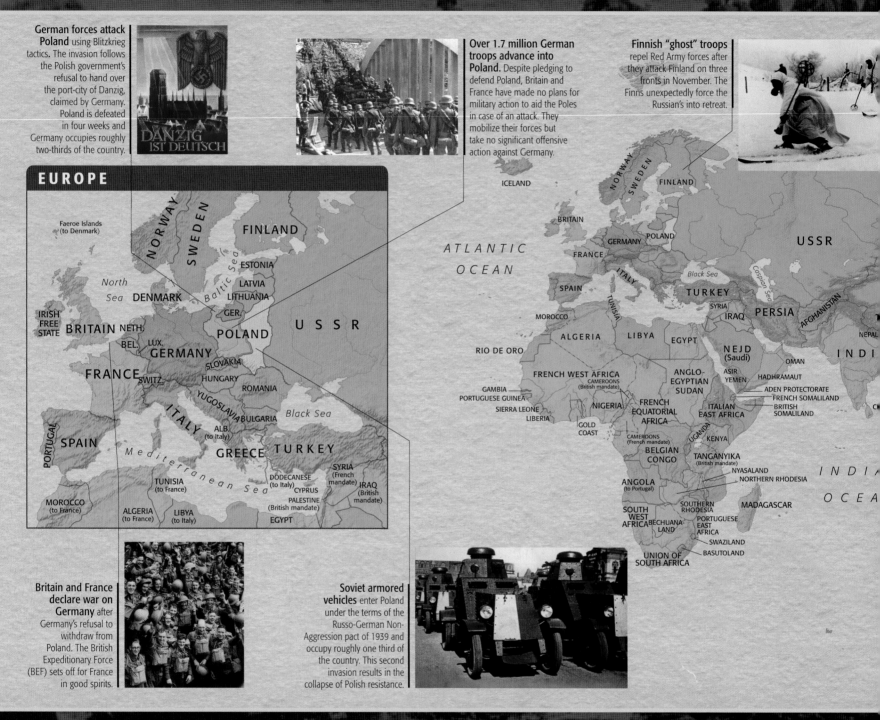

German forces attack Poland using Blitzkrieg tactics. The invasion follows the Polish government's refusal to hand over the port-city of Danzig, claimed by Germany. Poland is defeated in four weeks and Germany occupies roughly two-thirds of the country.

Over 1.7 million German troops advance into Poland. Despite pledging to defend Poland, Britain and France have made no plans for military action to aid the Poles in case of an attack. They mobilize their forces but take no significant offensive action against Germany.

Finnish "ghost" troops repel Red Army forces after they attack Finland on three fronts in November. The Finns unexpectedly force the Russian's into retreat.

EUROPE

Britain and France declare war on Germany after Germany's refusal to withdraw from Poland. The British Expeditionary Force (BEF) sets off for France in good spirits.

Soviet armored vehicles enter Poland under the terms of the Russo-German Non-Aggression pact of 1939 and occupy roughly one third of the country. This second invasion results in the collapse of Polish resistance.

At the beginning of 1939 there was still hope that a major war in Europe might be avoided. But Hitler's relentless aggression at last goaded the British and French governments into taking a stand. After German troops occupied Prague, Czechoslovakia, in March, the Western democracies committed themselves to support Poland, which was the next nation to come under pressure. Hitler knew that to fight the Poles, British, and French at the same time would be a gamble, but found a valuable ally in Joseph Stalin, who decided that a cynical deal with the Nazis, though they were his ideological enemies, offered the best prospects for Soviet security.

The Nazi–Soviet Pact in August opened the way for the German invasion of Poland on September 1. Reluctantly, Britain and France honoured the letter of their obligations to Poland and declared war on Germany two days later, though they did nothing to prevent

1939

Japanese forces bomb the Chinese city of Chungking killing 5,000 people. The two countries have been at war since 1937 and many more Chinese will to lose their lives during World War II.

Alaska
(to US)

CANADA

NEWFOUNDLAND

Albert Einstein sends a letter to US President Roosevelt regarding developing the atomic bomb before the Germans and the other Axis power can do so.

OLIA

NA

MANCHUKUO

PACIFIC OCEAN

UNITED STATES OF AMERICA

KOREA   JAPAN

Formosa

MEXICO

DOMINICAN REPUBLIC
VIRGIN ISLANDS
LEEWARD ISLANDS

ATLANTIC

CUBA
HAITI

OCEAN

RENCH
OOCHINA

PHILIPPINE
ISLANDS
(to US)

GUAM

Mariana
Islands
(Japanese mandate)

BRITISH HONDURAS
GUATEMALA
EL SALVADOR

HONDURAS
NICARAGUA

WINDWARD ISLANDS
BARBADOS
TRINIDAD AND TOBAGO
BRITISH GUIANA
DUTCH GUIANA
FRENCH GUIANA

BRITISH
BORNEO
BRUNEI

Marshall Islands
(Japanese mandate)

Caroline
Islands
(Japanese mandate)

COSTA RICA
PANAMA

VENEZUELA

ARAWAK

Nguru
(British mandate)

Gilbert
Islands
(to Britain)

COLOMBIA

ECUADOR

DUTCH EAST INDIES

TERRITORY
OF NEW GUINEA

Solomon
Islands
(to Britain)

Ellice
Islands
(to Britain)

WESTERN
SAMOA
(NZ mandate)

AMERICAN
SAMOA

As a result of the **Battle of the River Plate**, the first major naval battle of the war, the pocket battleship *Graf Spee* is scuttled. Having been followed to the port of Montevideo, escape was deemed impossible but capture was out of the question.

P
E
R
U

BRAZIL

PORTUGUESE
TIMOR

PAPUA

New
Hebrides
(to france
and Britain)

Fiji
(to Britain)

BOLIVIA

PARAGUAY

AUSTRALIA

New
Caledonia
(to France)

C
H
I
L
E

URUGUAY

ARGENTINA

NEW
ZEALAND

Following Britain's declaration of war on Germany on September 3, many Commonwealth governments, including Australia, take steps to provide men and aid for the war effort.

THE WORLD IN DECEMBER 1939

Germany
German conquests to Dec 1939
Japanese Empire
Japanese conquests to Dec 1939
Allied states
Neutral states
Territory occupied by USSR
Frontiers Sep 1939

Poland being overrun by German forces, abetted in the east by the Soviets. The atrocities committed by both the Nazis and the Soviets in conquered Poland were but a foretaste of the wider horrors that World War II held in store.

While Poland suffered, the British and French endured the minor inconveniences of the "Phoney War." Although civilian life was disrupted by blackouts and the evacuation of cities, there were neither battles on the Western Front nor bombing raids on London or Paris. The most dramatic action was at sea, where German U-boats and surface raiders threatened Allied shipping. When Finland was attacked by the Soviet Union in November, Britain and France were almost tempted to send their idle forces to intervene in defense of the Finns. Meanwhile, the United States stood on the sidelines, rooting for Britain and France but hoping to keep out of any fighting.

TIMELINE 1939

Spanish Nationalists capture Barcelona ▪ **German troops occupy Prague** ▪ **Germany invades Poland** ▪ **Russia invades eastern Poland** ▪ Britain and France declare war on Germany ▪ British Expeditionary Force is sent to France ▪ **The Winter War** ▪ Battle of the River Plate

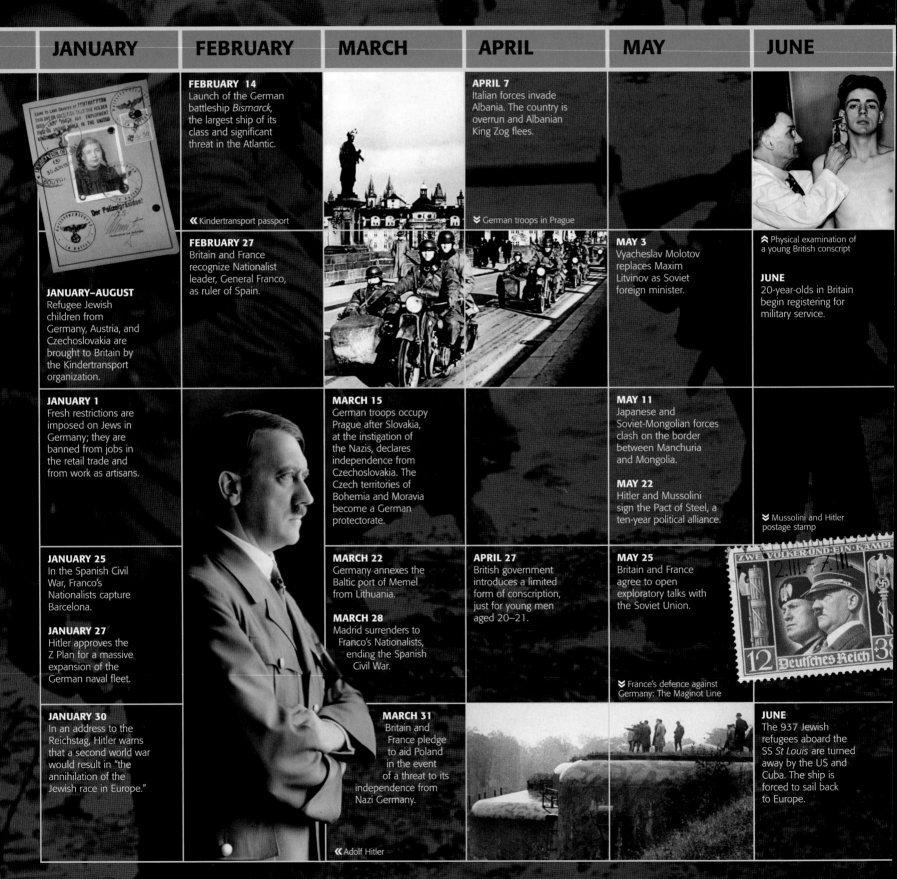

JANUARY	FEBRUARY	MARCH	APRIL	MAY	JUNE

« Kindertransport passport

FEBRUARY 14
Launch of the German battleship *Bismarck*, the largest ship of its class and significant threat in the Atlantic.

APRIL 7
Italian forces invade Albania. The country is overrun and Albanian King Zog flees.

⌄ German troops in Prague

⌃ Physical examination of a young British conscript

JANUARY–AUGUST
Refugee Jewish children from Germany, Austria, and Czechoslovakia are brought to Britain by the Kindertransport organization.

FEBRUARY 27
Britain and France recognize Nationalist leader, General Franco, as ruler of Spain.

MAY 3
Vyacheslav Molotov replaces Maxim Litvinov as Soviet foreign minister.

JUNE
20-year-olds in Britain begin registering for military service.

JANUARY 1
Fresh restrictions are imposed on Jews in Germany; they are banned from jobs in the retail trade and from work as artisans.

MARCH 15
German troops occupy Prague after Slovakia, at the instigation of the Nazis, declares independence from Czechoslovakia. The Czech territories of Bohemia and Moravia become a German protectorate.

MAY 11
Japanese and Soviet-Mongolian forces clash on the border between Manchuria and Mongolia.

MAY 22
Hitler and Mussolini sign the Pact of Steel, a ten-year political alliance.

⌄ Mussolini and Hitler postage stamp

JANUARY 25
In the Spanish Civil War, Franco's Nationalists capture Barcelona.

JANUARY 27
Hitler approves the Z Plan for a massive expansion of the German naval fleet.

MARCH 22
Germany annexes the Baltic port of Memel from Lithuania.

MARCH 28
Madrid surrenders to Franco's Nationalists, ending the Spanish Civil War.

APRIL 27
British government introduces a limited form of conscription, just for young men aged 20–21.

MAY 25
Britain and France agree to open exploratory talks with the Soviet Union.

ZWEI VÖLKER UND EIN KAMPF

12 Deutsches Reich

⌄ France's defence against Germany: The Maginot Line

JANUARY 30
In an address to the Reichstag, Hitler warns that a second world war would result in "the annihilation of the Jewish race in Europe."

MARCH 31
Britain and France pledge to aid Poland in the event of a threat to its independence from Nazi Germany.

« Adolf Hitler

JUNE
The 937 Jewish refugees aboard the SS *St Louis* are turned away by the US and Cuba. The ship is forced to sail back to Europe.

"It is evil things that **we shall be fighting** against, **brute force**, bad faith, injustice, **oppression and persecution**. And against them I am certain that the right will prevail."

BRITISH PRIME MINISTER NEVILLE CHAMBERLAIN'S SPEECH, DECLARING WAR ON GERMANY, SEPTEMBER 3, 1939

JULY	AUGUST	SEPTEMBER	OCTOBER	NOVEMBER	DECEMBER	»

JULY
British government publishes a public information leaflet: *Your Gas Mask And How To Use It*. Most of the population, including children, have now been issued with masks.

SEPTEMBER 1
Germany invades Poland.

OCTOBER 6
End of Polish military resistance; Hitler makes peace offer to Britain and France that is swiftly rejected.

OCTOBER 7
Deployment of British Expeditionary Force in France completed.

NOVEMBER 1
Western Poland formally annexed into the German Reich.

NOVEMBER 4
Warsaw ghetto established: the city's Jews are forced into a single area.

AUGUST 20–31
The Soviets, led by General Zhukov, defeat the Japanese at the Battle of Khalkyn Gol.

OCTOBER 14
German U-boat sinks British battleship *Royal Oak* in naval base at Scapa Flow.

NOVEMBER 4
The US Neutrality Act is amended to allow the delivery of war supplies to Britain and France on a cash-and-carry basis.

« French newspaper seller on day war is declared

> British child's gas mask

AUGUST 23
Nazi Germany and the Soviet Union sign a non-aggression pact, secretly agreeing to divide Poland between them.

SEPTEMBER 3
Britain and France declare war on Germany. The liner *Athenia* is sunk by a German U-boat.

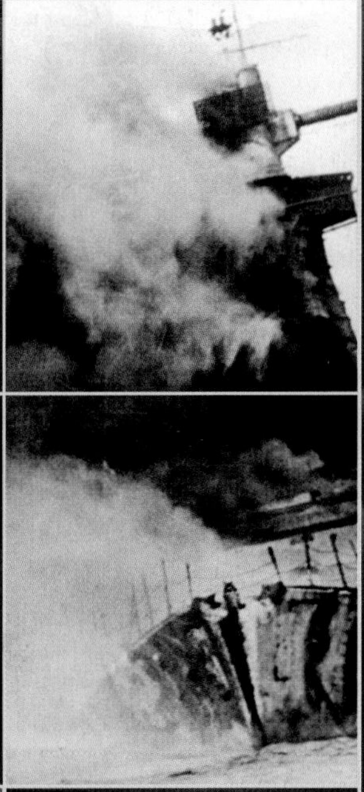

> The battleship *Graf Spee* is scuttled by its crew

DECEMBER 11
Finns halt Soviet advance at Suomussalmi.

DECEMBER 13
Battle of the River Plate. The German battleship *Graf Spee* is damaged and takes refuge in Montevideo, Uruguay.

AUGUST 25
Britain and France sign a formal agreement to defend Poland; Mussolini informs Hitler that Italy intends to remain neutral.

SEPTEMBER 5
President Roosevelt reaffirms the neutrality of the United States.

SEPTEMBER 17
Soviet troops invade eastern Poland.

SEPTEMBER 27
Fall of Warsaw.

« The ruins of Warsaw

NOVEMBER 24
Japanese capture the southern Chinese city of Nanking.

DECEMBER 17
Graf Spee is scuttled outside Montevideo harbor.

DECEMBER 18
Fifteen RAF bombers are lost in a daytime raid on German port of Wilhelmshaven.

» German and Soviet officers meet after the invasion of Poland

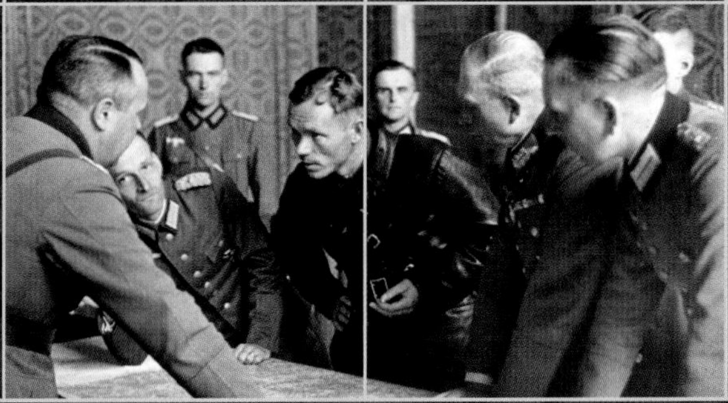

JULY 17
Molotov suggests direct military discussions between the Soviets and the British.

JULY 27
British and French military missions embark by sea for the Soviet Union.

NOVEMBER 30
Soviet Union invades Finland. Start of the Winter War.

> Finnish anti-tank rifle

49

BEFORE «

The Munich Agreement of September 1938 « 42–43 handed over the Sudeten area of Czechoslovakia to Germany.

"PEACE FOR OUR TIME"
Assured by Hitler that the Sudetenland was to be the "last territorial demand in Europe" made by Germany, British prime minister, **Neville Chamberlain**, announced that the agreement meant "peace for our time."

NIGHT OF ATROCITIES
On November 9/10, 1938, **Jewish shops, homes, and synagogues** across Germany and Austria were attacked by the Nazis. This event became known as *Kristallnacht* (Crystal Night, because of the shattered window glass) « 42–43. Almost 100 Jews were murdered and between 20,000 and 30,000 were taken away to **concentration camps**. These atrocities severely damaged Germany's international reputation, especially alienating opinion in the United States.

HITLER'S POLISH DEMANDS
Partitioned between Russia, Prussia, and Austria in the late 18th century, Poland had been restored as an independent state after World War I. Under the terms of the **Versailles Treaty** « 18–19, Poland was given a strip of territory linking it to the Baltic. This **"Polish Corridor"** separated East Prussia from the rest of Germany. The seaport of Danzig (Gdansk), largely German in population, was declared an **autonomous "Free City."** In 1939 Hitler demanded land access to East Prussia across the Polish Corridor..

The Path to War

Hitler's greed and aggression were not satisfied by his gains under the Munich Agreement. His next target was Poland, once again using the pretext of setting right the "unjust" Versailles Treaty. Britain and France wanted Poland to make a deal with Hitler—but events took a different course.

The tide of events in Europe turned decisively toward war on March 15, 1939. On that day German troops marched unopposed into Prague, completing the destruction of Czechoslovakia begun the previous year at the Munich Conference. The Czech lands of Bohemia and Moravia were put under Nazi occupation as a "Protectorate," while Slovakia became, in effect, a German puppet state.

Hitler had correctly calculated that Britain and France would take no military action in response, but he underestimated the shock effect that the destruction of Czechoslovakia would have on international opinion. Up to this point Germany's demands for a revision of the allegedly unjust Treaty of Versailles had helped to

Czechoslovakia falls
German troops entering Prague on March 15, 1939. Czechoslovakia had first gained its independence only 20 years before, in the aftermath of World War I, and would have to endure six years of brutal Nazi occupation before being reestablished.

Rescue mission
Shortly before war was declared, around 10,000 mostly Jewish, children were evacuated by train and boat from Nazi-occupied territory to Britain in an operation known as Kindertransport (children's transport).

conceal Hitler's expansionist ambitions. The march into Prague revealed his naked aggression.

Europe was already in the grip of an accelerating arms race. In February, for example, the British government had authorized the maximum expansion of military aircraft production without

1,500 The estimated number of German aircraft that bombed Warsaw on September 24, 1939. The Poles had a total of only 600 modern aircraft at this time.

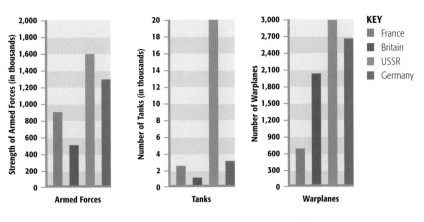

KEY
- France
- Britain
- USSR
- Germany

Armed Forces · Tanks · Warplanes

Military strength of the combatants

In 1939 the combined forces of Germany and Russia overshadowed those of France and Britain. It was, however, the German Luftwaffe, with its imposing fleet of modern aircraft, that was most prepared for war.

regard for cost. The breakneck pace of Hitler's rearmament program was pushing the German economy to its limits too. But the Western democracies still hoped to avoid war, while Hitler had not anticipated a major conflict in 1939.

When German troops entered Prague, however, British prime minister Neville Chamberlain belatedly decided that he and his government must be seen to take a stronger line with Hitler. They offered Poland, among others, a guarantee of support against possible German aggression. The French government of Edouard Daladier did likewise, dragged along in the wake of its British allies.

The invasion of Poland

Just as Hitler had not understood the impact of the occupation of Prague upon the Western democracies, the British government did not foresee the effect of its guarantee to Poland upon Hitler. The enraged Führer immediately told his army commanders to draw up plans to invade Poland, with a provisional target date of September 1, 1939.

Although making preparations for war, the British and French governments were still determined

> ## "We in Poland do not know the concept of **peace at any price**."
>
> GENERAL JÓZEF BECK, SPEECH, MAY 5, 1939

to avoid war if they possibly could. They wanted the Poles to negotiate with Nazi Germany to avoid a conflict. But the Polish government, dominated by General Józef Beck, was determinedly nationalistic and unwilling to bow to any German pressure.

Hitler had, in any case, no genuine interest in negotiating an agreement with Poland. He had felt cheated of a war over Czechoslovakia in the previous year and, having decided upon an invasion of Poland, he did not intend to be denied

the chance of military glory a second time. He did still hope, however, to avoid having to fight the British and French at the same time as the Poles.

The tide of events in Europe appeared to be flowing in Germany's favor. In March 1939 General Franco's forces completed their victory in the Spanish Civil War. Hitler made a further small advance by absorbing the Baltic city of Memel (present-day Klaipeda) into the Reich, while in the Adriatic Mussolini occupied Albania. The alliance between Hitler and Mussolini was confirmed by the declaration of a Pact of Steel between Italy and Germany in May.

The United States' government watched developments in Europe with concern but no possibility of intervention, given the strength of American isolationist feeling. The US was simply not a factor in the diplomatic and military equation.

The attitude of the Soviet Union, by contrast, was of critical importance. Moscow would become the focus of the final diplomatic maneuvers of peacetime in the summer of 1939.

"DANZIG IS GERMAN"

On August 23, 1939, Nazi Germany and the Soviet Union signed a pact, secretly agreeing to partition Poland between them.

POLAND CRUSHED

Following the German invasion of Poland on September 1, 1939, **Britain and France declared war on Germany two days later 54–55 »**. Unable to resist the might of the German forces, the **Poles were forced to surrender 58–59 »** after just four weeks.

DANZIG

Danzig was annexed by the German Reich on September 2, 1939. After the war the **city became part of Poland**. Most of the German population was driven out and replaced by Poles. Under its Polish name of Gdansk, the city was the focus of strikes by the **Solidarity trade union** against Poland's Communist government in the early 1980s.

Expanding Germany's borders

The spurious need for *Lebensraum*, or "living space", informed Hitler's plans for war. Up to 1939, Germany's expansion concentrated on neighboring territories with ethnic German populations.

KEY
- Germany 1933
- Area of German expansion Mar 1935–Mar 1939
- --- German defensive lines 1939

Rifles

The rifle was the basic infantry weapon of World War II. Bolt-action repeater rifles were widely used, as they had been in World War I, but these appeared increasingly outdated alongside self-loading semi-automatic rifles such as the Gewehr 43 and the M1 Garand.

1 Karabiner 98k, an improved version of the 1898 Mauser, was introduced in 1935 as the standard German infantry rifle. **2 7.92 mm x 57 cartridge**, the standard rifle round of the German Army in both World Wars, used in the Karabiner 98k and Gewehr 43. **3 Gewehr 43**, a German Walther-designed semi-automatic rifle introduced in 1943. It had a gas-operated self-loading mechanism and 10-round detachable box magazine. **4 Lee-Enfield No. 4 with grenade launcher**. Grenades were fired from standard infantry rifles from World War I onward, propelled by a blank cartridge. **5 .303 cartridge**, the standard British cartridge from the late 19th century to beyond the end of World War II. **6 Oil bottle and pull-through**, used to clean the British Lee-Enfield rifle. **7 Lee-Enfield No. 4**, a direct descendant of the rifle adopted by the British Army in 1885. The No. 4 version was first introduced in 1939 and became standard issue from 1941. **8 7.62 mm x 54R cartridge**, introduced at the same time as the Mosin-Nagant bolt-action rifle in 1891, was standard Soviet ammunition throughout World War II. **9 Mosin-Nagant 1891/30**, the standard-issue Soviet

infantry rifle of World War II, was also an excellent sniper rifle when fitted with a telescopic sight. **10 7.7 mm x 58 cartridge**, the round fired by the Japanese Arisaka Type 99 rifle, larger than the 6.5 mm x 50 round used by the older Arisaka Type 38. **11 Arisaka Type 99**, a Mauser-style bolt-action rifle issued in 1939 as an improvement on the outdated Japanese Arisaka Type 38, which still remained in use throughout the war. **12 Tokarev SVT-40**, a Soviet semi-automatic rifle. Over a million were produced early in the war, but it was considered too difficult to maintain for standard infantry issue. **13 Mosin-Nagant Carbine**, a Soviet rifle, was shorter than the Mosin-Nagant rifle but otherwise similar. **14 M1 Garand**, a semi-automatic rifle adopted by the United States Army in 1936, served as the basic American infantry weapon in World War II. **15 M1 Carbine**, also of American manufacture, was a more compact version of the M1 Garand, used by airborne and support troops and in jungle warfare. **16 .30 caliber cartridge**, the ammunition developed for the American M1 Carbine, was sometimes criticized as underpowered.

1 KARABINER 98K (GERMANY)

4 LEE-ENFIELD NO. 4 WITH GRENADE LAUNCHER (BRITAIN)

6 OIL BOTTLE AND PULL-THROUGH (BRITAIN)

9 MOSIN-NAGANT 1891/30 (USSR)

10 7.7 MM X 58 CARTRIDGE (JAPAN)

11 ARISAKA TYPE 99 (JAPAN)

12 TOKAREV SVT-40 (USSR)

13 MOSIN-NAGANT CARBINE (USSR)

2 7.92 MM X 57 CARTRIDGE (GERMANY)

3 GEWEHR 43 (GERMANY)

5 .303 CARTRIDGE (BRITAIN)

7 LEE-ENFIELD NO. 4 (BRITAIN)

8 7.62 MM X 54R CARTRIDGES (USSR)

14 M1 GARAND (US)

15 M1 CARBINE (US)

16 .30 CARTRIDGE (US)

Declarations of War

Backed by his new ally, the Soviet Union, Hitler plunged Europe into war on September 1 1939 with his attack on Poland. On September 3 Britain and France ended their hesitation and declared war on Germany. A new global conflict had been unleashed.

On the night of August 31, 1939, the Nazi SS faked a Polish raid on a German radio station at Gleiwitz on the border with Poland. Some prisoners from a concentration camp were killed and their bodies, wearing Polish uniforms, were shown to the press. Announcing that it was responding to this "Polish attack," at 4.35am the following morning, Germany sent troops into Poland, beginning World War II in Europe.

The invasion came after a summer of diplomatic activity focused on the Soviet Union. When Britain and France promised to guarantee Poland against

German aggression in April 1939, they had no plans to give the Poles actual military assistance. They did nothing to reinforce Poland's defenses, nor did they plan to attack Germany from the west. They did, however, try to draw the Soviet Union into a commitment to defend Poland.

Negotiations between Britain and France and Joseph Stalin's Soviet regime made slow progress. The British government was reluctant to do a deal with a Communist dictatorship, while the Poles adamantly rejected the idea of allowing Soviet troops into Poland under any circumstances. For his part, Stalin was doubtful of the motives of the Western democracies, suspecting them of wishing to deflect Nazi aggression against the Soviet Union.

Hostility between the Communist Soviet Union and Nazi Germany was such a fixed and apparently deep-

International news
French newspaper headlines on the early evening of September 3 announce Britain's declaration of war that morning. France's own declaration of war was to follow the same day.

Naval bombardment
The veteran German coast-defense ship *Schleswig-Holstein* in action against the Polish naval base at Westerplatte near Danzig early on September 1, firing the first shots of World War II in Europe.

rooted aspect of European politics that an alliance between the two seemed unthinkable. Yet they had persuasive shared interests in the short term. Determined to make war on Poland before the autumn rains set in, Hitler needed to reduce the number of enemies he might have to fight

simultaneously. Stalin, for his part, was tempted by the chance to extend his rule westward at the expense of Poland and the Baltic States.

Serious discussion between the Nazi and Soviet regimes began secretly in late July. On August 21 Germany announced that its foreign minister, Joachim von Ribbentrop, had been invited to Moscow. Two days later an astonished world learned of the signing of a Nazi–Soviet Pact. One of its secret terms provided for Germany and the Soviet Union to divide Poland between them.

« **BEFORE**

In April 1939 the governments of Britain and France promised to come to the aid of Poland if the country were attacked by Germany, while Hitler was secretly making invasion plans.

FASCISM AND COMMUNISM
Throughout the 1930s **Nazi Germany and the Soviet Union were ideological enemies**; Soviet dictator Stalin denouncing Nazi "Fascism" and Hitler uttering torrents of invective against the evils of Soviet "Bolshevism."

TRADITIONAL ENEMIES
Poland was bitterly hostile to the Soviet Union; the **Poles traditionally regarded Russians as potential oppressors**. Most of Poland had been a Russian province before World War I and after the conflict, **in 1920, the country defeated the Soviets** in a war to secure its independence. The USSR formally recognized the new boundary of Poland in the 1921 Peace of Riga.

> The first civilian ship to be hit by a German U-boat was the SS *Athenia*, carrying over 1,000 people of whom 300 were American. The sinking, within nine hours of the British declaration of war, caused a furore in Allied circles.

With the agreement with Stalin in his pocket, Hitler ordered that the long-planned invasion of Poland should begin on August 26. However, at the last moment, he hesitated. Britain and France assured Germany that they really did intend to go to war if he attacked the Poles—a formal military alliance between Britain and Poland was signed on August 25.

Final maneuvers

At the same time, Mussolini told Hitler that, despite its Pact of Steel alliance with Germany, Italy intended to stand on the sidelines. Faced with the prospect of taking on France, Britain, and Poland unaided, Hitler took the decision to countermand the order for the invasion.

Through the last week in August a flurry of diplomatic initiatives was launched to avert war. Hitler made a grandiose peace proposal to the British—including a patronizing offer to help defend the British Empire. Birger Dahlerus, a Swedish friend of the prominent Nazi Hermann Goering, acted as a private emissary shuttling between Berlin and London with various proposals for a settlement of Germany's factitious differences with Poland. But last-minute hopes for peace were illusory. The Poles would not make any concessions, and Hitler did not want them to accept his demands over Danzig and the Polish Corridor. These were pretexts to justify attacking Poland. His delay had been an attempt to undermine British and French support. He rescheduled the invasion for September 1. There was no further postponement and Hitler expected the Allies to back off.

Despite their commitment to Poland, Britain and France did not respond to the German invasion with immediate declarations of war. French military leaders pleaded with their government for more time to complete mobilization before war was declared. Britain called for the withdrawal of German forces from Poland, although this was "not to be considered as an ultimatum." The French and British still clung to the hope that, as in the Czech crisis of 1938, peace would be saved by an international conference, possibly brokered by Mussolini.

> "I cannot forecast to you the action of Russia. It is a riddle wrapped in **a mystery inside an enigma**."
>
> WINSTON CHURCHILL, RADIO BROADCAST, OCTOBER 1939

The British House of Commons eventually forced the issue. After a debate on the evening of September 2 in which Members of Parliament strongly expressed hostility to the hesitations of the government, it was clear to Prime Minister Neville Chamberlain that he would either have to honor the agreement with Poland or resign. At 9am on September 3, Britain therefore delivered an ultimatum to Germany, demanding an immediate end to hostilities in Poland. The ultimatum expired at 11am. Forced into action, Chamberlain then made a broadcast to the nation on the radio, announcing in dignified but melancholy tones that "this country is at war with Germany." France, which had delivered its own ultimatum to Hitler, declared war at 5pm the same day.

A new world war

British and French colonies were automatically also at war with Germany. Britain's Dominions, however, had to make their own decision whether to join in. Australia and New Zealand declared war unhesitatingly. Canada, where the issue was more controversial, followed suit on September 10. In South Africa the war caused a governmental crisis; Jan Smuts took over as prime minister and declared war on September 6. In

Dividing the spoils

Soviet and German officers meet in Brest-Litovsk on September 22 at the junction of what would become their respective occupation zones in Poland, as secretly agreed in the Nazi–Soviet Pact a month before.

Danzig returns to German rule

German troops and officers of the mainly German Danzig police demolish a border post around the former Free City, September 1, 1939.

the United States, President Roosevelt promised in his Labor Day radio speech to keep America out of the war.

Unlike the scenes that greeted the declarations of war in 1914, when streets were filled with cheering crowds, Europe entered the war in a deeply somber mood, expecting death and destruction on a massive scale.

AFTER »

Poland was defeated in little over a month's fighting, while the Western Allies failed to do anything to help the Poles.

SOVIET EXPANSION
The Soviet Union followed a **policy of expansion** on its western borders in 1939–40, occupying eastern Poland, Lithuania, Estonia, and Latvia, as well as parts of Romania and Finland. This policy led to the **Winter War** with **Finland 64–65 »**.

THE PHONEY WAR
In Western Europe major **fighting did not break out until the spring of 1940**. The period from the declarations of war to the German **invasion of Denmark and Norway 74–75 »**, when the Allies became engaged, is known as the **Phoney War 60–61 »**.

SS RECRUITING POSTER FOR OCCUPIED NORWAY

GERMAN DICTATOR Born 1889 Died 1945

Adolf Hitler

"Germany's **problem** could only be **solved by force**"

ADOLF HITLER, NOVEMBER 1937

No individual played a larger role in causing and shaping World War II than German dictator Adolf Hitler. Yet for the first 30 years of his life this son of a minor Austrian official seemed destined to a life of total insignificance. Until 1914 Hitler was a rootless drifter who had failed in his ambition to be an artist and could find no place in society for himself. In World War I he served in the German Army, although he did not acquire German nationality until 1932. He was by all accounts a brave soldier—earning the Iron Cross twice—but struck no one as possessing any special leadership qualities, only attaining the rank of corporal. The intense experience of four years of trench warfare, followed by the shock of Germany's defeat, colored the rest of his life.

Postwar resentment

Like many embittered ex-servicemen lost in the chaos of postwar Germany, Hitler slipped into extremist politics. He discovered a hitherto unrealized talent for whipping up the emotions of a disillusioned public with his fiery speeches, and imposed his leadership upon the small but radical Nazi Party. The political ideas that Hitler proposed were not original; they were a variant on standard right-wing German nationalism, but he invested these ideas with exceptional emotional power. Desperate for an excuse to explain his country's defeat in war and his personal lack of success in life,

Man of destiny

The official image of Hitler in Nazi Germany was of an intense and powerful figure who would lead the country to victory.

Political memoirs

The first volume of *Mein Kampf* (*My Struggle*) consists of a mythologized version of Hitler's early life, along with a presentation of Nazi thought, including anti-Semitism and the solution of Germany's problems by conquest.

he adopted with passionate sincerity the belief that the German people were victims of a "stab in the back" by socialists and Jews, and of an "international Jewish conspiracy."

The failure of the *putsch* (coup) he mounted in Munich in 1923 might have ended Hitler's political career, but instead he exploited his trial to publicize his views and used his subsequent time in prison to dictate his political memoirs, *Mein Kampf.*

"I will go down as the **greatest German in** history ..."

HITLER, MARCH 15, 1939

A naturally egotistic and narcissistic personality, he had developed an absolute conviction that he was the historic leader who would one day save the German people. This belief sustained him through a period when the Nazis were marginal to German politics, but really began to resonate with the German public during the late

Longtime companion
Hitler's relationship with Eva Braun, whom he met in 1929, was not made known to the public. The pair were only married on April 29, 1945, as the Red Army closed in on Berlin. One day later the couple committed suicide.

"Any **alliance whose purpose is not** the intention **to wage war** is senseless and **useless**."

HITLER IN "MEIN KAMPF", 1925

1920s when high inflation and mass unemployment were crippling the economy, creating opportunities for extremist parties. A complete cynic in his political tactics, Hitler operated as a vote-winning politician in democratic electoral politics, while being hell-bent on establishing a dictatorship.

Defeating the opposition
Hitler's opponents consistently underrated him, both before and after his rise to power, finding his histrionic personality hard to take seriously. The conservative German politicians who allowed him to become chancellor in 1933 thought they would be able to control him and were astounded to find their country a single-party Nazi state within months of his appointment. The German officer corps swore allegiance to him because he offered them military resurgence, but found themselves unable to moderate his aggressive ambitions. Hitler's sense of messianic purpose took stronger hold of him as events led to the fulfilment of his wildest ambitions. His success in restoring Germany's military strength and overturning the Versailles Treaty without provoking a war proved

him a master of manipulation. He played on his opponents' hopes and fears, exploiting his neurotic capacity for sudden rages as a method of intimidation, deploying a skilled gambler's instinct for brinkmanship and sudden decisive action. Yet

peaceful victories did not satisfy Hitler. He believed that it was morally good for the strong to triumph violently over the weak, and longed to fulfill the role of successful war leader.

Early military successes
Hitler can take much of the credit for Germany's military successes in the early stages of World War II. His belief in mobility and shock as tactical principles made him back radical proponents of Blitzkrieg over more conservative commanders in the German Army. His estimate of the weakness of morale among his enemies was correct. But spectacular early victories confirmed his growing belief in his own infallibility. As the war progressed he lost all faith in his generals and insisted upon taking personal control of the details of all military operations, to disastrous effect.

When the tide of war turned against Germany, Hitler's grasp on reality weakened. His mental and physical state deteriorated and he withdrew to a life spent in command bunkers, never seen and rarely heard by the German people. His survival when an assassin's bomb exploded alongside him at Rastenburg in July 1944 was taken by him as further evidence of destiny protecting its chosen instrument. He accepted no personal responsibility for the catastrophe that he had brought upon the German people, ascribing his failure to disloyalty and betrayal.

A vote for Hitler
In 1932 Hitler and his Nazi Party offered Germany a "government of freedom and peace." Though he did not win this election, Hitler eventually made Germany a one-party state and plunged Europe into war.

The Führer speaks
Propaganda played an important part in Hitler's hold on power. Rallies of the Nazi Party membership, such as this one held at Dortmund in 1933, allowed Hitler to personally inspire the masses who chose to follow him.

HITLER DURING WORLD WAR I

‹‹ BEFORE

In April 1939 the German Army began detailed planning for "Fall Weiss" (Case White), the invasion of Poland.

RAPID VICTORY
The German chief of the general staff, General Franz Halder, told his commanders that **victory would have to be achieved in "record speed"** and that it must be "liquidated." He anticipated a **victory in three weeks**, and dismissed the Poles as "not serious opponents."

BRAVE STANCE
Guaranteed the support of Britain and France in case of a German attack, the Polish government **refused to give way to German demands ‹‹ 50–51** for the annexation of the Free City of Danzig and access routes to East Prussia across the "Polish Corridor" in Pomerania.

HITLER'S NEW ALLY
Stalin signed a Nazi–Soviet Pact **‹‹ 54–55** in Moscow on August 23, 1939. A secret clause provided for **the partition of Poland between the Germans and Soviets**.

Poland Destroyed

Nazi Germany's first military campaign was a triumph for Hitler's leadership. With the Soviet menace in the east seemingly neutralized by the Nazi–Soviet Pact, the German armed forces crushed Polish resistance in a matter of days, with a potent combination of air power and tank forces.

German military operations against Poland began at 4:40am on September 1, 1939, with Luftwaffe air strikes across the border. German troops began advancing into Poland at 6am.

Always a bold risk-taker, Hitler had left only 44 divisions of his army to defend Germany's western border against France—where the French could theoretically deploy around 100 divisions. What is more, almost all Germany's tanks and aircraft were sent to the Polish front. Hitler guessed correctly that the French would fail to mount a serious offensive in Poland's aid. This gamble allowed him to deploy overwhelming force against the Poles.

German superiority
Poland's armed forces were far from negligible in size, but lacked modern aircraft, tanks, and transport vehicles. The Germans fielded six armored divisions and 10 divisions of mechanized infantry, alongside some 40 divisions of more conventional infantry advancing on foot. With a large fleet of modern aircraft, the Luftwaffe had no difficulty achieving command of the air. Polish pilots fought bravely and skillfuly,

Polish cavalry
In addition to 30 infantry divisions, the Polish Army included 11 cavalry brigades but only two mechanized brigades in 1939. They had no answer to the Germans' more modern weapons.

but their aircraft were too few and a generation out of date. The Luftwaffe acted with devastating effect, sowing panic among civilians and disrupting the Polish Army's lines of communication.

Polish commanders were perhaps over-optimistic about their ability to resist a German offensive, and placed reliance on the readiness of Britain and France to come to their aid by attacking Germany from the west. Poland had more than 1,400 miles (2,300 km) of border exposed to German attack.

Unevenly matched
Poland's richest mining and industrial areas were situated close to Germany, and the Poles were determined not to sacrifice any national territory. They chose to defend their long frontiers, rather than position most of their forces on a more defensible line along the rivers Vistula and San. Polish troops, thinly spread and pushed too far forward, found themselves exposed to penetration and encirclement by a faster-moving enemy.

Despair among the ruins
The German bombardment of Warsaw was relentless, with many buildings, including hospitals, razed to the ground. By the end of the war about 85 percent of the city had been destroyed.

KATYN MASSACRE

In 1940 the Soviet secret police executed 22,000 Poles who were being held in Soviet camps. They included army officers captured in September 1939 and others rounded up after the Soviet annexation of eastern Poland. They were shot and buried in mass graves. In 1943 the Nazis found some of the mass graves in Katyn Forest near Smolensk, then under German occupation. The Russians denied responsibility for the crime until 1990.

Les mŕtvuych v Katyne

AN ANTI-SOVIET GERMAN POSTER PUBLICIZING THE KATYN MASSACRE

> "In **starting and waging** a war it is not right that matters but **victory**."

ADOLF HITLER, 1939, QUOTED IN W.L. SHIRER'S "THE RISE AND FALL OF THE THIRD REICH"

The German forces were divided into Army Group North under General Fedor von Bock and Army Group South under General Gerd von Rundstedt. Bock's group attacked from the west and from East Prussia, swiftly cutting off the large number of Polish troops defending the disputed "Polish Corridor." Rundstedt's group made a succession of thrusts forward from German Silesia, and advanced units reached the outskirts of Warsaw by September 8. Polish troops inflicted a few local reverses on the Germans with courageous, if poorly coordinated, counterattacks, but were unable to reverse the tide.

Some Polish forces succeeded in withdrawing behind the Vistula to join reserves in defense of Warsaw, but further east a German enveloping move from north and south along the line of the Bug River left the city's defenders encircled. Germany repeatedly called on

4 MILLION The number of Polish civilians killed under Nazi rule, three quarters of whom were Jews murdered in the ghettos and camps.

the Soviet Union to join in the destruction of Poland, as secretly agreed in Stalin's pact with Hitler the previous month. On September 17, Soviet troops crossed Poland's eastern border. There were no Polish forces available to resist them. In despair, the following day the Polish government and high command sought refuge in neutral Romania. The fighting around Warsaw continued until September 28, when the city surrendered after sustaining heavy damage through German bombing and artillery shelling. The last serious military resistance ended on October 5.

Resounding victory

For Hitler, this awesomely swift victory confirmed his belief in his own military genius and his utter contempt for his enemies. The Western Allies had done next to nothing to aid a country that they had guaranteed to defend. Defeated in a month, the state of Poland had ceased to exist. Some areas in the west were absorbed into Germany itself. Territory east of the Bug River was annexed by the Soviet Union (land that Stalin held on to at the end of the war and that Poland would never regain). The rest of the country, where the vast majority of ethnic Poles lived, became the General Government to be ruled brutally according to Nazi racial theories. Before the end of 1939 Polish Jews, numbering around 5 million people, were being separated from the rest of the Polish population and herded into ghettos.

Germany and the Soviet Union had agreed that they would suppress any form of Polish "agitation." Both the aggressors interpreted this as meaning the massacre or imprisonment of any Poles who might provide leadership to a movement of resistance. By the end of the war Poland was to have lost a fifth of its population to military action, acute hardship, and extermination—the highest percentage population loss of any country in World War II.

Treatment of the Jews

The Nazis herded Jews into restricted areas known as ghettos and forced them to wear a yellow Star of David as identification. Thousands would soon die from starvation and ill treatment.

German and Soviet invasion

Poland's long borders made it almost impossible to defend. On September 17, 1939, Soviet troops advanced from the east, effectively squeezing Poland on all sides. Capitulation of the beleaguered country was inevitable.

KEY
- → German advance/operation
- → Soviet advance
- — German/Soviet demarcation line in Poland
- — Frontiers 1939

AFTER

Despite the relative ease of their victory, the Germans lost 13,000 killed and 27,300 wounded. The Soviet Union lost less than a thousand men in occupying eastern Poland.

THE AFTERMATH

For Poland the casualties were much higher, with **70,000 killed and 133,000 wounded**. More than 900,000 Poles became prisoners of war, 217,000 in the hands of the Soviets and 694,000 captured by the Germans.

CONTINUING THE FIGHT

Some 80,000 Polish servicemen escaped from Poland to neutral countries, later rejoining the war in the service of the **Polish government in exile 110–11 »**, first in Paris and then in London. After the German invasion of the Soviet Union in 1941, the Soviets released about 75,000 Polish prisoners of war, and they joined the Polish forces fighting with the Western Allies. Polish pilots played a major role in the **Battle of Britain 84–85 »**.

WARSAW UPRISING

The Polish resistance, the major part of which was known as the Home Army, carried out intelligence and sabotage operations in occupied Poland throughout the war. In 1944 the Home Army led an **uprising in Warsaw 272–73 »** but this was brutally suppressed by the Nazis.

The Phoney War

After the defeat of Poland, Britain and France faced a long period of inaction, largely because Hitler was frustrated in his desire for a swift offensive in the West. Adopting a defensive strategy, the French waited behind the seemingly secure Maginot Line, while both countries planned for German air attacks.

« BEFORE

In preparing for war the governments of Britain and France drew heavily on their experience in the 1914–18 conflict.

MAXIMIZING RESOURCES
World War I had shown that the **rationing of scarce commodities** would prove necessary and that governments would need to intervene in the **running of the economy** to maximize production for the war effort.

THE THREAT FROM THE SKY
World War I had also seen air raids by German aircraft on cities—London and Paris had both been bombed. **Fear of aerial bombing** had been reinforced by the spectacle of air attacks in the **Spanish Civil War « 38–39** and in **Japan's invasion of China « 40–41**. Governments were therefore ready with plans for "blacking out" lights as a **precaution against night air raids**, and had drawn up programs to provide shelter during raids and to **evacuate vulnerable citizens**.

GAS ATTACKS
Since poison gas had been widely employed in World War I it was expected to be used again. **Civilians in combatant countries** were issued with gas masks, as were military personnel.

When Britain and France declared war on Germany in September 1939, most people expected their country would face imminent death and destruction on a massive scale. However, while Poland experienced the horrors of modern warfare to the full, elsewhere the only significant military action happened at sea. The Western Allies found themselves stuck in a strange interim period of war without combat, soon dubbed the "Phoney War," which would last until April 1940.

Governments had had plenty of opportunity to get ready for war and preparations to cope with air raids had been especially thorough. Expecting that its cities would be devastated by bomb attacks, Britain began a mass evacuation of children from areas considered most at risk of air attack even before the declaration of war. In all, 3.5 million people left their homes. The French evacuated the entire population of the city of Strasbourg, on the border with Germany, to southwest France. Hospitals in British cities were emptied to free beds for bombing casualties. Entertainment venues were closed. The snakes in London Zoo were even killed for fear that a bomb might free them to roam the devastated capital.

When bombing failed to materialize and no great battles erupted on the Western Front, civilian life settled down again. Public entertainments and professional sports resumed, and many evacuees drifted back to their homes. Although ration books were issued, rationing itself was slow to develop—in fact, the first food rationing in Britain did not come into force until January 1940. Meanwhile, however, the preparations to meet air raids continued. More than a million Anderson air-raid shelters to be dug into people's back gardens were distributed free by the government of Britain. The blackout remained the most dramatic evidence of a war in progress. The evening ritual of putting up blackout blinds to stop light from seeping from houses was rigorously enforced by air-raid wardens. Car accidents during the blackout caused far heavier casualties than any military action in the last months of 1939.

Despite a feeling of anticlimax as the war failed to ignite, popular support for the war was general, if unenthusiastic. In order to broaden his government, Prime Minister Neville Chamberlain brought Winston Churchill, an outspoken opponent of appeasement, into the war cabinet, putting him in charge of the Navy. In France Edouard Daladier's government faced a more divided political situation and significant outspoken

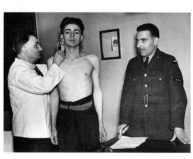

Testing conscripts

In answer to the conscription call, a young recruit undergoes a fitness examination. Britain introduced a limited form of compulsory military service in May 1939, but full recruitment was slow to take off.

Empire troops arrive in Britain

As in World War I, the dominions of the British Empire all declared war on the mother country's enemies. By 1940 Australian troops had arrived, here shown parading across Westminster Bridge in London.

The red rubber mask fitted snugly over the child's head, and was held in place with straps

Child's gas mask
The colorful "Mickey Mouse" gas masks were designed for two- to five-year-old children. They were so-called not because they resembled the cartoon character but to make them less intimidating to the very young.

A blue tin can with perforated holes held a block of asbestos that served to absorb poisonous chemicals

"Four months of **the strangest war** in history."

NEW STATESMAN MAGAZINE, DECEMBER 30, 1939

The German offensives of spring 1940, first in April against Denmark and Norway **74–75 »**, and then in May against France, Belgium, and the Netherlands **76–77 »**, decisively ended the Phoney War.

POLITICAL CHANGES

The French and British **governments fell** in spring 1940. Daladier was replaced as French prime minister by the more vigorous Paul Reynaud in March, and **Chamberlain gave way** to Churchill as British prime minister in May.

BOMBING

The German air bombing campaign against London and other British cities, expected at the outset of the war, actually began in September 1940 during the **Battle of Britain 84–85 »**. The most intense phase of the **Blitz 88–89 »** lasted until May 1941. Initially London was the primary target, with nearly **one million incendiaries** falling on the city **in the space of two months** from September 7.

Civilian air-raid shelters

A British family takes cover in an Anderson air-raid shelter. All seem to be carrying their gas masks—a legal requirement at all times. Families often spent hours in the shelters so many took in food and books, too.

defeatism. Yet both the French premier and Chamberlain firmly rejected a peace proposal from Hitler after his victory over Poland. The Phoney War did not result from a lack of commitment to war by the Western Allies, although it reflected their defensive mentality. In addition, Britain and France had both convinced themselves that time was on their side. They pinned their hopes on a naval blockade that would eventually bring Germany to its knees. Meanwhile, they prepared to meet a German offensive against France should it come.

Such an offensive was certainly Hitler's intention. If he had had his way, the Phoney War would have been brief. As soon as Poland was defeated, and even while he was making his public peace proposal, Hitler instructed his generals to prepare an invasion of France and Belgium.

This invasion was scheduled for November 1939 but it was postponed because of bad weather conditions. Hitler then ordered an offensive for the following January, but yet another postponement was needed after plans for the operation fell into Allied hands.

Troop build-up

These delays meant that the armies of the Allies had more time to organize, but they also faced a demoralizing

1 MILLION The number of coffins ordered for air-raid victims by the British Government at the war's start.

60 THOUSAND The number of Britons killed in air raids overall.

period of inactivity. While France, with its tradition of universal military service, was able to call into being a mass army in weeks, the build-up of the British Army was much slower. A modest British Expeditionary Force had taken up position in northern France by October, but was only gradually expanded. Conscription was slow to take effect in Britain as equipment and training facilities were lacking. All men between the ages of 18 and 41 were liable for military service, but even by May 1940 only those aged up to 27 had actually been called up. At the end of 1939 there were still more than a million unemployed in Britain.

Lull before the storm

Inaction at the Front and the absence of German air attacks bred a degree of complacency among the Allies. They were buoyed up by the modification of the Neutrality Acts by the US Congress, which allowed them to begin purchasing military supplies from the US. By early April 1940 Chamberlain was confident enough to assert that Hitler "had missed the bus." This was to prove the gravest delusion.

TECHNOLOGY

THE MAGINOT LINE

In 1930 France began constructing a line of fortifications along its eastern border with Germany. Named after war minister André Maginot it was intended to spare France a repeat of the bloodletting of the 1914–18 war by keeping the Germans off French soil. Subterranean concrete bunkers, forts, and observation posts were linked by communication tunnels and defended by machine-gun nests and artillery guns mounted in cupolas. A less elaborate Alpine Line further south confronted Italy, while scanter fortifications spread along France's border with neutral Belgium—the Belgians had their own fortified line facing Germany.

THE MAGINOT LINE

Construction of the Maginot Line absorbed much of the French pre-war military budget. In 1940 it proved irrelevant, bypassed by a German advance through the Ardennes.

BEFORE «

Regardless of the British and French declarations of war, Hitler and then Stalin overran Poland in about a month. Britain and France made no attempt to fight back.

HITLER'S NAVY

The size of Germany's navy had been severely restricted by the terms of the Versailles Treaty of 1919. However, in 1935 an Anglo–German naval agreement **gave Germany the right to expand its navy to 35 percent of Britain's naval strength**, including submarines and battleships, both previously banned. In January 1939 **Hitler approved the Z Plan for the huge expansion of the German Navy** proposed by his naval commander-in-chief, Admiral Erich Raeder, but this was not intended to deliver greatly increased naval strength until 1944.

PROTECTING CIVILIANS

When war broke out in September 1939, President Roosevelt called on all sides in the European conflict to **avoid the bombing of civilians or of undefended cities**. In order not to offend the United States, Britain, France, and even Germany at first complied with this request. The Germans, however, argued that their **bombing of Warsaw «58–59** was legitimate as the city was being actively defended by the Polish Army.

bombing of Warsaw «58–59

TECHNOLOGY

U-BOAT

The English term "U-boat" is derived from *Unterseeboot* (German for "submarine"). U-boats ran on diesel engines when on the surface and on special batteries when submerged, as the diesel engines otherwise sucked the oxygen from inside the submarine, depriving the men of air. Much later in 1943 U-boats began to be equipped with the *Schnorchel*, a pipe system of Dutch invention that allowed the diesels to run while submerged. U-boats could remain underwater for a day or more to wait out enemy attacks.

Early Skirmishes

To match the inactivity on land on the Western Front, air and naval actions in the first months of the war did not approach the intensity they were to reach later. There were dramatic small-scale successes for each side, especially at sea, but neither the Allies nor the Germans made any decisive gains.

The months following the outbreak of World War II in Europe were dubbed the "phoney war" because of the absence of major fighting. The French Army briefly marched 16 miles (25 km) into the German Saarland in September 1939, while Hitler was busy crushing Poland, but swiftly withdrew and took no further offensive action. The British Expeditionary Force (BEF) sent to France did not suffer its first casualty until December that year. Yet, during this period of inactivity on land, there were some very notable skirmishes in the air and also much action at sea.

Both sides were deterred from starting bombing campaigns against one another's cities by a desire to avoid escalating the war—raids would obviously provoke retaliation in kind from their enemy—and to avoid alienating the neutral United States. The ruthless attitudes of total war had not yet taken hold—Britain's air minister, Sir Kingsley Wood, rejected a plan to bomb German forests because they were private property.

To avoid the risk of damaging property or killing civilians, the RAF sent its bombers to attack German warships. Their orders were not to bomb any targets on land or any merchant ships. These early raids revealed serious defects in Britain's preparations for air war: bombers had difficulty in locating their targets; their bombs often did not explode; and the bombers, attacking in daylight, were shown to be hopelessly vulnerable to German defenses. Of ten aircraft that bombed warships at Wilhelmshaven on the second day of the war, seven were shot down. In two similar raids that took place in mid-December, 18 of the 36 bombers taking part were destroyed. Such losses were clearly unsustainable. Most RAF operations were restricted to minelaying at sea by day and the dropping of propaganda leaflets over Germany by night. According to Arthur Harris, future head of RAF Bomber Command, the RAF's leafleting campaign "supplied the Continent's requirement for toilet paper for the five long years of war."

The Luftwaffe also used its aircraft to attack shipping, but Germany's most striking offensive blows were delivered by U-boats. On the evening of September 3, 1939, just hours after Britain declared war, British passenger liner *Athenia* was sunk by a torpedo fired by *U-30*. Of the 112 passengers

> **189,000** The tonnage of Allied merchant shipping sunk in December 1939. Of the 73 ships lost, 25 were victims of U-boat attack; almost all the rest fell to mines. One U-boat was sunk.

Blenheim bomber

In 1935 the prototype Blenheim was faster than any RAF fighter but by 1939–40 it was outmoded, with weak defensive armament and a modest bombload.

killed, 28 were American. Deeply embarrassed, Germany denied that a U-boat had been responsible. The German response was very different two weeks later when *U-29* inflicted the first major loss on the Royal Navy, torpedoing aircraft carrier HMS *Courageous*.

Attacking Scapa Flow

The commander of the German Navy's U-boats, Admiral Karl Dönitz, next tried an even more spectacular coup, sending *U-47*, under Lieutenant Commander Günther Prien, to attack the Royal Navy's main base at Scapa Flow in the Orkney Islands, off the north of Scotland. Prien penetrated the harbor's defences on the night of 13/14 October and sank the battleship *Royal Oak* at its moorings.

These setbacks were disconcerting for Britain's new First Lord of the Admiralty, Winston Churchill. But,

Use of mines

Soviet sailors at work defusing a mine. Around half a million naval mines were laid during the war, by all nations. The most common types (like the one shown here) were activated by contact with a target ship.

> **"** After **such losses** it is assumed that the enemy will not give any more opportunities of **practice-shooting** at Wellingtons. **"**

FROM A GERMAN FIGHTER SQUADRON'S REPORT, DECEMBER 18, 1939

Germany's victories in Western and Northern Europe in the spring of 1940 ended the period of early skirmishes.

ADMIRAL GRAF SPEE'S PRISONERS
Before the River Plate episode, *Admiral Graf Spee* had passed some **300 captured merchant seamen** to a German tanker, *Altmark*, which was to take them to Germany. On February 16, 1940 the British destroyer *Cossack* **surprised and boarded** *Altmark* in neutral Norwegian waters. The prisoners were freed and **carried to Britain**.

STRATEGIC BOMBING
The RAF first attacked inland targets on May 15, 1940, bombing **oil installations and railways** in the Ruhr. Both sides began bombing cities in early autumn 1940 **88–89 »**. After the **fall of France 82–83 »** the Germans stepped up the U-boat offensive from bases on France's Atlantic coast.

CAPTAIN OF *ADMIRAL GRAF SPEE*, HANS LANGSDORFF

as in World War I, the key issue was whether Britain could keep open the sea routes that brought vital food and other imports from North America and the British Empire.

German U-boats—at this time few in number and based far from the Atlantic sea lanes—were only one of the hazards for Allied merchant ships. They also suffered heavy losses to magnetic mines, a menace eventually negated by the widespread degaussing of ship's hulls to neutralize their magnetic fields from late 1939. They were also prey to German aircraft and marauding long-range surface warships.

Battle of the River Plate
The most successful German raider during the early part of the war was the pocket battleship *Admiral Graf Spee*.

50 The percentage of RAF bombers that were shot down during the daylight raid on ships around the port of Wilhelmshaven on December 18, 1939, an unsustainable rate of attrition.

It sank nine ships in the Indian Ocean and South Atlantic. On December 13, 1939 the Royal Navy cruisers *Exeter*, *Ajax*, and *Achilles* located *Admiral Graf Spee* off the estuary of the River Plate. The Allied squadron was outgunned but succeeded in damaging the ship, forcing it to put into port at Montevideo, in neutral Uruguay, for repairs. Believing himself trapped by a superior force, on December 17 the German captain, Hans Langsdorff, scuttled *Admiral Graf Spee* in the River Plate estuary.

The victory at the River Plate was a boost to British morale and reflected well on Churchill, identified as the most bellicose member of the British war cabinet. Yet, both at sea and in the air, Britain had mostly had the worst of its early skirmishes with Germany.

Burning wreck
The *Admiral Graf Spee* aground and burning after being scuttled by its crew off Montevideo. Pictures of the ship's radar aerials (visible at the top of the mast) gave British experts information about German progress in this field.

The Winter War

The Nazi–Soviet Pact set Stalin free to expand Soviet influence along his country's western borders. Stalin trusted nobody and territorial expansion was seen as much as a buffer against a future attack by Hitler as an absolute gain for Soviet power. He did not get all his own way with Finland, however.

« BEFORE

In 1917–18, during the Russian Revolution, Finland and the Baltic States of Estonia, Lithuania, and Latvia declared themselves independent of Russian rule.

OUTSIDE THE SOVIET UNION
In the ensuing years the revolutionary **Bolshevik regime succeeded in reasserting authority** over most of the former Russian Empire, but Finland and the Baltic States managed to uphold their independence.

MILITARY PURGE
In May 1937 **eight senior commanders** in the Soviet Red Army, including Marshal Mikhail Tukhachevsky, were arrested by the Soviet secret police. The eight were **accused of plotting** to collaborate with a German invasion of the Soviet Union that would allow them to overthrow Stalin. All of the men were executed. A **wholesale purge of the Soviet officer corps** followed in which 45 percent of all senior army and navy commanders were killed or fired.

UNLIKELY ALLIES
The **Nazi–Soviet Pact of August 1939 « 54** and an agreement between the Germans and the Soviets after their partition of Poland gave the Soviet Union the green light to **extend its influence over Finland and the Baltic States.**

At the end of November 1939, while the Phoney War still prevailed in Western Europe, a shooting war broke out further east between Finland and the Soviet Union. The Soviet–Finnish conflict followed directly from the Soviet accord with Nazi Germany and the absorption of eastern Poland into the Soviet Union. Estonia, Latvia, and Lithuania, with no hope of any outside support, were forced to sign treaties of "mutual assistance" with the Soviet Union, giving the Soviets the right to establish bases on their territory.

Finland under threat
At the same time Finland was asked to cede some territory near Leningrad (St. Petersburg), as well as various naval and air bases. In compensation, the Soviets offered Finland a chunk of largely worthless land in Karelia. The Finns refused the Soviet offer and negotiations broke down in mid-

November. Stalin then decided that Finland was to be conquered and incorporated into the Soviet Union.

On November 30, 1939, Soviet troops launched an assault across the Finnish border. Almost half a million Soviet

430,000 The number of Finns who lost their homes and their land in the territory taken by the Soviets at the end of the Winter War.

troops confronted around 130,000 Finnish soldiers. The Finnish air force was outnumbered ten to one. The Soviet commander, Marshal Kliment Voroshilov, promised a swift victory. The Finns, however, were in no mood to give in. The bombing of Helsinki at

Field Marshal Gustav von Mannerheim
A national hero for his role in securing Finnish independence at the end of World War I, he returned from retirement to lead the Finnish Army in 1939–40.

Finnish machine-gun position

Well-camouflaged Finnish troops in action with an M32 machine gun. This gun was based on a Russian design but had been improved for winter use by the Finns.

the start of the war aimed to undermine the Finnish will to resist, but it only strengthened their resolve.

Finland had constructed a formidable system of fortified positions along the southern stretch of its border, known as the Mannerheim Line. Attacked by the Soviets with an unimaginative frontal infantry advance supported by artillery, the defenses held firm, and heavy casualties were inflicted on the invaders. Soviet soldiers were not equipped to fight in the ice and snow while the Finns were used to the conditions, deploying ski troops who wore white winter camouflage. The Soviet's technological advantage was negated as Finnish snipers picked off officers and "Molotov cocktails"— bottles of burning gasoline— were lobbed into tanks. By the start of 1940 the invasion had stalled.

International opinion

The spectacle of a small country defending itself gallantly against a powerful invader inevitably attracted widespread sympathy and admiration.

but the Norwegian and Swedish governments refused to co-operate. Churchill, the most aggressive of British ministers, advocated using the expeditionary force primarily for an invasion of Norway and Sweden, which would cut off German supplies of iron ore, carried from Swedish mines via the Norwegian port of Narvik. In March 1940 the British and French

Helsinki bombed

Soviet air attacks on Helsinki and other Finnish cities caused international outrage in 1939, but were feeble by comparison with later events in World War II; reportedly fewer than 100 Finns were killed.

The threat of Allied action against Norway and Sweden, made apparent during the Soviet–Finnish War, was partly responsible for Hitler's decision to occupy Norway.

MORE SOVIET GAINS

On June 17, 1940, Soviet troops **occupied Estonia, Latvia, and Lithuania** and incorporated them into the Soviet Union. Hundreds of thousands of their people were **executed or sent to prison camps** in Siberia.

FINLAND STRIKES BACK

In June 1941 **Germany invaded the Soviet Union 134–135 »**. Finland joined in the attack to recover territory it had lost in 1940. The Finns called this the **Continuation War**, to emphasize its link with the Winter War.

A MOLOTOV COCKTAIL

" ... the enemy attacks resembled **a badly directed orchestra** with every instrument **ignoring the beat**."

FIELD MARSHAL MANNERHEIM DESCRIBING THE INITIAL SOVIET OFFENSIVE

The moribund League of Nations roused itself to expel the Soviet Union. In Britain and France there was a clamor for intervention in defense of the Finns. Since the Soviet Union was at this time acting as a loyal ally of Germany, the idea of fighting the Soviets did not seem unreasonable. At least it offered the prospect of an end to the inertia of the Phoney War.

The British and French governments agreed to assemble an expeditionary force for dispatch to the Baltic. But there were many difficulties in the path of such an operation. The only realistic way to send troops to Finland was across neutral Norway and Sweden,

governments agreed to send the troops and violate Norway's and Sweden's neutrality. But before the force could embark, Finland had to sue for peace.

Finnish defeat

The military situation had been reversed by the dispatch of 27 extra Soviet divisions to the Finnish front and the replacement of Voroshilov by the more effective Marshal Semyon Timoshenko. The Soviets battered through the Mannerheim Line, leaving Finland exposed to certain defeat. Soviet losses had been heavy—some 127,000 killed—and Stalin was prepared to abandon his

conquest of Finland in return for a swift end to the fighting. The Finns had to cede the territory and bases demanded by the Soviet Union, but retained their independence.

Having assembled a force to defend Finland and then failed to send it in time, the Western democracies were once more discredited. The debacle led directly to the fall of the Daladier government in France, the more pugnacious Paul Reynaud taking over as French premier.

In the Soviet Union the revealed deficiencies of the Soviet Army led to military reforms that proved their worth later in the war. Both in Germany and the West, however, the impression remained that the Soviet Union were militarily incompetent and unlikely to offer effective resistance to a German invasion.

Furious resistance

Alone and unsupported, the bold and courageous Finns held off the Soviet offensive for two months until overwhelmed by vastly superior manpower and being forced to fight on an extended front.

Lahti L-39 20 mm anti-tank rifle

This Finnish anti-tank rifle, nicknamed the "Elephant Gun," saw limited service in the Winter War. Anti-tank rifles generally were soon replaced during the war by larger and more powerful anti-tank artillery weapons.

Barrel

10-round magazine

Cheek rest helped the firer take advantage of the rifle's long-range accuracy

Ski-type mounting for use on snow

5 Feb 25 1939
Slow Soviet progress in the far north halted at Nautsi

Barents Sea

Petsamo

Nautsi

Murmansk

14TH ARMY

3 Dec 11 1939
Finns halt Soviet advance on Suomussalmi

Kandalaksha

Kemijarvi

Markajarvi

9TH ARMY

1 Nov 30 1939
Soviets invade at several points on the border simultaneously

Oulu

Kem

Suomussalmi

Kuhmo

U S S R

SWEDEN

F I N L A N D

8TH ARMY

Joensuu

Lake Onega

2 Dec 6 1939
Soviets make first of several attempts to break through the Mannerheim Line

KARELIA

Lake Ladoga

Turku

Viipuri

13TH ARMY

Hanko

Helsinki

Leningrad

7TH ARMY

Gulf of Bothnia

Tallinn

E S T O N I A

4 Feb 1 1940
Massive Soviet offensive against Mannerheim Line

Baltic Sea

L A T V I A

6 Mar 13 1940
Soviet attack on Viipuri forces Finns to agree to peace terms of Treaty of Moscow

L I T H U A N I A

EAST PRUSSIA

N

0 ___ 300 km
0 ___ 300 miles

KEY

→ Soviet advance
→ Finnish advance
---- Mannerheim Line
— Frontiers 1939

DICTATOR OF THE SOVIET UNION Born 1878 Died 1953

Joseph **Stalin**

> "**This war** is not as in the past; whoever **occupies a territory** also imposes on it his **own social system.**"

JOSEPH STALIN, APRIL 1945

Stalin was born Iosif Vissarionovich Dzhugashvili in a town in Georgia, then a part of the Russian Empire. Brought up in poverty, he was educated at a theological college, but instead of entering the priesthood he became involved in radical politics. Joining the Bolshevik faction of the Russian Social Democratic Labor Party, he adopted the revolutionary pseudonym Stalin ("Steel"). His subversive activities won the admiration of the party leadership and he was made a member of their central committee in 1912.

From the Bolshevik seizure of power in October 1917 to the establishment of the Soviet Union as the world's first communist-ruled state in December 1922, Stalin was a hard-working and ruthless member of the revolutionary

leadership, though often overshadowed by his more flamboyant, intellectual colleagues. However, when a struggle developed over succession to the Soviet leadership, Stalin proved superior to them all in his cunning, sure-footed political maneuvers, and grasp of the realities of power. Exploiting his position as Communist Party general secretary to establish an iron grip on the party and the state, by 1929 he had made himself the undisputed master of the Soviet Union and leader of the worldwide communist movement.

Man of Steel

At the height of his power, Stalin almost always appeared in uniform. Every Soviet victory in the war was attributed to his military genius.

Young activist

In 1902 Stalin was arrested for organizing strike actions by workers at oilfields in his native Georgia. This photograph of the 23-year-old political activist was taken by the tsarist police for their files.

Kindly leader

A 1930s propaganda poster portrays Stalin as the benign leader of Soviet peasants, workers, and armed forces. Such images were produced while Stalin enslaved and murdered millions of his people in the name of progress.

Rather than believing in the possibility of an imminent world revolution, Stalin was obsessed with ensuring the survival of the Soviet Union in a hostile world. He saw himself as the ruler of a weak and backward country that needed to be transformed at breakneck pace from an archaic peasant society into a modern industrial state. Only this would enable the Soviet Union to defend itself against its enemies. Stalin was prepared to use any degree of terror to achieve the transformation of Soviet society and to defend his own grasp on power against potential rivals.

Transforming the Soviet Union

Throughout the 1930s Stalin drove the Soviet Union forward in a rush for economic growth that was horrifyingly wasteful of human lives. Millions of ordinary citizens were used as slave labor, starved in man-made famines, or killed by the apparatus of state terror. Thousands of members of the Soviet elite, including party leaders and commanders of the armed forces, were arrested by the secret police and executed after show trials.

At the same time, as the situation in Europe grew increasingly dangerous, Stalin moved cautiously in international affairs. At first inclined to see Nazi Germany as no different from any other capitalist state, by 1938 Stalin was concerned enough about German ambitions to think about cooperation with the Western democracies. He always suspected, however, that Britain and France would try to turn Hitler against the Soviet Union, and in August 1939 Stalin decided that a deal with the Nazis offered the best potential for Soviet security.

> ## "It is time to **finish retreating**. Not one step back!"
>
> ORDER FROM STALIN, 28 JULY 1942

БУДЕМ ДОСТОЙНЫМИ СЫНАМИ И ДОЧЕРЬМИ НАШЕЙ ВЕЛИКОЙ ПАРТИИ ЛЕНИНА-СТАЛИНА

> ## "**History** shows that there are **no invincible armies** and that there **never have been**."
>
> RADIO BROADCAST BY STALIN, JULY 3, 1941

Marshal's insignia

Stalin took the rank of Marshal of the Soviet Union in 1943, wearing this insignia. In 1945 he was declared Generalissimo, a rank created for him alone.

Stalin was therefore caught off guard when the Germans invaded in 1941. The catastrophic defeats suffered by the Soviet Union could have brought his downfall, yet Stalin reasserted his leadership of the "Great Patriotic War," using a mix of exhortation and terror to inspire heroic resistance by the Soviet people. His military policy of "no retreat, no surrender" was immensely costly, but unlike Hitler he came to trust his generals more as the war went on, sensibly bowing to their military expertise. Stalin handled the wartime alliance with the United States and Britain in masterly fashion. Never trusting his allies, he successfully sustained a working relationship with Roosevelt and Churchill on the basis of temporary mutual interest, while never wavering in his single-minded dedication to extending the power of the Soviet Union.

Postwar anxieties

Victory over Germany did nothing to relax Stalin's paranoia. His extension of the Soviet system to Eastern Europe and his suspicion of the Western powers led to the "Iron Curtain" division of Europe and the Cold War confrontation with the United States. Yet his cautious nature and persistent sense of the vulnerability of the Soviet Union made him avoid direct armed conflict with the West. Despite the fact that he was responsible for destroying the lives of millions of Soviet citizens, his death in 1953 was genuinely mourned by the majority of his people.

Lying in state

Stalin's death in 1953 was the occasion for a huge display of public mourning. In Moscow Soviet citizens lined up for hours to file past his body.

3

GERMANY TRIUMPHANT

1940

The German "Blitzkrieg" unleashed in Denmark, Norway, the Netherlands, Belgium, and France seemed unstoppable. As Britain found itself the next target of Hitler's war machine, Italy, Germany's ally, seized its moment to open new theatres of war in Africa and the Mediterranean

...twaffe begins ...ritish cities on ... 7. The attacks ...ate on London ...ndustrial areas like Coventry.

At Dunkirk the Royal Navy, assisted by many small civilian boats, evacuates over 330,00 British and French troops from Northern France.

The Germans invade Denmark and Norway in April. Denmark falls without a fight, but Norwegian partisans fight until June 10.

...OPE

ICELAND

NORWAY

SWEDEN

FINLAND

oe Islands ...enmark)

ESTONIA

LATVIA

LITHUANIA

North Sea DENMARK

Baltic Sea

...TAIN

GER.

NETH.

POLAND

USSR

BEL. LUX.

GERMANY

SLOVAKIA

FRANCE

SWITZ.

HUNGARY

ROMANIA

YUGOSLAVIA

BULGARIA

Black Sea

ITALY

ALB. (to Italy)

...PAIN

M e d i t e r r a n e a n   S e a

GREECE

TURKEY

DODECANESE (to Italy)

SYRIA (French mandate)

IRAQ (British mandate)

TUNISIA (to France)

CYPRUS

PALESTINE (British mandate)

...CO ...ce) ALGERIA (to France)

LIBYA (to Italy)

EGYPT

ATLANTIC OCEAN

NORWAY

SWEDEN

FINLAND

BRITAIN

POLAND

GERMANY

FRANCE

ITALY

Black Sea

SPAIN

TURKEY

SYRIA

IRAQ

PERSIA

AFGHANISTAN

Caspian Sea

MOROCCO

TUNISIA

NEPAL

ALGERIA

LIBYA

EGYPT

NEJD (Saudi)

OMAN

INDIA

RIO DE ORO

FRENCH WEST AFRICA

ANGLO-EGYPTIAN SUDAN

ASIR

YEMEN

CE...

GAMBIA

PORTUGUESE GUINEA

CAMEROONS (British mandate)

SIERRA LEONE

NIGERIA

FRENCH EQUATORIAL AFRICA

ITALIAN EAST AFRICA

FRENCH SOMALILAND

LIBERIA

GOLD COAST

CAMEROONS (French mandate)

UGANDA

KENYA

BRITISH SOMALILAND

BELGIAN CONGO

TANGANYIKA (British mandate)

NYASALAND

NORTHERN RHODESIA

ANGOLA (to Portugal)

SOUTHERN RHODESIA

MADAGASCAR

SOUTH WEST AFRICA

BECHUANA-LAND

PORTUGUESE EAST AFRICA

UNION OF SOUTH AFRICA

SWAZILAND

BASUTOLAND

The Italians invade British Somaliland from Abyssinia. They also make small incursions into Kenya and Sudan.

...rmans launch ...ive against the ...ries and France ...10. By June 14

Italy enters the war on the side of Germany on June 10, and declares war on Britain and France. Italian troops

1940

In the Sino–Japanese War, the Japanese do not undertake any great new offensives, but continue to bomb Nationalist towns and bases around the capital Chungking.

President Roosevelt wins an historic third term. Despite his close relationship with Britain, he is still reluctant to join the war in Europe.

The United States agrees to send Britain 50 old destroyers, mainly for use as convoy escorts. In exchange it receives land in various British possessions on which to build bases.

General Wavell's Western Desert Force enjoys great success against the Italians, capturing thousands of them. The fighting in North Africa will intensify when the Germans under Rommel are obliged to come to the Italians' aid.

THE WORLD IN DECEMBER 1940

- Axis powers (Germany and Italy) and allies
- Axis conquests to Dec 1940
- ◆ Vichy France and colonies
- Japanese Empire
- Japanese conquests to Dec 1940
- Allied states
- Allied conquests to Dec 1940
- Neutral states
- Territory occupied by USSR
- Frontiers Sep 1939

over Britain gave way to a nine-month night-bombing campaign against British cities and war industry. By the time the Blitz came to an end in May 1941, Hitler's plans for the invasion of the Soviet Union, under consideration since July 1940—were well advanced.

For the British, 1940 provided a few crumbs of comfort, not least preservation from a German invasion and a strengthening of national morale during the Blitz. Material support from the United States was a welcome boost, although this aid had come at a price. In North Africa in the fall of 1940, victory over the Italians by Western Desert Force, the British and Commonwealth forces under the command of General Wavell, provided a welcome respite from the litany of Allied defeats which had marked the early part of the summer. Unlike the Axis, however, the British seemingly had few strategic options as the year came to an end.

TIMELINE 1940

Scandinavia invaded by Germany ▪ **Blitzkrieg: Invasion of Luxembourg, Belgium, the Netherlands, and France** ▪ Escape from Dunkirk ▪ **The Battle of Britain** ▪ **The Blitz** ▪ British bases exchanged for US backing ▪ **Italy enters the war**

JANUARY	FEBRUARY	MARCH	APRIL	MAY	JUNE
JANUARY 8 Rationing introduced in Britain. The first foodstuffs to be rationed are bacon, butter, and sugar.	❯ A box of British wartime eggs		**APRIL 9** Germany invades Denmark and Norway. Their troops land at major ports and drop by parachute. **APRIL 10** British destroyers attack German shipping in fjord leading to Narvik.		**JUNE 6** German panzers break through the French defences on the Somme. **JUNE 10** Norway surrenders to Germany. ≪ Stuka dive-bomber
			APRIL 13 Second battle of Narvik. Germans lose eight destroyers. **APRIL 16–19** British, French, and Polish troops land at Harstad for an attack on Narvik.	**MAY 10** Start of Germany's *Blitzkrieg* invasion of Luxembourg, Belgium, the Netherlands, and France. **MAY 10** Winston Churchill becomes British prime minister.	
JANUARY 8 Major victory by Finnish forces over Soviets at Suomussalmi.	**FEBRUARY 11** The Red Army finally breaches the Finnish Mannerheim Line.	⌃ German paratroops landing in Norway **MARCH 12** Treaty of Moscow brings the Winter War between the USSR and Finland to an end. The USSR makes a number of territorial gains.	**APRIL 30** German forces seize Dumbas, a key center of the railroad network, and Norwegian resistance collapses.	**MAY 13** Three German Panzer divisions cross the Meuse near Sedan. **MAY 14** Bombing of Dutch city of Rotterdam. **MAY 15** The Netherlands surrender.	
⌃ Finnish machine-gun crew		**MARCH 16** German bombing raid on British naval base at Scapa Flow in the Orkney Islands, Scotland.		**MAY 27–JUNE 3** Dunkirk evacuation. Despite constant German bombing raids, more than 330,000 British and French troops are ferried to safety in Britain from Dunkirk.	⌃ Italian military parade **JUNE 10** Italy declares war on France and Britain. **JUNE 14** German troops enter Paris.
	FEBRUARY 16 Royal Navy forces board the German steamer *Altmark* and free 299 prisoners of war. Norway protests as the incident takes place in neutral Norwegian waters.	**MARCH 21** Following the resignation of Edouard Daladier, Paul Reynaud becomes prime minister of France and forms a new cabinet.		**MAY 28** Surrender of Belgium.	**JUNE 22** France, now led by Marshal Pétain, signs armistice with Germany.

❯ Winston Churchill

" … the Battle of France is over. I expect that the **Battle of Britain** is about to begin … The whole **fury and might** of the enemy must very soon be turned upon us.**"**

WINSTON CHURCHILL IN A SPEECH TO PARLIAMENT, JUNE 18, 1940

| JULY | AUGUST | SEPTEMBER | OCTOBER | NOVEMBER | DECEMBER | » |

SEPTEMBER 2
The US gives Britain 50 old destroyers in exchange for bases in the Caribbean and Newfoundland.

SEPTEMBER 7
Start of the Blitz. Port of London attacked by 354 German bombers.

NOVEMBER 5
Roosevelt reelected for a third term as US president.

NOVEMBER 11
Successful British raid on Italian port of Taranto by torpedo bombers from aircraft carrier *Illustrious*.

DECEMBER
Greeks push the invading Italian forces back over the Albanian border. The Germans are forced to send 50,000 troops to bolster Italy's position.

⌃ Spitfire

JULY 10
Start of the first phase of the Battle of Britain. The German Luftwaffe and the RAF battle in the skies above the English Channel.

AUGUST 3
Italian forces enter British Somaliland in East Africa. The small British garrison withdraws.

AUGUST 14
Britain and US agree on Lend-Lease scheme.

⌃ British poster boosting morale during the Blitz

OCTOBER 5
Daylight air attacks on Britain come to an end.

⌄ Surveying bomb damage in London

DECEMBER 9
Start of Operation Compass, British offensive in the Western Desert. Tens of thousands of Italians surrender as their forces are driven out of Egypt.

Beat 'FIREBOMB FRITZ'

BRITAIN SHALL NOT BURN

BRITAIN'S FIRE GUARD IS BRITAIN'S DEFENCE

AUGUST 15
Luftwaffe launches five big attacks, chiefly against Fighter Command airfields.

AUGUST 23–24
First German bombing raids on Central London.

⌃ Italian troops in retreat across the Egyptian desert

NOVEMBER 14–15
Massive German bombing raid on Coventry, England.

DECEMBER 29
Roosevelt's "Arsenal of Democracy" speech, urging Americans to help arm Britain.

DECEMBER 29–30
Devastating firebomb raid sets much of the City of London ablaze.

⌃ Air raid warden's handbooks

JULY 16
Hitler orders preparations for the invasion of Britain to begin.

AUGUST 25–26
The British launch a retaliatory raid on Berlin.

SEPTEMBER 17
Hitler calls off Operation Sealion, the invasion of Britain.

SEPTEMBER 27
Germany, Italy, and Japan sign Tripartite Pact.

OCTOBER 18
Britain reopens the Burma Road, a vital supply route for Chinese forces fighting the Japanese. It had been closed since July.

NOVEMBER 20
Hungary joins the Tripartite Pact.

NOVEMBER 23
Romania, under threat from Russia, joins the Tripartite Pact.

» US factory producing aircraft parts for Britain

JULY 23
USSR occupies Latvia, Lithuania, and Estonia.

SEPTEMBER
Renewed evacuations of children from London with start of the Blitz.

OCTOBER 28
Italy invades Greece.

OCTOBER 29
Draft lottery in the US to select the first men to do military service.

« Young evacuee leaving London during the Blitz

The Invasion of Denmark and Norway

In April 1940 two neutral nations were suddenly attacked and overrun by Germany. Throughout the short-lived campaign, Anglo–French forces were revealed as ill-prepared, poorly equipped, and badly led, presaging the disasters that were shortly to follow in France.

On February 21, 1940, Hitler tasked General Nikolaus von Falkenhorst, who was in command of the XXI Corps during the Polish campaign, with the invasion of Norway. Armed with a simple travel guide, Falkenhorst came up with a plan and a list of operational requirements. Within just one week Hitler had added the occupation of Denmark to Falkenhorst's duties as an afterthought, in order to provide a land bridge to Norway.

Hitler believed, correctly, that Britain and France were planning to send troops across northern Norway and into Sweden, ostensibly to help the Finns in their Winter War with the Soviet Union but in fact to cut off Germany's large iron ore imports from northern Sweden. Although the Finns had to surrender in March, Anglo–French plans to block the iron ore traffic continued to be developed. The British intended in early April to lay mines in Norwegian territorial waters ("the Leads") to force the ore ships into international waters where Allied vessels could attack them.

Qualification badge
German paratroopers received this token once they had completed their training.

Missing the target

On April 7, the German invasion force set sail carrying eight divisions. On the same day the Royal Navy was beginning its operation to mine the Norwegian Leads. Although the German forces were spotted by British reconnaissance aircraft, the sighting was misinterpreted by the Admiralty, which was convinced that the German fleet was readying itself for a breakout into the Atlantic. The British Home Fleet therefore set sail on an interception course with a nonexistent foe while the German fleet remained unmolested.

Norway's response

The Norwegian government, however, was warned what was afoot, although its ability to respond was limited. Its 15,000-strong army was capable of only local defense, and the government

Fierce battles at Narvik
German warships and transport ships burn in Narvik harbor after the second British naval attack. The narrow waters of Ofotfjord leading to Narvik meant that the naval battles there were short-range deadly affairs.

placed unwise store on its neutrality—it thought that Britain's naval superiority would make a German attack impossible.

Nevertheless, in the Norwegian capital, Oslo, there was stiff resistance. The elderly guns of the harbor fort sank the heavy cruiser *Blücher*, and this check enabled the Norwegian royal family to escape north to Trondheim. Falkenhorst had to improvise, air-landing 3,000 troops at Oslo's airport, Fornebu, and seizing control of it.

The Germans had an easier time when they came ashore at a number of points along Norway's coast, at Kristiansand, Stavanger, Bergen,

« **BEFORE**

Norway was important to Hitler as a strategic springboard for aerial attacks against Britain.

VITAL RESOURCES

The British naval blockade **threatened the route of German supply ships** bearing iron ore from Sweden through the **port of Narvik**. Hitler was also advised that Danish airfields would be needed to support the invasion of Norway and therefore decided that **Denmark should be occupied simultaneously**.

GERMAN PREPARATIONS

For the occupation of Denmark, the German high command allotted **two motorized brigades to drive up the Jutland peninsula** to seize airfields that had been captured in parachute landings, as had the vital bridges between the islands. The **old battleship *Schleswig-Holstein*** was to force the entrance of Copenhagen harbor and **land troops to take the capital**. In Norway German troops were to make five widely separated landings on the Norwegian coast, backed by parachute drops.

"There are six Chiefs of Staff and three Ministers who have voice in Norwegian operations. But **no one is responsible for the creation of military policy.**"
WINSTON CHURCHILL, FIRST LORD OF THE ADMIRALTY, 1940

The beginning of airborne warfare
German parachute landings in Norway allowed the capture of key strategic points before consolidating forces arrived. These attacks, the first of their kind, proved highly effective.

Trondheim, and as far north as Narvik. By now, however, they were opposed not only by the Norwegians but also by the British and French who, because of their preparations to intervene in Finland, had contingents ready to sail for Norway. By April 18, the British 146th Infantry Brigade had come ashore north of Trondheim and 148th Infantry Brigade had landed south of the city. They were soon engaged by the Germans who were moving north from Oslo up the Gubrandsdal and Osterdal valleys. The British did not fare well. Badly equipped, ineptly led, and under constant air attack, they could make no headway, and by May 3 both brigades had been evacuated from the ports at which they had landed.

Battles for Narvik

To the north the situation remained fluid. In the first naval battle of Narvik, fought on April 10, the Royal Navy's 2nd Destroyer Flotilla, commanded by Captain B.A.W. Warburton-Lee, sailed into Ofotfjord, sinking seven German

10 The number of destroyers the Kriegsmarine lost at Narvik. Other major ships were sunk or damaged off Norway, weakening the German navy before the planned invasion of England.

troop transports and two destroyers, and damaging three more, while losing two of his destroyers. Warburton-Lee was mortally wounded and was awarded a posthumous Victoria Cross.

In the small hours of April 13 a Royal Navy squadron, commanded by Vice-Admiral W.J. Whitworth and consisting of the battleship *Warspite* and nine destroyers, arrived to complete the destruction of the German naval force, reducing the German navy's effective destroyer force by half.

In the two battles of Narvik the Royal Navy had destroyed the major part of General Eduard Dietl's 3rd Mountain Division, and its commander had escaped ashore with only 2,000 troops and 2,600 sailors with whom to fight some 25,000 Allied troops. From April 14 Dietl, one of Hitler's favorite generals, found himself besieged in Narvik, which was for the moment out of range of German air cover. He was eventually forced to retreat to the Swedish border, which he reached at the end of May. By then the collapse

Rescued sailors
First Lord of the Admiralty Winston Churchill inspects the surviving crew of the destroyer *Hardy*, which was lost at Narvik.

Wrong-footed
As well as a streamlined command structure, the Germans enjoyed air superiority that overpowered Allied and Norwegian resistance.

4 Apr 10 & 13
Royal Navy inflicts heavy losses on German destroyers and supply ships at Narvik

7 Apr 16
Start of landings of force of British, French, and Polish troops at Harstad

11 Jun 8
Allied evacuation from Narvik

2 Apr 9
German seaborne troops land at Kristiansand, Bergen, Trondheim, and Narvik

9 Apr 24
Norwegians attack Germans south of Narvik, but are forced to retreat

6 Apr 16
British and French troops land at Namsos for attack on Trondheim

10 May 2
Germans force Allied evacuation from Namsos

5 Apr 16
British and French troops land at Andalsnes

8 Apr 20
German and British troops clash around Lillehammer

3 Apr 9
During landings at Oslo, German cruiser *Blücher* is sunk, but city is soon in German hands

1 Apr 9, 1940
German forces invade Denmark

Harstad, Narvik, Bodo, Namsos, Steinkjer, Trondheim, Storen, Andalsnes, Dombas, NORWAY, Lillehammer, Bergen, Oslo, Stavanger, Kristiansand, Stockholm, SWEDEN, FINLAND, Gulf of Bothnia, ESTONIA, LATVIA, LITHUANIA, Baltic Sea, Scapa Flow, Rosyth, North Sea, BRITAIN, Aalborg, DENMARK, Copenhagen, Wilhelmshaven, GERMANY, EAST PRUSSIA

0   300 km
0   300 miles

KEY
➡ German landing/advance
➡ Allied landing/advance
⬤ German airborne landing
— Frontiers 1939

of the Allied front in France had made the Allied campaign in Norway pointless and their forces in the country were withdrawn in early June. King Haakon VII and his ministers escaped to Britain to set up a government in exile.

The new prime minister

Before the French campaign had begun, the dithering, chaos, and half-measures that had unfortunately characterized Allied operations in Norway brought down Neville Chamberlain's British government. Ironically, as Britain's navy minister, Winston Churchill bore a large share of responsibility for the problems of the Norwegian campaign, but when the political maneuvering ended he was chosen to be the new prime minister. Churchill took office on May 10, the day Hitler attacked on the Western Front. He would soon transform Britain's war effort, but for the moment more troubles lay ahead.

AFTER

The Germans installed a puppet regime headed by a Norwegian Nazi, Vidkun Quisling, whose name was to become synonymous with traitor.

CONTACTS
From Britain the **exiled Norwegian leaders 110–111 ≫** maintained secret contacts with Norway, and there was two-way traffic by small craft across the North Sea. **Many Norwegians escaped to Britain** to fight on the Allied side. Norway's merchant navy was also a vital Allied resource.

NORWEGIAN WOMEN WITH GERMAN SOLDIERS

RESISTANCE
There was an **effective resistance movement within Norway** and Hitler kept large numbers of troops there until the end of the war. In Denmark King Christian remained in the country and became a focus for the **national opposition to Germany's anti-Semitic policies**.

FEW RECRUITS
The Nazis tried to **recruit Danes and Norwegians** into their armed forces but only about 5,000 answered the call, a fraction of those who remained loyal to their own country.

Stuka power
The Ju 87 dive bomber played a key role in Blitzkrieg, supporting the forces advancing on the ground. As it dived towards its target, it sounded a wailing siren.

Blitzkrieg

France traditionally had one of the strongest armies in the world, but in less than a month, from May 10, 1940, new German attack methods smashed the French forces, as well as their British, Dutch, and Belgian allies. None had any real answer to Germany's combination of fast-moving tanks and air power.

On the eve of the launching of the invasion of the Low Countries and France, General Maurice Gamelin, the Allied Commander-in-Chief, clung to the belief that the German attack, when it came, would be a mechanized version of the Schlieffen Plan of 1914, outflanking the Maginot Line with an attack through Holland and Belgium.

Competing plans
Gamelin planned to order the British Expeditionary Force (BEF) and 27 of the best divisions in the French Army to move north to support the Dutch and Belgian forces along the Dyle River.

The German invasion of Belgium and Holland, however, assigned to Bock's Army Group B, was intended precisely to draw the BEF and many of the most effective French formations north, enabling Rundstedt's Army Group A to break through the weakly held Ardennes to the south, cross the Meuse River and drive to the Channel, trapping the Allied forces in the north inside a huge pocket.

BEFORE

As soon as he had destroyed Poland, Hitler began planning an attack in the West, though this was repeatedly postponed during the Phoney War ❮❮ 60–61.

INITIAL PLANS
The original German plan had envisaged a drive through the Low Countries and a descent on Paris, reminiscent of the **Schlieffen Plan** of 1914. However, on January 10, 1940, two Luftwaffe officers carrying parts of the plan crash-landed in Belgium and **failed to burn the evidence**. There was an immediate reappraisal.

"SICKLE CUT"
Under the influence of Lieutenant General Erich von Manstein, the chief of staff to the commander of Army Group A, General Gerd von Rundstedt, an **alternative plan** was devised in which the main blow was to be delivered **through the Ardennes**, a wooded hilly area of eastern Belgium, which the French and British believed to be **wholly unsuitable for armored operations**. This more radical scheme aimed to exploit the mobility of Germany's Panzer divisions to throw the Allies completely off balance and win a rapid victory.

Von Leeb's Army Group C was to mount holding attacks in the south.

The BEF had 200 light tanks and 100 infantry tanks but included no dedicated armored formations, as Britain's only tank division, First Armored, was not yet combat ready. The French armored and motorized formations were of better quality than their infantry, and included tanks superior to and more numerous than those in the 10 German armored divisions (3,000 to 2,439), but over half were tied to slow-moving infantry units.

Holland overwhelmed
The German offensive was launched on May 10 as German paratroops and air-landing formations seized strategic locations in Holland. On May 14 the Luftwaffe bombed the center of Rotterdam, killing 1,000 inhabitants and making 78,000 homeless. The Dutch capitulated the next day.

On May 10 the linchpin of the Belgian defenses, the supposedly impregnable Fort Eben Emael, on the confluence of the Albert Canal and Maas River, was neutralized in a daring *coup de main*. Following Gamelin's plan, the BEF and French armies wheeled northeast on to the Dyle Line, while on the BEF's right

Capture of Eben Emael
This Belgian fortress, defended by 1,200 men, was captured by just 78 German airborne troops—pictured in action—who were landed on top of it by glider to destroy its defenses with explosive charges.

flank, in the Gembloux Gap, the first major tank battle of the war was fought on May 12–13 between German and French armored units.

Panzer breakthrough
However, the real danger for the Allies loomed to the south. Army Group A, spearheaded by Panzer Group Kleist, advanced through the Ardennes and, with heavy support from the Luftwaffe, secured three bridgeheads across the Meuse River. Thereafter, German tank formations drove through northern France on an 50-mile (80-km) front between May 16 and 21. For the Allies, the Battle of France was now lost.

AFTER

The Blitzkrieg advance across France was followed immediately by the evacuation from Dunkirk 78–79 ❯❯ and the complete defeat of France 82–83 ❯❯.

BRITISH DEFIANCE
Despite the **virtual destruction** of the largest and best-equipped part of its army, Britain decided to fight on, inspired by the newly appointed prime minister, Winston Churchill. Hitler's preparations to invade England came to nothing after the **Luftwaffe's failure in the Battle of Britain 84–85 ❯❯**.

NEW BLITZKRIEG ATTACKS
Germany made new conquests in 1941. In the spring German forces **overran Yugoslavia and Greece 132–133 ❯❯** in a matter of weeks, while in Africa one of the successful Panzer generals of France 1940, Erwin Rommel, led his tanks to **new victories over the British forces 124–125 ❯❯**. Hitler's main aim for 1941, however, was to **defeat the USSR** in **Operation Barbarossa 134–135 ❯❯**. Once again the German tank and air forces secured stunning early victories and rapid advances but ultimately they failed to convert these into a decisive victory.

AN EXHAUSTED FRENCH SOLDIER IN RETREAT

TECHNOLOGY
PANZER DIVISIONS

The German term *Blitzkrieg* means "Lightning War" and is said to have been coined by an American journalist in 1939 to describe the techniques whereby Hitler's forces won their early victories. A combination of tank units (right) with close air support from the Luftwaffe was key to success on the ground. In France in 1940 Germany had no more and no better tanks than their enemies, but German tanks were concentrated into mechanized formations—Panzer divisions—committed to rapid movement and shock effect. And throughout the German forces, all arms—tanks, infantry, artillery, and air support—linked by radio communication, worked together far more effectively than those of their opponents.

BEFORE

The German advance to the Channel coast **« 76–77** and the defeat of the Allied forces in Belgium and the Netherlands virtually ensured the collapse of France.

CRUCIAL DECISIONS

At the beginning of the third week in May 1940, the British war cabinet was **considering a partial but not total evacuation** of the British Expeditionary Force (BEF) from northern France. However, its freedom of maneuver was to be overtaken by events. Thereafter, the **German decision to halt their armor**, which had suffered heavy losses in men and material in the previous two weeks of fighting, enabled the bulk of the BEF to **withdraw into the defensive perimeter around Dunkirk.**

GOERING'S BOASTS

On the insistence of Hermann Goering, the **Luftwaffe assumed responsibility for the annihilation of the BEF** and the fall of the port itself. Hitler, still fearful of a strong Allied counterattack, readily **agreed to commit his air force** to execute the *coup de grâce* in a campaign in which, until that point, **the ground forces had played the dominant role**. He also considered that any further narrowing of the Dunkirk pocket by German armored formations would make the Luftwaffe's task that much more difficult to complete. The combined orders from the German high command rendered an **appalled General Heinz Guderian**, one of the leading tank commanders, "utterly speechless."

Dunkirk

During the Dunkirk evacuation Churchill worried that it would be the greatest military disaster ever suffered by Britain. In the event, German errors and brilliant naval organization on the Allied side did just enough to give Britain a fighting chance of continuing the war, even if France was defeated.

At 7pm on May 20 German armored formations reached Abbeville, at the mouth of the Somme River, effectively dividing the Allied armies into two. An hour later tanks of XIX Corps were on the Channel coast at Noyelles. On the same day General Maxime Weygand succeeded Gamelin as the Allied commander-in-chief. Hitler was also busy on the 20th, reviewing plans for the drive into the heart of France that would complete the destruction of the French Army.

Preparing the evacuation

The British war cabinet was also making an important decision. It decided that part of the BEF might have to be evacuated from the Channel ports and so instructed the Admiralty to begin assembling small ships on the south coast to take the troops off. The operation, codenamed "Dynamo," was not as yet intended to be a full-scale evacuation—the cabinet hoped that most of the BEF would be able to break through the Panzer corridor in

Allied wounded leaving Dunkirk
British and French troops board a ship during the Dunkirk evacuations on May 27. Far more troops were evacuated from the port, as here, than from the beaches.

northern France to join hands with the surviving French armies on and south of the Somme River. An Allied attack at Arras on May 21 was briefly to keep this forlorn hope flickering.

Lord Gort, the commander of the BEF, now conducting a fighting withdrawal in Belgium, was more

340,000 The estimated number of men, one third of them French, saved by the time the evacuation of Dunkirk ended on June 4, principally by the Royal Navy.

realistic. On May 23 he withdrew from Arras the force that had dented Rommel's Seventh Panzer Division. The commander of British II Corps, General Alan Brooke, wrote in despair that, "Nothing but a miracle can save the BEF now."

There was a miracle, of sorts, on May 24. Hitler, fretting about the vulnerability of his Panzer formations in the coastal lowlands laced with dykes and canals, halted his armor for two days. It enabled the BEF, and a substantial number of French troops, to withdraw behind the "Canal Line" to the port of Dunkirk. The Luftwaffe had the task of destroying them.

At midnight on May 27 Belgium capitulated. Behind the defended perimeter at Dunkirk the evacuation was under way. Planned by Vice-Admiral Bertram Ramsay, it began

Operation "Sickle Cut"

Germany's rapid advance from the Ardennes region to the Channel coast cut the Allied armies on the Western Front in two and confined the BEF and substantial French forces to the Dunkirk area.

at 7pm on May 26. Ramsay had assembled over 1,000 vessels,including destroyers and other warships,cross-Channel ferries, pleasure steamers, and even craft as small as cabin cruisers manned by civilian crews.

The Dunkirk miracle

On the night of May 26/27, 8,000 troops were taken off; on May 28 the figure rose to 19,000. On May 31, the day Gort left for England, 68,000 made their escape. The Royal Navy played the greatest role in the event, but "little ships" were also involved. Throughout the evacuation the town, beaches, and coastal waters came under heavy attack from the Luftwaffe, and the contracting perimeter was under constant pressure. Six British and three French destroyers were sunk and 19 badly damaged. Some 217 other craft were sunk, among them 161 of the "little ships."

Unjust criticism

The RAF's Fighter Command attracted criticism for its apparent absence from the skies. In fact it had broken up many of the Luftwaffe's attacks further inland, downing over 100 aircraft of all types in fierce air battles and losing a similar number of aircraft itself.

The BEF left all heavy equipment. Many British soldiers remained too. Bombardier J.E. Bowman of the 4th Infantry Division recalled: "Discarded equipment littered the beach and all along there were rifles sticking up in the sand with tin hats on top to show where the owner had been hastily buried."

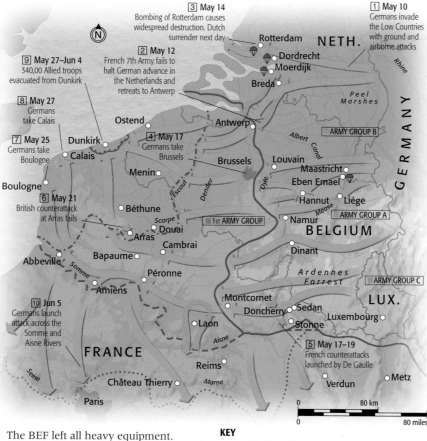

KEY

——	Allied front line May 16
– · –	Allied front line May 21
┬┬┬	Allied defensive line May 28
– –	Allied front line Jun 4
· · · ·	Allied front line Jun 12
⇨	German advance
⇨	Allied movement
⊗	Airborne assault
——	Frontiers 1939

AFTER

Churchill called the evacuation from Dunkirk an escape not a victory, though it was a huge boost to British morale.

BRITAIN FIGHTS ON

The scale of the evacuation undoubtedly surprised the German high command. The Luftwaffe, prevented by bad weather, had **failed in the strategic aim of destroying the BEF**. Although the **British army was critically weakened**, there remained a nucleus with which to continue the war. Hitler was compelled to **improvise a plan for the invasion of England**, which would be thwarted by the RAF in the **Battle of Britain 84–85 》**.

A GERMAN FILM UNIT AT DUNKIRK

The beaches at Dunkirk

Thousands of Allied troops stand or sit in orderly lines as they await evacuation, despite the fact that they were in constant danger of air attack. Sand deadened the impact of Luftwaffe bombs, but the lack of cover exposed the troops to strafing aircraft.

The Evacuation of Dunkirk

A flotilla of some 1,000 naval and civilian ships crossed the English Channel to rescue more than 330,000 British and French troops from Dunkirk. Under constant attack, troops waded into shallow waters to board small boats that ferried them to larger ships. Soldiers often had to make several attempts before being taken off. Many were evacuated, not from the open beaches, but by larger craft like destroyers which came alongside the eastern mole at the entrance to Dunkirk harbor. The sea was surprisingly very calm ...

"The picture will always remain sharp-etched in my memory—the lines of men wearily and sleepily staggering across the beach from the dunes to the shallows, falling into little boats, great columns of men thrust out into the water among bomb and shell splashes. The foremost ranks were shoulder deep, moving forward under the command of young subalterns ... As the front ranks were dragged aboard the boats, the rear ranks moved up, from ankle deep to knee deep, from knee deep to waist deep, until they, too, came to shoulder depth and their turn. The little boats that ferried from the beach to the big ships in deep water listed drunkenly with the weight of men. The big ships slowly took on lists of their own with the enormous numbers crowded aboard."

CREWMAN ARTHUR D. DIVINE, WHO MANNED ONE OF THE BOATS THAT RESCUED SERVICEMEN FROM DUNKIRK

"We got on the ship's deck, with very little trouble, but saw several weary men topple back into the sea below. No sooner had we settled down below, than there was an almighty noise—the Stukas and Dorniers had returned with their bombs. Later we learned that this was to be the last daylight evacuation and turned out to be HMS *Worcester*'s 6th and last journey. She had carried over 5000 servicemen to safety and this last trip she suffered 350 dead and 400 wounded ... From the instant I settled down below decks on HMS *Worcester*, a great burden of responsibility seemed to fall from my shoulders."

MAJOR TOM AVERILL OF THE BRITISH EXPEDITIONARY FORCE, ON BEING EVACUATED FROM DUNKIRK IN OPERATION DYNAMO

Homeward bound
Most of the rescued troops were exhausted on the crossing of the Channel from Dunkirk to Britain; some of them had spent many days on the beach waiting to be evacuated. Royal Navy destroyers took most of the troops off.

‹‹ BEFORE

Hitler's troops had already knocked the Netherlands and Belgium out of the war, destroyed the British Expeditionary Force, and smashed the strongest and best-equipped parts of the French Army.

TOO LITTLE, TOO LATE

On May 21 the French high command proposed that encircled Allied forces north of the German line should **coordinate convergent attacks** on the Panzer corridor with the French armies still operating to the south. This would have been the correct way to deal with the **Blitzkrieg ‹‹ 76–77** tactics but the means and authority with which to deliver such a blow no longer existed. General Weygand's **remaining 49 divisions** extended from the Channel to the Maginot Line over a front of some 230 miles (370 km).

BATTLEFIELD REFLEXES

The Germans were also exhausted but, unlike the French, they were exultant and displayed **enormous drive and flexibility** in swinging around from their northern advance to drive south and southeast to the Somme and Aisne rivers. The **supply movements** for this maneuver were highly complex but were accomplished with exemplary efficiency.

The Fall of France

After the stunning victories of May it took Hitler's armed forces scarcely a couple of weeks more to finish off their campaign. No one had imagined that France, recognized as one of Europe's great powers, could be completely overwhelmed after a mere six weeks of fighting.

> " In three weeks England will have **her neck wrung** like a chicken."
>
> GENERAL WEYGAND, JUNE 1940, PREDICTING THAT BRITAIN'S DEFEAT WOULD FOLLOW THAT OF FRANCE

After the Dunkirk evacuation, General Weygand's hopes rested on the so-called "Weygand Line," an imaginative attempt to carry out a last-ditch defense of France. The line ran from the Channel coast, following the Somme and Aisne rivers, to the Maginot Line at Montmédy. It was to consist of a linked checkerboard of heavily defended "hedgehog" positions (a system later copied by

155,000 The number of German losses in France in 1940 from dead, wounded, and missing: a third of the total in the single battle of Verdun in World War I.

NATO in the 1970s to deal with an attack by the Red Army), which could continue to resist even if bypassed.

In practice many of the "hedgehogs" collapsed on their first brutal contact with the enemy. Their defenders lacked anti-tank weapons and had no air cover. The Luftwaffe completely dominated the skies. Some French units held on with great courage, even when isolated from the main body of the retreating French Army. On June 9 Army Group A, led by Panzer Group Guderian, went on the attack on the River Aisne. It encountered heroic resistance from the French 14th Division, led by General de Lattre de Tassigny, but the German drive rolled

MARSHAL PHILIPPE PÉTAIN

In World War I Pétain's defence of Verdun made him a national hero. He became the French president on June 16, 1940 and, convinced that it was in France's best interests to cease fighting and that Britain was close to defeat, offered the Germans an armistice on June 22. His Vichy government collaborated with the Germans, although in December 1940 he dismissed his prime minister, Pierre Laval, who wanted France to join the Axis. What little power Pétain exercised was removed when the Germans occupied the Vichy-controlled area after the Allied landings in North Africa in November 1942. Pétain claimed to have done his best to protect the French people from the Nazis but after the war he was sentenced to death for treason; he was later given a reprieve but died in prison.

Unusual tourist
Hitler poses in front of the Eiffel Tower in Paris on June 23, 1940. On the left is his court architect and later armaments minister, Albert Speer, and on the right is his favorite sculptor, Arno Breker.

Surrendering French soldiers

The infantry shown here fleeing the German onslaught were among the two million French prisoners of war who after the Battle of France were to go into indefinite German captivity.

on. Guderian later recalled that 1st Panzer Division advanced "as though this were a maneuver."

The aged Marshal Pétain, the hero of the Battle of Verdun in 1916, who had been brought out of retirement to be deputy prime minister, was now begged by his former chief of staff to bring President Roosevelt into the imminent armistice negotiations before Italy joined the war. But Roosevelt had already told French prime minister Paul Reynaud that he had no power to influence the situation and could offer no more material aid.

Paris abandoned

On June 10, the day on which Italy declared war on France, Reynaud moved the French government from Paris to Tours, on the Loire River, where he met with Churchill for a final conference the next day. Churchill urged Reynaud to defend Paris but the latter had already taken the decision to declare the capital an open city.

Many Parisians were now fleeing from the Germans, who arrived on June 14. Two days later Churchill offered to declare an indissoluble union between Britain and France, an idea that had also been proposed by the junior French defense minister, Brigadier-General Charles de

German hand grenade

The German Model 24 "potato masher" grenade had been in use since World War I. It could be thrown up to 130 ft (40 m) and was very effective against infantry positions, less so against armored vehicles.

Gaulle, who had arrived in London as an exile on June 17. The French cabinet rejected Churchill's proposal, seeing it as a humiliating subordination to the British. Now they would have to submit instead to the Germans.

At Tours a glum Weygand told Churchill, "C'est la dislocation" ("It's total breakdown"). Nevertheless, the garrison of the Maginot Line—40,000 strong—continued to ignore all calls to surrender. Only one small section of its defenses was ever taken by attack. But resistance was now pointless. As if to prove it, on June 12 the British landed 52nd Lowland Division and the Canadian Division at Cherbourg, in a bid to help French troops open a new front in the west. Both divisions had to be evacuated almost as soon as they arrived.

In the small hours of June 17, Pétain, now France's new president, approached the Germans, via the Spanish ambassador, to open armistice

> General Weygand, France's commander-in-chief in 1940, was present at the 1918 Armistice negotiations as chief of staff to Marshal Foch, then the Allied supreme commander.

negotiations (Pétain had until recently been ambassador in Madrid). A new humiliation awaited Pétain's emissaries. They had to sign the armistice terms in the railway coach near Compiègne in which Marshal Foch had dictated peace terms to the Germans in 1918.

Harsh terms

An exultant Hitler observed the arrival of the French delegation and was filmed stamping his feet in excitement. The armistice terms presented by General Wilhelm Keitel, who was Hitler's armed forces chief of staff, were harsh. Even though Pétain's government—shortly to be removed to the spa town of Vichy—was to remain notionally sovereign, Paris, the whole of northern France and its Atlantic coast were to become a German occupation zone. The costs of the occupation forces were to be met by the French. Alsace and Lorraine were incorporated into Germany itself. France's colonies were to remain under Vichy control along with the French Navy, which was to be demilitarized. Germany was to retain indefinitely all French prisoners taken during the

After Hitler's vaunted "glorious victory," life in occupied France became hazardous, especially for the Jewish population, while Vichy cooperated with the Nazi regime.

GERMAN GAINS

The defeat and occupation of much of France gave Hitler a number of **important strategic gains**, not least the acquisition of U-boat bases on France's Atlantic coast to add to those in Norway. The German Navy could now broaden the scope of its operations and develop its attacks in the **Battle of the Atlantic 118–19 ▶▶**.

VICHY AND OCCUPATION

Marshal Pétain's **Vichy regime** emphasized conservative values—**"Work, family, country"** replaced "Liberty, equality, fraternity" as the national slogan. Despite its collaborationist stance, in late 1942 the Germans moved into Vichy France to occupy the whole country. France remained under German control until after the **D-Day Landings 258–59 ▶▶**.

VICHY MEDAL

AIDING THE GERMANS

Meanwhile, the Vichy regime helped the Germans deport Jews to the death camps and forced hundreds of thousands of French people to work in Germany for the German war effort. By 1944 Vichy's paramilitary forces were joining the Germans to fight the **French Resistance 222–23 ▶▶**.

six-week campaign, including the garrison of the Maginot Line. The Armistice was signed on June 22 and, along with France's separate armistice signed with Italy, was to come into force on the morning of June 25.

Germany's victory, brilliantly conceived and ruthlessly executed, cost the Third Reich 27,000 killed, 110,000 wounded and 18,000 missing. By contrast France suffered 90,000 dead

> **80** The number of French Members of Parliament who voted against the setting up of Vichy. Many were arrested as "traitors" on Pétain's orders and five died in concentration camps.

and 200,000 wounded, and 1,900,000 of its soldiers had been taken prisoner or were missing—one quarter of the country's young male population.

The French were prostrate, but the British monarch, George VI, comforted himself with the pragmatic observation, "Personally, I feel happier that we have no allies to be polite to or to pamper." Churchill was less sanguine. On June 18, in somber mood, he told the House of Commons, "The Battle of France is over. I expect the Battle of Britain is about to begin."

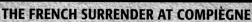

THE FRENCH SURRENDER AT COMPIÈGNE

Hitler was determined to reverse the Treaty of Versailles following the end of World War I. He therefore chose the site of the Armistice signing, on November 11, 1918, for the French surrender ceremony in 1940 (right). The Compiègne site and the railway carriage in which the Armistice signing took place had been preserved as a memorial. After the Battle of France Hitler had the railway carriage taken to Germany (where it was later destroyed) and the site itself cleared so that no reference to Germany's previous defeat survived.

« BEFORE

Germany's lightning victories in Poland, Norway, and France were all based on a combination of air power and the strength of their forces on the ground.

MAKING GOOD THE LOSSES

In the **Battle of France ‹‹ 82–83** both the **Luftwaffe and the RAF were badly hit**. In the fighting between 10 May and 20 June **the RAF lost 940 aircraft**, including 386 Hurricane and 67 Spitfire fighters. The serious loss of fighter pilots left Fighter Command 25 per cent below establishment. In the same period the **Luftwaffe lost 1,100 aircraft**, including 200 Me 109 fighters and 500 He 111 medium bombers. **Both sides needed to regroup** before the Battle of Britain could begin.

PRODUCTION RACE

By July 1940, before the Battle of Britain was fully under way, Britain was producing **more fighter aircraft than Germany**, narrowing the lead Germany had gained before the war.

An unwise tactician
Head of the Luftwaffe, Reichsmarschall Goering, seen addressing his aircrew, had been an ace pilot during World War I. During the Battle of Britain, however, he forced his fighter pilots to follow inappropriate tactics, tied too closely to the bomber-escort role.

The **Battle of Britain**

By early summer Hitler seemed to have the war all but won; by the autumn the RAF had delivered a blow to that possibility. While German military power was not seriously undermined, the battle was of great importance in scoring a first and decisive defeat of the Luftwaffe.

Reichsmarschall Hermann Goering was confident that it would take less than a week to destroy the major part of the Royal Air Force's Fighter Command. After the Luftwaffe's triumphs in Poland and France, he was sure that Britain could be brought to its knees by air power alone. At his disposal were some 2,000 operational aircraft deployed in three *Luftflotten* (air fleets). The two strongest, Luftflotte 2 and 3, had their bases in France and Belgium within easy flying distance of southern England. Luftflotte 5 was based in Norway and Denmark and was tasked with attacking targets in the north of England and Scotland.

RAF Fighter Command, led by Air Chief Marshal Sir Hugh Dowding, had approximately 700 fighters organized in four Groups: 11 Group in the crucial southeastern sector; 12 Group covering the Midlands and East Anglia; 10 Group, which from mid-July defended the west of England; and 13 Group, defending the north of England, Scotland, and Northern Ireland.

The RAF deployed roughly the same number of fighters as the Luftwaffe but had the significant advantage of a well-prepared radar and control system to bring them into action. In contrast, the Luftwaffe was hampered by a number of key deficiencies. It badly underestimated the vulnerability of its bombers, and discounted the limited range of its main fighter, the Messerschmitt 109E.

In the first stage of the battle, until the end of July, the Luftwaffe launched attacks on ports on the south coast and on shipping in the Channel. After heavy shipping and aircraft losses the British curtailed all Channel convoys. On August 12 a German raid put the radar

> **60** The percentage of successful Fighter Command pilots of 1940 who survived the war. The higher a pilot's kill score, the better his statistical chances of survival.

station at Ventnor on the Isle of Wight out of action for 11 days, but the loss was concealed from the Luftwaffe by radar coverage continuing elsewhere. On August 15 Goering unwisely concluded that further attacks on radar stations would be of little or no use.

All-out combat

That same day the Luftwaffe initiated the most intensive phase of the battle. For the only time all three air fleets combined to throw five successive waves against targets as widely separated as Portland in the southwest and Tyneside in the northeast. On what its aircrew dubbed Black Thursday, the Luftwaffe lost 69 aircraft and 190 aircrew, while Fighter Command lost 34 aircraft and 13 pilots.

RAF Hawker Hurricane fighters

Hurricanes of 111 Squadron in 1939–40. Hurricanes were the more numerous of the two main RAF fighter types in 1940 and shot down more enemy aircraft than the more famous Spitfire.

TECHNOLOGY

RADAR

Radar is an acronym for "Radio Direction and Ranging" – itself a term coined in the United States in 1940. The original British term was RDF ("Radio Direction Finding"). Radar sets transmit pulses of radio energy that may be reflected back by distant objects to give accurate measurements of these targets' positions. In the 1930s all major nations made technical advances in the field but Britain did the most to fit these into a well-organized air defence scheme. By 1940 Britain's Chain Home system of 30 coastal radar stations could quickly feed reports back to Fighter Command HQ. This information was cross-checked with information from ground observers and other sources and the "filtered" results were then transmitted onwards to the stations actually involved in controlling the fighter squadrons. Radar was likewise of vital importance in tracking and directing naval operations (right).

With the prize still eluding its grasp, the Luftwaffe narrowed its aim in late August to focus on the destruction of 11 Group's seven sector stations. Several were badly damaged and it seemed as if the Germans had gained the upper hand. Yet both sides were feeling the strain. In the first six days of September the Luftwaffe lost 125 aircraft, while Britain's reserve of experienced aircrew was running dangerously low. Fighter Command had received 476 new aircraft – but they would be useless without experienced pilots to fly them. On September 7 the Luftwaffe changed tactics again and launched its first mass daylight raid on London. Luftwaffe intelligence thought, mistakenly, that Fighter Command now had only 100 aircraft and was set to be finished off. But on 15 September the Germans suffered a crushing reverse when two heavily escorted waves of bombers ran into nearly 300 British fighters over London. By the end of the day the Luftwaffe had lost 55 aircraft to Fighter Command's 28. Air superiority had been decisively denied the Luftwaffe and September 30 saw the last major daylight raids. By the end of October the Luftwaffe had run out of ideas. Victory in the Battle of France had been a triumph for the Luftwaffe's army co-operation role, for which it was prepared and equipped. But in the Battle of Britain the Luftwaffe had to undertake a hastily prepared strategic offensive with both unsuitable aircraft and poor intelligence about its opponent. In the months from July to November 1940, the Luftwaffe lost 1,537 aircraft against the RAF's 925. Britain survived to fight on.

AFTER

With the defeat of the Luftwaffe, Hitler postponed, indefinitely, Operation Sealion, the planned invasion of Britain. Plans for Operation Barbarossa, the invasion of the Soviet Union, gathered momentum.

FURTHER AIR OFFENSIVES
The setbacks of the Battle of Britain did not prevent the Luftwaffe quickly winning **total air superiority in the Balkans 132–33 »**, and during **Operation Barbarossa 134–35 »**.

NEW AIRCRAFT TYPES
Even before the Battle of Britain was over, the **competing air forces** were frantically developing **new versions of their best combat aircraft**. In 1940 the Spitfire I and Me 109E were **fairly evenly matched**; the slightly

35,000 **The number of Messerschmitt 109s built during the war. Like its Battle of Britain counterpart, the Spitfire, the Me 109 remained in front-line service throughout the war.**

later 109F was superior to the next major Spitfire variant, the Mk V, but the later **Spitfire IX and XIV could outpace the 109G**. In the aftermath of the Battle of Britain, **the Blitz 88–89 »** enabled the RAF to build up its strength.

A MESSERSCHMITT 109F, AS USED IN NORTH AFRICA IN 1941–42

Scramble!
RAF Spitfire pilots and their groundcrews run to their aircraft for an emergency "scramble" take-off in July 1940. Although Britain's radar and control system was advanced, other RAF facilities in 1940 were primitive. Many airfields, like this one, had grass rather than all-weather surfaces.

> "Of course we were **as scared as anyone else** would have been. But we knew that we had **the whole country behind us**."
>
> FLYING OFFICER DENNIS DAVID, 87 AND 213 SQUADRONS

BRITISH PRIME MINISTER Born 1874 Died 1965

Winston Churchill

"I have nothing to offer but blood, toil, tears and sweat."

CHURCHILL, ON BECOMING PRIME MINISTER, MAY 13, 1940

Signing for victory
Winston Churchill making the "V for Victory" sign that was one of his wartime trademarks. For the war cabinet he wore a pinstriped suit; elsewhere he donned his Blitz "siren suit.".

Winston Churchill became prime minister of Britain in 1940, on the same day that Germany invaded Belgium. He was already 65 years old, and widely distrusted in political circles, but during the course of his term he silenced his critics to become an extraordinarily inspiring and successful wartime leader.

Churchill first entered politics in 1900 as a Conservative Member of Parliament (MP). Four years later he crossed the House to join the Liberals; however, in 1923 he went back to the Conservatives. Neither party trusted him and this distrust extended to the Labour Party when, in 1910, he took strong measures against striking workers. Churchill held various cabinet posts between 1911 and 1929, but though considered to be an extremely clever man, he also had a reputation for recklessness, particularly after supporting the disastrous Gallipoli campaign of World War I in 1915.

Herald of war

By 1931 Churchill was out of office. Most people believed his political career was over. But he was not a silent backbencher. From 1933 he warned that Germany was rearming "secretly, illegally, and rapidly," and called for Britain to strengthen its air force and work with the League of Nations to prevent a war that he believed was coming. He had powerful supporters, both inside and outside the party, but his warnings were ignored and he became increasingly isolated for his outspoken criticism of the government's appeasement policy. Following Hitler's march into Czechoslovakia, Churchill's popularity began to grow and there were calls for his return to public office. When war broke out Churchill was appointed First Lord of the Admiralty. He threw himself into

The first war
Churchill visiting dockyards in 1918 when he was minister of munitions. He was always popular with the British public.

action, insisting that naval vessels be equipped with radar, merchant ships be armed, and plans be drawn up to send a naval force to the Baltic. Events moved quickly: Hitler invaded Belgium, prime minister Neville Chamberlain resigned, and Churchill replaced him at the head of a coalition government. Politicians were wary, but the British public was delighted.

In his first speech to the House of Commons, Churchill pledged "victory at all costs" and never deviated from this goal. As well as being prime minister he was also minister for defence, responsible for military strategy in conjunction with his hand-picked chiefs of staff. One of his first decisions was to order the evacuation of stranded troops from Dunkirk that began on May 26, 1940. He also flew to France to try to encourage the French to continue fighting, but without success.

Following the fall of France on June 25, 1940, Britain stood alone, facing possible invasion. In a number

HOLDING THE LINE!

Bulldog determination
Often described as having bulldog-like qualities, Churchill, a staunchly patriotic man, was frequently portrayed as a British bulldog. This 1940 cartoon shows him holding the line against Nazi Germany.

Inspiring speeches
Churchill's wartime speeches inspired and informed the nation, helping to dispel dangerous rumors. Without fail troops and families tuned in to hear "Winnie" speak.

> ## "We will **fight them on the beaches** ... we shall fight in the fields and in the streets ... we shall **never surrender.** "
>
> WINSTON CHURCHILL, JUNE 4, 1940

of stirring and patriotic speeches, Churchill galvanized the British public, rallying the whole population to the defence of Britain. Opinion polls indicated that over 80 percent of the population supported him. A man of colossal energy, he visited coastal towns, strode through bombed-out streets, and met with troops, becoming a visible and unmistakeable leader.

American allies
From the outset of the war Churchill believed that US intervention was essential, and worked hard to persuade President Roosevelt to come in on the Allied side, but the American people were against getting involved. After the attack on Pearl Harbor on December 7, 1941, however, the US was forced to fight.

Victory in Europe Day
Churchill, with distinctive Havana cigar, waves to cheering crowds in London on V-E Day, May 8, 1945.

The first two years of Churchill's leadership were marked by military defeats. His standing with the public remained high but there were many who criticized his leadership and interference in military decisions, particularly after defeat in Greece. However, in November 1942, victory at El Alamein in North Africa helped to turn the tide, and criticism of his leadership abilities soon died away.

The "Big Three" leaders—Churchill, Roosevelt, and Stalin—met in Tehran in 1943 to discuss plans for an Allied invasion of occupied Europe, but by this point it was clear that Churchill wielded less influence than the other two. He had favored invasion through the Mediterranean but Roosevelt argued for a cross-Channel invasion, which was eventually adopted.

Final years
Following the Allied invasion of Normandy Churchill's influence over grand strategy continued to decline. In May 1945 there was a general election in Britain. Despite Churchill's huge popularity, a Labour government was voted in. In 1951 the Conservatives regained power with Churchill as prime minister, but now in his late seventies, and in poor health, he resigned four years later. He died in 1965.

TIMELINE

November 30, 1874 Churchill is born at Blenheim Palace, Oxfordshire. His father is Conservative politician Randolph Churchill, his mother American heiress Jennie Jerome.

1895 Having been educated at the Royal Military Academy, Sandhurst, he is commissioned in the 4th Queen's Royal Hussars light cavalry regiment.

1896–98 Serves in India and Egypt, combining his military career with journalism.

1899 Covering the Boer War for the *London Morning Post*, he is captured by Boers but escapes, becoming a national hero.

1900 Enters parliament as Conservative Member of Parliament (MP) for Oldham.

1904 Churchill leaves the Conservatives and joins the Liberal Party.

1908 Elected MP for Dundee, and marries Clementine Hozier.

1910 Promoted to the Home Office; sends troops to Tonypandy, Wales, against striking miners.

1911 Appointed First Lord of the Admiralty with a brief to modernize the Royal Navy.

1915 Dismissed from Admiralty following disastrous Dardanelles Campaign of World War I. Resigns from government and commands a battalion on the Western Front (until May 1916).

1917 Returns to government as minister of munitions.

1921 Appointed Colonial Secretary, but loses parliamentary seat in 1922.

CHURCHILL'S REMINGTON

1924 Rejoins the Conservative Party and is elected MP for Epping, a seat he holds until 1964. Appointed Chancellor of the Exchequer.

1931 Resigns from the shadow cabinet in protest against proposals for Indian self-rule.

September 1939 Takes up the position of First Lord of the Admiralty in the war cabinet.

May 1940 Chamberlain steps down and Churchill takes over as prime minister at head of coalition government. He orders the retreat from Dunkirk, and round-up of "enemy aliens."

August 1941 Churchill and Roosevelt issue the Atlantic Charter; their aims for the postwar world.

January 1943 Casablanca Conference: Churchill and Roosevelt agree to accept only unconditional surrender from Axis powers.

February 1945 Yalta Conference: Churchill, Roosevelt, and Stalin determine shape of postwar Germany and Poland.

July 1945 Defeated by Labour in General Election: becomes leader of the opposition.

1951 Conservatives return to power with Churchill as prime minister.

1955 Churchill resigns premiership but remains an MP until 1964.

January 24, 1965 Churchill dies nine days after suffering a severe stroke. His body lies in state in Westminster Abbey for three days.

The **Blitz**

In World War II, more than in any other previous conflict, civilians were thrust into the front line. Germany's Blitz of Britain's cities in 1940–41 was the first sustained attempt to destroy a country's industries and terrorize its people by bombing from the air. It would not be the last.

German bombing inspection
Armorers inspect the payload of a Luftwaffe bomber. In 1940 German light case bombs were twice as destructive as British equivalents. But aircraft bombloads were modest compared with those later carried by British bombers.

« BEFORE

Neither Britain nor Germany bombed enemy cities by night in the early months of the war, though both had used night bombing in World War I.

ELUSIVE VICTORY
By the end of August 1940 the Luftwaffe seemed to be winning the **Battle of Britain ‹‹ 84–85**, but not fast enough. **Autumn gales threatened** the safe passage of the invasion barges across the Channel. The Luftwaffe decided to **shift the focus of attack** from Fighter Command's airfields to London. Hitler, who still **hoped to bring Churchill to the conference table**, had thus far withheld permission to bomb the capital. Now he ordered his forces to make "disruptive attacks on the population and air defences of major British cities, including London, by day and night."

FINDING TARGETS
Both Britain and Germany had discovered in smaller operations earlier in the war that their existing types of bomber aircraft could not fight their way to targets **without a fighter escort** during daytime. It remained to be seen how well their **crews' navigational skills and equipment** would stand up to the demands of bombing accurately at night.

O n Saturday, September 7, 1940, the Luftwaffe launched its first major raid on London. The "Blitz," as Germany's bombing campaign became known in Britain, was about to begin. That day 300 aircraft dropped more than 300 tons of bombs on London's docks and the densely packed streets of the East End. The fires they started lit the way for 250 more bombers, which attacked between 8pm and dawn.

London's ordeal
For two months, between September 7 and November 12, London was spared bombing on only 10 nights. Some 13,000 tons of high explosive and a million incendiaries fell on the city, killing 13,000 people and leaving over

250,000 homeless. The cost to the Luftwaffe was negligible. Only a handful of the RAF's night fighters were fitted with a primitive form of airborne radar. Nor had the Luftwaffe much to fear from the capital's anti-aircraft defences.

In addition, the Germans had a secret weapon. Dubbed *Knickebein* ("Crooked leg"), it consisted of two radio beams directed from stations in Europe. The bombers would fly along one beam and release their bombs when the first

Air-raid rattle
British air-raid wardens carried rattles to warn of gas attacks. Unlike a whistle, the rattle could be used while the warden was wearing a gas mask.

beam was intersected by the second. Rashly, the Luftwaffe had tested *Knickebein* over England in March 1940, when they had no plans to mount a night bombing campaign against Britain. The examination of a crashed He 111 bomber enabled British scientists to unlock the secrets of *Knickebein* and start to develop countermeasures. By the autumn of 1940, when the Luftwaffe turned its attention to industrial centers in the Midlands, it had perfected a more sophisticated version of *Knickebein*, *X-Verfahren* ("X-system"), which employed four beams and a clockwork timer on board the aircraft that was linked to the beams and the bomb release. A crack unit, known as

40 The percentage of Londoners who went regularly to an air-raid shelter at night during a raid. This surprisingly low figure was revealed in a survey of November 1940. The majority of the population stayed in bed or under the stairs.

Kampfgruppe (KGr) 100, was formed to act as pathfinders for the main bombing force, marking the target with incendiaries.

Late in the afternoon of November 14, the British detected an X-beam crossing the Midlands. Less than two hours later the first He 111s of KGr 100 arrived over Coventry to mark the target. They were followed by 449 bombers that devastated the center of the city and badly damaged a score of factories. Yet the city recovered quickly from its ordeal, and within days most of its factories were back in business.

Britain under pressure
Throughout January and February 1941 the Luftwaffe strove to maintain the pressure on London, the industrial Midlands, and Britain's western ports, the last link in the Atlantic supply

KEY
※ Major air raids or towns suffering repeated bombing
☼ Other important air raids
▬ Main British industrial areas
⊕ British fighter base
✈ German air base

1 Mar 16, 1940
Bombing of Scapa Flow naval base. First British civilian casualty of the war

5 Mar 13/14, 1941
Luftwaffe attacks Clydebank in attempt to destroy its shipyards

4 Nov 14/15, 1940
449 German bombers devastate Coventry, leaving one third of its inhabitants homeless

3 Sep 7, 1940–Nov 12, 1941
Raids over London kill over 15,000 and make more than 250,000 homeless

6 May 1–7, 1941
Luftwaffe subjects Liverpool to seven successive nights of heavy raids

2 Jul 10, 1940
In first major attack, Luftwaffe bombs Swansea docks and Royal Ordnance factory at Pembrey

7 May 10, 1941
London suffers largest raid to date. Thousands left without electricity, gas, or water

German bombing attacks on Britain
Initially Luftflotte 3, based in France, carried out most of the night bombing attacks but soon the whole of Germany's bomber force was committed. All of Britain's larger cities, industrial areas, and ports were targeted.

Beat 'FIREBOMB FRITZ'

BRITAIN SHALL NOT BURN

BRITAIN'S FIRE GUARD IS BRITAIN'S DEFENCE

Warnings of fire

Incendiaries were probably more dangerous and destructive than explosive bombs. In the Coventry raid of November 14, 1940, over 40,000 incendiary bombs were dropped by some 450 aircraft.

chain. By now the air defenses had improved. In March night-fighters shot down 22 bombers and AA guns claimed 17 more. In May the fighters claimed 96 kills, the guns 32.

The final phase of the Blitz began on April 16, 1941, and reached a climax on May 10 with a raid on London that left one third of the capital's streets impassable and 1,400 civilians dead. But by now Hitler's strategic priorities had changed and the build-up to the invasion of the Soviet Union was gathering momentum. As a result, two thirds of the Lufwaffe was transferred to Eastern Europe.

Hitler's bombing campaign against Britain had failed. The Luftwaffe's principal weapon, the He 111, did not pack a big enough punch to bomb the British into surrender. Coventry had been targeted just once, and London's sheer size had saved it. Civilian morale had not crumbled—in the saying of the time, Britain could "take it."

AFTER »

Germany's bomber force did not return to attack Britain in comparable strength at any later stage in the war, while the British and Americans would retaliate in kind.

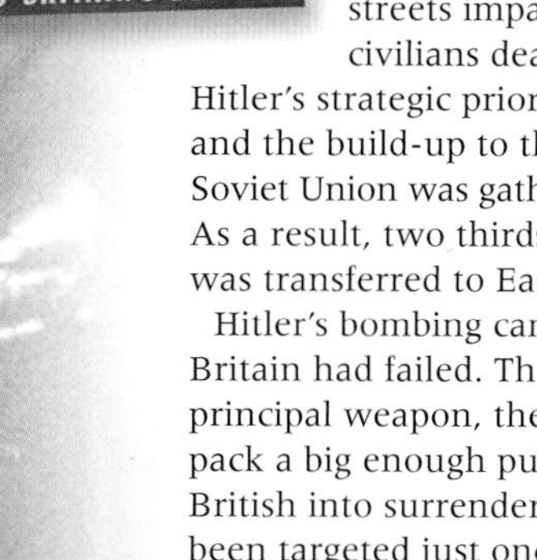

LESSONS

The Blitz had caused human suffering and material damage but it had **not destroyed civilian morale nor dealt a significant blow** to Britain's war-making capacity. Bombing was about the only effective way Britain could in turn **strike back at Germany**, and the government planned **a huge expansion of the RAF bomber force**. By 1943 Bomber Command would have **Germany's cities** in its sights 214–17 »

COVENTRY CATHEDRAL DEVASTATED

ROCKET ATTACKS

The nearest German equivalent to the massive Anglo-American bombing campaign were the unmanned **V-weapons attacks on London** 278–79 » in 1944–45.

London in flames

Members of the Auxiliary Fire Service battle a blaze in the City of London in December 1940. Fighting fires caused by air raids was especially difficult when bombing often destroyed water mains.

Refuge from the Blitz

When the Blitz began, tens of thousands of Londoners took to sleeping in Underground train stations. Conditions were poor, with serious overcrowding and no sanitary facilities, although the authorities slowly introduced improvements such as bunk beds on platforms. The "tube" was not necessarily a safe haven from the bombing—for example, 111 people died when a bomb struck Bank station in January 1941.

"On benches on each side, as though sitting and lying on a long street-car seat, were the people, hundreds of them. As we walked on they stretched into thousands.

In addition, there was a row of sleeping forms on the wooden floor of the tube, stretched crosswise. Their bodies took up the whole space, so we had to watch closely when we put our feet down between the sleepers.

Many of these people were old—wretched and worn old people, people who had never known many of the good things of life and who were now winding up their days on this earth in desperate discomfort ...

... There were children too, some asleep and some playing. There were youngsters in groups, laughing and talking and even singing. There were smart-alecks and there were quiet ones. There were hard-working people of middle age who had to rise at 5:00am and go to work.

Some people sat knitting or playing cards or talking. But mostly they just sat. And though it was only 8:00pm, many of the old people were already asleep.

It was the old people who seemed so tragic. Think of yourself at 70 or 80, full of pain and of dim memories of a lifetime that has probably all been bleak. And then think of yourself now, travelling at dusk every night to a subway station, wrapping your ragged overcoat about your old shoulders and sitting on a wooden bench with your back against a curved steel wall. Sitting there all night in nodding and fitful sleep.

Think of that as your destiny—every night, every night from now on."

US WAR CORRESPONDENT ERNIE PYLE, DESCRIBING LONDONERS SHELTERING FROM THE BLITZ IN LIVERPOOL STREET UNDERGROUND STATION

Sleeping on the tracks
A few sections of the Underground, such as Aldwych station shown here, were used purely as shelters. In most places, though, sleepers shared stations with passengers and trains until services stopped running at 10:30pm.

Britain Organizes for Total War

◀◀ **B E F O R E**

Rationing, air raids, civilian mobilization, conscription, and government regulations brought war directly into people's lives and homes. From 1940 British civilians were moved onto a total war footing, with women, men, and even children mobilized for war more thoroughly than in any other nation.

The British government planned for war before 1939 but moves to mobilize the public were slow at first.

EMERGENCY POWERS

In August 1939 **Parliament introduced the Emergency Powers (Defence) Act**, giving the government sweeping powers over the British people to ensure public safety. **Military conscription** came in May 1939 for men aged 20–21, later extended to men aged 18–41. During the **Phoney War ◀◀ 60–61** security measures were implemented, but it was **Dunkirk ◀◀ 78–79** and **the Blitz ◀◀ 88–89** that brought a sense of urgency to the Home Front.

SLOW ECONOMIC CHANGE

In 1939 the British economy was not fully organized for war. **Armament production increased slowly** and Britain imported 70 percent of its food. By May 1940 the labor force had only increased by 11 percent and **one million people were still out of work**.

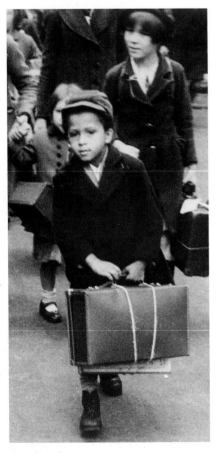

Away from home
From 1939 to 1944 almost one million children were evacuated at least once from British cities to escape the bombing. Not knowing where they would end up, they were housed with strangers, often far from home.

Organizing Britain for total war was no easy task. In May 1940 Winston Churchill replaced Neville Chamberlain as prime minister and the pace of change quickened. Propaganda urged all citizens to play their part, new government ministries were set up, and the government used its emergency powers to control all aspects of daily life, from food supplies through to industry and home defense. Income tax was raised, volunteers were recruited for the Home Guard, military conscription was extended, and nonessential industries were wound down to shift resources into producing weapons, aircraft, and other necessities. In a particularly draconian measure, so-called "enemy aliens"—Germans and Italians living in Britain—were rounded up and interned in designated areas.

> **22 MILLION** The number of British women and men who were in the armed services, war industries, and civil defense positions in 1943.

Rationing and austerity

Wartime Britain was a mass of rules and regulations. Everyone had to carry an identity card, and supplies of food, gasoline, and water were restricted. Food rationing was introduced in January 1940, initially for butter, sugar, bacon, and ham, but from 1941, when U-boat attacks disrupted imports, rationing was extended to most foodstuffs. Intent on keeping the

population fed, the government set up a Ministry for Food under Lord Woolton, whose name was jokingly given to a wartime vegetable-and-oatmeal pie. Every household was issued with a ration card, which by law was registered with local shops. The Ministry of Agriculture used its powers to direct food production, fix prices, and force farmers to bring unproductive land into cultivation.

A government-inspired "Dig for Victory" campaign urged people to grow vegetables, and food gardens sprang up. Bread was never rationed, but the wartime loaf, known as the National Loaf, was a peculiar gray. "British Restaurants" were set up to provide nourishing, low-cost meals for

Working on the land

By 1943 over 80,000 women, members of the Women's Land Army were producing 70 percent of Britain's food. Many lived in cities and had never before worked in agriculture.

Island prisoners of war

Some 300,000 Italians and Germans, including refugees from Nazi Germany, were held captive behind barbed wire. These former boardinghouses on the Isle of Man became internment camps until 1941.

workers. Each child was given a daily milk allowance. By and large, the public thought rationing was fair, and some people ate better than they had during the Depression.

As shortages grew, clothing too was put rationed. Each person was allowed only one new outfit a year and, encouraged by a "Make Do and Mend" campaign, women unpicked and re-knitted sweaters and reused old clothes. Stockings, cosmetics, and other consumer goods disappeared. The government laid down rules for

WOMEN OF BRITAIN

COME INTO THE FACTORIES

ASK AT ANY EMPLOYMENT EXCHANGE FOR ADVICE AND FULL DETAILS

clothing and furniture production, setting up a "Utility" label. Soap was limited, the use of water for washing was controlled, and people were urged to collect scrap for aircraft manufacture.

Women in the workforce

Under Ernest Bevin, minister for labor, the workforce was directed where it was most needed. Some 200,000 men were kept in reserved occupations, such as farming, but the government knew that women were crucial and they entered the laboor force in their thousands, many for the first time. Initially the government relied on women to volunteer, but 1941 introduced conscription. A year later all women aged 18–60, married or single, had to register for war work and could be assigned to factories, agriculture, or the auxiliary services. Women entered all areas of the workforce, but despite their invaluable contribution, women were not given equal pay with men.

Calling all women

Recruitment posters encouraged women to enter factories. Work in munitions was skilled and could be dangerous, but wages were higher than before the war. Many women found it hard to leave when war ended.

AFTER ›»

The war years had a profound and lasting impact on the British public.

DESTRUCTION

The Blitz ended in 1941 but bombing raids continued throughout the war. In 1944 British civilians suffered again when **flying bombs 278–279 ›»** hit cities in southern England.

RATIONING AND REFORM

Food and fuel shortages continued after the war and rationing did not end until 1954, by which time even bread had been rationed. However, the postwar years saw the start of the **Welfare State**, with benefits such as free health care and family allowances.

WOMEN

By the time war ended, the number of women workers had grown by two million and they made up more than 43 percent of the labor force **170–71 ›»**. Settling back into domestic routine was hard and divorce rates soared.

2 TOY SOLDIERS (GERMANY)

3 WARTIME CHILDREN'S
CARD GAME (BRITAIN)

AIR RAID
ALARM

Fanny Fuzzy

Polly Puffer

Percy Puffer

1 LONDON FIRE BRIGADE
TEDDY BEAR (BRITAIN)

4 EVACUEE'S
SUITCASE (BRITAIN)

EMP

5 PARACHUTE SILK
BRIDESMAID'S DRESS (BRITAIN)

The Home Front
in Europe

All over Europe civilians had very similar experiences of the war: rationing, the black market, the spirit of "make do and mend," civil defense duties, strict identity controls, the perils of air raids, and the evacuation of children.

1 **This teddy bear** wears the insignia of the volunteer fire guards whose main duty was watching for fires. 2 **Toy soldiers**, like this proud Nazi unit, helped breed a spirit of patriotism in the next generation. 3 **This children's card game** is a wartime variation on the old British game of "Happy Families." 4 **An evacuee child's suitcase** was usually made of cheap materials. This one is leather, but many were just cardboard. 5 **Parachute silk** was much sought after for making women's clothes. This dress was made for a bridesmaid at a soldier's wedding in 1945. 6 **This German gas mask** claims that its filter protects against all known chemical weapons. It was never put to the test as gas attacks did not take place. 7 **Tobacco** and cigarettes were not rationed, but there were periods of scarcity. The military were better supplied than civilians. 8 **Air raid wardens' whistles** warned people to take shelter during a bombing raid. 9 **Sealing tape** was stuck to window panes so that broken glass did not fly about in a bomb blast.

10 **British Fire Guards wore helmets** when assisting the Fire Brigade in dangerous situations. 11 **A German meat ration card** was divided into cut-out coupons for 50g (about 2oz) of meat. By July 1944 the ration had fallen to 250g (about 10oz) per week. 12 **Tea** was rationed in Britain from 1940, everyone over the age of five being entitled to just 2 oz (56 g) a week. 13 **Cocoa** was very popular in Britain following the rationing of chocolate. 14 **This French clothing coupon** entitled the bearer to one pair of women's shoes. 15 **Clothing coupons** were introduced in Britain in 1941. Every article of clothing was worth a certain number of points. 16 **A health certificate** was issued to boys in the Hitler Youth. With membership compulsory, there were eight million members by 1940. 17 **This cookie cutter** enabled cooks to reward children with a sweet version of Germany's military honor. 18 **A Nazi Party membership card** often gained the bearer extra privileges. 19 **This card entitled French mothers** with three children under 14 or two under four to priority service in shops and government offices.

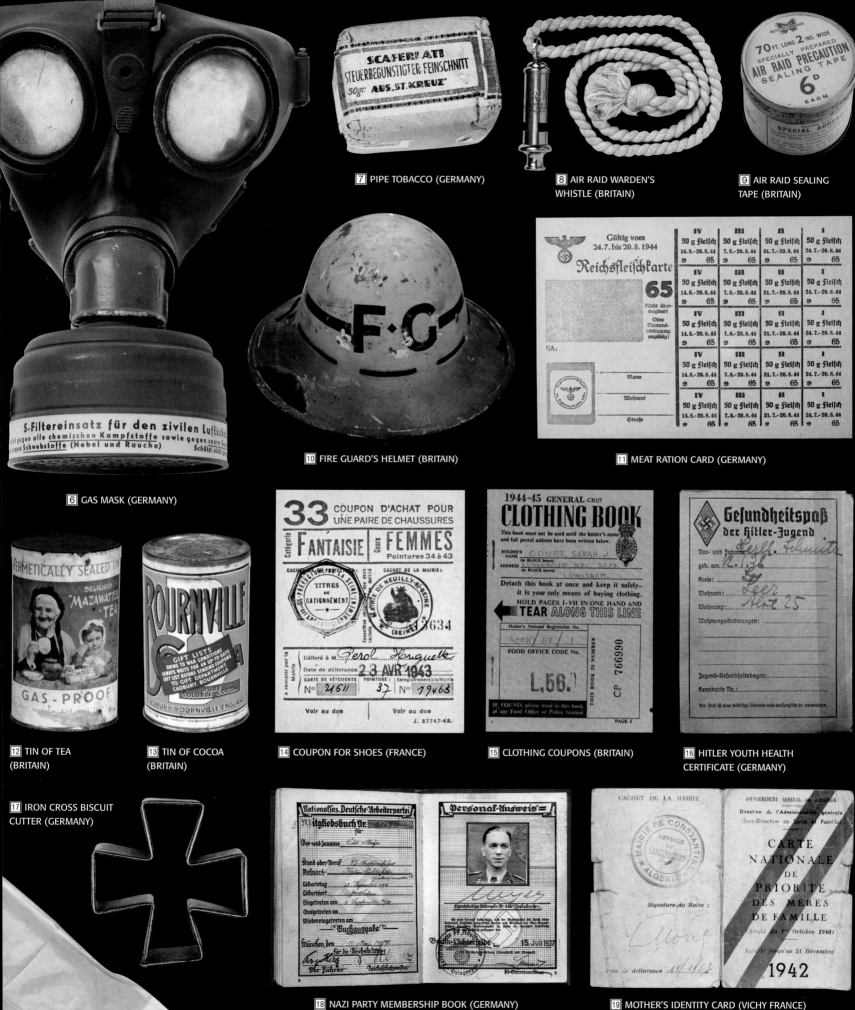

7 PIPE TOBACCO (GERMANY)

8 AIR RAID WARDEN'S WHISTLE (BRITAIN)

9 AIR RAID SEALING TAPE (BRITAIN)

10 FIRE GUARD'S HELMET (BRITAIN)

11 MEAT RATION CARD (GERMANY)

6 GAS MASK (GERMANY)

12 TIN OF TEA (BRITAIN)

13 TIN OF COCOA (BRITAIN)

14 COUPON FOR SHOES (FRANCE)

15 CLOTHING COUPONS (BRITAIN)

16 HITLER YOUTH HEALTH CERTIFICATE (GERMANY)

17 IRON CROSS BISCUIT CUTTER (GERMANY)

18 NAZI PARTY MEMBERSHIP BOOK (GERMANY)

19 MOTHER'S IDENTITY CARD (VICHY FRANCE)

America Backs Britain

In the mid-1930s the President Franklin Delano Roosevelt had been quick to grasp the threat posed by Germany, Italy, and Japan. However, deep-seated isolationist and pacifist opinion at home left him with little room to maneuver on the international stage. The Lend-Lease Act was to change everything.

Britain's Atlantic lifeline
From 1941 to 1945 the United States was supplying nearly one third of Britain's food requirements, providing everyday staples, such as flour—seen here being unloaded—and rice. Britain imported over a million tons of food and material a week.

> "I have seen war … **I have seen the dead** … I have seen children starving … I hate war."
>
> FRANKLIN D. ROOSEVELT, SPEECH AT CHAUTAUQUA, NEW YORK, 1936

In 1935 the US Congress passed the first in a series of Neutrality Acts—measures that prohibited material or financial aid to nations at war.

Poland's rapid collapse in September 1939 came as a shock, and President Roosevelt reacted by asking Congress to amend the Neutrality Acts so that arms could be supplied to the British and French. A six-week debate finally produced an amendment that allowed belligerents to buy war materials on a "cash and carry" basis.

By late June 1940 the situation in Europe had worsened. Britain, its forces evacuated from France, faced a German invasion. On June 22, 1940, Congress passed the National Defense Tax Bill and would soon assign $37 billion to produce a "two ocean" navy and an expanded army and air force.

The Lend-Lease Act

In July 1940, as the Battle of Britain began in earnest, the new British prime minister, Winston Churchill, appealed to Roosevelt for 50 old destroyers. In an act that was technically illegal, Roosevelt agreed, but at the price of 99-year leases on a number of sea and air bases in the British West Indies and Bermuda.

Roosevelt was reelected in November 1940 for an unprecedented third term as president. When Congress met in January 1941, he sought support for the nations that were fighting to defend what he called the Four Freedoms: freedom of speech, freedom of religion, freedom from want, and freedom from fear.

What the British needed, however, was not fine words but arms on easier terms than those of "cash and carry." Roosevelt's solution was the Lend-Lease Act, passed by Congress in March 1941. The Act enabled the British to borrow war supplies from the United States against the promise of later repayment. By the end of the month, Congress had voted Lend-Lease a colossal $7 billion.

> **In 1940 the United States produced only 346 tanks. In 1944 some 17,500 rolled off the production lines.**

Coming to the aid of the Allies
President Roosevelt signs the Lend-Lease Act, which was to provide billions of dollars worth of aid to US Allies during the war—from building the tracks for Soviet railroads to tanks for British armored divisions.

Crisis talks

Roosevelt had taken "all steps short of war." At the end of March 1941 Axis ships in US ports were seized. In April US warships escorted convoys bound for Britain. In May 50 oil tankers were diverted to the British. At the end of the month, after the US freighter *Robin Moor* was torpedoed, Roosevelt declared a state of emergency. Axis credit in the United States was frozen and Axis consulates closed. In July US Marines replaced the British garrison in Iceland, which the British had occupied after the fall of Denmark. On August 9 Roosevelt and Churchill met for talks in Newfoundland. The destruction of Germany was given priority and they issued the Atlantic Charter, which embodied the four freedoms. Yet these joint pledges of action meant little until the US was at war with Germany.

The push to action

Hitler seemed unlikely to oblige—his attention was concentrated on the Eastern Front. Roosevelt told his Secretary of the Treasury, Henry Morgenthau, "I am waiting to be pushed into the situation." When the shove came, it was from an entirely different direction: the Far East.

«« 24–25

BEFORE ««

Despite pressing economic issues and huge anti-war sentiment, Roosevelt was well aware of the implications surrounding a British defeat at the hands of Germany.

ROOSEVELT WALKS A TIGHTROPE
From the mid-1930s President Roosevelt, although mindful of the threat from Germany, Italy, and Japan, devoted his energy to reviving the ailing US economy after the **Great Depression** «« 24–25.

ANTI-WAR
Roosevelt had to deal with strong isolationist sentiment at home. The America First Committee sought to **enforce the Neutrality Acts**; one of its leading spokesmen was the airman Charles Lindbergh, whose **anti-war stance** made him one of the committee's leading members. However, Roosevelt knew that it would **not be in US interests for the British to be defeated.**

CHARLES LINDBERGH

AFTER AFTER

Fleet Admiral Isoroku Yamamoto had first-hand experience of the might of the US economy and knew that an all-out Japanese victory was a pipe dream.

THE ARSENAL OF DEMOCRACY
The help that the United States gave the Allies in the early part of the war greatly helped to **revive the US economy from the Great Depression** and placed it on a firm footing to enable it to join the fight against the Axis 148–49 »». When unleashed, **the almost limitless power of the US economy** provided one of the principal planks in the Allied victory.

INDUSTRIAL POWER
The possibility of such a victory was all too evident to Fleet Admiral Isoroku Yamamoto, the commander-in-chief of the Japanese Combined Fleet, who had served as a naval attaché in the US before the war and was **an admirer of its native industrial genius**. It was for this reason that he would only **guarantee the Japanese emperor six months of victory** in the Far East and Pacific after the outbreak of war. He feared that in order to achieve victory over the US, the Japanese would have to "march into Washington and sign the treaty in the White House".

Shipments of arms
Machine guns for Allied warplanes await shipment.
The colossal industrial strength of the US underpinned
the Allied war effort. American productive muscle and
Soviet manpower were the keys to Allied victory.

Italy Enters the War

When Benito Mussolini annexed the small Adriatic kingdom of Albania in April 1939, he was imitating Hitler's annexation of Czechoslovakia. On June 10, 1940, as German victory in the Battle of France was beyond doubt, Mussolini declared war on France. This would become a pattern over the next two years.

An uneasy alliance
Mussolini and Hitler savor triumph at Munich in June 1940, but the faultlines in their alliance were soon exposed. Hitler's influence on Rome did not sit well with the Italian people—even the Vatican protested.

In June 1940 the Italians attacked France with 28 divisions across the Alpes-Maritimes. Four French divisions replied by inflicting 5,000 casualties for a loss of only eight dead.

Mussolini's prize for this inglorious passage of arms was an occupied zone stretching 50 miles (80 km) into France from the Italian border. Hitler regularly tried to restrain his fellow dictator and when this failed, loyalty obliged him to bail out "Il Duce." In the geopolitical game at which Hitler had proved a master, Mussolini was the weak link.

A force to be reckoned with

In October 1940 the Romanian dictator, General Ion Antonescu, allowed the country to be occupied by the German army. Mussolini had not been told and in a fit of pique announced that he would "occupy" Greece, launching an invasion from Albania on October 28. The 162,000 men of the Italian army were checked by the mobilizing Greeks and by the year's end had been driven back into Albania, half of which fell into Greek hands. By March Hitler was reviewing plans to invade Greece via Yugoslavia and Bulgaria.

The fall of France in June 1940 meant the Italian navy had become the largest force in the Mediterranean. Centrally placed, its six battleships could outpunch the two British fleets, which were tactically placed to protect the convoy routes: Force H, based at Gibraltar, with two battleships and one aircraft carrier; and the British Mediterranean Fleet, based in Alexandria, with four battleships and one aircraft carrier.

The aircraft carrier was the decisive weapon. On November 11, 1940, the British escorted the carrier *Illustrious* to within 200 miles (320 km) of the naval base at Taranto on the heel of Italy, where all six battleships lay at anchor. Torpedoes launched from *Illustrious* crippled three battleships and two cruisers for the loss of just two aircraft.

War in the desert

Mussolini further complicated the strategic problems of the Axis by opening up new areas of war in the Western Desert of North Africa and in East Africa—the only places after the fall of France where Allies' ground forces were able to get to grips with the Axis. Commanders in Egypt and Libya were prisoners of geography and climate, like their counterparts in the Soviet Union. The Western Desert was an arid wasteland yielding nothing. The coastal plain confined the armies to a narrow 40-mile (65-km) coastal strip. The war

> **The Italian commander at Bardia in Libya was General Annibale Bergonzoli. The bearded General was dubbed "Electric Whiskers" by British troops.**

> **"I am stopped in the middle of 200— no, 500—men with their hands up … Send up the bloody infantry!"**
> BRITISH TANK COMMANDER ON ITALIAN SURRENDER, DECEMBER 1940

« BEFORE

Mussolini's overwhelming desire for glory was not sustained by his country's declining military strength.

EXPANDING ECONOMY
Italy's dictator, **Benito Mussolini « 22–23**, had an unbridled desire for military glory that had led him to expand the country's economy and industrial capacity to an unsustainable level. Italy's **economy could support barely one tenth** of the German military expenditure.

AN ARMY IN DECLINE
Mussolini's desire for aggrandizement also meant that **Italy had renewed its armory too early** and was unable to compete with its British equivalents. This came at a time when **Italian military strength was declining absolutely**, sapped by emigration to the US and Mussolini's obsession with his Blackshirt formations. Il Duce was always **running to catch up with Nazi Germany** and in the process over-reaching himself. Finally, in 1940 the rapidity of **Germany's victory in the West « 76–83** spurred Mussolini into a declaration of war as French resistance was crumbling.

A sinking in Taranto
Oil leaks from Italian warships after the British attack in 1940. Two waves of Swordfish torpedo bombers left the *Illustrious* and swept through Taranto harbor, shifting the balance of power in the Mediterranean.

in North Africa was marked by a series of advances and retreats along this 1,200-mile (1,930-km) long strip, stretching from Tripoli to Alexandria, along which a chain of small ports were the only points of military value. The war took the form of dashes from one point of maritime supply to the next, with the aim of depriving the enemy of water, fuel, ammunition, reinforcements, and food—all the essentials of desert warfare.

In 1940 the British had things their own way. In September the Italians launched an offensive into Egypt from their North African colony in Libya. Although

heavily outnumbered, the British Western Desert Force went on the attack on December 9, driving the Italians back 500 miles (800 km) to El Agheila, taking 130,000 prisoners and a massive haul of equipment.

Mussolini's East African empire consisted of Italian Somaliland, Eritrea, and Abyssinia. These territories threatened the entrance to the Red Sea and Britain's adjacent African colonies. It fell to General Wavell, the British commander-in-chief in the Middle East, to tackle Italian forces here. They outnumbered the British but remained strategically isolated, while the British brought in reinforcements through the ports on the littoral of the Indian Ocean.

The final push

The campaign was the last conflict of high empire, featuring camel corps, native levies, and rugged terrain, and saw none of the armored formations of the Battle of France. The Italians quickly overran British Somaliland but

Exploding devil
Italian Mod.35 hand grenades were highly dangerous when found unexploded. They were nicknamed "Red Devils" by British and Commonwealth troops.

remained on the defensive. The British launched a counter-stroke from Kenya into Italian Somaliland in January 1941. Mogadishu was captured on February 25, forcing the Italian armies out. The local British commander, General Sir Alan Cunningham, pushed into Ethiopia and took the capital, Addis Ababa, on April 6 after an advance of 1,000 miles (1,600 km).

Action in the north

In a separate campaign, the Italians were driven into Eritrea, while in northwest Ethiopia a small unit of Sudanese and Ethiopian guerrillas took on seven Italian brigades. The Italians retreated to Keren, where they resisted doggedly for eight weeks before being ousted. Asmara, the Eritrean capital, fell to the British in April and the port of Massawa soon after. Mopping-up operations continued until November.

Erratic performance
The Italian military looked impressive on parade but its weaponry was a generation out of date. Many troops lacked the motivation to fight, though some divisions displayed outstanding skill and resourcefulness.

AFTER »

Although Mussolini wanted to ally himself with Hitler, his people had other ideas. The German dictator was also harboring doubts about the alliance.

FRIEND OR FOE?
Far from being an asset to the Axis, **Italy became an embarrassment**, relying on German support as one catastrophe succeeded another, as in the **war in the desert 124–25 »**. The enemies Mussolini chose were Hitler's but they were not foes against whom the Italian people harbored any animosity.

A JUNIOR PARTNER
The Italian upper classes were for the most part **Anglophiles**; the Italian peasantry and working classes were admirers of the US. However, out of **misplaced loyalty**, Hitler was obliged to stand by his fellow Fascist dictator, whose value as an ally was **at best dubious and at worst disastrous**. With the **Allied landings in Italy 210–13 »**, the tide of war began to turn.

武運長久

稲垣春男

橋本房雄

中川栄

後藤

長坂

富山

4

THE WIDENING WAR

1941

Yugoslavia, Greece, and Crete fell to Germany, but most German resources were conserved for the huge offensive against the unsuspecting Soviet Union. After Japan's surprise attack on Pearl Harbor, the United States entered the war against both Japan and Germany.

THE WIDENING WAR

Leningrad was besieged by the Germans from September 1941 until 1944. In winter supplies could be driven across ice-covered Lake Ladoga, but more than a million starved to death.

The Bismarck presented such a threat to shipping in the Atlantic that the British deployed almost every available ship to hunt it down. The battleship was finally sunk on May 27.

Operation Barbarossa, Hitler's invasion of the USSR, made huge gains through the summer. But, as the Germans neared Moscow and winter closed in, they met stiffer Soviet resistance.

EUROPE

Faeroe Islands (to Denmark)

NORWAY
SWEDEN
FINLAND

North Sea
Baltic Sea
ESTONIA
LATVIA
LITHUANIA

IRISH FREE STATE
DENMARK
BRITAIN NETH.
BEL. LUX.
GER.
POLAND
USSR

FRANCE SWITZ.
GERMANY
SLOVAKIA
HUNGARY
ROMANIA

YUGOSLAVIA
ITALY
ALB. (to Italy)
BULGARIA
Black Sea

PORTUGAL
SPAIN
Mediterranean Sea
GREECE
DODECANESE (to Italy)
TURKEY
SYRIA (French mandate)
IRAQ (British mandate)
CYPRUS
PALESTINE (British mandate)

MOROCCO (to France)
ALGERIA (to France)
TUNISIA (to France)
LIBYA (to Italy)
EGYPT

ICELAND

NORWAY
SWEDEN
FINLAND

BRITAIN
GERMANY
POLAND
FRANCE
ITALY
Black Sea
Caspian Sea
USSR

SPAIN
TURKEY
SYRIA
PERSIA
AFGHANISTAN

MOROCCO
TUNISIA
PALESTINE
IRAQ

ALGERIA
LIBYA
EGYPT
NEJD (Saudi)
OMAN
HADHRAMAUT
INDIA

RIO DE ORO
FRENCH WEST AFRICA
ANGLO-EGYPTIAN SUDAN
ASIR
YEMEN
ADEN PROTECTORATE
FRENCH SOMALILAND
BRITISH SOMALILAND

GAMBIA
PORTUGUESE GUINEA
SIERRA LEONE
LIBERIA
NIGERIA
CAMEROONS (British mandate)
FRENCH EQUATORIAL AFRICA
ABYSSINIA

GOLD COAST
CAMEROONS (French mandate)
UGANDA
KENYA
ITALIAN SOMALILAND

ATLANTIC OCEAN

BELGIAN CONGO
TANGANYIKA (British mandate)
INDIAN OCEAN

ANGOLA (to Portugal)
NYASALAND
NORTHERN RHODESIA

SOUTH WEST AFRICA
BECHUANA-LAND
SOUTHERN RHODESIA
PORTUGUESE EAST AFRICA
MADAGASCAR

SWAZILAND
UNION OF SOUTH AFRICA
BASUTOLAND

After a coup by pro-German Rashid in April, Britain se force from India invade Iraq and reins a pro-British goverm

The Axis invasion of Yugoslavia in April was ruthlessly efficient. The Yugoslav air force was destroyed while still on the ground, then mechanized columns completed the conquest in less than two weeks.

Erwin Rommel and the Afrika Korps were sent to Libya in February to reinforce the Italians, who were in danger of defeat. In his subsequent desert campaigns Rommel won the respect of friend and foe alike.

I n 1941 the war in Europe and North Africa spread to the Balkans, the Middle East, and, most significantly, the USSR. In preparation for Hitler's long-planned invasion of the USSR, Axis forces first took control of Yugoslavia, Greece, and Crete. The Germans also went to the aid of the Italians in Libya. Although the latter were defeated in Abyssinia and lost all their other possessions in East Africa, the new combined German-Italian force under Rommel

proved more than a match for the British in Egypt, threatening to advance across the Western Desert to take the Suez Canal. The British also had to deal with the threat of hostile Vichy French forces in Syria and Lebanon, and a pro-German miltary coup in Iraq.

In late June the focus moved to Eastern Europe when Hitler launched the invasion of the USSR. Axis forces poured across a 1,000-mile (1,600-km) front from the Baltic to the Black Sea

1941

Japan's surprise attack on **Pearl Harbor** was designed to put the US Pacific Fleet out of action. Five battleships were sunk, but the all-important aircraft carriers were at sea.

Roosevelt and Churchill met for the first time on a ship off Newfoundland in August. There they drew up the Atlantic Charter, a blueprint for the postwar world.

President Roosevelt responded swiftly to the Japanese bombing of Pearl Harbor, declaring war on Japan on December 8, and on Germany and Italy three days later. Here he looks over the joint Congressional declarations of war against Germany and Italy.

When the Japanese **invaded Malaya,** the British warships *Prince of Wales* and *Repulse* sailed to intervene, but were sunk by torpedo bombers on December 10.

THE WORLD IN DECEMBER 1941

Axis powers (Germany, Italy, and Japan) and allies
Axis conquests to Dec 1941
Area under Japanese control, Dec 1941
Vichy France and colonies
Allied states
Allied conquests to Dec 1941
Neutral states
Frontiers Sep 1939

Stalin and the Soviet forces were totally unprepared. German armies swept forward along the whole front, taking hundreds of thousands of prisoners, and by December were within striking distance of Moscow.

With Europe's attention focused on Germany, Japan decided that the time had come to execute its plan to take over the British, Dutch, French, and American colonies in Asia. Their offensive began with the surprise attack on Pearl Harbor to neutralize the US Navy.

By the end of 1941 Germany had conquered vast swathes of Europe, and the Japanese were in the process of doing the same in Asia and the Pacific. But the Axis had awakened two sleeping giants. The USSR's seemingly inexhaustible reserves of manpower would make it a far more formidable foe than Hitler had imagined, while the US would now put all its vast economic and industrial potential into combating not only the Japanese in the East, but also Nazi Germany in Europe.

TIMELINE 1941

War in North Africa ▪ Lend-Lease ▪ **The U-boat War** ▪ Secret Warfare ▪
German Invasion of Yugoslavia and Greece ▪ Hunting the *Bismarck* ▪ **Operation Barbarossa** ▪ War in the Middle East ▪ Siege of Leningrad ▪ **Pearl Harbor**

JANUARY	FEBRUARY	MARCH	APRIL	MAY

⌃ Italian soldiers surrender near Bardia, Libya

MARCH 1
Bulgaria signs Tripartite Pact, becoming part of the Axis.

MARCH 4
British attack on oil facilities at Narvik, Norway.

APRIL 2
Anti-British general Rashid Ali seizes power in Iraq and cuts off oil supply to the Mediterranean.

APRIL 6
German, Italian, and Bulgarian troops invade Yugoslavia and Greece.

JANUARY 5
Australian troops capture the town of Bardia in Libya, just across the border with Egypt.

FEBRUARY 6
General Rommel ordered to Libya to help beleaguered Italians.

FEBRUARY 7
Italian 10th Army surrenders at Beda Fomm. The British take Benghazi.

MARCH 7
British forces arrive in Greece.

MARCH 9
Start of final unsuccessful Italian offensive against Greece.

⌄ Roosevelt signing the Lend-Lease Act

APRIL 10
US occupies Greenland, a step closer to supporting Britain in the Atlantic.

APRIL 10
Rommel attacks Tobruk; 24,000 Allied troops besieged.

⌃ Enigma machine

JANUARY 22
Operation Compass: surrender of the Libyan port of Tobruk to the Allies.

FEBRUARY 12
Rommel lands in Tripoli to take command of the Afrika Korps.

8 MAY
Enigma encoding machine obtained from *U-110*, which is captured by British off Iceland.

20 MAY
German paratroopers land on Crete in Operation Mercury.

FEBRUARY 25
Mogadishu, capital of Italian Somaliland, falls to the British.

MARCH 11
US President Roosevelt signs Lend-Lease Act. This allows the US to supply Britain and other Allied countries with arms while, in theory, remaining neutral.

APRIL 17
Yugoslavia surrenders to the Nazis. A government-in-exile is formed in Britain.

APRIL 18
Anglo-Iraqi War begins as Britain challenges pro-Axis government.

⌃ The *Bismarck*

MARCH 24
Rommel retakes El Agheila in Libya in a surprise attack.

MARCH 27
Coup in Yugoslavia overthrows the pro-Axis government.

APRIL 23
King George II and Greek government evacuate to Crete.

APRIL 27
German troops occupy Athens.

24 MAY
German battleship *Bismarck* sinks British battlecruiser *Hood*.

27 MAY
Sinking of the *Bismarck* after relentless pursuit by Royal Navy.

« General Erwin Rommel

> "**No matter how long** it may take us to overcome this premeditated invasion, the **American people in their righteous might** will win through to **absolute victory**."
>
> PRESIDENT ROOSEVELT IN HIS SPEECH TO CONGRESS FOLLOWING PEARL HARBOR, DECEMBER 8, 1941

JULY	AUGUST	SEPTEMBER	OCTOBER	NOVEMBER	DECEMBER
JULY 3 Stalin calls for "scorched earth policy." **JULY 7** US occupies Iceland. **JULY 14** Allies overthrow Vichy French government in Syria.	**AUGUST 5** Germans capture Smolensk. **AUGUST 7** Stalin appoints himself Generalissimo, leader of the Red Army.	**SEPTEMBER 3** Auschwitz gas chambers used for first time. **SEPTEMBER 8** 900-day siege of Leningrad begins.	**OCTOBER 2** Germans launch Operation Typhoon against Moscow. **OCTOBER 15** First heavy snowfalls of Russian winter recorded.		**DECEMBER 7** Japan bombs US naval base at Pearl Harbor. US and Britain declare war on the following day.

» US propaganda poster

| | **AUGUST 9**
Roosevelt and Churchill meet aboard ship off Newfoundland coast and sign Atlantic Charter, setting out their vision for the postwar world. | | **OCTOBER 16**
Soviet government evacuates Moscow and moves to Kuibyshev. | **NOVEMBER 15**
Germans begin final push toward Moscow. | |
| **JULY 24**
Japan occupies French Indochina.

JULY 31
Goering asks Reinhard Heydrich for "final solution" of the Jewish problem. | **AUGUST 12**
Hitler shifts forces away from Moscow to strike south through Ukraine to the Crimea. | | **OCTOBER 18**
War minister Tojo Hideki becomes prime minister of Japan. | **NOVEMBER 18**
Operation Crusader launched. British relieve troops trapped in siege of Tobruk, Rommel forced to withdraw to El Agheila. | **DECEMBER 11**
Germany and Italy declare war against US.

DECEMBER 13
Germans retreat from Moscow to form "winter line." |

ꙮ Menorah monument to the victims of Babi Yar

ꙮ General Tojo Hideki

| | **AUGUST 25**
Germans engage Soviets around Kiev to stop them retreating. The operation successfully encircles almost half a million troops east of the city. | **SEPTEMBER 29**
German SS troops kill thousands of Jews at Babi Yar, a ravine on outskirts of Kiev. | | **NOVEMBER 26**
As Japanese fleet sets sail for the Hawaiian Islands, US delivers an ultimatum to Japan to withdraw from the Axis. | |
| | **AUGUST 25**
Britain and USSR invade Iran to protect oilfields from Axis. | | **OCTOBER 19**
Official "state of siege" declared in Moscow.

OCTOBER 21
Mass slaughter of Serbs carried out by Ustaša fascists in Yugoslavia. | **NOVEMBER 27**
Panzers reach the outskirts of Moscow.

NOVEMBER 28
Hitler meets Grand Mufti of Jerusalem and gives approval for Arab actions against British. | **DECEMBER 19**
Hitler becomes commander-in-chief of the German Army.

DECEMBER 25
Hong Kong surrenders to Japanese. |

ꙮ German soldiers braving the Russian winter

« Exhausted Soviet troops

Life under the Swastika

By 1941 most of Europe was under the control of Nazi Germany. Only five states—Ireland, Portugal, Spain, Sweden, and Switzerland—remained neutral. Otherwise millions of people were living under German rule. Most resigned themselves to occupation, some collaborated, some resisted.

Visible signs of Nazi occupation included the presence of German troops, swastikas flying over public buildings, curfews, rationing, identity cards, and intense Nazi propaganda. Government of the occupied lands varied, although all directives came from the Reich. In some areas, the Germans retained existing governments, finding it more effective to work through collaborators and pro-Nazis such as Vidkun Quisling in Norway, or extreme right-wing groups in Belgium and Hungary. In Poland, the Baltic States, and the western USSR, Germany imposed total rule, setting up military governments headed by Nazi officials, such as Governor-General Hans Frank in Poland. Military governments were installed in Belgium and northern France. Uniquely, King Christian X of Denmark was left alone to rule his country, largely because Hitler considered the Danes Aryan and

Life in the ghetto
Nazi soldiers arrest Jews in the Warsaw ghetto, 1942. From 1939 Polish Jews were herded into ghettos where they were intended to starve to death. Disease was rife, food rations were limited, and unemployment was high.

hoped the country would support him in his fight against Communism. The king, however, honorably refused to collaborate and in 1943 Germany took control of Denmark. Throughout occupied Europe, Berlin relied on force or the threat of force to ensure co-operation, and on the compliance of mayors, police, and other local officials.

Shortages and hardships

Impact of occupation on civilian life varied. On the surface, Nazi occupation in Western Europe appeared benign. According to Hitler's view of the world, Western Europeans were similar to Germans and could therefore be treated in a reasonably civilized fashion. However, resistance was punished, and although citizens tried to live normally, there were big changes. Both curfews and censorship were widely imposed, movement was restricted, and there was the ever-present threat of being stopped and searched. Food, clothing, and fuel rationing were introduced and Germany stripped countries of resources, either to meet the needs of the occupying forces or for the war effort within Germany. As normal

The yellow star
Jews in most occupied areas were made to wear a six-pointed yellow star—often bearing the word "Jew." The star above is Dutch; Jews in Germany wore "Jude" and in France "Juif."

foodstuffs vanished, food lines appeared and local people had to make do with alternatives. In France casein, a white protein, and ersatz coffee, made from acorns, entered the diet, wooden shoes replaced leather ones, and people used bicycles or charcoal-burning vehicles instead of gas-driven cars. A black market thrived where goods could be bought for a price. But coal and firewood disappeared, as did soap. Shortages were worst in the cities but as war continued, hardships intensified. Thousands starved in Greece during 1941–42, and in Holland during the winter of 1944–45 an estimated 6,000 people died of starvation. The impact of occupation was worst of all in Eastern Europe. Hitler and the Nazi

13,152 The number of Jewish women, men, and children rounded up in Paris on July 16–17, 1942 by the French authorities. They were then deported to Auschwitz.

regime considered the Slavic peoples— the Poles, the Russians, and the citizens of the Baltic States—and all Jews to be subhuman and dispensable. In the Nazi view they should be removed to create what was known as *Lebensraum* ("living space") for the German "master race." Occupying forces in Eastern Europe treated local populations with great brutality, ignoring their civil rights, forcibly evicting people from their homes to make way for German settlers, and rounding up those deemed "undesirable," such as Communists, Roma, and Jews. All over the occupied territories, local people were either encouraged or forced to go to Germany to work.

Resistance and collaboration

There were many cases of direct collaboration as people, either fearful or supportive of the Nazis, acted as informers or used German occupation

to their advantage. In 1941 and 1942 Hitler appeared invincible and punishment for resistance was severe, so that for most individuals despair gave way to reluctant cooperation.

Even so, people in all occupied countries found ways and means of resisting. It was forbidden to listen to BBC broadcasts, but thousands of people did so in secret and by 1942 the BBC was broadcasting in 24 languages, often sending coded messages to the French Resistance. Dutch citizens walked out of Nazi propaganda films, patriotic graffiti appeared on public walls, and the citizens of Denmark wore RAF colors. Certain courageous individuals frequently risked severe punishment or even death to help

« BEFORE

Even before war broke out, Germany had annexed Austria and Czechoslovakia. Once war was declared, German troops marched further into Europe.

OCCUPYING TERRITORIES
Between 1939 and 1940 **German forces occupied western Poland « 58–59**, invaded **Denmark and Norway « 74–75**, and went on to occupy **Belgium, Holland, and France « 76–77**. By June 1940, northern France had fallen and the Vichy government had been set up in non-occupied France. In 1940 **German forces also occupied the Channel Islands.**

PERSECUTION OF JEWS
In 1939 more than nine million Jews lived in Europe, many in Poland and more than 500,000 in Germany. The Nazi persecution of Jews had started with the **"Nuremberg Laws"** passed in 1933, which **stripped Jews of their citizenship** and began the process of segregating them. In November 1938 in a pogrom that became known as **Kristallnacht (Crystal Night, or the Night of Broken Glass) « 42–43**, Jewish businesses, cemeteries, and synagogues were attacked.

Liberation from Nazi rule did not begin until 1944. For people living in occupied Europe conditions worsened although resistance increased.

RESISTANCE AND LIBERATION

By the summer of 1942 German-occupied territories extended **from the Channel Islands to Moscow**, but from 1943 **the tide began to turn**. Allied secret services aided resistance movements and from 1942 the **French Resistance 222–23 ⟫** intensified its activities, while partisans in Albania and Yugoslavia harried occupying forces. In 1944 the Allies landed in France, beginning the **Liberation 268–69 ⟫**.

THE HOLOCAUST

From 1942 Nazi persecution of the Jews escalated into the **Final Solution 176–77 ⟫**. Jews everywhere were rounded up and **deported to extermination camps** such as Auschwitz. By 1945 the Jewish population of Europe had dropped to about three million—**at least six million had been murdered**. Figures vary, but it is likely that about another five million people perished in and outside the camps. They included Roma, Communists, homosexuals, disabled people, and so-called "undesirables."

HOLOCAUST VICTIM (1929–1945)

ANNE FRANK

One of the best-known victims of the Holocaust, Anne Frank was a German-born Jewish girl whose family left Germany for Holland in 1933. In 1940, when Anne was nearly 11, German forces marched into Holland. Two years later, as Nazis began rounding up Dutch Jews, the family went into hiding, helped by friends. They survived for two years in what Anne called their "secret annex," during which time she kept a diary of her experiences. In 1944 the family were betrayed and deported. Anne died in Bergen-Belsen, aged 15. Her diary survived and was published after the war.

---

members of the French Resistance or to come to the aid of Allied soldiers who arrived behind enemy lines.

Treatment of Jews

Jews were persecuted throughout Nazi-occupied Europe. After the arrival of occupying forces, local officials were ordered to provide lists of Jews, who were then stripped of their civil rights and banned from schools, restaurants, and public spaces. Soon Jews were

rounded up and forced into ghettos or deported east to concentration camps. In many areas, Jewish Councils were set up to work with Nazi officials, something that has since been argued over. The move to deport Jews in France was slower, but from 1941 they too were being deported. The pattern was the same in every occupied country. Some brave individuals risked their lives to hide Jews or help them to escape. Persecution was worst in Eastern

On the surface
After the occupation, daily life apparently returned to normal in Paris. Restaurants and bars reopened and German troops sat side-by-side with Parisians. Swastikas and increasing civilian hardship gave the lie to normality.

Europe where killing squads called *Einsatzgruppen* carried out mass extermination on a daily basis. Jewish ghettos were created in Poland in 1939, and from 1942 thousands were sent to their deaths in concentration camps.

> "One day this terrible war will be over ... **we'll be people again and not just Jews**."

ANNE FRANK WRITING IN HER DIARY, APRIL 11, 1944

Life under German Occupation

In May 1940 German troops began their occupation of Western Europe. Moving swiftly, German troops occupied the Netherlands, Belgium, Luxembourg, and France. On June 14, 1940 German forces entered Paris. Caught off guard by the speed of the German advance, the French Army and the people of Paris offered little resistance.

"We first became aware that Germans were in occupation of the city when Paris fire trucks, manned by Frenchmen, stopped below our hotel on Friday morning and we watched them haul down the four big French flags which encircled the Rond-Point des Champs Elysées. Then they began to tear down posters which urged Frenchmen to buy armament bonds. We went out then to meet the incoming troops, advancing along the Rue Lafayette, past the Madeleine [church] into the Place de la Concorde ... it was startling to observe the nonchalance with which those Germans marched through the heart of Paris. They were still at war with France, but they did not even bother to assign guards along the boulevards through which they advanced.

Those first German troops were young and alert and freshly shaved ... We stood at the Madeleine on that sunny morning amid small clusters of Frenchmen and watched the Germans pass. They looked about them with a lively curiosity at the beautiful city which most of them were viewing for the first time ... The French people around us watched the procession in silence, bearing themselves with that dignity and sang-froid which their authorities had recommended.

For several days after the occupation the German army authorities simply ignored the population of Paris ... We had curfew at nine o'clock and the blackout continued ... Paris ... took on the appearance of a military city. There were continuous troop parades up and down the boulevards, there were military band concerts, there was the incessant roar of planes flying low over the city ... On the afternoon of the second day of occupation .. the first French prisoners went by in trucks through the Place de la Concorde. The crowds had become larger then, and they surged towards the defeated men. Girls and women ran after them, a few weeping ... Sunday the sixteenth, the third day of the occupation, was a cool sunny day. By this time Paris had become accustomed to the steady roll of army vehicles, carrying German troops and guns ... "

JOURNALIST DEMAREE BESS, OBSERVING GERMANS OCCUPYING PARIS, JUNE 1940

Life as normal

German officers and Parisians in a café on the Champs Elysées on Bastille Day, July 14, 1940. Cafés and restaurants had reopened and life in Paris had all but returned to normal despite the German occupation.

‹‹ BEFORE

In the summer of 1940, Hitler's troops swept through the Low Countries and into France. Most of Europe fell under Nazi rule.

POLAND

Perhaps 100,000 **Polish servicemen escaped** to neutral countries in 1939 when their nation was overrun by **Germany and the Soviets** **‹‹ 58–59**. Twice as many ended up as prisoners in the USSR, where thousands, many of them army officers, would be **murdered by the Soviet secret police (NKVD)**.

GERMAN CONQUESTS IN 1940

In April 1940 **Hitler conquered Denmark and Norway ‹‹ 74–75**. The Danish government and king remained in the country throughout the war, **collaborating as little as possible** with the Nazis. The Danish merchant navy and the overseas possessions of Greenland and the Faroe Islands **came under Allied control**. Norway's king and government led a futile defense against the Nazi attack and then **went into exile in Britain**.

THE LOW COUNTRIES AND FRANCE

All of northwest Europe was occupied during May and June 1940 ‹‹ 76–83. The Dutch and Luxemburg governments went into exile in Britain. **Belgium's top politicians escaped** but ended up for a time in Vichy France, from where a number went to London to set up a true exile government. France itself was an entirely different matter. **Marshal Pétain's Vichy regime** remained in theory the legitimate government of France after the surrender. Few in 1940 believed that de Gaulle's **Free French would in time take over that role**.

Governments in Exile

As the German grip on Europe tightened, thousands fled their homelands and escaped abroad. Among the refugees arriving in Britain were the monarchs and politicians of occupied countries, as well as their soldiers, sailors, and airmen, all determined to fight Nazi aggression on the side of the Allied forces.

Early on the morning of April 9, 1940, the German cruiser *Blücher* slipped quietly into Oslofjord in Norway. The German plan was to arrest the Norwegian king and his cabinet, and force the country to capitulate to their attack. Instead, the *Blücher* was hit by torpedoes from a Norwegian coast defense fort

20 **The number, in percentage terms, of the world's oil tankers that belonged to Norway in 1940. More than one third of Britain's wartime oil imports came in Norwegian ships.**

and sunk. King Haakon VII and his family escaped to carry on the fight, eventually fleeing their country in June when defeat was inevitable.

King Haakon VII was not the only national leader to sidestep capture in a dramatic fashion. By the summer of

Training for the return home
Czechoslovakian troops training in Britain in 1942. A Czech armored brigade fought in France in 1944 and helped lay siege to the German garrison in Dunkirk. Czech units also served with the Red Army in 1944–45.

1941 London was home to the monarchs, governments, opposition leaders, and resistance movements of a dozen occupied nations, all of them seeking an early return to their homelands and the restoration of legal rule there.

Polish ministers had established a government in exile in Paris, after the disasters of September 1939. When Germany invaded France in May 1940, they escaped to London. The Dutch royal family, headed by the formidable Queen Wilhelmina, also fled to the safety of Britain.

When Belgium fell, King Léopold III surrendered, but the country's political leaders later transferred government operations to London. On June 17 1940, with French defeat imminent,

Rally to the cause
General de Gaulle meets volunteers from the French colony of Saint Pierre and Miquelon, in London, 1942. The islands, off the coast of Newfoundland, joined the Free French cause in 1941 after previous loyalty to Vichy France.

Charles de Gaulle, a very junior general who had briefly been a government minister, escaped to London. De Gaulle strongly opposed the newly established Vichy government

Flying for freedom
Polish fighter pilots fought effectively with the RAF from 1940 to the end of the war. A Polish squadron, No. 303, claimed the highest number of "kills" in the Battle of Britain.

had also set up a second (Communist) Polish government in exile and ensured that this had the dominant role after the war ended.

One of the obvious roles that all exiled governments played was to keep in touch with their people and inspire them to resist the German occupation. Queen Wilhelmina's broadcasts on

> **15,000** The number of Polish army officers murdered by the Soviets at Katyn and elsewhere in 1940. The Nazis publicized their discovery of the mass graves in 1943.

Radio Oranje were eagerly awaited by her people back home in the Netherlands, who had to listen to them secretly (in the German-occupied zone, it was illegal to listen to broadcasts from Britain). The British Special Operations Executive (SOE) worked with all the exiled governments to ferry agents into the occupied countries and set up resistance groups. One of the reasons why General de Gaulle's Free French came to be accepted as the legitimate leadership of France was that they created a National Resistance Council actually in occupied France to coordinate resistance activities.

Armed forces
Many trained servicemen escaped with their governments and were formed into fighting units to serve alongside the British and other Allied forces. Over 19,000 Poles served within the British RAF, a Polish army corps fought in Italy, and an armored division in northwest Europe. The Dutch forces comprised many warships that were berthed in the East Indies in May 1940. However, most of these were sunk in early combats against the Japanese in 1941–42.

The largest exile forces were French. At first de Gaulle had few supporters but he gradually won over various French colonies in Africa. Following the Torch invasion of northwest Africa in November 1942, the large French forces there, previously loyal to Vichy, came over to the Allied side. In August 1944 the French First Army played a full part in the invasion of southern France, and in the same month General Leclerc's French armored division led the liberating Allied troops into Paris.

POLISH NATIONALIST (1881–1943)
WLADYSLAW SIKORSKI

General Sikorski had been prime minister of Poland in the 1920s. He became head of government and commander-in-chief of Polish exile forces first in France and then from London. When Germany attacked the USSR he negotiated a deal with Stalin for Polish prisoners in the USSR to be released to fight Hitler, but received no promise from Stalin that Polish territory would be restored after the war. Sikorski died in an air crash in 1943. Allegations of sabotage surround his death.

AFTER

Some governments in exile returned home with honor to play a full part in the future political life of their nations. Others were not so fortunate.

GENERAL CHARLES DE GAULLE
President of the French National Committee set up the Headquarters of the Free French Forces here in 1940
GREATER LONDON COUNCIL

LONDON'S DE GAULLE PLAQUE

WESTERN EUROPE
The exile governments from Western Europe returned to **restore civilian democratic rule** in their countries. There were inevitably political changes—King Léopold of Belgium was eventually **forced to abdicate** because of his wartime role, for example. All countries faced the **problem of integrating** the huge resistance forces who had fought hard at home with the leaders and other exiles who had served abroad.

EASTERN EUROPE
Both Czechoslovakia and Poland had postwar governments for a time that included London exiles and Communists aided by the Soviets. By 1947–48 the **Communists had seized control** in both countries by brutality and fraudulent elections. For Yugoslavia the wartime exile government had been **discredited by its internal squabbling**. Since the country had then largely been freed by Tito's Communist partisans, it was they who became the new government.

and made a series of radio broadcasts from the BBC urging his countrymen to fight on: "France has lost a battle but France has not lost the war!"

Carrying on the fight
Some of the governments in exile had few resources and depended entirely on the support of the Allies, first from Britain and later also via Lend-Lease from the US. Other governments were able to pay their way: the Dutch and the Norwegians had large incomes from their merchant navies, and the Belgians had the mineral wealth of their African colonies. For the Allies there was never any question that some, like the Dutch and the Norwegians, were the legitimate governments of their nations; for others the situation was far more complicated. General de Gaulle's Free French Forces were only formally recognized by Britain and the US as the provisional government of France in October 1944, after most of the country had been liberated from the Germans.

In the meantime there had been much political maneuvering to merge the Free French with

> In 1939, when the captain of the Polish submarine *Orzel* became sick, its crew, unable to return home, docked in neutral Estonia. They were arrested but escaped with their boat, sinking a Nazi troop transport off Norway.

politicians and armed forces from the French territories freed by the Allies in their advances since 1941. General de Gaulle gradually won these political battles, while at the same time successfully asserting France's right to an independent national role.

The scene in the East was different. The war ended with the Soviets holding on to the whole zone, which Stalin was going to rule as he saw fit regardless of the consequences.

Resistance tactics
The various London governments in exile had broadly democratic aims, and often a strong anti-Communist bias. Stalin had no intention of letting them return home and take control of their countries.

Poland was perhaps the most notable victim of Stalin's ruthless tactics. Thousands of Poles escaped through Romania to the West when their country was overrun in 1939, but tens of thousands more went into Soviet captivity where many were murdered. Eventually a large number were allowed to leave the Soviet Union to join their compatriots fighting alongside the Western Allies. However, other Poles were formed into army units under Soviet control. By the time the Red Army reached Polish territory Stalin

"This war is not over as a result of the Battle of France. This war is a worldwide war."

CHARLES DE GAULLE, IN A RADIO BROADCAST FROM LONDON, JUNE 18, 1940

LEADER OF THE FREE FRENCH Born 1890 Died 1970

Charles de Gaulle

"The **flame of French resistance** must not and **shall not die**!"

CHARLES DE GAULLE'S FIRST BROADCAST FROM LONDON, JUNE 18, 1940

Patriotic, individualistic, and often difficult to work with, General de Gaulle was leader of the Free French forces and head of the French government in exile.

Committed to the military from an early age, de Gaulle served under Colonel Philippe Pétain in World War I. He was wounded at Verdun and spent 32 months as a prisoner of war. Always an intellectual, his postwar career included lecturing at the French War College and distinguished service in Poland. He was appointed secretary to the National Defense Council and should have had a glittering career, but in the 1930s he antagonized politicians and high-ranking military

only French commander to achieve a German retreat during their relentless invasion. Now a brigadier-general, he was appointed undersecretary of state for national defense, and suggested an Anglo-French union for the duration of the conflict. The French cabinet rejected his proposal. By now Pétain was prime minister and de Gaulle, who fiercely opposed the armistice and collaboration with Germany, flew to London on June 17, 1940, where the following day he broadcast to the French people urging resistance. His hope, and that of Winston Churchill, was that others would join him. Pétain branded him a traitor and sentenced him to death in his absence.

Resistance leader
The flag of the Free French, chosen by de Gaulle, consisted of the Cross of Lorraine set against the tricolor. The cross symbolized resistance against invaders of France.

personnel by his outspoken criticism. His chances of promotion ceased, and he slipped into obscurity.

When World War II broke out, de Gaulle was a tank commander in Alsace. He had predicted a German advance through Holland and Belgium and championed the need for more tank units, but his views were largely ignored. He attacked advancing German forces at Montcornet and Caumont, where he became the

The Free French

From now on de Gaulle's role was more political than military. His aim was to build up a Free French movement that he would lead from London. Winston Churchill backed him but President Roosevelt, was wary, believing that de Gaulle's main concern was to restore France's independence rather than the wider Allied war aims.

De Gaulle's Free French forces initially included only those French troops who had escaped the occupation of France, but gradually colonial territories in sub-Saharan Africa, such as Chad and Cameroon, rallied to de Gaulle, as did French Indochina and other smaller regions. From 1941 Free French forces were fighting with the Allies in Libya, Egypt, Syria, and Lebanon.

The Free French movement gathered momentum when an underground resistance movement was established within France. De Gaulle naturally felt that he should be the nominal leader of this movement, which he named the Fighting French Forces. He sent an emissary to France to try to unify

Le grand Charles
Dressed in a general's uniform and standing 6 ft 4 in (1.94 m) tall, de Gaulle was an imposing and dignified figure.

the various resistance groups under his leadership, which was partially achieved in 1943 with the National Council of the Resistance.

In 1943 de Gaulle left London and set up his base in Algiers, where he formed the French Committee of National Liberation (FCNL) jointly with General Henri Giraud, commander-in-chief of the Free French forces in North Africa. Later, de Gaulle skillfully maneuvered Giraud into a subordinate role.

Tensions and liberation

By June 1944 Free French forces had grown to more than 300,000 regular troops, and de Gaulle's popularity in France was on the rise. But there were tensions between de Gaulle and the Allied leaders, many of whom saw him as a loose cannon. His determination to restore France's glory was seen as a deviation from the main war effort. To his annoyance, he was often sidelined in decision-making and was suspicious of Britain and the United States' attempts to influence France's future.

Matters came to a head in 1944 when de Gaulle announced that the FCNL was to be known as the provisional government of France, with him at its head. Roosevelt and Churchill were

Flame of resistance
Charles de Gaulle made his first broadcast to the French people from the BBC studios after the fall of France on June 18, 1940.

Appeal of June 18, 1940
De Gaulle's famous words, "France has lost a battle. But France has not lost the war!", were not part of the official script for the BBC broadcast of June 18.

furious; they refused to recognize de Gaulle's action and excluded him from the planning of Operation Overlord, the invasion of Normandy. On August 25, 1944, de Gaulle, preceded by the 2nd Armored Division and the US Army, entered Paris. The French greeted him as their new leader and by October the Allies recognized him as France's leader.

Significantly, de Gaulle was not invited to the Yalta Conference in February 1945, where the "Big Three"—Stalin, Churchill, and Roosevelt—debated the shape of postwar Europe; nor was he invited to the subsequent Potsdam Conference, where the future of Germany was determined. Within France, however, de Gaulle was a hero. He headed the immediate postwar government, but resigned in 1946. He returned as president in 1958, and during his term of office dealt with two uprisings in Algeria, agreed France's independent nuclear capacity, and worked toward a unified Europe.

> "Since they whose duty it was to wield **the sword of France** have let it fall … I have taken up **the broken blade**"
>
> SPEECH GIVEN BY DE GAULLE, JULY 13, 1940

Leadership rivals
General de Gaulle arrives in North Africa for talks with General Giraud, commander-in-chief of the Free French forces (shown left). Roosevelt favored Giraud as leader of postwar France.

TIMELINE

- **November 22, 1890** Born in Lille, France, into a literary upper middle-class family.

- **1912** Having shown an early and keen interest in military matters, graduates from the Saint-Cyr Military Academy.

- **1913** Joins an infantry regiment as a second lieutenant serving under Colonel Pétain.

- **March 1916** Promoted to captain during World War I. Captured at the Battle of Verdun, he makes several unsuccessful attempts to escape.

- **1919–21** Fights against the Red Army on a military mission to Poland, and gains Poland's highest military decoration.

- **1923–25** Lectures at the French Staff College and publishes his first book, *Discord Among the Enemy* (1924), about German politics. Promoted to the staff of the Supreme War Council.

- **1934** Publishes *The Army of the Future*, in which he argues for a professional standing army and mechanized warfare, using tanks and planes.

- **1939** Takes over command of the 5th Army's armoured vehicle force in Alsace.

- **May 15–28, 1940** Made commander of the 4th Armored Division. Attacks German forces at Montcornet with tanks, forcing the German infantry to retreat. Promoted to brigadier general.

- **June 6, 1940** Appointed undersecretary of state for national defense by French prime minister.

- **June 17, 1940** Marshall Pétain becomes prime minister of France; de Gaulle flies to Britain.

- **June 18, 1940** Broadcasts an appeal from London to the French people.

- **July 4, 1940** In his absence, sentenced to four years imprisonment by a court martial in Toulouse. On 2 August he is sentenced to death.

- **June 1943** With Henri Giraud, sets up the French Committee of National Liberation (FCNL).

- **May 26, 1944** Announces that the FCNL is to be known as the Provisional Government of the French Republic.

FRENCH NEWSPAPER HERALDING THE LIBERATION OF PARIS

- **August 25, 1944** Enters liberated Paris with US troops; in October Allies recognize him as the head of the French government.

- **November 13, 1945** Elected head of the French government. Resigns in January 1946.

- **December 1958** Elected president of France's Fifth Republic, during the Algerian crisis.

- **April 1969** Steps down as president of France and retires from public life.

- **November 9, 1970** Dies suddenly at home in Colombey, and is accorded a small funeral at his local church, as specified by his last wishes.

1 WARNING AGAINST "CARELESS TALK" (US)

2 IMPENDING ALLIED DESTRUCTION OF NAZI GERMANY (US)

7 RECRUITING POSTER (ITALY)

3 NAVY RECRUITING POSTER (CANADA)

4 CALL TO THE WORKERS TO JOIN THE WAR EFFORT (CANADA)

5 CELEBRATING EARLY VICTORIES AT SEA (JAPAN)

6 SHOW OF AERIAL MIGHT (JAPAN)

Propaganda

Propaganda was a powerful way of uniting the people and furthering a particular cause. It could manipulate public opinion, help with recruitment, stir patriotism, advertise ideologies and beliefs, and provide the public with safety information.

1 An American "careless talk" poster highlights the danger of enemy agents. Citizens of Japanese descent were interned as a precaution after Pearl Harbor. **2** An anti-Nazi poster fosters public support for the US's allies and their cause. **3** A Canadian navy recruitment poster urges "Do it well … do it quickly … their victory will be yours." The Royal Canadian Navy went from having only six destroyers to being the world's third largest navy by the war's end. **4** A poster for war production in Canada affirms "It's our war." The decision to declare war alongside Britain was initially controversial in Canada. **5** The Japanese air force is celebrated in this poster, which emphasizes how "Aircraft can be the difference between winning and losing the battle." **6** A war bond poster asks the Japanese public to buy war bonds in support of the 1937–45 Sino-Japanese War effort. **7** An Italian recruitment poster inspires men to enrol in the anti-aircraft artillery. The figure loading the gun closely resembles Mussolini. **8** This poster warning against spies was used in both France and Britain. The public was reminded not to discuss ship sailings, war production, or troop movements. **9** British leaflets dropped over Burma aimed to demoralize

Japanese troops, warning that "Without modern weapons you are doomed." They were written in several languages to persuade the Burmese people not to side with the Japanese. **10** A poster of Soviet and Allied cooperation in overcoming the Nazis portrays the Soviet Union as doing the lion's share. **11** A Soviet arms industry poster illustrates the direct contribution of the factory worker to the war effort. Tens of thousands of Soviet women were employed in production. **12** Soviet anti-Nazi propaganda portrays the enemy as inhuman, galvanizing the Soviet people to action. The strength of Soviet nationalism surprised the Germans. **13** A Free French poster depicts the Free French as the anvil on which the Nazis will be crushed by the hammer of the Allies. **14** A German blackout poster reminds civilians to observe blackout regulations: "The enemy sees your light!" **15** This Nazi anti-Soviet, anti-Jewish poster shows the exhumation of mass graves in the Ukraine. The figure presiding over the corpses is a Jewish-Bolshevik commissar. Many Ukrainians fought for Germany against the Soviets. **16** An anti-Soviet poster depicts Germany as the saviour of Europe, protecting it from the evil Soviet influence.

11 CELEBRATION OF HEROIC EFFORTS OF THE ARMS INDUSTRY (USSR)

8 WARNING AGAINST SPIES (BRITAIN)

9 LEAFLETS DROPPED TO DEMORALIZE
JAPANESE TROOPS (BRITAIN)

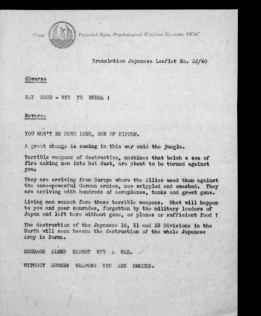

ALLIED COOPERATION STRANGLING HITLER (USSR)

12 CALL TO EXTERMINATE HITLER'S BEASTS (USSR)

13 "BETWEEN THE HAMMER … AND THE ANVIL"
(FREE FRENCH)

The Secret War

Throughout the war Allied and Axis powers used codes and ciphers to pass sensitive military and diplomatic information around the world. Behind the scenes an army of codebreakers worked in absolute secrecy to intercept and interpret the information. By and large, the Allies had the edge.

Germany's greatest asset was the "Enigma" machine. Developed for commercial purposes, the German Navy adopted one version in 1926, and the German Army later adopted another. By 1935 Enigma machines were standard equipment for all Germany's armed forces. Able to encipher messages in millions of ways, Enigma was ideal for the rapid enciphering and deciphering of military instructions that proved so useful for Germany's Blitzkrieg tactics. In 1939 three Polish cipher experts managed to replicate Enigma and passed their knowledge on to Britain and France just weeks before war began.

The Enigma was a fiendishly complex piece of equipment. It had three main parts: a keyboard to type in the plain letters; a scrambling unit of three, later four, alphabetical rotors to turn the plain letters into code; and an illuminated lamp-board for displaying enciphered letters. A plug-board containing six cables sat below the keyboard.

Enigma's security derived from the way it was set up. The rotors could be arranged in a different order, aligned in any position, and set to rotate at varying speeds. Likewise, the cables could be plugged in many different combinations. All these settings were changed daily, according to a monthly code book.

The Germans believed the Enigma code was unbreakable. In response, the British government assembled a team of outstanding mathematicians,

Sending in code

German soldiers use Enigma to encode a message. One worked the machine, a second called out the enciphered letters, the third wrote the message.

Enigma machine

Enigma looked like an ordinary typewriter but was an electromechanical device that scrambled sentences into completely illogical sequences of letters, using pre-set moving rotors. It could encipher a message in over 10,000 million, million ways.

linguists, and scientists to form the Code and Cipher School at Bletchley Park, Buckinghamshire. Here, Alan Turing (see opposite) designed an electromechanical machine based on an earlier Polish version that could break the Enigma code. Using a procedure that was known as traffic analysis, it was possible to identify which type of machine had enciphered a message, thus reducing Enigma's many variables.

Luckily for the Allies, Enigma had a flaw: it could not encipher any letter as itself. Also, some messages were very similar; for example, a six-letter cipher text, sent out at 6:05am each day, turned out to be the six letters of *Wetter*, announcing the day's weather forecast. Clues such as these, together with procedural errors in setting the machines up each day, and the capture of codebooks, gave Bletchley the help they needed. From 1941 they were deciphering all German naval Enigma messages, and the vital intelligence gained—codenamed "Ultra"—proved crucial in revealing the location of U-boats

> ## 12
> The number of years that the war was shortened by—as some historians believe—after the British deciphered the German Enigma code in 1941.

« BEFORE

Skills in codebreaking—cryptography—developed considerably during World War I, with the British deciphering German codes.

BRITISH INTELLIGENCE

German military and diplomatic messages were sent by a **complex number code**. In early 1917 **British codebreakers** working in Room 40 of the Admiralty in London **deciphered** a major communication between the German foreign secretary, **Arthur Zimmermann**, and his ambassador in Washington D.C. for onward transmission to Mexico, offering that country American territory if it **declared war on the US**. The release of the message to the US press did much to bring the United States into the **war against Germany ‹‹ 16–17** in April 1917.

MORSE CODE

Russia **did not encipher** its messages, but sent them in **Morse code**. Early German victories in 1914 were the result of **interception** by the German Signals Intelligence Service.

MORSE CODE TRANSMITTER

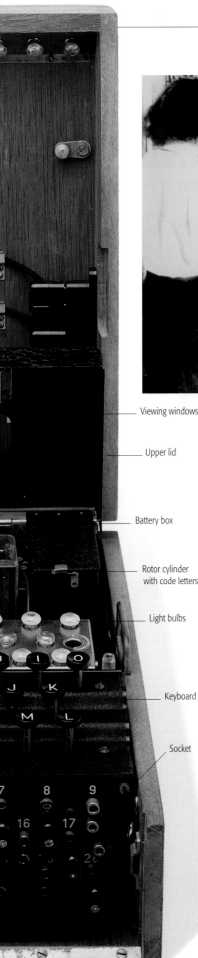

Viewing windows

Upper lid

Battery box

Rotor cylinder
with code letters

Light bulbs

Keyboard

Socket

Front
panel

Colossus calculating machine

Developed at Bletchley Park, the Colossus broke the most complex Lorenz codes used in high-level German communications. Ten machines worked full time to reveal the contents of 600 top-secret messages a month.

in the North Atlantic, helping Allied shipping to evade their attacks. Churchill saw the Ultra intercepts as a secret weapon, calling them "golden eggs."

Codebreaking in the US

Across the Atlantic, the Americans were working on Japan's "Alphabetic Typewriter 97," first used to encipher diplomatic messages in 1939. It was

William Friedman, intercepted one message that had been enciphered on both machines. They also discovered the telephone technology behind Purple. Armed with these two insights, they broke the code in September 1940 and then reconstructed a Purple machine to decipher Japanese diplomatic messages. It was through Purple that the US government learned that Japan was about to break off peace negotiations prior to the attack on Pearl Harbor, but they never completely broke the naval code JN-25 and were caught unaware when Japanese naval bombers attacked the US Pacific Fleet.

MATHEMATICIAN (1912–54)

ALAN TURING

After studying mathematics at Cambridge University, Turing, at the age of 24, wrote a theoretical paper detailing the principles of modern computing. This envisaged a universal computing machine that could be programd to solve certain mathematical problems. One of the chief codebreakers at Bletchley Park, Turing provided some crucial breakthroughs in deciphering the Enigma code. The secrecy necessarily surrounding Turing's wartime achievements meant that his genius has only recently been fully acknowledged.

"The geese that laid the **golden eggs** and never cackled."

WINSTON CHURCHILL, ON THE TEAM AT BLETCHLEY PARK

codenamed "Purple" because it was based on an earlier machine that the Americans had already cracked, which was codenamed "Red."

The Purple code was created by a machine that consisted of two electric typewriter keyboards connected by wires and switches based on standard telephone switchboard technology. Not every Japanese embassy had the new machine, however, so many messages were sent using the old Red technology. Fortunately, the codebreakers of the US Army Signals Intelligence Service, led by

While the Japanese used machines, Americans used code talkers, specifically Navajo Native American. Recruited to work with US forces in the Pacific, they sent and received military messages in their own, unique language. The benefit of using Navajos was that they worked at the speed of speech, an improvement on the previous laborious system of enciphering and deciphering messages using a cipher machine.

The "Purple" machine

"Purple," the Japanese cipher machine, differed from Enigma in having telephone switches rather than rotating scramblers to encipher and decipher its messages.

AFTER »

The work of the British codebreakers at Bletchley Park remained top secret until many years after World War II.

IN THE NAME OF SECRECY
Ultra files were locked away and, although the Colossus was the world's **first programmable, electronic computer**, the machines were broken and their **blueprints destroyed**.

HELPING TO WIN THE WAR
Breaking Rommel's codes aided Montgomery in the **North African campaign 182–83** ». Using Ultra enabled the Allies to divert ships away from danger during the **Battle of the Atlantic 204–05** », and helped to reveal **the size and location** of German forces in Normandy before **D-Day 254–55** ».

NAVAJO CODE TALKERS

‹‹ BEFORE

Before the French surrendered in June 1940, both Britain and Germany achieved scattered successes in the war at sea.

BRITAIN'S SUPPLY LINE

In 1939 Britain **imported roughly half its food**, all its oil, and many other raw materials. In World War I Germany's submarines had tried to cut Britain's supply lines and almost succeeded. However, at the start of World War II the **German Navy had relatively few submarines** in service and manufacturing new ones was not high on the country's priority list.

BRITISH EXPANSION

As on land, combat at sea in 1939–40 was very infrequent. Germany's U-boats achieved some successes—**sinking the battleship *Royal Oak* ‹‹ 62–63** in the Royal Navy's main fleet base, for example—but **Germany's attacks on British trade had limited results**. In effect, Britain was given a breathing space to get its convoy system up and running and set about greatly expanding its anti-submarine forces. Norway's large merchant navy, previously neutral, went over to the Allies when **Norway itself was attacked ‹‹ 74–75**, more than offsetting the initial sinkings by German U-boats.

U-BOAT ACE (1912–1998)

OTTO KRETSCHMER

After joining the German navy in 1930, Kretschmer became the most successful submarine commander of any navy during World War II, sinking 47 ships, mostly merchantmen but also warships. This earned him honors in Germany and the popular title, "Wolf of the Atlantic." In March 1941 his *U-99* was sunk during a convoy battle, Kretschmer was taken prisoner, and he spent six years in Allied captivity. After the war he became an admiral in the West German navy.

The **U-Boat War**

The Battle of the Atlantic was a fight for Britain's very survival. Without supplies brought by sea, Britain would starve and its army would have no fuel for its tanks, ships, or planes. Hundreds of ships needed to sail to and from British ports every month. Germany's U-boats had plenty of targets to choose from.

For the first year of the war, German U-boat activity against British supply lines was effective, but limited. This all changed with the fall of France. Germany moved its submarine bases to ports in western France, giving the boats direct short-range access to the main Atlantic sea lanes.

Vulnerable under water

U-boats sank dozens of Allied ships each month between June 1940 and the end of the year. Admiral Karl Dönitz, the head of the U-boat force, introduced the "wolf pack" system where submarines hunted in groups, attacking the convoys on the surface at night.

At the start of the war the Royal Navy placed great faith in its ASDIC detection equipment, now usually known as sonar. This used sound waves to detect

Tracking the enemy
A U-boat captain at the periscope sets his sights on an enemy ship, while his officers take instrument readings that will be used to aim the torpedoes.

submerged submarines. However, it could not locate a submarine on the surface. At night or in bad weather a surfaced submarine was very hard to spot visually. The Navy could use radar for the job but this was only gradually being introduced. During the second half of 1940, by exploiting this weakness, U-boats regularly

> " The only thing that ever **really frightened me** during the war was the U-boat peril."
>
> WINSTON CHURCHILL

Sinking of merchant ships month by month, Jan 1940–December 1941

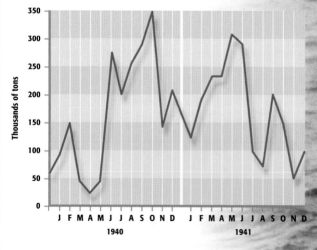

Battle of the Atlantic 1940–41
Sinkings rose alarmingly when the Germans acquired new U-boat bases in France in 1940, but fell in 1941 when the British and Canadians began using escorts.

Refuelling at sea
To keep the maximum number of combat submarines on patrol, a few large boats, like the former minelayer *U-116* (top), were used to refuel and resupply smaller attack boats, like *U-406*, a Type VIIc.

Torpedo calculator
Submarine crews of all nations used complicated devices like this one to set the speed and path of their torpedoes for firing, based on estimates of the target ship's course and speed.

penetrated right inside convoy formations, sinking up to half a dozen ships in a frantic hour or two before escaping into the darkness. A small band of U-boat "aces," like Otto Kretschmer, Günther Prien, Erich Topp, Joachim Schepke, and other U-boat captains inflicted terrible damage.

Improving tactics

For the British during this time, it was a simple matter of survival. To combat the U-boat threat, merchant ships traveled in convoy, but convoys could only move as fast as the slowest ship, and it took time to assemble them

before sailing. Ships heading for Britain were almost invariably heavily laden with supplies; when one was hit, it went down like a stone. Less than half of all merchant seamen survived the sinking of their ships. One convoy, in October 1940, was spotted by six U-boats, four of them commanded by "aces." Seventeen Allied ships were lost, along with their vital cargoes.

German attacks such as these forced the British to supply convoys with naval escorts for greater stretches of their journey to and from North America, but there was a critical shortage of these potentially life-saving escort vessels. Gradually, however, British tactics improved. New ships called corvettes were developed. These were small warships of less than 1,000 tons,

which, although slow and horribly uncomfortable for their crews in bad weather, were designed to carry effective anti-submarine weapons.

The problem of air cover

The British also steadily introduced more air support for the convoys, both from land bases and aircraft-carrying ships, but there was never enough. Both sides used radio intelligence and codebreaking information to initiate and avoid attacks. The Germans had the advantage in this respect but Britain managed to gain the upper hand for some months from the spring of 1941.

Throughout the year the United States, although still officially neutral, became increasingly committed to fighting in the Atlantic. Although most Americans did not realize it, "neutral"

60 **The percentage of cargo received by Britain during the war—40 percent of its usual peacetime cargo was lost. This meant that rationing of food and other essentials had to be tightened.**

US Navy warships were in effect fighting alongside the Allies from the middle of 1941, at a time when codebreaking information had revealed that Hitler did not then intend to go to war with the United States. Even so, several American warships were damaged or sunk in the fall of 1941. In the aftermath of the surprise attacks on Pearl Harbor on the morning of December 7, 1941, Hitler foolishly changed his mind and declared war on the United States, making his own final defeat certain. However, for the first six months of 1942 German U-boats attacked coastal shipping, running amok off America's east coast.

Because of astonishing command failures at the top of the US Navy, it took many months for a properly escorted convoy system to be introduced in the western Atlantic and Caribbean. While German submarines were not well suited to operations so far from home, U-boat commanders scored success after success. By the middle of the year the Allies were fighting back more effectively, but it was clear that the U-boat menace in the Battle of the Atlantic was far from over.

AFTER

The Battle of the Atlantic continued to the last day of the war but the Allied victory was inevitable by the middle of 1942.

SHIPYARD BATTLE
During July 1942, for the first time in World War II, **more Allied merchant ships were launched than were sunk** by German U-boats. In the middle of 1943, **the United States' huge ship-building program 168–69 >>** meant that the total Allied merchant stock now **exceeded the level of 1939** and would continue to grow throughout 1944 and 1945.

BADGE WORN BY A U-BOAT CREWMAN

GERMAN LOSSES
Germany's U-boats were doomed to failure. Growing Allied escort forces and their advanced technology confirmed this in **the Battle of the Atlantic 204–05 >>**. From 1945 onward, most U-boats were sunk before their first patrols. **Three quarters of men who served in U-boats died.**

Life on a U-boat

Sometimes described as "iron coffins," German U-boats were mainly deployed to attack Allied shipping convoys. Crews lived and worked in the confined spaces on board for up to three months at a stretch. Provisions were good—though food often went moldy—but the air became foul and water was at a premium, so washing and shaving were discouraged. U-boats were extremely effective in the early stages of the war, but by May 1943 the Germans were suffering mounting losses, while their attacks were becoming less successful.

"We were now battling our way through the February storms, the severest of the winter. The sea boiled and foamed and leaped continually under the lash of gales that chased one another across the Atlantic from west to east. *U-230* struggled through gurgling whirlpools, up and down mountainous seas; she was pitched into the air by one towering wave and caught by another and buried under tons of water by still another. The cruel winds whipped across the wild surface at speeds of up to 150 miles per hour ... When we were on watch, the wind punished us with driving snow, sleet, hail, and frozen spray. It beat against our rubber diver's suits, cut our faces like a razor, and threatened to tear off our eye masks ... Below, inside the bobbing steel cockleshell, the boat's violent up-and-down motion drove us to the floor-plates and hurled us straight up and threw us around like puppets ...

Shipboard routine had replaced the excitement of the chase and the battle. And it was a maddening routine. The small ship rolled and slapped, listed and shuddered endlessly. Utensils, spare parts, tools, and conserves showered down on us continually; porcelain cups and dishes shattered on the deck-plates and in the bilges as we ate our meals directly out of cans. The men, penned up together in the rocking, sweating drum, took the motion and the monotony with stoicism. Occasionally, someone's temper flared, but spirits remained high. We were all patient veterans. Everyone aboard looked alike, smelled alike, had adopted the same phrases and curses. We had learned to live together in a narrow tube no longer than two railroad cars. We tolerated each other's faults and became experts on each other's habits—how everyone laughed and snarled, talked and snored, sipped his coffee and caressed his beard. The pressure mounted with the passage of each uneventful day, but it could be relieved in an instant by the sight of a fat convoy."

U-BOAT COMMANDER HERBERT E. WERNER, DESCRIBING LIFE ON BOARD U-230

Cramped conditions
U-boats carried a crew of around 40 men, who shared cramped conditions among the torpedoes and food supplies. They also shared bunks: as one man got up to start his four-hour watch, another took the bunk.

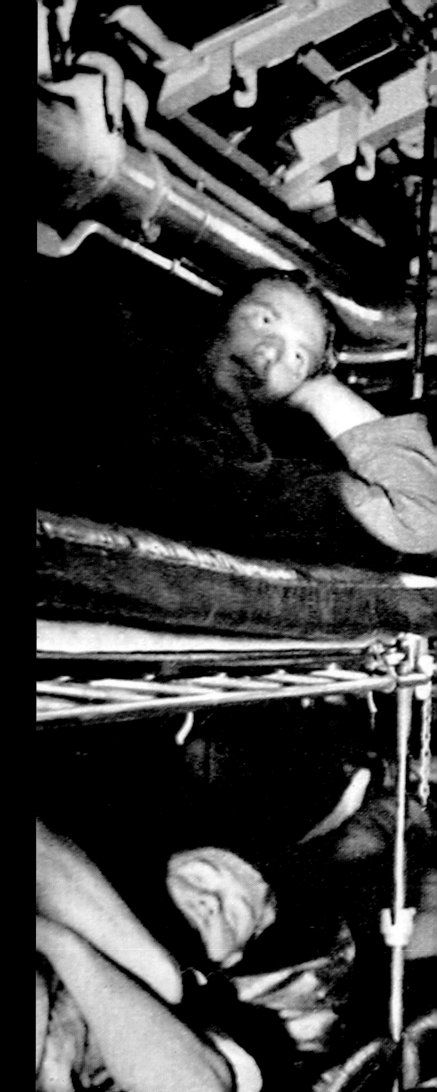

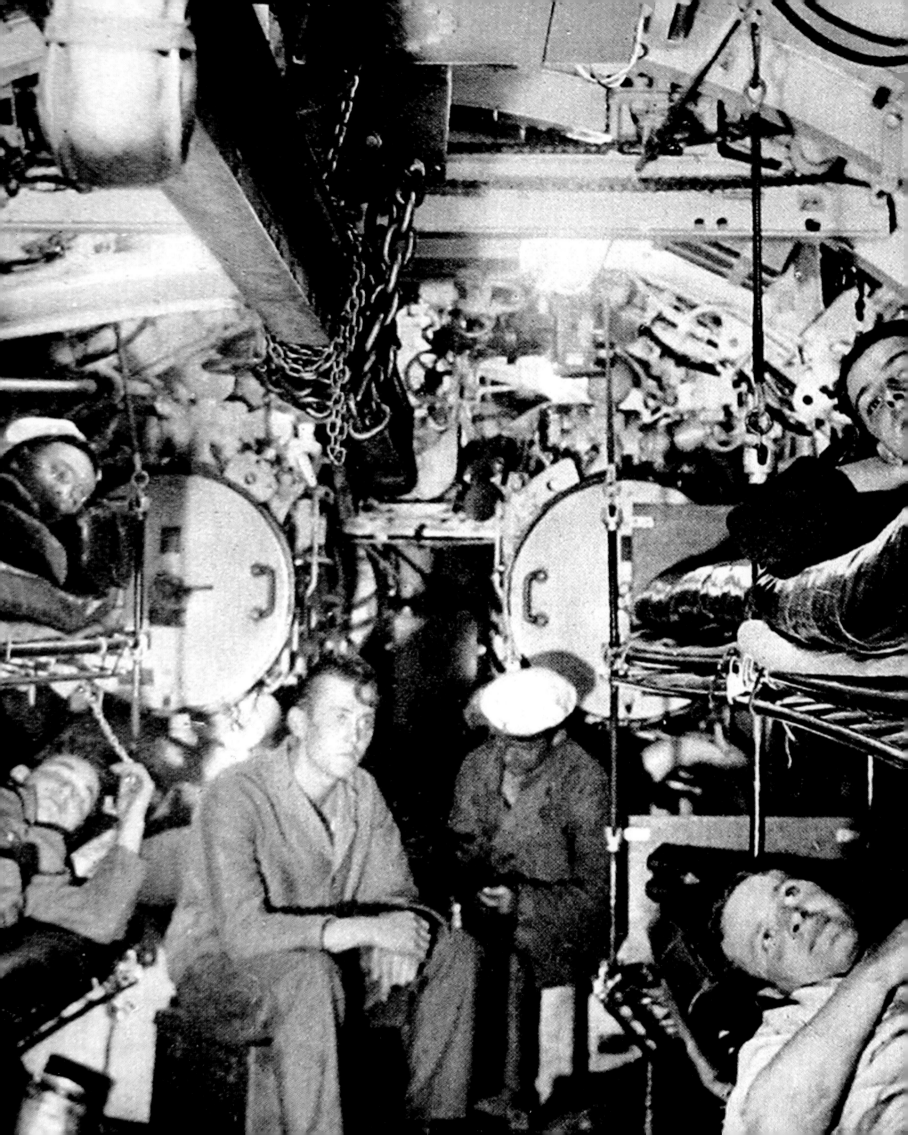

Hunting the Bismarck

By the spring of 1941 Germany's major surface warships had caused extensive damage and disruption to Britain's vital supply routes. Now a new battleship, the *Bismarck*, was ready, and more dangerous than anything that had gone before. One of the Royal Navy's tasks would be to hunt down the *Bismarck*.

As Germany's navy the *Kriegsmarine* was rebuilt during the 1930s, it was clear that it would take considerable time to expand it to the point where it could challenge Britain's Royal Navy in a fleet battle. Admiral Raeder's pre-war "Z Plan" envisaged having the forces needed to do so by around 1944. In the meantime, as well as attacking Britain's trade with U-boats, the *Kriegsmarine* would deploy their surface vessels for long-distance raids on British commerce.

As war loomed, Britain was aware of the German threat but was still constrained by the inter-war naval disarmament treaties. Thus the new

Scanning the horizon
Able Seaman Alfred Newall on lookout duty aboard HMS *Suffolk*. Newall was reportedly the man who first sighted the *Bismarck* as it sailed through the Denmark Strait.

battleships of the *King George V* class that Britain had started manufacturing in the late 1930s were designed to the limit of 35,000 tons. Germany's big ships all flagrantly breached the treaty limits.

In late 1940 and early 1941 the pocket battleship *Admiral Scheer* and the battlecruisers *Scharnhorst* and *Gneisenau* made successful raids in the Atlantic and Indian Oceans. By the spring of 1941 the newest of the German ships, the 42,000-ton *Bismarck*, more formidable than any British vessel, was ready for operations, along with the heavy cruiser *Prinz Eugen*. Hitler had always been reluctant to risk his navy's most prestigious vessels but Admiral Raeder persuaded him that the time was right to launch the *Bismarck* and its smaller consort into combat. The *Scharnhorst* and the *Gneisenau* were at the French port of

Brest preparing for new operations and would make a dangerous combination if they could link up with the *Bismarck*. Vice-Admiral Günther Lütjens, who was to command the whole operation, wanted to wait until the other ships

> ## "We shall **fight to the last shell**. Long live the Führer."
> **ADMIRAL LÜTJENS, LAST RADIO MESSAGE FROM THE "BISMARCK"**

could join them, but he was overruled by Raeder. The German squadron set sail on May 18, 1941 from the eastern Baltic toward the North Sea.

Intelligence information from the Swedish Navy and air reconnaissance off Norway told the British that the

Bismarck was on the move. All Allied heavy ships were put on alert and scouting forces hurried to cover the routes by which the *Bismarck* could reach the main Atlantic shipping lanes.

Battle of the Denmark Strait
The German warships were sighted again northwest of Iceland and shadowed southwestward through the Denmark Strait. The battleship *Prince of Wales* and battlecruiser HMS *Hood* were the nearest of the unavoidably scattered major British vessels and were sent to intercept.

On the morning of May 24, the big ships met and within minutes HMS *Hood* was attacked. An explosion tore the battlecruiser in two, killing all but three of its 1,418 crew. The *Prince of Wales*, even newer than the *Bismarck* and not yet fully ready for battle, was badly damaged and retired to safety.

Although rather old and outdated, the *Hood* had been regarded as the pride of the Royal Navy and its loss was a major blow. Now more than ever it was vital to sink the *Bismarck* before it could run amok in the convoy routes. Fortunately for the Allies, the ship had not escaped unharmed. Two shells from the *Prince of Wales* had caused a fuel leak, and Lütjens decided to head for the safety of western France for repairs. With major British warships closing in on all sides, the German ships separated and for a time shook off their many pursuers. On May 26 the *Bismarck* was once again spotted by a patrol plane just 30 hours from the safety of the French

« BEFORE

Germany knew that its modest surface fleet was no match for the British one and sought other naval means to undermine the Allied war effort.

HITLER'S NAVY
At the outbreak of the war, Germany's Grand Admiral Erich Raeder knew that his surface ships **could not win a full-scale fleet engagement** with the much larger British Royal Navy. Hitler had told him that he did not expect to have to fight Britain until the mid-1940s—by then Germany's fleet would be much larger.

KRIEGSMARINE ENSIGN

COMMERCE RAIDING
Instead of seeking an all-out battle, when war began the German Navy (the *Kriegsmarine*) used its large ships for long-distance raids against British trade. The pocket battleship *Admiral Graf Spee* was sunk on such a mission in 1939 **« 62–63** but its sister ships and Germany's battlecruisers and cruisers made several damaging voyages up to early 1941. As well as sinking Allied ships, they **forced the British to halt or divert convoys**, delaying the delivery of vital cargoes and significantly disrupting Britain's war effort.

Pursuit and sinking of the Bismarck
Britain's best chance of finding the *Bismarck* was in its voyage from Norway into the main Atlantic shipping lanes, but even then a vast area east and west of Iceland had to be covered. British forces were therefore widely spread and came into action at different times.

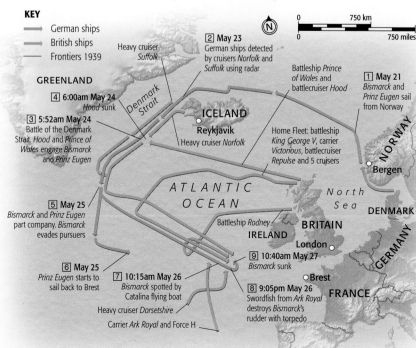

KEY
— German ships
— British ships
— Frontiers 1939

GREENLAND

Denmark Strait

4 6:00am May 24
Hood sunk

3 5:52am May 24
Battle of the Denmark Strait. *Hood* and *Prince of Wales* engage *Bismarck* and *Prinz Eugen*

Heavy cruiser *Suffolk*

2 May 23
German ships detected by cruisers *Norfolk* and *Suffolk* using radar

Battleship *Prince of Wales* and battlecruiser *Hood*

1 May 21
Bismarck and *Prinz Eugen* sail from Norway

ICELAND
Reykjavik
Heavy cruiser *Norfolk*

Home Fleet: battleship *King George V*, carrier *Victorious*, battlecruiser *Repulse* and 5 cruisers

NORWAY
Bergen

ATLANTIC OCEAN

North Sea

5 May 25
Bismarck and *Prinz Eugen* part company. *Bismarck* evades pursuers

Battleship *Rodney*
BRITAIN
IRELAND
London

DENMARK
GERMANY

9 10:40am May 27
Bismarck sunk

6 May 25
Prinz Eugen starts to sail back to Brest

7 10:15am May 26
Bismarck spotted by Catalina flying boat

Heavy cruiser *Dorsetshire*

Carrier *Ark Royal* and Force H

Brest
8 9:05pm May 26
Swordfish from *Ark Royal* destroys *Bismarck*'s rudder with torpedo
FRANCE

The warship in action
Soon after sighting the *Bismarck*, the Royal Navy opened fire but they were no match for the *Bismarck's* 15-in guns. HMS *Hood* sank within three minutes. The cause—a single shell that pierced its magazine.

coastline. Swordfish torpedo aircraft from the carrier *Ark Royal* were sent on a last-chance attack. One of the two hits they scored jammed the *Bismarck's* rudder. The ship could only move slowly in a helpless circle and was an easy target. The British battleships *King George V* and *Rodney* arrived the next morning and pounded the *Bismarck* into a wreck. Multiple torpedo hits extended the damage but it is possible

714 The number of 14-inch (*King George V*) and 16-inch (*Rodney*) shells fired in the final action. About 80 were hits but the *Bismarck's* main armor was probably not penetrated.

that in the end the *Bismarck* was actually scuttled by its own crew. Only 115 of the 2,222 men on board were saved. HMS *Hood* had been avenged and one great threat to Britain's Atlantic lifeline cancelled out. But the *Bismarck's* sister ship *Tirpitz* was nearly ready for action.

German survivors rescued
Many of the *Bismarck's* crew took to the water when their ship went down. Only a few were rescued by Allied ships, including by HMS *Dorsetshire* as shown, before a U-boat scare forced the British rescuers to leave.

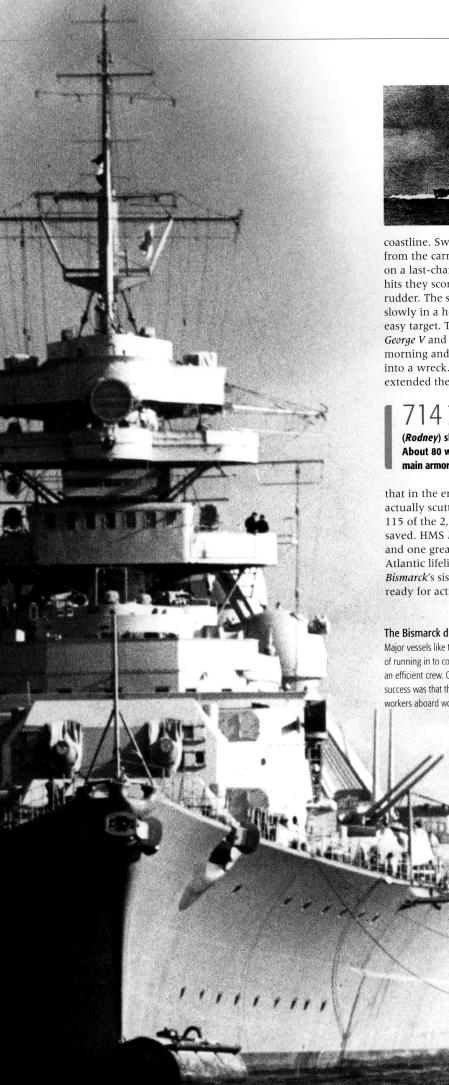

The Bismarck during training, 1940
Major vessels like the *Bismarck* needed a lengthy period of running in to correct manufacturing defects and train an efficient crew. One of the reasons for *Bismarck's* initial success was that the *Prince of Wales* still had dockyard workers aboard working on gun-turret problems.

AFTER »

In naval affairs, as in land warfare, Hitler became increasingly convinced that he knew better than his top commanders.

PRINZ EUGEN
After splitting from the *Bismarck*, the *Prinz Eugen* should have continued its raiding operations alone, but **engine trouble forced it to abandon its mission** and head for France.

NORWEGIAN BASES
The loss of the *Bismarck* turned Hitler against using his capital ships for **risky long-range raiding**. He became convinced, too, that the Allies intended to invade Norway and ordered his navy to send all its big ships there, so that **they would also be able to attack Allied supply convoys to Russia**.

CHANNEL DASH
The German ships in western France were bombed by the RAF, but the *Prinz Eugen*, the *Scharnhorst*, and the *Gneisenau* made a **daring daylight escape up the English Channel** from their base in Brest in February 1942. Damage from the RAF attacks limited the force sent to Norway, however, and the *Scharnhorst* and the *Tirpitz* were both eventually sunk in Norwegian waters.

The War in the Desert

The fighting in North Africa saw swings of fortune unmatched in any other theater of the war. First one side then the other had the upper hand, forcing their enemies into long and sometimes panicky retreats. Largely roadless and waterless, the desert was a hostile environment in which to fight.

Italy was not well prepared to fight in World War II when Mussolini joined the conflict in June 1940. For all Mussolini's boasting, his country's economy was weak and its armed forces, though impressive in size, had many weaknesses. Few ordinary Italian soldiers had much enthusiasm for the fight and their training was very poor. Their generals spent more time enjoying a luxurious lifestyle than preparing for battle and the soldiers' weapons were second rate. Much the same applied at sea and in the air. Many Italian naval guns were inaccurate because of unsatisfactory manufacturing standards and the air force relied on outdated biplane fighters and bombers dating back well before the war. The Italian economy was too weak and ill-run to rectify these problems.

Italy's empire

In 1940, Italy had important colonies in North and East Africa. Modern Libya was then Italian ruled while in the horn of Africa, Eritrea, and Italian Somaliland (the southern part of

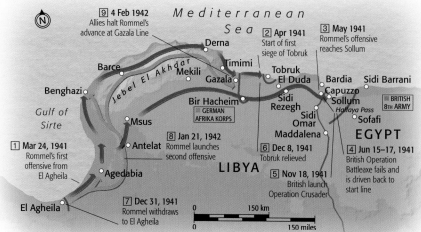

9 4 Feb 1942
Allies halt Rommel's advance at Gazala Line

2 Apr 1941
Start of first siege of Tobruk

3 May 1941
Rommel's offensive reaches Sollum

1 Mar 24, 1941
Rommel's first offensive from El Agheila

8 Jan 21, 1942
Rommel launches second offensive

6 Dec 8, 1941
Tobruk relieved

4 Jun 15–17, 1941
British Operation Battleaxe fails and is driven back to start line

5 Nov 18, 1941
British launch Operation Crusader

7 Dec 31, 1941
Rommel withdraws to El Agheila

KEY

→ Rommel's first offensive Mar–May 1941
→ Rommel's second offensive Jan–Feb 1942
— British defensive line
— Axis defensive line

Changing fortunes in the battle for Libya
At the end of 1940, and again in late 1941, Allied forces advanced hundreds of miles west to El Agheila only to be thrown back in subsequent weeks by renewed German-led Axis offensives.

modern Somalia) had been the bases for the Italian pre-war conquest of Abyssinia, now modern Ethiopia. Both were potentially well-placed to attack Britain's vital imperial lifeline through the Suez Canal in British-controlled Egypt. British land and air forces in the Middle East were small and could expect little reinforcement at first after the disasters in France and with the threat of German invasion.

On September 23, 1940, Italy's 250,000-strong Tenth Army advanced into Egypt from Libya then stopped cautiously. British Empire

Italian troops surrendering
Australian troops take some of the 36,000 Italians who surrendered at Bardia in January 1941. Thousands more would surrender as the Allied desert offensive continued.

forces in Egypt (from India, Australia and New Zealand as well as Britain), although less than a quarter as strong, still prepared a counter-offensive.

Hitler intervenes

The British attack began on December 7 and was immediately very successful. All the Italian front-line positions were almost instantly overrun and a second phase of attacks from the start of January began penetrating deep into Libya. The Italian troops were in full retreat with thousands of men being captured daily.

Hitler could not allow Italy, his main ally, to be defeated so easily so he sent an ambitious young general, Erwin Rommel, to Libya with a small force to block any further British advance.

At the same time as Rommel was arriving, British strength in North Africa was diminishing. Some of the British Middle East Command's resources in early 1941 were devoted to conquering the Italian possessions in the horn of Africa, a process which was

<< **BEFORE**

When Italy entered the war on Hitler's side, it opened up new and dangerous fronts in the Mediterranean and Africa.

ITALY ENTERS THE WAR
In June 1940 **Italy declared war on Britain and France** << **98–99**. Italy had a large Mediterranean fleet and colonies in North and East Africa. The British army had troops in Egypt, **guarding the Suez Canal**, the link to the British Empire in Asia and Britain's Arabian oil supplies.

EARLY ITALIAN MOVES
The Italian Tenth Army, badly trained, **poorly equipped, and appallingly led**, advanced a short distance into Egypt from Libya in September 1940, but then halted and went over to the defensive despite hugely **outnumbering the opposing British force**.

ITALIAN BAYONET

German observation post in the desert
A soldier uses rangefinding binoculars to check for Allied movement in typically open and featureless desert terrain, well-suited to tank maneuvers and long-range anti-tank gunnery.

88MM GUN

Germany's 88 mm gun was the most powerful anti-tank weapon used in the desert war. The wide open spaces of the desert terrain emphasized long-range anti-tank gunnery and the "88", originally designed as an anti-aircraft gun, had the high muzzle velocity and flat trajectory that made it ideal for this role. German tactics were to draw Allied tanks into range of hidden anti-tank guns. These were often other German weapons but the much-feared "88" was credited with many of the resulting tank "kills".

> "We have a very **daring and skilful opponent** against us, and, may I say … **a great General.**"
>
> WINSTON CHURCHILL ON GENERAL ROMMEL

effectively complete by April though the final Italian surrender did not come until November. More importantly, other Allied units were withdrawn from Africa and sent to support Greece in what would be a fruitless battle against German invasion.

Rommel attacks

This combination gave Rommel his chance. Realizing that the forces opposing him were very weak he attacked on March 24, 1941. Within a month his forces had recaptured all the ground the British had recently won except for the port of Tobruk which remained in Allied hands

> The British Cruiser Mk VI Crusader tank was faster and more mobile than the German Panzer IV but its lightweight 2-pounder gun and insufficient armor proved to be inadequate against the Panzers' superior gunnery.

though isolated behind German front-lines. It would go on to endure an eight-month siege.

For the moment Rommel, at the end of a long and tenuous supply line, could go no further. German forces were easily able to beat off two minor British attacks in May and June after which both sides settled down to build their strength for the battles to come.

In November the Allied forces struck first. For three weeks there was a confused series of tank battles between the Egyptian frontier and Tobruk. The British forces frittered away much of the numerical superiority with which they began the battles but the German and Italian resistance was gradually

worn down. Tobruk was relieved and Rommel fell back to El Agheila. Once again the British forward positions were relatively weak, in part because British resources that might have come to Africa were being sent east to face the Japanese. Rommel's troops were reinforced with tanks, supplies, and air support. They attacked on January 25, 1942, the Allies drew back, and by the start of February the Germans had retaken most of the territory they had just lost.

AFTER »

Although Rommel would make further advances in early 1942, overwhelming Allied resources condemned him to defeat at El Alamein later that year.

THE END IN AFRICA
El Alamein was followed by the **Anglo-American Torch landings 186–87** » in northwest Africa. **General Montgomery's forces advanced steadily west** from Egypt. The First Army from Algeria moved east with difficulty, but by May 1943 the **last Italian and German forces in Tunisia had been defeated**.

DEATH OF THE DESERT FOX
After the final Axis defeat in Africa, Rommel's next major command was in France in 1944, preparing the German forces to resist the **D-Day invasion 258–59** ». He was wounded in an Allied attack in July and while he was convalescing, it was discovered that he had known something of the conspiracy to overthrow Hitler. **Rommel was forced to commit suicide**.

Medicine in the field

New weaponry caused horrific injuries and took a terrible toll on life during World War II. The warring countries were desperate for troops and improved medical techniques and drugs helped soldiers return quickly to duty after injury.

1 An American Red Cross badge. The International Red Cross was neutral and helped all those caught up in the conflict. **2** This armband identified German medical personnel. **3** This pennant marked the location of a field medical unit on D-Day. All the places where the unit served subsequently are written on the pennant. **4** A water bottle was essential in the heat of the Russian summer, when many soldiers were treated for dehydration. **5** Japanese water purification kit. In the tropics, ground water had to be sterilized before it was safe to drink. **6** This British tablet tin contained painkillers, sedatives, and antiseptics for use by medical officers. **7** These German dental records found in Arnhem include an x-ray. Mobile dental units were vital to the health of troops. **8** This US Army steel helmet has red crosses painted on all four sides. This form of identification was first used in North Africa in 1943. **9** This haversack, carried by NCOs of the Royal Army Medical Corps, held drugs, bandages, splints, and dressings. **10** The shell dressing was introduced into the British Army in 1915 as a result of the large wounds caused by shell fragments. **11** The first field dressing pack

contained two dressings in a waterproof wrapper and safety pins. It was usually carried in a special pants pocket. **12** This field dressing was carried by all members of the Japanese armed forces. **13** A Japanese thermometer and case. Fevers in tropical regions were caused by malaria, dysentery, and yellow fever. **14** The tin holds a tourniquet used to control excessive bleeding from a limb. **15** Drug ampules and hypodermic needles in paraffin wax casings were carried by doctors in this safe, handy tin. **16** This 3/4fl oz (20 ml) syringe is a good-quality doctor's instrument. **17** This instrument roll contains an assortment of probes, forceps, and other instruments for field surgery. **18** This field sterilizer consists of a small alcohol-fueled burner and a tray for boiling water to sterilize medical instruments. **19** Medical orderly's pouch. German army medical orderlies carried two of these on their belts. They contained dressings and drugs. **20** This morphine ampule is a one-use injection carried by medical personnel and sometimes by soldiers. **21** This Japanese medical kit contains various dressings, pills, and medicines, including a powder for use in gas attacks.

CONTENTS OF TABLET TINS
(1941 PATTERN)

A	Tablet	Aspirin, gr. 5		No. 6
B	,,	Calomel, gr. 1		,, 2
C	,,	Cathartic :— *SENOKOT*		
		Calomel, gr. 1		
		Ext. Coloc. Comp., gr. 2½	in each	
		Ext. Hyoscy. Sicc., gr. 1/2		
D	,,	Cough :—		
		Codeine Phosphate, gr. 1/8		
		Benzoic Acid, gr. 1/2	in each	
		Ammonium Chloride, gr. 2		
		Ext. Glycyrrh., gr. 2		
E	,,	Dover Powder, gr. 5		
F	,,	Lead and Opium POISON D.D.A. :—		
		Lead Acetate, gr. 2	in each	
		Opium in Powder, gr. 1		
G	,,	Morphine Tartrate, gr. 1/4		
		POISON D.D.A.		
H	,,	Potassium Permanganate, gr. 2		12
		To be dissolved in water before administration		
I	,,	Quinine Hydrochloride, gr. 4		
J	,,	Sodium Bicarbonate, gr. 10		
K	,,	Sodium Bromide, gr. 5		
		To be dissolved in water before administration		
L	,,	Sodium Salicylate, gr. 5		

1 RED CROSS BADGE (US)

2 RED CROSS ARMBAND (GERMANY)

4 WATER BOTTLE (USSR)

3 RED CROSS FLAG (BRITAIN)

5 WATER STERILIZATION OUTFIT (JAPAN)

除毒包

6 TABLET TIN (BRITAIN)

7 DENTAL DOCUMENTS OF SS SOLDIER (GERMANY)

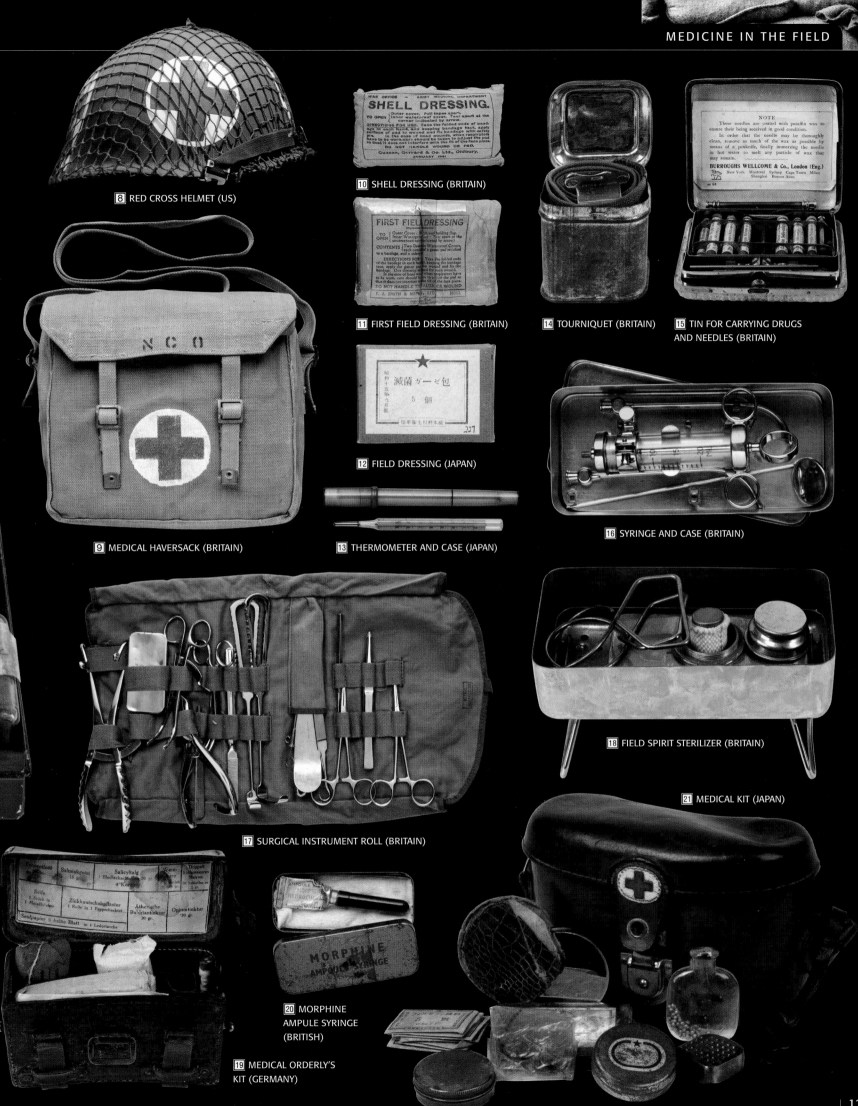

8 RED CROSS HELMET (US)

10 SHELL DRESSING (BRITAIN)

11 FIRST FIELD DRESSING (BRITAIN)

14 TOURNIQUET (BRITAIN)

15 TIN FOR CARRYING DRUGS AND NEEDLES (BRITAIN)

12 FIELD DRESSING (JAPAN)

16 SYRINGE AND CASE (BRITAIN)

9 MEDICAL HAVERSACK (BRITAIN)

13 THERMOMETER AND CASE (JAPAN)

18 FIELD SPIRIT STERILIZER (BRITAIN)

21 MEDICAL KIT (JAPAN)

17 SURGICAL INSTRUMENT ROLL (BRITAIN)

20 MORPHINE AMPULE SYRINGE (BRITISH)

19 MEDICAL ORDERLY'S KIT (GERMANY)

GERMAN GENERAL Born 1891   Died 1944

Erwin Rommel

"Don't fight a battle if you don't gain anything by winning."

ERWIN ROMMEL, IN HIS BOOK "INFANTERIE GREIFT AN", 1937

Field Marshal Erwin Rommel earned his fame as a commander of mobile armored forces in Europe and North Africa from 1940 to 1943. He was unique in being praised by both sides in the war—in the summer of 1942 British prime minister Winston Churchill, described him as "a very skillful and daring opponent" and "a great general," and in Germany he was known as the "people's marshal."

Rommel's rise to prominence was due, in part, to his association with the Nazi Party who held him up as an example of a "good German." A much decorated junior infantry officer in World War I and an advocate of bold, aggressive tactical doctrines, Rommel was exactly the kind of military tactician who appealed to Hitler. In the late 1930s the Führer drew Rommel from the relative obscurity of a military academy into his entourage, giving him command of his personal escort battalion. The pair's respect and admiration was mutual—in 1940 Rommel described Hitler as "a military genius."

The invasion of France

Although Rommel had no experience with tanks, his personal influence with the Führer won him command of an armored division for the invasion of France in May 1940. He more than justified the choice. His 7th Armored Division earned the nickname "the Ghost Division" because the speed of its advance from the Ardennes region to the Channel coast caused even

Mutual respect
Hitler was a huge fan of Rommel and regularly promoted him. Although Rommel was not involved in the plot to kill Hitler, he was implicated by a conspirator and committed suicide to keep his family safe.

the German high command to lose track of its movements. Rommel's absolute determination to maintain forward momentum, despite the risks of exposed flanks and outrunning supplies, played a decisive part in the early German victory. He ended the campaign as one of its heroes and was promoted to major-general in 1941.

The desert general

As well as being promoted, Rommel was further rewarded for his impressive contribution to the successful invasion of France by being sent to the North African desert, first as the leader of the German Afrika Korps and subsequently as commander of all Axis forces in North Africa. The location and conditions of the Desert War were particularly suited to Rommel's strengths. With control of his own show—he was uncomfortable in his relation to higher command—he was often presented with opportunities for rapid movement and maneuver. Rommel was above all else a flexible tactician, commanding from the front and improvising imaginative responses to a constantly changing battlefield situation. From the first moment of his arrival in Libya, he proved that, even with limited strength at his disposal, he

Honored commander
Rommel in the full dress uniform of a German general displays his panoply of decorations, including born Knight's Cross of the Iron Cross at his throat.

The Desert Fox

From August 1941 Rommel was given command of the German and Italian forces in the Western Desert of North Africa. His skill at conducting armoured warfare in Libya earned him the nickname "the Desert Fox."

could outwit and outmaneuver the slower-moving British forces. He molded his armored forces into a highly motivated team, winning the loyalty and respect of his subordinates, and swiftly weeded out any officers whom he deemed not up to scratch. The ultimate failure of the Axis forces in the Desert War was largely due to elements beyond Rommel's control. Yet even after his forces were held in July 1942 at El Alamein, stopped in September at Alam Halfa, and finally defeated in November at the second battle of El Alamein, he had demonstrated his outstanding skills as a battlefield commander in a series of ultimately doomed fighting withdrawals and counterattacks.

Back in Europe

After the Axis surrender in North Africa in 1943, the Nazi regime did not know what to do with Rommel. Goebbels's propaganda machine had made Rommel into a German icon, but the shadow of defeat in Africa tarnished his reputation, and his health had deteriorated under the strain of war. Eventually given responsibility for the defense of the French coast, his efforts ensured that the defenses of Normandy were improved, but the success of

> ## "I would be rather more **happy** had he given me **one more division.**"
>
> COMMENT AFTER RECEIVING THE RANK OF FIELD MARSHAL FROM HITLER, 1942

Hero of the Reich

Rommel's reputation as a military genius was exploited by the Nazi propaganda machine. Here he is featured on the cover of the mass-market magazine *Signal*.

Operation Overlord— the Allied invasion in June 1944—showed the accuracy of his prediction that, once a beachhead was established, it would prove impossible to dislodge.

Disillusionment and death

Rommel's personal reputation was untarnished by responsibility for massacre or atrocity, and his treatment of Allied prisoners of war was exemplary, but he was never an opponent of Nazi ideology. He was, however, increasingly critical of the regime for the failings of its military

leadership. By 1944 Rommel could see that his country was heading into an abyss. He played no part in the plot to assassinate Hitler in July 1944, but his off-the-record criticisms of the conduct of the war brought him under suspicion. Convalescing after being wounded in Normandy, Rommel was offered the choice of taking poison—in which case his family would be spared from Hitler's vengeance—or face prosecution as a traitor. He chose suicide, allowing the regime to claim that he had died of his wounds, maintaining his status as a war hero. His tragedy was the same as all those patriotic Germans who welcomed the opportunities the Nazi regime offered, and who realized their mistake far too late.

Leading from the front

Rommel liked to keep up with the action, exercising command from a tank or staff car while maintaining radio contact with his headquarters.

Conflicts in the Middle East

In 1941 a new threat to the Allies emerged from the Middle East. Nationalists in Iraq sought to ally themselves with Germany, the Vichy regime was about to welcome Nazi troops into Syria, and Iran's neutrality threatened vital supply channels. For the British, the cost of defeat in the oil-rich region was unthinkable.

By early 1941 Britain was fighting the Italians (and presently Nazi Germany) in Africa and was sending increasing military assistance to Greece. The British government saw its control of Egypt and the Suez Canal as a crucial link between its empire in Australasia and Asia and the home country. Iran and Iraq also provided much of Britain's oil supplies. Direct

11 MILLION
Number of tons of oil produced annually by Iran and Iraq, and available to the Allies if they kept control of these countries.

threats to the oil stocks or via other territories in the region would be fiercely challenged.

In 1939 Iraq had a pro-British government but many leading Iraqi soldiers were pro-Nazi. In April 1941 Rashid Ali el-Ghalani seized power in a military coup. El-Ghalani stopped

« **BEFORE**

Before World War II much of the Middle East was ruled by Britain and France under League of Nations mandates dating from the aftermath of World War I « 18–19.

END OF THE OTTOMAN EMPIRE
During World War I the Ottoman Empire in Turkey fought as an ally of Germany and was defeated. **Britain had promised its Arab allies that it would support their independence** after the

> **In the 1917 Balfour Declaration British foreign minister, Arthur Balfour, wrote to Jewish leaders saying that Britain would support the establishment of a Jewish "national home" in Palestine.**

war and also made a vague commitment to setting up some sort of Jewish homeland. In the event, to the anger of Arab nationalists and Zionists, **Britain and France took control of most of the former Ottoman Empire**.

IRAQ
Iraq was ruled as a British mandate in the 1920s but became independent in 1932 by a treaty with the British. **Britain retained oil rights** and kept military bases in the country.

Grand Mufti Hadj Amin el-Husseini in Berlin
After reaching Berlin from Iraq in 1941 the Mufti helped the Germans recruit Muslim volunteers for their armed forces. The Waffen SS eventually included numerous Muslim troops recruited in Albania and Yugoslavia.

British troop movements through Iraq from the vital oil port of Basra in the south. All the fuel needed by the British forces in the Middle East flowed along pipelines running through Iraq and Syria to Haifa (in present-day Israel). Claiming that the Anglo-Iraqi Treaty had been violated, the Allies landed troops at Basra on April 18.

March on Baghdad
The British also had intelligence that the Nazis were sending military support to Iraq via Vichy French Syria, though in fact Hitler was too busy with his planned Russian invasion, and sent little support to the Iraqi cause. Despite this, el-Ghalani pressed on with plans to attack the British airbase at Habbaniya (near Baghdad). Habbaniya was only guarded by half-trained pilots and instructors but held out all the same. Britain rallied a 5,800-strong intervention force (Habforce) in Transjordan for a march on Baghdad. Iraq's army proved no match for the British, and, dispirited by the lack of Axis support, the Iraqi leader fled to Iran, and then on to Germany.

Because the Vichy authorities had allowed German aircraft to use bases in Syria en route to Iraq, Britain decided to invade Syria. Operation Exporter began on the morning of June 8, 1941. British, Australian, and

French camel "cavalry" in Syria in 1940
France maintained camel units as part of its colonial army in North Africa and Syria before the war. The troopers were locally recruited but officers and many NCOs were from metropolitan France.

Free French troops were to overthrow the French garrisons that had been loyal to the Vichy regime. On July 12, after six weeks of fighting, the leader of the Vichy troops, General Henri Dentz, signed an armistice at Acre.

When Germany invaded Russia on June 22, 1941, the Allies needed to transport supplies across officially-neutral Iran to the Soviet Union. Iran (then often known as Persia) refused to expel its considerable German community, so from August 25, 1941, British and Soviet forces occupied the country, meeting little resistance. Eventually, almost a quarter of Allied Lend-Lease supplies sent to the Soviet Union passed through Iran.

Events in Palestine
Before the war British control of Palestine had been disrupted by the growing confrontation between the region's Arab and Jewish populations and by the so-called Arab Revolt of 1937–39. As war approached the fundamental British objective was to avoid further troubles in the region.

The No.27 ammunition limber could carry 32 rounds of 25-pounder ammunition. The crew rode in the tractor and a small additional amount of ammunition could also be carried here.

Muzzle brake

Breech

Gunshield

The CMP "Quad" artillery tractor was one of the various vehicles used by British and Empire forces to tow artillery weapons. Many, like the Canadian-built Chevrolet 8440 (shown), evolved from the British Morris C8 Quad.

The 25-pounder gun had a shell weight,of 25 lb (11.3 kg). This was a lighter weapon than equivalents in other armies but it had good range of 13,400 yd (12,250 m). It was 87 mm (3.45 in) caliber.

Circular firing platform for quick traversing

"The Arabian Freedom Movement in the Middle East is **our natural ally against England."**

ADOLF HITLER, MAY 23, 1941

25-pounders in service
The 25-pounder was Britain's principal divisional artillery weapon throughout the war. An 8-gun 25-pounder battery was usually allocated to each infantry or armored brigade but would also be available to fire in support of other units too.

Therefore, in 1939, to appease Arab opinion, Jewish immigration was virtually halted by the British, just when European Jews were desperately trying to escape from persecution.

4.2 MILLION The amount in tons of Lend-Lease supplies shipped to the Soviet Union via Iran, almost exactly the same quantity transported by the dangerous Arctic convoys.

This placed Jewish leaders in a dilemma: if they challenged the British authorities in Palestine they would indirectly be helping the Nazis.

In the event Jewish-owned agricultural and industrial businesses in Palestine supported the British war effort and thousands of Jewish people fought in the British forces as part of the Palestine Regiment. They acquired arms and undertook military training which would be of use in their own campaign for independence after the war. Jewish leaders also did all they could to support illegal Jewish immigration into Palestine, especially after early 1942 when they had definite information about the Holocaust. Called *Aliyah Bet* in Hebrew, this mass immigration grossly flouted the British quotas.

Britain's aim of keeping the Arab population of Palestine acquiescent was achieved for the most part. Influential leader, Hadj Amin el-Husseini, the Grand Mufti of Jerusalem, had helped inspire the Arab Revolt but had fled to Switzerland in 1937. He eventually ended up in Berlin, broadcasting for the Germans to the Muslim world and condemning British and Jewish influence in the Middle East in vitriolic speeches.

AFTER »

After World War II most countries in the Middle East became more truly independent than before and were joined by a new nation, Israel.

PALESTINE AND ISRAEL
The Holocaust 176–77 » transformed the position for Palestine's Jews and the Zionist movement. **After the war many survivors came to Palestine**, seeking a Jewish homeland. **Israel achieved its independence in 1948 344–45 »**, following a terrorist campaign

470 THOUSAND Jews lived in Palestine prior to the start of World War II.

250 THOUSAND Nazi victims went to Palestine between 1945 and 1948.

conducted against the occupying British forces. In November 1944 Lord Moyne, **the British deputy resident minister of state, was assassinated** in Cairo by Zionist terrorists.

THE ARAB LEAGUE
Although the Middle East was under Allied control from 1941–45, all the regional countries either **gained or reasserted their independence after the war.** Egypt, Lebanon, Syria, Transjordan, and Iraq were founder members of the Arab League in 1945. Among other things this called for an **independent Palestinian state.**

THE BRITISH DEPUTY MINISTER OF STATE, LORD MOYNE

« BEFORE

Hitler intended to control southeastern Europe and Italy's Fascist leader Benito Mussolini saw Greece as an easy conquest.

ITALY IN ALBANIA AND GREECE
Italy annexed Albania in the spring of 1939. In October 1940 **Mussolini began an invasion of Greece** from Albania without first informing Hitler of his plans. Greece fought back effectively and by early 1941 Greek forces had pushed Mussolini's troops back into Albania. At the same time Italians forces in North Africa were in retreat.

2.9 MILLION
The tonnage of Romanian oil used by Germany in 1941. This was a vital resource to be defended at all costs.

BARBAROSSA AND THE BALKANS
Hitler's secret plan for 1941 was the attack on the USSR. But before beginning the campaign on the Eastern Front **he needed to secure his southern flank in the Balkans**—either by diplomacy or conquest.

ITALIAN ARMORED CARS

The Balkans Invaded

A German column advances into Yugoslavia
German armored cars and transport vehicles in a Yugoslav town. Many of the vehicles have German flags displayed to prevent "friendly fire" attacks from the Luftwaffe, which dominated the skies above.

In April 1941 Hitler conquered Yugoslavia and Greece to secure Germany's flank for the invasion of the Soviet Union. Mussolini was on the retreat in Albania and British troops and bombers were arriving in Greece, all too near Romania's oilfields—threats Hitler could not ignore.

Even before the German failure in the Battle of Britain Hitler was planning to fulfil his long-held ambition to destroy the Soviet Union and seize new territories for the German people in the east. This attack was scheduled for the summer of 1941 but first Hitler wanted to ensure that his southern flank was secure. In the winter of 1940–41 Hungary, Romania, and Bulgaria were all pressured into, in effect, becoming allies of the Germans.

In the meantime, Benito Mussolini's attack on Greece from Albania had gone badly wrong. By early 1941 half of Albania was in Greek hands. Hitler could not let his ally be humiliated in this way. Worse still, British air and ground forces were arriving to help the Greeks, which posed a potential threat to Germany's vital oil supplies from Romania. Hitler's only option was to attack Greece.

In March 1941 the Yugoslavian ruler Prince Paul signed the Tripartite Pact. He had reluctantly agreed to join the German bloc, but at the end of the month was overthrown in a coup. Hitler was furious and ordered his forces to invade both Yugoslavia and Greece as soon as possible.

Conquering Yugoslavia
Germany's attack began on April 6, 1941, with the first of a number of air raids on the Yugoslav capital, Belgrade. All in all some 17,000 Yugoslav civilians died in these attacks. As well as being totally outmatched in the air, the Yugoslavian forces on the ground were weak and scattered throughout the country. They couldn't compare with the attacking German troops.

Germany's first ground advance into the country came from Romania on April 8 and was joined over the next few days by other units from Hungary and Austria plus an Italian force in the far north. They met little resistance. The Yugoslavs surrendered on April 17. The whole country was conquered at a cost of only 150 German dead.

Fighting for Greece
The Allied forces never established a coherent plan for the defense of Greece. British commanders wanted the Greek military forces to withdraw from their northernmost provinces and pull back from their gains in Albania to set up a defence line, the "Aliakmon

Sights

Ammunition feed, by belt or drum

Folding bipod

German MG34 7.62 mm machine gun
The MG34 was a standard German machine gun throughout World War II. It could be used by maneuvering troops with a bipod mount (as shown here) or on a tripod in prepared positions.

Pivoting trigger to select full automatic or semi-automatic fire

Line," in the mountains a little to the south. The Greeks, however, did not try to carry out this important strategy until too late.

Three Australian and New Zealand divisions, along with other British ground and air units, had been sent from North Africa to Greece—far too few troops to hold a determined

German attack. However, their departure from the North African desert had left the remaining Allied Front vulnerable and given General Rommel the chance to make his first decisive move forward.

In Greece, the German troops were soon advancing rapidly. On April 21, with the northern half of

the country already lost, the British command decided to evacuate Greece. The Germans entered Athens on April 27. By the 29th the Allied evacuation was complete; 50,000 troops had left. Thousands more were captured.

Airborne attack on Crete

The last stage in the campaign was a German attack on Crete. Many of the Allies from the mainland had been sent there but they had few heavy weapons. When German paratroops landed on the island on May 20 the garrison fought back. For a time it looked as if the enemy might fail but the Germans took the vital Maleme airfield and poured in reinforcements in transport aircraft.

Yet again the Allies evacuated. Over 11,000 men were captured and nine vital Royal Navy warships were sunk.

Germany had crushed Yugoslavia and Greece in little more than a month. The forces soon headed north to join the attack on the USSR which was not held up at all by the battle in the Balkans.

German conquest of the Balkans, 1941
Germany deployed six Panzer divisions and over 1,000 aircraft to lead their attacks, a combination the Allies were helpless to resist. Improvised Allied defense lines were soon outflanked.

AFTER

Yugoslavia and Greece both suffered greatly from German occupation, a resistance struggle, and internal conflicts.

RESISTANCE IN YUGOSLAVIA
Two main resistance groups emerged: the mainly Serbian Četniks led by Draža Mihailović and the Communist partisans led by Josip Broz (usually known by his adopted name, Tito). In addition, in Croatia the **Ustaša movement set up a semi-independent government** which massacred many Serbs and Bosnians.

The Yugoslav groups fought viciously among themselves as well as against the Germans. Britain and the United States finally decided that the **partisans were the most valuable allies**. In 1944–5, with Soviet help, **Tito took control of the country 276–77 》**.

GREECE
The Germans left in October 1944 and **the British moved in**. Hundreds of thousands of Greeks, many of them Jews, died under Nazi rule.

USTAŠA DICTATOR PAVELIĆ

276–77 》

GERMAN 2ND ARMY · HUNGARY

ITALIAN 2ND ARMY · Trieste

HUNGARIAN 3RD ARMY

6 Apr 11–12 Hungarian army overruns part of northern Yugoslavia, which is then annexed by Hungary

0 · 150 km
0 · 150 miles

Zagreb · CROATIA · Sava · Fiume

Belgrade · ROMANIA

1 Apr 6, 1941 Heavy bombing of Belgrade. Yugoslav high command paralysed

Zara (to Italy) · YUGOSLAVIA · Bucharest

Sarajevo · Drina · Uzice · Morava · Danube

2 Apr 6 First Panzer Corps invades from Bulgaria and reaches Belgrade on the 12th

7 Apr 16 Fall of Sarajevo · Nis · SERBIA

Dubrovnik · Sofia · BULGARIA

ITALIAN 9TH ARMY · Scutari · Skopje · Vardar · GERMAN 12TH ARMY · Plovdiv

3 Apr 9 Germans take Salonika, trapping Greek troops defending Metaxas Line

4 Apr 9 German motorized corps reaches Monastir · ALBANIA (to Italy) · Durazzo · Tirana · Monastir · Strumo · Nestos · Metaxas Line

ITALY · **5 Apr 10** British start to fall back from Aliakmon Line · Pogradec · Edessa · GREEK 2ND ARMY · Thasos

ITALIAN 11TH ARMY · Florina · Aliakmon Line · Samothrace · TURKEY

Himara · **8 Apr 20** Greek First Army surrenders · GREEK 1ST ARMY · BRITISH W FORCE · Salonika · Larissa · Lemnos · Lesbos

GREECE · Aegean Sea

9 Apr 24 Germans break through British positions at Thermopylae · Thermopylae · **10 Apr 24–30** British evacuation from Piraeus and ports in the Peloponnese

Cephalonia · Khios

11 Apr 25 German paratroops take Corinth · Patras · Peloponnese · Corinth · Athens · Piraeus · Dodecanese (to Italy)

Nafplio · Kalamata · **12 May 20** German airborne invasion of Crete

Monemvasia · Mediterranean Sea · GERMAN 5TH MOUNTAIN DIV

Canea · Suda · Rethymno

KEY · GERMAN 7TH PARACHUTE DIV · Maleme · Heraklion · Crete

N · **13 May 28–Jun 1** British and Commonwealth troops evacuated from Sphakia to Alexandria · Sphakia · BRITISH CREFORCE

KEY

→ Axis advance

Parachute/glider landing

Allied defensive position April 6, 1941

KEY MOMENT
CAPTURE OF MALEME AIRFIELD ON CRETE, MAY 20–21

Like all airborne forces German paratroops attacking Crete had only light arms and limited supplies. When they encountered opposition heavier than expected they faced total defeat. The only way for the paratroops to be reinforced was to capture the airfield at Maleme. Fortunately for them a breakdown in communications on the Allied side led to New Zealand troops being withdrawn from the vital Hill 107 overlooking the airfield. The Germans captured Maleme in fierce fighting and began flying in supplies and reinforcements. It was the turning point in the battle but even so, German paratroop casualties had been so heavy that Hitler forbade any similar parachute operations in the future.

Operation Barbarossa

Hitler's decision to invade the Soviet Union ushered in the bloodiest conflict in history. The battles on the Eastern Front would make up the decisive campaign of the war and would be fought with the utmost brutality. Hitler thought it would be an easy conquest, but it proved to be the Nazis' undoing.

« BEFORE

After his lightning victories in Western Europe in 1939–40, Hitler turned to his greatest project, the complete destruction of Stalin's Soviet Union.

SOVIET AND GERMAN EXPANSION
Hitler's and Stalin's foreign ministers agreed an **uneasy alliance in August 1939 « 54–55**, under the terms of which they cooperated to overrun Poland the next month. From 1940–41 **both dictators extended their influence into other areas of Eastern Europe**. Hitler dominated Hungary and Romania and conquered Yugoslavia and Greece. **Stalin attacked Finland « 64–65**, annexed the Baltic States, and grabbed territory from Romania. Both were preparing for an eventual conflict.

HITLER'S PLANS
Hitler believed that the **German race should be supreme in Europe** and that its greatest threat were Jews and Communists. He also coveted the USSR's economic assets. In the summer of 1940 he planned an attack on the east.

In the early hours of June 22, 1941, more than three million German, Hungarian, and Romanian soldiers were ready to turn against the Soviet Union; 3,350 tanks and 2,270 aircraft led the attack. It was the largest military force ever assembled. Army Group North was to attack through the former Baltic States, to take Leningrad. Army Group South was to head for the Ukraine, and Army Group Center was to target Minsk and Smolensk. As dawn broke, a huge German wave poured across the 1,900-mile (3,000-km) front from the Baltic to the Black Sea. Within hours the Luftwaffe

625,000 The number of horses used by the German army to invade the USSR. Most of the German forces relied in large part on horse transportation.

had practically wiped out the front-line Soviet air units. On the ground Panzer divisions led the advance, with infantry following behind. Russian positions were quickly overrun. Although they had ample intelligence information of their own and had been warned of the coming attack by Britain and the United States, the Soviet Union's forces were caught off guard. Stalin believed the Allied intelligence to be propaganda and so had forbidden his generals to make effective defensive preparations.

Rapid German advances
Army Group Center was the strongest German force, with two of the four groups of Panzer divisions. Within days they had reached Minsk in a pincer movement, cutting off some 300,000 Red Army troops to be taken prisoner by the following infantry. Army Group North began a relentless advance towards Leningrad. Army Group South made slower progress at first against more effective Soviet resistance.

Stalin had panicked when the attack began but finally rallied, and on July 3 made a radio broadcast to his people, announcing a "scorched earth policy" and appealing to Russian nationalism. On July 13 Britain and Russia signed

Retreating Soviet soldiers
The German advances threw the Soviet military system into chaos. Thousands of troops were separated from their units, and many, like these, lost their weapons in the course of their desperate retreat.

German tank and infantry
German infantry accompany a Panzer III tank. The secret of the German success was not the power of their tanks as such but the way they were used in close cooperation with all the other sections of their army.

a mutual assistance pact, and both Britain and the US began sending supplies to the Soviet Union.

Throughout the planning of Operation Barbarossa Hitler and his generals were unsure what should be their main objective. One obvious target was Moscow, the enemy capital; another option was Leningrad, the birthplace of the Communist regime; a third was the Ukraine, with its great agricultural and mineral resources, and beyond that were the oilfields of the Caucasus.

During July and August, Army Group North drove forward to Leningrad. By the end of August it was only 30 miles (50 km) away. In the meantime Army

> Adopting a "scorched earth policy," Soviet forces would start fires to hinder the Germans' advance. In July 1941, an Axis command post was almost completely destroyed by a fire in a pine forest near the Luga River.

Group Center had surged on to Smolensk and seemed poised to continue on to Moscow. Hitler now intervened and ordered much of Army Group Center's tank force to change direction and attack south to help the slower-moving Army Group South in its advance on Kiev.

Soviet losses
At first it seemed that Hitler had made the right decision. Army Group South took the city of Kiev after brutal fighting and strong resistance from the Soviets. Some 600,000 troops from the Red Army were captured, nearly the entire southwestern front of the army. With this considerable loss, the Soviet Union had few reserves left to defend the capital, Moscow.

While the fighting around Kiev was continuing, the Soviets mounted a desperate defense on the approaches to Leningrad. With resources being

> " When Operation Barbarossa is launched, **the world will hold its breath**."
>
> ADOLF HITLER'S EVE-OF-BATTLE MESSAGE TO HIS TROOPS, JUNE 21, 1941

Operation Barbarossa, 1941

Time and again the Germans smashed the Russian defences and time and again their deft tank units surrounded huge numbers of troops. But the distances involved and Russia's huge manpower reserves made final success elusive.

KEY

— German front line Jun 21
–·– German front line Sep 1
– – German front line Nov 15
···· German front line Dec 5
— — Pocket of Soviet troops
➤ German advance

FINLAND

Gulf of Finland

Baltic Sea

5 Jul 10
Start of Finnish offensive against Soviet Union in support of the Germans

8 Sep 8
Start of siege of Leningrad

Lake Ladoga

Tallinn
Narra
Leningrad

ESTONIA

Luga

Novgorod

NORTHWEST FRONT

3 Jul 1
Germans take Riga

Riga

LATVIA

1 Jun 22, 1941
zer Group crosses an and penetrates iles (80 km) into Soviet territory

Memel

Tilsit

LITHUANIA

Dvinsk

Dvina

6 Jul 16
Germans take Smolensk, but pockets of resistance hold out till 5 Aug

11 Oct 2
Operation Typhoon, the assault on Moscow, begins in the north

18 Dec 5
German forces take up defensive positions 15 miles (25 km) from Moscow

Kalinin

ARMY GROUP NORTH

EAST RUSSIA

ARMY GROUP NTRE

Kaunas

1 Jun 22, 1941
2nd and 3rd Panzer Groups make rapid breakthrough toward Minsk

Moscow

WEST FRONT

Mozhaisk

13 Oct 23
Soviet troops in Vyazma pocket surrender

Vyazma

Smolensk

Kaluga

Białystok

Minsk

Volkovysk

Bug

BYELORUSSIA

Tula

12 Oct 14
Soviet troops in Bryansk pocket surrender

Warsaw

Pripet Marshes

9 Sep 16
Soviet forces trapped in pocket east of Kiev. City falls to the Germans three days later

Bryansk

15 Nov 15
Germans resume drive to Moscow from Tula area

Brest-Litovsk

Vistula

Pripet

Orel

2 Jun 26
Large numbers of Soviet troops encircled at Białystok

4 Jul 3
Germans claim to have taken 324,000 prisoners after encircling Soviet forces west of Minsk

GERMANY

POLAND

Kowel

ARMY GROUP SOUTH

Lutsk

1 Jun 22, 1941
Army Group South encounters Soviet resistance in advance toward Kiev

Kursk

10 Sep 30
Operation Typhoon, the assault on Moscow, begins in the south

Przemysl

Tarnopol

U S S R

Kiev

Belgorod

14 Oct 24
Kharkov falls to Germans

Kharkov

7 Jul 19
Soviet forces encircled around Uman

UKRAINE

SOUTHWEST FRONT

HUNGARY

Dniester

Uman

Prut

1 Jun 22, 1941
Two Romanian armies take part in German drive into Ukraine

Bug

17 Nov 27
Germans forced to abandon Rostov, which they had taken on Nov 21

Rostov

ROMANIA

Odessa

Kherson

Black Sea

Sea of Azov

CRIMEA

Kerch

Sevastopol

16 Nov 16
Start of siege of Sevastopol

---

committed elsewhere the German advance slowed to a crawl. Rather than embroil his tanks and infantry in a bloody battle in the city itself, Hitler decide to starve the city into surrender. The siege was to last 900 days.

The road to Moscow

Hitler ordered Army Group Center to resume its march on Moscow in Operation Typhoon. Even with the delay imposed by the Kiev operations, the road to Moscow seemed to be open. Stalin recalled Marshal Zhukov, his ablest general, from Leningrad to command the defense of Moscow. Even so, by October 13 German forces were only 90 miles (150 km) from the capital, but their advance slowed dramatically with the arrival of the *rasputitsa*, torrential autumnal rains that turned the roads into seas of mud.

Hitler had thought the war was lost for the Soviet Union, but he had underestimated the resistance. In fact, as the German advance on Moscow finally ground to a halt in freezing weather, Soviet reserves, assembled from their forces in the Far East, were poised to counterattack. The war on the Eastern Front was far from over.

AFTER

The German victories seemed endless but in reality their forces were struggling, worn out by Russia's vast distances and increasingly fierce Soviet resistance.

A BRUTAL WINTER

The German Army never made it to Moscow. Stalin's troops defended it ferociously and **forced the Germans back 140–41 》**. Germany was completely unprepared for the hazards of winter warfare. Many **soldiers suffered from frostbite** in the coldest winter in 140 years. The German retreat infuriated Hitler and he lost trust in his generals. But in 1942 **Germany would attack again 190–91 》**.

SIEGE OF LENINGRAD

The siege of Leningrad lasted until January 1944. Supplies of water, food, energy, and utilities were interrupted, causing wipespread starvation among the beleaguered civilians. By the time the siege was finally lifted **about a million civilians had died** and a further 1.4 million evacuated.

СМЕРТЬ ФАШИСТСКОЙ ГАДИНЕ!

SOVIET POSTER "KILLING THE NAZI SNAKE"

Leningrad Besieged

The siege of Leningrad lasted from September 1941 until January 1944, but the first, bitter winter was the worst. Despite rationing, thousands starved to death—5,000 a day by January 1942. People ate cats, dogs, and birds, and there were reports of cannibalism. Bombing and freezing conditions destroyed the sewage system and water supply. Conditions slowly improved from March 1942.

"9 and 10 November 1941. We haven't been able to buy our full rations in this ten-day period: we are due 400 grams of cereal, 615 grams of butter, and 100 grams of flour—but these items are nowhere to be found. And where they do come on sale, huge queues form, hundreds and hundreds of people out in the street, in the bitter cold, and the amount delivered is usually just about enough for 80 to 100 people. So people stand there, get chilled to the bone, and leave with nothing to show for it. People get up at four in the morning, queue outside the shops until nine in the evening, and still come away with nothing ... At the moment there is an air-raid alert in force. It has already lasted for about two hours. Need and hunger drive people out to the shops, in the freezing cold, to join the long queue, the crush of people.**"**

DIARIST YURA RIABINKIN, AGED 16, WHO PROBABLY DIED IN LENINGRAD AFTER HIS FINAL DIARY ENTRY ON JANUARY 4, 1941

"I had lost so much weight that there was no flesh on my legs at all. My chest was like a man's—just nipples ... The children were also very skinny, and my heart would falter when I saw their bony little arms and their transparent little faces and huge eyes ... There was nothing to heat water with or cook anything. Rosa told me that they had a little coal in the basement, but that it was a terrible place to go to, because they had been piling the dead bodies there ... We took buckets and went. There were indeed a number of corpses there. We tried not to look at them ... Once I went out for bread while the shelling was going on, because the queues were shorter ... and I came under heavy shellfire ... I constantly went about in my husband's felt boots and wore two overcoats: my own and my husband's on top of it. Everyone else was bundled up like that too.**"**

DIARIST LIDIYA GEORGIEVNA OKHAPKINA, MOTHER OF TWO SMALL CHILDREN, AND SURVIVOR OF THE SIEGE

Bombed out
Citizens of Leningrad, muffled against the extreme cold, leave a bombed-out building with whatever possessions they can carry. The Germans bombed and shelled the city daily from September 1941.

BEFORE

The invasions of Poland and the Soviet Union gave the Nazis the chance to implement their vision of a racial utopia.

MEIN KAMPF
In his book, *Mein Kampf*, written while he was in prison in the 1920s ≪ **20–21**, Hitler had explained how he **blamed Communists and Jews for Germany's problems** and how he intended to eliminate them.

DEATH SQUADS IN POLAND
As in Russia in 1941, the **German forces invading Poland in 1939** ≪ **58–59** were followed by SS murder squads. **They rounded up and killed anyone who was likely to resist** the German conquest: political leaders, intellectuals, priests, and others. Many Polish Jews were also killed at this time but **most were herded into ghettos** in the major cities to be dealt with later.

SS COLLAR TAB

Victims of a Nazi massacre
Russian survivors search for relatives and mourn their dead. Massacres of civilians by roaming Nazi murder squads or *Einsatzgruppen*, rare in other war theaters, were common on the Eastern Front.

Nazi Massacres

Hitler's war in the East was to be different from any that had gone before. As German troops penetrated deep into Russia, they waged an unprecedented campaign of slaughter against Communists and Jews. Prisoners of war on both sides were treated brutally and regularly shot out of hand.

Although Germany's Jews were viciously persecuted before the war and hundreds murdered, mass killing was not then Nazi policy. The conquest of Poland in 1939 brought millions more Jews under Nazi control; thousands of Jewish (and non-Jewish) Poles were killed in the following months but most of Poland's Jews were herded into ghettos, where they could be put to work for the German war effort. Many died of various cruelties, but there was not yet a program of official systematic killing. The planned invasion of the Soviet Union, however, would bring yet more Jews into German hands. Here, a more determined and deliberate policy would be introduced.

Invasion and atrocity
Hitler told his generals that the attack on Russia would be a war of annihilation targeting "Jewish Bolshevism." His Commissar Order of March 1941 spelled this out and added that international law did not apply because the Soviets had never ratified the Hague Convention.

As in Poland in 1939 the German armed forces were to be tracked by *Einsatzgruppen* (or Special Action Groups), SS units that were to carry out the killings. Although some German army leaders had misgivings, army commanders generally concurred with Hitler's orders and cooperated fully with the SS killers.

There were four *Einsatzgruppen*, of some 3,000 men in all, operating all along the Eastern Front. Some of the killing was assisted by local civilians, notably in parts of the Ukraine and Lithuania, where anti-Semitism was already deep-seated.

The killing escalates
In summer meetings between Hitler and senior officials, the Nazi policy grew clearer. All measures were to be taken to cleanse the Soviet Union of Jews and Bolsheviks. These victims were rounded up and taken to secluded sites to be shot and buried in ditches or quarries, notably at Babi Yar near Kiev where, over two days toward the end of September 1941, thousands of civilians were massacred. It also became common to lock Jews in their synagogues and set them alight. And all this was carefully reported by the SS units. Their own records list the murder of some 600,000 Jews in 1941.

Soviet prisoners of war also suffered. They were denied medical care, beaten, starved, and shot if too ill to march. The Nazis captured 3.8 million Soviet troops in 1941; around 3 million did not survive their captivity or the years of slave labor in Germany that followed. Much of the ill-treatment in the first stages probably arose from the German Army simply being unable to cope with the volume of prisoners.

However, as Slavs, Nazi ideology saw the Soviet people as *Untermenschen,* or sub-humans, whose

> **33,771** The number of Jews killed at Babi Yar near Kiev, Ukraine, in September 1941. They were rounded up, made to undress, led to a ravine, forced to lie down, and shot.

lives were valueless. Some Ukrainians initially welcomed the Nazis and looked forward to gaining their independence. But the Nazis regarded the Ukraine as a source of food, iron, coal, and slave labor. As many as seven million Ukrainians died in the war, a sixth of the population. Among the many cruelties, the German Army destroyed numerous villages in murderous reprisals for Soviet partisan activity.

Across the Soviet Union, increasingly barbaric acts were carried out on an unimaginable scale. In 1941, however, Hitler's main worry was that, despite the vast numbers dying every day, the killing techniques were too clumsy. New methods of mass murder were needed.

Slaughter of the masses
Unlike the death camp mass executions, the Nazis did not hide their activities in 1941. Many German troops and even some civilians saw what was being done in their name.

AFTER

Although perhaps one million people had been murdered by the Nazis in the East by the end of 1941, this was only the beginning.

THE HOLOCAUST
The *Einsatzgruppen* had killed many Jews by the end of 1941 but the process was too slow for the Nazis. **Death camps would now take over** the fulfillment of the **"Final Solution" 164–65** ≫.

THE WAFFEN-SS
As well as dealing with the "Jewish problem," the SS had its own army, the Waffen-SS, commanded by Heinrich Himmler. In 1941 this was only a small part of the German forces but it would increase substantially later—from six divisions to nearly 40. **Waffen-SS units rarely took prisoners** on the Eastern Front and were known for their ruthless determination in attack. They were responsible for many atrocities on all fronts.

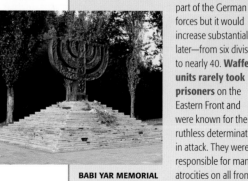

BABI YAR MEMORIAL

> **"The struggle is one of ideologies** and racial differences and will have to be waged with … **unmerciful and unrelenting harshness** … my orders must be followed without complaint.**"**

ADOLF HITLER, "COMMISAR ORDER," MARCH 1941

Moscow Saved

Operation Typhoon—Germany's offensive against the Soviet capital, Moscow—should have been another spectacular success for Hitler. Instead, the outcome was the first major reverse for the German Army, proving that Hitler was not invincible after all.

When Germany launched its Soviet offensive, Operation Barbarossa, in June 1941, Hitler expected the campaign to be over in just 10 weeks. At the end of September, having sent its forces deep into the Soviet Union, Germany's high command launched what was hoped

would be a final decisive offensive, to capture the city of Moscow and break the Red Army. Many German generals had wanted to begin this attack more than a month before, when they were likely to have better weather, but Hitler had overruled them. Instead, German forces were gathered from across the entire Eastern Front. Germany's army supply system was failing to cope with the Soviet Union's vast distances and difficult roads, however, and it now had few reserves left.

German troops took the important cities of Bryansk and Vyazma, and captured hundreds of thousands of Soviet prisoners, but it was becoming clear that the weather was worsening while Soviet resistance was stiffening. Every year, for a few weeks in

spring and fall, heavy rain creates a muddy terrain in Russia, this would have made military operations all but impossible. This *rasputitsa* season almost halted the German advance. It made life hard for the Red Army, too, although Soviet defenses were being strengthened by hurriedly organized militia forces and troops transferring from the far eastern border, which it was now clear Japan had no plans to attack.

By the end of October the German attack had been halted. Their troops were exhausted. Even so, in mid-November, despite the doubts of the

front-line commanders, they attacked again. Winter had now set in completely and, with the ground frozen solid, vehicles were able to move once again.

Germany loses the advantage

Hitler had been so confident of a quick victory that his troops were completely unprepared for the severity of the Russian winter. They had little warm clothing, yet the winter of 1941 was the worst in about 140 years. Many troops suffered from frostbite; over 14,000 had limbs amputated. Hot food was a rarity, while washing became impossible. Many sentries simply froze to death. Tank crews often had to light fires under their vehicles in the morning to warm the engines enough for them to start.

The German offensive began on November 15. Just six weeks before, they had amassed a substantial numerical superiority on the Moscow front, but now numbers were nearly equal. Furthermore, Soviet troops were supplied with new, highly effective equipment, including T-34 and KV-1 tanks, and Katyusha artillery rocket launchers.

For all their losses and increasing hardship, the German advance again began well. By the end of November German troops were fighting in the northeastern suburbs of Moscow itself, within 18 miles (30 km) of the city center. But they could go no further.

It was now clear—and not just on the Moscow front—that Germany's attacking power was

BEFORE

Germany planned to annihilate the Soviet Army in a brutal and rapid assault. Initially, the German campaign went to plan.

OPERATION BARBAROSSA
Germany's **invasion of the USSR** began on June 22, 1941. **Within weeks,** the Germans had captured **hundreds of thousands** of Soviet troops and vast swathes of territory **《 134–35**.

JAPANESE–SOVIET NEUTRALITY PACT
Japan and the Soviet Union **fought numerous battles** on their far eastern borders in the 1930s but, in April 1941, they signed a **neutrality pact**. Japan was tempted to abandon this when Hitler attacked the USSR but instead kept to its new **policy of southern expansion 《 146–47**.

GERMAN GENERAL (1888–1954)

HEINZ GUDERIAN

A leading expert in tank operations, Guderian helped to create the armored "Panzer" divisions that led the German Army to its early victories. He commanded Panzer units to great effect in Poland in 1939, then France in 1940, and his troops won some of Germany's biggest victories in Russia, in 1941. However, Guderian was fired that same winter after failing to reach Moscow. He did serve later as inspector general of Panzer forces and chief of the general staff, but by that time Hitler chose to ignore his advice.

7.62 mm Tokarev TT-33
Like all Soviet weapons, the Tokarev automatic pistol was robust. It had an 8-round magazine and could also use German 7.63 mm ammunition.

ОТСТОИМ МОСКВУ!

"Let's Defend Moscow"
Soviet wartime propaganda was very successful in inspiring its citizens to fight fiercely in what it called the Great Patriotic War.

> **"** Moscow will be defended **to the last**."
>
> JOSEPH STALIN, ORDER OF THE DAY, OCTOBER 19, 1941

exhausted. The cracks were beginning to appear. At the southern end of the front, Army Group South retreated from Rostov. Hitler fired General von Rundstedt, its commander, for allowing

918,000 The number of Axis casualties suffered in Russia in 1941—almost one third of the force's initial strength.

this; the German Army commander-in-chief, two of the three army group commanders, and two of the three top tank leaders would all be fired before the winter was out.

Soviet counter-offensive
The German attack on Moscow had failed and they now hoped to stand where they were, on the defensive, through the winter. The Soviets had different ideas, however. At 3am on the morning of December 5, the Russians launched a major counter-

German troops struggle to keep warm
As well as lacking effective winter clothing, German troops found much of their equipment inadequate for coping with the intense Russian cold. Lubricating oil in weapons and vehicle engines often froze solid.

offensive, in which some 88 divisions would attack the German Army along a 500-mile (800-km) front. The Siberian troops emerged from ferocious snowstorms, clad in white camouflage uniforms. Panic immediately spread among the German troops, who were forced to pull back. They continued to retreat rapidly for a week or so. Hitler was furious and commanded his troops to hold their positions. Stalin ordered his men to develop new attacks, but his troops lacked strength and Germany was able to rebuild its front.

Moscow had been saved, and Hitler did not try to take the city again. He had the resources to rebuild his army for new campaigns but, with almost one million casualties to date, Germany would never be as strong as it had been in 1941, able to attack along the whole of the Eastern Front. Far from being out of Russia before the winter set in, the Germans would now have to attempt new attacks in the summer of 1942.

German soldiers surrender to the Russians
German prisoners of war in Soviet hands suffered as badly as Red Army troops held by the Germans. Tens of thousands died from ill-treatment and the last of the survivors were not released until well into the 1950s.

AFTER »

Despite suffering heavy losses, the Germans were able to rebuild their forces for new attacks on the Eastern Front in 1942.

GERMAN WITHDRAWAL
The **Soviet attacks** forced the Germans to retreat up to 175 miles (280 km) from Moscow but the Soviet reserves **were exhausted**, while confidence returned to the Germans.

SOVIET ARMY HAT

HITLER'S VOWS
Hitler had **argued repeatedly** with his commanders during the battles of 1941 and, following the **failure to capture** Moscow, he **dismissed the army's commander-in-chief** and a range of other

During the battle for Moscow—from early October 1941 to January 1942—some 650,000 soldiers from the Red Army died. The figure represents about 50 percent of the men fighting on the Eastern Front at the time.

top generals. From now on, he would make all the **major military decisions** himself, many of which proved to be serious mistakes.

GERMANY'S NEXT OFFENSIVE
Germany's targets for 1942 were **Stalingrad and the Caucasus 190–91 »**. Hitler, however, never decided clearly which wing of the attack was more important. **Both failed disastrously.**

America on the Brink

President Roosevelt wanted, if at all possible, to keep America out of full-scale participation in the war. But Japan and Germany posed a threat to US interests and both were ruled by brutal, morally repugnant governments. Preventing their victory and yet staying out of war was a difficult challenge.

Chinese Nationalist troops armed by the US
The US sent substantial shipments of arms to the Chinese Nationalists later in the war, but outside help was not as important as the Japanese thought in preventing their victory in China before December 1941.

O n the eve of Pearl Harbor the United States was still officially neutral but had in fact moved a long way from the neutrality that it had maintained in September 1939. The legal restrictions imposed by the Neutrality Laws of the late 1930s had been greatly eased. Not only were countries at war able to obtain arms and other supplies from the US, but the United States' government was paying for much of them under the Lend-Lease scheme introduced in the spring of 1941. By the summer of 1941, the US Navy had in effect joined the British and Canadians in the fight against Germany's U-boats in the western Atlantic. And in the Pacific the United States had imposed drastic economic sanctions against Japan, cutting off its oil supplies and most of its foreign trade.

All of these measures followed from President Roosevelt's policy to give all possible aid, short of declaring war, to Britain and its allies so that they might defeat Germany. At the same time, Roosevelt wanted to deter Japan from going to war until America's own rearmament had built up the country's strength to a level the Japanese would not dare to attack. British and French arms orders in 1939–40 had helped expand America's military manufacturing capabilities, but the real impetus came after the fall of France when the US military budget was vastly increased, notably in the "two-ocean navy" plans. These gave the US forces the capability to fight a major war simultaneously in both the Atlantic and Pacific theaters. This measure was really a response to the German threat but the Japanese saw it as a direct challenge to their expansionist aims. The next step was a compulsory military draft for young men—the first time this had occurred

> **1** The slender majority in the United States House of Representatives following the vote on August 12, 1941, in favour of extending the term of service of American draftees from one year to 30 months.

‹‹ BEFORE

Americans were overwhelmingly anti-war, but Japanese aggression meant that conflict looked increasingly inevitable.

AMERICA AND THE EUROPEAN WAR
From the outbreak of the European war to the autumn of 1941, **the US gave increasing aid to its British allies** but was still determined to avoid going to war with Germany if at all possible.

Japan's feeble pretext for going to war with China in July 1937 ‹‹ 40–41 outraged many Americans. Washington was not yet prepared to go to war with Japan but instead began exerting economic and diplomatic pressure. Events in the European war also led

ROOSEVELT AND CHURCHILL AT THE "ATLANTIC CHARTER" CONFERENCE IN AUGUST 1941

to **large-scale strengthening of American armaments** from the summer of 1940, which the **Japanese took as a threat to their expansion** plans. From then the tensions escalated, with Japan trying new advances and the United States responding with embargoes and other economic measures.

in the US in peacetime. Congress approved the US Conscription Bill in September 1940.

US weaknesses

American military planning was also greatly developed. Secret talks with the British in Washington D.C. in early 1941 established a basic framework for military coordination. Both Roosevelt and Churchill agreed that, in the event of the US being at war with both Germany and Japan, defeating Germany would be a higher priority for the Allied countries.

Despite all this there were still weaknesses. It would take considerable time to train the first draftees and to make the weapons they needed. US land and air power had been neglected between the wars. The US Navy was better preparedw but it would take many months before the ships

Oil embargo on Japan
Barrels of oil intended for Japan are held in the US following the introduction of the oil embargo in August 1941. Fears over their dwindling oil supplies helped bring the Japanese government's decision to go to war.

ordered in 1940 were available to the naval fleet. Cooperation between the US Army and Navy was also notoriously poor and, although the US had good intelligence on Japanese plans, an organization to put this to good use was sadly lacking.

There was a growing acceptance by the American people that they might well be forced to join the fight, but in the summer of 1941 opinion polls still showed that most of the United States' population wanted to avoid war. American politicians were likewise unsure. When Roosevelt asked Congress to extend the draft in August 1941 his plans were only narrowly passed after fierce debate.

Atlantic combats

By the summer of 1941 the Pan-American Neutrality Zone set up by the US extended roughly halfway across the Atlantic. Warships of non-American countries could be attacked inside that area but because Canada was part of the same continent as the US, and part of the British Commonwealth, British warships were exempt. The US Navy was also escorting convoys to the US Marine garrison in Iceland, so clashes with Germany's U-boats were inevitable. On September 4 a US destroyer was

The Japanese attack on Pearl Harbor was almost immediately followed by Hitler's declaration of war on the United States.

PEARL HARBOR
By December 1941 all attempts at a peaceful settlement between the US and Japan had failed. On December 7 **Japanese forces went on the offensive** with a surprise attack on Pearl Harbor, an American naval base on the Hawaiian island of Oahu. The following day President **Roosevelt asked Congress to declare war on Japan 148–49 »**. On December 11 **Hitler foolishly declared war on the US**, making the war a truly global conflict.

AMERICAN RESOURCES
Although American rearmament had begun in earnest following the fall of France in 1940, it took time for the various production programs to gather speed. However, by 1945 **the US had supplied not only its own armed forces but also a quarter of British requirements** and some 10 percent of Soviet needs. A range of government agencies, like the War Production Board and the Office of War Mobilization, oversaw every aspect of the economy. **The US made huge amounts of equipment** in every category—300,000 aircraft, for example. These were the sort of figures that **neither Germany nor Japan could hope to match**.

"The structure of world peace … must be a peace which rests on the cooperative effort of the whole world."

PRESIDENT ROOSEVELT'S ADDRESS TO CONGRESS, MARCH 1, 1945

attacked by a U-boat. The destroyer fired back but neither was hit. However, in mid-October, 11 men of the US Navy died when the USS *Kearny* was struck by a torpedo, and 100 more men were killed when the USS *Reuben James* was sunk at the end of that month.

The people of America were not fully aware of just how far their government had committed them to the fight. President Roosevelt portrayed these incidents as the result of German aggression, which was far from true. Hitler had in fact ordered his U-boats

2 | **The years that it was estimated Japan's oil stocks would last its troops, unless new fields were taken or a deal made with the US.**

to avoid incidents with the Americans, as Roosevelt knew from codebreaking information passed on by the British.

Although President Roosevelt was clearly taking the United States to the brink in the actions he ordered against Germany's U-boats in the Atlantic Ocean and in the aggressive sanctions he brought into effect against the Japanese, he was also well aware that both potential enemies had a record of starting wars whenever it suited them.

President Roosevelt's policies were designed to guarantee that, if the United States decided on war, it was likely to begin in circumstances that were as favorable as possible for the country. In the end, when the United States did go to war it was by Japan's and Germany's choice.

US equipment for the Allies
British Army mechanics at work preparing a US-made M3 Stuart light tank for service "somewhere in England" in 1941. In updated forms the Stuart would remain in US and Allied service until the end of the war.

PRESIDENT OF THE UNITED STATES Born 1882 Died 1945

Franklin D. Roosevelt

"We must be the **great arsenal** of **democracy**."

F. D. ROOSEVELT, DECEMBER 29, 1940

When Japan bombed Pearl Harbor on December 7, 1941, Franklin Delano Roosevelt was already serving his third term as US president—the only president to serve more than two terms. He had won popularity as the man who brought the US out of the Depression; he went on to lead the US through World War II, playing a major role in defeating the Axis powers and determining the shape of the postwar world.

Always a Democrat, Roosevelt entered politics in 1910, when he won a seat in the New York State Senate. He gave his support to Woodrow Wilson, who, as US president, subsequently appointed Roosevelt Assistant Secretary of the Navy. The post gave Roosevelt valuable naval and administrative experience, and during World War I he gained even more experience in military naval planning.

In 1921 Roosevelt was diagnosed with polio and became completely paralyzed. He made a slow recovery but never regained the use of his legs. Encouraged and assisted by his wife, Eleanor, he fought to resume his political career and in 1928 was elected Governor of New York. The following year the Wall Street Crash marked the beginning of a long economic depression in the US, and the world. Roosevelt ran as the Democratic presidential candidate, promising an interventionist program of "relief,

recovery, and reform." Elected in 1932, he introduced a raft of progressive social legislation, known as the New Deal, which enabled much needed social welfare. He also initiated his famous "fireside chats," where he spoke directly to the nation via radio broadcasts. By now immensely popular, Roosevelt's reward was a second victory in 1936.

War approaches

By the late 1930s, with the Depression almost over, foreign policy became the major issue in the US. Roosevelt had always advocated a policy of military preparedness and he clearly saw the threat posed by Nazi Germany and Japan. The mood of the country,

Long-serving president

Franklin Delano Roosevelt, often known as FDR, was the 32nd President of the United States. Widely admired, he served his country continuously from 1933 to 1945.

Declaration of war

FDR. signs the declaration of war against Japan on December 8, 1941. Roosevelt had provided support to Britain and other Allies but the Japanese attack on Pearl Harbor brought America irrevocably into the war.

Quebec Conference
At the conference held in Quebec in August 1943, Roosevelt, Churchill, and Canadian prime minister Mackenzie King (top left) agreed to intensify bombing raids on Germany and build up US forces in Britain.

however, had been isolationist since the 1920s, and Congress, which had passed the Neutrality Act in 1935, advocated neutrality for the United States. However, when Britain declared war on Germany in 1939, Roosevelt stated that although the US might remain neutral, it could not remain inactive. He persuaded Congress to support Allied efforts with "all aid short of war," while at the same time strengthening US defenses. Roosevelt increased the US contribution by providing warships in exchange for naval bases, and in one of his fireside chats urged the public to consider further involvement.

> ## "The **United States** can accept no result save **victory**."
> **ROOSEVELT DECLARES WAR ON JAPAN, DECEMBER 8, 1941**

One of Roosevelt's first moves in his historic third term as president was to pass the Lend-Lease Act, which allowed the United States to provide military aid to Britain, China, and the Soviet Union. In August 1941 Roosevelt met with British prime minister Winston Churchill in the first of many wartime meetings. They issued the Atlantic Charter setting out an 8-point charter of aims for the postwar world. They also pledged their two countries to "see the final destruction of the Nazi tyranny."

The US enters the war
Many Americans saw World War II as a European affair, but there was another threat to American neutrality—Japan.

Fourth-term president
Roosevelt speaks at his inauguration ceremony in January 1945. Despite his declining health, he defeated Thomas E. Dewey comfortably, but died after only three months in office.

In 1940 Japan joined the Axis powers and consequently relations between Japan and the United States worsened. Roosevelt was aware of Japan's hostility and in 1941 cut US supplies of oil to Japan, while continuing diplomatic negotiations. However, on December 7, 1941, Japan attacked Pearl Harbor. The mood of the country changed completely and Roosevelt now had its full support. The following day in a speech to Congress, he famously described December 7 as a "day of infamy" and declared war on Japan. A few days later Germany and Italy declared war on the United States. With the US now in the war, Roosevelt immediately became a very active Commander-in-Chief, appointing military commanders and working on strategy. Despite the attack on Pearl Harbor, Roosevelt prioritized Germany's defeat and, appointing General MacArthur to fight in the Pacific, concentrated on achieving victory in Europe. To this end he held

"We want FDR again"
Roosevelt's popularity led to his nomination as Democratic presidential candidate for an unprecedented third term in 1940.

a series of meetings with Winston Churchill and other Allied leaders, at Cairo, Tehran, and Casablanca, in which the progress of the war was decided. As the balance of the war shifted, Churchill and Roosevelt discussed plans for the invasion of France. The two men were not always in agreement: Roosevelt favored a direct invasion of France; Churchill preferred a more indirect approach from the Mediterranean. In the event it was Roosevelt's plans that were adopted and he appointed General Dwight D. Eisenhower to lead the Allied command. Roosevelt sought to establish a close alliance of all the Allied nations, working with Soviet leader Joseph Stalin and Chinese leader Chiang Kai-shek. As early as December 1941 Roosevelt was planning for the postwar world, and in the Declaration of the United Nations laid the foundations for the modern United Nations, which was set up in 1946. It was work that Eleanor Roosevelt continued after Roosevelt's death, when she drafted the UN Declaration of Human Rights.

Ill health
War took its toll on Roosevelt and by 1944 his heath was quickly deteriorating. However, he was in good enough health to secure a fourth term of office as US president, and attended the Yalta Conference in 1945 where the "Big Three" decided the shape of postwar Europe. By this time he was obviously exhausted and suffering from advanced arteriosclerosis. Roosevelt died on April 12, 1945, less than a month before the German surrender and victory in Europe, and with defeat of the Japanese imminent.

TIMELINE

- **January 30, 1882** Franklin Delano Roosevelt is born in Hyde Park, New York, into a wealthy family. He is second cousin to former president, Theodore Roosevelt.

- **1903** Having studied history at Harvard, he begins studying law at Columbia University.

- **1905** Roosevelt marries Anna Eleanor Roosevelt, niece of Theodore Roosevelt. They go on to have six children.

- **1908** Having passed his bar exam, Roosevelt joins a prominent Wall Street law firm.

- **1910** Enters politics as a Democrat and is elected to the New York State Senate; he is re-elected in 1912.

- **1913** President Woodrow Wilson appoints him Assistant Secretary of the Navy, a position he holds until 1920.

- **1918** Tours European battlefields.

- **1920** Enters politics full time and is chosen as vice-presidential candidate to James M. Cox in the presidential election. They run on a pro-League of Nations ticket but are defeated.

- **August 1921** Contracts polio and is paralyzed from the waist down.

- **1932** The Democrat Party elects Roosevelt as its presidential candidate.

- **March 1933** Is inaugurated as the 32nd President. He implements the New Deal program of social and economic reforms and delivers his first "fireside chat."

- **1936** Is re-elected president.

- **February 1941** Roosevelt achieves an historic third term as president. He makes his famous "Four Freedoms" speech (freedom of expression and religion; freedom from want and fear).

- **March 1941** Roosevelt signs the Lend-Lease bill to provide arms and financial help to Britain and other Allied nations.

- **August 1941** The Atlantic Charter: Roosevelt and Winston Churchill commit to destroying Nazi Germany.

- **December 8, 1941** Delivers his "Infamy Speech" to Congress urging a declaration of war on the Japanese empire.

- **1943** Roosevelt and Churchill meet at Casablanca: they determine to accept only unconditional surrender from Germany.

- **August 1943** Quebec Conference: Roosevelt and Churchill plan the Normandy invasion

- **November–December 1943** Cairo Conference: Roosevelt, Churchill, and Chiang Kai-shek discuss strategy in the Far East.

- **April 12, 1945** Suffers massive cerebral hemorrhage and dies at "Little White House," his cottage in Warm Springs, Georgia.

THE FIRST LADY

Japan Gambles on War

Many Japanese leaders were convinced that it was their national destiny to rule in Asia. But they were still struggling to win the war in China and Japan's lack of natural resources was as threatening as ever. They decided that the only way forward was new attacks that would somehow make all come right.

BEFORE

Japan's attempts to expand its empire in China were met with trade sanctions by Western powers, sending Japan looking elsewhere for allies and new conquests.

WAR IN CHINA
Japan had annexed and begun to exploit **the Chinese** province of Manchuria in the early 1930s, setting up the puppet state of Manchukuo. In 1937 Japan started **full-scale attacks on China ‹‹ 40–41**. By 1939 the Japanese controlled large areas of northern and eastern China and had more than a million troops in action. The process was brutal, with

250,000 The lowest likely estimate of the number of Chinese killed in the Japanese Army's rampage of pillage, mass rape, and murder in Nanking.

the most notorious incident being the "rape of Nanking" in 1937–38. This agression and **such atrocities brought widespread condemnation** from the US and the European countries with Asian colonies and interests in China.

EMPIRE EXPANSION
Most Japanese leaders believed that they could solve the country's problems by **expanding its empire** and accessing raw materials for industry. They wanted to create an anti-imperialist "Greater East Asia Co-Prosperity Sphere" from which **all native Asians would benefit**. In fact, the empire was more brutal than those it attacked.

JAPANESE POSTER EXTOLLING THEIR (ALLEGEDLY) PEACEFUL COOPERATION WITH MANCHUKUO

NORTH OR SOUTH?
Japan's dilemma was which direction to attack in. During the 1930s **Japan fought various battles with the Soviets** along the borders of the far eastern USSR. In 1939 **Japan was badly defeated** in a crucial campaign in Mongolia. From then on **Japan would look further south for new conquests**.

Japan's invasion of China from 1937 did not lead to decisive results. At the outbreak of the European war in 1939, for all its victories, Japan was bogged down. As the war dragged on, it used up valuable manpower and resources. The United States had responded to the invasion by imposing trade restrictions on exports to Japan of scrap metal and iron. Japan needed these supplies to continue the war and build an empire; almost a third of Japanese imports came from the US. When Germany conquered the Low Countries and France in 1940, the Japanese government saw new opportunities to resolve their problems.

Japan's long history of conflict with Russia and the USSR had continued in the 1930s but Japan had been badly defeated in 1939. This put an end to all attempts of expanding the Japanese empire northward on mainland Asia. But gains to the south were a different matter. With the Netherlands and France defeated, and Britain menaced by Hitler, their colonies seemed ripe for the picking—and they had vast resources. The Dutch East Indies had oil, and British Malaya had rubber, tin, and much more. For Japan, it was too good an opportunity to miss.

The fateful decision
In July 1940 the Japanese government adopted a new policy. They would win their war in China by blocking supplies reaching the Chinese through British Burma and French Indochina and they would gain control of the resources of Malaya and the East

> ## "If we yield to America's demands, it will destroy the fruits of the China incident."
>
> GENERAL TOJO HIDEKI, OCTOBER 14, 1941

Indies, by war if necessary. The first step was to move troops into northern Indochina in September 1940. At the same time Japan agreed the Tripartite Pact with Germany and Italy. From Japan's point of view this was aimed at limiting US involvement in Asian affairs. But the Japanese had miscalculated and the United States were not at all intimidated by Japan's new alliance. Instead, the Americans introduced an embargo on metal exports to Japan.

The next big development came in July 1941 when the Japanese sent troops into southern Indochina. The US immediately froze all of Japan's assets, and embargoed the sale of oil. This action was soon followed by the British and the Dutch. It meant a loss of 90 percent of Japan's oil imports.

One reason for the US's tough line was that American codebreakers were reading many Japanese diplomatic messages. They thought that Japan was at the point of no return and only drastic measures might stop war, and

Richard Sorge, a German spying for the Soviet Union in Japan, told the Russians in September 1941 of Japan's decision to attack south. Stalin moved armies from the Far East just in time to defend Moscow that winter.

if Japan was going to start a war anyway then an embargo would weaken them in the meantime.

Failed diplomacy
Negotiations of a sort between the United States and Japan continued in the later months of 1941. The US government knew how difficult they were making life for the Japanese but they did not think the Japanese sincerely wanted peace. In fact, the Japanese had not truly made up their minds. The country stepped up preparations for war but also continued their attempts to negotiate, in part because Emperor Hirohito made it clear that he did not want conflict.

In October a new prime minister, General Tojo Hideki, took over in Japan. He and his government thought it inconceivable for Japan to withdraw from China, as the US demanded.

Athough war with the United States was a great risk, the Japanese still had a chance if they stopped hesitating and attacked immediately. The Japanese army and navy had plans for rapid conquests already prepared and on November 29 the government decided to go to war. Emperor Hirohito gave his formal permission on December 1 and the attack orders went out. The Japanese would remove the United States from the Pacific in one devasting blow. All that remained was the delivery of a final diplomatic note to the Americans immediately before the attack on Pearl Harbor began.

It was typical of the indecisiveness of Japan's approach to war that this last step was bungled. The note was delivered late, after the bombs had started hitting Pearl Harbor and after the Americans already knew its contents from their efficient codebreaking service.

JAPANESE GENERAL AND PRIME MINISTER (1884–1948)

TOJO HIDEKI

Born in Tokyo to a military family, Tojo was a hardliner who became one of the most important generals in the Imperial Japanese Army in the 1930s. He advocated attacks on China, and in 1940, as army minister, helped create the Tripartite Pact with Germany and Italy. In October 1941 he succeeded Prince Konoe as prime minister and led Japan into war. In the opening months Tojo held enormous power but repeated military disasters brought about his resignation in 1944. He was arrested as a war criminal by the Allies in 1945, brought to trial, and executed in 1948.

Japanese troops training on bicycles
Western powers greatly underrated Japanese training and technology. Using "low-tech" transport like these bicycles during their invasion of Malaysia, for example, made the Japanese more mobile than their opponents.

AFTER »

The Japanese attacked British, American, and Dutch territories in Asia and the Pacific in December 1941, making World War II a truly global conflict.

JAPAN'S OFFENSIVE

The attack on **Pearl Harbor 148–49 »** started at 7:55am on December 7, local time. The Japanese achieved total surprise. In less than an hour, **the American Pacific Naval Fleet was crippled**. The US was at first appalled, then angry at what was felt to have been a "sneak" attack. **No formal declaration of war had been made by Japan**. Japanese landings in Malaya began on December 8, before the Pearl Harbor raid started. **Strikes on the Philippines, Hong Kong, Guam, and Wake Island followed 158–59 »**.

AXIS ALLIANCE

Hitler declared war on the United States on December 11, 1941, but Germany and Japan never cooperated effectively. In addition, the **Allies were able to decode signals from Japanese diplomats** in Berlin to learn important information about secret German plans.

GERMAN AND JAPANESE GENERALS DISCUSS MILITARY STRATEGIES IN MARCH 1941

Japanese Army aircraft
Mitsubishi Ki-21 bombers on the ground and Nakajima Ki-27 fighters above. Both types of aircraft served effectively in Japan's attack on China but were less successful in later combats.

BEFORE

As Japan's ambitious plans for expansion in Southeast Asia met with opposition, it had no alternative but to prepare for war.

NEGOTIATIONS BREAK DOWN

The Japanese military, bogged down in its **war with China since 1937 << 40–41**, now badly needed raw materials and oil. Western powers with **territorial interests in Southeast Asia** disapproved of attacks on China and halted trade with Japan. Attempts were made to negotiate a peaceful settlement, but Japan **refused to back down << 146–47**. By late November 1941, diplomacy was failing and **war in the Pacific** seemed inevitable. **The United States now expected attacks** on Malaya, or possibly the Philippines, to begin at any time.

JAPANESE DOUBTS

Admiral Yamamoto Isoroku was **opposed to war** with the US. He said that his fleet could win victories for six months or so, after which **Japan would be crushed**. His prediction proved to be correct. Even so, he dutifully planned the attack on Pearl Harbor, **drawing on lessons** learned from the British attack on the **Italian fleet base at Taranto** in November 1940 **<< 98–99**.

JAPANESE ADMIRAL (1884–1943)
YAMAMOTO ISOROKU

Yamamoto was commander-in-chief of the Japanese Combined Fleet during 1941–43. Before the war, he became Japan's top expert in naval air power and planned the attack on Pearl Harbor, despite his belief that Japan was foolish to attack the United States. His strategy was less successful in the Battle of Midway in 1942, when his plan was discovered by US codebreakers. Admiral Yamamoto was killed on April 18,1943 when his plane, heading for Ballalae Airfield in the Solomon Islands, was ambushed by American fighter pilots and shot down over the jungle of Bougainville. The Admiral's death was a major blow to Japanese morale.

Pearl Harbor

While negotiating peace, Japan was preparing for war. In November 1941 an aircraft carrier strike force secretly set sail toward the American naval base at Pearl Harbor, Hawaii. The attack, which devastated the US Pacific Fleet, ensured that the US would become a major player in the war.

On November 26, 1941, the six aircraft carriers of Japan's First Naval Air Fleet left the Kurile Islands in northern Japan and sailed across the Pacific. For several months prior to leaving, the carriers' airmen had trained for an attack on the main base of the US Pacific Fleet at Pearl Harbor. Now they were getting ready to carry it out.

The Japanese government met with military chiefs on November 29, and discussed the pros and cons of war at length. In the event, however, they decided it would be humiliating to give in to the United States' latest demands. Emperor Hirohito formally accepted his government's

> **5** The number of Type A midget submarines that attacked Pearl Harbor. The two-man boats may have made one torpedo hit but all five vessels were lost.

decision on December 1, and Japan's aircraft carriers received the signal to carry out their attack on the US Fleet in Pearl Harbor as planned.

Japan's main strategy was to seize territory in Southeast Asia that could provide natural resources that were not found in Japan. This would give the Japanese Empire the ability to win its war in China and defend itself against enemies. The armed forces of the European colonial powers in the area were weak and could be easily defeated. The Philippines, then a US commonwealth, stood on the flank of the proposed advance so it, and other American possessions, would be hit as well. The US land and air forces were

negligible but the US Navy was a more serious threat to Japan's plans and so, by this roundabout reasoning, became their primary target. Although several Japanese leaders warned otherwise, it was generally assumed that the United States was weak and decadent and would give up after a few defeats.

Japan's surprise attack

Strict radio silence was maintained as Japan's strike force headed eastward. Mainly using codebreaking information, Western intelligence picked up that the fleet had sailed, but no one could say

Bombing of Oahu

As well as the ships in the fleet anchorage, the Japanese bombed airfields on the island of Oahu. The destroyer *Shaw* can be seen exploding in the background of this view of the wreckage at the Ford Island seaplane base.

The news reaches New York's Times Square
Most Americans were unaware how badly US–Japanese relations had deteriorated by late 1941. In New York and elsewhere, December 7 seemed a typical peacetime Sunday—until the news from Hawaii arrived.

where it was. On the morning of December 7, 1941, at 5:50am the Japanese carriers were in position north of Oahu. Torpedo bombers would strike at the American fleet, before a second wave would finish the job and bomb the shore installations.

America had expected an attack from Japan somewhere but, at Pearl Harbor, commanders were more worried about sabotage from the people of Japanese descent living on the Hawaiian islands.

At any rate, the port was not on high alert. The anti-aircraft guns were not manned, all ammunition was locked away, and combat aircraft were parked in lines out in the open so that sentries could guard them easily. Since it was a peacetime Sunday, many sailors had shore leave and very few were on duty. A total of 366 Japanese bombers and fighters struck the naval base at Pearl

> **3** The number of US warships sunk or damaged at Pearl Harbor that were total losses and could not be refloated, repaired, or put back into service.

Harbor. The US battleship *Arizona* was blown up. The *Oklahoma* capsized and a further six battleships were badly damaged in the attack. A total of 188 US aircraft were destroyed and another 150 damaged. In all, 2,403 Americans were killed. The Japanese lost just 55 men and only 29 planes. On the face

A cowardly attack?
Japan's attack on Pearl Harbor was particularly resented because it came before a declaration of war had been delivered. There was little else that Japan could have done to anger the American people more.

vital oil storage facilities, the naval dockyard, and submarine pens also emerged unscathed. It would not be long before the naval base was restored to its former efficiency.

The US at war
The following day President Roosevelt addressed a joint session of Congress. Seething at the late delivery of the note that broke off peace negotiations with Japan, the president called December 7, 1941 "a date which will live in infamy", further describing the attack as "unprovoked and dastardly". Without hesitation, Congress voted for war against Japan. That same day, Britain also declared war on Japan.

Although the attack on Pearl Harbor was a crushing defeat for the US, it had achieved something that many months of pleading from Churchill had failed to do—isolationism was now over. The American nation, shocked and bitterly dismayed by events at Pearl Harbor, were now united in their commitment to go to war. When Hitler heard about

AVENGE PEARL HARBOR

OUR BULLETS WILL DO IT

> "That the Pearl Harbor attack should have **succeeded in achieving surprise** seems a **blessing from heaven**."
>
> JAPANESE PRIME MINISTER TOJO

of it, Admiral Yamamoto's bold attack appeared to have gone like clockwork, although this was not the case.

The US Pacific Fleet's three aircraft carriers were out at sea that morning, and so were saved. Their survival forced American commanders to make air power their main weapon in the war against Japan, which proved to be the best route to victory. At Pearl Harbor,

the Japanese attack on Pearl Harbor, he was jubilant. Now that Japan was an ally, he felt it was impossible to lose the war. In perhaps his greatest error of judgement, Hitler now declared war on the United States. This poor decision ensured that the US was forced to bring its military might to Europe and as such, it was a decision that would ultimately lead to Germany's defeat.

AFTER ≫

The attack on Pearl Harbor ensured that America would fight until Japan had been totally defeated by the Allies.

GLOBAL WAR
Hitler was under no treaty obligation with Japan to declare war on America but, on December 11, 1941, he pitted **Germany against the might of the United States** and the war became a genuine world conflict.

AMERICAN FLEET RECOVERS
Most of the battleships damaged at Pearl Harbor were repaired to serve later in the war. By then, however, the **US Navy's attack** was led by its aircraft carriers. Their survival in 1941 pointed the **way to victory 162–63 ≫**.

HITLER DECLARES WAR ON THE UNITED STATES

Attack on Pearl Harbor

On December 7, 1941, Japanese planes, taking off from aircraft carriers some 217 miles (350 km) north of Oahu, bombarded the US Pacific Fleet at Pearl Harbor. The attack, which had been meticulously planned, involved fighter and bomber planes, and caught the Americans completely unaware. The first wave of planes, led by Commander Mitsuo Fuchida, hit Pearl Harbor just before 8am. Within a short space of time five out of the eight American battleships stationed there were sunk or sinking.

"I peered intently through my binoculars at the ships riding peacefully at anchor. One by one I counted them. Yes, the battleships were there all right, eight of them ... It was 7:49am when I ordered my radioman to send the command 'Attack!'. He immediately began tapping out the prearranged code signal: 'TO, TO, TO ...'

Leading the whole group, Lieutenant Commander Murata's torpedo bombers headed downward to launch their torpedoes, while Lieutenant Commander Itaya's fighters raced forward to sweep enemy fighters from the air. Takahashi's dive-bomber group had climbed for altitude and was out of sight. My bombers, meanwhile, made a circuit toward Barbers Point to keep pace with the attack schedule ...

The attack was opened with the first bomb falling on Wheeler Field, followed shortly by dive-bombing attacks upon Hickam Field and the bases at Ford Island ... Lieutenant Commander Murata ... released torpedoes. A series of white waterspouts soon rose in the harbour.

Lieutenant Commander Itaya's fighters, meanwhile, had full command of the air over Pearl Harbor. About four enemy fighters which took off were promptly shot down. By 8am there were no enemy planes in the air, and our fighters began strafing the airfields ...

As we closed in, enemy anti-aircraft fire began to concentrate on us. Dark grey puffs burst all around. Most of them came from ships' batteries, but land batteries were also active ... While my group circled for another attempt, others made their runs, some trying as many as three before succeeding. We were about to begin our second bombing run when there was a colossal explosion in Battleship Row. A huge column of dark red smoke rose to 1,000 metres. It must have been the explosion of a ship's powder magazine [This was the battleship *Arizona*]. The shock wave was felt even in my plane, several miles away ... "

JAPANESE COMMANDER, MITSUO FUCHIDA, DESCRIBING THE ATTACK ON PEARL HARBOR

Being briefed
Japanese pilots receive their instructions before setting off to attack Pearl Harbor. Their planes included fighters and torpedo, dive, and high-level bombers.

5
THE SHIFTING BALANCE
1942

Conflict became truly global with the Japanese conquest of Southeast Asia, but US entry into the war was to prove a turning point. The Allies saw victories in North Africa, and in the Soviet Union, the titanic struggle turned in the Soviets' favour with the heroic defense of Stalingrad.

THE SHIFTING BALANCE

Auschwitz II (Birkenau) is completed in 1942 as the first camp becomes overcrowded. The largest of the Nazi extermination camps, it becomes the final destination of Jews from all over Europe, as well as anti-Nazis, and Romany gypsies.

US forces land in Casablanca in November as part of Operation Torch. Its first objective is to win control of Morocco and Algeria from Vichy France.

Operation Uranus, a major Soviet offensive, is launched in November to trap the German troops in Stalingrad. The success of the operation leads to the surrender of the German Sixth Army.

EUROPE

The island of Malta is bombed relentlessly by the Germans. The only British naval base between Gibraltar and Egypt, it survives the onslaught and remains an active threat to Axis convoys to North Africa.

The German city of Cologne suffers the first of many massive air raids. A number of Allied leaders, notably Sir Arthur "Bomber" Harris, put their faith in a strategy of bombing Germany into submission.

El Alamein, where Rommel is defeated by Montgomery in November, proves the decisive battle of the Desert War.

In 1941, what had begun as an essentially European conflict became a world war. In the six months from December 1941, the Japanese conquered swathes of the central Pacific and the Far East, and humiliated the British, the Dutch, and the United States.

In the aftermath of the attack on Pearl Harbor, on December 7, 1941, Hitler declared war on the United States. Churchill correctly recognized this as a turning point in the war, although much hard fighting lay ahead. The Japanese then attempted to secure their vast perimeter by luring into battle and destroying the US Pacific Fleet, but in two crucial naval encounters (Coral Sea and Midway—May and June 1942 respectively) they were first halted and then decisively defeated. They were now obliged to defend an ocean empire which might be attacked at any point by the gathering might of the American war machine.

1942

US naval forces intercept the Japanese fleet at Midway and stop its advance across the central Pacific. It is the loss of four aircraft carriers that most damages the Japanese.

The US government begins a program of forcible relocation and internment of both Japanese Americans and Japanese nationals following the attack on Pearl Harbor.

The USS Wasp is torpedoed while supporting US troops on Guadalcanal. Fighting on the island continues for six months before the Japanese withdraw.

Allied air and naval forces are based in Australia's Northern Territory. Its capital Darwin is the target of two bombing raids in February and March.

The Battle of the Coral Sea in May is a boost for the US. It loses one carrier, the *Lexington*, but proves that the Japanese navy can be halted.

THE WORLD IN DECEMBER 1942

- Axis powers and allies
- Axis conquests to Dec 1942
- Allied states
- Allied conquests to Dec 1942
- Area under Japanese control, Dec 1942
- Neutral states
- Frontiers Sep 1939

The point which the Americans chose to attack was the Solomons chain. On August 7, 1942, US Marines stormed ashore at Guadalcanal, the first move in an epic struggle that marked the beginning of the American reconquest of the Pacific.

The initiative was gradually, but definitely, passing from the Axis to the Allies. Guadalcanal was secured on February 9, 1943. In Germany six days earlier, Hitler had declared four days of national mourning following the destruction of Sixth Army at Stalingrad. In North Africa, the "Torch" landings by the Allies in Morocco and Algeria, and the British victory at El Alamein (November 1942), were followed by a protracted fight for Tunisia that was not concluded until May 1943. The Allies were victorious, capturing thousands of German and Italian prisoners. Hitler had now suffered a second Stalingrad, this time on the shores of the Mediterranean.

TIMELINE 1942

Japanese Conquests in Asia and the Pacific ▪ The Final Solution ▪ Malta and the Mediterranean ▪ New Guinea and the Solomon Islands ▪ **Midway** ▪ Battle of the Atlantic ▪ **El Alamein** ▪ Torch Landings in North Africa ▪ **Guadalcanal** ▪ **Stalingrad**

JANUARY	FEBRUARY	MARCH	APRIL	MAY	JUNE
JANUARY 2 Japanese forces capture Manila in the Philippines. **JANUARY 11** Germans begin Operation Drumbeat, aimed at destroying shipping along the east coast of America.	**FEBRUARY 7** President Vidkun Quisling abolishes the Norwegian constitution and establishes a dictatorship. ❯ Japanese Arisaka rifle	**MARCH 8** The Avro Lancaster enters service. It will become the principal bomber used on night raids over Germany. **MARCH 8** Japanese forces capture Rangoon, the capital of Burma.		**MAY 5** Japanese forces land on Corregidor, the island fortress in the Philippines, which surrenders the following day. ❮ Japanese celebrating the fall of Corregidor	
JANUARY 20 The Red Army attacks Axis forces along the Eastern Front.	**FEBRUARY 8** Japanese forces based in Siam begin the invasion of Burma.	**MARCH 11** General Douglas MacArthur leaves the Philippines, with his staff, declaring, "I shall return."	**APRIL 15** King George V awards the island of Malta the George Cross for its "heroism and devotion" in the face of relentless German and Italian bombing raids. ❯ German bomb damage in Valletta, Malta	**MAY 7** Battle of the Coral Sea. Drawn battle fought between US and Japanese carrier aircraft to the east of New Guinea. Japanese call off intended landings at Port Moresby. ❯ US carrier *Yorktown* on fire at Midway	
JANUARY 20 At a secret conference at Wannsee, chaired by Reinhard Heydrich, key Nazi ministries discuss the "Final Solution" to the Jewish problem. **JANUARY 26** The first US troops land in Britain.	**FEBRUARY 15** Despite claims of impregnability, Singapore falls to the Japanese. 70,000 soldiers are captured. ❯ Surrender of Singapore to the Japanese			**MAY 12** Axis armies smash the Soviet counter-offensive along the Kharkov Front. **MAY 26** In North Africa, Rommel attacks the Gazala Line. ❯ Japanese navy sextant	**JUNE 4–7** Battle of Midway. Japanese attempt to win control of the island of Midway, but are heavily defeated, losing four carriers to the US Navy's one.
	MARCH 17 General Douglas MacArthur is appointed commander of the combined Allied forces in the Southwest Pacific by Roosevelt.	**MARCH 17** General Douglas MacArthur is appointed commander of the combined Allied forces in the Southwest Pacific by Roosevelt.	**APRIL 18** Doolittle Raid, launched from US carrier *Hornet*, bombs Tokyo. **APRIL 21** First "Milch cow" U-boat, *U-459* heads for the Atlantic carrying supplies for other U-boats.	**MAY 30** The first 1,000-bomber raid by the RAF devastates Cologne. ❯ Doolittle Raid, first US bombing raid on Japan	
	FEBRUARY 23 Arthur "Bomber" Harris takes over Bomber Command. He is a keen proponent of the area bombing of Germany's centers of population.	**MARCH 20–23** British convoy from Alexandria to Malta suffers heavy losses as it nears its destination.			**JUNE 10** Germans launch major offensive in Ukraine to gain access to the oil reserves in the Caucasus region. **JUNE 25** Eisenhower appointed commander-in-chief of US forces in Europe.

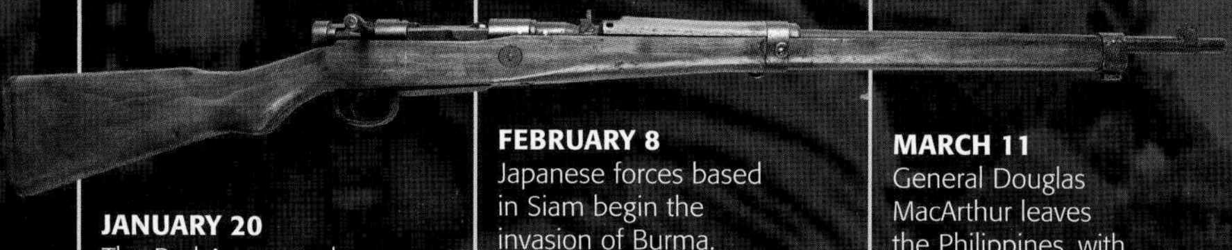

"If I am told to **fight regardless of the consequences**, I shall **run wild** for **the first six months or a year**, but I have utterly **no confidence** for the second or third year."

ADMIRAL ISORUKU YAMAMOTO, COMMANDER OF THE JAPANESE COMBINED FLEET, PREDICTING THE COURSE OF THE WAR TO PRIME MINISTER KONOYE, SEPTEMBER 1940

JULY	AUGUST	SEPTEMBER	OCTOBER	NOVEMBER	DECEMBER

JULY 9
Chinese Nationalist forces defeat the Japanese in Jiangxi Province.

JULY 15
Resupply air bridge to China, operated by General Claire Chennault's "Flying Tigers," gets under way.

AUGUST 7
US First Marine Division lands on Guadalcanal in the Solomon Islands.

≫ German U-boats in the mid-Atlantic

SEPTEMBER 12
Battle of Bloody Ridge on Guadalcanal. US troops repel concerted Japanese attack.

⌃ Australian submachine-gun for jungle warfare

SEPTEMBER 12
British liner *Laconia* carrying Italian POWs is sunk off Africa by *U-156*. Many of the survivors are rescued by the U-boat.

OCTOBER 13–18
German Sixth Army occupies most of Stalingrad.

OCTOBER 23
The Allies are victorious at the second battle of El Alamein.

NOVEMBER 8
Allied invasion of North Africa (Operation Torch) begins with landings in Morocco and Algeria.

⌃ Troops and ships at the Torch landings

DECEMBER 12
Germans launch Operation Winter Storm to relieve the Sixth Army.

JULY 27
First clash between Australians and Japanese on Kokoda Trail, New Guinea.

AUGUST 13
Roosevelt gives the go-ahead for the Manhattan Project—research into building the atom bomb.

AUGUST 13
Remnants of Pedestal convoy reach Malta from Strait of Gibraltar.

SEPTEMBER
Germans advance slowly through the ruins of Stalingrad. They are met by fierce Soviet resistance as buildings change hands several times in the course of a day.

DECEMBER 21
As German attempts to relieve the Sixth Army come to nothing, Hitler refuses to allow General Paulus to attempt to break out from Stalingrad.

≪ Monty, Rommel's new opponent in Egypt

AUGUST 13
Montgomery assumes command of the British Eighth Army.

AUGUST 19
British and Canadian raid on French port of Dieppe is a failure.

SEPTEMBER 15
US carrier *Wasp* torpedoed off Guadalcanal by Japanese submarine.

OCTOBER 26
Drawn naval battle off the Santa Cruz Islands. The US carrier *Hornet* is sunk.

⌃ M3 Grant tank used in North Africa

10 NOVEMBER
German troops start to occupy Vichy France.

19–22 NOVEMBER
Operation Uranus. Soviet offensive encircles German Sixth Army at Stalingrad.

DECEMBER 31
Japanese decide to evacuate their troops from Guadalcanal.

≫ Vicious streetfighting in Stalingrad

AUGUST 23
Germans enter suburbs of Stalingrad. Bombing has already reduced much of the city to rubble.

AUGUST 30
Rommel launches attack on British Eighth Army south of El Alamein.

SEPTEMBER 22
The Soviet defenders of Stalingrad, already confined to a narrow strip of land along the west bank of the Volga, are split in two by the German advance.

OCTOBER 30
British boarding party recovers German codebooks from sinking *U-559*.

The Japanese Onslaught

Japan's imperial designs in the Pacific were based on a simple calculation: the United States had to be presented with a fait accompli that would be too difficult to reverse. This did not allow for the fact that the Americans would fight back, and that their economic and military power would overwhelm Japan.

Triumph of the Rising Sun
In spite of plentiful evidence from the Sino-Japanese War, the colonial powers in the Far East underestimated the strength and expert coordination of the Japanese campaign in the Far East and the Pacific.

BEFORE

To coincide with the Pearl Harbor strike, the Japanese planned simultaneous offensives in the Far East and the Pacific, heading both southeast and southwest.

IMPERIAL JAPAN
Japan's desire to build an empire had been evident as early as September 1931, with its **invasion of Manchuria ‹‹ 32–33** and, subsequently, **China ‹‹ 40–41**, in 1937.

PLAN OF ATTACK
The idea now was to **advance southwest** down the **Malayan peninsula**, before branching right and left into **Burma and the Dutch East Indies**. From Formosa a second principal thrust would **aim southeast** through the Philippines to link with the southwest thrust in the East Indies. **Subsidiary drives** would secure Guam in the Marianas, Wake Island, north of the Marshalls, and would **extend Japanese control** to the Gilbert Islands.

ULTIMATE CONTROL
The **overriding Japanese aim** was to secure primacy in its chosen sphere of influence, to **defeat the Western colonial powers** and, if necessary, Russia. China was to be subdued and **incorporated into the Japanese Empire**, while other Asian states were to exist within an Asian **Co-Prosperity Sphere ‹‹ 146–47** under Japanese leadership. Asia was to be wrested back from Western colonialists, demonstrating the **huge industrial and economic strides** being made by Japan.

As one Japanese fleet made for Pearl Harbor, a second one headed for southern Thailand and northern Malaya. At dawn on December 8, 1941, two divisions of General Yamashita's 25th Army landed at Singora and Patani, in southern Thailand, and a third in Khota Baru, in northern Malaya.

British commanders in Malaya had foreseen the possible Japanese use of Singora and had planned to move into Thailand to forestall them. But the Japanese caught them fatally off-balance and they never recovered.

The Japanese enjoyed complete command of the air. Command of the sea was secured on December 10 when Japanese aircraft sank the battleship *Prince of Wales* and the battlecruiser *Repulse* (Force Z) as they attempted, without air cover, to break up Japanese landings on the east coast of Malaya.

Little resistance
The Japanese were now able to mount additional seaborne invasions on the west coast of Malaya to harry and cut off the retreating British. The General Officer Commanding (GOC) Malaya, Lieutenant-General Arthur Percival, proved ineffective. Morale was further undermined by the sheer speed and relentless pressure of the Japanese advance, which carried them to the naval base at Singapore in just 58 days. Singapore surrendered on February 15, with the loss of 138,000 troops from

the British Commonwealth. It was to be the greatest and most humiliating military defeat in British history.

On December 25 the British colony of Hong Kong had surrendered to Major General Sano's 38th Division. The Japanese celebrated their victory with an orgy of killing and rape. The Dutch were Japan's next colonial target in the Pacific. Dutch possessions

included Java, Sumatra, Timor, Borneo, the Celebes, and the western half of New Guinea, all of which fell within the American, British, Dutch, and Australian (ABDA) command under General Wavell. The Japanese landed at will, had command of the air, and, having defeated an Allied naval squadron at the Battle of the Java Sea on February 27, 1942, dominated the sea. Victory in the Java Sea accelerated the conquest of the Dutch East Indies, whose civil administration surrendered unconditionally on March 8.

Advance to the Philippines
To the north of the Dutch East Indies, the Japanese invaded the Philippines, a US possession, though largely self-governing, on December 8. The combined US and Filipino forces, commanded by General MacArthur, could not check the Japanese advance and withdrew into the Bataan peninsula, where they held out until April 1942. Nearly 80,000 US and Filipino troops went into captivity,

KEY MOMENT

THE FALL OF SINGAPORE

On February 15, 1942, General Percival joined the flag party for a rendezvous at General Yamashita's headquarters, set up in Singapore's Ford Motor Factory. In the lunchroom, which was packed with Japanese camera crews and journalists, Percival agreed to a ceasefire and signed the instrument of surrender. He spent the rest of the war as a POW in Manchuria, but was present on board the battleship *Missouri* to witness the final Japanese surrender, on 2 September 1945.

> **"The drop-outs became more numerous. They fell by the hundreds in the road … "**
> SERGEANT SIDNEY STEWART ON THE BATAAN DEATH MARCH OF APRIL 1942

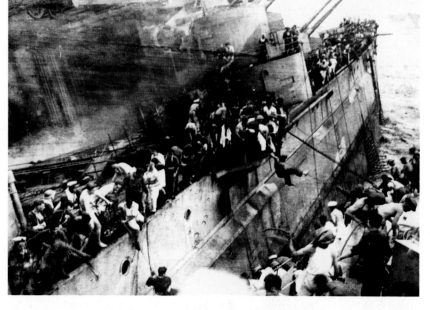

Sinking of HMS Prince of Wales
The *Prince of Wales'* crew abandoned ship on December 10, 1942, after an attack by Japanese bombers and torpedo-bombers of XXII Air Flotilla.

many of them dying in the subsequent "death march" out of Bataan. The last United States' stronghold, the island fortress of Corregidor, in Manila Bay, finally surrendered on May 6, 1942.

Less than a month before the surrender of Singapore, the Japanese 15th Army invaded Burma with the hope of gaining vital resources, such as rubber and oil. Opposing them were two weak

Japanese shell

The relentless bombardment of Singapore by Japanese troops implied that they had a huge supply of shells. This was a dangerous overestimate but Singapore capitulated nevertheless.

divisions, which withdrew to the rivers Salween and Sittang, until they were forced to abandon them in February. In early March 1942 the British Lieutenant-General Alexander took command. He decided to abandon the capital, Rangoon, and retreat with "Burcorps," as his army was called, overland to India. It was the longest retreat in British military history.

The British and Indian troops were exhausted and short of supplies, while the Burmese troops had begun to desert in droves. In this epic endeavor Alexander was assisted by the Chinese Fifth and Sixth Armies, under the

> A vital weapon in Japan's initial conquests in the Far East was the highly mobile, lightly armored, Type 95 tank. It had a crew of three, top speed of 28 mph (45 kph), and a main armament of one 37 mm gun and two 7.7 mm machine-guns.

American General Stilwell. They had entered Burma to secure the Burma Road, which was their only land link with China. Also joining forces were the tanks of the Seventh Armoured Brigade, which had arrived in Rangoon shortly before the city was evacuated. On May 19, having covered 600 miles (960 km) in nine weeks, the survivors of "Burcorps" crossed the Indian frontier at Tamu, in the Chin Hills. The long withdrawal was halted at last by the monsoon, which, however, also prevented the Japanese armies from advancing into India.

AFTER

Within just six months, and with feeble resistance from the Allies, the Japanese were in control of a substantial area of the Pacific Ocean by April 1942.

CONSOLIDATING POWER

To the north the Japanese **threatened the Aleutians** and the approaches to Alaska; in the west they were encamped on the **borders of India**; to the south **they menaced Australia 166–67 ≫**. Now they needed to consolidate the enormous **defensive perimeter** on the boundaries of their conquests. They gambled that, faced with the scale of the **Japanese Blitzkrieg**, the United States would **abandon any hope** of fighting back **162–63 ≫**.

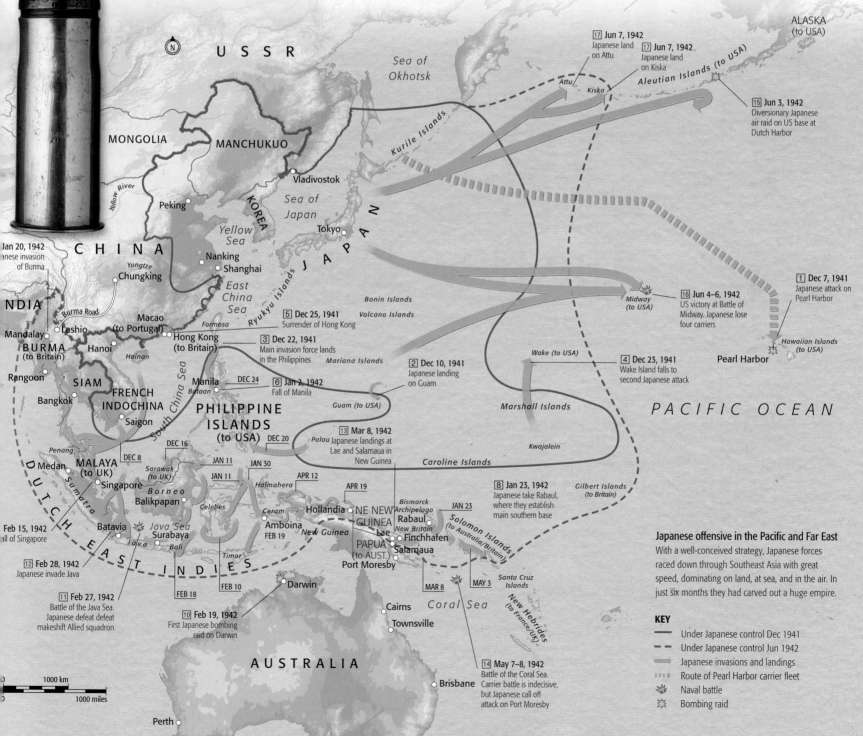

Jan 20, 1942 Japanese invasion of Burma

[5] Dec 25, 1941 Surrender of Hong Kong

[3] Dec 22, 1941 Main invasion force lands in the Philippines

[6] Jan 2, 1942 Fall of Manila

[2] Dec 10, 1941 Japanese landing on Guam

[4] Dec 23, 1941 Wake Island falls to second Japanese attack

[13] Mar 8, 1942 Palau Japanese landings at Lae and Salamaua in New Guinea

[8] Jan 23, 1942 Japanese take Rabaul, where they establish main southern base

Feb 15, 1942 Fall of Singapore

[12] Feb 28, 1942 Japanese invade Java

[11] Feb 27, 1942 Battle of the Java Sea. Japanese defeat defeat makeshift Allied squadron

[10] Feb 19, 1942 First Japanese bombing raid on Darwin

[14] May 7–8, 1942 Battle of the Coral Sea. Carrier battle is indecisive, but Japanese call off attack on Port Moresby

[17] Jun 7, 1942 Japanese land on Attu

[17] Jun 7, 1942 Japanese land on Kiska

[15] Jun 3, 1942 Diversionary Japanese air raid on US base at Dutch Harbor

[16] Jun 4–6, 1942 US victory at Battle of Midway. Japanese lose four carriers

[1] Dec 7, 1941 Japanese attack on Pearl Harbor

Japanese offensive in the Pacific and Far East

With a well-conceived strategy, Japanese forces raced down through Southeast Asia with great speed, dominating on land, at sea, and in the air. In just six months they had carved out a huge empire.

KEY

——	Under Japanese control Dec 1941
- - -	Under Japanese control Jun 1942
⇒	Japanese invasions and landings
▪▪▪▪	Route of Pearl Harbor carrier fleet
✺	Naval battle
✺	Bombing raid

Japanese soldiers celebrate
Jubilant Japanese troops claim a captured US artillery piece as they celebrate the fall of Corregidor on May 6, 1942. An island fortress in Manila Bay, in the Philippine Islands, Corregidor had been the last US stronghold to surrender to the Japanese invasion.

The New Japanese Empire

On the face of it, the inhabitants of the Greater East Asia Co-Prosperity Sphere had simply exchanged one set of masters—the colonial powers—for another, their Japanese conquerors. Each nation held its own views on the new leadership but rarely did this prove a challenge for the Japanese authority.

BEFORE

By the time the Japanese had control in the Pacific Ocean, they had already gained a good 10 years' experience in administering conquered territory in Manchuria.

IMPERIAL GAINS
Now the islands of Guam and Wake, the Philippines, French Indochina, Burma, Thailand, Malaya, the Dutch East Indies, most of New Guinea and Papua, the Bismarck archipelago, and parts of the Gilbert and Solomon Islands were **also in Japanese hands ‹‹ 158–59**.

JAPAN'S EMPIRE THEORY
The drive toward a **"Greater East Asia Co-Prosperity Sphere" ‹‹ 146–47**, which had been promoted by the Japanese armed forces and in **nationalist circles** before the war, did contain a genuine belief in the mission of Japan, as the first **Great Power in Asia**, to lead other Asians to independence from foreign rule.

Conquest brought with it a host of administrative difficulties. Order had to be maintained, government machinery replaced, markets supported and stimulated, and economies placed on a footing that benefited the conqueror.

Japan promised much but delivered absolutely nothing. The Co-Prosperity Sphere was merely a convenient mask for Japanese imperial ambition, and none of its populations drew any material benefit from association with Japan. In fact, the much-vaunted "prosperity" flowed only one way—toward the Rising Sun. Nor did the representatives of the occupied peoples—all of whom were chosen by the Japanese—carry equal weight in the eyes of their conquerors.

Indeed, some were more "equal" than others and very soon it became clear who those people were. This came to light in November 1943 at the first, and only, Greater East Asia Conference held in Tokyo, Japan.

During this conference, which lasted two days, it transpired whose side the visiting representatives supported. Chang Chung-hui, the prime minister of Manchuria— effectively a Japanese colony since 1930—was a puppet of the Japanese. This was also true of Wang Ching-wei, the premier of Japanese-occupied China. The Indian nationalist Subhas Chandra Bose, the Bengali founder of the Indian National Army, was in a different political position but no less

12	**THOUSAND of the 61,000 prisoners of war employed on the Burma Railway died.**
90	**THOUSAND of the 270,000 Asian laborers died—a third of the total first employed.**

dependent on the Japanese. The Thai prince Wan Waithayakon was, nominally, the representative of an independent state that was allied with Japan and, as a reward, had been granted territory from neighboring Laos and Burma.

Declaration of war
The head of state of occupied Burma, Ba Maw, was initially a genuine enthusiast for the Co-Prosperity Sphere, declaring war on both Britain and the United States on August 1, 1943. This would have been greeted with a hollow cheer in the parts of Burma and Thailand where thousands of the local population were used as slave labor, alongside Allied prisoners of war, on the construction of the Burma Railway. Huge numbers of these men died completing the task. The head of state of the occupied

Philippines, José Laurel, had been urged by the legitimate president Manuel Quezon, who was in exile, to feign cooperation with the Japanese, but had gone over to them and declared independence from the United States.

However, the majority of the Filipino population harbored little ill-feeling toward the Americans and took pride in their Westernized culture—in the Japanese victory parade one Filippino band had played *Stars and Stripes Forever*. The Philippines was the only occupied territory that saw large-scale guerrilla resistance to the Japanese.

Japan's problem areas

Among the colonies excluded from the Greater East Asia Conference in Tokyo were Indochina—which remained under Vichy French administration— Malaya, and the Dutch East Indies. Malaya's large Chinese population, which included a small but effective Communist guerrilla movement, deterred the Japanese from allowing them to experiment with self-rule, no matter how contrived it might be.

Meanwhile, the Muslim Malays, who were not hostile to the Japanese, were fobbed off with vague promises of future independence, as were their co-religionists in the Dutch East Indies.

The continuing campaign in New Guinea against the Americans and Australians precluded a similar promise, although a handful of nationalists, among whom was the

INDIAN NATIONALIST LEADER (1897–1945)
SUBHAS CHANDRA BOSE

In 1939 Bose was president of the Congress Party but two years later he went to Germany to seek recruits for his Indian National Army (INA) among Indian prisoners of war. Bose arrived in Japan in 1943 on a German submarine and continued to seek new recruits from Indian troops who had been taken prisoner while fighting for Britain in Malaya and Burma. Nevertheless, it was the Japanese who retained control of the INA, not the Indian politician. Bose died in a plane crash in roughly 1945—the exact date is disputed.

future President Sukarno of Indonesia, were offered a role in government in the fall of 1943. A number of strategically important territories, including Hong Kong and Singapore, were meanwhile absorbed into the new empire and run by the military.

The Japanese had been halted at the gates of India, an obvious target after the invasion of Burma. Under the British Raj, the subcontinent, with a population of 350 million, had needed a security force of only 250,000 troops, and most of those were stationed on

> ## "For them there was **only one way** to do a thing, **the Japanese way;** only one goal and interest, **the Japanese interest**."
>
> BURMESE PRESIDENT, BA MAW, ON THE FAILURE OF THE CO-PROSPERITY SPHERE

Support for Britain
Indian troops arrive in Singapore in December 1941: After the fall of Singapore, some of them were persuaded to join the Indian National Army.

the Northwest Frontier. From the onset of war, both Indian princes and the vast majority of the population had backed Britain overwhelmingly. Over two million Indians—making up the world's largest volunteer army—had joined the armed forces and served with distinction in Africa, the Middle East, Italy, and Burma. But following the disasters in Malaya, Singapore, and Burma, the leader of the National Congress Party, Mahatma Gandhi, demanded that the British leave India.

Britain's refusal to accede to this demand led to calls for a "non-violent" rebellion, followed by the arrest of the Congress leaders in August 1942. It took 57 battalions two and a half months to restore order. This was proof, if indeed proof were needed, that at the end of the war the anticipated independence for India would have to be honored.

The initial enthusiasm prompted by Japan's six months of conquest in 1941–42, was rapidly dissipated by the reality of cynical, brutal, and arbitrary Japanese rule.

CHINA'S WAR YEARS
The model, established in Japanese-occupied China in 1937, had **systematically exploited for profit** those territories in which Japanese armies were strong enough to **impose their control**. The majority of Chinese suffered under **Chinese Nationalist corruption**, Communist austerity, or **Japanese "rice offensives."**

BENGAL FAMINE
By mid-May 1942 the **British had been driven out of Burma**. Fearful of a Japanese invasion of India by way of Bengal, **the British stockpiled food** for themselves and burned crops on the

STARVING BENGALI WOMAN AND CHILD, 1943

Burmese border. In October Bengal was **hit by a cyclone** that **ruined the harvest**. Rice prices soared, and some **2.5 million Indians died**. In the event, the Japanese **invasion of India was averted by the Allies 248–49 ≫**, and the Bengal famine need not have happened.

THE INDOCHINA WAR
The French colony of Indochina comprised modern Vietnam, Cambodia, and Laos. During World War II **the Communist guerrilla movement of the Viet Minh**, led by Ho Chi Minh, received Allied support in fighting the Japanese. After the **Japanese surrender in 1945 326–27 ≫**, Ho Chi Minh set up the **Democratic Republic of Vietnam**. In 1946 the French returned to their colony, and in the

HO CHI MINH

ensuing Indochina War **the Viet Minh fought resolutely for independence**, forcing out the French in 1954. **Vietnam was divided between north and south**, and before long the United States had involved itself in the area.

« BEFORE

Having conquered its vast empire in the Pacific Ocean, the Japanese high command now had to find some way of consolidating its extensive defensive perimeter.

THE DOOLITTLE RAID

On April 18, 1942, 16 B-25 **Mitchell bombers**, under the command of Colonel James Doolittle, took off from the carrier *Hornet*, sailing north of **Midway Island**, some 650 miles (1,000 km) away from Tokyo, and flew on to **bomb the Japanese capital** and three other targets.

The aircraft had been stripped of much equipment and given auxiliary fuel tanks. But when the *Hornet* was spotted by a Japanese patrol vessel, **the raid was launched early**. After dropping their bombs, **the aircraft ran out of fuel** before they could reach their intended landing strips in China.

THE DOOLITTLE RAID

THE MIDWAY KEYHOLE

The raid settled a **strategic argument** in the Japanese high command. The *Hornet*'s launch point had been in the **Midway "keyhole"** in the Japanese perimeter **« 158–59**. The gap had to be closed, so an **offensive against Midway** was to be launched immediately.

Coral Sea and Midway

To secure their vast Pacific perimeter, the Japanese sought to lure into battle and destroy the US Pacific fleet. In the two crucial naval encounters of Coral Sea and Midway, in May and June 1942, the Japanese were first halted and then decisively defeated by US carrier task forces.

The Coral Sea was the gateway to Port Moresby in New Guinea, control of which would isolate Australia from the Allies. While the Japanese Invasion Group took troop transports to Port Moresby, covered by the light carrier *Shoho*, the Carrier Striking Force, under command of Admiral Yakagi and comprising the carriers *Shokaku* and *Zuikaku*, was to cruise into the Coral Sea and past the Solomon Islands to prevent any US attempt to interfere with the invasion. Thanks to the American interception and decryption of Japanese JN25 naval signals traffic, which was codenamed "Magic," the US Navy was fully aware of the thrust of the Japanese plans.

Initial clashes

Admiral Chester Nimitz, commander-in-chief of the US Pacific Fleet, ordered a concentration of forces in the Coral Sea, which comprised Admiral Fletcher's Task Force 17, with the carrier *Yorktown*, Admiral Fitch's Task Force 11, with the carrier *Lexington*, and Admiral Crace's Task Force 44, with US and Australian cruisers and destroyers.

Nimitz intended to concentrate his forces by May 4. But the Japanese moved first, on the previous day, occupying Tulagi in the Solomons,

The Douglas SBD Dauntless fighter bomber

Sailors on board a US carrier service a Douglas SBD Dauntless dive bomber. In the Pacific war, the Dauntless sank more shipping than any other weapon and was the US Army's main dive bomber until 1943.

which they aimed to use as a base for seaplanes to cover the Port Moresby operation. On May 4 Fletcher launched air strikes on the landings at Port Moresby before turning south to join the *Lexington*.

For the next two days, Japanese and US carriers hunted each other with no success. But on May 7 the Japanese found and attacked Task Force 44, assigned to harass the Invasion Group off Port Moresby, sinking a destroyer and a tanker. At 11am on the same day, 53 Douglas SBD Dauntless dive bombers from the *Lexington* and *Yorktown* found the light carrier *Shoho*, and sank it. The next morning, both sides found each other and launched air strikes immediately.

The *Lexington* and *Yorktown* were bombed by 33 Aichi D3A dive bombers (codenamed "Val" by the Allies). The *Lexington* suffered a hit that sliced through four decks. At midday it was torpedoed twice. Ninety minutes after that, it was racked by a huge explosion, abandoned, and sunk by a US destroyer. The Japanese carrier *Shokaku* had also been hit, putting it out of action for the next six months. The US carrier *Yorktown* had also been heavily damaged but was repaired at Pearl Harbor in just 45 hours. For the first time in naval history, two fleets had fought a battle without even seeing each other, at a range of nearly 200 miles (320 km).

Japan's next move

The Japanese had won a tactical victory—with only one small carrier lost, they had fared better than the Americans—but they had been forced to abandon their attack on

Japanese heavy cruiser *Mikuma*

The hulk of the Japanese heavy cruiser *Mikuma*, which was abandoned on May 6 following three air strikes from the carriers *Enterprise* and *Hornet*. This was the last Japanese casualty in the Battle of Midway.

Port Moresby. The Japanese also believed that both of the American carriers had been sunk at Coral Sea, which encouraged Admiral Yamamoto, the Japanese commander-in-chief, to press on with his plans to capture the island of Midway, in the central Pacific, which offered a base within striking distance of Hawaii.

Yamamoto's plans were complicated and failed to integrate his four carriers with the rest of his major surface units. He dispersed his forces with the aim of luring the US into a trap and launching a surprise attack, but he remained ignorant of American dispositions. On the other hand, thanks to "Magic" intercepts, Admiral Nimitz had a clear picture of his enemy's dispositions. Assembling northeast of Midway with the carriers *Hornet*, *Enterprise*, and the patched-up *Yorktown*, Nimitz set his own trap for the four Japanese carriers, under the command of Admiral Nagumo. In the small hours of June 4, still unaware of the approach of the US carrier task forces, Nagumo launched an air strike on Midway to soften up its defenses.

It was not until 8:20am that Nagumo received news of the US carrier force to the northeast, and changed course. The first US carrier strike failed to find its target as a result. A second attack, by 41 unescorted Douglas TBD-1 Devastator torpedo bombers, was intercepted by Nagumo's fighters with the loss of all but six of the bombers.

The final showdown
But this apparently suicidal attack had pulled the Japanese fighters down almost to wavetop level. At 10:30am, with Nagumo's decks still a hive of activity, criss-crossed by fuel lines, dive bombers from all three American

The horizon mirror is divided in two, vertically. One side has clear glass for sighting the horizon; the other side is mirrored, to reflect the sun.

Japanese sextant
An invaluable navigational aid, a sextant can be used to determine one's geographical position. It works by using two mirrors to calculate the sun's altitude at noon, which then produces a reading on the scale on the arc.

USS Yorktown
Smoke billows from the bridge of USS *Yorktown* following a direct hit by Japanese dive bombers launched by the carrier *Hiryu*, on June 4, 1942.

carriers arrived overhead. Within five minutes the *Kaga*, *Akagi*, and *Soryu* were put out of action. The next day the *Akagi* was abandoned and sunk; the *Kaga* was abandoned at 4:40pm; the *Soryu* had sunk ten minutes earlier, ripped apart by massive internal explosions, taking with it 718 sailors. Only the *Hiryu* survived to launch an attack on the *Yorktown*, which set the carrier ablaze. A second attack from the *Hiryu* scored two hits on the *Yorktown*'s port side. The crew were forced to abandon

ship. On 7 May a Japanese submarine I-168 finally sank the beleaguered American carrier while under tow.

The *Hiryu*'s moment of triumph was brief, however. The carrier was found by US dive bombers from the *Enterprise*, hit repeatedly, and set ablaze. Its crew abandoned ship after a huge explosion, and the *Hiryu* was sunk by Japanese destroyers the next day. The initiative, both at sea and in the air, had passed to the US naval forces.

The telescope points to the horizon mirror. The sun, sighted in the index mirror, now appears in alignment with the horizon, and a reading can be taken.

AFTER

The Battle of Midway saw the US Navy emerge clear-cut victors over the Imperial Japanese Navy. That victory was counted in one currency alone—aircraft carriers.

A SEVERE BLOW TO JAPAN
In one day the **balance in the Pacific had been restored.** The Japanese had mistakenly believed that the Americans **would give up**, and that the war in the Pacific would be a short one 166–67 **》**. From now on, **US expertise** and productive capacity would prove **more than a match for Japanese staying power.**

US SUPREMACY IN THE PACIFIC
By January 1943 **US front-line air strength** in the Pacific had overtaken that of Japan and, in November of that year, **Admiral Koga lost 75 percent of the bombers** he despatched against the American **landings in the Solomons 165–66 》**. By 1944, the US were deploying **11,442 aircraft** against a Japanese total of **4,050**. In **the campaigns of that year 230–31 》**, US air power **remorselessly chewed up the Japanese** bomber arm.

The arc of a sextant is 60° of a circle. (In Latin *sextans* means one sixth.) A scale is marked along the edge, which can determine both latitude and longitude to within 200 m (0.1 nautical mile).

The index arm slides along the sextant's arc until the sun is located in the index mirror and, therefore, appears in the horizon mirror.

3,500 Japanese sailors and airmen were killed at the Battle of Midway.

300 American sailors and airmen were killed at the Battle of Midway.

« **BEFORE**

Despite greater losses to the Japanese at the Battles of the Coral Sea and Midway, American superiority on the ground in the Pacific remained marginal.

PLAN FOR ATTACK

General MacArthur was keen to take over most of the US Navy and **hit the main Japanese base at Rabaul**, on the New Guinea island of New Britain. The navy, however, opted for a **more modest approach**.

NEW PLAN

MacArthur's proposal would force the navy to take unnecessary risks in confined waters. Instead the navy favored a **step-by-step advance** up the Solomon Islands, to the east, while MacArthur took on the northeastern side of New Guinea. The two would then **converge on Rabaul** in a bid to **overcome the Japanese**.

DIVISION OF COMMAND

The relevant **areas of command** in the Pacific were established at the start of July 1942. Task One, allotted to the US Navy, involved the **capture of the Solomon island of Guadalcanal**, where the Japanese were building a new airfield.

Guadalcanal

Commanded by Lieutenant-General Vandegrift, the First Marine Division landed on Guadalcanal on August 7. The small Japanese garrison was swiftly overcome and the US marines gained control of the airfield. The retaking of the island immediately became the utmost priority for Japanese high command.

Guadalcanal was surrounded on three sides by other islands. Together, these formed a confined channel, which US sailors nicknamed the "Slot." Once the troops were ashore, the US Navy had to resupply them in these dangerous, confined waters.

On the night of August 8/9, off Savo Island, the Japanese surprised the US fleet covering the landings, sinking four ships and damaging another two. Their superiority in night-fighting techniques and the destructive power of their Long Lance torpedoes—the most advanced of the time—gave them the edge.

The US retaliates

Ten days later the Japanese began to pour reinforcements into Guadalcanal, supported by naval guns and aircraft, which pounded the airfield, now

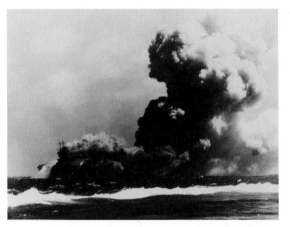

American carrier in flames
The USS *Wasp* was torpedoed by the Japanese submarine *I-19*, south of Guadalcanal, on September 15, 1942. She had taken two direct hits, narrowly missing one more. The crew abandoned ship and she was sunk by USS *Landsdowne*.

named Henderson Field in honor of a marine killed at Midway. On August 24 the second major naval engagement of the campaign—the Battle of the Eastern Solomons—took place east of

Guadalcanal, when the Americans intercepted a Japanese fleet bringing reinforcements. They sank a carrier, a cruiser, and a destroyer, and downed some 60 enemy aircraft for the loss of 20 of their own. On land there was also ferocious fighting, not least for a feature near Henderson Field which the Marines dubbed "Bloody Ridge." Meanwhile

American M3 light tank on Guadalcanal
The M3 tank entered service with the US Army in 1941 and also saw service with the British and other Allied armies during World War II. Its main armament was a 37mm gun plus four machine-guns.

Task One: the capture of Guadalcanal

The island lay at the southernmost tip of the group, and was just outside the Japanese area of control. The departure point for the operation was, therefore, New Zealand, which offered a fairly safe approach.

the nightly convoys of Japanese destroyers bringing reinforcements to Guadalcanal continued. On the night of October 11/12, in the Battle of Cape Esperance, an American cruiser and destroyer force surprised a Japanese cruiser squadron, opening fire at the pointblank range of 5,000 yds (4,570 m). The battle was not an unqualified victory, but did much to restore battered US morale.

Changing fortunes

On October 26 two larger fleets clashed during the Battle of Santa Cruz, in which four Japanese carriers lost 100 of their aircraft. Of the two US carriers involved, *Enterprise* was badly damaged and *Hornet* sunk.

The Japanese also launched a series of heavy attacks on the Marines defending Henderson Field. They flew in aircraft based elsewhere, but the Marines held out and, after reinforcement, even counterattacked. Battleships *Hiei* and

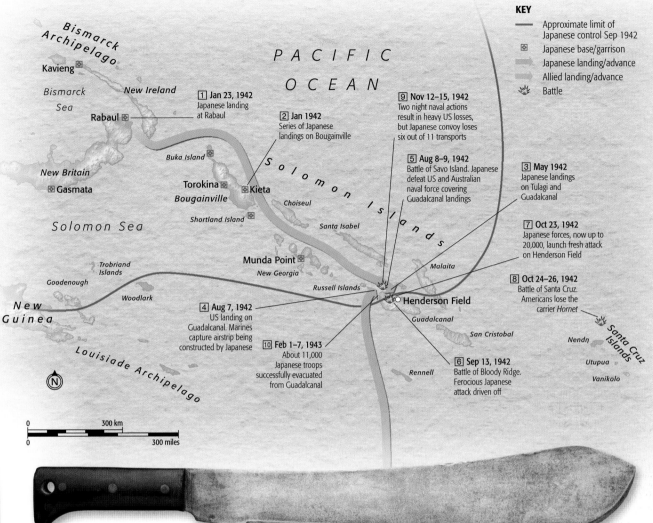

KEY
- Approximate limit of Japanese control Sep 1942
- Japanese base/garrison
- Japanese landing/advance
- Allied landing/advance
- Battle

PACIFIC OCEAN

Bismarck Archipelago
Kavieng
Bismarck Sea
New Ireland
Rabaul
New Britain
Gasmata
Buka Island
Torokina
Kieta
Bougainville
Shortland Island
Solomon Sea
Trobriand Islands
Goodenough
Woodlark
New Guinea
Munda Point
New Georgia
Russell Islands
Choiseul
Santa Isabel
Solomon Islands
Malaita
Henderson Field
Guadalcanal
San Cristobal
Rennell
Nendö
Utupua
Vanikolo
Santa Cruz Islands
Louisiade Archipelago

1 Jan 23, 1942 Japanese landing at Rabaul

2 Jan 1942 Series of Japanese landings on Bougainville

9 Nov 12–15, 1942 Two night naval actions result in heavy US losses, but Japanese convoy loses six out of 11 transports

5 Aug 8–9, 1942 Battle of Savo Island. Japanese defeat US and Australian naval force covering Guadalcanal landings

3 May 1942 Japanese landings on Tulagi and Guadalcanal

7 Oct 23, 1942 Japanese forces, now up to 20,000, launch fresh attack on Henderson Field

8 Oct 24–26, 1942 Battle of Santa Cruz. Americans lose the carrier *Hornet*

4 Aug 7, 1942 US landing on Guadalcanal. Marines capture airstrip being constructed by Japanese

10 Feb 1–7, 1943 About 11,000 Japanese troops successfully evacuated from Guadalcanal

6 Sep 13, 1942 Battle of Bloody Ridge. Ferocious Japanese attack driven off

0 300 km
0 300 miles

Kirishima, with an escort of a cruiser and 14 destroyers, were also sent to bombard the airfield on November 12. American codebreakers and radar gave warning of their approach and they were engaged by a US squadron. The Japanese lost two destroyers and the battleship *Hiei*. The Japanese kept up the pressure the following night, their warships plastering Henderson Field with over 1,000 shells. But the airfield

> **Coastwatchers, planters, traders, and colonial officials, living in the Solomons during Japanese occupation played a vital role, reporting enemy naval and air movements by radio.**

remained operational and the next day its fighter-bombers attacked the withdrawing Japanese fleet and sank seven out of 11 troop transports.

On November 14/15 a Japanese task force clashed with an American task force, whose major units were the battleships *Washington* and *South Dakota*. A savage mêlée ensued, in which *Washington* scored enough hits on the battleship *Kirishima* for her to have to be scuttled the next day.

The four surviving Japanese troop transports were run aground, landing only 2,000 men—a trivial return for so great an investment. The two battles of

Machete
US marines based on Guadalcanal were issued with machetes for cutting through vegetation. It was so dense in places, that it took a handful of men several hours to clear a path of just a few metres.

Guadalcanal proved to be decisive. One last attempt to land troops was made, on November 30, before the Japanese high command decided not to risk any more heavy units or transports on bombardment or reinforcement missions. This, and the fact that the United States were now building up their own men and supplies, meant that the defeat of the Japanese ground forces was only a matter of time.

Spoils of war
US troops display a Japanese flag on Guadalcanal. The island was cleared of the enemy by February 7, 1943, exactly six months after the first marines landed there.

AFTER »

In January 1943, the Japanese commander on Guadalcanal moved his headquarters to the neighboring island of Bougainville. By February the Japanese cut their losses and quit Guadalcanal altogether.

MASS EVACUATION
Starved of reinforcements and supplies the Japanese troops on the island had lost heart. The climate and conditions in the jungles were very poor and, as rations dwindled, the men fell prey to **tropical disease**. The **"Tokyo Express"**— a name invented by American sailors for the **nightly convoy of Japanese destroyers** that brought in reinforcements to Guadalcanal—was **running in reverse**, taking off the sick and the wounded. In an operation that rivaled the Allied evacuation of the Gallipoli peninsula in January 1916, the Japanese removed some **12,000 starving survivors** from Guadalcanal.

FINAL PUSH
Yet again, the Japanese had begun as the **stronger combatant** but had frittered away their initial advantage in a series of piecemeal initiatives. Neither did they fare well against MacArthur's troops in New Guinea, in their bid to **secure Port Moresby 166–67 »**.

« **BEFORE**

New Guinea offered the Japanese an anchor for their southern perimeter and a base from which to threaten the Allies' strategically significant port of Darwin.

FLAWED STRATEGY

The initial Japanese plan—**to occupy and secure** Port Moresby on New Guinea's southeastern tip—had been checked by the Allies at the battles of Coral Sea and Midway « **162–63**. Already, the underlying strategic dilemma facing the Imperial high command was having an impact: in order to secure the Japanese perimeter they had no choice but to **destroy the US Pacific fleet** in a major battle, and this they had so far failed to do.

A NEW APPROACH

Determined to continue, the Japanese were forced to **develop another strategy**. In July 1942, they landed on the northern coast of New Guinea and struck out, **overland this time**, for Port Moresby in the south.

KEY MOMENT

DARWIN BOMBED

Although the Japanese had no plans to invade Australia—they feared the task was beyond the capacity of their military—they saw the continent as an obstacle to their objectives in the Pacific.

In particular, they feared the threat posed by Darwin, the only major port capable of reinforcing the Allies as they resisted the Japanese advance. With Darwin out of action, the Japanese believed they stood a greater chance of maintaining their hold on the region.

On February 19, 1942, Japanese carrier-borne aircraft attacked Darwin, sinking the US destroyer *Peary* and seven transports. Despite a number of such attacks, lasting well into 1943, Darwin remained a vital source of supply in the Pacific until the end of the war.

9 mm barrel

Barrel shroud

Side-loading magazine

Pistol grip

Defending Australia

The Japanese never intended to invade Australia. However, they were aware that the capture of Port Moresby, New Guinea, would isolate Australia from the US, while securing an important stretch of Japan's defensive perimeter. It would also provide a major strategic route between the Indian Ocean and the Pacific.

The Japanese drive through the Pacific in the months following the attack on Pearl Harbor led to a conviction among Australians that their nation was a target for invasion. Their military therefore underwent a rapid expansion and, by mid-1942, Australia had raised 11 infantry and three armored divisions.

American aid

The British collapse in the Far East meant that Australia was forced to turn to the United States and, from February 1942, the Americans assumed strategic responsibility in the Pacific. A month later General MacArthur arrived to assume command of the Southwest Pacific Area, and all of Australia's combat units in the theater were placed under his command.

The Australian General Thomas Blamey, nominally commander of the Allied Land Forces, effectively had no control over US strategy and few Australians served on MacArthur's staff. By 1945 nearly a million US service personnel had passed through Australia, with many US military bases

having been built in the Northern Territory as well. The Americans had already frustrated the Japanese navy's efforts to capture Port Moresby and thereby to secure a strategic route between the Indian and Pacific Oceans, when they defeated them at the Battle of the Coral Sea, and at Midway a month later.

Japanese military losses forced the high command to abandon any immediate plans to alight on the southeastern tip of the island. However, on July 22, 1942, they tried again, when elements of the Japanese 18th Army landed on the north coast of New Guinea, at Buna and Gona. One of the largest islands in the world, New Guinea was divided between Dutch and Australian administrations and much of it was still unexplored. The Japanese plan was to capture Port Moresby by means of an overland advance through the passes of the Owen Stanley range of mountains, which separate New Guinea's north and south coasts. The range was crossed by the Kokoda Trail, a 60-mile (95-km) track rising to a height of over 7,000 ft (2,000 m). Even today, crossing the

> **Native bearers offered vital logistic support to the Allies. They came to the aid of the troops, carrying heavy supplies and escorting injured soldiers down the Kokoda Trail to safety.**

American presence in Australia

The US forces maintained a big presence in Australia throughout the Pacific campaign. Here, US Army Air Force fighter pilots, based in Northern Territory, inspect a map before going out on patrol.

trail is a daunting prospect. Days of sweltering heat and humidity are followed by freezing nights, while endemic tropical diseases present a constant threat to health.

Clash on the Kokoda Trail

General MacArthur was equally concerned with New Guinea. He decided to build up forces on the island as a necessary prelude to an offensive against the main Japanese base at Rabaul, in New Britain. However, the Japanese forces on New Guinea were now probing inland, and on June 22 they encountered and clashed with a battalion of native troops.

The build-up gathered momentum on both sides. The Allies sought to deny the airstrip at Kokoda to the Japanese, who seized it on July 29. Some 2,500 Japanese troops, commanded by Major General Tomarito Horii, then advanced on Port Moresby along the Kokoda

Japanese jungle boots

The going was often tough, through dense, boggy jungle terrain. Soldiers were issued with lightweight jungle boots, with quick-drying canvas uppers and rubber soles.

Austen sub-machine-gun

The Australian-produced Austen (from "Australian" and "Sten") had the barrel, body, and trigger mechanism of the Sten combined with features of the German MP 40. It could fire single shots or fully automatic rounds.

Folding stock

Shoulder rest

Trail. Horii's forces outnumbered the Allied defenders by five to one. By August 12 he was within 30 miles (50 km) of his objective but was meeting increasingly tough resistance. The fighting on the trail was bitter. The Japanese tactical manual had changed little since the campaign in Malaya. Pinning the enemy with frontal attacks, they felt for the flanks, aiming to engage them from the rear. But Horii had a strict timetable, which left him little or no time to outflank his Australian and American enemy.

Prolonged assaults on the outnumbered Allies were the order of the day. On both sides, however, the majority of the casualties were claimed by tropical disease. Quinine, still the principal anti-malarial drug in use by the Australians, was in short supply. The art of air-dropping supplies was in its infancy and enormous quantities were "free-dropped" (without parachutes) in the wrong places. Meanwhile, the passage of so many troops reduced the trail to a fetid quagmire.

Japanese withdrawal

Horii never reached Port Moresby. He withdrew partly under Allied pressure and partly because his superiors wanted him to establish a jungle fortress at Buna and Gona. At the end of August a secondary Japanese landing at Milne Bay, on the eastern tip of New Guinea, was fended off by two Australian brigades reinforced by two squadrons of fighter aircraft. This proved the first time in World War II that the Japanese had experienced a reverse on land. Moreover, the Japanese high command had decided to concentrate on the fight for Guadalcanal. Horii did not survive the withdrawal. Along with several of his senior officers, he drowned while crossing the Kumusi River.

The Japanese around Buna and Gona defied the exhausted Australians and Americans throughout November. The arrival of a new commander on the ground, Lieutenant General Robert Eichelberger, revitalized the offensive. Gona was taken in early December and Buna fell just under a month later.

Cautious advance

An Australian infantryman armed with a Bren gun moves forward on the Kokoda Trail, which saw some of the most savage fighting in the most inhospitable terrain encountered in the war in the Pacific.

AFTER »

Victory in New Guinea ended the threat to Australia and now cleared the way for General MacArthur to focus on the great Japanese stronghold of Rabaul.

MACARTHUR'S DEMANDS CHALLENGED

MacArthur wanted **more men and materials** for his advance through the Solomon Islands and the Bismarck archipelago. However, this started a **bitter interservice dispute** in Washington, which lasted until March 1943, when **Operation Cartwheel 230–31 »** was put into action.

NEW AREAS OF COMMAND

Scheduled to begin in June 1943, Operation Cartwheel **redefined the command responsibilities** in the Pacific. **Admiral Nimitz** was made **overall commander for the entire theater**; General **MacArthur** was responsible for the **Southwest Pacific Area**; and Admiral **Halsey** was entrusted with **operations in the South Pacific Area**, including an advance on

12,000 The number of **Japanese troops killed on the Kokoda Trail in 1942.**

2,850 The number of **Allied troops lost on the Kokoda Trail. The majority of them were Australian soldiers.**

MacArthur's flank. **Rabaul remained the ultimate target** for Operation Cartwheel, but by the time most stages had been successfully carried out, the Allies deemed the taking of the base **no longer necessary**, and that it should be isolated and neutralized instead.

America Organizes for Victory

Following the attack on Pearl Harbor, the United States swung into action, mobilizing troops and reorganizing its economy, industry, and civilian population for war—and victory. A wave of patriotism swept the country and by 1942 America was on a war footing, and experiencing massive social and economic changes.

◀◀ BEFORE

When war began in 1939, the United States was ill-prepared, but as Hitler's armies stormed through Europe, America began to shift from its neutral position.

EMERGING FROM DEPRESSION

In 1939 America was **emerging from economic depression**. Unemployment, stemming from the massive global downturn, was still high and manufacturing depressed. Following **the fall of France ‹‹ 82–83**, a peacetime draft was introduced and from March 1941 **America provided arms and supplies** to Allied nations through the **Lend-Lease Act ‹‹ 142–43** and edged closer to war. On December 7, 1941, the

8 MILLION The number of unemployed in the US in 1940. This reduced the consumption of goods, which raised the levels even further.

Japanese attacked **Pearl Harbor ‹‹ 148–49**. The following day **the US declared war** on the Axis powers of Germany and Japan.

EMPLOYMENT RESTRICTED

In 1939 married women were not expected to work. In some communities, laws **prohibited married women from working** in banking, local government, insurance, and teaching. Black Americans faced severe discrimination. They made up less than 10 percent of the labor force, and were **restricted to low-paid, low-status work** in both the southern and northern states.

Probably the biggest change war brought to the United States was economic. The need to produce the necessities of war—tanks, shells, aircraft, landing craft, and warships—galvanized industry and moved the country out of economic depression into a boom economy. Using a series of War Power Acts to override state and local authorities, President Roosevelt shifted industry onto a total war footing.

Working hours grew from an average of 38 hours a week in 1939 to 47 hours in 1943, factories operated a three-shift system, and millions were recruited into the labor force, so much so that by 1943 unemployment had disappeared. Small workshops and manufacturing businesses were transformed into high-tech factories, where mass production enabled weapons and armored vehicles to be produced by the thousand. Production soared, rising by nearly 30 percent between 1941 and 1945 and by 1944 the US was producing more than 40 percent of the world's armaments, so fulfilling Roosevelt's aim to make America "the arsenal of democracy."

100 THOUSAND armoured vehicles were produced from 1940-45

300 THOUSAND aircraft were produced from 1944-45

41 BILLION rounds of ammunition were produced from 1941-45

Visible women

At the start of the war, US armed forces were small in number and poorly equipped. Unlike some other Allied nations, the US had no tradition of peacetime conscription. Even so some 12 million men and women were

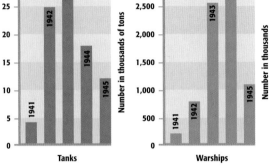

drafted into the armed forces and sent around the world to fight. One of the most marked social changes was the increased visibility of women. Some 200,000 joined the armed forces, serving in the Women's Army Corps (WAC) or as pilots with the newly formed WASP (Women's Airforce Service Pilots), ferrying military aircraft from factories to airbases, or in the navy. On the home front, millions of women entered the labor force, many of them for the first time, particularly married women and those with children. Most went into the defense industries, working in shipyards, military aircraft manufacture, and munitions factories, doing skilled work such as welding and riveting—something previously thought of as unsuitable for women. "Rosie the Riveter" and "Wanda the

Soaring production rates

US industrial output soared between 1941 and 1945. Mass-production techniques from the auto industry were applied to munitions so that thousands of tanks, jeeps, and warships rolled off the production line.

Welder" became iconic images used for recruitment purposes during the war, but despite the importance of women's war work, they were consistently paid far less than men.

Prejudice and patriotism

The demands of war also brought black Americans into more skilled jobs for the first time, as black people in their thousands moved north and west to work in the new factories. Prejudice, however, was rife. Black Americans saw distinguished service in all the armed forces but in a racially segregated military many were placed in menial jobs and barred from the same facilities as white service personnel. Despite the establishment of a federal Fair Employment Practices Committee by executive order in June 1941, black defense workers were often paid far less than white workers.

19 MILLION The number of women in the labor force in 1944. For many the work was physically tiring and low paid, but "Rosie the Riveter" and her call "We can do it!" galvanized US women.

The influx of some 700,000 black Americans into white urban areas also caused racial tensions and conflict. Matters came to a head in 1943 when race riots broke out in Detroit, Michigan, and in New York City, foreshadowing the problems that would appear again after the war. In April 1942 Roosevelt spoke of how

KEY MOMENT

THE INTERNMENT OF JAPANESE AMERICANS

When World War II broke out there were approximately 120,000 Japanese people living on the west coast of the United States, most of them in California. However, following the surprise attack on Pearl Harbor, a vitriolic anti-Japanese mood swept the country. In response, Roosevelt agreed that Japanese Americans should be classed as "enemy aliens," and in February 1942 Executive Order 9066 was passed that enabled the US Army to remove Japanese inhabitants from certain areas thought to be vulnerable to Japanese attack. As a result, all Japanese Americans living on the west coast

were forced to sell their property and businesses and were moved to internment camps or relocation centers. Some Japanese Americans protested this action through the courts but without success. By 1944 the mood was changing. Japanese Americans were fighting with Allied troops and, following a Supreme Court ruling that stated that internment of people whose loyalty was not in question was unconstitutional, American relocation camps were closed and families began to return home. Anti-Japanese feeling continued for some time after the war but in recent years, many people have received compensation.

Riveting Rosie
Millions of women entered the American labor force during the war. Some worked in more traditional areas of women's work such as assembling radios; others worked as welders and riveters.

everyone in the United States—"every man, woman, and child"—was in action on the home front. Government propaganda urged every American to do their part by joining up, entering war industries, or recycling and saving resources. Rationing was introduced and people threw themselves into the war effort. As silk stockings vanished, women stained their legs and drew "seams" up the back of their calves. Wartime skirts grew shorter to save material and zippers disappeared as the metal was needed for the military. Waging war was costly and Americans were told to buy war bonds and victory stamps to meet the costs. Hollywood also assisted. Stars such as Clark Gable and Frank Sinatra added their voices to the drive to buy war bonds and entertained troops who were serving abroad. By 1945 the US public had given some $135 billion in war bonds.

AFTER »

The war cost the United States billions of dollars and nearly 416,800 lives but it was to turn it into a superpower.

GLOBAL DEFENSE
America came late into the war but US forces fought in every theater, including the **Pacific 230–31 »**, Europe, and **Asia, 312–13 »**. The cost was partly financed through war bonds, which people were constantly urged to buy.

NEW TECHNOLOGY
Within the US, **war stimulated new developments** in weapons technology, and led to the creation of the **atomic bomb 322–23 »**.

US WAR BONDS POSTER

Women in Industry

More than 6 million American women joined the factory workforce during World War II, many working as welders, engineers, and machine operators in the aircraft, shipbuilding, and munitions industries. In Britain, the figure was about 2 million. Working in munitions was particularly dangerous: in the US some 37,000 women were killed and 210,000 permanently disabled.

"I loved getting into the challenge of getting dirty and getting into the work. I did one special riveting job, hand riveting that could not be done by machine. I worked on that job for three months, ten hours a day, six days a week, and slapped three-eighth- or three-quarter-inch rivets by hand that no one else would do. Our department had a majority of women. Many of them had no training at all, particularly the older women. We had women in our department who were ex-schoolteachers, artists, housewives. I'd sit them down and show them how to use the drill press, the size drill to use, the size of screw, the kind of rivets ... Then I would go back and check to see if the riveting was okay, and if there were any bad rivets, they had to take them out.**"**

AMERICAN RIVETER RACHEL WRAY, ONE OF THE FIRST WOMEN HIRED AT CONSOLIDATED AIRCRAFT (CONVAIR)

"I was told I had to go to work on Group One. That group was nicknamed the Suicide Group on account of the many workers who had been blown up, killed, maimed or blinded ... I would be working with highly explosive gunpowder for making detonators ... Eleven went to Group Five Powder but I had to wait for a guide to take me to Group One. It was then I noticed that she only had one hand and a finger missing off that. I asked her what had happened and she made up some story or other. I later found that she had had them blown off when she went to work on Group One ...

... Outside we had to leave our coats, shoes, bags, money, hairclips, and anything metal in the Contraband Place ... One day I was given a red box to carry with one person in front and behind carrying red flags walking along the clearways, taking them to be stored in magazines to be used later. I didn't know what I was carrying. There was a massive explosion and I dropped the box and was shocked to see a young woman thrown through a window with her stomach hanging out. Luckily the box, which contained detonators, did not explode or we would have had our legs blown off ... **"**

BRITISH FACTORY WORKER MABEL DUTTON DESCRIBING WORK AT RISLEY ROYAL ORDNANCE FACTORY, WARRINGTON

A wartime workforce
Wearing trousers and snoods for safety, women check the nose cones of Douglas A-20 planes in a US factory. War production brought women into jobs previously only held by men, and their contribution was enormous.

BEFORE ◄◄

In 1939, an incident occurred on the Dutch-German border that compromised Britain's intelligence networks in Europe.

FATAL DISCLOSURE

Two officers of the British Secret Intelligence Service (SIS) were lured over the border by **SS men masquerading as Allied sympathizers**, under the command of Colonel (later General) Walter Schellenberg. The SIS men were taken prisoner and under heavy pressure, **disclosed vital information** about British intelligence operations. This compounded the difficulty of **gathering information** inside occupied Europe after the German **Blitzkrieg ◄◄ 76–77.**

SIS RESISTANCE

The **Special Operations Executive** was perceived as the answer, but its establishment caused severe problems within British intelligence. SIS, whose remit was **low-profile information-gathering**, regarded the new agency as amateurs whose sabotage activities with resistance movements would **attract unwanted attention** from German **military intelligence**. From the outset, the two agencies regarded each other with **mutual suspicion**.

Secret Armies

The Special Operations Executive (SOE) was formed in July 1940 at the behest of Winston Churchill, who instructed its agents to "set Europe ablaze." SOE's primary purpose was to undertake sabotage and broadcast and disseminate "black propaganda" in occupied territories.

The principal purpose of Churchill's brainchild was to support the resistance movements in those countries of Europe and the Far East that were occupied by Germany and its allies. By the summer of 1944, SOE employed some 10,000 personnel, approximately 50 percent of whom were either agents in the field or those waiting to be dispatched.

An ideal role for women

Just under one third of SOE's total personnel were women. Selwyn Jepson, who was SOE's chief recruiting officer until 1943, accorded female recruits in the field absolute equality with men, observing, "In my view women are very much better than men for the work. Women, as you know, have a far greater capacity for cool and lonely courage than men."

In the field, an SOE network, or "circuit," depended on three key figures—a courier, a radio operator, and an organizer. Most of the female field agents in France worked as couriers, who traveled around as messengers and liaison officers. Because they were constantly on the move, the couriers ran the highest risk of being stopped and arrested. In this situation, women usually found it easier to invent plausible cover stories and tended to attract less attention than men, who, from early 1942, were liable to be picked up by the Germans on the streets and sent to Germany as forced labor. Women were also less likely to be searched than men were, and thus could more easily secrete messages.

German infiltration

Circuits always ran a risk of infiltration by German counter-intelligence, even more so if they became unmanageably large. One of the worst disasters to befall SOE was the betrayal of the "Prosper" circuit around Paris, by its French field air-transport officer, Henri Déricourt, which led to the arrest and execution of a number of agents.

> " The **question of relations** … is delicate. Various **secret services** were trying to do different things, but sometimes had to do them in the same places; **rivalry was the inevitable result**."
>
> PROFESSOR M.R.D. FOOT, HISTORIAN OF SOE

ECCO il NEMICO

Know your enemy

Entitled "Here is the Enemy," this US-produced poster (1942) depicts the cold face of a Nazi officer, in whose monocle is reflected the silhouette of a hanged man. Anti-Nazi propaganda like this targeted civilians in the hope that they would join the fight against the Axis.

Portable radio

Agents' radios were often modular, like this three-part German example (receiver, power supply, transmitter), which made them easier to assemble, disassemble, and transport.

Unrifled barrel

Cocking mechanism

Trigger guard

The single-shot pistol was cheaply made. It weighed 1 lb (450 g) and had a 4 in (102 mm) barrel. At times OSS agents used the pistol to get better weapons from their enemy.

Hollow pistol grip for storing spare ammunition

Liberty pistol
The .45 caliber Liberty pistol was made in huge quantities—one million in total—in the US. The pistols were intended for use by OSS agents and resistance fighters in Axis-occupied territories.

Now It Can Be Told
Former SOE agents Jacqueline Nearne and Captain Harry Rée play Felix and Cat as they reenact their wartime activities with the French Resistance in the 1944 film, *Now It Can Be Told*, made by the RAF film unit.

Another example of Axis infiltration occurred in Holland, where captured SOE agents were forced to maintain communications with headquarters in London, as if they were still at large. In their training, the agents had been instructed that, if captured, they should plant code words in such messages. This they did, but SOE chose to ignore the warning signals. As new SOE agents parachuted into Holland, they found the Germans waiting for them. The Germans called this deadly and one-sided intelligence battle the *Englandspiel* (England game).

SOE victories
SOE nevertheless had a number of significant successes. In 1943 SOE agents led by Knut Haukelid were parachuted into Norway to sabotage Germany's program to develop an atomic weapon with the "heavy water" produced by the Norsk Hydro plant. The plant was subsequently flattened by Bomber Command, and the last stocks of heavy water were sent to the bottom of a Norwegian lake by Haukelid's men, who sank the ferry on which they were carried.

In Greece, Italy, and France various SOE teams successfully derailed trains and brought down railroad bridges. In France, in June 1944, this activity was a significant factor in frustrating German attempts to reinforce their troops fighting to contain the Normandy bridgehead.

America's secret army
In 1942 the Americans set up the Office of Strategic Services (OSS), modeled on SOE and run by much-decorated World War I hero and postwar lawyer, General William "Wild Bill" Donovan. Early recruitment for OSS was mostly from fashionably connected men and women on the East Coast, earning

Resistance weapon supplies
Members of the French Resistance gather to study the use and maintenance of various weapons dropped by parachute. They include a Sten MKII; Ruby, Colt, and Le François pistols; and Colt and Bulldog revolvers.

the agency the nickname "Oh So Social." OSS used fewer women than SOE as field agents. A notable exception was Virginia Hall, who had the rare distinction of working in the field for both agencies. She also had a prosthetic foot, the result of a shooting accident in the 1930s. While on the run from the

470 SOE agents were sent into the field in France.

39 of the SOE agents in France were women.

118 of these SOE agents failed to return, 13 of them women.

Gestapo during her SOE days in France, Hall signaled the agency's Baker Street headquarters that she hoped "Cuthbert" would not be a problem. London flashed back, "If Cuthbert troublesome, eliminate him." The agency had clearly forgotten that "Cuthbert" was the codename for Hall's prosthetic foot.

AFTER

SOE was wound up at the end of the war, but many of its personnel found a postwar home in MI6, the British agency charged with gathering intelligence abroad.

SOE AGENT PEARL WITHERINGTON

DOUBLE AGENTS
The postwar employment of SOE agents in MI6 led to a **succession of disasters**, as the SOE had been **infiltrated by agents** working for the Soviet Union, among them Kim Philby. Attempts to send agents behind the **Iron Curtain 340–41 ≫**, employing SOE methods in the new **Cold War 348–49 ≫**, were thus doomed from the outset as some agents had already been identified. Just as had happened with the *Englandspiel*, **Soviet intelligence** was waiting for them or, as often happened, allowed agents to remain at large until they had **further compromised MI6**. Then they were pulled in. Similar problems occurred in the US, where **former OSS agents** worked for its postwar successor, the **Central Intelligence Agency (CIA)**.

RESISTANCE STAMP

Espionage

The British Special Operations Executive (SOE) and the American Office of Strategic Services (OSS) developed a wide range of communications equipment and an arsenal of ingenious weapons. Other agencies also developed an imaginative array of clandestine equipment; notable in this endeavor were the British MI9 and its American equivalent, MIS-X, which were established to aid the activities of escapees from prisoner of war camps and those personnel who were trying to avoid capture in occupied Europe.

1 False German identification document produced for the head of OSS, General William "Wild Bill" Donovan, to demonstrate the US agency's expertise. **2 Handkerchief map,** on which the map would only become visible once it was soaked in urine. **3 Suicide pill** carried by British SOE agents, concealed in an item of jewelry. The so-called L-Pill (L for lethal) took just five seconds to take effect when swallowed. **4 Ring with concealment,** possibly used to hide microdot plans. **5 Playing cards with concealed maps** that could be exposed by soaking. **6 SOE transceiver,** a device that could send and receive messages, with earth, headphones, and battery pack. **7 Clandestine blade kit** used by SOE and also acquired by OSS operatives trained in Britain. **8 Battery-powered radio** used by a German Abwehr espionage agent in Britain—hence the English labeling. **9 .25-caliber Webley belt pistol,** worn on a belt hidden under clothing. The trigger was activated by a length of cable that ran to the user's hand. **10 Pencil pistol,** a 6.35 mm weapon that fired its bullet straight from the cartridge, located in the top section of the pencil. **11 Hidden knife** inside a pencil developed by MI9, the escape and evasion agency; designed to be overlooked during an initial search. **12 SOE pipe pistol,** which was fired by removing the mouthpiece and twisting the bowl while grasping the barrel. **13 SOE concealment insoles** that enabled the wearer to hide escape aids such as a knife blade and gold coins. **14 OSS "Beano" grenade,** designed to explode on impact. **15 SOE lapel knife,** which could be hidden inside a patch on the underside of a jacket lapel. **16 .38-caliber glove pistol,** designed for self-defense by US naval intelligence. It was fired at point-blank range by pressing the plunger into an opponent's body while striking a blow.

6 SOE TRANSCEIVER (S-PHONE) MK IV (BRITAIN)

1 FALSE GERMAN IDENTIFICATION DOCUMENT MADE BY OSS (US)

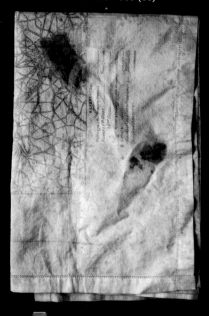

4 RING WITH CONCEALMENT (BRITAIN)

3 SUICIDE PILL (BRITAIN)

5 PLAYING CARDS WITH

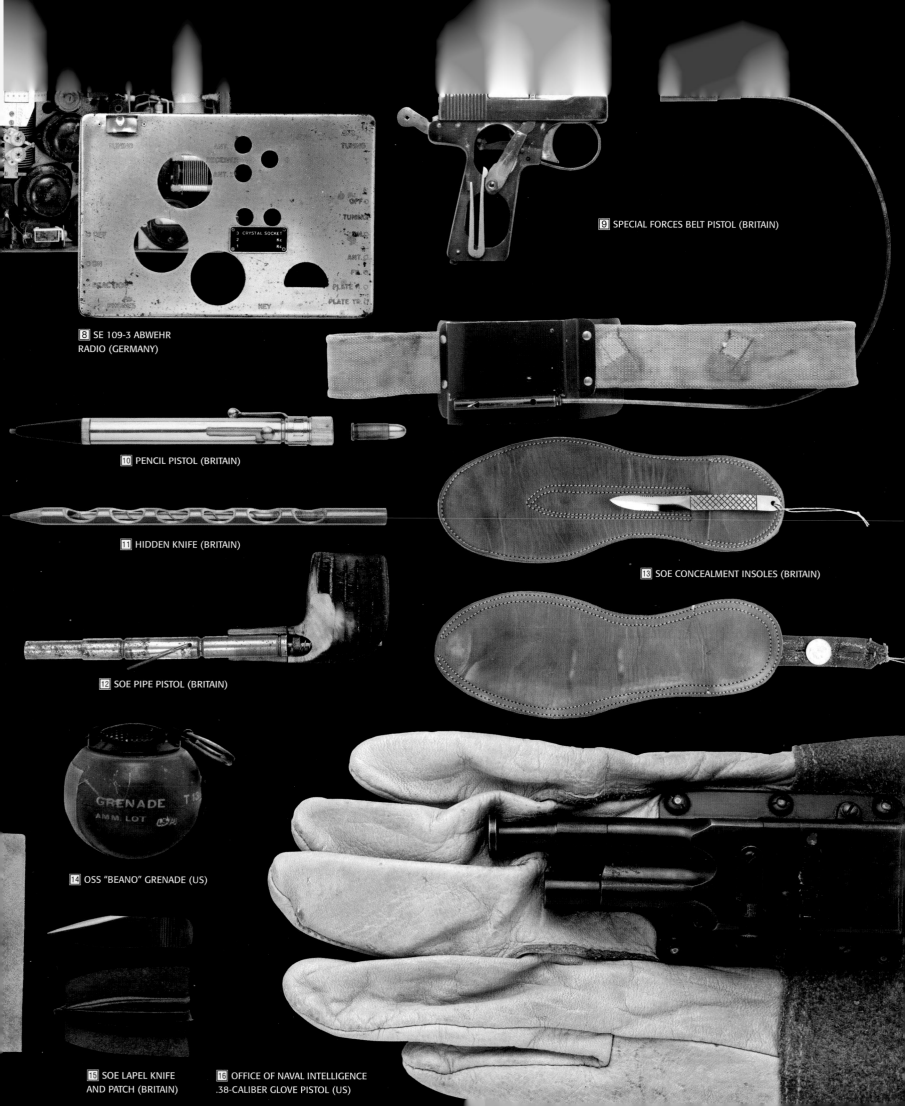

8 SE 109-3 ABWEHR
RADIO (GERMANY)

9 SPECIAL FORCES BELT PISTOL (BRITAIN)

10 PENCIL PISTOL (BRITAIN)

11 HIDDEN KNIFE (BRITAIN)

13 SOE CONCEALMENT INSOLES (BRITAIN)

12 SOE PIPE PISTOL (BRITAIN)

14 OSS "BEANO" GRENADE (US)

15 SOE LAPEL KNIFE
AND PATCH (BRITAIN)

16 OFFICE OF NAVAL INTELLIGENCE
.38-CALIBER GLOVE PISTOL (US)

BEFORE

Hitler's obsessive anti-Semitism can be traced back to racial theories prevalent in Austria and Germany during the late 19th century, which he absorbed in the years before World War I.

NATIONALIST TENDENCIES
In the **immediate postwar years ≪ 20–21** these beliefs were the common currency of all the parties of the **German nationalist Right**.

THE JEWS OF EASTERN EUROPE
The **Third Reich** secured diplomatic and **military victories in 1938–39 ≪ 58–59**, which placed millions of Eastern European Jews under Nazi control. Millions more were engulfed by **Operation Barbarossa ≪ 134–35**.

HIMMLER'S HENCHMEN
From June 1941 the systematic mass murder of Jews began on the Eastern Front, sanctioned by Himmler and carried out by *Einsatzgruppen* (SS killing units). These squads rounded up and shot thousands of Jews on a daily basis, and were responsible for at least two million civilian deaths.

The Holocaust

At the start of his own political career in the 1920s, Hitler did not place overriding emphasis on his anti-Semitism but, by the early 1930s it formed the bedrock of National Socialist philosophy. Once Hitler became the German chancellor in 1933, it came to shape all aspects of the Party's program.

The advantage of hindsight leaves no student of the period in any doubt about the implications of Hitler's writing and speeches, or about the impact of Nazi racial legislation following his rise to power. But it is debatable whether a comprehensive program for the complete physical destruction of the entire Jewish population of Germany had been set out in any detailed form by 1939.

The Final Solution
What is beyond dispute, however, is the fact that German military victories in the first two years of World War II delivered into Hitler's hands the Jewish population of much of Europe. In the early stages of the conflict the Germans had created numerous Jewish ghettos in Poland. The largest was in the capital, Warsaw, where at least 40,000 Jews died of starvation in 1941.

The huge territorial gains made by Germany in the summer of 1941, when it invaded what Hitler called the "Jewish-Bolshevik" Soviet Union and overran most of European Russia, produced the so-called "Final Solution," a Nazi euphemism for the extermination of European Jewry (*die Endlösung*). The phrase came from a statement made by Himmler to Rudolf Höss, the commandant of Auschwitz, in early summer 1941, that Hitler had given orders "for the final solution of the Jewish question."

Killing units and death camps
In the East, the massacres had at first been undertaken by *Einsatzgruppen*, mobile killing units, often helped by Latvian, Ukrainian, Lithuanian, and other local allies. At Odessa in fall 1941, for example, up to 80,000 Jews were killed by men of *Einsatzgruppe D* and troops from Germany's ally, Romania, into which Odessa had been incorporated. These units were soon deemed inefficient, however, and an alternative sought.

In January 1942, at a secret meeting in Wannsee chaired by Reinhard Heydrich, deputy head of the SS, the Final Solution was systematized.

Death camp inmates
The inmates of Auschwitz-Birkenau, an extermination camp, await liberation by the Red Army at the end of January 1945. At least two million Jews died in this terrible place, together with another two million Russian prisoners of war.

Heydrich industrialized the killing, establishing extermination camps based on the existing system of concentration camps. Clusters of camps were built in Poland—among them Treblinka, Belzec, Majdanek, Sobibor, and Auschwitz-Birkenau.

Another SS technocrat, Adolf Eichmann, and his subordinates organized the transportation to these and other camps of Jews, Slavs, Red Army prisoners of war, Roma

Arbeit macht frei
The train tracks lead straight up to the forbidding main gates at Auschwitz-Birkenau in southern Poland. Over the entrance, as at other extermination camps, the sign reads *Arbeit macht frei*—"work brings freedom."

SS AND GESTAPO CHIEF (1900–1945)

HEINRICH HIMMLER

Himmler joined the Nazi Party in its early days and, in 1928, was asked by Hitler to assume command of the *Schutzstaffeln* (SS). A close confidant of Hitler, Himmler soon became the second power in the Nazi state, heading the Gestapo and the Foreign Intelligence Service. In 1943 he became minister of the interior and, in 1944, commander-in-chief of the Home Army. A fanatical anti-Semite, Himmler was responsible for the execution of the "Final Solution." Captured by the British Army on May 23, 1945, he committed suicide by biting on a poisoned capsule.

Sites of the Nazi death camps

The Nazis had over 40 death camps, of which at least eight were used for mass murder. In the cities, Jews were forced to live in ghettos before being transferred by rail.

KEY

○ Concentration camp
● Extermination camp
◻ Site of mass killing
✳ Ghetto
(8,000) Estimated number of Jews killed
— Frontiers Nov 1942
▨ Greater Germany Nov 1942
▨ Axis controlled territory
▨ Allied territory
▨ Neutral territory

(Gypsies), political prisoners, and homosexuals. The inmates of the death camps came from every part of occupied Europe, their meticulously logged railway movements providing somber detail for historians. The camps were sometimes linked to industrial complexes run by the SS, and those capable of work on arrival were usually given a temporary stay execution. The rest—the old, the infirm, and children—were gassed. In April 1943 there was a rmass escape of prisoners from Treblinka. That month, there was an uprising in the Warsaw ghetto, and those Jews who survived the fighting were sent to extermination camps.

> " … we asked whether our life was not a **living nightmare**, so **unreal** did this life appear in **all its horror**."
>
> MARIE-CLAUDE VAILLANT-COUTURIER, CONCENTRATION CAMP SURVIVOR, AT THE NUREMBERG TRIALS, JANUARY 28, 1946

AFTER »

As early as 1942, the routine removal and transportation of the Jews to the death camps was a fact known to every inhabitant of Nazi-occupied Europe.

LIVING IN FEAR

The knowledge in itself was a **chilling deterrent** to any individual who considered opposing the Third Reich and its allies, whether by violent or non-violent means. If arrested, the same fate that had **overtaken the Jews 178–79 »** would almost certainly befall them.

THE FULL HORROR

By degrees, the Western Allies gathered a picture of the **Final Solution** from intelligence sources and refugees. But it was not until the summer of 1944, when the advancing **Red Army** overran the abandoned camp at Majdanek in Poland, where some **1.4 million Jews had been killed**, that the true extent of the horror was presented to the Allied leaders.

AUSCHWITZ LIBERATED

In the following months, the **litany of liberated camps 300–01 »**, with their mounds of corpses and emaciated survivors, revealed the **depths of Nazi degradation**. At 3pm on January 27, 1945, **Soviet troops reached Auschwitz-Birkenau**, where they found 648 corpses and 7,000 survivors, 1,200 at Auschwitz main camp and 5,800 at Birkenau. Those who could walk had already left on a forced march.

THE SHOES OF HOLOCAUST VICTIMS

WAR CRIMINALS

The years that followed the end of World War II saw the establishment of the **Jewish state of Israel**, in 1948, and the subsequent identification and hunting down of **Nazi war criminals 338–39 »** by the Israeli intelligence services and other international agencies. **All too few of the perpetrators were caught** and placed on trial but death has now claimed many.

6 MILLION The number of Jews who died during the Third Reich—about 40 percent of the world's Jewish population— and probably five million more people deemed undesirable by the Nazis.

Rounding up the Jews

Jews in Eastern Europe, particularly Poland, were treated with appalling brutality. Initially herded into ghettos, from 1942 they were rounded up from the ghettos and either murdered or sent to death camps such as Treblinka and Belzec. Between July 22 and September 12 1942, some 265,000 Jews were rounded up from the Warsaw ghetto and sent to the gas chambers at Treblinka.

"Monday 27 July. The 'action' still continuing at full strength. People are being rounded up. Victims on Smozca Street. People were dragged from the trams and shot. One hundred dead (old people and the sick) at the *Umschlagplatz* [Jewish cemetery]. Huge numbers of dead at Ogrodowa Street. The remaining occupants were taken out, no notice was taken of their papers ... Shooting all day. Dead on Pawia and other streets ... How high will the numbers of deported become?

Thursday 30 July. The ninth day of the 'action' that is continuing with all its fearfulness and terror. From five in the morning we hear through the window the whistles of Jewish police and the movement and running of Jews looking for refuge ... From midday yesterday onwards the shooting has not stopped next to our building. A soldier stands at the corner of Zamenhof and Nowolipie Streets and abuses the passers by ... By midday 4,000 people had been rounded up ...

Saturday 1 August ... The 11th day of the 'action' that gets progressively more terrible and brutal. Germans are in the process of emptying whole buildings and sides of streets. They took about 5,000 people out of 20–2 and other buildings on Nowolipie Street. The turmoil and terror is appalling. There is a general expulsion of all the occupants of Nowolipie Street ... The nightmare of this day surpasses that of all previous days. There is no escape and no refuge. The round-ups never cease ... Mothers lose their children. A weak old woman is carried onto the bus. The tragedies cannot be captured in words ...

Friday 28 August. The acts of terror are continuing ... Today we had a long talk with Dowid Nowodworksi, who returned from Treblinka .... His words confirm once again and leave no room for doubt that all the deportees...are taken to be killed and that no one is saved ... Yesterday about 4,000 people were driven from Warsaw to their deaths ... God! Are we really to be exterminated down to the very last of us?"

JEWISH DIARIST, ABRAHAM LEWIN, WHO PROBABLY PERISHED IN JANUARY 1943.

Deportation
Armed members of the SS force Jews out of the Warsaw ghetto in May 1943 for deportation to the death camps. This round-up followed a heroic armed resistance by those in the ghetto, which was ultimately defeated.

Malta and the Mediterranean

The inhabitants of Malta found themselves under constant attack as the campaign in North Africa intensified. First the Italians, and then the Germans, from their bases in Sicily, launched incessant bombing raids on the island—but on the ground the resolve not to capitulate grew ever stronger.

Following Italy's first bombing raid in June 1940, the threat to Malta from the air increased from January 1941, when the Luftwaffe moved into bases in Sicily. On January 10, 1941, Ju 87s from Sicily attacked the dockyard at Valletta and damaged the carrier *Illustrious*, which was in the harbor. This marked the beginning of a siege that was to last over two years, and which saw losses of over 2,000 aircraft to the Royal Air Force, the Luftwaffe, and the Regia Aeronautica collectively.

Defending the island was difficult at best, but the British had to keep both garrison and population supplied. Every convoy to Malta needed a strong naval escort, and in the two years up to the summer of 1942, over one third of the merchant vessels that were sent failed to reach the island. This left food in desperately short supply and Malta's population endured severe rationing

Luftwaffe aerial view of Malta
Frequent air attacks were the basis of the Axis offensive against Malta. In the two-year siege, some 3,000 raids were made in total. The Allies claimed to have shot down over 800 Axis aircraft, with a loss of 1,100 themselves.

◀◀ BEFORE

The Crown Colony of Malta lay 50 miles (80 km) from the southern coast of Sicily. Strategically important from the start, its significance grew as the conflict widened.

AXIS AGGRESSION
Axis leaders were quick to see **the potential** of the island: whoever controlled Malta would also **control the Mediterranean**. In seizing Malta, the Axis forces would deny the British the central Mediterranean and **remove a major threat** to their own supply lines to North Africa. The first bombs fell on Malta just a few hours after **Italy entered the war ◀◀ 98–99**, on June 10, 1940, marking the beginning of a long, relentless siege.

BRITISH DEFIANCE
Threats of **an aerial attack** had persuaded the British to move its **Mediterranean fleet** from Malta to Alexandria in the 1930s. However, the island remained the **only British base** between Gibralta and Egypt. As long as the **campaign in North Africa ◀◀ 124–25** continued, the British were **determined to keep hold of Malta**, even though they knew the price of doing so would be very high.

as the bombs rained down. Another threat to the island came from the sea. During the night of July 25/26 1941, the harbor in Valletta became the target of Italian torpedo boats and "human torpedoes"—torpedoes modified to carry a detachable explosive charge. The attack was aimed at the submarine anchorage, and a convoy thought to be in the port, but was driven off by the shore defenses in the only major coastal defense action fought by the British during the war.

Renewed Axis efforts
The aerial bombardment eased, temporarily, in June 1941, when the majority of Luftwaffe aircraft were thrown into the opening phase of Hitler's offensive against Russia, Operation Barbarossa. But six months later bombing was back to its earlier intensity.

Nevertheless, the British submarines and aircraft based in Malta continued to disrupt the Axis supply lines. Field Marshal Kesselring, German Commander-in-Chief South, was intent

on breaking Malta's tough resistance. Based in Rome from December 1941, the field marshal had some 400 aircraft under his command. He used these to inflict huge losses on Allied shipping in the Mediterranean. He also laid dense minefields around Malta, virtually cutting the island off from supply.

By August 1942 General Rommel was at the height of his success in North Africa, having driven the Allied forces back to El Alamein in northern Egypt. Losing Malta at this critical stage in the war would be a disaster for the Allies—almost certainly leading to their defeat in North Africa—and yet such a loss now looked imminent.

Operation Pedestal
Malta was at the end of its fuel and food resources. One last push would have to be made if the Allies were going to save the island and stay in the game. On August 3, 1942, a British convoy set sail from the Clyde River to relieve Malta.

Codenamed Pedestal, the convoy comprised 14 fast merchantmen and the oil tanker *Ohio*, and was to be escorted by 24 destroyers, three aircraft carriers, two battleships, seven cruisers, and eight submarines. The plan was for the heavy ships to turn back when the group reached the Sicilian narrows. Thereafter, Pedestal would be protected by four cruisers and 12 destroyers.

Seven days after leaving Britain, as the convoy was passing through the Straits of Gibraltar, it was spotted and shadowed. A savage battle ensued, starting with the German *U-73* sinking the British carrier *Eagle* on August 11. From the next day, the convoy was under constant attack from air and naval units, which included aircraft

The George Cross
The George Cross—the highest award for civilian gallantry—was given to the people of Malta in 1942.

Bomb damage in Valletta
Malta's capital, Valletta, was a primary Axis target, not least because its dockyard harbored Allied naval craft. The bombing of Malta was so intensive that the island became the war's most-bombed area.

flying from bases in Sardinia and Sicily, 21 U-boats, and squadrons of S-boats deployed off the coast of Tunisia. The convoy also had to contend with freshly laid minefields.

Malta saved
On the afternoon of August 13, three of the convoy's survivors arrived at Malta. The tanker *Ohio*, barely afloat but with her vital cargo of oil intact,

> **6,000** The tonnage of bombs that were dropped by the Luftwaffe on the island of Malta between March 20 and April 28 1942, in a total of 11,819 sorties.

limped in the next day. The feat of seamanship that brought it there earned the tanker's master, Captain D.W Mason, the George Cross. What

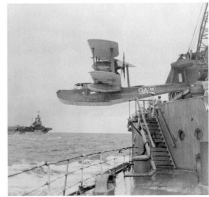

HMS Warspite
A seaplane launches from the deck of the battleship HMS *Warspite*. Deployed in the Mediterranean from 1940 to 1941, the ship escorted many supply convoys from Egypt to Malta, and back again.

restored. Two more convoys reached Malta by the end of the year, and the island lived to fight another day.

Allied victory at El Alamein and the subsequent capture of Axis airfields in Libya further eased the situation. The siege of Malta was not yet over but the island had been held against the odds, and food and other essential supplies were now reaching its defenders and citizens on a regular basis.

King George V awarded the George Cross to the island in April 1942, in recognition of the heroism of its population. This was the only time that it has been awarded collectively.

> "This **poor old hooker** hasn't got many minutes now. I **hope** to God **she lasts long enough**."
> CAPTAIN DUDLEY MASON, COMMANDER OF THE TANKER *OHIO*, ON REACHING VALETTA HARBOR

remained of the merchantmen and warships in the convoy had taken heavy punishment in the battle: two of the cruisers and a destroyer had been sunk; another two cruisers had been badly damaged, as had the aircraft carrier *Indomitable*. Despite such heavy losses, however, Operation Pedestal had been a success and Malta's ability to resist the force of the Axis onslaught had been

AFTER

The tremendous resolve of the Maltese inhabitants, together with the concerted efforts of Allied forces, had kept Malta from falling during the Axis offensive.

THE WAR IN NORTH AFRICA
Royal Air Force operations from Malta were now **a vital factor** in the campaign against the **Axis forces in North Africa 182–83 »**, attacking not only their land troops but also the essential supply convoys that were sent to **reinforce Rommel's Afrika Korps**.

MALTA'S NAVAL BASE RESTORED
The eventual **defeat of Axis forces** in North Africa **186–87 »** and the **invasion of Sicily 210–11 »** and, subsequently, **the Italian mainland 212–13 »**, removed the Axis air

Civilian casualties on Malta were relatively light thanks to its excellent air-raid shelters, which were dug into the island's soft sandstone rock.

threat **once and for all**. This meant that, from the summer of 1943, Valetta could once again be used by the Allies as a **major naval base**.

TECHNOLOGY
HUMAN TORPEDO

Nicknamed the *maiale* (pig) because its operators found it so difficult to steer, the Italian "human torpedo" was a modified torpedo with a detachable explosive charge in place of a normal warhead. A two-man crew sat astride the craft's casing in specially designed diving suits. On arriving beneath their target vessel, the crew detached the charge, fixed it to the ship's bottom like a limpet mine, and set a time fuse. On December 19, 1941, the Italians launched a daring raid of three human torpedoes on the harbor at Alexandria, damaging the British battleships *Queen Elizabeth* and *Valiant* so badly that they were out of action for several months.

BEFORE

The Western Desert Campaign began toward the end of 1940, with an Italian invasion of Egypt. Since that time, the advantage had passed first to the Allies, then to the Germans and Italians.

INITIAL CONFLICT
Although the Allies were successful in forcing an **Italian retreat in February 1941**, this had not been enough to secure their victory outright. Instead they now came face to face with **General Erwin Rommel's Afrika Korps ‹‹ 124–25**.

ROMMEL'S FIRST OFFENSIVE
Despite having orders to stay **on the defensive**, Rommel immediately took advantage of what he saw to be a **weak Allied defence** and launched a series of attacks that resulted in **driving the Allies** out of Libya. **One stronghold** remained, Tobruk, which was immediately besieged.

OPERATION CRUSADER
With the **balance of power** constantly shifting from one side to the other, **the year ended with Allied efforts to relieve Tobruk**. Although they were successful, yet again, the **victory fell short** of ending the conflict for good.

Advancing British tanks
A British Valentine infantry tank raises a cloud of sand. Valentines were extremely reliable and a number of them motored over 3,000 miles (4,800 km) on their own tracks in the pursuit of the Afrika Korps, having defeated the Axis forces at the Battle of El Alamein.

El Alamein

The campaign in the Western Desert reached a stalemate, and both sides paused to make good their losses. The offensive resumed in May 1942 for the last time. The following fall Rommel was to face an enemy who commanded a more numerous, better-equipped, and better-motivated army.

Rommel moved first and attacked on the night of May 26/27. The battle line ran south for 35 miles (55 km) from Gazala on the coast to Bir Hacheim, a fortified box held by the First Free French Brigade. Rommel caught the British off guard south of Bir Hacheim as 21st Panzer Division overran Third Indian Motor Brigade's position, while two more panzer divisions fanned out across the desert, wheeling in a northeast direction, toward Tobruk.

Versatile artillery
The German 88 mm anti-aircraft gun was used to great effect in targeting aircraft. The gun proved deadly when the Germans used it as an anti-tank weapon against the Allies during the Western Desert Campaign.

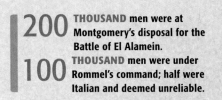

200 THOUSAND men were at Montgomery's disposal for the Battle of El Alamein.
100 THOUSAND men were under Rommel's command; half were Italian and deemed unreliable.

In the center of the Gazala Line, Rommel personally led an armored drive, confident that enemy minefields would protect his flanks and rear. By nightfall on the 27th, however, he had been pushed back onto the minefields and the box held by 150th Brigade.

Rommel considered asking the British field commander, Lieutenant-General Neil Ritchie, for terms, but his situation eased when the Trieste Division opened a corridor through the minefields.

Rommel was still caught in a position known as the "Cauldron." The British delayed with fatal results, and it was not until June 5 that Ritchie attacked the Cauldron at Sidra Ridge and Aslagh Ridge; both attacks were repulsed.

Back on the offensive on June 6, Rommel overran two Indian brigades and destroyed the artillery of the Fifth Indian Division. After the Free French

withdrew from Bir Hacheim Rommel was able to pentrate the Gazala line in strength and resumed his northeast thrust toward Tobruk. Recognizing that the battle was lost, Ritchie reinforced the Tobruk garrison and withdrew into Egypt. On June 20–21, Rommel stormed Tobruk, taking 33,000 prisoners; the loss of Tobruk was the Eighth Army's worst defeat.

New Allied command
Following the fall of Tobruk, General Auchinleck, the commander-in-chief in the Middle East, then took personal command of Eighth Army and, during the course of July, halted Rommel's drive into Egypt at the First Battle of

LANDMINE

Minefields were a vital "area denial" weapon. The simplest type was a small canister with a few ounces of explosive. Buried in the ground with just its sensor exposed, it reacted if it was stepped on. A "bounding" mine contained fragments of metal and was buried underground in a steel mortar tube. On being fired, the mine was blown into the air where it was detonated at waist height. Large anti-tank mines were detonated by the pressure of a tank passing over them. The most basic method of mine clearing was by hand. A slow and dangerous process—well-laid minefields were covered by defensive fire—this often happened at night.

Advance at El Alamein
British infantry burst through a smoke screen with fixed bayonets. The ground is marked by the tracks of the tanks which advanced ahead of them.

El Alamein. By July 27, having fought themselves to a standstill, both sides were digging in, preparing to regroup. The British held a crucial advantage: operating nearer their base meant that reinforcements and supplies reached them sooner than those of the Afrika Korps, whose supply lines were now dangerously overextended, some 1,200 miles (1,930km) from Tripoli. Rommel was now also restricted to a narrow front of some 40 miles (65 km),

stretching from the sea to the Qattara Depression, a salt marsh at the bottom of a line of cliffs. It was clear he would attack as soon as he felt strong enough.

Montgomery's plan
Churchill now replaced Auchinleck with General Harold Alexander as commander-in-chief in the Middle East, and appointed General Bernard Montgomery to command the Eighth Army. Montgomery was quick to show his mettle by halting the latest offensive, launched by Rommel on October 30/31, to the south of Alam Halfa Ridge. Montgomery employed a coordinated defense of tanks, artillery, anti-tank guns, mines, and ground-attack aircraft. Rommel broke off the offensive on September 2. He now found himself in a strategic double bind. He could neither advance nor retreat, while his enemy was preparing to go on to the offensive.

Montgomery's plans for battle differed markedly from those employed earlier in the campaign. Rather than playing Rommel at his own game of Blitzkrieg, for which British armored formations exhibited no great flair, he aimed to destroy his enemy, once and for all, in a grinding set-piece battle. It would open with an infantry-artillery assault, supported by heavy tanks, whose task it was to destroy the fixed defenses of the Afrika Korps and their garrisons. Only after the conclusion of this "dogfight" would the main body of armor march forth into the battle. On October 22, 1942, Eighth Army fielded nearly 200,000 men, 1,000 front-line tanks, 2,300 artillery pieces, and 530 serviceable aircraft. The Afrika Korps numbered some 100,000 men with 520 tanks, nearly 300 of them Italian, 1,200 artillery weapons, and some 350 serviceable aircraft, mostly Italian. The Afrika Korps had also lost Rommel as its commander, since he had been invalided back to Germany with a stomach ailment.

The Second Battle of El Alamein
The battle began on October 23 with an artillery bombardment of 450 guns, which preceded a main push along the coastal road and a diversionary attack to the south. The Afrika Korps was not distracted by the diversionary attack and held fast on the coast. Rommel returned

> **10,000** men of Afrika Korps were killed, and 15,000 wounded.

> **2,350** men of the Eighth Army were killed and 8,950 were wounded.

to the campaign in North Africa on October 26, the day that Montgomery threw in more tanks to reinforce his main thrust. After a week of bitter fighting, the Afrika Korps had been reduced to a strength of 35 tanks, and Montgomery had hacked through the center of Rommel's front. By November 2 he was ready to retreat, but Hitler forbade withdrawal, forcing Rommel to commit the last of his armor to block the northern corridor.

Throughout the battle Montgomery had been receiving virtually "real time" information on Rommel's dispositions, via Enigma intercepts. Confident in the knowledge that the Germans were now counterattacking in the north, Montgomery concentrated his main effort on the corridor in the south. By mid-afternoon on November 7, Montgomery's armor was driving up into the Afrika Korps' rear, forcing Rommel to order a full withdrawal along the coast road. The retreat was to continue for 2,000 miles (3,200 km).

In November 1942, following defeat at the Second Battle of El Alamein, Rommel was forced to retreat toward Tunisia.

ROMMEL'S "GOLDEN BRIDGE"
Montgomery **184–85 ≫** pursued cautiously, but **failed to outflank** his retreating enemy. The task was **furter hampered by heavy**

> **25** PER CENT The casualties among Montgomery's infantry at El Alamein. Tank and artillery crews and engineers also suffered.

rain, which made off-road movement difficult. Moreover, the **British losses** sustained at El Alamein had been heavy and a **pell-mell pursuit** might have given Rommel the chance to turn on the Eighth Army, **inflicting more damage**. Thus Rommel was given a **"golden bridge,"** the coast road to Tunis. By this time, however, **Operation Torch 186–87 ≫** was well under way, and **eventual Axis surrender** just a matter of time.

GERMAN PRISONERS AT EL ALAMEIN

> "We are going to finish with this chap Rommel once and for all. It will be quite easy. There is no doubt about it. **He is definitely a nuisance.**"
>
> GENERAL BERNARD MONTGOMERY, AUGUST 1942

BRITISH FIELD MARSHAL Born **1887** Died 1976

Bernard **Montgomery**

> ## "**Our mandate** … is to **destroy the Axis forces** in North Africa … It can be done, and it **will be done!**"

MONTGOMERY ADDRESSING HIS TROOPS IN NORTH AFRICA, 1942

Possibly the best known of the British generals of World War II, Bernard Montgomery, often known simply as "Monty," had been a professional soldier for more than 30 years when Britain declared war with Germany in 1939.

After training at the Royal Military College, Woolwich, London, he joined the Royal Warwickshire Regiment in 1908 and first witnessed active service in World War I. What he saw on the battlefields of France and Belgium had a profound influence on his approach as a commander. Not only was he seriously injured early in the war but he also witnessed the horrific conditions and pointless casualties that confirmed his belief that successful campaigns needed careful preparation and tactical training of the men rather than sheer force and repetitive drill.

> ## "The capacity and will to **rally men and women** to a common purpose."
> **MONTGOMERY'S DEFINITION OF LEADERSHIP**

At the conclusion of World War I Montgomery had been promoted to the rank of temporary lieutenant colonel, but his unconventional and sometimes arrogant approach often antagonized his superiors. His skill as an officer, though, was seldom in doubt and when war broke out in 1939, he commanded the 3rd Infantry Division.

Escape from Dunkirk

Montgomery and the 3rd Division spent the early months of World War II in Belgium, forming part of the British Expeditionary Force (BEF). There was very little fighting, but Montgomery foresaw a possible defeat and prepared his men for a tactical retreat—and was proved right when German troops advanced into the Netherlands in May 1940, forcing the British and French to retreat to Dunkirk (see p.78) and then across the Channel to England.

In 1942, taking control of North Africa was crucial to opening up the Mediterranean to Allied shipping. The German army, under General Erwin Rommel, was advancing toward Alexandria, on the northern coast of Egypt, and the uncoordinated tactics of the Eighth Army was doing little to stop it. After he was appointed commander of the Eighth in 1942,

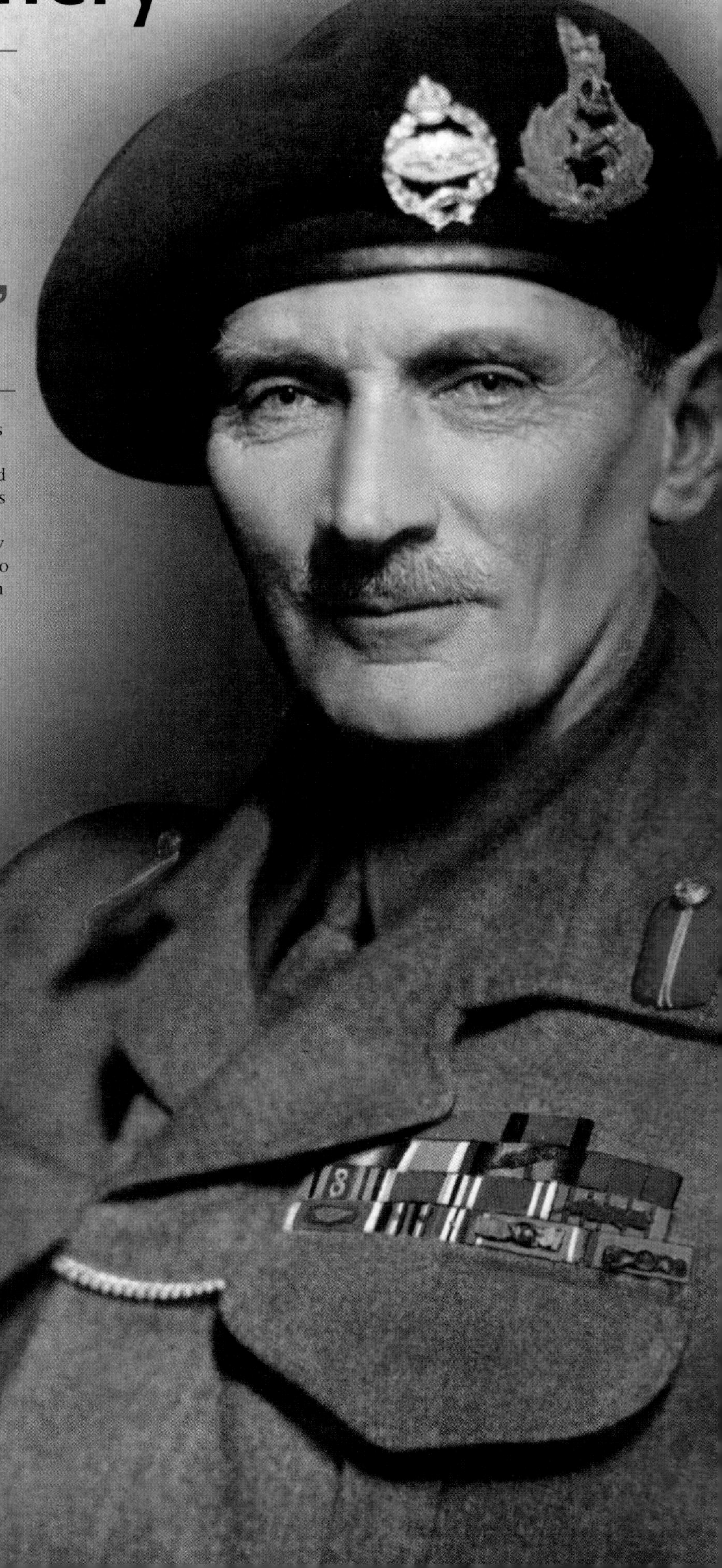

"Monty"

Field Marshal Sir Bernard Law Montgomery in May 1945, wearing his trademark battledress and beret with the badge of the Royal Tank Regiment alongside his field marshal's badge.

Montgomery managed to transform the campaign by designing cohesive, coordinated battle plans for both the army and air units. He also made it his business to improve morale, personally visiting as many of the units as he could, and replacing his officer's cap with an informal beret.

El Alamein

Once his forces were in place he established a reinforced stronghold at Alam Halfa, west of Alexandria, and once again his foresight saved the day. Rommel attacked Alam Halfa at the end of August 1942, a couple of weeks after Montgomery's arrival, but was forced back. Monty resisted the temptation to attack the retreating Germans, and was criticized at the time for indecision, but he used the time to plan a major offensive, which drew on plans devised by his predecessor, Claude Auchinleck.

This came in October, when he judged the time right to fight at El Alamein (see p.182). After 12 days of intense fighting, the Battle of El Alamein proved to be decisive, allowing Montgomery to go on to capture Tobruk and Tripoli, and forcing the Axis surrender in Tunisia. As a result he was knighted and promoted to the rank of full general.

Preparing for D-Day

From North Africa, Montgomery turned his attention to the invasion of Sicily and southern Italy, which was also vital to securing the Mediterranean for the Allies. There was tension between him and the American commanders, Patton and Bradley, which left him frustrated at the lack of planning, and the Americans angered by his high-handedness and caution. Nonetheless, Allied troops advanced through Italy in the fall of 1943; but by the end of the year the advance had slowed because of bad weather and poor communication between the British and American forces.

Montgomery's experience was then needed back in Britain for final preparations for the invasion of Normandy (see p.254 and p.258). As commander of the 21st Army Group, he improved the Allied invasion plan, Operation Overlord, in June 1944. He was always to argue that his scheme for the breakout from Normandy succeeded, but victory owed as much

Lüneburg Heath
As commander of the 21st Army group, Montgomery reads the terms of surrender to delegates of the German forces on Lüneburg Heath, in northern Germany, on May 4, 1945.

The desert war
Montgomery watches the advance on German lines in North Africa in 1942. He used the tank for forward observation in the Western Desert Campaign, and in the invasion of Italy.

Combined forces
The US provided Sherman and Grant tanks. The tank shown here is Montgomery's Grant M3A3 tank.

to the determination of Allied soldiers and German strategic over-expansion as to his generalship. And with US troops now forming the majority of the Allied forces in Europe, it was General Eisenhower who took personal command of ground forces.

Still in command of the 21st Army Group, however, and now promoted to field marshal, Montgomery led Operation Market Garden (September 1944)—the campaign to capture bridges in the Netherlands and to push on into Germany's industrial heartland. Unusually, however, the operation was poorly planned and executed, which led to the defeat at Arnhem, further tensions with the Americans, and losing the chance to advance in to Germany that year.

Final years
In May 1945 Montgomery accepted the surrender of the Germans in northern Germany, Denmark, and the Netherlands. After the war he continued to serve as Chief of the Imperial General Staff, and later as deputy supreme Allied commander until his retirement in 1958.

> "With **stout hearts**, and with **enthusiasm** for the contest, let us go **forward to victory**."
>
> MONTGOMERY TO TROOPS ON THE EVE OF D-DAY, JUNE 5, 1944

Torch Landings

Operation Torch was the largest Allied amphibious operation of the war thus far. Conceived in London, in July 1942, it marked the beginning of the final stages of the campaign in North Africa, which culminated in the surrender of the Axis forces in Tunisia, in May 1943.

T he Torch landings consisted of three Task Forces—Western, Central, and Eastern—landing respectively at Casablanca, Oran, and Algiers. The size of the operation was immense, involving over 100,000 men and 120 vessels. Sailing at high speed, under formidable air cover, the convoys reached their pre-assault positions without being intercepted by U-boats.

German intelligence failed to appreciate the significance of this Allied armada. Until Central and Eastern Task Forces passed through the Straits of Gibraltar during the night of November 5/6, the Germans had assumed that this was another attempt, in the style of Operation Pedestal, to run supplies to Malta. Doubts now crept in, with a new intelligence assessment envisaging a landing at Tripoli, in Libya. On November 7 intelligence concluded that there would be landings in North Africa, although Hitler, who believed

> **The US troops of Western Task Force, who landed at Casablanca, waded ashore carrying the Stars and Stripes under the illusion that the French colonial troops would not fire on them. In fact, heavy fighting ensued until November 11.**

that such a strategy would only drive the Vichy government further into the Axis camp, did not agree. The landings were launched on November 8, 1942.

All three met with varying degrees of resistance, but on November 9, Admiral Darlan, the Vichy High Commissioner, ordered a ceasefire after being taken into protective custody by the Allies. In spite of counter-orders from Vichy, the greater part of the French forces obeyed Darlan. Now it was the Allies' turn to be taken by surprise. Field-Marshal Albert

Kesselring dispatched troops from the island of Sicily to hold Tunisia, toward which General Rommel was retreating, shadowed by Montgomery.

British airborne troops were dropped ahead of the Anglo–American First Army, but they failed to link up with ground troops, enabling the Germans to establish a strong defensive line. The Allies had been hoping to make a swift

BEFORE

The Torch landings in North Africa were agreed by the Americans and British in the absence of an alternative—they were still unprepared for a cross-Channel invasion.

MAINTAINING PRESSURE
The landings marked a **third significant stage** in the Allies' campaign in North Africa, which had already seen desert action in **Libya ‹‹ 124–25** in 1940 and, more recently, at the **battles of El Alamein ‹‹ 182–83**.

A SECOND FRONT
The Allies still planned for a **Second Front**, in 1943, but in the meantime the Torch alternative would provide **employment for the growing US Army** in Britain and also for a substantial part of the British home reserve, which could **take on an offensive role** now that the danger of a German cross-Channel invasion had receded.

American troops come ashore
Behind American troops landing at Arzeu, near Oran, is a landing craft assault (LCA). This small craft had quiet engines and would have carried about 35 fully equipped infantry for this initial assault on an enemy-held beach.

British mountain howitzer
Allied troops often found themselves held up by strong German positions in rugged, mountainous terrain. Mortars and howitzers were vital in dislodging them.

SPAIN

6 Nov 8, 1942
Western Task Force lands in Morocco. After overcoming resistance by local French forces, begins eastward advance

6 Nov 8, 19
Centre Task Force attempt land at Oran, but does secure beachhead until 10

Gibraltar

Tangier

SPANISH MOROCCO

US CENTRAL TASK FORCE

US WESTERN TASK FORCE

Port Lyautey

Rabat

Casablanca

Melilla

Tiemse

Fez

Safi

MOROCCO

Marrakesh

thrust through Tunisia to join hands with the Eighth Army, advancing from El Alamein, but the rapid build-up of German reinforcements ensured that the Tunisian campaign now became a bitter slogging match.

Final offensive

In January 1943, having completed his withdrawal to Tunisia, Rommel planned a spoiling attack that would destroy the Allies' offensive capacity and consolidate the German hold on Tunisia. On February 14 General von Arnim's Fifth Panzer Army launched an attack on the inexperienced US II Corps at Sidi Bou Zid, while Rommel's Afrika Korps advanced through the Kasserine Pass, and on toward the Tebessa province. It was a rude baptism of fire for the raw Americans, who were very roughly handled by von Arnim and Rommel. Fortunately for

Mareth Line casualty
Stretcher bearers of the Indian Medical Service come to the aid of a Gurkha wounded in the assault on the Mareth Line, April 1943. The tough Gurkha troops had a fearsome record of bravery with the British Eighth Army.

KEY MOMENT
VICHY FRANCE

The rump French government, formed by Marshal Pétain after France surrendered to Germany on June 20, 1940, was based in the spa town of Vichy, 75 miles (120 km) northwest of Lyon. (Paris was still the official capital.) It controlled about two fifths of unoccupied France and the French colonies. Pro-collaboration, Pétain's administration was known as the "Vichy government." It survived until the Torch landings, after which the whole of France came under German control in Operation Attila. Most of the Vichy French clung to the terms of the armistice, which had been signed with Germany in the summer of 1940, only as long as Hitler remained the master of Europe. At the first indication of the shrinking of his power, they held themselves ready to defend the long-term interests of France in a swift change of allegiance.

VICHY POSTER RECRUITING FRENCH PEOPLE TO WORK IN GERMANY

the Allies, the two German leaders were uneasy partners and their offensive lost momentum.

On February 22 Rommel conducted a skillful withdrawal, leaving 6,000 American casualties. This was the last German offensive in North Africa.

Thereafter it was a matter of squeezing the life out of the Axis forces, a task tailor-made for Montgomery, who now became subordinate to the Allied commander in North Africa, the US General Eisenhower. Montgomery's adversary at Alamein, Rommel, now left the theater on grounds of illness, leaving General Hans-Jürgen von Arnim to hold on behind the Mareth Line, the German fortifications running from the shores of the Gulf of Gabes to the slopes of the Matmata Hills, a distance of some 30 miles (50 km). After failing with a frontal assault, Montgomery outflanked the Mareth Line, but the Axis managed to extricate most of their forces to a defense line hinged on the Wadi Akarit, which was breached by 4th Indian Division on April 5/6. For two weeks the Allied and Axis forces traded punches as the Axis perimeter around Tunis inexorably shrank. The final Allied attack opened on April 22. Tunis fell on May 7; Bizerta, 45 miles (72 km) to the northwest, was taken on the same day. Final resistance collapsed on May 13, when the Italian First Army laid down its arms and surrendered to the Allies. More than 250,000 prisoners were taken. Hitler, who had for a long time considered North Africa a sideshow, had reinforced the Afrika Korps too little and too late.

39 THOUSAND Allied soldiers came ashore at Oran in Algeria.

35 THOUSAND Allied soldiers landed at Casablanca in Morocco.

33 THOUSAND Allied soldiers came ashore at Algiers in Algeria.

The North African arena
The Allies invaded North Africa from the west, landing on the Atlantic coast of Morocco and the Mediterranean coast of Algeria. The Germans sent troops to Tunisia to prevent these troops from linking up with the British Eighth Army.

AFTER »

The Tunisian campaign had exposed the frailty of US troops and their senior commanders when faced with battle-hardened veterans of the Afrika Korps.

STRONG LEADERSHIP
One American commander, General Patton, who took command of II Corps after the reverse at Kasserine, exhibited **qualities of leadership** that marked him out for command of US Seventh Army in the **invasion of Sicily 210–11 »**.

NEW THREAT TO AXIS
For the Axis, the Tunisian campaign exposed the **bankruptcy of Hitler's strategy**. The capture of eight Axis divisions, kept there **at the Führer's insistence**, left Italy and its offshore islands with no immediate prospect of adequate defense, while **major Allied forces were now available** for operations across the entire sweep of the Mediterranean. The only question was, where would they choose to land?

ITALY
Sardinia

6 Nov 8, 1942
Eastern Task Force meets with only light resistance during landings at Algiers

7 Nov 10, 1942
Germans land in Tunisia

■ GERMAN 5TH ARMY

16 May 10, 1943
Having withdrawn to Cape Bon, Axis forces surrender

■ US EASTERN TASK FORCE

Sicily
Cape Bon

Algiers
Blida Bougie
Philippeville Bône
Constantine
Bizerta
Tunis
Enfidaville

■ US 1ST ARMY
Kasserine Sbeitle
TUNISIA
ALGERIA Biskra Sidi Bou Zid
Gafsa Maknassy Sfax

13 Feb 22, 1943
US forces halt Axis counter-offensive in Kasserine Pass

15 May 7, 1943
Allied forces capture Tunis

Malta
(to Britain)

Crete

12 Feb 4, 1943
8th Army reaches Tunisian border

Gabes
Mareth Medemine
Tripoli
Homs
Buerat

11 Jan 23, 1943
8th Army enters Tripoli

14 Mar 22–26, 1943
New Zealand and British force outflanks Axis defenders of the Mareth Line

9 Nov 23–Dec 13, 1942
Rommel makes stand at El Agheila, but is eventually outflanked by 2nd New Zealand Division

10 Dec 26, 1942–Jan 16, 1943
Rommel makes stand near Buerat, but is again outflanked

El Agheila

LIBYA

1 May 26, 1942
Start of Rommel's offensive against the Gazala Line

Mediterranean Sea

8 Nov 13, 1942
8th Army recaptures Tobruk

Derna Gazala
Benghazi Jebel El Akhdar Tobruk Sollum Sidi Barrani
El Adem Mersa Matruh
Bir Hacheim

GERMAN AFRIKA KORPS

5 Nov 4, 1942
8th Army starts pursuit of retreating Axis forces

2 Jun 21, 1942
Germans and Italians take Tobruk

4 Oct 23–Nov 2 1942
Allied victory at El Alamein

Alexandria
El Alamein
BRITISH 8TH ARMY
Cairo

Qattara Depression

3 Aug 30, 1942
Rommel's attack on El Alamein halted

EGYPT

0 300 km
0 300 miles

N

KEY
— Allied advance/landing
┉ Gazala Line
— Axis advance/landing
— Axis front line October 23, 1942
– – Axis front line March 20, 1943
···· Axis front line May 3, 1943
┬┬┬ Mareth Line

"One Day of War"
A Red Army soldier feeds a small child in a devastated village retaken from the Germans. This still is from "One Day of War in the Soviet Union" a propaganda film shot on June 13, 1942, by a team of 160 Russian cameramen.

Saving the Soviet Union

Operation Barbarossa, Germany's invasion of the Soviet Union in 1941, had done much to reduce the country's productive capacity, striking significant blows to its steel and coal industries. Thanks to its almost limitless resources and huge Allied aid, however, the Soviet Union was able to survive.

From June 1941 to November 1942, the Red Army's strength at the front grew considerably from 2.9 to 6.1 million men. Mere manpower, however, would have been meaningless without Russia's ability to preserve an industrial base with which to equip, arm, and continuously sustain the Red Army.

In August 1941, Hitler had switched his main effort from the center to the south of the Soviet Union and, in the process, had dealt a potentially crippling blow to its coal and steel production, which declined in the winter of 1941 by 63 percent and 58 percent respectively.

In turn, this change of focus placed the central Moscow-Upper Volga region beyond the reach of the German Army. After the German retreat from Moscow in December 1941, the Soviet Union retained the central region, which, along with the industrial regions of the Urals and the Kuznets Basin, in western Siberia, was sufficient to provide the Soviet Union with the manufacturing resources that decided the outcome of the war. It was nevertheless, a close-run thing.

BEFORE

The Germans had planned for the invasion of the Soviet Union as early as December 1940, their initial objective being to defeat the Red Army in the field.

HITLER'S AIM
Operation Barbarossa ≪ 134–35, had it succeeded, would have **swallowed colossal tracts** of the Soviet Union's agricultural land and the greater part of its **strategic industries** for the Third Reich. Victories in the opening weeks of the war in the East threatened just that.

FATAL DECISIONS
The severity of the Russian winter had **hampered Germany's advance** in 1941 and this, coupled with the Soviets' determination to defend their land and people displayed during the **German drive on Moscow ≪ 140–41**, spurred on further resistance. At the same time, the Soviets focused on saving their war economy, aided by prewar planning, ruthless organization, and heroic self-sacrifice.

Propaganda poster, 1942
Emotive posters were printed, in which the population of the USSR were exhorted to make heroic sacrifices to aid the war effort in the name of Lenin and Stalin.

As soon as the Panzers moved off their start lines in June 1941, a special Russian unit had begun to move heavy industry lock, stock, and barrel, from the western and central areas of European Russia beyond the Ural mountains, out of reach of German armor and aircraft. The problems raised by this huge effort were eased by a prewar program for the strategic relocation of heavy industry, aimed at balancing the output of traditional industrial centers with that of the raw-material and new manufacturing zones that lay beyond the Urals.

Combining resources
Thus it was possible to "marry" evacuated plants with factories in the eastern regions of the Soviet Union. For example, at the beginning of July 1941, the armored plate mill at Mariupol, in the southern Ukraine, was moved to the new industrial complex at Magnitogorsk, east of the Urals; and the huge tank plant at Kharkov was transferred to the tractor factory at Chelyabinsk, which also accommodated part of the Kirov plant evacuated from Leningrad. It became popularly known as "Tankograd." Just ten weeks after

the last engineers left the Kharkov works, "trudging along the railway tracks," the first 25 T-34s rolled off the Chelyabinsk production lines.

A slow and harsh recovery
The men and women who migrated with their factories suffered immense hardships. Discipline was harsh. An edict of December 26, 1941, made absence without leave punishable by up to eight years imprisonment. It is not surprising that, in spite of heroic efforts, there was a sharp fall in total industrial output by some 50 percent. Even by 1945, coal and steel production had not returned to the levels of 1940. Nevertheless, in 1942 Soviet armaments production, exploiting huge stocks accumulated before the war, surpassed that of Germany: 24,400 Soviet tanks and armored fighting vehicles to 4,880 German; 21,700 aircraft to 14,700; 4 million rifles to 1.4 million. This could not have been achieved without US aid to the Soviet Union through Lend-Lease. By May 1945 the Americans had shipped over 16 million tons of supplies, including locomotives, rails, and machine tools. American agriculture also provided five million tons of food, enough to give each Red Army soldier rations for every day of the war.

> **Under the terms of the "Lend-Lease Act," the United States supplied the Soviet Union with three quarters of its total copper requirements between 1941 and 1943. Much came via the Trans-Siberian railway.**

AFTER

The price of survival was costly. The Germans had occupied and pillaged European Russia, while the Soviet Union had ruthlesssly stripped its own territory for the waging of war.

CIVILIAN HARDSHIP
Elderly men, women, and children **worked punishing hours** sustained by the **most meager rations**. In a characteristically Soviet contradiction between the development of sophisticated technology and the most primitive living conditions, scientists in Moscow were working on an **atomic bomb 348–49 ≫** while collective farm workers were tilling fields with methods little changed since the Middle Ages.

A PRICE WORTH PAYING
Despite such hardship, the huge civilian effort contributed to the devastating **German defeat at Stalingrad in 1943 192–93 ≫** that marked the beginning of Hitler's decline.

SOVIET CIVILIAN MEDAL

Arctic convoys
A chilly watch on a British cruiser escorting an Arctic convoy to the Soviet Union. This lifeline, opened in August 1941, ferried thousands of tanks, trucks, and aircraft around North Cape to Archangel and Murmansk.

TECHNOLOGY

THE T-34

The mainstay of the Soviet Union's tank armies, the T-34 was a superb machine, which went through the war without any major modification. It was fast and agile, with broad tracks that reduced ground pressure to a minimum. It had a range of 186 miles (300 km), nearly twice that of the German Panther and three times that of the Tiger. Its design was hugely influential, with later Panthers adopting its excellent sloping armor, which offered greater protection against gunfire.

The German Drive to the East

In June 1942 Hitler launched his summer offensive against the Soviets. Ignoring Moscow, he ordered his armies to advance southeast towards the oilfields of the Caucasus. They made steady progress across the steppes of Ukraine until August when they reached the city of Stalingrad on the Volga.

In May 1942 Stalin ordered the Red Army's Southwest Front to retake Kharkov by attacking from the Izyum salient. This bulge in the German front had been created during the Soviet counter-offensive in January 1942. The Southwest Front was commanded by Marshal Timoshenko, who launched his attack on May 12. But the Germans contained the Soviet thrusts and, on May 17, delivered a counterblow with converging attacks into the Izyum salient, which cut off the Soviet spearheads. Over 250,000 prisoners were taken and every Soviet armored formation in the pocket was destroyed.

At the southern end of the Eastern Front was the Black Sea port of Sevastopol, bypassed in Barbarossa, then isolated by a five-division blockade and units of the German Navy. In May 1942 the city was besieged by the Eleventh Army with 10 infantry divisions and 120 batteries of artillery, including the 800 mm "Gustav" railway gun.

The infantry assault on Sevastopol took place on June 7, after five days of artillery bombardment and air strikes. It was not until June 30 that the Germans broke into the city, occupying it on July 3. In the Soviet withdrawal, many of the defenders were evacuated by small boats, a Dunkirk-like "miracle" on the Black Sea.

Operation Blue

Hitler had every reason to be buoyed by the tide of events. He was determined to take what had been denied him in 1941. There would be no more talk of withdrawal. He was convinced that the Red Army was on the verge of collapse but chose to ignore the simultaneous seepage of Germany's strength in the East in order to bolster its position in the West. As a consequence, the German Army in the East would have to depend increasingly on the unreliable troops of Germany's allies, the Romanians, Hungarians, Italians, Spaniards, and Slovaks.

Germany's summer offensive, Operation Blue, was launched on June 28, 1942. Field Marshal von Bock's Army Group B was to advance toward Voronezh and down the grasslands between the rivers Don and Donets (the Don-Donets corridor) in the direction of Stalingrad, while Field

Crossing the Don River
German infantry cross the Don River during the drive to Stalingrad and the Caucasus. Following the devastating defeat at Stalingrad, German Army Groups A and B were forced to withdraw well to the west.

> ## "It was … the most **desolate and mournful region**."
> A NAZI ON THE DON-DONETS CORRIDOR

Fold-down windshield

◀◀ BEFORE

Hitler's strategic plans for 1942 were ambitious and included seizing the oil fields in the Middle East, so destroying the basis of British power in the region.

FIRST BATTLE OF KHARKOV
This spectacular example of geopolitical overreach began with **Operation Barbarossa ◀◀ 134–35**, when the Soviet Union **lost its third city**, Kharkov, which fell to the **German Sixth Army** on October 24, 1941.

OPERATION BLUE
The **summer campaign of 1942** was codenamed Operation Blue. In **Führer Directive No.41**, Hitler stated that the principal

> **British codebreakers got wind of German plans and notified Stalin, but he dismissed it as disinformation.**

aim of the campaign, having destroyed the Soviet Union's defense potential, was to "**cut them off**, as far as is possible, from their most important **centers of war industry**."

Tow hook

Watertight hull

Based on the Volkswagen Type 1, this amphibious vehicle was suited to all kinds of terrain. It had four-wheel drive—the front wheels doubling as rudders in water—and a propeller to the rear.

TECHNOLOGY

KATYUSHA ROCKET

The nickname "Little Katie" was given to the Red Army's fin-stabilized rockets, which were launched from rails mounted on heavy trucks. A Katyusha division was capable of firing a barrage of 3,840 projectiles (230 tons of high explosive) up to a range of 3.5 miles (5.5 km). Although the launchers were slow to reload, they were mobile, which meant that they could be easily relocated before the enemy had a chance to return fire.

Marshal List's Army Group A drove for the Don crossings east of Rostov. By 6 July Army Group B had reached the River Don opposite Voronezh. The advance seemed like a rerun of the summer of 1941, with the Red Army falling apart on the first armored impact. Von Bock, however, fretted that fresh Red Army formations might attack his exposed left flank from Voronezh. He obtained permission from Hitler to secure the city with armored formations detached from General Friedrich Paulus's Sixth Army.

But determined Red Army resistance drew von Bock into a slogging match that threatened to dislocate Operation Blue's timetable. On July 13 Hitler

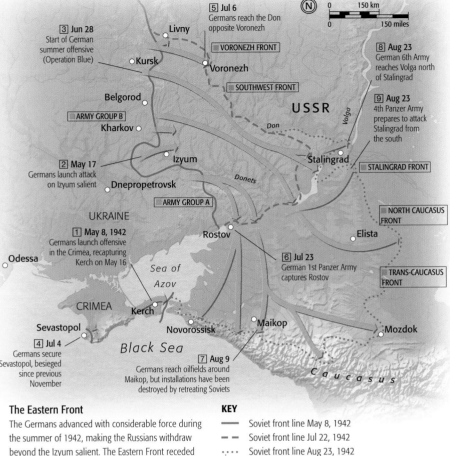

The Eastern Front

The Germans advanced with considerable force during the summer of 1942, making the Russians withdraw beyond the Izyum salient. The Eastern Front receded well into the Caucasus and on toward Stalingrad.

KEY
— Soviet front line May 8, 1942
-- Soviet front line Jul 22, 1942
···· Soviet front line Aug 23, 1942
⇒ German advance

German Schwimmwagen
The *Schwimmwagen* (literally "swimming car"), designed by Ferdinand Porsche, could tackle snow, mud, and water obstacles, and so was ideal for the Russian campaign.

Each vehicle came equipped with a snow shovel for tackling large snow drifts, and a paddle, which came in useful for steering the *Schwimmwagen* should the engine fail when in water.

intervened, replacing von Bock with Field Marshal von Weichs. Meanwhile, General Paulus was ordered to turn east toward Stalingrad, providing further protection for the German left flank.

In the Don-Donets corridor the Red Army was now threatened by a series of encirclements on the scale it had suffered in Operation Barbarossa.

> Vital delays in the proposed schedule of Operation Blue gave the Red Army an opportunity to develop an effective strategy for the defense of Stalingrad.

With enormous difficulty, the recently appointed chief of the Soviet general staff, Marshal Vasilevsky, persuaded Stalin that more orders to "stand fast" regardless of the strategic situation invited further catastrophe, and that it was vital for the Soviet forces in the corridor to withdraw.

Threat to Stalingrad mounts

On July 23 Rostov, which the Red Army had lost and then retaken in the fighting of the winter of 1941–42, fell to Army Group A almost without a fight. Hitler ordered Army Group A and First Panzer Army to drive for the oilfields in the Caucasus, while Army Group B advanced toward Stalingrad. Neither side could have foreseen the horror that would face them there.

AFTER

On August 9, just six weeks after the start of Operation Blue, First Panzer Army had reached Maikop, 320 km (200 miles) southeast of the town of Rostov.

OILFIELD DISAPPOINTMENT
The Germans captured the Soviet Union's most westerly oilfields, only to find that they had been **wrecked by the retreating Red Army**. They now lacked the fuel to maintain the **momentum of their advance**, and were **never to reach** the principal sources of oil beyond the Caucasus.

1 MILLION The total number of German soldiers who fought the Soviets in the wider battle of Stalingrad. Almost one tenth were later taken prisoner.

THWARTED INTENTIONS
Operation Blue had started well, but was delayed because of stiffening **Red Army resistance** and Hitler's obsessive shuffling and reshuffling of his forces over an **increasingly extended front**. German forces were reorganized and redeployed, resulting in substantial logistical difficulties. Troops desperately needing to sustain the drive into the Caucasus were, instead, committed to **the fight for Stalingrad 192–93 ≫**.

5.6 MILLION men were deployed on the Eastern Front by the Soviet Union.

6.2 MILLION men were deployed by Germany and the Axis powers during the war.

Soviet Triumph at Stalingrad

The battle for Stalingrad, was to become one of the most savage conflicts of World War II. Neither dictator—Hitler or Stalin—could afford to lose the city whose name was so inextricably linked with Soviet pride. Defeat for either side would mean a crippling, perhaps fatal, blow to morale.

While the German First Panzer Army was bearing down on Maikop, in the Caucasus, its Sixth Army—much of whose transport had been temporarily transferred to Army Group A—was moving slowly down the Don-Donets corridor toward Stalingrad, an industrial city that straggled for some 20 miles (16 km) along the west bank of the Volga River.

> " Stalingrad is no longer a town … it is an enormous cloud of **burning, blinding smoke**. "
>
> AN OFFICER OF THE GERMAN 24TH PANZER DIVISION, OCTOBER 1942

Germans taken prisoner
Over 100,000 German troops surrendered at Stalingrad. Losses and casualties suffered by the Sixth Army were dwarfed by those among the Italian and Romanian armies screening the flanks of the Stalingrad pocket.

The first assault
By August 19 General Paulus, now reinforced by Fourth Panzer Army, was poised to begin his assault on the city. Four days later, following a raid by 600 aircraft, German troops entered the outskirts of Stalingrad and also carved out a salient to the north of the city along the western bank of the Volga. At Hitler's forward headquarters at Vinnitsa, in the Ukraine, the mood was jubilant. Morale was boosted once more on September 5, when a Russian counterattack, designed to drive off the German forces north of Stalingrad, was thrown back with heavy losses.

Soviet counterattack
Stalin remained determined to hold Stalingrad, whatever the cost. On September 13 he sanctioned a plan presented to him by Zhukov, who in August had been appointed First Deputy Supreme Commander-in-Chief of Soviet Armed Forces and was now in overall command of the entire Stalingrad sector. His plan envisaged a wide encirclement of the Axis forces on the Lower Volga and the destruction of the Sixth Army in Stalingrad.

On the same day, the immensely tough and able General Chuikov was appointed as the new commander of the Soviet 62nd Army in Stalingrad. Fighting in the city intensified, and the battle for Stalingrad now became every

≪ BEFORE

After the start of Operation Blue, Army Group B was inexorably drawn deeper into the quagmire at the center of which lay the industrial city of Stalingrad.

RETREAT AND DEFENSE
As **Operation Blue ≪ 190–91** came to an end, early in September, Army Group B's spearhead **closed in on Stalingrad**. Here, the advance stopped; the Red Army had retreated as far as it was going to. By November 1 there were **five Russian armies** defending Stalingrad and two German armies—**Sixth and Fourth Panzer**—fighting their way into the city.

HEAD TO HEAD
The Germans were on the brink of a battle for a major Soviet city, which Stalin had vowed to **defend to the last**—in this he was resolute. Hitler, meanwhile, appeared to be **mesmerized by the city** that bore the name of his **rival dictator**. Departing from the **policy of Blitzkrieg ≪ 76–77**, he committed his army to one of attrition. The decision proved to be a disaster for the **German Sixth Army**.

soldier's nightmare, a bloody, house-to-house fight in which the advantage passed to the men of the Red Army.

The Germans edged painfully toward the steep western banks of the Volga. Attrition replaced Blitzkrieg, which had proved so effective in the summer and fall of 1941, and at the beginning of 1942, the Germans had given the Soviet Union the opportunity to prepare for the conflict and to mount effective resistance against the enemy.

The Germans weaken

Paulus established his headquarters in a huge department store a few hundred yards from the Red Army ferry points that plied back and forth at night, bringing out some 35,000 wounded

13,500 guns were brought in by the Soviets.

1,400 aircraft were used to defend Stalingrad.

894 tanks were used in the counterattack.

during the battle and returning 65,000 reinforcements. By November the Germans had chopped Chuikov's command on the western bank into four groups, forcing communications

SURRENDER OF PAULUS

By promoting Paulus to field marshal on January 30, Hitler intented to stiffen his resolve—no German field marshal had ever surrendered in the field. Paulus was exhausted, however, his nerve shredded. On the morning of January 31, staff officers of General Shumilov's 64th Army arrived at Paulus's headquarters to discuss surrender terms with his chief-of-staff, General Schmidt. Two hours later, Soviet General Laskin arrived to take Paulus's formal surrender, marching him and other staff officers to Shumilov's headquarters.

between them to be carried out on the east bank. The Germans reached the river itself, at the southern edge of the city, 11 days later. But the battle had by now become, for them, a struggle whose cost far exceeded its strategic or tactical value, remorselessly sucking in units that were essential for sustaining the dwindling hopes of a breakthrough in the Caucasus. By mid-November Sixth Army had shot its bolt.

At the same time German intelligence was becoming aware of a Red Army build-up on the northern and southern flanks of the Stalingrad salient, which were screened by Romanian, Italian, and Hungarian armies of dubious value. Zhukov's preparations for the counterblow, codenamed "Operation Uranus," had been characteristically rigorous and ruthless. The lives of the defenders of Stalingrad had been traded for time, while the Soviet high command waited for the arrival of a frost to harden the ground for armor and for the Allied landings in North Africa to tie down German reserves in Western Europe. By November 18

450,000 **The number of men from those countries allied to Germany who lost their lives on the Eastern Front—a high price to pay for supporting Hitler.**

Street fighting in Stalingrad

Red Army soldiers advance cautiously over mounds of rubble in Stalingrad. So fierce was the fighting that troops rarely exposed themselves to enemy fire in this fashion.

Zhukov had assembled a counterattack force of over one million men, amply armed with new guns, tanks, and aircraft. The next day these were released against the German flanks of the Stalingrad salient.

Destruction of Axis forces

By November 23 the Soviet forces had closed their trap, after which time they concentrated on blocking the efforts of Army Group Don to break through to the Sixth Army captured within. With this done, in January 1943 the Red Army began the systematic destruction of the forces trapped inside Stalingrad. On January 31, having been promoted to field marshal by Hitler just the day before, Paulus gave up; German losses in the Stalingrad pocket amounted to 20 divisions and over 150,000 men. Of the 108,000 who surrendered and were marched into captivity, only 5,000 survived to see the end of the war. Six more divisions, including two Luftwaffe formations, had also been destroyed outside the area of encirclement.

For their part, Germany's allies on the Eastern Front—the Hungarians, Italians, and Romanians—had lost four entire armies, and with them, possibly, any desire they might originally have felt to play an active role in Russia.

AFTER

A major turning point in World War II, the Battle of Stalingrad was the worst defeat the German Army had suffered up to that time and it delivered a heavy blow.

LOW GERMAN MORALE

For three days, German radio broadcast an uninterrupted program of **solemn music**. The Germans **decided not to release the letters** sent by the survivors from Soviet POW camps, which were **intercepted and destroyed**.

SOVIET FUTURE SECURED

The **boost to the Soviets** was immeasurable, giving them the impetus to overcome the Germans again at **Kursk 226–27 ≫** in 1943. They owed their success, in part, to **General**

2 MILLION **The estimated number of casualties to Russian and Axis forces during the 199-day battle.**

Zhukov 228–29 ≫, whose military genius had secured the fate of the Soviet Union. It was Zhukov who later captured **Berlin and the Reichstag in 1945 304–05 ≫**.

Stalingrad

Between August 1942 and February 1943 German and Red Army forces fought in the streets of Stalingrad. Fighting centered on a massive grain silo, the train station, a giant department store, and Mamayev Kurgan hill overlooking the city. Initially German troops had the upper hand but ordered by Stalin to take "not one step back," Red Army soldiers defended their city fiercely.

"13 September. A bad date, our battalion was very unlucky. The katyushas [Soviet rocket launchers] inflicted heavy losses this morning: 27 killed and 50 wounded. The Russians fight with the desperation of wild beasts; they won't allow themselves to be taken prisoner, but instead let you come up close and then they throw grenades. Lieutenant Kraus was killed yesterday, so we have no company commander.

16 September. Our battalion is attacking the grain elevator with tanks. Smoke is pouring out of it. The grain is burning and it seems the Russians inside set fire to it themselves. It's barbaric. The battalion is taking heavy losses. Those are not people in the elevator, they are devils and neither fire nor bullets can touch them."

GERMAN SOLDIER WILLI HOFFMAN, OF THE 94TH INFANTRY DIVISION, ON THE BATTLE FOR THE GRAIN ELEVATOR

"An attack began in the morning [19 September] and lasted 48 hours. The enemy was moving inexorably towards the summit in six files. At times it seemed to us that they were invincible. But the sixth file did not hold out under our fire, and we rushed into the attacks ... Most of the German soldiers appeared to be drunk and threw themselves in a frenzy at the summit. After each round of bombing there would be a moment of dead silence ... But then the hill would come alive again like a volcano, and we would crawl out of the shell holes and put our machine guns to work. The barrels of the guns were red-hot and the water boiled inside them. Our men attacked without waiting for orders ... It was mass heroism. We lost many men as a result of direct hits on shell-holes ... The slopes of the kurgan were completely covered in corpses. In some places you had to move two or three bodies aside to lie down."

RUSSIAN SOLDIER NIKOLAI MAZNITSA, OF THE 95TH RIFLE DIVISION, ON THE DEFENSE OF MAMAYEV KURGAN

A ruined city

The aerial bombardment by the Luftwaffe in August 1942 had left Stalingrad in ruins. Then in September that year, fighting began inside the city, with combatants battling in shattered buildings and factories.

6
THE ALLIES TURN THE TIDE
1943

In the USSR fierce fighting continued as the Germans retreated. Meanwhile the US battled Japan in the Pacific, while Allied air and sea power secured the North Atlantic. The Allies took the offensive, invading Italy and bombing Germany cities.

THE ALLIES TURN THE TIDE

The Allies launch raids to disrupt specific German targets. This includes raids in Northern Europe, as well as on dams and industrial targets in the Rhineland.

Despite constant bombing Albert Speer is able to increase German war production. He moves production underground and further east, out of the range of Allied bombers.

A successful counter-offensive by the Red Army at Kursk effectively ends the possibility of a German victory in the east.

EUROPE

Faeroe Islands (to Denmark)

NORWAY
SWEDEN
FINLAND
North Sea
Baltic Sea
ESTONIA
LATVIA
LITHUANIA
DENMARK
GER.
IRISH FREE STATE
BRITAIN
NETH.
BEL.
LUX.
GERMANY
POLAND
U S S R
FRANCE
SWITZ.
SLOVAKIA
HUNGARY
ROMANIA
YUGOSLAVIA
BULGARIA
Black Sea
ITALY
ALB. (to Italy)
PORTUGAL
SPAIN
Mediterranean Sea
GREECE
TURKEY
DODECANESE
SYRIA
IRAQ
MOROCCO (to France)
TUNISIA (to France)
ALGERIA (to France)
LIBYA
CYPRUS
PALESTINE
EGYPT

ICELAND
NORWAY
SWEDEN
FINLAND
BRITAIN
GERMANY
POLAND
USSR
ATLANTIC OCEAN
FRANCE
ITALY
Black Sea
Caspian Sea
SPAIN
TURKEY
PERSIA
MOROCCO
TUNISIA
SYRIA
IRAQ
AFGHANISTAN
ALGERIA
LIBYA
EGYPT
NEJD (Saudi)
OMAN
NEPA
INDI
RIO DE ORO
FRENCH WEST AFRICA
ANGLO-EGYPTIAN SUDAN
ASIR
YEMEN
ADEN PROTECTORATE
GAMBIA
PORTUGUESE GUINEA
CAMEROONS (British mandate)
SIERRA LEONE
LIBERIA
NIGERIA
FRENCH EQUATORIAL AFRICA
ABYSSINIA
FRENCH SOMALILAND
BRITISH SOMALILAND
ITALIAN SOMALILAND
GOLD COAST
CAMEROONS (French mandate)
UGANDA
KENYA
BELGIAN CONGO
TANGANYIKA (British mandate)
NYASALAND
ANGOLA (to Portugal)
NORTHERN RHODESIA
INDIA
OCEA
SOUTH WEST AFRICA
BECHUANA-LAND
SOUTHERN RHODESIA
PORTUGUESE EAST AFRICA
MADAGASCAR
SWAZILAND
UNION OF SOUTH AFRICA
BASUTOLAND

The French Committee of National Liberation in Algiers is founded by the Free French. It becomes the French Provisional Government-in-Exile on June 2 with de Gaulle at its head.

After victories in North Africa the Allies shift their attention to the invasion of Sicily. Following the conquest of the island in August, the Italian government signs a secret armistice with the Allies.

Roosevelt, Churchill, and Stalin meet in Tehran to discuss the Allied wartime strategy and postwar planning.

The beginning of 1943 marked the geographical high point of Nazism. But in February the remnants of the Sixth Army surrendered at Stalingrad. That summer, Hitler gambled on a massive tank battle to eliminate the Russians from Kursk, but failed. US marines continued the perilous, laborious task of retaking the islands of the Pacific that began in 1942. At first the Japanese defenders fought for every scrap of beach and jungle, but the Americans

dislodged them from one island after another: Woodlark Island, New Georgia, Bougainville, and so on. In August US troops landed on the Island of Kiska only to find that the Japanese had already left.

In the Atlantic, the U-boats had been mauling British convoys since 1940. But in the spring of 1943 Allied sea and air power drove the U-boats out of the North Atlantic: the highway between Britain and the US was now secure, and preparations for D-Day could begin.

1943

Chiang Kai-shek is elected President of the Republic of China. His prestige rose in 1943 when he attended the Cairo Conference with Roosevelt and Churchill.

Allied success against German U-boats forces the Germans to suspend their operations in the Atlantic.

Alaska (to US)

CANADA

NEWFOUNDLAND

MANCHUKUO

LIA

KOREA

JAPAN

CHINA

Formosa

US troops recapture Attu in the Aleutian Islands in May, after their navy defeats the Japanese off the Komandorski Islands on March 24.

UNITED STATES OF AMERICA

ATLANTIC OCEAN

MEXICO

CUBA

DOMINICAN REPUBLIC
VIRGIN ISLANDS
LEEWARD ISLANDS
HAITI

BRITISH HONDURAS

GUATEMALA
EL SALVADOR

HONDURAS
NICARAGUA

WINDWARD ISLANDS
BARBADOS
TRINIDAD AND TOBAGO

Mariana Islands

ENCH
CHINA

PHILIPPINE ISLANDS

GUAM

Marshall Islands

COSTA RICA
PANAMA

VENEZUELA

BRITISH GUIANA
DUTCH GUIANA
FRENCH GUIANA

BRITISH
BORNEO
UNEI

Caroline Islands

COLOMBIA

AWAK

Gilbert Islands

ECUADOR

PACIFIC

BRAZIL

UTCH EAST INDIES

TERRITORY OF NEW GUINEA

Nauru

OCEAN

PERU

PORTUGUESE TIMOR

PAPUA

Solomon Islands

Ellice Islands

BOLIVIA

AUSTRALIA

New Hebrides

WESTERN SAMOA

Fiji

AMERICAN SAMOA

PARAGUAY

New Caledonia

CHILE

URUGUAY

NEW ZEALAND

ARGENTINA

As part of the South Pacific Offensive US Marines land on Bougainville and the resultant victory paves the way for the US attack on the Philippines.

THE WORLD IN DECEMBER 1943

	Axis powers and allies
	Axis conquests to Dec 1943
	Area under Japanese control, Dec 1943
	Allied states
	Allied conquests to Dec 1943
	Neutral states
—	Frontiers Sep 1939

Meanwhile, a smaller invasion of Europe took place. In July 1943 a combined British-American-Canadian force struck at Sicily—"the underbelly of Europe," as Churchill called it—and from there, an assault of the Italian mainland was launched. The underbelly was not as soft as the prime minister had hoped. German forces, bolstered by Italian troops, mounted strong resistance, and clung on to positions far from the Alps and the borders of the Reich.

But the Reich was not beyond reach. Throughout the year German cities were pounded night and day by the airborne artillery of Bomber Command and the US Eighth Air Force. The Ruhr Valley, situated in Germany's industrial heartland, was pummeled night after night; the city of Hamburg was razed to the ground; and Berlin itself became a regularly attainable target for the heavy bombers as the Allies gradually began to take control of the skies.

TIMELINE 1943

German surrender at Stalingrad ▪ Allied victory in Tunisia ▪ **German U-boats withdrawn from the Atlantic** ▪ **Strategic bombing of Germany** ▪ German war production ▪ **Battle of Kursk** ▪ Island-hopping in the Pacific ▪ **Invasion of Italy**

JANUARY	FEBRUARY	MARCH	APRIL	MAY

JANUARY 10
Soviet armies launch Operation Ring, tightening the noose around the surrounded German Sixth Army at Stalingrad.

APRIL 7–18
Japanese air offensive over the Solomons and eastern New Guinea is defeated.

MAY 11
US landings on Attu Island in the Aleutians. The Island is secured by the end of the month.

⌃ US troops on Guadalcanal with captured Japanese flag

JANUARY 27
The United States launches its first air raid on Germany. The cities of Emden and Wihelmshaven are bombed during the day.

FEBRUARY 1–7
Japanese soldiers are successfully evacuated from Guadalcanal.

MARCH 2–4
Battle of the Bismarck Sea. US B-25s sink 12 Japanese ships bound for New Guinea.

⌃ British Avro Lancaster heavy bomber

JANUARY 31
Field Marshal Friedrich Paulus, of the German Sixth Army, disobeys Hitler's instructions and surrenders at Stalingrad.

FEBRUARY 4–7
Convoy SC-118 from Halifax attacked in mid-Atlantic by 20 U-boats. Thirteen merchantmen are sunk.

APRIL 18
Operation Vengeance. Acting on intelligence, US fighters intercept Admiral Isoroku Yamamoto's plane over Bougainville and shoot it down. Yamamoto, the man who planned the Japanese attack on Pearl Harbor, is killed.

MAY 13
Italian 1st Army surrenders in Tunisia. The Allies capture 240,000 Axis soldiers.

≫ US General Dwight D. Eisenhower

FEBRUARY 7
It is announced by President Roosevelt that General Eisenhower is to command Allied operations in North Africa.

MARCH 26–27
Axis troops evacuate the Mareth Line in southern Tunisia, after being attacked frontally and outflanked by Montgomery. They fall back to Wadi Akarit north of Mareth.

MAY 16–17
Dambusters raid. "Bouncing bombs" are used against the Ruhr dams in Germany's industrial heartland. Two of the three dams attacked are breached.

FEBRUARY 14–22
Battle of Kasserine Pass, Tunisia. Rommel and von Arnim combine to force an Allied withdrawal.

≫ British 3.7 in mountain howitzer

MAY 24
Karl Dönitz (commander-in-chief of the German *Kriegsmarine*) withdraws almost all U-boats from the North Atlantic after record losses during the month of May.

≪ The surrender of Field Marshal Paulus at Stalingrad

"We demand from the fascist tyrannies **unconditional surrender** ... they must yield themselves absolutely to our **justice and mercy**."

WINSTON CHURCHILL, JUNE 30, 1943

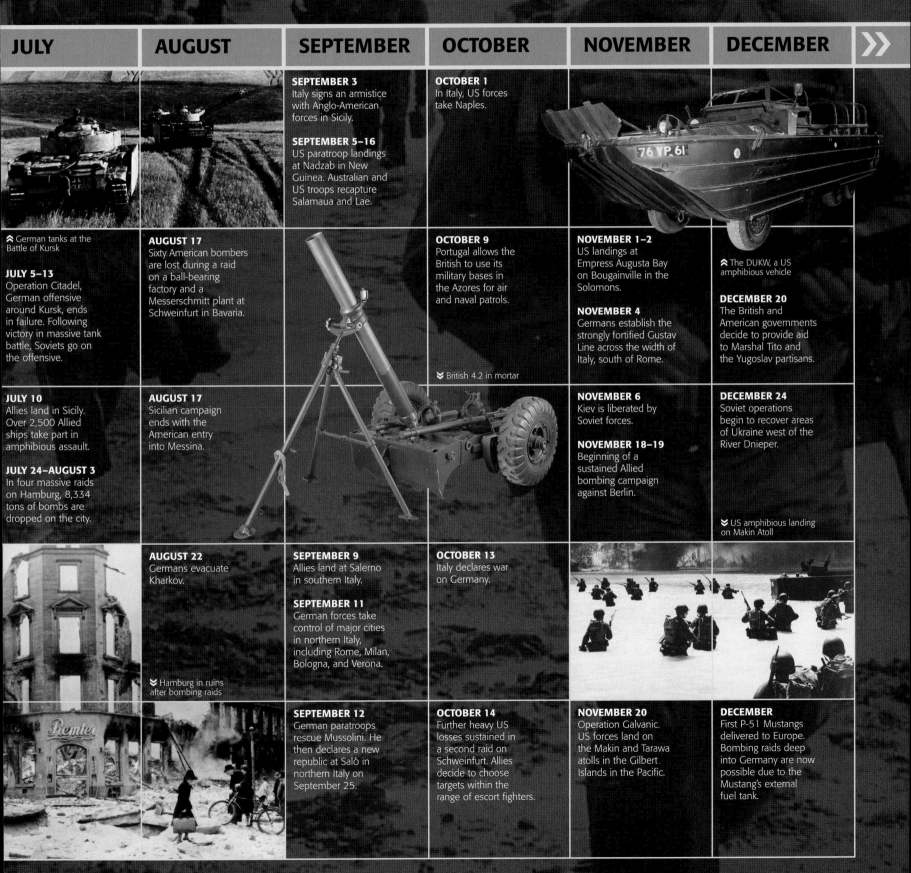

JULY	AUGUST	SEPTEMBER	OCTOBER	NOVEMBER	DECEMBER	»

SEPTEMBER 3
Italy signs an armistice with Anglo-American forces in Sicily.

SEPTEMBER 5–16
US paratroop landings at Nadzab in New Guinea. Australian and US troops recapture Salamaua and Lae.

OCTOBER 1
In Italy, US forces take Naples.

⌃ German tanks at the Battle of Kursk

JULY 5–13
Operation Citadel, German offensive around Kursk, ends in failure. Following victory in massive tank battle, Soviets go on the offensive.

AUGUST 17
Sixty American bombers are lost during a raid on a ball-bearing factory and a Messerschmitt plant at Schweinfurt in Bavaria.

OCTOBER 9
Portugal allows the British to use its military bases in the Azores for air and naval patrols.

⌄ British 4.2 in mortar

NOVEMBER 1–2
US landings at Empress Augusta Bay on Bougainville in the Solomons.

NOVEMBER 4
Germans establish the strongly fortified Gustav Line across the width of Italy, south of Rome.

⌃ The DUKW, a US amphibious vehicle

DECEMBER 20
The British and American governments decide to provide aid to Marshal Tito and the Yugoslav partisans.

JULY 10
Allies land in Sicily. Over 2,500 Allied ships take part in amphibious assault.

JULY 24–AUGUST 3
In four massive raids on Hamburg, 8,334 tons of bombs are dropped on the city.

AUGUST 17
Sicilian campaign ends with the American entry into Messina.

NOVEMBER 6
Kiev is liberated by Soviet forces.

NOVEMBER 18–19
Beginning of a sustained Allied bombing campaign against Berlin.

DECEMBER 24
Soviet operations begin to recover areas of Ukraine west of the River Dnieper.

⌄ US amphibious landing on Makin Atoll

AUGUST 22
Germans evacuate Kharkov.

SEPTEMBER 9
Allies land at Salerno in southern Italy.

SEPTEMBER 11
German forces take control of major cities in northern Italy, including Rome, Milan, Bologna, and Verona.

OCTOBER 13
Italy declares war on Germany.

⌄ Hamburg in ruins after bombing raids

SEPTEMBER 12
German paratroops rescue Mussolini. He then declares a new republic at Salò in northern Italy on September 25.

OCTOBER 14
Further heavy US losses sustained in a second raid on Schweinfurt. Allies decide to choose targets within the range of escort fighters.

NOVEMBER 20
Operation Galvanic. US forces land on the Makin and Tarawa atolls in the Gilbert Islands in the Pacific.

DECEMBER
First P-51 Mustangs delivered to Europe. Bombing raids deep into Germany are now possible due to the Mustang's external fuel tank.

Allied Leaders Plan for Victory

In 1943 it became increasingly clear that the high tide of Nazism was passing, and that—sooner rather than later—the war would end in defeat for Germany. So now the leaders of the Allied nations began to plan for victory, and to stake their separate claims in the postwar world.

International heavyweights
Stalin, Roosevelt, and Churchill met together in one room only twice during the war: first at Tehran, in 1943 (above), and then at Yalta, in 1945, when the war was all but over.

BEFORE

Summit meetings between national leaders were a new tool in the diplomatic armory, and air travel was the innovation that made their engagements possible.

FREQUENT MEETINGS
In no previous conflicts had national leaders, their generals, and diplomats **consulted so frequently** or so regularly.

THE WESTERN ALLIES
Winston Churchill ≪ 86–87 was always eager to journey far and wide to make the British case to his **American and Russian allies.** For him, these trips seem to have been a diversion from the **daily grind of wartime leadership.**

President Roosevelt ≪ 144–45 also saw the benefits of regular face-to-face contact and attended numerous summits with Churchill; he was the **first American president** ever to leave his country during wartime.

JOSEPH STALIN
Sole dictator of his country and deeply suspicious by nature, **Stalin ≪ 66–67** never liked to leave his home turf. He received **Churchill at the Kremlin** in 1942, but was **not persuaded** to meet **Roosevelt and Churchill together** until the end of 1943, at Tehran.

A llied conferences were the board meetings of global war. Many of the significant decisions about the conduct of the war, and about the shape of the world at the end of the war, were thrashed out in face-to-face meetings between representatives of what Winston Churchill liked to call the "Grand Alliance"—the anti-Nazi coalition of Britain, the United States, and the Soviet Union.

The Big Three
Churchill, President Roosevelt, and Soviet premier Joseph Stalin were profoundly different characters, but each considered his own personality to be a valuable asset to his country. Whenever they met, they came to the conference table like poker aficionados, and were prepared to play as skillfully as possible the hands they were dealt by the vagaries of war. 1943 was a year

46 The number of countries that signed the Declaration of the United Nations, each committing to fight until the Axis was defeated, and not to negotiate a separate peace with Germany or Japan.

for conferences. The first talks of the year took place during January in Casablanca. This was a significant venue, chosen to underline the fact that French North Africa was newly in Allied hands. Joseph Stalin was invited but declined to attend. The Red Army was, at the time, engaged in the battle for the possession of Stalingrad, and he felt he could not leave his post.

Churchill turned out to be a good advocate for Soviet war aims at Casablanca, insisting that aiding the USSR must be a priority, as "no investment could pay a better dividend," and that, collectively, the Allies "cannot let Russia down."

Disappointingly from the Russian viewpoint, the British delegation persuaded the Americans that no invasion of Europe could practically be launched that year. D-Day, the long-awaited second front, was officially postponed to the spring of 1944. In the meantime, Roosevelt and Churchill agreed that the best way to take the fight to Hitler was to bomb German cities from the air. This was backed up with some fighting talk: at the end of the

conference, President Roosevelt surprised Churchill by declaring that the Allies' policy could be nothing less than the complete "unconditional surrender" of Nazi Germany. That policy was extended to Fascist Italy at the following meeting between the two leaders, which took place in May in Washington. The Allied invasion of Sicily was about to begin, and the Americans and British were, rather too optimistically, expecting a rapid end to resistance in the Italian peninsula.

In the event, Allied troops had only just ended the conquest of Sicily when Roosevelt and Churchill met again— in Quebec in the middle of August.

An Anglo-American agenda
The Quebec meeting, codenamed Quadrant, was very much an Anglo-American affair. Stalin was not invited; instead, he was one of the subjects under discussion. The American troops on Sicily were, it was noted, almost exactly the same distance from Berlin as the Red Army soldiers battling for the city of Orel. Roosevelt said that he wanted British and American soldiers "to be ready to get to Berlin as soon as

Before the battle
The 1943 invasion of Sicily was to be undertaken by an American army under General Patton, and a British force commanded by General Montgomery, seen here addressing his troops on the eve of the attack.

KEY MOMENT
THE UNITED NATIONS

The United Nations is an international organization born of World War II. It has its origins in the "Atlantic Charter," a document drafted and signed by both Churchill and Roosevelt at the Placentia Bay Conference, in Newfoundland, in 1941. That document called for the collaboration of all countries in the fight against Fascist tyranny. It also expressed a hope for a peace that would give all nations "the means of dwelling safely within their boundaries" and that would allow all the citizens of the world to "live out their lives in freedom from fear and want." These aspirations were officially adopted by the delegates attending the San Francisco Conference in 1945, and at which the United Nations Organization officially came into being.

did the Russians." This comment was the first intimation that the cooperation between the US and the USSR was set to turn into a competition. And it was with the race to Berlin in mind that the two Western leaders set a provisional date for D-Day—May 1, 1944.

But for now, Stalin remained a vital ally. In October the foreign ministers of the Big Three, Anthony Eden for Britain, Cordell Hull for the United States, and Vyacheslav Molotov for the Soviet Union, met in Moscow to prepare the ground for a grand summit to be held at the end of the year. The three men also held the first discussions about the postwar settlement—the opening remarks in a debate that would later dominate the great-power conferences of 1944 and

of the second front. Churchill showed British appreciation of the Red Army's efforts by presenting the Soviet leader with a ceremonial sword, forged from Sheffield steel and inscribed with the words "To the steel-hearted citizens of Stalingrad." Stalin, for his part, could not resist teasing Churchill at dinner with the suggestion that 50,000 German staff officers should be executed as war criminals. Churchill was so outraged at the idea (and he knew Stalin was perfectly capable of it) that he stormed out of the room. Stalin then had to seek Churchill out and insist that he had only been joking.

Stalin was deadly serious, however, when he demanded that a swathe of eastern Poland, roughly tracking the Curzon Line, be surrendered to the Soviet Union—the Poles were to be compensated by the addition of a strip of German territory on their country's western border. Churchill agreed to this westward transposition of Poland's borders—to the subsequent horror

"We ... have **shaped and confirmed** our common policy."
DECLARATION OF THE THREE POWERS, TEHRAN, DECEMBER 1, 1943

Churchill's hot line
This telephone was used by Churchill at RAF headquarters to speak to his commanders. Churchill knew how to use his powers of oratory to inspire his men in the field.

1945. For now, all they decided was that Austria should be detached from the German Reich and reconstituted as a fully independent nation.

Restoration of the prewar world order was on the agenda again in November, when Churchill and Roosevelt held a meeting in Cairo. The main subject of the talks was the war in the Far East. Churchill was clear that one of his primary war aims was to restore Britain's imperial colonies in the Far East: Malaya, Burma, Hong Kong, and Singapore. This was something to which Roosevelt could not agree; still less was he prepared to risk American lives shoring up the British Empire. The issue was still rankling at the end of the month, when the two Western leaders set off for Tehran in Iran.

Stalin comes to the table
The Tehran Conference marked the first time that Churchill and Roosevelt met jointly with Joseph Stalin. The Soviet leader arrived buoyed up by recent Russian victories, and was glad to be given a firm date for the opening

of the Polish government in exile in London. It had been to protect Poland's integrity, after all, that Britain had gone to war in the first place.

Now, the Polish territory ceded in the east—and, in effect, new postwar Poland itself—were to become part of the vast buffer zone that protected the Soviet Union's western border.

AFTER »

The Big Three did not meet again until Yalta in February 1945. By this time, the war was in its final stages, and discussions centered on a settlement for Germany.

THE OCCUPATION OF GERMANY
Britain, the US, France, and the Soviet Union were each to have their **own zones of occupation in Germany 338–39 »**. Berlin, although in the Russian zone, was to be subjected to the **same four-way split**.

SOVIET STRENGTH
Stalin used his pre-eminence to argue that all the republics of the Soviet Union should have seats at the incipient United Nations. Bartered down to **just three seats—**for Russia, Ukraine, and Byelorussia—this was still a huge diplomatic coup for Stalin. The battle lines of the **Cold War 348–49 »** were slowly taking shape.

A foothold in Italy
American troops fought a hard and exhausting campaign in Sicily. Although the soldiers did not yet know it, they and their British comrades were now in a race to get to Berlin before Stalin's Red Army.

BEFORE

At the start of the war, Admiral Karl Dönitz, commander of the U-boat fleet, devised a strategy for gaining control of the Atlantic.

AN ATTACK ON BRITISH SHIPPING
Dönitz estimated that, if Germany could sink **750,000 tons** of British shipping per month, then the country would be brought to the brink

In June 1942 the German U-boat force sunk 637,000 tons of British shipping—a greater total than in any previous (or subsequent) month. The kill rate amounted to 359 tons for each German submarine at sea.

of starvation and would have to **sue for peace**. He reckoned that he required **300 submarines** to achieve this, but over the first winter of the war a mere **27 were available**. The result was that the U-boats lost their first and best chance to **sever the transatlantic link**, while Britain stood alone against Nazi Germany and **the Royal Navy was at its weakest ≪ 118–19**.

SCENE SET FOR A SHOWDOWN
By 1943 Dönitz had **all the U-boats he needed**. In January, ominously for the Allies, Hitler appointed him head of the entire German Navy (the *Kriegsmarine*). The stage was now set for a **decisive clash** between German U-boats and the British convoys in the North Atlantic.

Showdown in the Atlantic

The fight for control of the Atlantic Ocean, which had begun in the first days of the war, reached a climax and a turning point in the spring of 1943. German U-boats, which had preyed on Allied shipping for years, suddenly found that they were no longer the hunters, but the hunted.

The Battle of the Atlantic was a ruthless, seaborne game of cat and mouse. The aim of the Allied convoys was to slip across the ocean undetected, while the goal of the U-boat wolfpacks was to destroy as many ships as they could. Both sides measured success or failure on the same scale: the volume of tonnage of shipping dispatched, month by month, to the bottom of the sea.

German supremacy
Tactically, the Germans had the upper hand for more than three years. Their naval intelligence had broken the code of the British merchant navy, so they often had a good idea when a convoy was due. Armed with this information, the submarines would track back and forth across the shipping lanes. When a captain detected a convoy, he radioed to all the other U-boats in the area. The assembled wolfpack would then attack at night and in force, slipping through the protective cordon of escort ships

and torpedoing the freight-carrying ships at will. The U-boats would often be far astern of the convoy before the armed escort could react.

By June 1942 the damage caused to British shipping by the German U-boat force—supplemented by surface ships and mines—had reached a record high, and the rate of loss was unsustainable for the Allies. Churchill met President Roosevelt at the beginning of 1943. The two leaders agreed that the Atlantic must be their main priority for that year. All other war aims depended

The charge was controlled by water pressure. When it reached a preset depth, a trigger inside the charge detonated the explosive.

Surge tank

Firing mechanism

An exploding cartridge inside this chamber forced gas rapidly into the larger expansion chamber, driving up a piston and hurling the depth charge into the air.

The Mark VII depth charge weighed 410 lb (185 kg) and carried explosive weighing 396 lb (179 kg). It sank 10 ft (3 m) per second and had a maximum operational depth of 300 ft (91 m).

A hydraulic arrestor was mounted on each side of the expansion chamber. These stopped the arbor (the tube on which the depth charge was mounted) from flying off with the depth charge.

Expansion chamber

High water
U-boats could travel twice as fast on the surface of the ocean as under water. Above the waves, however, they were much more vulnerable to detection and attack. The submarines generally remained below sea level during the hours of daylight.

The depth charge was the typical armament of British anti-submarine warships. One great advantage of this as a weapon was that the launchers could be mounted on the deck of almost any ship with ease.

Mark IV depth charge launcher
Depth charge launchers similar to this model had been in use since World War I. A primitive alternative to such launchers was simply to roll charges off the back of the ship like barrels.

on being able to move men, material, and food by sea from the US to Britain—and also from Britain to the Soviet Union. Military and scientific experts in Britain and the United States were ordered to look at ways of countering the Germans' superiority. An intensive effort led to a series of tactical advances and technological innovations that were to gradually tip the balance of the battle away from the Germans and back toward the Allies.

New strategies for the Allies

One simple, yet effective, procedure emerged from a study of the figures for shipping losses. An analysis conducted late in 1942 threw up the surprising fact that the wolfpacks generally sunk the same number of ships in each attack—no matter how many targets they had. The obvious response was to make the convoys as large as possible: better to sacrifice six ships for every hundred that survived, than six for every fifty.

The Allies also realized that air attack was an effective deterrent. The German submarine commanders preferred to operate inside the so-called "air gap"—the area of ocean that was out of reach of long-range planes. Measures were taken to shrink the air gap and so limit the U-boats' area of operations. Aircraft carriers were attached to the convoy escorts; the planes flying ahead of the ships as scouts. A number of VLR ("very long range") B-24 Liberators also became available to Coastal Command.

Dramatic change of fortune
This chart shows the losses to both British shipping and German U-boats in the Atlantic Ocean from 1942–43. An almost complete reversal occurred from the start of 1943, when the British adopted a series of new tactics.

> **72** The total number of kills credited to some 40 B-24 Liberators that were requisitioned by RAF Coastal Command in a bid to weaken the German U-boats during April and May of 1943.

The increase in Allied air power was supplemented by ingenious inventions such as the Leigh Light, an airborne radar that coordinated with a strong searchlight that suddenly illuminated a targeted U-boat as a plane—a Liberator or a Wellington bomber—came in to attack. The Leigh Light now meant that U-boats were no longer safe on the surface at night. Improvements in Allied sonar (the underwater radar known as Asdic) made it easier to see the enemy below the surface too: the depth as well as the position of a submerged U-boat could now be ascertained.

What is more, Allied planes and ships were better armed in 1943 than ever before. One of the new weapons was the "hedgehog," a salvo of 24 mortar bombs that was fired forward from a ship's bows. A bomb exploded on impact, setting off the other 23, and

Deep impact
The explosion of a depth charge was less deadly than it looked, because its force was greatly dissipated under water. What is more, the turbulence caused by the blast rendered sonar ineffective for up to 15 minutes.

increasing the probability of a kill. This deadly device, was far more effective than the depth charges used in the early days of the Atlantic battle. Aircraft now flew into battle equipped with homing torpedoes that could seek out a U-boat beneath the waves. The U-boats were no longer invisible: they could be sought out and destroyed.

Turning the tide
These technological innovations had an impact all at once, in the spring of 1943. Suddenly there was a complete reversal of fortunes: in March 82 ships were sunk for the loss of 12 U-boats; in April 39 ships were lost to 15 U-boats; and in "Black May," as the U-boat crews called it, the Allies lost 34 ships in the Atlantic, while 43 U-boats—a fifth of the fleet—were destroyed. From now on, instead of dodging U-boats, the convoys and their escorts went looking for them, knowing they were stronger. Dönitz, for his part, saw that he had been defeated by the ruthless, inexorable arithmetic of attrition. He simply could not afford to take the losses and withdrew his battered U-boats from the Atlantic.

Spine of the hedgehog
A single hedgehog spigot mortar could sink a German U-boat. They were launched 24 at a time, and exploded on contact rather than at a set depth, so any explosion indicated a hit.

The U-boats returned to the Atlantic in the fall of 1943, but they never regained their former position of supremacy.

MORE GERMAN LOSSES
The Germans were **never able to sink** enough British ships to imperil the supply lines between the US and Britain, and **the price paid** in lost U-boats and crews sunk rose at **an inflationary rate** throughout 1944. This was due in part to

SQUID DEPTH CHARGE LAUNCHER

increasingly sophisticated weaponry such as the "squid," a **three-barreled depth charge launcher.** It fired depth charges that **automatically exploded** at a depth taken from sonar readings.

ALLIES PLAN FOR D-DAY
The fact that the sea routes were now **relatively secure** made it possible for the Allies to build up an invasion force in Britain, and so **to prepare seriously for D-Day 254–61 ≫**. (Significantly, the German U-boats **did not manage to sink** a single US troop ship during the entire war.)

Admiral Dönitz hoped that Germany's **new and, now faster, submarines** (Types XII and XIII) would turn the battle at sea back in his favor, but by the time they came into service, in 1945, it was **too late for them make a difference.**

ADMIRAL DÖNITZ

THE PRICE OF DEFEAT
When **the end of the war was declared in 1945 306–07 ≫**, 156 German U-boat crews surrendered to the Allied forces; a further 221 German captains preferred to **scuttle their ships**, consigning them to the depths, rather than bow down and **hand them over** to the Allies.

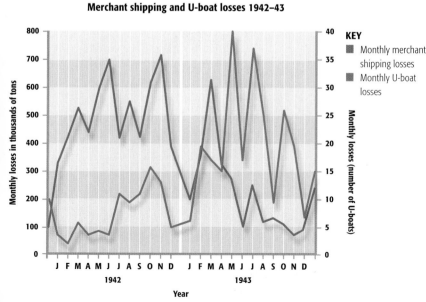

Merchant shipping and U-boat losses 1942–43

KEY
- ■ Monthly merchant shipping losses
- ■ Monthly U-boat losses

(Left axis: Monthly losses in thousands of tons — 0, 100, 200, 300, 400, 500, 600, 700, 800)
(Right axis: Monthly losses (number of U-boats) — 0, 5, 10, 15, 20, 25, 30, 35, 40)
(X axis: J F M A M J J A S O N D 1942 — J F M A M J J A S O N D 1943)
Year

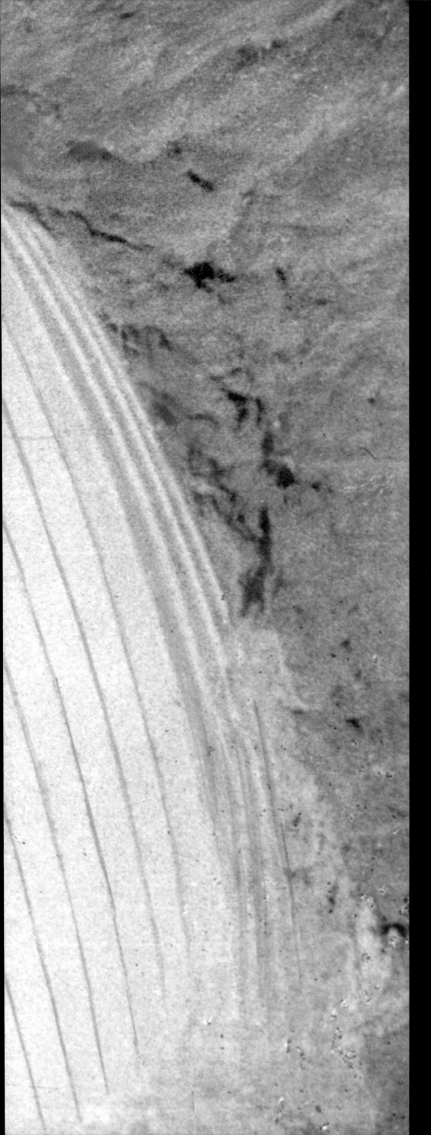

Sinking of merchant ships

Allied merchant shipping transported food, fuel, weapons, troops, and passengers throughout the war. Merchant ships, which were crewed by civilians, varied from luxury liners through oil tankers and tramp steamers. Crossing the Atlantic either solo or in convoy, they were vulnerable to attacks by U-boats and Luftwaffe. Some 30,000 merchant seamen lost their lives during the war.

"... at about 9 o'clock I decided to turn in for the night and was partially undressed when there was a terrific explosion from the starboard side which was immediately followed by another. I jumped out of the bunk, rushed to the cabin door, which came away in my hands, saw that the mess was ablaze, and started to run down the alley way. I saw the apprentice ... We rushed back into my cabin, smacked the door back into position to prevent the fire entering, undid the thumb-screws to the porthole, opened it up ... and ran to the focs'lehead ... By this time the ship was ablaze from bridge to stern, the whole sky being lit up by the flames ... I saw the starboard life boat had crashed into the sea but the port life boat was still hanging on the davits ... As we were running along the foredeck to the bridge, this boat also crashed into the sea ... We had to jump from the shelter deck to the falls about 6 feet [1.82m] and slide down them. Three other men threw themselves into the boat in desperation ... I ... noticed men running round the poop who were on fire, throwing themselves into the sea which was itself on fire ... We were about 40ft [12m] from the ship's side when the 3rd officer came running along the fore-deck ... He dived over the side and we picked him up ... Slowly the ship drew ahead of us whilst we struggled to keep clear of burning sea. We heard some screams for help and rowed over and pulled out of the water a fireman who was terribly burned ... we heard two other cries for help and found in the water an able seaman ... shortly after we picked up a pumpman ... We tried to pursue the ship, looking for survivors, but it was an impossible task because those in the boat were so gravely injured and collapsing, leaving only three to row against the wind and sea ... The third officer and I attended to the wounded and were horrified at the extent of their injuries. There seemed no further signs of life anywhere so we hoisted sail and set course for Trinidad ... "

CHIEF OFFICER CAPTAIN T.D. FINCH, ONE OF SIX SURVIVORS FROM THE OIL TANKER SAN EMILIANO, SUNK BY U-BOAT ON AUGUST 9, 1942

Abandoning ship

Survivors from the merchant ship *Laconia*, which was sunk on September 12, 1942, managed to cling to a upturned lifeboat for several days before being rescued by a French ship. Sometimes U-boat crews assisted merchant seamen forced to abandon their ships.

1 TELEPHONE OPERATOR'S BADGE (GERMANY)

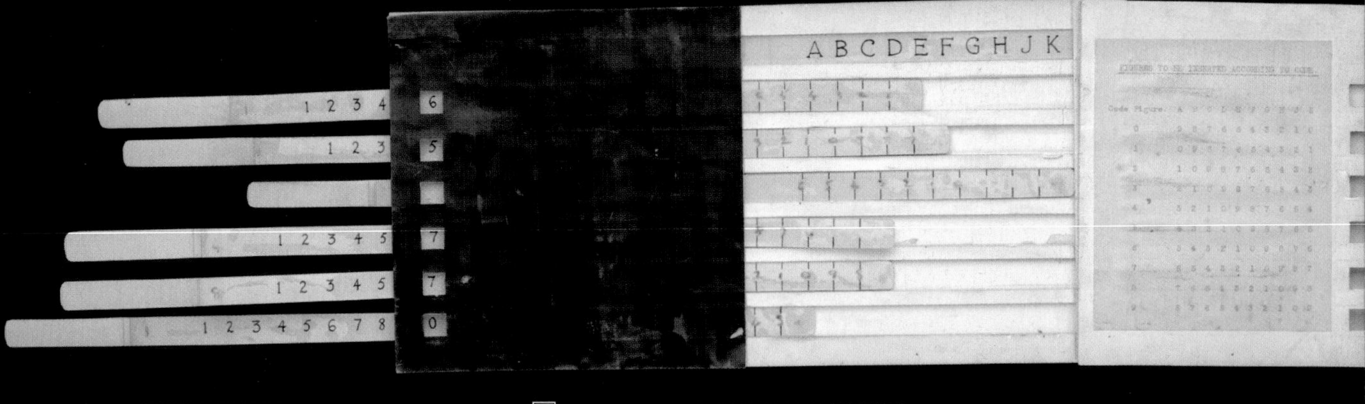

ABCDEFGHJK

2 TACTICAL ENCRYPTION WALLET (BRITAIN)

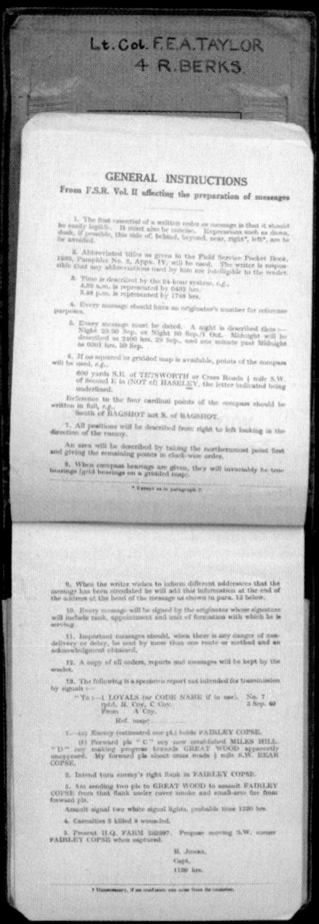

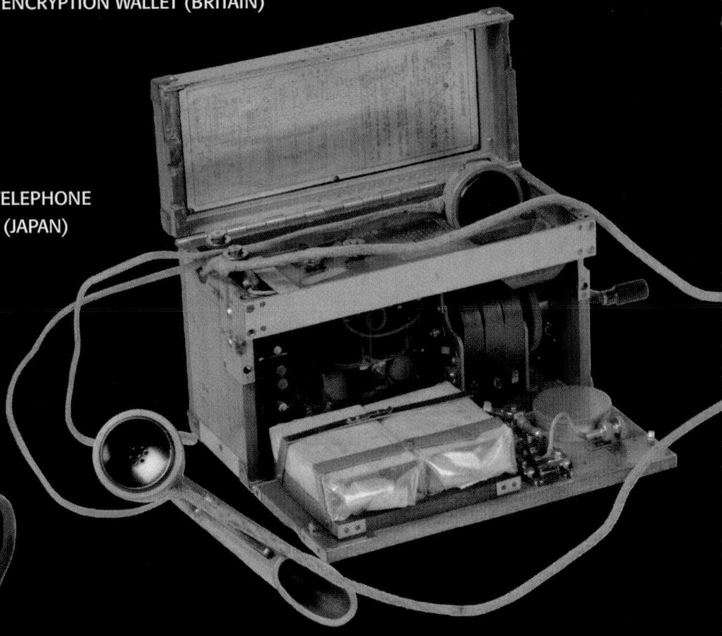

5 FIELD TELEPHONE MODEL 92 (JAPAN)

3 FIELD MESSAGE BOOK (BRITAIN)

4 EE-8 FIELD TELEPHONE (US)

Communications

In World War II efficient and secure communications could make the difference between victory and defeat. Top-level strategic communications were routinely enciphered, and adversaries would attempt to crack hostile codes and ciphers.

1 Badge of a German telephone operator, whose function in the German armed forces was usually fulfilled by a noncommissioned officer. **2** British tactical encryption wallet. The device enabled sliding strips to be aligned, in a specified but frequently changed sequence, to enable low-level information like map references to be encrypted and decrypted. **3** Field message book. This British booklet furnished commanders with a message pad, whose covering pages, seen here, gave a reminder of the army's rules on message-writing. **4** This American EE-8 field telephone was widely used for battlefield communications throughout the war. It had a range of 10–15 miles (16–24 km). **5** Japanese field telephone model 92, used for local operations. This example was captured by the Allies during the advance on Mandalay in Burma. **6** British pigeon

parachute. Thousands of homing pigeons were parachuted into France. The hope was that anti-Nazi citizens would send them back with useful information. **7** Mark II suitcase radio that was used by Oluf Reed Olsen, a Norwegian agent working for Britain in occupied Norway. Radios were a key tool of resistance movements in occupied Europe. **8** British Type A Mark III radio, the smallest transceiver of the war, and one of the best. It could make contact over a distance of 500 miles (800 km). **9** German Kryha cipher machine developed to encrypt commercially sensitive information. Its cipher was easily broken, but it was nevertheless used by the diplomatic corps of several nations, including Germany. **10** This US Converter M-209 cipher machine could fit in a case about the size of a lunchbox, and was secure enough for tactical use on the battlefield.

6 PIGEON PARACHUTE (BRITA

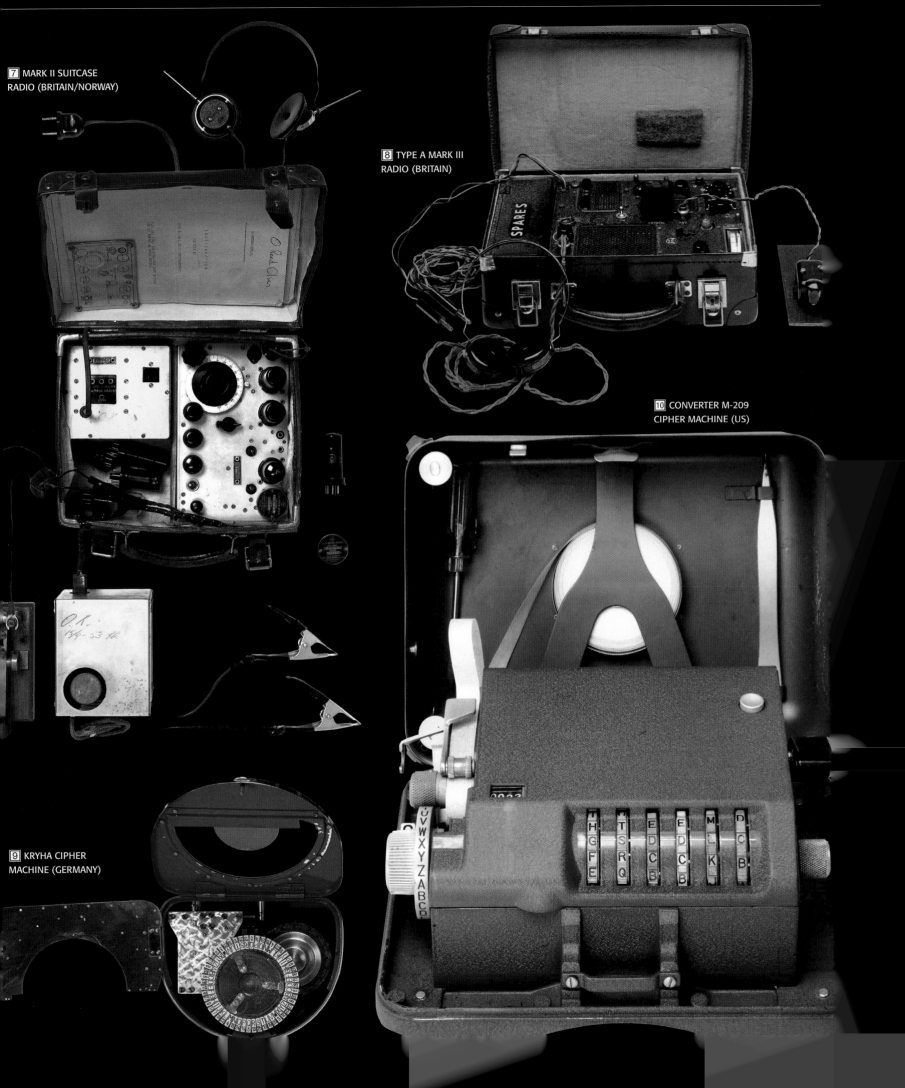

7 MARK II SUITCASE
RADIO (BRITAIN/NORWAY)

8 TYPE A MARK III
RADIO (BRITAIN)

10 CONVERTER M-209
CIPHER MACHINE (US)

9 KRYHA CIPHER
MACHINE (GERMANY)

The Invasion of Sicily

The Allied leaders decided to follow up victory in North Africa by invading Sicily and then mainland Italy. This succeeded in knocking Italy out of the war but profiting from this success was not simple. Britain and the US had different ideas about how to take the Mediterranean campaign forward.

The Allied invasion of Sicily in July 1943 was codenamed Operation Husky and involved air and sea landings on an huge scale, with more troops engaged than in the Normandy invasion the following year. Some 150,000 soldiers took part in the initial landings, with over 3,000 ships and landing craft and around 4,000 aircraft.

The landings

This mighty blow fell upon a poorly prepared enemy. Allied deception plans convinced the Axis leaders that Greece or Sardinia were likelier targets for an invasion. Distrust and dislike between the Nazis and Italians also hampered preparations. Mussolini limited the Axis forces in Sicily and insisted that they remain under the command of Italian general, Alfredo Guzzoni.

Allied commanders nonetheless approached the operation with caution. The American Seventh Army and the

Italian prisoners
Truckloads of Italian prisoners fill the streets of Messina as Sicily falls to the Allies on August 17, 1943. The demoralized Italians were often content to surrender, but their German allies fought with skill and tenacity.

British Eighth Army were ordered to land on adjoining stretches of coast on the southeast of the island. This tactic would enable them to support one another against any counterattack. The operation was under the overall command of General Eisenhower, with Patton leading the American ground forces and Montgomery the British.

Heading for Sicily on July 9, the Allied force ran into a summer storm that came close to aborting the entire operation. For troops on board landing craft, many facing their first experience of combat, seasickness compounded anxiety. The bad weather added to the difficulties experienced by troops of the British 1st Airborne and US 82nd Airborne Divisions, carrying out the

were put off guard, believing no landings could be expected in such terrible conditions.

Beginning on the morning of July 10 the Allies came ashore with only light casualties. There was an awkward moment when first Italian tanks and then German Panzers attacked. But the Axis armor was seen off by a combination of naval gunfire and the use of captured Italian

4.2 in mortar

Both British and American infantry received fire support from 4.2 in mortars during the invasions of Sicily and Italy. This is the British version.

> **100,000** The number of German and Italian troops successfully evacuated from Sicily to mainland Italy in August 1943 despite the Allied air and naval supremacy.

first Allied airborne operation of the war. Sent in by parachute and glider to land behind the beaches on the night of July 9/10, the paratroopers were widely scattered and many of the gliders came down disastrously in the sea. Yet the freak weather did not work entirely to the Allies' disadvantage. The scattered airborne troops spread confusion in the enemy rear and coastal forces

BEFORE

The Axis defeat in North Africa in spring 1943 opened the way for the Allies to strike across the Mediterranean with an invasion of the Italian island of Sicily.

CASABLANCA CONFERENCE
Meeting at the conference in Casablanca in January 1943 **‹‹ 202–03**, Churchill and Roosevelt discussed their future strategy. **Churchill favored an advance through Italy**, striking at what he called "the soft underbelly of Europe." **The US wanted operations in the Mediterranean to be limited** in order not to divert resources from the **planned invasion of northern France**. But they eventually agreed that victory in North Africa would be followed by an invasion of Sicily. **The capture of the island** would make sea communications through the Mediterranean more secure and **might drive Italy out of the war**.

DEFEAT IN THE DESERT
In mid-May 1943 the Axis forces in North Africa, by then cornered in Tunisia, surrendered **‹‹ 186–87**. **The loss of a quarter of a million German and Italian troops,** many sent into Tunisia by Hitler in a late, futile attempt to stave off defeat, **left the defenses of other Axis-held territories** in the Mediterranean, including those on Sicily, **severely depleted**.

> "When we meet the enemy **we will kill him.** We will show him **no mercy**."
>
> US GENERAL GEORGE S. PATTON, JULY 1943

Barrel

Sight mounting

The unrifled barrel of the British mortar contrasted with the rifled barrel of the American M2. Both were simple and rugged weapons that proved highly effective in combat.

Elevation control

The 4.2 in mortar was derived from the British Stokes mortar of World War I. Originally designed for firing smoke shells, the mortars were adapted to fire high-explosive fragmentation rounds.

Tripod support

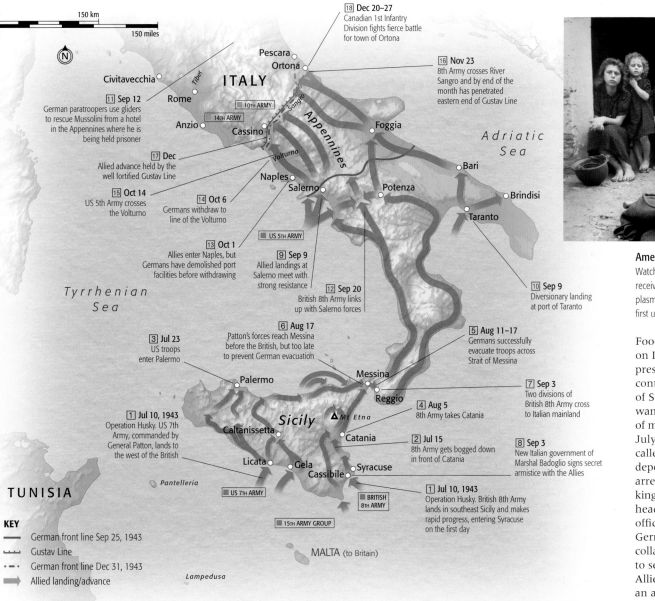

Map: The campaign in Sicily and Italy, 1943

18 Dec 20–27
Canadian 1st Infantry Division fights fierce battle for town of Ortona

16 Nov 23
8th Army crosses River Sangro and by end of the month has penetrated eastern end of Gustav Line

11 Sep 12
German paratroopers use gliders to rescue Mussolini from a hotel in the Appennines where he is being held prisoner

17 Dec
Allied advance held by the well fortified Gustav Line

15 Oct 14
US 5th Army crosses the Volturno

14 Oct 6
Germans withdraw to line of the Volturno

13 Oct 1
Allies enter Naples, but Germans have demolished port facilities before withdrawing

9 Sep 9
Allied landings at Salerno meet with strong resistance

12 Sep 20
British 8th Army links up with Salerno forces

10 Sep 9
Diversionary landing at port of Taranto

6 Aug 17
Patton's forces reach Messina before the British, but too late to prevent German evacuation

5 Aug 11–17
Germans successfully evacuate troops across Strait of Messina

3 Jul 23
US troops enter Palermo

7 Sep 3
Two divisions of British 8th Army cross to Italian mainland

4 Aug 5
8th Army takes Catania

1 Jul 10, 1943
Operation Husky. US 7th Army, commanded by General Patton, lands to the west of the British

2 Jul 15
8th Army gets bogged down in front of Catania

8 Sep 3
New Italian government of Marshal Badoglio signs secret armistice with the Allies

1 Jul 10, 1943
Operation Husky. British 8th Army lands in southeast Sicily and makes rapid progress, entering Syracuse on the first day

KEY
— German front line Sep 25, 1943
⊢ Gustav Line
–·– German front line Dec 31, 1943
⇒ Allied landing/advance

American medic in action
Watched by local people, a wounded American private receives blood plasma on Sicily in August 1943. Blood plasma transfusions were a new life-saving technique first used by US forces earlier in the war.

Food shortages, Allied bombing raids on Italian cities, and the unpopular presence of German troops all contributed to unrest. The invasion of Sicily was a final blow to the Duce's waning prestige. He had lost the support of many of his closest associates. On July 24 the Grand Council of Fascism called on King Victor Emmanuel to depose their leader. Mussolini was arrested and taken to Abruzzo and the king appointed Marshal Pietro Badoglio head of government. Italy remained officially committed to fight alongside Germany, but its war effort was collapsing and the government began to seek a separate peace with the Allies—the two eventually signed an armistice on September 3, 1943.

anti-tank guns. The British then quickly took the port of Syracuse almost without a fight, and Montgomery was tasked with advancing up the east of Sicily while Patton defended his flank—a lesser role to which he did not take kindly. Montgomery's advance north soon bogged down as the Germans brought in more troops, demoting the predominantly unenthusiastic Italians to a subsidiary role. It was not long before General Patton seized the opportunity to take over the initiative, staging a triumphal progress up the west of Sicily to Palermo, his path cleared by local Mafiosi whose contempt toward Mussolini made them greet the US soldiers as liberators. But the Germans were able to pull back in good order around the key port of Messina, from

which they succeeded in evacuating almost all of their 40,000 troops to the Italian mainland, along with most of their equipment and some 60,000 of their Italian allies.

Mussolini deposed

Patton took a fierce competitive pleasure in seeing his forces enter the port of Messina on the morning of August 17 hours ahead of the British forces. Yet for the Allies it had been a wasted opportunity. Bolder use of their command of sea and air could have trapped the crucial German divisions. Their escape contributed greatly to the hard fighting the Allies would face later in the campaign on the Italian mainland.

The invasion of Sicily was, however, wholly successful in its psychological impact upon the Italian Fascist regime. Since the spring Mussolini had been facing mounting popular discontent.

The wheeled baseplate on the British 4.2 in mortar was designed to make it easier to move around. This was a feature that was not found on the equivalent American weapon.

Barrel rest for traveling

The campaign in Sicily and Italy, 1943
The Allies conquered Sicily in July–August 1943 and invaded the Italian mainland in September. The Germans mounted a stubborn defense, holding the Allied advance south of Rome until summer 1944.

AFTER

After capturing Sicily, the Allies landed on the Italian mainland 212–13 ≫. On September 8, 1943, the Italian government announced its surrender, but the Germans took over the defense of Italy.

MUSSOLINI'S REPUBLIC
Four days after the Italian government announced its surrender, **German paratroopers freed Mussolini** from captivity. Forces loyal to his Italian Social Republic **fought alongside the Germans** until the end of the war. Mussolini himself was caught and **executed by Italian partisans** in April 1945 306–07 ≫.

A COSTLY CAMPAIGN
Italy did not turn out to be the soft target anticipated by Churchill. Foul weather, harsh terrain, and determined and resourceful German defense made **every advance costly and difficult**. Allied forces took until June 1944 to reach Rome 252–53 ≫.

Held by the Gustav Line

Napoleon once said that because Italy was shaped like a boot the way into it was from the top. Allied troops in 1943–44 would have understood what he meant. Harsh terrain, bitter weather, and ferocious German defense meant some of the hardest fighting of the war for the "D-Day dodgers in sunny Italy."

The Italian campaign in the second half of 1943 was an excruciating disappointment for the Allies. In August the situation seemed ripe for major gains. Italy's newly installed government of Marshal Badoglio was secretly seeking an armistice, while publicly continuing to assure Germany of its commitment to the war. The Allied commanders planned landings in mainland Italy to coincide with an

3,618 The number of bridges built by British engineers in the course of the Italian campaign. As the Allied forces advanced they repeatedly had to attack across fast-flowing rivers.

Italian surrender. Both the political and military moves were, however, too slow to catch the Germans off balance. While the Allies organized their invasion forces, German troops took up key positions in Italy, so that they could

Neapolitan welcome
Italian civilians in Naples run forward to greet Allied soldiers entering the city on October 1, 1943. The population had staged an uprising against the Germans, forcing them to withdraw before the Allies arrived.

> "The **stagnation** of the whole campaign on the Italian front is becoming **scandalous** …"
>
> PRIME MINISTER WINSTON CHURCHILL, TO THE BRITISH CHIEFS OF STAFF, DECEMBER 1943

take over the defense of the peninsula if the Italians decided to surrender.

On September 3, 1943, Montgomery's Eighth Army crossed the Straits of Messina from Sicily into Calabria unopposed. On the same day the Italian government signed an armistice—in effect an unconditional surrender. But the surrender was not made public until September 8, the announcement timed to coincide with a second wave of Allied landings, on

beaches in the Gulf of Salerno. Reacting swiftly, German forces under General Karl Student occupied Rome, although failing to capture Marshal Badoglio and his government, which had fled to Brindisi.

The Salerno operation went badly. A US and a British corps, comprising General Mark Clark's US Fifth Army with Montgomery's Eight Army, went ashore in the early hours of the morning of September 9. The Germans under General

« BEFORE

In summer 1943 the capture of Sicily and the collapse of the Fascist regime in Italy offered the Allies a golden opportunity for rapid advances on the Italian mainland.

LANDINGS IN SICILY
Between July 10 and August 17 1943 Allied forces invaded and captured Sicily **« 210–11**. They failed, however, to trap **German forces**

The Allies fighting in the Italian campaign in 1943 included Poles, Indians, Algerians, Moroccans, French, Canadians, and New Zealanders, as well as British and Americans.

defending the island. This enabled the Germans to **withdraw with their equipment intact** to the Italian mainland. **British and American leaders had already fought** over the plans and objectives for the Sicilian operation. **Further disputes would follow** as the Italian campaign developed.

FALL OF MUSSOLINI
On July 24 Italian Fascist leader **Benito Mussolini was deposed** and replaced as head of the Italian government by **Marshal Pietro Badoglio**, who had opposed Italy's alliance with Nazi Germany.

Heinrich von Vietinghoff used limited forces to such good effect that four days later the Allied troops were still trapped in a shallow beachhead—by when, according to their original plan, they should have been in occupation of Naples. With German Panzers thrusting to within one mile of the beaches in places, the Allies had to mount a major reinforcement effort to save the landings from disaster.

New German defenses

By September 15 Vietinghoff had to accept that the landings could not be repulsed, but he was able to stage a fighting withdrawal to defensive positions further north. Allied troops finally entered Naples on October 1, greeted as liberators by a population that had evicted the Germans in sharp fighting three days earlier.

The Italian defection from the Axis created a confused military and political situation. Tens of thousands of Italian troops surrendered to their former allies and were carried off as prisoners to Germany, where they spent the rest of the war providing forced labor for the Reich. On the Greek island of Cephalonia, where Italian troops resisted the German forces, 1,600 Italians died in the ensuing fighting and 5,000 more were shot in cold blood after being taken as prisoners of war.

Italy joins the Allies

On October 13 Marshal Badoglio's government declared war on Germany. But by then Benito Mussolini had been freed to set up his Italian Social Republic based at Salò on Lake Garda in northern Italy. Italians loyal to the Badoglio government subsequently fought with the Allies, while Mussolini supporters continued to fight alongside the Germans, and Italian partisans

The Allies eventually fought their way to Rome in June 1944, only to face more stubborn German resistance further north.

STRUGGLE FOR MONTE CASSINO
From mid-January to mid-May 1944 the **Allies fought four battles** before they dislodged the Germans from the heights of Monte Cassino.

ANZIO LANDINGS
On January 22, 1944, the Allies carried out **landings at Anzio** between the Gustav Line and Rome. Contrary to plan, they remained **hemmed in to their beachhead** until May.

FALL OF ROME
Allied forces entered Rome on June 4, 1944 **252–53 »**. The **Germans pulled back northward to the Gothic Line** and other defensive positions between Florence and Bologna, holding them over the following winter.

German motorbike
The Zündapp K800 was the standard German military motorbike of World War II. It was much admired by Allied troops when they captured examples in Italy.

fought against both Mussolini and the German occupation forces. The Allies, progress northward in the last three months of 1943 was grimly described by British General Harold Alexander as "slogging up Italy." The mountainous terrain well suited the defensive strategy pursued by Field Marshal Albert Kesselring. The Germans fell back on a series of fortified lines, the most formidable of which was the Gustav Line which stretched across Italy along the Garigliano and Sangro rivers, with Monte Cassino as its key strongpoint. By December the Allied forces were stuck in a costly struggle for these fortified positions, with no immediate prospect of a breakthrough.

Landing at Salerno
US infantry wade ashore during the Salerno landings in September 1943. The first wave of US troops came under heavy fire as they approached the beaches.

KEY MOMENT

MUSSOLINI ESCAPES

Arrested by the Italians after his fall from power in July 1943, Benito Mussolini was held in a hotel at Gran Sasso, high in the Apennine mountains. On September 12 ,1943, a German force, commanded by Waffen-SS officer, Otto Skorzeny, crash-landed gliders on to the mountain. Mussolini was flown off in a light aircraft. The bold rescue was a propaganda coup for the Nazis and enabled them to install Mussolini as puppet ruler of northern Italy, heading the Italian Social Republic.

Bombing Germany by Night

In 1943 the RAF waged three separate campaigns against Germany. First the bombers went for the industrial heartland of the Ruhr; then Hamburg was hit, becoming the first city to endure a "firestorm"; and later on in the year, the bombers turned their destructive power against the German capital, Berlin.

With the bleak irony of fighting men everywhere, the crews of RAF Bomber Command referred to the Ruhr as "Happy Valley." The area surrounding the Ruhr River was a densely populated belt of grimy cities, with Essen, Dortmund, Duisburg, and Bochum, making up the industrial engine of the nation. The significance of the Ruhr made it an obvious target—especially since the region's westerly location placed it well inside bomber range. But the Germans were keenly aware how vulnerable the area was to attack and from the very beginning, the entire valley was forested with anti-aircraft guns and was alive with searchlights.

The Battle of the Ruhr began in March 1943, and lasted until July. The first target was Essen, a city full of essential steel mills and armaments factories. Pathfinder Mosquitoes preceded the main wave, dropping colored flares to stake out the attack area. They were followed by waves of Stirlings, Wellingtons, and Lancasters, which

High flyer
The Lancaster was much-loved by the crews that flew in it. Nicknamed the "Lankie," it had a high ceiling of 20,000 ft (6,000 m), which made it a difficult target for German fighters.

unloaded their bombs over the city center. About 60 ha (160 acres) of Essen were flattened. This pattern was repeated across the Ruhrland night after night, and even cities as far away as Munich and Stuttgart were attacked. This ringing of the changes was a tactical necessity, since to return to the same places night after night would have allowed the Luftwaffe to amass too many of its guns and fighter planes in the target area. As it was, the flak was sometimes so thick that, as the cliché went, "you could have got out and walked on it."

Keeping the Germans guessing about the target had a downside for the Allies, too. Every night of respite gave the Nazis time to clear up the battered factories and get them working again. The only way to put them permanently out of action was to bomb them incessantly.

Firestorm in Hamburg

However, the RAF simply did not have enough planes to bomb the factories non-stop. But Britain's bombing strength was growing rapidly and though aircraft losses were high, new ones were coming on stream in even greater numbers. The

total availability of RAF bombers on any given day rose from less than 6[?] in February to almost 800 in Augu[st]

On July 24 the might of Britain's bomber fleet was unleashed on Hamburg. The tactics used were the same as before: the first wave would drop high-explosive bombs to blow out doors and windows; subsequent waves would drop incendiaries, ligh[t] legions of rapidly-spreading fires. T[he] scale of this attack was vast. On the first day, 2,300 tons of bomb[s] fell in little over an hou[r,] five times more ordnan[ce] than the heaviest air ra[id] on London. The fires lit the RAF were fanned by strong wind, and stoked by the tinder-dry conditions. Single bla[zes] soon merged to form an inferno[.]

The raids were reprised three days [later,] and this time the flames caused a gi[ant] updraught that sucked in air to crea[te a] hot gale. This was the "firestorm" th[at] killed 42,000 civilians and obliterate[d] the city center. "It was a catastrophe[,]" wrote Goebbels in his diary, "the

> ## 2.7 MILLION
> **The total tonnage** of bombs dropped on Europe by the Allied forces. Two thirds of these were unloaded after D-Day on June 6, 1944.

Britain's nocturnal bombing strategy was born of necessity in the first years of the war. After the fall of France ≪ 82–83, long-range bombing was the only way that Britain could strike at Germany.

BEFORE

Britain's nocturnal bombing strategy was born of necessity in the first years of the war. After the fall of France ≪ 82–83, long-range bombing was the only way that Britain could strike at Germany.

NIGHT FLIGHTS
Daylight raids past the range of escorts would make the bombers prey to German Me 109s and anti-aircraft guns. At night, the bombers were harder to spot; but it was **hopeless to target anything smaller than a whole town**.

IN PURSUIT OF AREA BOMBING
British military leaders were faced with a choice—abandon all offensive action against Germany or bomb city centers in the hope of **damaging German industry** and the morale of the German people. Britain chose the second option—"area bombing"—and pursued it with ever-increasing ferocity.

> ## "It will cost us 500 aircraft. It will cost the Germans the war."
> ARTHUR "BOMBER" HARRIS ON THE BOMBING OF BERLIN, NOVEMBER 1943

HEAD OF RAF BOMBER COMMAND (1892–1984)
ARTHUR "BOMBER" HARRIS

Arthur Harris, the head of Bomber Command, believed that bombing alone could bring Germany to its knees, and render a land invasion of Europe unnecessary. To this end, he systematically obliterated German cities. It was a pitiless use of air power, but to Harris's mind there was poetic justice in it: "The Nazis entered this war under the rather childish delusion that they were going to bomb everyone else, and nobody was going to bomb them. At Rotterdam, London, and Warsaw, they put their theory into operation," he said. "They sowed the wind, and now they are going to reap the whirlwind."

AFTER ››

DAMBUSTER RAID

On May 16, 1943 a squadron of Lancaster bombers launched a daring attack on the dams of the Mohne and Eder rivers in the Ruhr valley. 617 Squadron struck with specially designed "bouncing bombs." These, dropped from a height of only 60 ft (18 m), skipped across the water's surface, sank at the dam wall, and exploded. Power supply merely dipped temporarily, but massive flooding devastated farmland for miles around. The success of this ingenious operation was also a huge propaganda coup for the Allies.

dearly and did not break Germany. Still, the price paid by Berliners was high; 14,000 civilians were killed or injured, with many more bombed out of their homes. To Harris, this was not regrettable collateral damage, but a positive result of area bombing—as was anything that drained Axis resources. Bomber Harris was pitiless: "It should be emphasized," he told the British

> Bomber Command's unofficial motto was "press on regardless," something bomber pilots had to do in the crucial moment of every mission, as they flew straight and level into storms of flak toward their nocturnal targets.

extent of which simply staggers the imagination." Bomber Command's codename for the attack was horribly apt: Operation Gomorrah.

Collateral damage

No German city was ravaged like this again until the end of the war. However, the failure to repeat the gruesome success of the Hamburg raids was not

for want of trying. As winter loomed, Air Officer Commanding-In-Chief, Arthur Harris, declared his aim to strike at the enemy's capital, "to burn his black heart out," as he told his crews. This was his last chance to prove that aerial bombing alone could bring down the Nazis. But the Battle of Berlin, which lasted throughout the winter of 1943–44, cost Bomber Command

cabinet in 1943, "that the destruction of houses, public utilities, transport, and lives, the creation of a refugee problem on an unprecedented scale, and the breakdown of morale both at home and at the battle fronts by fear of extended and intensified bombing, are accepted and intended aims of our bombing policy. They are not by-products of attempts to hit factories."

Ghost town

The destruction of Hamburg began at 12:55am on July 27, 1943. In the next hour or so, 2,326 tons of bombs were dropped on the city. Temperatures reached 1,500°F (800°C) in the ensuing firestorm, setting fire to asphalt on the streets. The devastation was total.

Despite the huge area bombing campaigns of 1943, the Allies failed in their main aims. But this did not stop Britain from continuing in its destruction of Germany.

GERMAN RESILIENCE

The area bombing campaigns of 1943 did not cripple Germany's war industries; in fact, under Albert Speer's energetic leadership, **the output of German fighter aircraft increased significantly 220–21** ››. Nor did the destruction of major cities like Hamburg undermine the people's will to fight; **German civilians proved to be just as resilient** and stoical as the British public had been in the worst days of the Blitz.

DRESDEN BURNS

The Allied area bombing campaign went beyond anything that the Luftwaffe had inflicted on Britain ‹‹ 88–91. The strategy was taken to logical (and morally questionable) extreme in July 1945 with **the fire-bombing of Dresden 294–95** ››. During the final few weeks of the war, the Allies mounted four separate attacks that devasted the city. Ironically, since the USAAF was never convinced of the effectiveness of the RAF's wartime approach, **the carpet-bombing techniques later used by American forces in Vietnam** and Cambodia sought to wreak destruction on a massive scale and can be seen as an adaptation to jungle warfare of the area bombing idea.

KEY

✳ German cities and towns subjected to major bombing raids

✩ Other targets of Allied raids

◭ Major RAF bomber base

◭ Major USAAF bomber base

— Range of Spitfire as fighter escort May 1943

- - - Range of Mustang P-51D as fighter escort May 1944

9 Dec 13, 1943
54 Mustangs escort US raid on Kiel and defend bombers for 40 minutes over target

1 Mar 28/29, 1942
234 bombers devastate historic city of Lübeck. In retaliation Hitler orders bombing of English cathedral cities of Exeter, Bath, and Norwich—the "Baedeker raids"

4 Jan 27, 1943
First USAAF raid over Germany targets port of Wilhelmshaven

6 Jul 24–Aug 3, 1943
Operation Gomorrah devastates Hamburg, killing 40,000

8 Nov 18, 1943–Mar 30, 1944
Series of raids on Berlin and other major cities—the "Battle of Berlin"

10 Mar 6, 1944
First major USAAF raid on Berlin

3 Jun 1/2, 1942
956 bombers take part in raid on Essen. Hazy atmosphere over Ruhr; disappointing results

2 May 30/31, 1942
Operation Millennium—the first 1,000-bomber raid—inflicts serious damage on city of Cologne

5 May 16/17, 1943
Dambusters raid on Möhne, Eder, and Sorpe dams

7 Aug 17, 1943
USAAF raid on Schweinfurt (center of ball-bearing industry) and Regensburg, where Messerschmitt fighters are built, suffers heavy losses—60 out of 376 bombers bombers are lost

Round-the-clock raids

American forces often attacked German cities the morning after a British raid, giving the enemy no respite from the nighttime bombing raids.

> "**Germany is a fortress**, but it is a fortress **without a roof.**"
>
> PRESIDENT FRANKLIN D. ROOSEVELT, 1944

Bombing Germany by Day

The US Eighth Air Force, based in Britain from late 1942, adopted a strategy of precision bombing against targets in Germany. This meant that US crews had to fly their missions by day, when specific factories and installations could be identified. But in broad daylight, US bombers were themselves targets.

BEFORE

If the US could take out pivotal Nazi "choke points," with a strategy superior to the British one, then Germany's capacity to carry on would be ruined.

GERMANY'S "CHOKE POINTS"
The US **concept of bombing**, set up before the war, stated that the German economy relied on 150 or so **key installations**. If these "choke points" could be hit accurately, then Germany's ability to fight on **would be undermined**.

NATIONAL PRIDE
Some US strategists also thought that **precision bombing** was a morally superior way of going about the job compared to **Britain's area bombing strategy ‹‹ 214–15**. "It is contrary to our national ideals," said one US general, "to make war on civilians." US air commanders believed that they had both the **technology and the expertise** to make precision bombing work in a clinical, humane way; that they could **accomplish with a sharp scalpel** what the RAF was clearly failing to do with a **big, blunt club**.

The US Eighth Air Force arrived in Britain in 1942, but flew only a few missions that year. None of those early sorties were directed against targets in Germany and on all of the missions the bombers flew with an RAF escort. It was not until 1943 that the practice of precision bombing was put to the test in the skies over the Reich.

The US role in the campaign against Germany arose from the 1943 meeting between Churchill and Roosevelt in Casablanca. The leaders' joint edict asked for "every opportunity to be taken to attack Germany by day to destroy objectives that are unsuitable for night attack." In response, General Ira Eaker, commander of the American bomber force in Britain, drew up a list of "pinpoint" targets inside the Reich. On his list were ball-bearing plants, oil refineries, aircraft factories, and U-boat yards. Individual buildings or industrial complexes, rather than whole cities, were the Americans' goal. Two complementary but separate plans were

pursued—a US one by day, and a British one by night. The Combined Bomber Offensive was not so much an alliance, but a competition to see whose methods would break Germany first.

Overcoming problems

Once the B-17s went into action it soon became clear that it would be difficult to achieve pinpoint accuracy in daylight. The Norden bombsight "could drop a bomb in a pickle barrel from 30,000 feet," but this was only true if the target was seen in its optical lens. All hinged on this reading, but it was often impossible to take in Europe's gray skies. US aircraft were blind in cloud and so their bombs missed frequently.

A separate issue arose from the fact that no fighters were capable of escorting the bombers. In order to protect themselves, B-17s flew in tight formations called "boxes." This meant that every plane in the box could cover every other one. However,

> **50,000** The estimated number of American aircrew killed or captured in the bombing campaign over Europe—roughly the same rate of loss as sustained on the missions flown by RAF Bomber Command.

TECHNOLOGY
NORDEN BOMBSIGHT

The Norden bombsight was designed by the engineer Carl Norden, and was an extremely sophisticated, top-secret targeting device—a kind of flying mechanical computer. A bombardier (bomb aimer) would input data such as airspeed and altitude, which the Norden would use to calculate the trajectory of the bomb about to be dropped. Close to the target the Norden functioned as an autopilot, keeping the approach straight and level and releasing the bomb at the right instant. In ideal conditions, the Norden could place a bomb dropped from a height of 20,000 ft (6,100 m) within 90 ft (27 m) of the target.

The Flying Fortress

Nicknamed the "Flying Fortress," the American B-17 bomber was equipped with 10 machine guns and four dedicated gunners—more firepower than any German or British bomber in service at the time.

every plane had to fly straight to avoid colliding and so were easy targets for anti-aircraft gunners. The German pilots soon figured out how to unlock the "boxes," and as the Eighth Air Force was not at full strength (the US could barely muster more than 100 aircraft at a time and the formation worked best with 300), the Germans' task was easier.

Airborne disasters

The critical mass of 300 was reached in the summer of 1943, and in August the Eighth Air Force attacked Schweinfurt. Most of Germany's ball-bearing factories were based there, and ball-bearings were vital for hardware. The raid was a disaster. Fighters and anti-aircraft guns wrought havoc in the US boxes; many of the B-17s missed their targets, and 36 of them were lost.

US bombers hit Schweinfurt again in October but bad weather made flying in formation difficult. The main force got there late to find the Germans waiting in ambush. Sixty of the 291 bombers committed were lost on that "Black Thursday." Worse still, the raids failed to strip Germany of ball-bearings.

After "Black Thursday" daylight raids into Germany were shelved and the US looked for new ways to make the B-17s impervious to an airborne siege.

AFTER

The US offensive paid dividends in 1944 with the arrival of the Mustang Fighters.

KING OF THE AIR

In the first half of 1944 the US bombing offensive was directed at rail depots in France—**vital groundwork** for the **invasion of Europe 258–59 》**, and precision bombing was the best way to attack without causing civilian casualties.

US raids on Germany resumed. The new **Mustang fighter** protected B-17s on long-distance raids—it carried enough fuel to **escort B-17s** to the most distant targets, and rivalled the **Messerschmitt 109**. The Germans had a dilemma: take on the Mustangs, or hang back. Either way, the Germans were losing the capability to fight in the air.

A MUSTANG FIGHTER

USAAF raid on Schweinfurt

During July and August 1943 B-17 Flying Fortresses and B-24 Liberators of the US Eighth Air Force set off from bases in East Anglia, England, in a series of bombing raids on industrial targets in Germany. RAF sorties took place at night, but the USAAF (United States Army Air Force) flew their raids during the day. The bombers came under constant attack and losses were severe, particularly during the Schweinfurt raid in August 1943.

"At the briefing we were told that the target was a complex of ball-bearing plants and the war would be shortened by six months if we pulverized it. F-47 Thunderbirds were to escort us to the German border ... and when we got there they waggled their wings in salute and peeled away. Within minutes we were under attack by swarms of enemy fighters.

There were deadly 109s and FW 190s joined by ... Me 110s and Ju 88s; the Germans were throwing everything they had at us. A 20mm shell ploughed through our right wing, missing the gas tanks by inches, and the bombardier called out what looked like .30mm holes in the cowling of the No. 2 engine ...

The box formations out on the far left and right seemed to be getting most of the attention, and Fortresses were falling everywhere. As they dropped out of the protection of the formation, the enemy fighters roared in for the kill. Parachutes started peppering the sky as American airmen jumped from their burning B-17s; what sickened me ... was the Fortresses that exploded in mid-air, giving the crews no chance of escape.

We bombed the ball-bearing works at 1511 hours and turned for home; from the fires and smoke it appeared the bombers had devastated the target. Then the Me 109s and FW 190s swooped in again. Our aircraft suffered no hits on the return journey, but B-17s in other formations were being pounded unmercifully ... as American parachutes filled the air and more B-17s plunged to earth or became fireballs.

The surviving aircraft—many with wounded men aboard—landed at their bases at about 1800 hrs ... it turned out that, of the 194 B-17s that crossed the enemy coast, 36 were shot down with the loss of 360 crew members. The Eighth's 'acceptable loss rate' ... was 5 per cent. The Schweinfurt loss rate was 20 per cent."

EDDIE DEERFIELD, 303RD BOMB GROUP, USAAF, ON A BOMBING MISSION TO A BALL-BEARING PLANT IN SCHWEINFURT, NORTHERN BAVARIA

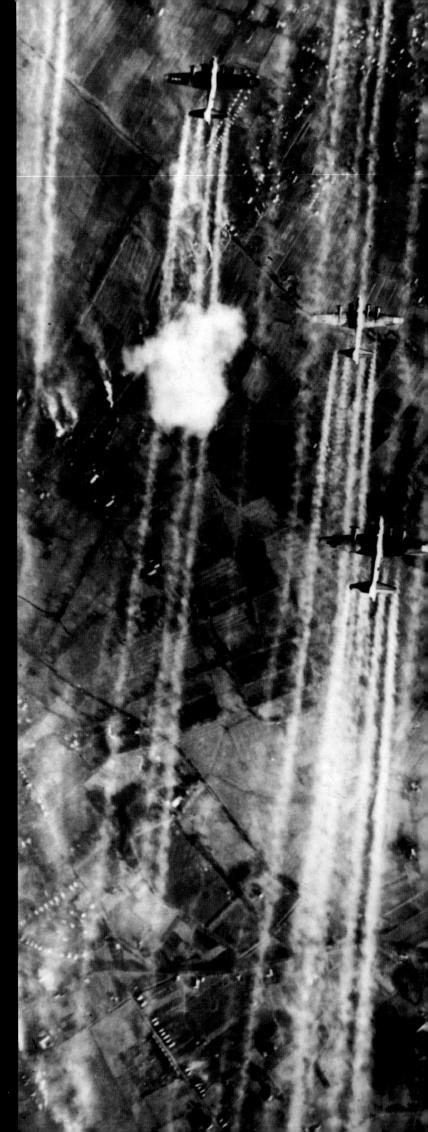

Deadly payload
Bombs from a US Eighth Air Force bomber fall toward their target. B-17s carried a crew of 10 men and a bomb load of 6,000 lb (2,720 kg). As bombers approached the target they were met by intense anti-aircraft fire, or flak.

The German War Industry

By 1943 the tide of war was turning against Germany. Victories had given way to defeats, more men were needed to fight and there was an urgent need for armaments. The country was finally mobilized for total war and, under armaments minister, Albert Speer, production rose dramatically.

Underground factories
Uncovered by American troops, this aircraft factory was built underground in a salt mine at Tarthun, near Schönebeck. Six fuselages were produced every day by some 2,400 slave laborers, mainly concentration camp inmates.

BEFORE

Germany had been rearming for several years before the war began, and as a result was better prepared for war than the Allied nations.

GERMAN WAR FOOTING

Following **Hitler's rise to power ‹‹ 24–25**, in 1933, the German economy was effectively put onto a war footing. **Arms production increased under Nazi rule ‹‹ 26–27** and, by 1939, Germany had a well-developed industry, a skilled labor force, and substantial reserves of

NAZI PENNANT

coal, oil, and rubber. Over the next two years Germany achieved **rapid victories**, with little strain on the country's economy, while resources poured in from Nazi-occupied countries.

Germany was not equipped for a long war, and the drain of men and equipment, especially on the **Eastern Front ‹‹ 192–93** put the country's economy **under serious strain**.

Until 1942, the Germany economy was not organized for a long war, largely because Hitler believed that blitzkrieg tactics and plundering occupied territories would bring the war to a speedy close, while providing the requirements of war. However, by 1942, it was clear that this would not be the case. Two thirds of Germany's labor force worked on war orders, but output was slow and failed to meet the needs of what had become total war. One problem was that, under the Nazi regime, the economy was poorly run and suffering from waste, inadequate planning, and military interference.

In 1942, therefore, Hitler appointed his chief architect, Albert Speer, to oversee war production with the aim of hugely increasing Germany's weapons output. Speer immediately implemented several major changes: he established a Central Planning Board, liaised directly with Hitler, and reduced military interference, bringing in skilled industrialists and engineers. As a result, despite Allied bombing raids on industrial centers, ball-bearing plants, and armaments factories, production of arms soared, with output of aircraft alone almost quadrupling from 11,000 in 1941 to more than 39,000 in 1944.

Foreign labor

Speer's so-called economic "miracle" was not achieved simply by more stringent planning; it was also the result of extensive exploitation of foreign labor. Between 1939 and 1944 the number of German men in the labor force dropped by more than 10 million—from 25.4 million in 1939 to 13.5 million in 1944—as increasing numbers were sent to fight. To fill shortages in factories and on the land, Nazi Germany brought in workers from the occupied territories, so that, by 1944, one in five of all workers in Germany came from outside. During the course of the war, as many as 12 million workers came to Germany from Poland, France, Belgium, Czechoslovakia, Serbia, Russia, and the Ukraine to work in the war industries, repairing bomb damage, or on the land. Some came voluntarily, responding to recruitment drives, while far more were deported from their own countries by force. Their treatment varied, with those from Eastern Europe used as virtual slave labor by industrial concerns such as Krupp, Siemens, and I.G. Farben.

The Nazis also used POWs and inmates from death camps, many of whom labored in underground factories, built to withstand bombing raids. One such example was the V-2 assembly plant in Nordhausen, which was constructed by inmates from Buchenwald, many of whom starved or died from overwork.

Life in Germany

Life did not change dramatically for non-Jewish civilians living in Germany during the first few years. Blackouts and

Women workers
Despite the Nazi emphasis on the woman's role as a homemaker, thousands of German women worked in munitions factories and in aircraft production. Many were also involved in the air defense of the Reich.

rationing were introduced, but news of victories and the influx of luxury and other goods from the occupied territories kept the mood of the country buoyant. Industry continued to produce several consumer durables and, unlike many other warring nations, women were not recruited into the war industries until after 1941. Hitler's view, and that of the Nazi Party, was that women belonged in the home, and that the primary role of a woman was to be a good wife and mother. In fact, owing to generous war pensions and these Nazi views, the number of women in the workforce declined by some 440,000 during this time.

> **7.5 MILLION** The number of foreign workers employed in Germany in 1944—most of whom were brought in from the occupied areas.

Total mobilization

Following defeats at Stalingrad and in North Africa, and with the arrival of round-the-clock bombing, however, the mood of the country became more desperate. Shortages began to bite, food rationing intensified, some civilians were evacuated from cities, and the civilian death toll started to rise. In February 1943 propaganda minister, Joseph Goebbels, announced total war measures. All men aged between 16 and 65 had to register for war work, or join the *Volkssturm* (home guard); women were actively recruited into munitions factories, and members of the Hitler Youth and the League of German Girls took up work in hospitals, with postal and transport services, and on the land. By 1944 the population had been mobilized but, by then, it was too late.

KEY
■ Annual production of aircraft
■ Annual production of tanks

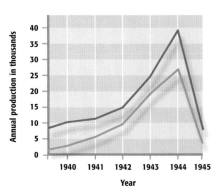

War production
Military output more than trebled from 1942 to 1944, with arms production accounting for 30 percent of all industry. After 1944 production dropped sharply.

Morale boost
Joseph Goebbels bombarded the nation with posters like this, stressing the unity between industrial workers, farmers, women in uniform, and the men at the front. This poster reads: "Total war is the shortest war."

HITLER'S ARCHITECT (1905–81)
ALBERT SPEER

Albert Speer joined the Nazi Party in 1932. Two years later he designed and organized the dramatic Nuremberg Rally. Between 1942 and 1945 he oversaw and directed Germany's economy, bringing in major reforms and achieving remarkable increase in munitions productivity—his architectural and economic skills meant he would become a member of Hitler's inner circle. Tried at Nuremberg after the war, Albert Speer disassociated himself from Hitler but did accept "collective responsibility" for war crimes. He served a 20-year sentence and died in London. Speer's claim that he was merely an architect, and knew nothing of the Holocaust, has been hotly disputed.

AFTER »

From 1944 living conditions for civilians in Germany were deteriorating rapidly and continued to worsen until the war ended.

HOMELESS AND STARVING
Allied bombing devastated cities, including Cologne, Hamburg, and **Dresden 166–67 »**, **leaving thousands homeless**. By 1945 many city dwellers were foraging for food. **Rationing had intensified**; by April 1945 an adult's weekly **meat ration** had dropped from 15½ oz (437 g) in May 1943 to 4¾ oz (137 g).

GERMANY DIVIDED
Following the end of the war, **the country was divided 340–41 »** between the Communist Eastern sector, and what became West Germany.

BEFORE «

The French Resistance was a movement born of defeat. Almost as soon as German troops overran the northern part of France, clandestine fighters began to engage in spontaneous acts of sabotage.

DE GAULLE LIGHTS THE RESISTANCE FLAME
Resistance fighters, or "soldiers of the night" as the writer André Malraux later called them, were **French civilians fighting Nazi occupation**. The first green shoots of resistance were nurtured by **General de Gaulle << 110–11**, who in June 1940 told his countrymen: "Must hope disappear? Is defeat final? No! Believe me when I tell you that nothing is lost for France. **Whatever happens, the flame of French resistance must not be extinguished** and will not be extinguished." De Gaulle wanted a professional army formed outside France. But many French civilians took him at his word, and began **fighting the Nazis individually, on their doorstep**.

The French Resistance

Some French people made it their business to fight back against Nazi occupation. At first, resistance was passive, taking the form of information-gathering, anti-Nazi propaganda, and aid to downed Allied airmen. But in 1943 armed struggle, assassination, and guerrilla warfare became their primary activites.

The French Resistance was not a single organization. There was a variety of separate networks, many built on a shared political or social outlook. In occupied France (as opposed to Vichy France in the south) socialists and trade unions formed the backbone of *Libération-Nord,* the main resistance network; the *Front National* was largely organized by pro-Soviet Communists; and the group known as *Résistance* was made up mostly of Roman Catholics. In the south of France there was a small faction called the *Armée Juive,* or the Jewish Army, consisting of French Zionists. They hid fellow Jews from the Nazis and smuggled them across the Pyrenees into neutral Spain.

In the first phase of the occupation, subversion was the only means of resistance. In France and Belgium as many as 1,000 underground newspapers and tracts were published during the war. Some were handwritten, others printed using rubber stamps or home-made presses. It was common practice for people to make two or three copies of any newsheet that came into their hands and pass them on. This ingenious mode of distribution—the chain letter—could not be stamped out by

> The SOE developed a range of specialist equipment for their agents to use. These devices included the "welrod" (a silent pistol), incendiaries hidden inside everyday objects, and lethal suicide tablets disguised as coat buttons in case of capture.

the Nazis so long as a single copy stayed in circulation. Even the names of these publications were a call to arms: *France, libère-toi!* (France, Free Yourself!); *Sous La Botte* (Under the Heel of the Jackboot); *Franc-Tireur* (Irregular).

A more hazardous way of hitting back was to become a link in the escape line for Allied aircrew shot down over France or Belgium. More than 2,000

Female fighters
The first armed resistance fighters hid themselves in remote parts of the French countryside. But as the Nazi hold on France grew weak, city dwellers—both men and women—took up arms and fought the Nazis on the streets.

London calling

The *maquis* did all they could to co-ordinate their actions with Allied operations. On June 5 resistance groups were alerted to the coming invasion by a coded radio message: "The die is cast, the die is cast."

partisans on the Eastern Front. These groups were large. A division of 4,000 based on the alpine plateau of Vercors harrassed the Germans throughout the winter of 1943. After D-Day they

> **220,000** The number of people who were honored by the postwar French government for their role in the Resistance, but the total number of fighters is impossible to know.

engaged in a month-long battle with more than 10,000 Nazi troops before being crushed by an airborne assault on their stronghold. In the wake of the battle, SS units slaughtered all the villagers of the Vercors plateau—not just the Resistance fighters, but the women and children too.

A village extinct

Massacres like this were part of a Nazi policy intended to deter attacks against their own. The SS often shot many innocent hostages in revenge for the wounding or killing of just one Nazi. One incident was the extinction of Oradour, a village in the Limousin region, apparently in reprisal for an officer's kidnapping. In July 1944 the village was sealed off and the men and women separated. The men were shot; the women and infants led to a church and set on fire. Oradour was razed to the ground and not rebuilt. Today, its ruins are a somber tribute, a reminder of the price France had to pay to maintain its resistance.

Allied airmen, having bailed out or crash-landed, were passed along these so-called "rat lines" and spirited out of the country. But the price was high—it has been estimated that the repatriation of every Allied evader was bought with the life of one *résistant*.

The escape lines could not have worked without the aid of the British military intelligence in London. Evasion was the responsibility of a department called MI9, but secret operations inside France were run by the "F Section" of the Special Operations Executive (SOE).

From its headquarters in Baker Street, SOE trained people for covert missions, arrranged drops of radios, arms, and bomb-making materials to groups of fighters inside occupied territory, and did its best to marshal the disparate efforts of the Resistance so that they dovetailed with the strategy of the British war cabinet. From May 1941 to August 1944, over 400 agents were sent to France to carry messages, make contact with resistance groups, or train local spies in the acts of sabotage.

Ways of the saboteur

Among the most able and inventive saboteurs were the *cheminots*, the French rail workers who joined resistance groups like the *Résistance-Fer*. The Germans depended on the French rail network, and during the summer of 1943 a war was waged—*la bataille du rail*—against German communication lines. The Nazis attached civilian passenger cars to their troop transports as protection, but so expert were the *cheminots* that they could time an explosion to destroy the Nazi carriages, leaving the others intact.

In 1943 the Nazis began conscripting French citizens to work in Germany. Many avoided this by fleeing deep into France's forests and inaccessible mountains. Here, they swelled the ranks of guerrilla bands known as the *maquis*, in the mold of the Russian

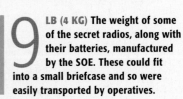

Badge of courage
In 1943 de Gaulle licensed a bronze medal to honor the courage of *Résistants*. The front shows the cross of Lorraine—their symbol.

Off the rails

The *Résistance-Fer* were specialized rail saboteurs and came into their own after D-Day. In the first month after the invasion they cut 3,000 train lines, hampering the Nazi efforts to bring reinforcements to the beachheads.

The French Resistance came into its own in 1944. On the eve of D-Day almost 1,000 sabotage actions were carried out and these continued until Liberation.

DISRUPTING THE NAZIS

By June 5, 1944, there was a secret army of 150,000 Frenchmen inside occupied France, trained, armed, and ready for action. Saboteurs set out to disrupt the German communication lines, to hobble the German response to

VERCORS FLAG

Operation Overlord: telegraph cables were cut, rail lines were blown up or stripped and locomotives were disabled. *Résistants* **delayed the deployment of the 2nd SS Panzer Division** to Normandy by two weeks by harrying the troops all the way from their base in Dordogne.

> **19 LB (4 KG)** The weight of some of the secret radios, along with their batteries, manufactured by the SOE. These could fit into a small briefcase and so were easily transported by operatives.

FIGHTING TO THE END

In the months that followed D-Day, during the long German retreat to the west and the **Liberation of France 268–69 ≫**, "terrorist" attacks and other **partisan actions had a deeply damaging effect on the morale of the Wehrmacht**, which never found an effective way to deal with the guerrilla tactics and clandestine activities.

Liberation of France 268–69 ≫

RESISTANCE FIGHTER (1899–1943)

JEAN MOULIN

Jean Moulin has become a symbol of French resistance to Nazi occupation. His role within the Resistance was to unite, or at least to coordinate, the various factions fighting against the Nazis. In May 1943 he called a secret summit of the heads of the various organizations. The meeting in Lyon was raided by German troops, and Moulin was captured. He was subjected to appalling torture by Klaus Barbie, the head of the Gestapo in Lyon, but died without giving anything away. Moulin was buried in Père Lachaise cemetery in Paris; in 1964 his remains were transferred to the Pantheon.

«

Prisoners of War in Europe

BEFORE

In theory, all prisoners of war had to be treated in accordance with the Third Geneva Convention, but many countries were not prepared for the sheer numbers involved.

THE THIRD GENEVA CONVENTION
The treatment of POWs was governed—in theory at least—by the **Third Geneva Convention** of 1929, which, with the exception of the Soviet Union, was signed by all the nations who later took part in the war. The Convention reiterated the Hague Conventions of 1899 and 1907, which stated that **fighting men who laid down their arms were to be decently treated**.

POW POPULATIONS
The Axis powers captured almost nine million enemy combatants in the course of the war, two thirds of whom were Russian soldiers who fell into German hands. **The Allies, for their part, took almost five million men prisoner** between the outbreak of war and VE Day. No warring country had ever had to deal with POW populations of this size, and both sides in the conflict struggled with the scale of the task.

The fate of POWs varied widely depending on the time and place of their capture, their rank, and nationality. For Allied officers, the main challenge of prison life was the open-ended tedium. For German or Russian soldiers on the Eastern Front, POW status often spelled death by starvation and neglect.

In the early days of the war, the Germans took far more prisoners than the Allies. The 50,000 British soldiers left behind in the retreat to Dunkirk spent a full five years being shuttled from one German camp to another. During that time there were incidents in which members of the British Expeditionary Force (BEF) were shot by their German captors. Later in the war, downed Allied bomber crews were occasionally lynched by angry German mobs. The first day or two of prisoner life—between surrender and consignment to a camp—was always the most hazardous time.

For the most part, the Nazis, and the Wehrmacht in particular, respected the codes of the Third Geneva Convention when dealing with British and American

In enemy hands
Airmen were especially aware of the possibilty of capture. But to many a POW's existence was a far better option than being stranded and exposed to other dangers. Fliers were over-represented in camps on both sides of the Channel.

prisoners. The Convention stated that POWs were to be promptly removed from the field of battle; they were to be given medical attention if wounded; they were to be housed and fed no worse than the garrison troops of the capturing power; and they were entitled to refuse to give any information to their interrogators but name, rank, and service number. While in captivity they had the right to correspond with family and friends, and if they escaped and were recaptured, then they were to be punished with nothing more severe than 30 days' solitary confinement.

Safe haven
Many German prisoners of war arrived in England after D-Day. Most were relieved to be out of the war and were happy to undergo the indignity of a delousing when they first arrived at their POW camp.

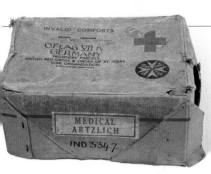

Prison lifeline
A Red Cross parcel was a lifeline for a prisoner of war. As many as 20 million packages were dispatched from Britain. They contained treasures such as jam, cocoa, dried fruit, tea, and powdered eggs.

The Convention also said that camps were to be open to inspection by members of the International Red Cross.

The Germans operated two types of POW institution—"Oflags" for enemy officers, and "Stalags" for NCOs and enlisted men. British and US Stalag prisoners were required to work in factories or on farms. The combination of regular exercise, fresh air, and plentiful food meant that the soldiers assigned to rural work often fared better than the POW officer class. Some even found the opportunity to forge relationships (both short- and long-term) with German women. The same phenomenon occurred among Italian prisoners of war in Britain,

11 The number of Axis POWs who made it back home. Luftwaffe pilot Franz von Werra escaped to the US from a camp in Canada. He traveled back to Germany from Mexico after evading arrest.

almost all of whom spent their time in captivity cultivating the land, working alongside British civilians.

The conditions under which some British and US officers were held allowed for no association with the local people. The inmates of Oflags were locked up at all times. They were not required to work, but they were given few comforts and meager rations. Until the end of 1944, when Himmler took over the running of the camps, a POW's food was supplemented with parcels from the Red Cross. These much-prized gifts not only kept inmates from malnutrition and hunger, they also allowed Allied POWs some surplus with which barter with the guards. Secret trade of this kind was one of the ways in which prisoners acquired the effects of escape—items of civilian clothing; samples of official papers; the tools of the forger, the digger, and the lock-picker, such as inkpads and trowels.

Escaping inmates
Many Allied prisoners felt duty-bound to escape because they saw it as the only contribution they could now make

Roll-call at Colditz
The courtyard at Colditz was the setting for the daily roll-call. It was also the venue for regular games of "stool ball," a boisterous version of rugby invented by British prisoners of war to while away the days.

corridors, that the inmates were free to explore, gave plenty of inspiration and opportunity for escape plans. POWs even managed to build and conceal a glider in the attic, but the castle was freed by US troops before they had a chance to use it.

No such inventive pastimes were available to POWs on the Eastern Front. Here the Geneva Convention meant nothing. The Wehrmacht scooped up more than three million Soviets in its first drive toward Moscow, from June

AFTER »»

For significant numbers of prisoners of war, imprisonment abroad turned into a form of emigration. Others became hostages during the first phase of the Cold War.

CITIZENS ABROAD
As many as 26,000 German prisoners of war found something to admire in the British way of life, and **elected to remain in Britain** rather than go back to Germany at the end of the war. Many of those sent to camps in the United States found wives in that country, and so swiftly became **citizens of the nation they had been fighting against 334–35 »**.

WAR CRIMINALS AND HOSTAGES
POWs of the Eastern Front fared much worse. Of the **90,000 Germans who had survived the Battle of Stalingrad, all but 6,000 died** in Soviet camps. Disease was rife, food scarce, and inmates were subjected to hard labor in terrible weather conditions. Those that survived were some of the million or more **German POWs who were deemed war criminals**. They were put to work repairing the Russian cities that their country had helped destroy. These men became, in effect, hostages of the first phase of the **Cold War 348–49 »**. The last of the survivors returned home—broken, and aged beyond their years—in 1956.

to December 1941 of these, two million were dead by the winter's end—shot out of hand or marched to death. The Soviets were just as brutal toward Germans. All the Axis troops in Soviet hands at the end of the war were shipped straight to the Gulags. They were joined by repatriated Soviet prisoners of war, who on their return were condemned as traitors for having allowed themselves to be taken prisoner by the Germans. This double incarceration—to be a prisoner first of Hitler, then of Stalin—was an ordeal that very few men survived.

"It was our duty to try to get out—and in so doing to cause as much trouble as possible."
CAPTAIN KENNETH LOCKWOOD, ALLIED ESCAPE COMMITTEE, COLDITZ

to the war effort. A handful of POWs let loose in the German countryside could divert the manpower of hundreds of police officers and reservists. So even if escapees were recaptured, a failed attempt could be said to have undermined the German war effort. But just as importantly, plotting escape gave Allied officers something to do—something more exciting and more meaningful than the amateur theaters, orchestras, and sports clubs that flourished in the Oflags.

A lucky few even managed to escape from Oflag IV-C—better known as Colditz—the medieval castle in Saxony to which the most recalcitrant escapees were sent. It was meant to be escape-proof, but its many hidden nooks and

BRITISH SOLDIER AND POLITICIAN (1916–1979)

AIREY NEAVE

A member of the Royal Artillery, Airey Neave was the first British officer to escape from Colditz. He had been wounded and was captured in 1940 while serving in France. The following year he made several escape attempts, so was sent to the high-security camp at Colditz Castle. In 1942 Neave marched out of the castle in a home-made German officer's uniform, accompanied by a fellow POW. It took them two days to travel by train to the Swiss border, which they crossed unnoticed. Neave became a member of parliament after the war and was assassinated by the IRA in 1979.

BEFORE

In the bitter winter of 1942, the Red Army halted the Germans at Stalingrad. More signficantly, they chased the Axis forces back across the snows.

RECEDING FRONT LINE
Relentless pressure from the Soviets forced the Germans into retreat ≪ 192–93 for the first time in the war. By the time the spring thaw came in 1943, the German front line had already receded far to the west.

OPERATION CITADEL
At Kursk, at the southern end of the Eastern Front, there was a deep Russian-occupied bulge in the line, a dangerous promontory into German-held territory. The German plan to eliminate the Kursk salient was codenamed Operation Citadel. It was the last blitzkrieg of the war—and the first blitzkrieg to fail.

FEAR OF ALLIED INVASION
It was hoped that Operation Citadel might force a summer stalemate on the Eastern Front. This would allow the Führer to divert some effort and resources to the West where, he was certain, an Allied invasion ≪ 202–03 was sure to come sooner or later.

Ideal tank territory
Armored columns could maneuver as freely as ships at sea in the open expanses of Russia. But, at Kursk, the Soviets forced the German Panther and Tiger tanks into narrow "killing zones," picking them off one by one.

The Battle of Kursk

The battle that raged around Kursk in July 1943 involved as many as 6,000 tanks, 4,000 planes, and two million infantrymen. It was a clash of armor, the like of which the world had never seen before, and it proved decisive to the outcome of the war on the Eastern Front.

In March 1943 the Soviet line at Kursk formed a deep bubble that was 112 miles (180 km) wide, and that protruded 63 miles (100 km) to the west of the city. Hitler knew that the Kursk bulge was a weakness in the German defenses, and that the Russians could use it to kick off a summer offensive. He and his generals decided that they needed to pinch it off using a fast-moving pincer attack from the north and south. The Soviet armies trapped inside the bubble could then be systematically killed in the German *Kesselschlacht* ("cauldron battle").

Kursk itself was an important rail hub, and so a prize worth winning. But this was only part of the hoped-for gain. If the German plan worked, the Soviet fighting capability in the sector would be severely weakened, and at the same time the German line across Soviet territory would be straightened and shortened. It might then be possible to fortify this line and hold the Russians at bay, forcing them to exhaust themselves against reinforced German defenses.

Hitler delays the offensive
The kind of attack that Hitler had in mind worked best when there was an element of surprise. But the Russians knew that an attack on Kursk had to come sooner or later. Field-marshal von Manstein, Hitler's commander in the field, wanted to launch the offensive in March, but Hitler ruled that it was better to wait out the Russian spring thaw, during which the landscape is a sea of mud, making troop movements

> **"The Russians exploited their victory** … There were to be no more periods of quiet on the **Eastern Front."**
> HEINZ GUDERIAN, 1943

GERMAN FIELD MARSHAL (1887–1973)
ERICH VON MANSTEIN

Erich von Manstein was an operational commander. He devised the plan which broke the British and French in 1940, but fought largely on the Eastern Front. After capturing the Crimea and the Kerch peninsula at the head of 11th Army, he went on to command Army Group Don. Although he supported the Kursk attack he felt it was delayed too long. Von Manstein was sacked by Hitler in 1944.

Top tank
The Russian T-34 was decisive at the Battle of Kursk. It is often said to have been the best tank design of the war. More than 57,000 were built between 1940 and 1945.

Defending Kursk

The Soviets made thorough preparations for a German attack on the Kursk bulge. The salient was protected with five or six concentric belts of trench lines and, in the east, six armies stood in reserve.

3,000 miles (4,800 km) of trenches. The lines of defense were laden with mines—hidden beneath the new summer undergrowth—and bristled with 20,000 artillery pieces. An army of more than one million men lay in wait, and vast quantities of men and armor were being held in reserve behind the lines. Much of this work had been concealed from the Germans, so the Kursk bulge was not just a fortress, it was also a trap: on July 5 two German Panzer armies rushed headlong straight into it. Even Hitler began to have doubts about the progress which, he remarked, "makes my stomach turn over," and he was right.

The 4th Panzer Army struck north from the Kharkov region, and the 9th Panzer Army headed south from Orel. The German offensive quickly ran into trouble. Many of the long-awaited Panther tanks broke down; many more were disabled by mines. These static targets were at the mercy of the Soviet anti-tank units, whose operating system was fiendishly efficient: one officer targeted a single tank with 10 guns at a time, before moving on to the next.

But many of the tanks that made it through the first line of defenses were equipped with the powerful 88 mm gun. This, and the tanks' heavy armor, helped them gain some ground in the first days of the battle. But therein lay another problem: the tanks often ran ahead of the infantry, and were caught like flies inside a Soviet defensive web. Here, amid swarms of foot soldiers, their firepower and thick steel plating was of little use to them: the Soviets found that the heaviest tanks could be stopped dead in their tracks with a close-range flamethrower blast to the radiator grill.

Victory for the Soviets

A week after Operation Citadel began, the northern prong of the attack was already coming to a standstill, while

almost impossible. Hitler delayed further, in April, when he decided to wait until June, when 300 new Panther tanks would be available. But in June the High Command received alarming reports of Soviet strength in the Kursk area, so Hitler decided to wait one more month in order that yet more Panthers could be shipped out to the front line.

The high price of delay

Hitler had seriously underestimated the strength and depth of Soviet defenses. While he delayed, the Russians built

| 1 MILLION | The number of anti-tank and anti-personnel mines the Soviets laid along the front at Kursk—more than 3,000 mines per 1,000 yards (1 km) of front. |

the southern prong, moving slowly but steadily, had advanced just 12 miles (20 km). On July 12 Stalin deployed his main reserve—the 5th Tank Army—against the southern wing. The

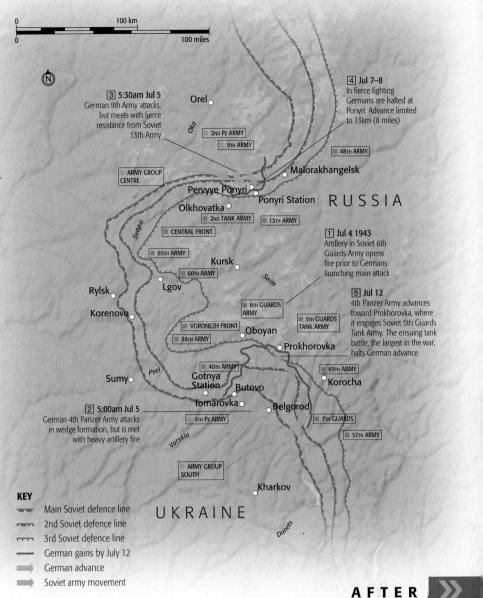

[3] 5:30am Jul 5
German 9th Army attacks, but meets with fierce resistance from Soviet 13th Army

[4] Jul 7–8
In fierce fighting Germans are halted at Ponyri. Advance limited to 13km (8 miles)

[1] Jul 4 1943
Artillery in Soviet 6th Guards Army opens fire prior to Germans launching main attack

[5] Jul 12
4th Panzer Army advances toward Prokhorovka, where it engages Soviet 5th Guards Tank Army. The ensuing tank battle, the largest in the war, halts German advance

[2] 5:00am Jul 5
German 4th Panzer Army attacks in wedge formation, but is met with heavy artillery fire

RUSSIA
UKRAINE

Orel, Malorakhangelsk, Pervyye Ponyri, Ponyri Station, Olkhovatka, Kursk, Rylsk, Lgov, Korenovo, Sumy, Gotnya Station, Butovo, Tomarovka, Belgorod, Oboyan, Prokhorovka, Korocha, Kharkov

2ND PZ ARMY, 9TH ARMY, 48TH ARMY, ARMY GROUP CENTRE, 2ND TANK ARMY, 13TH ARMY, CENTRAL FRONT, 65TH ARMY, 60TH ARMY, 6TH GUARDS ARMY, 5TH GUARDS TANK ARMY, VORONEZH FRONT, 38TH ARMY, 40TH ARMY, 69TH ARMY, 4TH PZ ARMY, 7TH GUARDS, 57TH ARMY, ARMY GROUP SOUTH

0   100 km
0   100 miles

KEY
- Main Soviet defence line
- 2nd Soviet defence line
- 3rd Soviet defence line
- German gains by July 12
- German advance
- Soviet army movement

two opposing tank formations clashed at Prokhorovka. Considered the pivotal moment of the battle, this engagement is often described as the biggest tank battle in history. Although the epithet is disputable, it was certainly a titanic conflict between the big German Tigers and the lighter, more nimble T-34s. The battle at Prokhorovka raged just as furiously in the air, where the increasingly skilled Soviet flyers denied the Germans the superiority to which they had been accustomed.

In numerical terms, the Russians fared worst: their losses were far higher than those of the Germans. But the Soviets could afford to take such losses, while the Germans could not. Hitler, usually insistent that his troops fight on, no matter what, suffered a loss of nerve and, on July 17, he called a halt to Operation Citadel. Possibly, he was distracted by the Allied landings in Sicily. At any rate, Germany was now fighting a war on two fronts. For all the battles still to be fought, this was a sure sign that the war in Europe was now approaching its endgame.

AFTER

After Kursk, the forces of the Soviet Union found themselves in total control of the war in the East. In the weeks following the battle, the Red Army took Kharkov, and captured the key city of Orel.

A NATION DEFEATED
Heinz Guderian, **the brilliant architect** of Germany's tank force, wrote: "We suffered a **decisive defeat** with the failure of Citadel. The armored formations, **re-formed and re-equipped** at so much effort, lost heavily in both **men and equipment**."

A NATION RETREATING
What this **Soviet victory** meant in effect was that, **from Kursk onward**, the Wehrmacht was fighting a **permanent rearguard action**. The Soviets drove the enemy west through the **burned-out expanses of the Ukraine**, and went on to **liberate Kiev** in November.
In 1944 a **Red Army offensive 270–71 »** pushed the Germans back **beyond the line** from which the **Barbarossa invasion** had originally been launched, in 1941.

SOVIET MARSHAL Born 1896 Died 1974

Georgy Zhukov

> "If we come to a **minefield**, our infantry attacks exactly as if it **were not there**."

GEORGY ZHUKOV, IN CONVERSATION WITH GENERAL EISENHOWER, 1945

A much decorated war hero and Soviet patriot, Georgy Zhukov was an outstanding military commander and a key figure in the Russian fight against Germany during World War II. He achieved remarkable victories at Moscow, Stalingrad, and Leningrad, and led the Soviet forces in the final assault on Berlin. A member of the Communist Party, Zhukov not only dared to challenge Stalin on military matters, but was also one of the few Bolsheviks to outlive him.

Planning tactics at Khalkin Gol
Zhukov conducted a brilliant counter-offensive at Khalkin Gol in Manchuria, inflicting dreadful casualties on the Japanese and preventing them from launching an attack on the Soviet Union later in the war.

Zhukov was born into an impoverished peasant family. Conscripted into the Imperial Russian Army, he served in World War I, winning two awards for bravery. Following the Bolshevik Revolution of 1917, Zhukov joined the Communist Party and the Red Guard, later commanding a cavalry division in the Russian Civil War. His bravery and ruthlessness brought him to the notice of Joseph Stalin, then a member of the government. Stalin encouraged him to study military science, which he did in Russia and Germany. The two men worked closely together after that, though not always harmoniously.

Rise under Stalin

Over the next few years Zhukov rose steadily through the ranks of the army, earning a reputation for strict discipline and absolute determination. When Stalin, now head of the Soviet Union, carried out a massive purge of Red Army officers between 1937 and 1938, Zhukov was safely far away on the

Leader of the Soviet forces

Soviet commander Georgy Zhukov led Soviet forces in some of their most significant victories of the war. Second-in-command only to Stalin during the Battle of Leningrad, Zhukov fell out of favor in the 1950s.

frontiers of Manchuria, where Soviet forces were battling the Japanese. In 1939 he led a successful counter-offensive at the Battle of Khalkin Gol, which resulted in massive casualties for the Japanese. A pioneer in the use of armored warfare, Zhukov achieved success by meticulous planning and skillful use of tanks. He applied classic cavalry tactics—massing his tanks, smashing a hole through the Japanese Army, and crushing the Japanese in a pincer movement—that characterized much of his later strategy. For his achievement, Zhukov was awarded the title Hero of the Soviet Union and promoted to general.

Hero of the Soviet Union
One of the most highly decorated generals in the Soviet Union, Zhukov was awarded the Hero of the Soviet Union medal four times.

Defending the Soviet Union
In June 1941 Germany invaded the Soviet Union. Unprepared in the face of advancing German forces, Stalin and Zhukov disagreed on strategy. Zhukov argued that troops should be withdrawn

Zhukov was also assisted by the Russian winter. He drove Germany out of the reach of Moscow, inflicting the first major German defeat on the Eastern Front.

Eastern Front victories
Zhukov was now back in favour with Stalin, who started listening to his generals as the war progressed. Zhukov effectively became Stalin's right-hand man when he was promoted to deputy commander-in-chief, and he was ordered to plan and coordinate military strategy over the entire Eastern Front. Zhukov was sent to direct the defense of Stalingrad, where in January 1943, using a mixture of utter ruthlessness—failure or desertion were punished by death—and brilliant military planning, he oversaw the encirclement and capture of the German Sixth Army. Soviet casualties were immense. Western commentators sometimes regarded Zhukov as far too ruthless, but Soviet warfare operated

Soviet Union and into Germany. As commander of the First Byelorussian Front, Zhukov led Soviet forces across Ukraine, through Byelorussia, into Poland and Czechoslovakia, and toward Berlin. Under Zhukov's management, Berlin was first encircled and then captured in April 1945, leading to the final capitulation and surrender of Germany. On May 8, 1945, Zhukov, on behalf of the Soviet High Command, received the German surrender.

Obscure final years
Following the end of the war, Zhukov remained in command of the Soviet occupying forces in Germany, and led the Soviet Victory Parade in Red Square, Moscow, where he inspected the troops and saluted Stalin. He later toured the Soviet Union with Allied Commander Dwight D. Eisenhower, who publicly acknowledged the debt owed to Zhukov, saying that victory would not have been possible without him.

Zhukov was a national hero in Russia and immensely popular, both within the military itself and with the general public. Unsurprisingly, Stalin now regarded him as a threat to his grasp on power. He removed Zhukov from

December 1, 1896 Born in the village of Strelkovka, about 62 miles (100 km) east of Moscow, into an impoverished peasant family.

1915 Conscripted into the Russian Imperial Cavalry. Promoted to sergeant and rewarded for bravery during World War I.

November 1917 Elected chairman of his squadron's Red Soldiers Committee when the Bolshevik's seize power in Russia.

1918–21 Fights in the Russian Civil War with the Red Army. Joins the Communist Party in 1919.

1923 Commands a horse cavalry regiment while stationed in Byelorussia.

ZHUKOV WITH STALIN

1930 Given command of Leningrad's 2nd Cavalry Division. Writes military manuals and advocates the use of tanks and mobile units for offensive maneuvers.

1939 Having escaped Joseph Stalin's purge of army officers, leads Soviet and Mongolian forces in the successful defense against Japanese invaders at Khalkin Gol. Awarded the title Hero of the Soviet Union for the first time.

1940 Promoted to full general and given the post of chief-of-staff of the Red Army.

July 1941 Argues that the Red Army should withdraw from Kiev when Germany invades the Soviet Union. Stalin disagrees; Zhukov loses post of army chief-of-staff.

September–December 1941 Put in charge of the defense of Leningrad; German advance is halted but siege begins. Assigned to defense of Moscow, and delivers the first German defeat.

August 1942 Becomes deputy commander-in-chief of Soviet armed forces under Stalin and works on plans for massive counter-offensive along the whole Eastern Front.

January 1943 Breaks through German blockade of Leningrad, opening a land corridor to the city.

July 4–15, 1943 Directs what will be the largest tank battle of the war at the Battle of Kursk.

1944 Directs Soviet offensive through Byelorussia.

March–April 1945 Meets with Stalin and plans the final assault on Berlin as the war in Europe draws to a close.

May 8, 1945 Represents the Soviet Union at Germany's formal surrender.

1946 Returns to Moscow a national hero. Stalin sees him as a threat and he is posted to Odessa.

1953 Recalled to Moscow on Stalin's death, and appointed deputy defense minister in 1955.

1957 Becomes a member of the Central Committee of the Communist Party but has a disagreement with First Secretary Khrushchev and is placed under house arrest.

1964 Restrictions on Zhukov are lifted after Khrushchev is deposed. Spends his final years writing his memoirs and recollections of the war.

June 18, 1974 Dies in Moscow at the age of 77, outliving both Stalin and Khrushchev.

> ## "If they **do not attack** until winter … then we will, and will **tear them to shreds!**"
>
> ZHUKOV ON THE GERMAN ARMY

as Kiev was indefensible; Stalin, however, insisted on defensive action. In the event, German forces overran Kiev and 500,000 Soviet troops were taken prisoner. Zhukov was sacked from his post as army chief-of-staff and sent to direct the defense of Moscow. Along with 88 infantry and 15 cavalry divisions and together with 1,500 tanks,

Toasting the Allies
Despite the mistrust held by Russia for the other Allies—and vice versa—generals Zhukov (center) and Eisenhower (second left) had a strong respect for each other that lasted beyond the end of the war.

on a massive scale: for Zhukov final victory justified heavy losses and he was highly regarded by his troops.

In early 1943 Zhukov directed the first breakthrough of the German blockade of Leningrad. At the Battle of Kursk in July 1943, Zhukov conducted what was to be the largest tank battle of the war, and gained a decisive victory. Turning his attention back to Leningrad, he orchestrated Operation Bagration in January 1944, an offensive that ultimately led to the city's liberation.

Following the Battle of Kursk, Soviet forces went on the offensive, driving the Germans back through the

Peace pact
Zhukov remained in Germany after the war ended, as commander of the occupied forces. He signed the pact that gave Allied forces supreme command over Germany.

Berlin and effectively banished him to a fairly insignificant posting in Odessa, in modern-day Ukraine, that had a limited troop deployment. Following Stalin's death in 1953, Zhukov was returned to prominence under First Secretary Nikita Khrushchev, and was appointed a member of the Politburo in 1957. However, after he opposed moves to reduce the size and power of the Red Army, he was expelled. In 1964 the new Soviet leader, Leonid Brezhnev, restored Zhukov to favor, but he never returned to political or military life. He spent his later years writing his account of the Soviet involvement in World War II and died in 1974. A million people filed past his body lying in state before he was buried with full military honors in the wall of the Kremlin in Red Square.

Island-Hopping in the Pacific

In the course of 1943 the US Navy and Marines began advancing across the Pacific, seizing Japanese-held islands in a series of amphibious assaults. The taking of these often tiny island bases was rendered costly by the fanatical determination of the Japanese defenders.

Prisoner on Tarawa Island
Very few Japanese were taken prisoner, partly because Japanese soldiers were urged by their officers to fight to the death, and partly because Allied troops were reluctant to allow a hated enemy to surrender.

BEFORE

In 1942 the tide of Japanese conquest was halted. But Japan still held a far-flung defensive perimeter.

SOLOMONS CAMPAIGN
American landings on Guadalcanal in the Pacific Solomon Islands in August 1942 brought a **vigorous response from the Japanese** on land and sea. By February 1943 Japan had been forced to withdraw from Guadalcanal, but **held on to other islands 《 164–65**.

NEW GUINEA
In the second half of 1942 Allied troops—mostly Australian—successfully **contained a Japanese invasion of Papua 《 166–67**. The Japanese maintained their positions elsewhere on the island of New Guinea and on New Britain.

NAVAL BALANCE
The American and Japanese navies fought a series of major battles during 1942. Despite the defeat of the main Japanese aircraft carrier force at **Midway in June 《 162–63**, neither side was able to impose its dominance at sea.

F uture United States strategy in the Pacific War was settled at a conference in Washington D.C. in May 1943. Unable to decide between the proposals of General Douglas MacArthur in the Southwest Pacific and the US Navy leaders in charge of the South and Central Pacific, the conference backed both. MacArthur was to advance along the north coast of New Guinea and capture the Japanese base at Rabaul on New Britain, while the Navy completed the conquest of the Solomons and thrust into the Central Pacific, initially to the Gilbert and Marshall Islands.

The Japanese remained confident of their ability to defend their Pacific perimeter, but their confidence was ill-founded. Their static garrisons and bases, scattered across a vast area of ocean, were vulnerable to being picked off one by one. The balance of forces was shifting inexorably against them. US factories and shipyards were now delivering a monumental expansion of war production, and fresh fighting men were pouring out of American training camps. The Japanese depended on the unbroken spirit of their men to impose heavy casualties on the Americans, but in a war of attrition the advantage lay overwhelmingly with the Allies.

The problems faced by the Japanese commanders were compounded by the Americans' superiority in signals

> **17** The number of Japanese who survived the Tarawa fighting out of a garrison of 3,000 troops and 1,000 construction workers. 129 out of 1,200 Korean forced laborers on the island also survived the battle.

intelligence. Decoding Japanese communications allowed the Allies to send land-based bombers to intercept a convoy of troop transports bound from Rabaul for New Guinea at the start of March 1943, sinking them all in the Bismarck Sea. It was a sign of the growing bitterness of the Pacific War that Japanese survivors were systematically machine-gunned in the water.

The first of the offensives envisaged at the Washington Conference got under way on June 30,1943. Codenamed Operation Cartwheel, it involved simultaneous advances in northern New Guinea and the Solomons, where landings were made on New Georgia and Rendova, islands located to the northwest of Guadalcanal. The operation soon ran into difficulties. On New Georgia, a large jungle-clad island, Allied troops struggled in the face of determined resistance by a garrison of more than 10,000 Japanese troops. In New Guinea progress was also slow and costly.

By August Allied commanders were adjusting their strategy. Instead of attempting to capture the most heavily defended Japanese positions, Allied forces would bypass them, leaving them, in MacArthur's adopted phrase, "to wither on the vine." So, in the

TECHNOLOGY

AMPHIBIOUS VEHICLES

While landing craft had to unload their men and equipment on the shoreline, amphibious vehicles were able to carry them onto the land. Unsurprisingly these vehicles played a large and growing part in the Allied landing operations in World War II. Introduced in 1943, the DUKW was "a truck that could swim." A six-wheeled vehicle, it could carry 25 men ashore or 2.5 tons of equipment. The other key amphibious vehicle was the Landing Vehicle Tracked (LVT), or Amtrac. LVTs were armored to turn them into assault vehicles to carry soldiers ashore under fire. Some were also fitted with turret guns, making them into amphibious tanks.

DUKW

Solomons, further landings were carried out on the islands of Vella Lavella and then, in November, on Bougainville, bypassing the heavily garrisoned island of Kolombangara. More importantly, the major goal of taking Rabaul itself was abandoned. After devastating attacks by US naval aircraft on the base in November, Rabaul was left behind as an impotent relic by the northward progress of the war, remaining in Japanese hands until the general surrender in September 1945.

New resources
The Central Pacific offensive did not get under way until November 1943. Only then did the United States have sufficient aircraft carriers and

Americans on Bougainville
The jungle terrain of the Solomon Islands created many difficulties for Allied troops. Although the Allies landed on Bougainville in November 1943, Japanese troops were still active on the island at the end of the war.

Makin Atoll
Soldiers of the US 27th Infantry Division wade ashore aon November 20, 1943. As at nearby Tarawa, assaulted the same day by Marines, a coral reef kept landing craft from reaching the beaches.

"It was painfully slow, wading … And we had 700 yards to **walk slowly into that machine-gun fire** … "

ROBERT SHERROD, WAR CORRESPONDENT, ON THE LANDING AT TARAWA

amphibious capacity for concurrent operations in the Southwest, South, and Central Pacific. The forces assembled for the landings on Makin and Tarawa in the Gilbert Islands were an impressive demonstration of the expansion of US naval power. Vice-Admiral Raymond Spruance had 17 aircraft carriers at his disposal, ranging from the latest Essex-class fast carriers to small escort carriers; in comparison, the Americans had fielded just three carriers at the battle of Midway. Twenty troop transports carried 18,000 men of the 2nd Marine Division bound for Tarawa and 7,000 troops of the 27th Infantry Division destined for Makin.

Bloody Tarawa

Both islands were tiny coral atolls ringed by reefs. Tarawa was about the size of New York's Central Park. Makin was relatively lightly held, but Tarawa had been heavily fortified by the commander of its 3,000-strong garrison, Rear-Admiral Keiji Shibazaki. He boasted that "it would take one million men one hundred years" to capture the island. In fact, it took the US Marines four days, from November 20 to 24, but the ferocity of the fighting in that short period was a foretaste of the larger struggles that lay ahead.

Despite a heavy bombardment from the sea and the air, the Marines came under fire as they went ashore. Those in LVTs (Landing Vehicle Tracked) were able to ride ashore over the coral, but the rest jumped in and had to wade through the water from the reef to the beach. Almost a third of the 5,000 Marines who landed on the first day were casualties. Many were hit before they even reached solid ground.

The defense of Tarawa ended with a series of suicidal *banzai* charges by the Japanese—taught to fight to the death, they charged at the Allies instead of surrendering; only 17 of the defenders survived. The Marines had lost more than 1,000 killed and over 2,000 injured. Island-hopping to Japan across the Pacific was not going to be a soft option.

KEY MOMENT

DEATH OF YAMAMOTO

On April 18, 1943, Admiral Yamamoto, commander-in-chief of the Japanese Combined Fleet, planned to fly to the island of Bougainville to inspect front-line bases. United States naval intelligence had decoded a message revealing details of Yamomoto's itinerary. A squadron of 18 US fighters, fitted with long-range fuel tanks, were sent from Guadalcanal to intercept Yamomoto's aircraft, the planes flying close to the water to avoid detection by radar. Yamamoto was shot down over the jungle and killed.

AFTER 》

In 1944 the Allied offensive reached the Marianas and the Philippines.

MARSHALLS AND MARIANAS
The Central Pacific offensive continued with landings on the Marshall Islands in February 1944. The **assault on the Marianas 238–89 》** followed, starting at Saipan in June 1944.

RETURN TO THE PHILIPPINES
Fighting continued in New Guinea and the Solomon Islands until the end of the war. Dominant at sea and in the air, the Allies were able to launch the long-awaited **invasion of the Philippines in October 1944 240–41 》**.

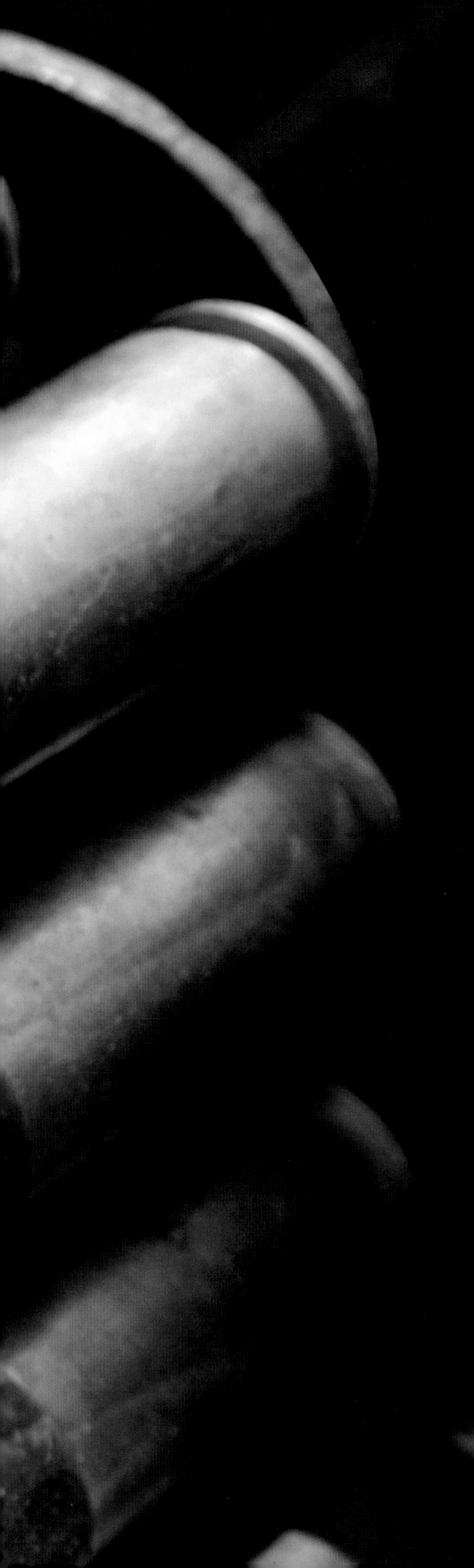

7
OVERWHELMING FORCE
1944

The Soviets drove the Germans from the USSR, advancing into Poland and the Balkans. The Allied D-Day landings created a second front, liberating France and Belgium, then meeting with a strong German counterattack. In the Pacific the Japanese navy was all but destroyed.

OVERWHELMING FORCE

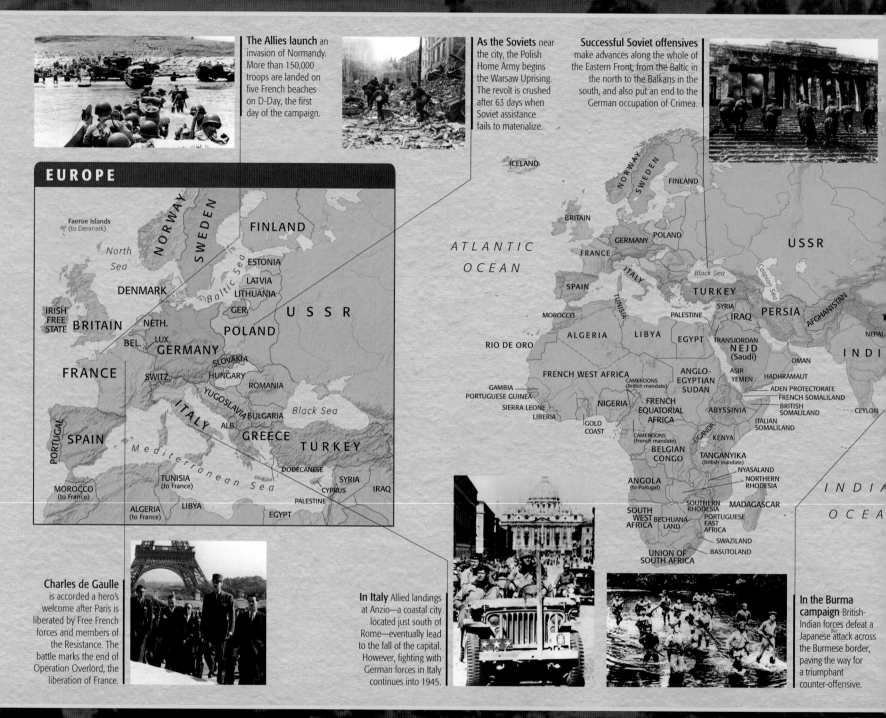

The Allies launch an invasion of Normandy. More than 150,000 troops are landed on five French beaches on D-Day, the first day of the campaign.

As the Soviets near the city, the Polish Home Army begins the Warsaw Uprising. The revolt is crushed after 63 days when Soviet assistance fails to materialize.

Successful Soviet offensives make advances along the whole of the Eastern Front, from the Baltic in the north to the Balkans in the south, and also put an end to the German occupation of Crimea.

Charles de Gaulle is accorded a hero's welcome after Paris is liberated by Free French forces and members of the Resistance. The battle marks the end of Operation Overlord, the liberation of France.

In Italy Allied landings at Anzio—a coastal city located just south of Rome—eventually lead to the fall of the capital. However, fighting with German forces in Italy continues into 1945.

In the Burma campaign British-Indian forces defeat a Japanese attack across the Burmese border, paving the way for a triumphant counter-offensive.

The year 1944 saw the Allies closing in on the German and Japanese homelands. On the Eastern Front the Russians liberated the remainder of the Soviet Union and advanced into Poland. Anticipating the Red Army's arrival, the Poles rose against their Nazi occupiers in Warsaw, but the Russians halted on the Vistula River and the uprising was in vain. In southern Europe the Russian advance forced the Germans to evacuate the Balkans.

As far as the Western Allies were concerned, the year's main event was the Normandy landings, which had been in preparation for more than two years. While France and much of Belgium were quickly liberated after the landings, hopes that the war in Europe could be ended in 1944 began to fade as supply problems ultimately slowed the advance of the Allies and enabled the Germans to recover to some extent. Indeed, in December they took the Allies

1944

Japan launches major offensives in central China, in response to the US using Chinese air bases to bomb Japanese targets.

General Douglas MacArthur makes good on his promise to return to liberate the Philippines from Japanese occupation.

The Dumbarton Oaks
Conference in Washington, D.C. lays the first foundations for an organization that eventually becomes the United Nations. Delegates from the US, Britain, the Soviet Union, and China attend.

The US secures the Mariana Islands from the Japanese. Air bases on the islands are then used by US bombers to attack the Japanese mainland.

Alaska
(to US)

CANADA

UNITED STATES
OF AMERICA

MEXICO

BRITISH HONDURAS
GUATEMALA
EL SALVADOR
COSTA RICA
PANAMA

CUBA
HAITI
DOMINICAN REPUBLIC
VIRGIN ISLANDS
LEEWARD ISLANDS
WINDWARD ISLANDS
BARBADOS
TRINIDAD AND TOBAGO
BRITISH GUIANA
DUTCH GUIANA
FRENCH GUIANA

HONDURAS
NICARAGUA
VENEZUELA
COLOMBIA
ECUADOR
PERU
BOLIVIA
PARAGUAY
BRAZIL
CHILE
URUGUAY
ARGENTINA

ATLANTIC
OCEAN

PACIFIC
OCEAN

MONGOLIA
MANCHUKUO
KOREA
JAPAN
FORMOSA
CHINA
FRENCH INDOCHINA
PHILIPPINE ISLANDS
BRITISH BORNEO
BRUNEI
SARAWAK
DUTCH EAST INDIES
PORTUGUESE TIMOR
PAPUA
TERRITORY OF NEW GUINEA
Volcano Islands
Mariana Islands
GUAM
Caroline Islands
Marshall Islands
Nauru
Gilbert Islands
Ellice Islands
Solomon Islands
New Hebrides
New Caledonia
WESTERN SAMOA
Fiji
AUSTRALIA
NEW ZEALAND

THE WORLD IN DECEMBER 1944
Axis powers and allies
Axis conquests to Dec 1944
Area under Japanese control, Dec 1944
Allied states
Allied conquests to Dec 1944
Neutral states
Frontiers Sep 1939

by surprise with a counter-offensive. Meanwhile, in Italy, there were grim battles before the Allies entered Rome in June, but the Germans again brought them to a halt before the year was out.

In Burma the Japanese launched a major offensive in early March, but this was repulsed and the Allies mounted an ultimately decisive counter-offensive. The Japanese also launched a series of offensives in China, forcing the Americans to withdraw their strategic bombers.

General Douglas MacArthur continued his island-hopping in the southwest Pacific, ultimately isolating the main Japanese base at Rabaul on the island of New Guinea. In the central Pacific Admiral Chester Nimitz secured the Marshall Islands and then went on to seize the Marianas. Thereafter, the two US drives converged with the landings in the Philippines. In the course of these operations the Japanese Navy was virtually destroyed.

TIMELINE 1944

Anzio Landings ▪ Turning Point in Burma ▪ **The Fall of Rome** ▪ **D-Day** ▪ Breakout from Normandy ▪
Return to the Philippines ▪ Flying Bombs ▪ **Hitler Bomb Plot** ▪ Liberation of France ▪ **Red Army**
Offensives ▪ **The Warsaw Uprising** ▪ Operation Market Garden ▪ **Battle of the Bulge**

JANUARY	FEBRUARY	MARCH	APRIL	MAY	JUNE

FEBRUARY 4
US secures Kwajalein in the Marshall Islands.

FEBRUARY 8
Revised plan for Operation Overlord (Normandy landings) formally approved.

≪ US troops landing in the Marshall Islands

MARCH 4
Merrill's Marauders begin operations in Burma.

APRIL 4
De Gaulle takes command of French armed forces.

APRIL 12
In the Crimea, Germans retreat to fortress of Sebastopol, but they hold out only until May 7.

JANUARY 16
Eisenhower, Commander-in-Chief of AEF (American Expeditionary Force), arrives in Britain.

FEBRUARY 11
US landings on Eniwetok Atoll in the Marshall Islands.

MARCH 7
Japanese launch a major offensive in Burma aimed at India.

MAY 15
Start of deportation of Hungarian Jews to Auschwitz.

MAY 15
In Italy, Germans withdraw from the Gustav Line to prepared positions closer to Rome.

⌃ D-Day landings

JUNE 4
Fall of Rome.

JUNE 6
D-Day landings in Normandy. By the end of the day, beachheads are established at all five landing sites.

JANUARY 22
Allied landing at Anzio behind the German Gustav Line in Italy. Determined German response traps US and British force in small beachhead until May.

FEBRUARY 17
Americans bomb Japanese naval base at Truk in the Caroline Islands, destroying almost 200,000 tons of shipping.

⌃ Germans in the Crimea fleeing from the Red Army

MAY 17
Monte Cassino finally taken by Polish troops.

≫ General Douglas MacArthur

≫ British 5.5in Howitzer

⌄ Allied troops landing at Anzio, Italy

FEBRUARY 19
Start of "Big Week," a bombing campaign against German aircraft production plants.

MARCH 15
Allies attack Monte Cassino for the third time, pounding it from the air and ground.

APRIL 18
Japan launches a new offensive in central China. Americans have to abandon some of their airbases.

MAY 27
As part of MacArthur's strategy of leap-frogging pockets of Japanese forces in New Guinea, US forces land on Biak Island.

MAY 31
Soviets launch attack into Romania.

JUNE 13
First V-1s launched against England.

JUNE 19
US landing on Saipan in the Mariana Islands.

JUNE 19
Battle of the Philippine Sea. Japanese suffer heavy aircraft losses.

MARCH 19
Hitler orders German occupation of Hungary.

MARCH 30
City of Imphal in eastern India besieged by the Japanese.

APRIL 28
During a rehearsal for the D-Day landings at Slapton Sands in southwest England, German torpedo boats attack US landing craft. A total of 749 soldiers and sailors are lost.

⌄ Soviet T-34 tank

"Only with great difficulty and by **using our last reserves** have we been able to **improvise new fronts**, both **east and west**. The sky over Germany grows **very dark**."

GERMAN FIELD MARSHAL ERWIN ROMMEL, SHORTLY BEFORE HIS DEATH, AUTUMN 1944

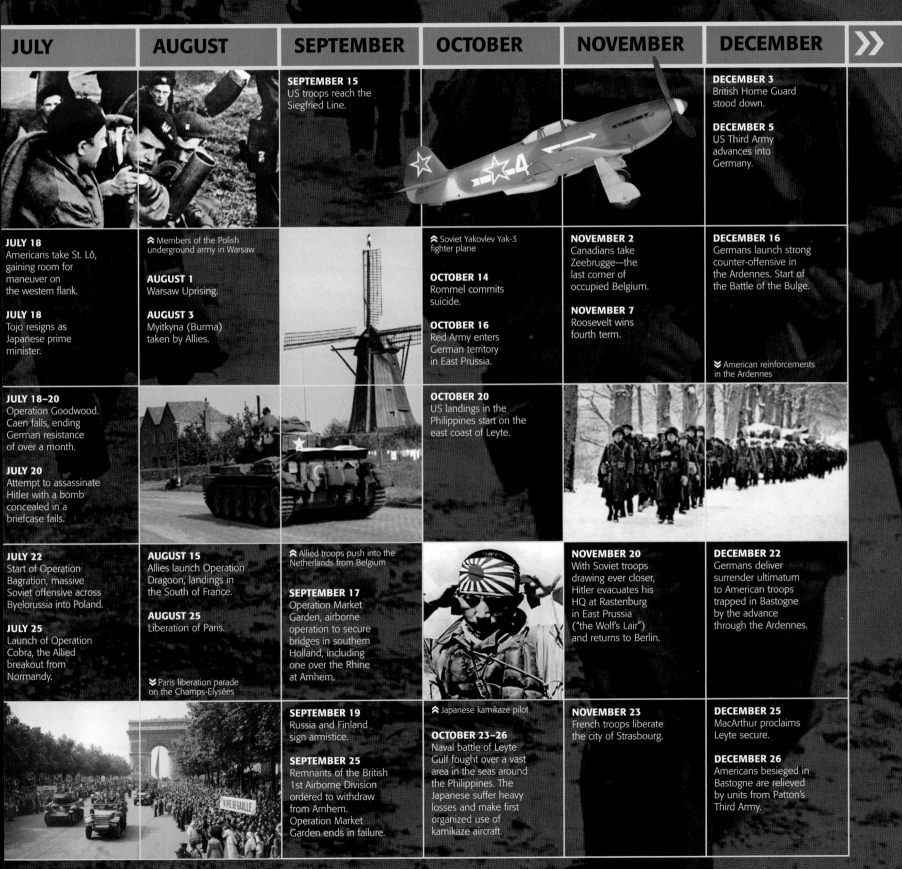

JULY	AUGUST	SEPTEMBER	OCTOBER	NOVEMBER	DECEMBER	»

SEPTEMBER 15
US troops reach the Siegfried Line.

DECEMBER 3
British Home Guard stood down.

DECEMBER 5
US Third Army advances into Germany.

JULY 18
Americans take St. Lô, gaining room for maneuver on the western flank.

JULY 18
Tojo resigns as Japanese prime minister.

⌃ Members of the Polish underground army in Warsaw

AUGUST 1
Warsaw Uprising.

AUGUST 3
Myitkyna (Burma) taken by Allies.

⌃ Soviet Yakovlev Yak-3 fighter plane

OCTOBER 14
Rommel commits suicide.

OCTOBER 16
Red Army enters German territory in East Prussia.

NOVEMBER 2
Canadians take Zeebrugge—the last corner of occupied Belgium.

NOVEMBER 7
Roosevelt wins fourth term.

DECEMBER 16
Germans launch strong counter-offensive in the Ardennes. Start of the Battle of the Bulge.

⌄ American reinforcements in the Ardennes

JULY 18–20
Operation Goodwood. Caen falls, ending German resistance of over a month.

JULY 20
Attempt to assassinate Hitler with a bomb concealed in a briefcase fails.

OCTOBER 20
US landings in the Philippines start on the east coast of Leyte.

JULY 22
Start of Operation Bagration, massive Soviet offensive across Byelorussia into Poland.

JULY 25
Launch of Operation Cobra, the Allied breakout from Normandy.

AUGUST 15
Allies launch Operation Dragoon, landings in the South of France.

AUGUST 25
Liberation of Paris.

⌄ Paris liberation parade on the Champs-Elysées

⌃ Allied troops push into the Netherlands from Belgium

SEPTEMBER 17
Operation Market Garden, airborne operation to secure bridges in southern Holland, including one over the Rhine at Arnhem.

NOVEMBER 20
With Soviet troops drawing ever closer, Hitler evacuates his HQ at Rastenburg in East Prussia ("the Wolf's Lair") and returns to Berlin.

DECEMBER 22
Germans deliver surrender ultimatum to American troops trapped in Bastogne by the advance through the Ardennes.

SEPTEMBER 19
Russia and Finland sign armistice.

SEPTEMBER 25
Remnants of the British 1st Airborne Division ordered to withdraw from Arnhem. Operation Market Garden ends in failure.

⌃ Japanese kamikaze pilot

OCTOBER 23–26
Naval battle of Leyte Gulf fought over a vast area in the seas around the Philippines. The Japanese suffer heavy losses and make first organized use of kamikaze aircraft.

NOVEMBER 23
French troops liberate the city of Strasbourg.

DECEMBER 25
MacArthur proclaims Leyte secure.

DECEMBER 26
Americans besieged in Bastogne are relieved by units from Patton's Third Army.

Battles for the Marianas

By summer 1944 Admiral Nimitz's advance across the central Pacific was making good progress. The next targets in his island-hopping campaign were the Marianas, 1,000 miles (1,600 km) west of the Marshalls. The Japanese, determined to hold on to the islands, devised a plan to thwart the Americans.

Admiral Nimitz issued orders for the assault on the Marianas on March 28, 1944. There were to be two attack forces: a northern force, consisting of two US Marine divisions coming from Hawaii, would take Saipan and Tinian; and a southern force, with one Marine division, was to land on Guam, using Guadalcanal in the Solomons as its mounting base. Two army divisions would provide the reserve. Saipan was to be attacked first on June 15, then Guam and Tinian.

Preparations for battle

The softening up of the Marianas began as early as February 23, before Nimitz had received his order to attack. Carrier aircraft struck at the four southernmost islands, knocking out 170 aircraft and sinking ships, losing just six US planes. A successful strike was also made against Truk that month. However, Nimitz was still concerned about Japanese interference from the Carolines. US planes based in the Solomons and Marshalls began to attack the islands in mid-March, with carrier aircraft mounting further attacks from the end of the month. These culminated in two days' worth of attacks on Truk at the end of April, which virtually destroyed the Japanese base.

While these operations were under way, Japan was also preparing. Apart from sending reinforcements to the Marianas, they hatched a plan designed to destroy the US Pacific Fleet. They hoped to lure the US ships to the western Carolines, where they would meet in a decisive battle against the Japanese Combined Fleet; based between Borneo and the Philippines, the Japanese fleet did not want to operate too far from its oil supplies in the Dutch East Indies (present-day Indonesia).

Marines on Saipan

US troops advance behind a tank during mopping-up operations on Saipan. The Japanese also had a few tanks, but they were quickly destroyed by the Allies.

Japanese honor

A dead Japanese soldier on Saipan. The troops were still imbued with the belief that to surrender was a disgrace and so few prisoners were taken in the Marianas.

Their plan meant that the Japanese would have to repulse any assault on the Marianas using the aircraft already based there. Unfortunately, by the end of May, there were only 170 planes available, thanks to US air attacks.

The assault force bound for Saipan started to leave Hawaii on May 26. Two weeks later, the pre-assault bombardment began. While carrier aircraft attacked Japanese airfields on the islands, surface ships bombarded Saipan. US frogmen were sent in to check the approaches to the selected landing beaches, but came under fire. The Japanese now knew where the landings were

550 The number of US craft which took part in the assault on the Marianas, making it the largest US amphibious operation in the Pacific Ocean at that time.

to be, on the west coast, and adjusted their own positions to improve their defense in time for the attack on Saipan, on June 15.

The battle heats up

Although the Japanese troops resisted fiercely, some 20,000 US Marines made it ashore, securing the beachhead. Their advance inland was slow, however. The Japanese fought with tenacity, and the landing of a US Army division on June 17 made little difference to progress.

While the battle for Saipan continued, there were dramatic developments at sea. When the American ships began their pre-assault bombardment, Admiral Soemu Toyoda, commander of Japan's Combined Fleet, ordered his ships into the Philippine Sea in order to destroy the US carrier force. US submarines spotted the fleet and surprise was lost.

Grenade discharger

A Japanese Model 89 grenade discharger. It had a rifled barrel of 2 in (50 mm) caliber and could fire a wide variety of projectiles. The Model 89 was fired from the kneeling position, giving it the nickname "knee mortar."

On June 19 the Japanese launched four air strikes from their carriers against those of the Americans. However, these were detected by radar en route and intercepted. Some 219 Japanese planes were shot down. It was no less damaging to the Japanese that two of their carriers

AFTER »

The capture of the Marianas by the Allies meant that the Japanese were now facing an eventual defeat.

NEW THREAT TO JAPAN
The outcome was also significant in that **B-29 bombers**, which would shortly be deployed to the islands, could now attack the **Japanese home islands 314–15 »** with ease.

MACARTHUR'S PROGRESS
Throughout this time US general Douglas MacArthur had been **advancing steadily in the southwest Pacific**. Having cleared the **Solomon Islands**, his forces had then dealt with the Japanese in the **Bismarck Archipelago**, eventually isolating the **main Japanese base** at Rabaul, on New Britain, rather than attempting **a direct attack** on it. Simultanueously, there had been a **series of landings** on the north coast of New Guinea.

AMERICA'S NEXT MOVE
MacArthur's drive, and that of Nimitz in the central Pacific, were about to join up. MacArthur **had his sights** set on the **Philippines as the next Allied target 240–41 »**.

were sunk by submarines. The Japanese commander was convinced that many of his missing aircraft had landed on Guam, and remained overnight in the area to recover them on board. Consequently, his force was attacked the following day by US carrier aircraft. They sank a carrier and shot down a

US and Japanese naval strengths 1941–45
Ship-building in the United States outstripped that of the Japanese from the very outset, and from 1942 onward, American production in aircraft carriers grew with significant speed.

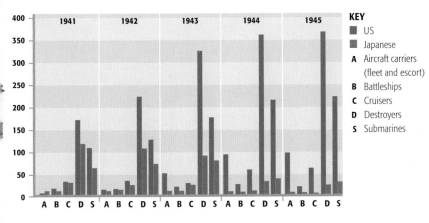

further 65 planes. The back of Japanese naval airpower had been broken in what was officially called the Battle of the Philippine Sea, but known more popularly by the Americans as the "Great Marianas Turkey Shoot."

America secures the Marianas
Better progress was now being made on Saipan. Its dominant peak, Mount Tapotchu, was captured on June 25 and, by early July, the island had been almost cleared. With defeat staring them in the face, the two senior Japanese

US aircraft strike the Marianas
A US Navy Grumman Avenger torpedo-bomber overflying Tinian during an air strike on the island prior to the landings.

commanders took their own lives on July 6. The following day the surviving Japanese made one last suicide attack and it was all over. Ninety percent of the Japanese garrison had been killed during the battles, at a cost of some 16,500 casualties to the US.

With Saipan secured, the Americans now turned to Guam and Tinian. The naval bombardment started on July 14 and the landings took place one week later. Again, the Americans got ashore successfully, but had to fight to enlarge the initial beachhead, and faced savage counterattacks from the Japanese.

Tinian was assaulted on July 24 and, again, Japanese resistance was bitter, but the outcome was never in doubt. The island was effectively in American hands by August 1, while the same situation was achieved on Guam nine days later. The Marianas had been won, although the final mopping up would take another three months.

TECHNOLOGY
SEABEES

By the time they had been secured, the infrastructure on the Pacific islands that had been in Japanese hands had been destroyed and needed to be repaired. The task fell to the US Navy's Construction Battalions, more informally known as the "Seabees" (from the acronym CB). Formed after the US entered the war, their ranks contained men skilled in all aspects of civil engineering. Landing as soon as a beachhead had been secured, they would begin by improving facilities for unloading supplies and equipment. Thereafter, the construction of airstrips, fuel storage tanks, roads, accommodation, and hospitals followed. Versatility was their watchword, and they lived up to their motto "We Build, We Fight."

BEFORE «

When General MacArthur left a doomed Philippines, in March 1942, he vowed to the Filipino people that he would return.

A PROMISE KEPT
In March 1944 the US **Joint Chiefs of Staff** (JCS) laid down that MacArthur was to assault the **southern Philippines** and then secure the **main island of Luzon**, while Admiral Chester Nimitz **tackled Formosa** (Taiwan).

However, **severe pressure on China** during that summer caused the JCS to consider **a direct invasion of Japan**. Both MacArthur and Nimitz insisted that the **Philippines must be dealt with first « 238–39**. The **JCS relented**, and so MacArthur **drew up his plans**.

FINALIZING PLANS FOR INVASION
MacArthur's intention had been to invade the **southernmost large island**, Mindanao, in mid-November, **landing on Leyte** a month later. Given the situation in China, he amended his plan, however. Now he would **bypass Mindanao**, assault Leyte in mid-October, and **land on Luzon** in December.

Return to the Philippines

The assault on the Philippines saw the American central and southwest Pacific drives finally join together. This also marked the last major sea battle in the Pacific Ocean and witnessed the debut of a new Japanese weapon—the kamikaze, or suicide, aircraft.

On October 12, 1944, Admiral "Bull" Halsey's Third US Fleet launched air strikes on Formosa and Luzon in preparation for the landings on Leyte. The Japanese plan was for any landings in the inner ring of islands protecting Japan to be met with immediate air and sea strikes. Admiral Toyoda, commander of the Combined Fleet, believed that Formosa and Luzon were the main US targets and launched a series of air attacks on the Third Fleet. These damaged some ships, but at a cost of around 500 planes to the Japanese.

Five days later US Rangers landed on Suluan Island at the mouth of the Leyte Gulf. They overwhelmed the Japanese garrison, but not before it had sent a warning message. Toyoda realized the true American target and now began to concentrate his fleet with a view to attacking the US invasion fleet. The landings themselves took place on October 20, as planned. The Japanese garrison was largely made up of new conscripts, and resistance was initially variable. The next day the US troops entered the capital of Leyte and the Japanese began to fight with greater determination. Meanwhile, the Combined Fleet was on the move. Toyoda's plan was to lure the American carriers northward, away from Leyte, by offering his four surviving carriers as bait, while the remainder of his fleet, divided in two, would pass through the Philippines

> ## 1 MILLION
> **The number of Filipinos killed during the war, the majority in the final year. A quarter of a million of them fought as guerrillas.**

The Leyte landings
US troops, having just landed on Leyte, take cover from Japanese snipers. Although the landings initially went well, Japanese resistance soon stiffened, producing some remarkably bitter fighting.

MacArthur wades ashore
General Douglas MacArthur joins his men as they wade ashore on the opening day of the Leyte landings. The pledge he made to the Filipino people in March 1942—that he would return—had been fulfilled.

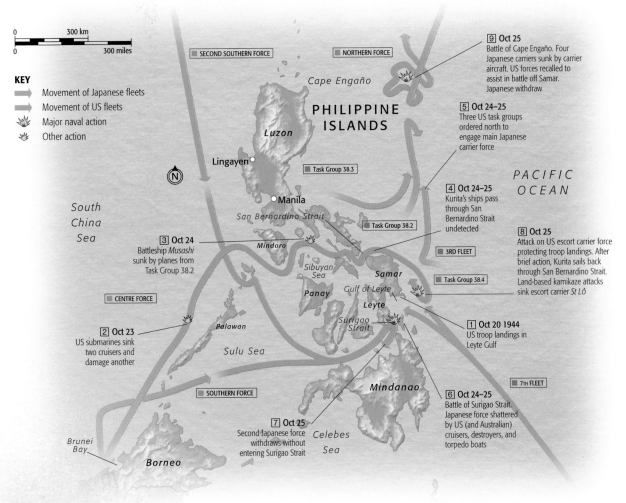

KEY
→ Movement of Japanese fleets
→ Movement of US fleets
✹ Major naval action
✾ Other action

9 Oct 25
Battle of Cape Engaño. Four Japanese carriers sunk by carrier aircraft. US forces recalled to assist in battle off Samar. Japanese withdraw

SECOND SOUTHERN FORCE

NORTHERN FORCE

Cape Engaño

PHILIPPINE ISLANDS

Luzon

Lingayen

5 Oct 24–25
Three US task groups ordered north to engage main Japanese carrier force

Task Group 38.3

Manila

San Bernardino Strait

PACIFIC OCEAN

4 Oct 24–25
Kurita's ships pass through San Bernardino Strait undetected

South China Sea

3 Oct 24
Battleship *Musashi* sunk by planes from Task Group 38.2

Task Group 38.2

Mindoro

3RD FLEET

8 Oct 25
Attack on US escort carrier force protecting troop landings. After brief action, Kurita sails back through San Bernardino Strait. Land-based kamikaze attacks sink escort carrier *St Lô*

Sibuyan Sea

Samar

Panay

Gulf of Leyte

Leyte

Task Group 38.4

CENTRE FORCE

Surigao Strait

1 Oct 20 1944
US troop landings in Leyte Gulf

2 Oct 23
US submarines sink two cruisers and damage another

Palawan

Sulu Sea

Mindanao

7TH FLEET

6 Oct 24–25
Battle of Surigao Strait. Japanese force shattered by US (and Australian) cruisers, destroyers, and torpedo boats

SOUTHERN FORCE

7 Oct 25
Second Japanese force withdraws without entering Surigao Strait

Celebes Sea

Brunei Bay

Borneo

Kamikaze pilot
A Japanese pilot prepares for his kamikaze mission, tying on his Rising Sun headband prior to departure. To die for one's country and the emperor was the ultimate glory for the Japanese warrior.

secured on December 25, but only after landings had been made on its northwest coast. MacArthur could now focus on Luzon, having made an initial landing on the island of Mindoro in mid-December. The initial assault was made in Lingayen Bay, on the west coast, on January 9, 1945. No opposition was met and the landing force began to advance toward Manila. Three weeks later, there were further landings at the base of the Bataan Peninsula and then at the entrance of Manila Bay, but more prolonged fighting lay ahead.

north and south of Leyte, destroying the shipping supporting the landings, thereby isolating the troops on shore. Initially, Toyoda's plan was successful, and Admiral Halsey was drawn north.

Japanese plans foiled

However, on October 23, US submarines intercepted the main strike force, sank two cruisers, and crippled a third. Halsey turned south again. The following day his aircraft engaged the Japanese fleet's Center Force between the islands of Mindoro and Luzon, sinking a battleship and crippling a heavy cruiser, although Halsey lost one of his carriers to an attack by planes based on Luzon.

Admiral Kinkaid's Seventh US Fleet, which had been protecting the shipping in Leyte Gulf, engaged the Southern Force and virtually destroyed it. This, however, left the amphibious shipping vulnerable, and the Center Force, undeterred by Halsey's initial attack, quickly sank an American escort carrier and three destroyers. Halsey, who had turned north once more to deal with the

Battle of Leyte Gulf

Japan's main striking force came from the Combined Fleet's base off the island of Borneo, but was reinforced by ships from Japan itself. The fleet's Northern Force represented the US carrier bait.

Japanese carriers, immediately turned about, leaving his own carriers to deal with the Japanese ones. Fearing that it was about to be cut off, the Northern Force hastily withdrew. Toyoda's four remaining carriers were all sunk.

Japan's new weapon

Leyte Gulf was the last fleet-versus-fleet action in the Pacific. The Japanese Combined Fleet had been left with no carriers and was in no position to challenge the US Navy any further. But there had been one disturbing feature of the battle. The Japanese unveiled a new weapon—aircraft packed with explosives and designed to sink Allied ships by diving onto their decks. The first kamikaze victim was the US escort carrier *St Lô*, which was sunk off Samar on October 25. On land, Leyte was

> ## "If only we might **fall—like cherry blossoms** in the spring—so **pure and radiant!**"
> FROM A POEM BY AN UNKNOWN KAMIKAZE PILOT

AFTER

It would take the remainder of the war to subdue the Philippines. Under Tomoyuki Yamashita, conqueror of Singapore and Malaya, the Japanese fought ferociously.

CONTINUED FIGHTING

Nowhere was this more true than on the **streets of Manila**. It took two weeks of intense struggle before it was finally secured, in early March 1945. By then the city was in **almost total ruin** and, worse, some **100,000 of its inhabitants** had been killed, many of them **victims of Japanese atrocities**. Thereafter, the fighting moved to the rugged hinterland. The smaller Philippine islands also had to be **liberated**.

CLOSING IN ON JAPAN

By March 1945 the campaign in the Philippines had become **a sideshow**, as had the eradication of the remaining Japanese forces in New Guinea. **The baton was handed to Admiral Nimitz**, who was given the task of dealing with the **last two stepping stones** to the Japanese mainland— **Iwo Jima and Okinawa 310–13 »**.

Landing in the Philippines

On October 20, 1944, General Douglas MacArthur, with General Kruger's Sixth Army, landed on Leyte Island, so fulfilling his promise to return to the Philippines. It was an historic event. The invading US fleet was the largest assembled in the Pacific. More than 200,000 troops were put ashore, as well as supplies and equipment. Initially the invading forces met minimal resistance but on October 23 the Japanese launched a full-scale naval attack.

" ... The *Nashville*, her engines bringing to life the steel under our feet, knifed into Leyte Gulf ... the blackness had given way to somber gray, and even as we saw the black outline of the shore .. the cloak of darkness began to roll back. On every side ships were riding toward the island ... I was on the bridge with Captain C.E. Coney. His clear, keen eyes and cool, crisp voice swung the cruiser first to port, then to starboard as he dodged floating mines ... then, just as the sun rose clear of the horizon, there was Tacloban [the capital of Leyte Island] ... Shortly after ... we reached our appointed position offshore. The captain carefully hove into line and dropped anchor. Our initial vantage point was 2 miles [3km] from the beaches, but I could clearly see the sandstrips with the pounding surf ... and the jungle-clad hills rising behind the town ... Across what would ordinarily have been a glinting, untroubled blue sea, the black dots of the landing craft churned toward the beaches.

From my vantage point, I had a clear view of everything that took place. Troops were going ashore at 'Red Beach' near Palo, at San Jose on 'White Beach', and at the southern tip of Leyte on tiny Panson Island ... At 'Red Beach' our troops secured a landing and began moving inland. I decided to go in with the third assault wave ... I took them [President Osmena, General Valdez and General Romulo] into my landing barge and we started for the beach ... As we came closer, we could pick up the shouts of our soldiers as they gave and acknowledged orders... The coxwain dropped the ramp ... and we waded in. It took me only 30 or 40 long strides to reach dry land, but that was one of the most meaningful walks I ever took ... "

GENERAL DOUGLAS MACARTHUR, LANDING ON LEYTE ISLAND, PHILIPPINES

A mighty force
Massive landing craft carry American troops and supplies toward the beach at Leyte Island. The invading force consisted of more than 730 transports and escorts, supported by aircraft carriers and 100 warships.

AMERICAN GENERAL Born 1880 Died 1964

Douglas MacArthur

"I said, to the people of the Philippines whence I came, I shall return"

MACARTHUR AFTER HIS ARRIVAL IN AUSTRALIA, MARCH 30, 1942

A flamboyant and controversial figure, Douglas MacArthur was one of the best-known American generals of World War II. He commanded Allied forces in the Southwest Pacific theater and administered Japan during its postwar occupation by the US.

Military heritage

MacArthur was born into the army. He once said that his first memory was the sound of bugles, and his early years were spent with his father, General Arthur MacArthur. Having graduated top of the class at West Point, he was commissioned to the US Army Corps of Engineers. He served his first tour of duty in the Philippines, marking a long association with the islands. Subsequently, he served as an aide to US president, Theodore Roosevelt, and during World War I he was chief-of-staff of the 42nd ("Rainbow") Division in France. By 1925 he had been made a major-general and in 1930 he was appointed US army chief-of-staff, the youngest man at that time to hold such a prestigious position.

Popular hero
In 1941, following the high drama of MacArthur's stand on the Bataan Peninsula, *Time* magazine featured the general as their "man of the year."

MacArthur's reputation suffered a blow in 1932 when he used force against a protest by war veterans in Washington. Three years later he went to the Philippines on the invitation of President Manuel Quezon to act as military adviser and create a defense force in the islands. One of his aides was Dwight D. Eisenhower. MacArthur retired from active service but soon came back into action in July 1941 when President Roosevelt appointed him commander of the US forces in the Far East. MacArthur focused on building up forces in the Philippines, although he had limited resources.

Defense of Bataan

On December 7, 1941, Japanese forces struck at Pearl Harbor. It was clear the Philippines would be next in line. There has been some debate about why MacArthur did not take what seemed to be appropriate action. In the event, when the Japanese attacked the Philippines, half of his air force was wiped out.

Fortress headquarters
MacArthur set up headquarters in a tunnel complex on Corregidor during the siege of the island. His withdrawal was well executed but he was unable to defend the island indefinitely.

Leader of the Pacific campaigns

Between the Allied retreat from Bataan in 1942 and the triumphant return to the Philippines in 1944, MacArthur commanded other campaigns throughout the Pacific, including the Battle of Los Negros in February 1944.

On December 22 Japanese forces took Manila. Always one to act on his own initiative, MacArthur, against the wishes of Washington, withdrew his forces—and his personal press pool— to the Bataan peninsula, setting up his headquarters on the island fortress of Corregidor. From there he conducted a highly publicized defense against the Japanese that made him a national hero. However, supplies were low and the defense had very little hope of success. Roosevelt ordered MacArthur to leave Bataan, which initially he refused to do. Taking into consideration MacArthur's popularity, which enabled him to have a powerful influence on military strategy, Roosevelt promised him his own theater of operations in the Pacific. In March 1942

"Our forces stand once again on Philippine soil"

MACARTHUR ON LANDING AT LEYTE ISLAND, OCTOBER 19, 1944

MacArthur was eventually ordered to escape by sea; his men, however, stayed on Bataan. They finally surrendered to the Japanese in April 1942 and many died on the Bataan "Death March."

Island-hopping in the Pacific

Once in Australia, MacArthur famously announced that he would return to the Philippines one day—and over the next two years that is what he worked toward. He was appointed Supreme Commander of the Southwest Pacific theater, working in conjunction with Admiral Chester Nimitz, commander-in-chief of the US Navy. The two men rarely saw eye to eye. Nimitz wanted to attack the Japanese through the islands of the central Pacific; MacArthur was determined to liberate the Philippines. The joint chiefs-of-staff adopted what was known as Operation Cartwheel, a two-pronged strategy aimed at isolating the major Japanese base at Rabaul.

While Nimitz advanced through the Solomon Islands, MacArthur advanced along the northeast coast of New Guinea, using an "island-hopping" or "leaping" strategy, bypassing main centers of Japanese force, leaving them to "wither on the vine," as he put it.

Return to the Philippines

By late 1944 MacArthur was ready to invade the Philippines. Neither Nimitz nor Washington approved, but as the idol of America, MacArthur was in a strong position and he was given the go-ahead. On October 19, 1944, in the full glare of publicity, MacArthur landed with his forces at Leyte Gulf, and over the following months, often against Washington's wishes, went on to fully liberate the Philippines. Recapturing the islands took longer than planned, but in 1945 MacArthur was present when the Allies finally took Manila.

MacArthur presided over the Japanese surrender in Tokyo Bay on September 2, 1945. After the war he oversaw the Allied occupation of Japan, with responsibility for restoring the economy and the demobilization of the military. In 1950 he was put in command of UN forces when the Korean War broke out but—after he was publicly critical of US President Truman's wish for a limited war—was relieved of his command. Thereafter he lived a fairly secluded life in New York until his death on April 5, 1964.

Commander of the Allied Powers

General MacArthur accepts the formal surrender of Japan aboard the USS *Missouri*. He went on to play a major role in the reconstruction of Japan after the war as Supreme Commander of the Allied Powers in Japan.

General MacArthur

Famous for smoking a corn cob pipe that he designed himself, MacArthur was criticized for self publicity and disregard of authority but praised for his bold, imaginative military strategy.

‹‹ BEFORE

China had been at war with Japan since 1937, but it was not until the end of 1938 that the West gave China any help, when the US loaned it money to buy arms.

AMERICAN AID

The Americans **increased their aid** in early 1941, when China, with Britain, became the first recipient of **Lend Lease ‹‹ 96–97**. Later that year, a group of **volunteer US airmen** under **Colonel Claire Chennault** were sent to China with their Curtiss P-40 Tomahawk fighters. Known as the **Flying Tigers**, the group soon began to **make quite an impression** on the Japanese.

CURTISS P-40 TOMAHAWK FIGHTERS

The Japanese 1944 offensive
A small group of Japanese officers observe Chinese positions from their hilltop vantage point and plan their next attack. The poorly led Chinese troops were no match for the Japanese forces.

Suffering China

China came under increased pressure as the Japanese launched a series of offensives. Chiang Kai-shek's troops proved incapable of holding them and the Americans were forced to remove their strategic bombers, which had begun attacking the Japanese mainland.

Initially, American aid had come to China via Burma but, by May 1942, Japan had overrun Burma, cutting off the Allied supply route. Henceforth, the only way that the aid could reach the Chinese was by air from India.

In February 1942 President Roosevelt had appointed General Joseph Stilwell to head a US military mission to China. He had much experience of the country, and was charged with improving the efficiency of Chiang's forces and overseeing the delivery of Lend-Lease material to them. Now, he took over command of a Chinese force that had been sent to help the British stem the Japanese invasion of Burma and led his men, on foot, into India.

Chiang Kai-shek's strategy
While General Stilwell was responsible for the re-equipment and training of the Chinese troops, he continued to advise and cajole Chiang Kai-shek, who was in Chungking, in an attempt to persuade the leader to take more positive action against the invading Japanese troops.

Chiang himself welcomed the aid he was receiving, but continued to believe that he would last longer than the Japanese and that their troops would eventually withdraw to face the growing American threat in the Pacific. Besides, his ultimate enemy continued to be Mao Zedong and the Communists.

While the Communists had joined forces with him to fight the Japanese, Chiang was determined to crush them once the Japanese had gone. Much to Stilwell's growing frustration, therefore, Chiang was more concerned with preserving his forces for this purpose than in running the risk of them being further severely

weakened by the Japanese. As it was, although some six million men strong, the Chinese Army remained relatively poorly equipped and trained. Endemic corruption and growing inflation—both of which were rife in the region of China controlled by the Kuomintang—also contributed to the army's plight.

> "The **advance of our forces** across the Pacific is swift. But this advance will be **too late for China unless you act now** and vigorously."
>
> ROOSEVELT TO CHIANG KAI-SHEK, SEPTEMBER 1944

It suited Chiang's strategy that the Communists were not beneficiaries of the Lend-Lease scheme, even though they were suffering Japanese pressure in those areas of the country that they controlled in the northeast, but were being more active than the Nationalists. The Communists' situation was not

Chennault's airfields
Numerous airfields were built in southeast China, under instruction from Colonel (later General) Chennault. Plant for such an undertaking was short and most of the airfields were built by hand using local peasantry.

helped by the fact that aid coming from the Soviet Union had dried up, because of the non-aggression pact it had signed with Japan in April 1941.

Japan on the offensive

Stilwell also clashed with Chennault, whose Flying Tigers were incorporated into the US Army Air Force in 1942, and who had become commander of the US 14th Air Force in China the following year. Stilwell was convinced that the Chinese soldier—with proper training, equipment, and leadership—was as good as any in the world. He worked hard both to prepare his Chinese troops in India, and within China itself, to equip and train 30 divisions, in accordance with his brief from Washington.

Chennault, on the other hand, was a firm believer in the omnipotence of air power. He argued that this could severely damage the Japanese forces in China and wreak havoc on the supply lines from resources-rich Southeast Asia to the Japanese homeland. To this end he organized the construction of numerous airfields in southeast China during 1942 and 1943, and demanded that the bulk of the Lend-Lease supplies be given to him. Chennault's strategy suited Chiang Kai-shek, since it would enable him to preserve his army, but Stilwell thought it would merely lead to the Japanese attacking the airfields.

Chinese evacuation
The war was a cause of constant upheaval in China. By late June 1944, families were fleeing their homes in large numbers, many of them evacuating by train in the face of the Japanese advance.

Stilwell's fears were confirmed when in April 1944 the Japanese launched a major offensive, using some 600,000 troops. Their aim was to capture the Allied airfields in southeast China and to establish a land supply route running from Indochina to Korea, in order to offset the grievous losses in Japanese merchant shipping to US submarines. Hunan province was quickly taken, and the advance headed southward. Chennault's planes did their best to delay the onrush, but the Chinese troops on the ground offered little resistance to the attack.

While this was happening in China, the US began to deploy their massive B-29 Superfortresses, and these made their first attack on the Japanese

650,000 The tonnage of supplies flown from India to China from July 1942. Many planes were lost en route owing to the hazardous flying conditions over a range of mountains nicknamed "the hump."

homeland in June. By now, Japanese troops had forced the evacuation of the US airfields in southern China. Chiang now demanded the return of the divisions that Stilwell was using in northern Burma to open the new land route from India to China. At the same time, he resisted requests from President Roosevelt to place all ground forces, including those of the Communists, in Stilwell's hands. Meanwhile, the Communists fighting in the northeast of the country had gained from the Japanese offensive, since it took much of the pressure off them, and enabled them to reorganize their forces. The poor efforts of the Nationalist troops resulted in growing disillusionment with the Kuomintang and increased support for Mao Zedong, whose troops had always fought much more actively—something that the US was slow to recognize.

Mixed fortunes

By the end of 1944, the Japanese had achieved their aims, and now had a continuous land corridor running from the southern tip of Malaya up through Indochina and China to Manchukuo. In stark contrast to the reverses that the Japanese forces were suffering on other fronts, the offensive in China had been an overwhelming success.

On the other hand, the disappointing performance by Chiang's forces during the Japanese offensive convinced the Western Allies that the Chinese were no longer in a position to take a decisive part in the defeat of Japan. From now on, therefore, China was merely seen as a means of tying down one million of the Japanese troops.

AFTER

In fall 1944 Roosevelt decided that China must now be considered a separate theatre of war from India and Burma.

STILWELL'S LEGACY
Roosevelt relieved Stilwell, whose relations with Chiang Kai-shek had **reached their nadir**, and engaged General Albert Wedermeyer in his place. However, Stilwell did prove that **the Chinese soldier could fight**. The troops that he had trained in India were now **advancing through northern Burma**, building a new Ledo Road 248–49 >> as they went.

US BOMBERS RETURN TO FIGHT
As for the **US bombers** that had been forced to evacuate China, the **capture of the Marianas in August 1944** enabled the aircraft to be redeployed, and they could now begin **bombing Japan in earnest** 314–15 >>.

FATE OF CHIANG KAI-SHEK
Chiang Kai-shek himself was to **turn on the Communists** again, after the **Japanese had surrendered**, but the outcome would be **disastrous for him** 346–47 >>.

US GENERAL (1883–1946)

GENERAL JOSEPH STILWELL

"Vinegar Joe" Stilwell served three tours in China between the two world wars, and was the US military attaché there during the first phase of the Sino-Japanese War. At the time of Pearl Harbor, he was a corps commander, and was posted to China in early 1942. His first task was to stem the Japanese advance into Burma; he also acted as Chiang's chief-of-staff. He became deputy to Lord Mountbatten, in 1943, after which time his Chinese troops, with US Special Forces, began building the Ledo Road in northern Burma. His relations with both the Chinese and British were difficult and he was recalled in 1944. But he was too good to leave unemployed, and he commanded the US Tenth Army during the Okinawa operations. He died of cancer in 1946.

Turning Point in Burma

The year 1944 witnessed a major change of fortune in Burma. In March, the Japanese launched a major offensive designed to take them into India. It was repulsed after bitter fighting and the British 14th Army began a counter-offensive that would prove decisive.

JAPANESE CANE KNIFE

Lord Louis Mountbatten became supreme Allied commander of the Southeast Asia Command in October 1943. He brought fresh purpose, while the British 14th Army, under General Bill Slim, had been undergoing rigorous training in jungle warfare. Mountbatten wanted to use amphibious operations to weaken the Japanese hold on Burma, but the priority of shipping lay with Europe and the Pacific, and there was virtually none to spare for Burma.

Even so, the British had begun to advance again into the Arakan, Burma's coastal region. Also, in north Burma, General Joseph Stilwell and his Chinese troops had begun their advance from Ledo, building a road as they went, to link up with the old Burma Road at Lashio. Mountbatten therefore agreed to mount a second Chindit expedition to tie down Japanese forces in the north and thus assist Stilwell's advance.

Japan on the offensive

The Japanese also had plans. They were to attempt an invasion of India in the expectation that the Indians themselves would then rise against their colonial master. The main attack would be made in central Burma, but they would also mount a diversionary attack in the Arakan. This opened on February 6, 1944. However, instead of withdrawing

BRITISH 2-IN MORTAR ILLUMINATING BOMB

as in the past, the British stood their ground and fought. Some elements were surrounded and were resupplied by air until they could be relieved and, after three weeks, the Japanese forces halted their attacks.

In the meantime, the first Chindit brigade had set off on foot and two more were flown into rough landing strips behind the Japanese lines in early March. The main Japanese offensive opened on the night of March 7/8. General Bill Slim had expected an attack, but not so early. His forces withdrew toward his main forward supply base at Imphal. Here, they resisted a succession of Japanese attacks. North of Imphal a crucial battle now developed at Kohima, the small hill village that guarded the road to Dinapur, the main railhead for supplies. The fighting, much of which was at close quarters, continued for two weeks until the British garrison could be relieved. The battle then

60 The percentage of Japanese troops in Burma that died during the campaign. The equivalent figure for the Allies was some 10 percent, including those who perished as prisoners of war.

continued, with the British gradually forcing the Japanese back. Meanwhile, the Chindits had been advancing north to link up with Stilwell, fighting some fierce actions as they did so.

Stilwell, too, was making good progress and, on May 11, Merrill's Marauders, the US Chindit equivalent, took Myitkyina airfield, although the Japanese in the town proved too strong for them. Simultaneously, forces from China began to advance down the old Burma Road.

Mogaung was captured by the Chindits at the end of June, but having spent months behind Japanese lines, the men were by now at their last gasp.

Japan on the defensive

The Japanese were also exhausted and had virtually run out of supplies. Hence, on July 11, they called off their offensive and began to withdraw, with

Jungle equipment

The 2-inch mortar was a British infantry weapon and could fire flares in the event of a night attack. All troops had machetes or similar tools to hack through the jungle or use for close combat. Fighting knives like the kukri were sometimes the only arms used by Gurkhas.

Slim's men following, to the Chindwin River. Three weeks later Stilwell finally secured Myitkyina, but by then the monsoon season had arrived, calling a halt to operations. Now forced onto the defensive, the Japanese drew up fresh plans. In the north they intended to prevent the link-up of the Ledo Road with the original Burma Road. In the center they planned to hold the British 14th Army on the Irrawaddy River, as well as stemming any advance west of the Irrawaddy to Rangoon.

While the advances in northern Burma continued, Slim began his offensive in early December with crossings of the Chindwin. Desperately short of supplies

Supplies dropped by parachute

Supplies are parachuted from a Douglas C-47 of the Tenth US Army Air Force on the 10 December 1944. The C-47 was the workhorse of Allied air transport, and the war in Burma could scarcely have been won without it.

BEFORE

In spring 1942 the British had been driven out of Burma and there was a general belief that the Japanese had proved themselves to be superior jungle fighters.

BRITISH UNEASE

Adding to **Britain's problems** was a growing independence movement in India and **a severe famine in Bengal ❮❮ 160–61**. At the end of 1942 the British launched **an assault in the Arakan**, Burma's coastal region, but it stalled. In February 1943, however, a brigade-sized force infiltrated Japanese lines and spent two months harassing Japanese communications. This concept of **long-range penetration** by Orde Wingate and his Chindits (see opposite) had **little strategic value**, but did demonstrate that the **British and Indian troops** could fight in the jungle **just as well** as the Japanese.

GURKHA KUKRI

"The **difficult** we will do at once, the **impossible** will take a little longer."

POPULAR SAYING IN THE BRITISH 14TH ARMY IN BURMA

ORDE WINGATE

Orde Wingate was an artillery officer, but came to prominence by organizing the Jewish "Special Night Squads" in pre-war Palestine and then leading a guerrilla force against the Italians in Abyssinia. His passion and eccentricity made him both friends and enemies, but in March 1942 Wavell ordered him to India, and he evolved his Chindit concept (named for the mythical Burmese beast the *chinthe*) for long-range penetration behind Japanese lines. He came to Churchill's attention after the first Chindit expedition, and he presented his ideas to Allied leaders in Quebec in 1943. On his return to India, he was allowed to increase his force to two divisions' worth. Wingate was killed in an air crash in 1944.

the Japanese were unwilling to give battle forward on their main defensive position on the Irrawaddy. Slim's plan was to trap the Japanese in the loop of the Irrawaddy based on Meiktila. Given the lack of Japanese resistance between the Chindwin and Irrawaddy, however, he amended it. Now his intention was to make the Japanese believe that his next objective was Mandalay, when in fact it was Meiktila, a key communications

Tropical diseases, epecially malaria and scrub typhus, affected both sides in Burma. At times, victims numbered 10-fold those of the battle's casualties. The Allies did reduce their sickness rates, by introducing preventative drugs.

center, which would also give him the ability to dash southwards to the ports of Rangoon or Moulmein. While this was happening, the advance down the Arakan continued, accompanied in January 1945 by a number of small amphibious operations designed to outflank the Japanese.

Burma liberated

In mid-January Slim's troops established bridgeheads across the Irrawaddy north of Mandalay, and Japanese forces spent the rest of the month trying to destroy them, but without success. Meanwhile, in northern Burma a momentous

event had occurred. On January 27 the forces advancing along the Ledo Road, under the command of General Stilwell, linked up with the Chinese troops that were advancing south, down the old Burma Road. Apart from mopping-up

Building the Ledo Road
A triumph of engineering, the Ledo Road ran 465 miles (750 km) from Ledo to the old Burma Road. It took two years to construct, through some of the country's most inhospitable terrain.

operations, the north of the country had now been liberated. Mid-February saw Slim's troops cross the Irrawaddy opposite Meiktila. The latter fell at the start of March, the Japanese having been convinced that Mandalay was the main objective, as Slim had hoped. Realizing their mistake, Japan launched a series of counterattacks against the town. The battle for Mandalay was taking place at the same time. The Japanese resistance was bitter, but finally, on March 20, Fort Dufferin, the last bastion in the town, fell. A week later the Japanese ceased their attacks on Meiktila and began to withdraw. Slim's sights were now set on Rangoon, some 300 miles (480 km) to the south.

The advance to Rangoon began on March 30. It followed the line of the Sittang River, brushing aside any Japanese opposition. The main concern was the approaching monsoon season. The Mango Rains, which preceded the monsoons, did arrive on April 20, but Slim's men remained undeterred.

To ensure that Rangoon was quickly seized, paratroops dropped at the mouth of its estuary on May 1, and Indian troops made an amphibious landing the next day. They entered the Burmese capital on May 3, a day after the Japanese had evacuated. Three days later, these forces joined up with the troops advancing down the Sittang.

AFTER ▸▸

In just 14 months, the Allied forces in Burma had repelled a major Japanese offensive threatening India and had then gone on to liberate much of the country.

JAPAN'S PREDICAMENT
The **remnants** of Japan's forces were now in two groups. Those east of the Sittang had **withdrawn to the Shan Hills** on the border with Thailand, while what remained of the Twenty-Eighth Army was **trapped west of the Sittang**. Neither group was fit enough to **withdraw to Malaya**.

MOUNTBATTEN PRESSES ON
Rather than concentrate on the final mopping up of these forces, Mountbatten was preparing for an **amphibious assault** to liberate Malaya and Singapore. The Japanese were expected to fight with their **usual ferocity** but, in the event, the dropping of **atomic bombs** and subsequent **Japanese surrender 322–27 ▸▸** meant that the landings **did not take place**.

Jungle Warfare in Burma

During the spring of 1944 the British, Gurkhas, and forces from China, East and West Africa, India, and the US fought the Japanese in India and Burma. The fighting was fierce and jungle warfare carried particular dangers, including heat, humidity, and tropical diseases. However, victories at Imphal and Kohima paved the way for the liberation of Burma in 1945.

"Every foot of progress had to be hacked out of trailing vines, creepers and spongy-leaved bushes. Giant teak trees, rising through the dense undergrowth, shut out the light. The column marched steadily and slowly through the dim twilight under a thick canopy of green. No sound broke the silence other than the patter of raindrops ... Torrential rain fell periodically; mist swathed and swirled in the valleys and round the towering peaks. In the bottom of the valleys swollen streams raged unabated, the noise of which could be heard thousands of feet above."

MAJOR JOHN SHIPSTER, 7TH/2ND PUNJABIS, ON MARCHING TO UKHRUL, EAST OF IMPHAL

"The rain now fell steadily. The Deep sector looked like Passchendaele—blasted trees, feet and twisted hands sticking up out of the earth, bloody shirts, ammunition clips, holes half full of water, each containing two pale huge-eyed men, trying to keep their rifles out of the mud, and over all the heavy, sweet stench of death, from our own bodies and entrails ... from Japanese corpses on the wire, or fastened, dead and rotting, in the trees. At night the rain hissed down in the total darkness, the trees ran with water and, beyond the devastation, the jungle dripped and crackled ...

With a crash of machine-guns and mortars the battle began. All night the Cameronians and the Japanese 53rd Division fought it out. Our machine guns ripped them from the new positions. Twice the Japanese forced into the barbed wire with Bangalore torpedoes [explosive charge at the end of a long piece of bamboo], and the blasting rain of the mortars wiped them out. At four a.m., when they launched their final assault to recover their bodies, we had defeated them ..."

MAJOR JOHN MASTERS, 111TH CHINDIT BRIGADE

Combined jungle forces
British, American, and local Kachin fighters wade across a stream in northern Burma. With few roads through the jungle, streams and rivers were often the only means of transporting men, weapons, supplies, and animals.

<< **BEFORE**

The initial success of the invasion of Italy turned to frustration when the Allies came up against the formidable Gustav Line.

OPERATION SHINGLE
At the beginning of **November 1943**, the Allied commanders in the Mediterranean came up with a plan to accelerate their **advance on Rome**. This was to carry out an **amphibious landing at Anzio**, some 30 miles (50 km) south of the Italian capital. However, the **failure to achieve** an early breakthrough of the **Gustav Line << 212–13** meant that the Anzio landing, **codenamed Shingle**, was put on hold and there was talk of cancelling it. In the end it was agreed that it would go ahead in January 1944.

The Fall of Rome

During the early months of 1944, the Allies fought a grim battle to break through the Gustav Line, forcing the Germans to withdraw in May. The Allies then entered Rome and continued their advance until halted once more in the mountains of northern Italy.

In the final months of 1943, after their hard-fought success in the Salerno landings, the Allied forces in Italy gradually pushed north toward Rome. The German commander-in-chief in Italy, Field Marshal Albert Kesselring intended to hold on for as long as he could, making the Allies fight all the way. He was greatly aided by the geography. As the Allies moved north they had to cross a succession of deep and fast-flowing rivers running to each coast from Italy's central spine, the Apennine Mountains. Each of these muddy valleys was overlooked by high and rugged hills, altogether ideal defensive terrain.

On the Allied side General Harold Alexander's 15th Army Group included US Fifth Army, attacking up the west side of the peninsula, and British Eighth Army on the Adriatic flank. Both armies had troops of several nationalities, not just the British and Americans implied by their titles.

In contrast to Kesselring's resourceful defense, the Allied commanders would not coordinate their forces well in most of the coming battles; nor would the Allied ground and air forces work together effectively.

The operations to break through the main German defenses, the Gustav Line, would be dominated by the

General Clark rides into Rome
This triumphant moment for General Mark Clark came at a price. His failure to follow the agreed plan enabled the German forces to withdraw north of Rome intact.

Anzio landings
Follow-up troops come ashore on the Anzio beaches. Bad weather held up the reinforcements for the first Allied landings, contributing to General Lucas's decision to delay the inland advance.

KEY MOMENT

THE FALL OF MONTE CASSINO

By May 1944 the historic Benedictine abbey of Monte Cassino had been reduced to rubble. As part of Operation Diadem, the task of capturing it was given to Polish II Corps, but their first attack on the night of May 11/12 failed. The German positions in and around the ruins high on the mountain (seen here in the background rising above the town of Cassino) were simply too strong. Further to the south, however, French troops managed to find a way through the Aurunci Mountains, which the Germans believed to be impassable, and could now overlook the Liri Valley, through which Highway 6 ran to Rome. A second attack on Monte Cassino by the Poles, on May 17, made some progress, but because of the French advance the German troops were already withdrawing from the whole Gustav Line. The following morning the Polish flag was finally hoisted over the ruins of the abbey.

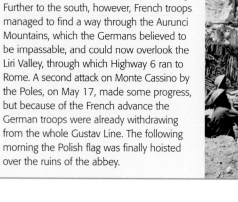

A split advance

The Apennine Mountains which represent Italy's spine, split the Allied advance northward, while helping the Germans to maintain their defense.

fighting in the area of Monte Cassino, rising above the town of Cassino on the banks of the Rapido River. Monte Cassino was crowned by an ancient Benedictine abbey, an historic treasure that the Allied commanders would controversially decide to bomb.

In mid-January 1944, in what is sometimes called the First Battle of Cassino, British, American, and French troops made a series of attacks on the Gustav Line defenses around the town of Cassino and to the north and south. These made only limited gains.

Allied forces land at Anzio

To help their forces break through the Gustav Line, Allied commanders also planned landings at Anzio further up the west coast, just south of Rome. The landings began on January 22, taking the Germans by surprise. But there was no clear plan as what to do next, and the local Allied commander, General Lucas, timidly decided to consolidate his beachhead before pushing inland.

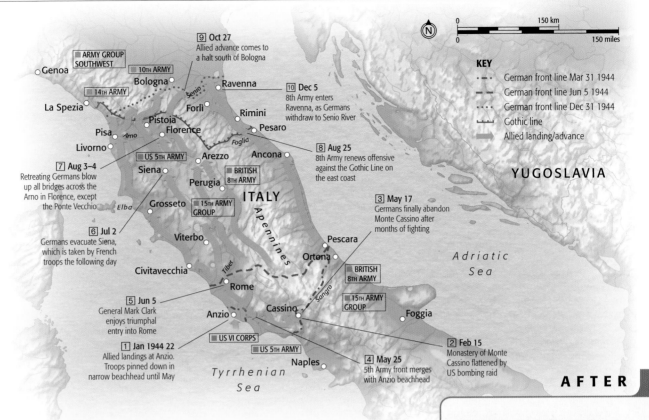

KEY
- German front line Mar 31 1944
- German front line Jun 5 1944
- German front line Dec 31 1944
- Gothic line
- Allied landing/advance

9 Oct 27 Allied advance comes to a halt south of Bologna

10 Dec 5 8th Army enters Ravenna, as Germans withdraw to Senio River

8 Aug 25 8th Army renews offensive against the Gothic Line on the east coast

7 Aug 3–4 Retreating Germans blow up all bridges across the Arno in Florence, except the Ponte Vecchio

6 Jul 2 Germans evacuate Siena, which is taken by French troops the following day

3 May 17 Germans finally abandon Monte Cassino after months of fighting

5 Jun 5 General Mark Clark enjoys triumphal entry into Rome

1 Jan 1944 22 Allied landings at Anzio. Troops pinned down in narrow beachhead until May

4 May 25 5th Army front merges with Anzio beachhead

2 Feb 15 Monastery of Monte Cassino flattened by US bombing raid

> ## "I had hoped [to hurl] a **wildcat** onto the shore, but [we got] a **stranded whale.**"
> WINSTON CHURCHILL ON THE ANZIO LANDING

Kesselring hurried up reinforcements and easily blocked the Allied advance when it eventually came. Far from the Anzio landing being a threat to the whole German position in Italy, as Churchill for one had hoped, the Allied force there was besieged.

A solid German defense

From early February there were renewed attempts to break through the Gustav Line. General Alexander transferred New Zealand and Indian troops from the Eighth Army to tackle Cassino once more. First he ordered the bombing of the monastery, since he wrongly thought that the Germans were using it as an observation post. Astonishingly, it was a full day before the initial air strike was followed up by

> The Allied forces deployed in Italy in 1944 were multinational and consisted of troops from the United States, Britain, Canada, France, India, New Zealand, Poland, and South Africa.

attacks on the ground. And Germans built even stronger fortifications in the rubble left by the bombing. The German defenders proved far too strong, both in this second battle of Cassino in

February and in an equally vicious third battle in March. Allied leaders then drew up a new plan, this time finally using their full resources, not just part of their armies. The bulk of the Eighth Army would capture Monte Cassino, while the Fifth Army attacked nearer the coast and the troops at Anzio cut communications between the Gustav Line and Rome. This offensive, codenamed Operation Diadem, was to be launched in the late spring.

In the meantime, a major air offensive, Operation Strangle, would target German supply lines further to the north. In the event this had only limited success.

Diadem itself was finally launched on the night of May 10/11. French troops of the Fifth Army finally unlocked the Gustav Line defenses, breaking through some 12 miles (20 km) south of

British 5.5 inch howitzer

This gun's ability to fire at high elevation was invaluable when engaging targets in the Italian mountains. It could fire a 100 lb (45 kg) shell up to 16,000 yds (14,600 m).

Cassino. Monte Cassino itself fell to a Polish corps serving with the Eighth Army. The Germans began retreating to the Caesar Line between Rome and Anzio and the Allies began their advance on Rome. On May 23 there was a breakout from the Anzio beachhead and, two days later, this advance linked up with the main body of the Fifth Army.

A misguided change of plan

The Fifth Army was then meant to cut off the retreat of the German forces from the Cassino area. But its commander, General Mark Clark, decided to head straight for Rome (his reason for this is still unclear).

By the time the Fifth Army broke through the Caesar Line, the threatened German forces had escaped. On June 5 Clark entered Rome, but even this pointless triumph was immediately overshadowed by news of the D-Day landings in France the next day. The Allies followed up the German forces north of Rome, but their withdrawal to new and tough defenses, the Gothic Line, was very skilful.

The task of the Allied forces became more difficult from the second half of July, when many French and American soldiers were withdrawn from the Italian front to take part in the landings in the south of France. From the fall of 1944 through to the spring of 1945, the Allied attacks would again be poorly coordinated. They would make slow and difficult progress against increasingly determined German defense.

AFTER

The Germans now built a new line of defense, the Gothic Line, again taking advantage of the natural barriers provided by mountains and river valleys.

ALLIED ADVANCES

The **British Eighth Army** managed to get through the German defenses, but several more river lines and the **autumn rains** slowed its advance. The **US Fifth Army** also penetrated the Gothic Line, but was halted by **heavy casualties**. By the end of the year, the British had come to a halt, too, and General Alexander decided to await spring before staging his **final offensive 304–05 ≫**.

BRITISH ITALY STAR

Preparing for D-Day

In the context of the war in Europe the Allies regarded the German invasion of Western Europe as their greatest challenge. They had to surprise an expectant enemy, overcome its formidable defenses, and grapple with the uncertain waters of the English Channel.

Sherman Duplex Drive tank
The Duplex Drive (DD) Sherman tank was a key element in the D-Day invasion. Using a collapsible canvas screen and driven by propellors, this tank could swim ashore and provide assault troops with armored support. However, it was vulnerable in choppy seas.

I n April 1943 the British general Frederick Morgan was appointed Chief of Staff to the Supreme Allied Commander (COSSAC) for the D-Day invasion. His commander had not yet been apppointed and he was given the task, with an Anglo-US staff, of drawing up the blueprint for the assault on Fortress Europe. Morgan inherited all the work that had been done previously by the British and agreed with their overall conclusions. Before drawing up his plan Morgan needed to know what forces would be available for the landings. But this was dependent on the amount of amphibious shipping. The forecast revealed that there should be sufficient numbers to transport three divisions for the initial Allied assault cross-Channel. Morgan finalized his planning in July 1943. He had considered both the Pas de Calais and Caen as possible landing areas while the former was very close to southern England, it was very heavily defended. Hence he opted for Caen.

Deception and development

The three assault divisions would disembark between Caen and the base of the Cotentin peninsula to the west. The flanks would be protected through the insertion of airborne forces. Once ashore the invasion force was to secure Cherbourg on the north coast of the Cotentin peninsula, clear Brittany, and sweep south across the Seine River.

Surprise was crucial, not just to enable the troops to get ashore, but also to prevent the Germans from sending significant reinforcements quickly from elsewhere. To this end, elaborate deception operations were developed. Foremost was to make the Germans believe that the landings would be in the Pas de Calais, and among the measures adopted would be the deployment of a fictitious force under the Allies' most thrusting general, George S. Patton, to southeast England. The Germans also feared an Allied invasion of Norway and retained

> **"We must go** unless there is a real and **very serious deterioration in the weather."**
>
> GENERAL DWIGHT D. EISENHOWER, JUNE 3, 1944

USN-702

BEFORE

When France fell ‹‹ 82–83, the Allies realized that Germany could not be defeated unless they re-entered mainland Europe.

PREPARING TO INVADE FRANCE

When the US entered the war it was agreed that preparations should be made for an invasion of Europe across the English Channel and that there would be a build-up of **US forces in Britain for this purpose ‹‹ 202–03**. The operation was originally planned for 1943, but the British wanted to **secure North Africa first ‹‹ 182–87** and then **knock Italy out of the war ‹‹ 210–11**. The cross-Channel invasion, initially codenamed Round Up, was postponed and a new date was set for Spring 1944.

37 THOUSAND US troops were in Britain in June 1942.

260 THOUSAND US troops were in Britain by November 1942.

790 THOUSAND US troops were in Britain by the end of 1943.

THE RIGHT LOCATION

The British had begun to **gather intelligence** on northwest Europe's coasts and had **conducted studies** on how and where such an assault might take place. They concluded that any landing area must be within range of fighter cover from Britain and needed to be near a port, but the **disastrous August 1942 Dieppe raid** had shown that ports were likely to be heavily defended. The Caen area of Normandy offered the best possibilities.

AFTER

The D-Day invasion was eventually fixed for June 5 ,1944—troops were briefed and ships prepared—but one factor that could not be controlled was the weather.

a large number of troops there. To play upon this, the fictitious British Fourth Army was established in Scotland.

Drawing on the experience of previous amphibious landings in the Pacific and the Mediterranean, the Allied invasion force introduced many technical innovations to the operation. As it might be a while before Cherbourg was operating as a port, temporary artificial "Mulberry" harbors were developed. To deliver fuel to the forces in France, a pipeline was built under the English Channel from the Isle of Wight. This was known as Operation Pluto—an acronym for Pipe Line Under The Ocean. In order to deal with obstacles and strongpoints, a family of specialized vehicles was designed—named, after their commander, Major

6,500 vessels took part in the D-Day invasion.
11,500 Allied aircraft faced 815 Luftwaffe planes.
194,000 Allied troops faced 57,000 Germans.

General Percy Hobart, "Hobart's Funnies." "Crab" tanks carried rotating flails to explode mines, "Crocodile" tanks mounted flamethrowers and other vehicles fired super-heavy "dustbin" charges to breach sea walls.

Morgan's plan was approved at the conference in Quebec on August 17 ,1943, but it was not until the start of December that same year that Eisenhower was made supreme Allied commander in Europe for the invasion, now codenamed Operation Overlord.

Ready for attack

Two weeks later Montgomery was given command of 21st Army Group—the ground force that would carry out the actual D-Day landings. Neither he

Naval Seabees in training
Seabees were US Naval Construction Battalions that built roads and bases for military use; the men were also trained in landing tactics and were given military training.

Commando dagger
This was the symbol of the British Commandos—elite units who were tasked with mounting nocturnal raids on occupied Europe to test the German defenses. Those who completed the rigorous training were awarded the dagger.

nor Eisenhower liked Morgan's plan because it was on too narrow a frontage. They therefore increased the Normandy assault force from three to five divisions. Meanwhile, across the other side of the English Channel, the Germans had not been idle. Fearing an Allied invasion from Britain, they had been working on a wide-ranging defense system along Europe's coasts ever since 1940.

By fall 1943 German coastal defenses, known as the "Atlantic Wall," were still poorly developed. Rommel, appointed to command Army Group B in what was to be the invasion sector, worked hard to improve them. A deadly assortment of anti-landing obstacles littered beaches and potential glider

Eisenhower addresses American troops
Dwight D. Eisenhower meets US paratroops on June 5, 1944; the troops were just about to board their aircraft on the eve of D-Day. It was an anxious time for Eisenhower, with success or failure hanging in the balance.

NATURE INTERVENES
By the end of May 1944, **British ports were clogged with ships** of all sorts, and assault troops had been moved to sealed camps close to their departure ports. It was there that the troops were briefed on their roles in the invasion.

On June 3 Eisenhower was told that the **weather for D-Day was likely to be stormy**. The next day he was informed that conditions would slowly improve over the next 36 hours so **he duly postponed the invasion by one day**. The Allies would now land on June 6. On the evening of the fifth, the invasion fleet set off across the English Channel.

THE AXIS CAUGHT UNAWARE
Meanwhile, **believing that conditions were too poor** for an invasion, many key German commanders had gone to Rennes for a map exercise, while **Rommel had returned to Germany** to plead for more troops. They were all about to have a rude shock 258–59 >>.

landing-fields, and concrete bunkers studded the coastline. In contrast, Rommel's superior, Gerd von Rundstedt, Commander-in-Chief West, argued that the defenses must simply hold long enough to enable the Germans to detect the Allied main effort, which could then be attacked by armored reserves.

In Britain the first few months of 1944 saw furious training activity. The assault divisions carried out practice landings on beaches resembling those in Normandy. In April there was a major scare when German E-boats hit an American convoy engaged in a rehearsal off the coast of Devon. The incident had to be hushed up. Meanwhile, Allied air forces had mounted a campaign both to destroy the Luftwaffe in France and to cut the routes leading into Normandy.

TECHNOLOGY
MULBERRY HARBORS

The need for artificial harbors to support an invasion force on shore had been recognized as early as 1942 and during 1943 prototypes were built. They consisted of an immovable breakwater formed by sinking blockships, with a floating breakwater to protect it. Floating roadways (right) ran from concrete pierheads and enabled vehicles to carry supplies ashore. Two Mulberry harbors were built, one to support the US beaches and the other the British ones. All the components had to be towed across the English Channel.

AMERICAN GENERAL AND PRESIDENT Born 1890 Died 1969

Dwight D. Eisenhower

"The eyes of the world are upon you. The **hopes and prayers** of liberty-loving peoples … **march with you**"

EISENHOWER'S ADDRESS TO US FORCES ON D-DAY, JUNE 6, 1944

A brilliant commander and military strategist, Dwight D. Eisenhower served as Supreme Commander of the Allied forces in Europe, organized the successful invasion of France in 1944, and went on to become the 34th president of the United States.

Yet, before 1941, Eisenhower was an unlikely choice for such a significant role. He had no combat experience, his promotions within the army had been gradual, and he was not well known, but he did have excellent negotiating and planning skills.

Eisenhower had also been in the army since his youth. A graduate of West Point, he was commissioned as a second lieutenant and during World War I commanded a tank training center. The war ended before he could be posted abroad. He continued his army career in peacetime, serving initially under George Patton, a pioneer of tank warfare, and was subsequently appointed chief-of-staff to Brigadier-General Fox Connor and sent to Panama. Heavily influenced by Connor, Eisenhower combined his duties with extensive studies in military planning and strategy. He also spent time in France, working under General Pershing and writing a guide to World War I battlefields, providing geographical knowledge that would become invaluable later.

Five-star general
Eisenhower started his military career as a West Point cadet. Even though he had no battlefield experience, he was made a five-star general in 1944, the highest rank in the US Army.

Skillful mediator
Eisenhower was an exceptional administrator. He was appointed chief-of-staff to General Douglas MacArthur and served with him in the Philippines, helping him to organize a defense force. It was not a post he particularly enjoyed but some historians have commented that the experience of working with MacArthur, who was an erratic man, may have been a useful one.

In 1939, shortly after Germany invaded Poland, Eisenhower returned to the United States. Made chief-of-staff of the Third Army, he came to the attention of General George Marshall, army chief-of-staff, because of his skills in planning war maneuvers. Marshall was impressed and in 1941, when the US joined the war, he sent Eisenhower to the army's war planning division in Washington D.C. From this point on Eisenhower's advancement was rapid. He particularly impressed Marshall

General "Ike"
Popularly known as "Ike," a nickname he gained in school, General Dwight David Eisenhower was widely admired, so much so that the slogan "I Like Ike" was used in his presidential campaign of 1952.

Q·Q·V

BACK UP EISENHOWER
WITH MORE G-E PRODUCTION

Home front propaganda
Eisenhower's distinctive image, along with those of other generals, was used on posters and other propaganda in the US to galvanize the national war effort on the home front into increasing production.

An inspiring leader

General Eisenhower addresses paratroopers of the US 101st Airborne Division in England, on the eve of D-Day. Bad weather had caused a delay, but on June 5, 1944, Eisenhower gave the go-ahead for the operations.

by his ability to deal with MacArthur, and in 1942 was appointed to plan the Allied invasion of North Africa. Though Eisenhower had no experience of high command, he had an outstanding ability to translate military strategy into practical action, and exceptional diplomatic skills. Planning Operation Torch, which was the first major Allied offensive of the war, involved handling some tricky individuals, such as Patton and Montgomery, who were forever at each other's throats. Eisenhower clearly showed he was able to mediate between them. In February 1943 he was promoted to four-star general and launched successful attacks on Tunisia, Sicily, and the Italian mainland.

Supreme commander

In December 1943 Eisenhower was chosen as Supreme Commander of the Allied Expeditionary Force and soon found himself in London, preparing for the invasion of Normandy. He had not been everyone's first choice—Roosevelt and Churchill had other preferred candidates—but his organizing and mediating skills made him the right one. In his memoirs, Montgomery described Eisenhower as a "military statesman" and claimed no one else could have welded the Allied forces into such a fine fighting machine. The invasion entailed coordinating land, sea, and air forces, involving something in the region of one million combat

alike, he had intended to retire at the end of the war, but President Truman appointed him chief-of-staff of the army. He directed the demobilization of the wartime army, then left active service to take up an academic post at Columbia University. In 1950 he returned to the international stage when Truman appointed him Supreme Commander of the newly formed NATO. Two years later, having been courted by both political parties, Eisenhower ran as the Republican presidential candidate. His

> ## "History does not long **entrust the care of freedom** to **the weak or the timid**."
>
> EISENHOWER'S FIRST INAUGURAL ADDRESS, JANUARY 20, 1953

troops and two million support services, and dealing with a variety of opposing views, proposals, and personalities. In the event, it was Eisenhower who on June 5, 1944, gambling on a break in bad weather, gave the order to launch what was known as D-Day the following day.

Popularity after D-Day

Eisenhower's responsibilities did not end with the D-Day invasion; he also supervised the Allied advance on Paris and the Battle of the Bulge, overseeing the events that eventually led to the German surrender in May 1945. He was criticized by some for allowing the Russians to capture Berlin but otherwise his achievements won him international acclaim and respect. Eisenhower was greeted as a hero when he returned to the US. Highly respected and liked by both the army and civilians

popularity brought him an easy victory and he was reelected for a second term in 1956. He left office in 1961 and retired to his home at Gettysburg Farm. He died eight years later.

Keeping the peace

Eisenhower's skills included the ability to smooth over personality clashes among his staff, such as those that occurred between Air Chief Marshal Tedder (right) and Field Marshal Montgomery.

TIMELINE

- **October 14, 1890** Born Dwight David Eisenhower in Denison, Texas.

- **1915** Graduates from West Point Military Academy. Commissioned as a second lieutenant.

- **1915–18** Commands a tank training center in Texas. Promoted to captain and receives the Distinguished Service Medal. World War I ends before he can be posted overseas.

- **1922–24** Assigned to the Panama Canal Zone. Influenced by his commander, Brigadier-General Fox Connor, he attends the Command and General Staff School, Fort Leavenworth, Kansas.

- **1927** Graduates from the Army War College, then serves with the peacetime army in France.

- **1929–33** Serves as executive officer to General George V. Mosley, Assistant Secretary of War in Washington D.C..

- **1933** Becomes an aide to General Douglas MacArthur, Army Chief-of-Staff.

- **1935** Goes to the Philippines with General MacArthur as assistant military advisor to the Philippine government and assists in the reorganization of the Philippine Army.

- **1939** Returns to the United States and serves variously as chief-of-staff to generals Thompson, Joyce, and Kreuger in Washington and Texas.

- **March 1941** Becomes a full colonel and in June is made chief-of-staff to the Third Army.

- **1941** Promoted to brigadier-general in September. He is appointed to the army's war plans division in Washington when the US joins World War II in December.

- **March 1942** Promoted to major-general, and appointed head of the War Department's operations division.

- **July 1942** Promoted to lieutenant-general and chosen to head Operation Torch, the Allied invasion of French North Africa.

- **February 1943** Promoted to full general, he directs the amphibious assault of Italy, which results in the fall of Rome in June 1944.

- **December 1943** Appointed Supreme Commander of the Allied Expeditionary Force. He goes to London to plan for the Normandy invasion.

- **June 6, 1944** D-Day landings go ahead on his order. Made a five-star general in December.

- **May 1945** Appointed Military Governor of the US Occupied Zone, Germany.

- **May 1948** Leaves active duty and becomes president of Columbia University, New York.

- **1950** President Truman appoints him Supreme Commander of the North Atlantic Treaty Organization (NATO).

- **1952** Runs as Republican presidential candidate against Democrat Adlai Stevenson.

- **1953** Elected 34th president of the United States. Serves two terms, being reelected in 1956.

- **March 28, 1969** Dies at Walter Reed Army Hospital, Washington D.C..

I LIKE IKE

PRESIDENTIAL CAMPAIGN BUMPER SIGN, 1953

D-Day Landings

The Normandy landings were the culmination of much preparation and represent the largest amphibious operation in the history of war. While not everything worked to plan, by the end of the day the Allied forces were firmly ashore and the liberation of Western Europe could begin.

BEFORE

Eisenhower's decision that the D-Day landings should go ahead on June 6 in spite of the questionable weather was a brave one 《 254–55. He knew only too well that if they failed it might be many months before the Allies could try again.

PREPARATIONS BEGIN

At 9pm on June 5 the BBC broadcast coded messages to the **French Resistance 《 222–23** (which was to play its part in disrupting routes leading to Normandy), alerting them that the invasion was on. Then two groups of RAF bombers took off for Boulogne and Le Havre. The planes dropped tinfoil strips (codenamed "window") to **confuse the German radar**

US PARACHUTE BADGE

into thinking that an invasion fleet was heading for the Pas de Calais. The paratroop element now arrived. Two US airborne divisions were dropped at the base of the Cotentin peninsula, while a British division landed east of the Orne River—both achieved their objective of **securing the Allied flanks**.

British balloon operators
Operation Neptune was the air and naval assault phase of Operation Overlord. Here, Royal Air Force balloon operators pull a winch across "King" beach, in Gold Sector, on the afternoon of the invasion.

There were five beaches selected for the landings—one for each of the assault divisions. The beaches were codenamed, from east to west, Sword (British), Juno (Canadian), Gold (British), Omaha (US), and Utah (US). Before the Allied troops could land it was essential to suppress the coastal batteries. To this end, the Allied air forces dropped 1,760 tons of bombs on them and they were subjected to an intense naval bombardment. Assault troops trans-shipped from transport vessels to their landing craft 7–11 miles (11–17 km) from the shore. There was a swell running and many were

seasick, while others had had little or no sleep. The weather was also murky, making conditions difficult.

The landings were to take place just after low water, on a rising tide, and local conditions meant that the Americans would have to land first, reducing the time available for bombardment. The first troops to go ashore were from the Fourth

US Infantry Division on Utah Beach at 6:30am. The current caused their landing craft to veer away from the correct beach and they landed 2,000 yds (1,830 m) south of it. This caused some bewilderment, with the troops having to wade 100 yds (90 m) to the shore, but it was a weak point in the German defenses and casualties were few. Assisted by

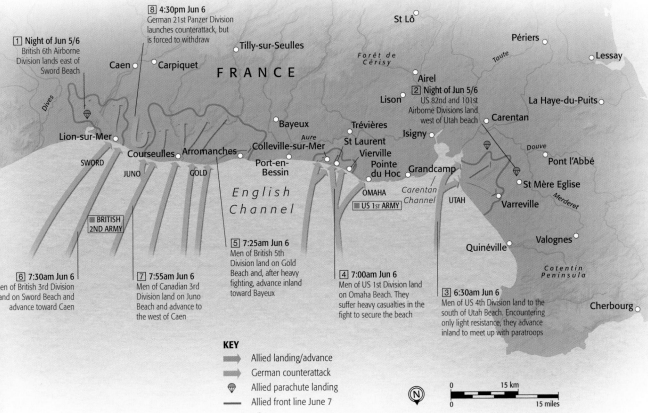

[1] Night of Jun 5/6
British 6th Airborne Division lands east of Sword Beach

[8] 4:30pm Jun 6
German 21st Panzer Division launches counterattack, but is forced to withdraw

St Lô

Périers

Lessay

Tilly-sur-Seulles

Forêt de Cérisy

Taute

La Haye-du-Puits

Caen · Carpiquet

F R A N C E

Airel

Lison

[2] Night of Jun 5/6
US 82nd and 101st Airborne Divisions land west of Utah beach

Bayeux · Trévières

Isigny

Carentan

Lion-sur-Mer

Aure

Colleville-sur-Mer

St Laurent
Vierville

Pont l'Abbé

Courseulles · Arromanches
Port-en-Bessin

Pointe
du Hoc · Grandcamp

St Mère Eglise

SWORD

JUNO · GOLD

*English
Channel*

OMAHA

*Carentan
Channel*

UTAH

Varreville

Merderet

Douve

BRITISH
2ND ARMY

US 1ST ARMY

Valognes

Quinéville

Cotentin
Peninsula

[6] 7:30am Jun 6
Men of British 3rd Division land on Sword Beach and advance toward Caen

[7] 7:55am Jun 6
Men of Canadian 3rd Division land on Juno Beach and advance to the west of Caen

[5] 7:25am Jun 6
Men of British 5th Division land on Gold Beach and, after heavy fighting, advance inland toward Bayeux

[4] 7:00am Jun 6
Men of US 1st Division land on Omaha Beach. They suffer heavy casualties in the fight to secure the beach

[3] 6:30am Jun 6
Men of US 4th Division land to the south of Utah Beach. Encountering only light resistance, they advance inland to meet up with paratroops

Cherbourg

KEY

➡ Allied landing/advance
➡ German counterattack
◆ Allied parachute landing
— Allied front line June 7

N

0 — 15 km
0 — 15 miles

The Normandy landings
Part of the German counterattack did reach the coast but, fearing being cut off by the 150,000 invaders, they were forced to withdraw.

> "You are about to embark upon the **great crusade.**"
>
> EISENHOWER TO HIS TROOPS, JUNE 5, 1944

the Sherman DD tanks that had moved ashore, the troops were able to link up with some of the US paratroops. By contrast, Omaha presented real problems. It was dominated by cliffs and was the most heavily defended of the beaches, with numerous underwater obstacles. Omaha was also much more exposed to the weather than Utah, but fears of fire from the German coastal batteries caused trans-shipping to take place 11 miles (17 km) from the shore. Many of the tanks sank, and landing craft were wrecked by the submerged obstacles or swamped by water. Some men also landed on the wrong beaches. The Germans maintained a heavy fire and those who got ashore were pinned down on the beach. By midday they had gained just a few precarious footholds.

Germans taken unaware
On Gold Beach the presence of rocks meant that the landing frontage was comparatively narrow. Even so, the 50th British Division was almost completely ashore by midday and had begun to advance inland. Only the village of Le Hamel on the right flank presented significant opposition but its defenses were weakened by the day's end. The Canadian Third Division on Juno also had to face extensive reefs, which meant a narrow approach to their beach. This delayed the landings by 25 minutes and caused congestion when the reserve brigade landed. The

Reinforcements come ashore
American infantrymen from V Corps, assigned to the US First Army, land dryshod from their LCVP landing craft on June 7, 1944. By 11 June the Allied forces had more than 300,000 men and 54,000 vehicles ashore.

only significant German resistance came in the center and meant that initially the Canadians had two separate beachheads. The division then advanced to Carpiquet airfield. On Sword Beach, just north of Caen, the British Third Division also got ashore, although heavy fire once the troops hit the beaches caused casualties. Commandos landing with the division were tasked with linking up with the paratroops on the Caen Canal and did so successfully.

On the German side the unusually long BBC message to the French Resistance resulted in a heightened alert, but at this stage it was widespread sabotage rather than the Normandy landings themselves that was the main concern for the Germans. In the very early hours of D-Day reports of airborne landings caused maximum alert to be instigated and absent commanders hurried back to their units. The troops actually defending the beaches were generally low grade and the Germans placed their main hopes on counterattacking with their armor to drive the Allied forces back into the

AFTER ➤➤

By the end of D-Day the Allies had landed **150,000 troops at a cost of 9,000 casualties,** considerably less than had at first been feared. Only Omaha had seen real problems.

GERMAN OBJECTIVES
The next task was to **link up the beachheads,** land reinforcements, and begin advancing inland. There would be some tough fighting ahead before **breaking out from Normandy 262–63 ➤➤**. For the Germans D-Day had been close to a disaster.

WOUNDED MEN ON OMAHA BEACH

Their plan to drive the Allies off the beaches had failed. They were also not sure whether this was the main assault or whether Calais would be next. **Deploying their armored reserves** was now a priority. But given the **Allied air supremacy** and disruption to the routes leading to Normandy, this would be no easy task.

sea. Unfortunately, the main Panzer reserve was under Hitler's control and when a telephone call was put through to his headquarters, von Rundstedt's staff were told that the Führer was asleep and could not be disturbed. Not until the afternoon did Hitler agree to

Handle

Magazine

Backsight

Barrel release
handle

Folding bipod

Butt

Bren light machine gun
Designed in Czechoslovakia, the Bren light machine-gun served the British infantry well throughout the war and for many years beyond. It was .303 caliber and had a range of 600 yds (548 m).

release the reserves. The one Panzer division in the area was scattered and it took time to concentrate. It initially attacked the British airborne troops, but then received orders to attack the British forces north of Caen. By then it was far too late.

Omaha Beach Landing

On June 6 1944 Allied forces—American, British, and Canadian—landed on five beaches on the Cotentin peninsula in Normandy, France. The worst casualties occurred on Omaha Beach, where American forces of the US 1st and 29th Divisions, supported by two special force battalions, encountered heavy opposition as they attempted to secure the 6-mile- (10-km-) long beach. Nearly 3,000 Americans were killed or injured in the landing.

"I didn't have any idea of how deep it would be, but I'm six foot one and the sea was up to my chest and it took me a while to find my feet ... I reached over and grabbed him [Sergeant Reed] by the jacket and pulled him out from under the ramp, otherwise he'd have been steamrollered by the landing craft. I pulled Reed out of the surf and maybe twenty yards up to the beach, and I said, 'OK, Sergeant, this is as far as I can take you now, I'll get the first-aid man over to you, I've got to go in with the rest of the platoon and complete our mission.' So I dropped him there and just then a mortar shell landed behind me, killed or wounded almost all my mortar section and knocked me flat on my face and I thought, what the hell I must be dead. All of a sudden sand was kicking up in my face and I said to myself, 'Ah, it's the German, he's shooting at me, he's trying to get my range, this is no place to be lying down.' ... Bodies lay still ... trickles of blood reddening the sand. Some of the wounded were crawling as best they could, some with a look of despair and bewilderment on their tortured and panic-racked faces. Others tried to get back on their feet, only to be hit again by enemy fire.**"**

LIEUTENANT SIDNEY SALOMON, C COMPANY 2ND RANGERS, ON LANDING ON OMAHA BEACH

A difficult landing
Amphibious tanks lead the way as American assault troops land at Omaha Beach. A high tide, heavy swell, and German snipers firing down from overlooking cliffs made the assault at Omaha a perilous operation.

Breakout from Normandy

While the D-Day landings had succeeded, the Allies faced six weeks of bitter fighting before they could break out from Normandy. By this time the German forces had all but been destroyed and those that remained hurriedly retreated across northern France, leaving just a few garrisons to hold on to ports.

The fighting in Normandy
British infantry prepare to attack a village with digging tools strapped to their backs. As soon as they reached their objective, they would dig in for protection against artillery fire and possible counterattack by the Germans.

BEFORE

Once ashore in Normandy **‹‹ 258–59** the Allies enjoyed significant advantages over the Germans. Air supremacy hindered the enemy advance, as did the French Resistance.

THE ROLE OF THE RESISTANCE
What concerned the Allies most was preventing the Germans from concentrating too much armor in Normandy enabling them to **mount a major counterattack**. Air power played a significant

SOE AGENT'S BRIEFCASE

part in slowing the move of the **Panzer and Panzer Grenadier divisions**, but so did the **French Resistance ‹‹ 222–23**. Their operations were coordinated by specially-trained **SOE agents ‹‹ 172–73**, and three-man teams parachuted into France during the days after D-Day. Disruption of routes and tying down German troops in the rear areas played their part. **Relentless Allied pressure in Normandy** itself also meant that these divisions found themselves being used to prop up the defense and **prevented a counterattack force** from being assembled.

During the period immediately after D-Day, the Allies succeeded in linking up their beachheads and began to advance inland. However, problems soon surfaced among the British forces in the east. The city of Caen had been a D-Day objective but Montgomery's forces had been unable to reach it, mainly because congestion on the beaches meant that the necessary armored support could not get forward in time. During the next week the British tried in vain to capture Caen but were held by the newly arrived 12th SS Panzer Division, which consisted of fanatical former members of the Hitler Youth. In the west the Americans had better success, and on June 18 they cut off the Cotentin peninsula from the rest of Normandy. The previous day Rundstedt and Rommel had met Hitler at Soissons to ask if they could evacuate the peninsula so as to shorten their line. But Hitler had refused, sealing the fate of the German troops there. He also ordered the port of Cherbourg to be

8	Allied armored divisions were in Normandy on 25 July.
23	Allied infantry divisions were in Normandy on 25 July.
1	Allied airborne division was in Normandy on 25 July.

defended to the last, but the Americans captured it on June 28, after a two-day battle. The harbor installations had been destroyed, however, and it would be some weeks before the port could receive ships. This was a blow to the Allies, since the previous week there had been a violent storm in the English Channel that had severely damaged both Mulberry harbors.

The Allies are hampered
At the end of June the British tried to break through west of Caen. They succeeded in advancing some 6 miles (9.5 km) but were then hit in the flank by SS Panzer troops and forced to partially withdraw. However, the continued pressure on the German forces was becoming hard for them to bear and so Rundstedt and Rommel met Hitler again, this time at his Alpine retreat. They appealed for more troops and permission to withdraw from Normandy, but Hitler refused,

> **"Make peace,** you fools, **what else can you do?"**
> GERD VON RUNDSTEDT TO HITLER'S STAFF, JULY 1, 1944

demanding instead that they liquidate the beachhead. Rundstedt, who felt that there was no alternative to making peace, was dismissed. He was replaced by Günther von Kluge.

The Americans now began to advance southwards toward St. Lô, but found the going difficult. A major reason for this was the nature of much of the Normandy countryside. Known as the "bocage," it consisted of woodland and small fields bounded by banks that were crowned by dense hedges. It was very claustrophobic and favored the defense over the attack, especially when it came to armored vehicles. Meanwhile, the British and Canadians were continuing to hammer their heads against Caen. RAF Bomber Command blasted the city's defenses with "carpet bombing" techniques. This enabled the ground

KEY MOMENT
THE BOMBING OF CAEN
The British and Canadians were held up by fortified villages north of Caen. On 7 July 447 RAF heavy bombers attacked. For fear of hitting their own, they dropped their 2,276 tons of bombs on the northern outskirts of Caen itself. The ensuing ground attack secured the northern part, but was impeded by the rubble from the bombing.

23 ft (7.06 m) barrel

forces to capture the northern half of the city, but yet again desperate German resistance foiled further progress.

On the threshold of victory
On July 10 Montgomery, who was controlling the battle, issued a new directive. The British Second Army was to launch a major attack just east of Caen to relieve pressure on the US First Army so that it could break out. A week later the Germans suffered a blow when Rommel was wounded by a fighter-bomber. Kluge took over Rommel's own command while retaining overall authority. On July 18 the British launched a major attack east of Caen. It ran out of steam short of its objectives, but helped pave the way for an eventual American breakout. The US forces were also now beginning to make progress, finally capturing the road-hub of St. Lô. On July 20 an assassination attempt against Hitler failed but distracted the Germans nevertheless.

The US began their breakthrough operation on July 25, with the town of Avranches being the initial objective.

Allied air power
A Douglas A–2 Havoc (called a Boston by the British) of the US Ninth Air Force attacking German supply dumps in Normandy. Overwhelming air supremacy was a crucial factor in the eventual Allied success in Normandy.

KEY

— German front line 25 July

-·-·- German front line 14 August

⟹ Allied advance

Breakout from Normandy

This map shows how the Allied forces cleared Brittany of the enemy and then broke out eastwards in pursuit of the shattered German armies.

Preceded by carpet bombing, it took two days to get through the German defenses. Avranches was liberated on July 31 and the breakout could begin. in the lead was George S. Patton's Third US Army, which had been arriving in Normandy over the past two weeks. Hitler was determined, however, that Kluge keep the Allied forces contained through spoiling attacks.

Final assault

Patton attacked on August 1, sending part of his army sweeping through Brittany, while the remainder advanced south and east. The Third Army overran Brittany in just a week. Hitler had, however, declared all ports to be fortresses that must not be given up and so the former U-boat bases of Brest, Lorient, and St. Nazaire had to be placed under siege. The US First Army was also pushing south and on the night of August 7/8 four Panzer divisions

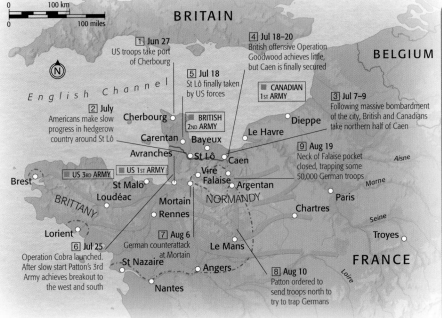

1 Jun 27 US troops take port of Cherbourg

2 July Americans make slow progress in hedgerow country around St Lô

4 Jul 18–20 British offensive Operation Goodwood achieves little, but Caen is finally secured

5 Jul 18 St Lô finally taken by US forces

CANADIAN 1ST ARMY

3 Jul 7–9 Following massive bombardment of the city, British and Canadians take northern half of Caen

BRITISH 2ND ARMY

9 Aug 19 Neck of Falaise pocket closed, trapping some 50,000 German troops

US 3RD ARMY **US 1ST ARMY**

6 Jul 25 Operation Cobra launched. After slow start Patton's 3rd Army achieves breakout to the west and south

7 Aug 6 German counterattack at Mortain

8 Aug 10 Patton ordered to send troops north to try to trap Germans

BRITAIN

English Channel

BELGIUM

Cherbourg · Carentan · Avranches · St Malo · Loudéac · Brest · Lorient · St Nazaire · Nantes · Rennes · Mortain · Vire · Falaise · Argentan · Bayeux · St Lô · Caen · Le Havre · Dieppe · Angers · Le Mans · Chartres · Paris · Troyes

BRITTANY · NORMANDY · FRANCE

Aisne · Marne · Seine · Loire

0 — 100 km / 0 — 100 miles

struck it in the flank near Mortain. The Germans were initially helped by poor visibility, which restricted air power, and the US lost some ground but once the skies cleared the attack was doomed. On the British flank, meanwhile, the Canadians mounted two set-piece attacks down the Caen-Falaise road, pushing the Germans back. By the middle of August the German forces in Normandy were in danger of being trapped. The US

94,000 The number of Allied troops that landed on the French Riviera on August 15, 1944. The invasion force consisted of the US Seventh Army and what would later become the French First Army.

advance had now swung eastward, while the British and Canadians were pressing south from Caen. Patton now began to direct part of his army north to close the trap, but General Omar Bradley, leader of the 12th Army Group, told him to halt at Argentan to avoid clashing with the British and Canadians. Realizing the danger, von Kluge told his forces to withdraw. The Falaise pocket was closed on August 19 and marked the end of the Battle of Normandy.

After the breakout, the Allies could begin the liberation of the rest of France and the Low Countries, the first target being Paris 268–69 ▶▶. Meanwhile, the Russians were launching their own offensive in the East.

AFTER FALAISE

Following the final battle of the **Falaise pocket**, Kluge was sacked by Hitler—he suspected Kluge of being implicated in the **bomb plot**

10 THOUSAND Germans were killed in the battle of the Falaise pocket.

50 THOUSAND Germans were taken prisoner in Falaise.

266–67 ▶▶. Called to Berlin to explain himself, Kluge committed suicide en route and was replaced by the politically reliable **Walter Model**.

RUSSIAN OFFENSIVE

There had, however, been other events that made people believe that the end of the war in Europe might be possible before the close of 1944. The Russians had launched a **major offensive in the East 270–71 ▶▶** and that was one reason why Normandy was **starved of German reinforcements**. They had been called eastward to try to stem the Red Army advance.

A US MILITARY POLICEMAN CONSULTS A PHRASE BOOK

DRAGOON

August 15 saw **Operation Dragoon** put into action. The Allies landed on the French Riviera and the forces, drawn largely from Italy, met with little resistance. On September 11, in less than a month, the troops joined up with Patton's Third Army near Dijon.

The breech mechanism in the original M1 version proved problematic and so was modified for the later M2. A rate of fire of some 40 rounds of ammunition per hour could be sustained.

The gun carriage was a split-trail design. The main road wheels were raised up when the gun was in action so that a solid firing platform could be created.

Limber, removed in action

US 155mm Long Tom

This heavy, 155 mm caliber field gun was the mainstay of American long-range artillery in the final months of the war. It fired 95 lb (43 kg) of a high explosive shell. Other ammunition available included smoke, chemical, illuminating, and even anti-armor types.

Trail

The firing platform was extremely stable, giving the Long Tom's 14-man crew good accuracy up to the gun's maximum range of 25,700 yd (23,500 m).

Personal gear

The fighting man required numerous items, apart from his weapons, to make him effective. Many of them were compact and light so that they could be carried on his person. They included the essentials of life, but they also maintained his morale.

1 This **Russian tank repair kit** enabled tank crews to carry out running repairs on their vehicles when in action. **2** A **waterproof flashlight** used by British Special Forces. It was battery operated and the lanyard or rope enabled it to be attached to the user. **3** A **Japanese tape measure**. The Japanese measured length in Ri (2.44 miles/ 4 km), Ken (5.97ft/ 1.8m), and Shaku (12in/ 30cm). **4** The **British sun compass** was the principal means of navigation in the desert; it worked on the sundial principle and was used in conjunction with a vehicle's mileometer. **5** This **Japanese compass** was an essential means of navigation, especially in the jungle. **6** A **British survival kit,** which was issued to all RAF aircrews for use if they had to bale out. It contained items ranging from high-energy candy, through water purification tablets, to a compass. **7** This **British penknife** was used especially by signalers when laying and repairing cable; it had a variety of blades and a wire-cutting tool. **8** This **British 24-hour ration pack** used by the troops in Southeast Asia provided food for one man. **9** **Invasion packs** issued to British troops contained general maps of the country, foreign currency, and phrase books. **10** A **mess tin and mug**. The British soldier

was issued with two mess tins, which could be used as cooking vessels, and an enamel mug. **11** **Cigarettes** that were issued to Canadian troops in Europe. Cigarettes were part of the field ration in most armed forces. **12** This **British anti-gas ointment** was to treat the effects of mustard gas. Chemical weapons were not, however, used on the battlefield during World War II. **13** This US **"blood chit"** was issued to US aircrews flying over territory under Russian control; it asked that the US Military Mission in Moscow be given the flier's particulars. **14** **British emergency rations** could not be consumed without the permission of a senior officer and contained processed meat. **15** **Pocket-sized novels** were issued to US troops. They were made small enough to fit into a breast pocket. **16** A **compendium of classic board games** for German army personnel. It was made of thin cardboard and the individual game counters and pieces had to be cut out. **17** A **Buddhist prayer card** which belonged to a Japanese Buddhist soldier. Religious faith often helped to provide strength and solace to those in combat. **18** A **razor and case** commercially produced with the British armed forces in mind, it also contains a shaving mirror.

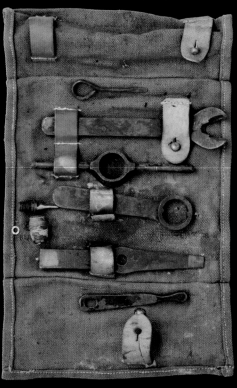
6 BRITISH SURVIVAL KIT ISSUED TO RAF AIRCREWS (BELOW LEFT AND RIGHT)

1 TANK REPAIR KIT (USSR)

3 TAPE MEASURE (JAPAN)

4 SUN COMPASS (BRITAIN)

7 PENKNIFE (BRITAIN)

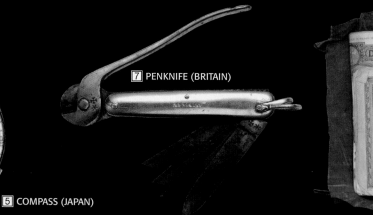
2 WATERPROOF FLASHLIGHT (BRITAIN)

5 COMPASS (JAPAN)

8 24-HOUR RATIONS (BRITAIN)

10 MESS TIN AND ENAMEL MUG (BRITAIN)

14 TWO TINS OF EMERGENCY RATIONS (BRITAIN)

Cigarettes
SWEET
CAPORAL
Kinney Bros

11 CIGARETTES ISSUED TO TROOPS IN EUROPE (CANADA)

B-55

THE
YEARLING

A NOVEL BY
Marjorie Kinnan
Rawlings

ARMED
SERVICES
EDITION

This book is intended for use by the United States
Armed Forces only, and is not to be reprinted
and is the property of the U. S. Government.
It has been published by the Council on Books
in Wartime, and is distributed by the Special
Service Division, A.S.F. for the Army and by the
Bureau of Naval Personnel for the Navy.

THIS IS THE COMPLETE BOOK—NOT A DIGEST

15 POCKET-SIZED NOVEL (US)

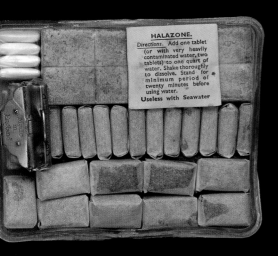

HALAZONE.
Directions. Add one tablet
(or with very heavily
contaminated water, two
tablets) to one quart of
water. Shake thoroughly
to dissolve. Stand for
minimum period of
twenty minutes before
using water.
Useless with Seawater

OINTMENT
ANTI-GAS Nº2
APPLY FREELY TO AFFECTED
PORTION OF SKIN
AS SOON AS POSSIBLE
RUB IN VIGOROUSLY FOR NOT LESS
THAN ONE MINUTE
KEEP AWAY FROM EYES

12 ANTI-GAS OINTMENT (BRITAIN)

Unterhaltungsspiele
für Soldaten

16 BOARD GAMES (GERMANY)

9 MONEY AND MAP FOR ARRIVAL
IN NORTH AFRICA (BRITAIN)

NORTH AFRICA
CONTAINING
CO, ALGERIA, TUNISIA, ITALIAN LIBYA
AND
SPANISH RIO DE ORO
SCALE

Я американец
"Ya Amerikánets" (Pronounced as spelt)
Пожалуйста сообщите
сведения обо мне в
Американскую Военную
Миссию в Москве

Please
communicate
my particulars
to American
Military Mission
Moscow

13 BLOOD CHIT (US)

17 WOODEN PRAYER CARD (JAPAN)

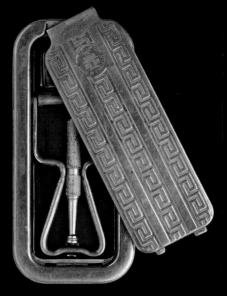

18 RAZOR AND CASE (BRITAIN)

Hitler Bomb Plot

There had been a number of plots to assassinate Hitler and make peace with the Allies, but the attempt made against his life on July 20, 1944, came closest to achieving its objective. In Berlin and Paris troops took over key buildings, but it proved premature, since Hitler, although shaken, was still very much alive.

BEFORE

The informal groups that were opposed to Hitler recognized that they would attract little popular support while the war was going well for Germany.

AN OPPORTUNITY ARISES
However, following the **debacle at Stalingrad** **‹‹ 192–95**, it became increasingly clear that Germany was **facing ultimate ruin**. With Hitler determined to pursue the war to **the bitter end**, opposing groups came to believe that the only way to save their country was **to remove him**.

A PERILOUS MISSION
Various groups formed a loose association, their members made up of middle-ranking army officers and Foreign Office officials. They **hatched a number of plots**, some of which they tried to put into effect, but which **failed** through lack of coordination, incompetence, and bad luck.

GERMAN STAFF OFFICER (1907–44)
CLAUS VON STAUFFENBERG

Born into an aristocratic family with a strong military tradition, Stauffenberg joined the cavalry and then qualified for the General Staff. Serving as a staff officer in the Polish and French campaigns, he then became responsible for recruiting Soviet prisoners. It was their treatment by the SS that sickened Stauffenberg, turning him against the Nazi regime, and he became involved with anti-Hitler groups as a result. In February 1943 he was sent to Tunisia, but was severely wounded, losing an eye, a hand, and part of his leg. It was on recovery from these injuries that Stauffenberg was posted to the Replacement Army in Berlin. He was shot on July 21, 1944, for his part in the plot.

The conspirators spent much time attempting to enlist the support of the leading field commanders. While the majority were now disgusted by Hitler, they considered it their duty to continue fighting and thought the conspiracy a distraction in the midst of their efforts to keep the enemy away from Germany's borders. It was also against their upbringing to break an oath and they had sworn loyalty to Hitler in person. As Field Marshal Erich von Manstein put it, "Prussian field marshals do not mutiny." The plotters had more success with the command of Germany's Replacement Army, which controlled the military forces at home and had its headquarters in Berlin.

The perfect plot
One of the leading plotters, Colonel Claus von Stauffenberg, was appointed chief-of-staff to the Replacement Army on July 1, 1944. Among his duties were trips to attend Hitler's conferences. He planned to take a briefcase bomb to one of these conferences. Once Hitler was dead the troops in Berlin would seize key buildings and a new government would be declared. The same would happen in Paris, whose commander was also one of the plotters. After two

> The first attempt against Hitler's life came in November 1939 when he was in Munich, celebrating the anniversary of his failed 1923 *putsch*. Artisan George Elser placed a bomb in the hall where Hitler was speaking. It detonated after he had left.

abortive attempts, Stauffenberg flew, with an aide, to Hitler's field HQ at Rastenburg in East Prussia, the so-called "Wolf's Lair," on July 20.

On arrival he attended a briefing and then retired to a cloakroom, where his aide handed him a briefcase containing two explosive devices. Stauffenberg had time only to prepare one of them, setting the timer for it to go off in 15 minutes. He then went to the hut in which Hitler's conference was to take place and arranged to sit close to him. He placed

Hitler visits the injured
Eleven men were badly injured by the blast, with three of them dying from their injuries. Hitler was lucky and suffered only a burst eardrum.

his briefcase by a leg of the table and asked to be excused to make an urgent telephone call. As he left the Wolf's Lair there was a loud explosion. Convinced that Hitler was dead, Stauffenberg flew back to Berlin.

News of the blast spreads
Meanwhile, chief of communications at Rastenburg, who was in on the plot, signaled Berlin, saying that there had been an explosion, but that Hitler was still alive. The plotters were now unsure whether to initiate the rest of the plan. Eventually, Stauffenberg arrived back saying Hitler was dead, but Goebbels was in Berlin and had heard he was still alive. Goebbels told the Berlin Guard Battalion to arrest the plotters.

The Paris plotters had already made arrests. But when Kluge, Commander-in-Chief West, heard that Hitler was alive, he ordered them to be released and the military governor of Paris was ordered to Berlin. He tried to commit suicide en route but was nursed back to health and was then executed.

AFTER

Many of those immediately involved in the plot, including Stauffenberg, were **shot within 24 hours of the bomb blast.**

THE FATE OF OTHER SUSPECTS
A series of **show trials** were conducted in Berlin, with all the defendants found guilty and then hanged on wire **suspended from meat hooks**; others were thrown into **death camps**. Rommel, who was implicated, **committed suicide.**

THE ALLIES CLOSE IN
Hitler **trusted his generals** even less after the bomb plot, personally **supervising operations** to an **ever greater degree**. In the meantime, rapid **Allied advances in the West and the East 268–71 ››** had to be faced.

TRIAL OF THE CONSPIRATORS

"Since the generals have up to now managed nothing, the colonels have now to step in."
COLONEL CLAUS VON STAUFFENBERG, 1944

The wrecked conference room
The damage caused by the bomb was extensive, but Hitler was saved by a stout table leg, which took the main force of the explosion. That same afternoon, he showed the wreckage to Mussolini.

Liberation of France and Belgium

« BEFORE

The Western Allies liberated France and much of Belgium in the late summer of 1944. The German armies appeared shattered and there seemed no reason why the Rhine could not be quickly reached and crossed. However, supplies increasingly could not keep up with the rapid advance, thus slowing it down.

The Allies had almost completely destroyed the German armies in Normandy, making their breakout and subsequent advance relatively straightforward.

THE ALLIED ADVANCE

The British and Canadians **thrust northward,** close to, and along, the coast of northern France, while the Americans **thrust further south**, with Paris being their immediate objective. Far to the southeast the **US and French forces**, which had landed in the south of France were **rapidly advancing northward** along the line of the **Rhône River ‹‹ 262–63**.

TROUBLED SUPPLY LINES

The French port of **Cherbourg had been destroyed** by its garrison. However, the United States were able to land much of their logistical requirement over open beaches. The further the Allied forces moved beyond Normandy, the longer their communication lines became. The **Red Ball Express convoy system**, running from Normandy to Chartres, worked wonders, but was no real answer.

> **By August 29 the trucks of the Red Ball Express were delivering 12,000 tons of fuel per day from Cherbourg to depots southwest of Paris. However, the trucks themselves were consuming 300,000 gallons (1 million liters) a day.**

Once across the Seine River, the US forces had Paris in their sights. On August 19, the same day that they established their first bridgehead over the river, there was an uprising in Paris, organized by the resistance and the French Forces of the Interior (FFI), an irregular army largely raised from the resistance. There was some bitter fighting with the German garrison, but thanks to the intervention of the Swedish consul-general, a temporary truce was arranged on August 23. On that same day, however, Hitler ordered the military governor, General Dietrich von Choltitz, to raze Paris to the ground.

A costly delay

With the Allies approaching the capital, von Choltitz decided to play for time. The Allies had originally intended to encircle Paris, rather than enter it, for

Paris is freed

Vehicles of the French Second Armored Division drive down the Champs Elysées from the Arc de Triomphe on August 25, 1944, marking the liberation of Paris. German snipers were still active in the city.

fear of causing too much collateral damage, but the uprising caused a change of heart. George S. Patton's Third US Army was tasked with liberating Paris and, on August 23, he sent two divisions, the Fourth US Infantry Division and the Second French Armored Division, toward the capital.

It became almost a race, but Philippe Leclerc's Free French were the first to arrive in Paris, entering the city late the following day, and using their local knowledge of the back streets. There was some resistance from the Germans, but on the afternoon of August 25 von Choltitz decided

Liberation of Brussels

Men of the Free Belgian Brigade, which was under British command, are wildly welcomed as they pass through the Belgian capital after its liberation by the Guards Armoured Division.

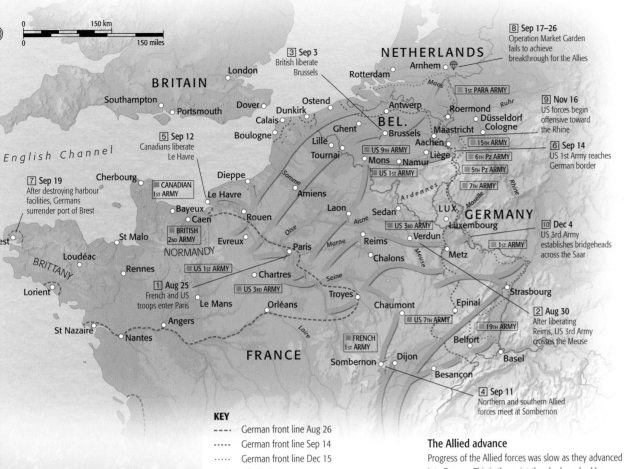

It was lack of fuel, rather than German resistance, that had slowed the Allied advance to a virtual halt.

NO END IN SIGHT
Now, as the **German forces** were able to draw breath to some extent, hopes of **defeating Germany** by the end of 1944 began to fade.

SLOWLY BUT SURELY
The one good piece of news was that the **Allied advance** from the south of France had made good progress. By **mid-September** they had **driven the German forces** facing them back almost into Germany. They had reached the Vosges Mountains and **linked up with Patton**.

DARING OPERATION
By then **Field Marshal Montgomery** had come up with a **daring plan 280–81 ≫** that might just break the growing stalemate, and enable a decision to be reached **before the end of the year**.

KEY
- - - - German front line Aug 26
· · · · German front line Sep 14
· · · · German front line Dec 15
➡ Allied advance
⛉ Allied airborne assault

The Allied advance
Progress of the Allied forces was slow as they advanced into Europe. This is the point they had reached by mid-December 1944, just before the Germans launched their surprise counter-offensive.

to surrender to Leclerc, despite some of his troops fighting on for longer. That evening de Gaulle entered Paris in triumph and, fearing a Communist coup, quickly formed a government. Paris had been just one factor in the plan. With the Germans retreating so rapidly across France a coherent strategy was needed.

Plan of attack
Eisenhower declared, on August 21, that he would take control of the ground campaign from September 1, and that his forces would advance on a broad front. But Montgomery objected, arguing that concentrated Allied forces should advance to the Ruhr via Antwerp in Belgium. This implied that Montgomery should lead the advance, but Eisenhower believed that the American public would not accept British command of US forces and insisted on his broad-front strategy.

On the German side, Walter Model had agreed to withdrawing from the Seine and was trying to establish a new defense line on the Somme and Marne rivers. Given the state of many of his divisions and the rapid Allied advance,

French five franc note
French currency was worth one sixth of its 1939 value and the French economy as a whole was in tatters following liberation.

this proved impossible. General Patton was advancing rapidly eastward to the south of Paris, and reached the Meuse River on August 31. On the same day the British in the north crossed the Somme. Fuel resupply was now a major problem, in spite of having set up a system of truck convoys on designated routes to bring supplies from Normandy.

Indeed, Patton had now halted because Eisenhower had agreed that priority for fuel should be given to the north so that Antwerp could be secured. It was freed on September 4, but could not function as a port until the Scheldt estuary, which connected Antwerp to the sea, had been cleared. Nothing could be done until October as most of Montgomery's resources were devoted to Operation Market Garden in the Netherlands. It was to be November before Antwerp's port was usable.

Further delays
The Germans, perceiving Patton to be the greatest threat, were concentrating their forces to oppose him. He managed to get across the Moselle, but this factor, added to his lack of fuel, brought his

advance to a halt once more. Courtney Hodges's First US Army on Patton's left flank sent patrols across the German border on September 11, but the fuel shortage meant that he could not exploit this. With the Canadians tied down in besieging the Channel ports, the British Second Army managed to liberate Brussels on September 3, but ran out of steam again, before it could reach the Dutch border.

FREE FRENCH LEADER (1902–47)
GENERAL PHILIPPE LECLERC

Leclerc was a regular officer who joined de Gaulle in Britain after the fall of France. De Gaulle sent him to bring France's African colonies to his aid, which he did. Leclerc then led a small force across the desert, linking up with the British Eighth Army in Tripoli in early 1943. After the end of the war in Europe, he commanded the French forces in the Far East, controversially favoring negotiation with the communist Viet Minh. He died in a plane crash in Algeria in 1947, and was posthumously created marshal of France.

Red Army Offensive

Summer 1944 saw the Russians continuing to drive the Germans back on all fronts. At the extreme ends of the Eastern Front, Finland and Romania were forced to sue for peace, while in the center, Operation Bagration almost tore the heart out of the German Army Group Center.

Liberated Slovaks
Slovak villagers greet their Red Army liberators in the fall of 1944. In terms of liberated terrain, this was a year of great achievement for Russian forces in Europe.

BEFORE

The failed attack at Kursk in the summer of 1943 had confirmed that the Red Army had become too strong for the Germans to do anything else but remain on the defensive.

SUSTAINED OFFENSIVE
The Russians had embarked on a series of **rolling offensives**. As soon as one began to lose impact they attacked elsewhere. This not only allowed the Germans **no breathing space**, but made it difficult for them to deploy reserves effectively.

A NEW DIRECTION
In January 1944 Leningrad was liberated after a **900-day siege ≪ 134–37** and the Red Army entered Estonia. Romania began to come under threat and the **Russian advance** reached its borders in the spring. German forces trapped in Crimea were **forced to surrender** in May. The Russians now planned **a major offensive** in the center to coincide with the **Anglo-American cross-Channel invasion ≪ 258–59**.

Joseph Stalin announced his plans for the summer on May 1, 1944. While the Red Army's main assault would be in the center, in Byelorussia (present-day Belarus), there would be a feint in the north designed both to knock Finland out of the war and to prevent the German Army Group North from going to the help of the main victim, Army Group Center. There would also be another feint in the south later on, to overrun Romania. The plans were drawn up in the greatest secrecy, and elaborate deception measures were put into effect in order to disguise both the time and the place of the main assault.

Germany left vulnerable
Army Group Center was, at the time, holding a long front, including a sizeable salient based on Orsha. As May wore on, the army's commander, Field Marshal Ernst Busch, became increasingly certain that the Soviets intended to attack him.

He asked Hitler's permission to shorten his line by withdrawing to the more defendable Beresina River. Hitler, who was convinced that the main Russian effort was to be in the south, refused this request, and Army Group Center was left vulnerable.

The Russian summer 1944 campaign opened on June 10, with the attack on Finland. The Finns were soon forced back, with the port of Viipuri falling on June 20. Two days after this, the main offensive, which was codenamed Bagration, opened, with the 1st Baltic Front striking south into the salient and enveloping Vitebsk. An entire German corps was lost when the city fell. On June 23 the 3rd Byelorussian Front joined in, attacking along the highway leading to Minsk. The two other Byelorussian fronts also entered the fray and

> The overall strength of the German Armed Forces fell by nearly 20 percent during 1944; much of this was caused by the army's devastating losses on the Eastern Front.

were soon across the Beresina River. Of Busch's armies, Third Panzer had been shattered, the Ninth Army had been encircled, and the withdrawing Fourth Army was in danger of being cut off. Yet, the desperate Busch still could not convince Hitler that his command had been torn open. Instead, Busch was sacked and replaced by Walter Model, but he could do little to stop the rot, and Minsk fell to the Russians on July 4. They had, by now, created yet

> "**Shattered** by the feeling that we can do nothing to help, **your old trailblazer** salutes his army."
> GENERAL VON TIPPELSKIRCH, COMMANDING FOURTH GERMAN ARMY, TO HIS TROOPS TRAPPED EAST OF MINSK, JULY 5, 1944

До верлина!

The Eastern Front

The Eastern Front changed beyond recognition between June and December 1944. Not only was the Soviet Union wholly liberated, but much of Eastern Europe was freed from German occupation as well.

another large pocket, which yielded some 57,000 German prisoners. Indeed, by this time, the German Army had lost the equivalent of 28 full divisions and only the wings of Army Group Center were still intact.

The Russian offensive continues

The Red Army pressed on regardless, entering Lithuania and Poland. Army Group North was also under severe pressure in Latvia and Estonia, and could do nothing to help Model. To increase the agony, the 1st Ukrainian Front now began to attack Army Group Center's southern neighbor, Army Group North Ukraine.

On July 20, the day of the bomb explosion at Hitler's headquarters at Rastenburg, the 1st Byelorussian Front reached the Bug River, which marked Poland's prewar border with the Russian Union and, three days later, entered Lublin. There it came across Majdenek, the first of the German extermination camps to be overrun.

Within another three days the 1st Byelorussian Front would reach the River Vistula, some 75 miles (120 km) southeast of Warsaw. The Poles in the capital had already risen against their German occupier in anticipation of this development. In spite of Hitler's orders to Army Groups North and Center to stand and hold their ground, nothing could stop the Russian onrush.

The T-34 tank was constructed using armor up to 4⅓-in (110-mm) thick. The design was such that the armor was sloped, providing more effective resistance to anti-tank weapons.

KEY
— German front line Jun 22
–·–· German front line Jul 25
– – German front line Sep 15
···· German front line Dec 15
⇒ Soviet /Bulgarian advance

Wider tracks gave the T-34/85 the advantage over the earlier T-34/76. It was able to cope better on very soft ground, making it less likely to become bogged down on the Eastern Front.

Russian T-34/85 tank

Upgunned from 76 mm to 85 mm, this version of the outstanding T-34 tank entered service in early 1944. Well armored, it was capable of speeds of 30 mph (48 kph).

AFTER »»

Operation Bagration produced a major crisis for the Germans and demonstrated just how much the Red Army had learned, transforming it into the highly effective fighting force that it had now become.

ROMANIA FALLS

Elsewhere on the Eastern Front, the long-awaited Russian **assault on Romania** began on August 20. Many Romanian formations, **tired of the war**, surrendered almost immediately. After three days King Carol declared **hostilities to be at an end**. The Russian troops seized the Ploesti oilfields and **entered the capital**, Bucharest. The 20 or so German divisions in the country scrambled

PREPARING FOR BAGRATION

out as best they could. Bulgaria, too, **hastily changed sides**. The Russians then went on to overrun much of Hungary and Slovakia.

FINLAND SURRENDERS

It was much the same story in Finland. On August 25 the Finns asked Moscow **for peace terms** and **sent a delegation** to discuss them. **An armistice** was signed on September 19 and

2.4 MILLION
The number of Russian troops, together with 5,200 tanks and 5,300 aircraft, committed to Operation Bagration.

the German forces in the country withdrew into Norway. The Russians also **overran the Baltic states** and reached East Prussia. It would not be long before the Red Army advanced into the **German Reich itself 298–99** »»

TECHNOLOGY

YAK-3 FIGHTER PLANE

This was the second Russian plane to be given the Yak-3 designation, the first never having progressed beyond prototype stage.

The second Yak-3 was conceived in 1941 as a fighter plane for ensuring air superiority over the battlefield. It was designed primarily for low-altitude combat. Problems during its development meant that it did not see any action until the pivotal Battle of Kursk in the summer of 1943, but some 5,000 aircraft were delivered

before production ceased in 1946. The Yak-3 fighter plane was armed with a 20 mm cannon and two 12.7 mm machine-guns. It was capable of reaching flying speeds of up to 367 mph (590 kph).

Map labels

FINLAND
Viipuri
Lake Ladoga
Helsinki
Gulf of Finland
Leningrad
Tallinn
KARELIAN FRONT
LENINGRAD FRONT
ESTONIA
Lake Peipus
3RD BALTIC FRONT
Pskov
2ND BALTIC FRONT
ARMY GROUP NORTH
Riga
LATVIA
Opochka
Memel
Dvinsk
Dvina
1ST BALTIC FRONT
LITHUANIA
Polotsk
Niemen
Vitebsk
Königsberg
Kaunas
3RD BYELORUSSIAN FRONT
EAST PRUSSIA
Vilna
Smolensk
ARMY GROUP CENTRE
Augustow
Orsha
Grodno
Minsk
Mogilev
2ND BYELORUSSIAN FRONT
Bialystok
BYELORUSSIA
Warsaw
Siedlce
Brest-Litovsk
Pripet Marshes
1ST BYELORUSSIAN FRONT
POLAND
ARMY GROUP NORTH UKRAINE
Lublin
Pripet
Kowel
Lutsk
Sandomiercz
1ST UKRAINIAN FRONT
Cracow
Kiev
Przemysl
Lwow
USSR
SLOVAKIA
Tarnopol
Dnieper
Vienna
ARMY GROUP SOUTH UKRAINE
4TH UKRAINIAN FRONT
Budapest
Lake Balaton
Dniester
HUNGARY
Prut
2ND UKRAINIAN FRONT
Debrecen
Carpathians
Bug
UKRAINE
Drava
3RD UKRAINIAN FRONT
Tiraspol
ROMANIA
Odessa
ARMY GROUP F
Transylvanian Alps
Belgrade
Galati
YUGOSLAVIA
Ploesti
Bucharest
Constanta
Danube
Black Sea
ARMY GROUP E
BULGARIAN ARMY
BULGARIA

Map timeline
1 Jun 10 — Offensive launched against Finland. Soviets take Viipuri on the 20th
10 Sep 22 — Russians occupy Tallinn
12 Oct 15 — Capture of Riga
3 Jul 3 — Liberation of Minsk. Large numbers of Germans encircled to the east of the city
5 Aug 1 — Poles launch uprising against Germans in Warsaw
9 Sep 14 — Russians reach outskirts of Warsaw
4 Jul 23 — Liberation of Majdanek extermination camp
2 Jun 23 — Operation Bagration is launched along 450-mile (700-km) front
14 Nov 4 — Russian forces reach outskirts of Budapest. Siege begins on 26 Dec
11 Oct 6 — 2nd Ukrainian Front launches offensive against Hungary
8 Sep 8 — Russian forces enter Bulgaria, which declares war on Germany
6 Aug 20 — Russian forces land at mouth of Danube and advance into Romania
13 Oct 20 — Belgrade falls to Russians after a week-long battle
7 Aug 31 — Russian forces enter Bucharest

Map scale: 0 — 200 km / 0 — 200 miles

Warsaw Uprising

With the Russian summer offensive rapidly liberating much of Poland and approaching the capital, the Polish Home Army rose against the Germans in Warsaw. The Red Army halted east of the River Vistula, however, and the Poles were left to fight on without support.

German troops in Warsaw

The uprising of the Polish underground movement was ruthlessly put down by the German forces present, with SS units being employed. This distraction cost the Germans some 17,000 lives in total.

Initially embracing all political factions, the Polish Home Army did not attack the Germans for fear of reprisals on the civilian population. This changed in 1942, when the Germans began to expel the Poles to make way for German colonists. The Home Army attacked the colonists, forcing the Germans to halt the expulsions.

Then, encouraged by the Red Army's progress, the Communists split from the Home Army and formed the National Council for the Homeland, at the end of 1943, just before the Russians reentered Polish territory. What then remained of the Home Army formed its own Council of National Unity, and both groups claimed to represent the Polish nation.

Soviet hostility

In 1942 General Sikorski had instructed the Home Army on what to do when the Red Army arrived. It was to offer the Russians assistance in dealing with the withdrawing Germans, but was not to allow Polish independence to be infringed. When the Russians crossed into Poland in January 1944 this strategy worked reasonably well, but soon some of its units were offered the choice of disbanding or joining the First Red Polish Army, which had been formed by the Russians. In cases where the NKVD, the Russian secret police, had taken over from the army, members of the Home Army were eradicated or sent to Gulags deep in the USSR.

The Home Army acts

As the Red Army began to close up to the River Vistula in late July 1944, the commander of the Home Army, General Tadeusz Komorowski, decided to rise up against the Germans in Warsaw. This would help the Russians get across the Vistula and politically it would help to ensure that a Polish government was in place when the Russians arrived. This he saw as essential since, on July 22, Radio Moscow had announced the formation of a Polish Committee for Liberation. This had also horrified the London Poles, who gave permission to attack the Germans. By July 29 the people on the eastern outskirts

Cross of Valor

Established in 1920, this Polish medal was reintroduced during World War II.

Home Army mortar crew

Home Army members operate a mortar. At the outset of the uprising, only around 15 percent of the insurgents were armed. However, over time, captured weapons helped to make good the shortfall.

of Warsaw could hear the sounds of battle as German forces counterattacked the 1st Byelorussian Front east of the Vistula. Two days later the Red Army was on the defensive. Unaware of this, Komorowski gave the attack order and the uprising erupted at 5pm on August 1.

The Germans did not have many troops in Warsaw, but they were able to prevent the Poles from seizing key buildings, although they did quickly gain control of several city districts. Komorowski, very short of arms, had to go onto the defensive and await help. The Western Allies asked Stalin to let aircraft use Russians airfields so that they could drop in supplies, but he delayed until mid-September. With civilian casualties rising sharply, the situation became desperate.

Eventually, on October 1, Komorowski accepted that there would be no concrete help coming from the Allies, so to save lives he was forced to surrender.

Resistance fighters surrender

A handful of Polish fighters, some wearing captured uniform, surrender to the German forces. Some 15,000 members of the Home Army were killed in action during the uprising, and many more civilians lost their lives.

Communist partisans being arrested

Arrested suspected Communist fighters pass British troops during the fighting in Athens, December 1944—two months before the civil war started.

Greece had been swiftly overrun by the Axis forces in April 1941 and came largely under Italian occupation.

SEEDS OF RESISTANCE

King George II and his government **fled to the Middle East ≪ 132–33** and a puppet regime was established in its place in Athens. Two major **resistance groups** were set up in Greece. The Communists formed the **National People's Liberation Army** (ELAS), while the moderates established the **National Republican Greek League** (EDES). Both took to the mountains of Greece, but while the two groups **shared**

BANKNOTE MADE DURING THE OCCUPATION

common ground in their aim to rid their country of its occupiers and their **mutual dislike** of the Greek monarchy, mistrust existed between the two from the outset.

SECRET ARMIES

The **Special Operations Executive (SOE) ≪ 172–73** had been taken by surprise by the **April 1941 invasion**, but did arrange for a few Greeks with radio sets to remain in the country and **pass information** to its Middle East HQ in Cairo. Knowledge of the resistance movements in Greece remained sketchy, however.

Resistance and Civil War in Greece

Combating the Axis occupation of Greece was bedevilled by enmity between the two main Resistance groups, although the Special Operations Executive (SOE) did its best to get them to cooperate with each other. When liberation came, a fierce civil war broke out as the Communists tried to take control.

In autumn 1942 the British identified the Gorgopotamos viaduct as a vital target. The viaduct carried the Salonika–Athens rail line and its removal would disrupt the Axis supply lines running down through Greece and across the Mediterranean to North Africa. A sabotage team was parachuted in to blow it up and make contact with both Greek resistance groups, ELAS and EDES, who were able to provide help in destroying the target in November.

Encouraged by this, the team was to continue its coordination efforts. It soon became clear that ELAS, or rather its political wing, the National Liberation Front (EAM), was bent on controlling all resistance activity to strengthen its position for taking over the country on liberation. Efforts were therefore made to boost EDES, thus ensuring them greater respectability from Britain.

Allied deception measures for the July 1943 Sicily landings included leading the Germans to believe that an attack on the Balkans was likely—achieved through widespread sabotage activity in Greece. Given the dominance of the communist ELAS, the SOE realized that it must work with them to bring this about. It therefore helped set up a joint Resistance HQ, with EAM/ELAS being given a dominant role. The operations were successful, and the Axis transferred two divisions to Greece to combat them.

Cooperation falters

This climate of cooperation between the resistance groups did not last long. In August 1943, a resistance delegation arrived in Cairo, accompanied by the

British Sten gun Mark V and magazine

This submachine gun was supplied to all resistance groups supported by the British. The more common version had a skeleton collapsible butt.

head of the British military mission to Greece. With EAM/ELAS delegates forming the majority it demanded that there be a plebiscite held in Greece on whether the king be allowed to return, and three government posts in the areas of Greece controlled by the resistance. The British refused both demands. Disgruntled, the delegates returned to Greece believing that the British intended to reimpose the monarchy

Forming the new Greek army
General Scobie, the British commander in Greece, in discussion with General Saphis, the commander of ELAS, and the bearded General Zervas, who led EDES.

by force. Fighting also broke out between ELAS and EDES. A truce was finally arranged in February 1944, after which EDES found its members restricted to just northwestern Greece.

A new prime minister for Greece

The EAM now created the Political Committee of National Liberation to govern the regions of the country that it controlled. However, the issue of whether this committee should play a part in any post-liberation government sparked mutinies within the Free Greek forces stationed in the Middle East. These discomfited the government in exile, who appointed anti-communist George Papandreou prime minister. He called a conference of all parties, in Lebanon, in May 1944, through which

> During the civil war, the British cut off arms supplies to ELAS, but this made little difference, since ELAS had obtained considerable quantities from the Italian occupation forces following the September 1943 Italian surrender.

he aimed to isolate the Communists. Greek communists rejected the proposal for a government of national unity and demanded Papandreou's removal.

Churchill's pact with Stalin

With the Red Army looking as though it would soon enter southeast Europe, Churchill agreed that Stalin would be allowed a free hand in Romania while Greece was to be in the British sphere of influence. This meant that EAM/ELAS could no longer expect support from Moscow. Thus, in August 1944, EAM agreed to join the Papandreou government, gaining some junior posts.

By September 1944 the Axis forces in Greece were starting to face the danger of being cut off by the Red Army, more so once their ally, Bulgaria, changed sides. They began to withdraw from southern Greece and British Special Forces made a number of landings.

"If we had not intervened, there would have been a **massacre**."

WINSTON CHURCHILL TO HIS WAR CABINET, DECEMBER 29, 1944

On October 12 the Germans evacuated Athens and, four days later, Papandreou arrived in the Greek capital. The British impressed on him that his priorities were reform of the currency, disarmament of all resistance groups, and the formation of a new Greek Army, to include former ELAS members. He also had to organize the reception of humanitarian aid for the, now starving, population.

A new currency was introduced and, on November 30, plans for the new army, which was to be an amalgam of troops that had fought under the British Army and units of the resistance, was announced. The Communists objected to the inclusion of certain elements and refused to disarm; their ministers resigned from government and they called a general strike.

On December 3 there were fatalities as Communist demonstrators clashed with the police in Athens. ELAS units also began to advance on the capital. Churchill ordered the British to use force to crush ELAS. The conflict spread to other parts of the country, but Stalin kept his word and did not interfere. The British failed to organize a ceasefire,

and Churchill himself arrived on Christmas Day to attend a conference for all parties, presided over by highly respected Archbishop Damaskinos. He then persuaded the Greek king to agree to the Archbishop becoming regent.

By the new year, the British forces had regained control of Athens and its port of Piraeus and, on January 4, a new Greek government was formed. Eight days later a truce was signed. This was confirmed by the Peace of Varkiza a month later. ELAS agreed to release civilian hostages it was holding, disarm its men, and cooperate in the formation of the National Army. All hoped that the reconstruction of the country could now begin.

The prime minister addresses his people
Newly appointed prime minister, George Papandreou, speaks to an Athenian crowd on his return to the capital on October 18, 1944. Not all citizens, by any means, welcomed his arrival.

AMERICAN ELECTION MONITOR'S BADGE

> The Greek Civil War had been short in duration, thanks to the military help given by the British, but it left unresolved issues.

CONTINUING NATIONAL UNREST
The question over the **future of the monarchy** had still to be decided and much needed to be done to **restore the Greek economy**.

LAW AND ORDER
Furthermore, while a general **amnesty** had been declared, it did not apply to any **criminal acts** committed under Axis occupation. This gave the **right-wing vigilante groups** an excuse to settle old scores with **former ELAS members**, and a number were murdered during the next year. The result was that **an increasing number** of communists took to the mountains once more with their weapons, **vowing to seek revenge**.

AN UNCERTAIN FUTURE
It therefore became **increasingly inevitable** that there would be a **second round** to the civil war **in the future**, especially once the **British forces** supporting the new government withdrew 340–41 ❯❯.

"Had there been **any longer delay** between the departure of the Germans and the arrival of the Greek government … EAM **would have seized power**."

HAROLD MACMILLAN, CHURCHILL'S REPRESENTATIVE IN GREECE, OCTOBER 18, 1944

BEFORE

The Axis occupation of Yugoslavia laid bare the fact that it was an artificially created state made up of diverse peoples.

THE SNAKEPIT

Dominant were the Serbs, who had the largest population and considered it their right to **rule the country**. The second largest group were the Croats, who were **predominantly Roman Catholic**, and resented the Serbs. The Slovenes did **respect the state**, but the **loyalty** of the Slav Muslims of Bosnia and Herzegovina **was questionable**. Macedonian Slavs tended to **look toward Bulgaria**, while many of the Montenegrins dreamed of their **independence being one day restored**.

AXIS OCCUPATION

Wooed by both the **Germans and the British**, Yugoslavia was **eventually overrun** by the Axis powers in a **lightning campaign in April 1941** **《 132–33** and King Peter and his government **fled to safety in Britain**.

EARLY RESISTANCE

A band of Serb royalists under **Draža Mihailović** began to fan the **flames of resistance**. Other **armed groups** also formed, but some were more **concerned with self-interest** than with **opposing the occupiers** of their country.

Balkan Snakepit

Resistance in Yugoslavia during the Axis occupation soon became fractured, revealing the lack of national unity among the country's peoples. Eventually, it was the Communists, under Tito, who provided the only effective opposition, and they played a key role in the liberation of Yugoslavia.

In the aftermath of the successful German invasion of Yugoslavia in the spring of 1941 it was natural that the British should back the royalist, Draža Mihailović, and his resistance organization—which became known as the Četniks—because Britain was harboring King Peter of Yugoslavia. The king's Serbian royalist stance was not to the taste of the majority of Yugoslavs but, initially, they flocked to his banner.

Many supporters came from Croatia, to which the Germans had granted independence as a puppet state, and which also now incorporated Bosnia and Herzegovina. The Germans had been encouraged to do this by Croatian

Equal in war

A sizeable minority of partisans in the Balkans were women and they were treated just like the men. Eventually, almost all of them were wearing British-supplied uniforms.

Nationalists, many of whom were pro-Fascist. Known as the Ustaša, these Croatian Nationalists had then begun a campaign of murder, expulsion, and forced religious conversion of the Serbs within Croatia's borders, driving many of them into the arms of Mihailović.

Tito and the Communists

Following the German invasion of the Soviet Union, another force came into play in the guise of the Communists under Tito (see opposite). In July 1941 Tito issued a national call to arms and his "partisans," as they became known, soon began to make their mark. In

Montenegro they captured some 5,000 Italian troops, and by September, had control over much of Serbia.

Mihailović's original policy had been simply to lie low and wait for the situation to improve. He was, however, swayed by Tito's call and the Četniks joined in the fight against the Axis powers. The German response was brutal; they declared that 100 Yugoslavs would be shot for every German soldier killed. This caused Mihailović to change his mind once more, since the German

TITO (JOSIP BROZ)

Born in Croatia, Josip Broz became a Communist revolutionary at an early age. He operated under various pseudonyms before eventually adopting that of "Tito" permanently. In the 1930s he spent much of his time in Moscow, working for the Communist International, or Comintern. He then returned to Yugoslavia in order to overhaul its Communist Party, and was made General Secretary in 1940. After World War II Tito was determined to keep Yugoslavia independent. Under him, the country remained neutral throughout the Cold War, practicing a more relaxed form of Communism than any found elsewhere. After his death, the unity he had forged in the country began to disintegrate.

repression convinced him that an armed uprising at this stage was premature. He therefore condemned what the Communists were doing, and even offered to fight them if the Germans would give him arms.

Britain backs Tito

The Germans themselves could now concentrate on Tito. From September 1941, Axis forces launched a series of drives against the partisans, forcing large numbers out of Serbia and into western Bosnia. Partisan casualties were heavy, yet they were growing in strength, and would reach 150,000 by late 1942.

That November, Tito convened the Anti-Fascist Council for the National Liberation of Yugoslavia in a bid to

> **15** The number of German divisions that Tito was able to keep tied down in Yugoslavia. These German troops could have been used by Hitler far more profitably elsewhere.

enlist the support of the Yugoslavian population as a whole, and to point out to the Allies that they should give him their full support. This was critical, as Mihailović was now turning actively against him. Indeed, during a further German offensive at the beginning of 1943, and in which the Partisans were driven into Montenegro, the Četniks and partisans clashed, with the former losing some 12,000 men.

Until now, the British had continued to support Mihailović, not least because he was still a minister in King Peter's government. In May 1943, however, a British officer visited Tito's headquarters

Captured partisans

Tito's partisans secured considerable areas of Yugoslav territory and the Germans made several attempts to drive them out. Here, German soldiers are seen guarding a group captured in the mountains in May 1943.

and was impressed with what he saw. At the end of July, Churchill therefore decided to give Tito firm backing and sent Brigadier Fitzroy Maclean to be a liaison officer with the leader. Even so, Allied support for Mihailović continued and was not finally withdrawn until May 1944. This fact always made Tito suspicious of British intentions. After the invasion of Italy and its surrender, Tito bolstered his strength by taking control of the arms of nine Italian divisions. Even so, the Axis powers continued to keep Tito's forces on the run. This culminated in May 1944 when an airborne assault was made on Tito's headquarters. He narrowly

9 mm Beretta
The partisans were partially armed with captured Italian weapons, such as this robust, semi-automatic Beretta pistol.

escaped capture and fled to a partisan-held airfield from where he was flown to Bari on Italy's Adriatic coast, which was also the headquarters of Force 133, responsible for coordinating support for Tito. In the meantime, he had agreed to the British establishing a Special Forces base on the Adriatic island of Vis.

A number of raids were then made on German-held islands. This eventually forced the Germans to deploy more of their troops to the Dalmatian coast, thus relieving pressure on the partisans on the mainland. Tito himself re-established his own headquarters on Vis and many of the raids were the combined effort of Anglo-Partisan forces.

Tito and the Soviets

In August 1944 Tito and Churchill met face-to-face for the first time in Naples. Tito assured the British prime minster that it was not his intention to establish a Communist government in Yugoslavia, but he also had other concerns. With the Germans starting to withdraw from the Balkans, and the Red Army having subjugated neighboring Romania, it was essential that Tito should reach an understanding with the Soviets. Therefore, and without telling Churchill, Tito flew to Moscow in September to visit Joseph Stalin. Between them, they coordinated the liberation of Yugoslavia and, on October 20, 1944, Tito's partisan forces and the Red Army entered the Yugoslav capital of Belgrade together.

With the Balkans now liberated from German occupation, Tito's priority was to rebuild Yugoslavia. The country had suffered terribly in the course of the war. More than a million Yugoslavs died, most of them killed by other Yugoslavs. Tito continued to have to walk a political tightrope, however. He still desperately needed material support from the Western Allies, but they did not want him to join the Communist camp after the war. On the other hand, while he wanted to create the ideal Communist state in Yugoslavia, he did not want to do so at the expense of becoming a Soviet satellite.

Liberation of Belgrade
Partisans and Soviet troops celebrate on October 20 1944. Although they had co-operated closely, relations between the two grew cold after the war.

AFTER

Tito created what undoubtedly became the most effective resistance movement of the war, especially in its ability to take on the German forces in open battle.

A COMMUNIST STATE
Tito's efforts **during the war** had combined the **disparate elements** in the country behind him as never before in its short history. Once **peace was declared**, it was not long before he was able to establish a **Communist state** in Yugoslavia.

TITO AND THE ALLIES
Immediately after the war in Europe, Tito **almost came to blows** with the Western Allies when he **declared** that the Italian port of Trieste should become **part of Yugoslavia**. At the same time, he remained concerned over Moscow's policy **toward his country 340–41 ❯❯**.

THE FATE OF MIHAILOVIĆ
Mihailović did reappear, and attempted to reform his **Yugoslav Home Army** from a number of **anti-Communist** groups, most of whom had **collaborated with the Axis**. In April 1945 he returned to Serbia to **lead a revolt** against Tito, but **his force was attacked** by Tito's Partisans en route. Mihailović himself was eventually **captured, tried, and executed**.

German Secret Weapons

As the noose began to tighten around Germany, Hitler declared that he was about to employ a new range of "miracle" weapons that would turn the tide. Chief among them were a new breed of U-boat, jet aircraft, and the V-weapons, but all of them arrived too late to alter the course of the war.

As far as Germany's V-weapons were concerned, development of them took place at an experimental site at Peenemünde, on the Baltic coast. The V-1 flying bomb and the V-2 rocket were developed in parallel, under the direction of the young rocket scientist Wernher von Braun (see opposite).

Britain intervenes

British intelligence began to receive information from agents at the end of 1942 that the Germans had some form of rocket program, especially after a first test-firing of the V-2 that October. Eventually, in August 1943, the RAF Bomber Command made an attack on the base at Peenemünde and inflicted a considerable amount of damage—so much so, that it forced the Germans to transfer their operations.

V-weapon production was relocated to the Harz Mountains, where slave labor was brought in to help. Although development work was still carried out at Peenemünde, test-firings now took

The V-1 flying bomb
A V-1 flying bomb in flight. It had an 1,875 lb (850 kg) warhead, could reach speeds of up to 420 mph (675 kph), and had a range of up to 125 miles (200 km).

made them difficult to bomb without running the risk of killing innocent civilians. Hence during the weeks leading up to D-Day, attacks were made on the missile supply depots instead.

London targeted

On June 13, 1944, just one week after D-Day, the first V-1s were fired at England. Just ten missiles were sent, of which four exploded on the launch ramps and two crashed into the sea. Of the remainder, just one caused casualties, killing six people in East London. There was now a short pause, during which the Germans improved their launch arrangements. The V-1 offensive then began in earnest, with an average of

V-2 rocket strike
Survivors trawl the rubble following another devastating rocket strike. The strikes were feared because it was impossible to give early warning of an approaching V-2.

‹‹ BEFORE

Hitler made his first public mention of a new breed of weapon as early as November 1942, in a bid to boost the morale of the German people. At the time, Germany was pursuing a number of separate projects.

SUBMARINE TECHNOLOGY
One concerned a **new type of U-boat**, which it was hoped would ensure victory for the Germans **in the Atlantic ‹‹ 204–05**. The Walter submarine was to overcome the **slow underwater speed** of conventional submarines, and the **need to surface** in order to **recharge the batteries** that powered it when submerged.

ROCKET POWER
The Germans were working on an entirely **new range of weapons**, which they referred to as their *Vergeltungswaffen* (**retaliation weapons**). More popularly known as **V-weapons**, these initially consisted of a **flying bomb and a rocket**, and the Germans intended to use them to great effect in countering the **Allied bombing of Germany ‹‹ 214–17**, which had dominated the **second half of 1943**. The Germans were also busy developing a number of **jet and rocket-powered** aircraft.

> " [The V-1 offensive] will make the British willing to **make peace** … "
>
> HITLER TO VON RUNDSTEDT AND ROMMEL, JUNE 17, 1944

place in Poland. It was at around this same time that the British began to be aware of the V-1, which was an offshoot of the German work on jet engines. Their concern over this increased in autumn 1943, when they identified launch sites being constructed in northern France. All of them seemed to

be pointing in the direction of London. Consequently, that December, the Allies launched an air offensive against the sites, codenamed Crossbow. By the time of the D-Day landings, all these fixed sites had been destroyed.

The Germans realized the vulnerability of this type of static launch ramp, which was largely built from concrete, and they introduced a new prefabricated type that could be dismantled and moved. Furthermore, they positioned these new ramps close to French villages, which

100 missiles being fired daily. Of those that reached England, many did fall on London and over one million of its inhabitants evacuated the city.

Anti-aircraft guns were the primary means of engaging the V-1s. They were mainly based just south of London, but to shoot V-1s down over built-up areas was counterproductive in that they would still cause as much ground damage when they exploded. Consequently, the guns were redeployed to the south coast,

where they immediately enjoyed greater success. Fighters, too, played their part, especially the RAF's first jet, the Gloster Meteor, which had entered service on July 12, just 12 days later than the first German jet, the Messerschmitt Me262.

The threat to Britain rises

By early September, with northern France liberated and the launch sites there overrun, the battle appeared to have been won. However, the Germans, had now introduced an air-launched version of their rocket fired from a Heinkel He111 bomber. Some 750 of

Biber midget submarine
At just 29½ ft (9 m) long, the *Biber*, or Beaver, midget submarine was a one-man vessel armed with two underslung short-range torpedoes. It could dive to a depth of 65 ft (20 m). In all, 324 were built.

21 in (53.3 cm) torpedo

Streamlined hull

The Germans had always been way ahead of the Allies in the fields of rocketry and submarine technology.

TECHNICAL INTELLIGENCE

In the immediate aftermath of the **war in Europe 338–39 »**, the Western Allies and the Soviets acquired vast quantities of German **technical intelligence**. Each followed the German lead in **U-boat technology** to develop new classes of submarine capable of **high sustained speeds** underwater, but with **better streamlining** and **more powerful batteries**.

THE SPACE RACE

Both the Soviets and the Americans used German **scientists and technicians** to work on rocket programs. This not only played a key part in their nuclear strategies during the **Cold War 348–49 »**, but also resulted in the **Space Race**. In modern terminology the V-1 was a **cruise missile** and the V-2 a **ballistic missile**. Direct descendants of these devices now feature in the **military arsenals** of every major nation.

CHEMICAL WEAPONS

Germany was the first to make so-called **nerve gases**. Because the factory producing these was situated in **eastern Germany** (now in Poland), the Soviets gained **most of their information** from the German research, although Britain and the US soon also **developed similar weapons** during the course of the **Cold War**.

---

these were launched over the next months, usually by night. In 1945 a long-range V-1 was introduced. Fired from Holland, the last of these to fly over England was shot down in March.

Throughout this time, however, the Allies had been fighting another threat. By the middle of the summer of 1944 they had gained a great deal of intelligence on the V-2. Since this was a free-flight rocket, developing considerably higher speeds than the V-1, it could not simply be shot down. Furthermore, it carried a larger warhead. Although the Allies knew that the V-2 was in production, all they could do was to wait for the next German offensive to begin.

V-weapon offensive fails

On September 9, 1944, one V-2 rocket struck the outskirts of Paris; a second then hit Chiswick in West London. Both were fired from Holland. The fact that they used mobile launchers, and that it only took 30 minutes to prepare for firing, launch the rocket, and leave meant that it was almost impossible to locate and destroy them. The only answer was to attack the rocket supply depots. As it was, the offensive carried on until late March 1945, with both Brussels and Antwerp suffering, as well as London. Only the destruction of the German transportation system, which meant that fresh rockets could not be delivered, finally halted the attacks. Had Germany's V-weapon offensive begun during the weeks leading up to the D-Day landings, it might have succeeded in causing serious disruption to the preparations for the invasion of France. Once the D-Day landings had taken place and the Allies had begun to sense their ultimate victory over Germany, however, the V-1 and V-2 offensives could be endured. In any event they were not sustained with sufficient intensity or over a long period of time.

It was much the same story with Germany's jet and rocket aircraft. As for the U-boats, the Walter type took too much time to perfect and, again, entered service too late.

The V-2 rocket

Bearing a 2,200 lb (980 kg) warhead, the maximum range of the V-2 was 200 miles (320 km). It reached a height of some 60 miles (96 km) before diving to earth at a speed of up to 2,500 mph (4,000 kph).

> **33,000** The number of people killed or injured by the 10,500 V-1s and 1,115 V-2s fired at England.

ROCKET PIONEER (1912–77)

WERNHER VON BRAUN

Von Braun developed a fascination for rockets when he was a boy. In 1932 he went to work on the German army's rocket program, and was the driving force behind the V-2 rocket. Throughout the war, he stayed at Peenemünde, latterly working on rockets of increased range. In March 1945 the Soviet advance caused him to leave the base and he surrendered to the Americans. After the war he went to the US, where he worked on missile programs before joining NASA and developing the rocket that helped put the first man on the moon in 1969.

BEFORE

With the Germans beginning to recover in the face of an ever-slowing Allied advance, hopes of ending the war before the year was out were fading fast.

MONTGOMERY DEVELOPS A PLAN
Newly promoted Field Marshal Montgomery had never been in favor of Eisenhower's **Broad Front strategy << 268–69**. Now he believed he saw a way of outflanking the main defenses protecting Germany, **the West Wall**, avoiding having to cross the Rhine River. His plan was to **seize a bridge** over the Lower Rhine at a Dutch town

A DUTCH SECRET RADIO

called **Arnhem**. This would require the Allies to capture bridges over other waterways **south of Arnhem**. Surprise was essential and Eisenhower approved Montgomery's plan of using the **First Allied Airborne Army**, which had been in England, unused, since **D-Day << 258–59**.

US paratroops
US airborne troops approach their destination, awaiting instructions to leave the aircraft. As well as main and reserve parachutes, each man also has a weapons container connected to him by a cord.

Operation Market Garden

By mid-September 1944 overstretched supply lines had slowed the Allied advance across France and the Low Countries. Something had to break the growing impasse. Field Marshal Montgomery's plan—to seize bridges over Dutch waterways and thrust into Germany—marked the beginning of a daring operation.

There were two major elements to Montgomery's plan. "Market," which concerned the airborne forces, called for the US 101st Airborne Division to secure crossings over canals at Eindhoven, while the 82nd Airborne Division secured bridges over the Maas at Grave and the Waal at Nijmegen. The British 1st Airborne Division was to drop at Arnhem and seize its bridge over the Lower Rhine. "Garden" would involve a ground force, General Sir Brian Horrocks's British XXX Corps, to link up with the paratroops on landing.

With the port of Antwerp still unable to function, Eisenhower agreed that priority of the limited supplies available should be given to Montgomery. It now looked as though the narrow-thrust approach that Montgomery had been advocating had been accepted by the supreme Allied commander.

Arnhem was obviously the critical part of the operation, being some 60 miles (95 km) away from the ground force start line. During planning, the RAF stated that it did not want to drop the paratroops too close to Arnhem, for fear of having too many of its transport aircraft shot down. A drop zone some 6 miles (9 km) away from the town was therefore chosen. Meanwhile, Dutch Resistance reported the presence of two SS Panzer divisions in the area, refitting after the Normandy campaign. This was disregarded by the planners.

A faltering start
The Allies' Operation Market Garden was launched on Sunday, September 17, 1944. The airborne drops did take the Germans by surprise, but not all went according to plan. The 101st seized the canal crossings and the 82nd took the bridge at Grave. But not all bridges were taken intact and the Germans often counterattacked fiercely. At Arnhem the British paratroops on the ground took four hours to reach the town, by which time the Germans had started to react. They destroyed the

En route to Nijmegen
A number of Cromwell tanks from the British Guards Armoured Division make their way along the road to the Dutch town of Nijmegen. Their intention was to link up with the US 82nd Airborne Division at the Waal River.

railroad bridge over the Lower Rhine and, while the British managed to secure one end of the road bridge, heavy fire prevented them from capturing the whole bridge at Arnhem.

Costly delays
The Garden part of the operation went more slowly than planned. One reason for this was that the British VIII and XII Corps, which were supposed to protect the flanks of XXX Corps, were overly cautious. Horrocks's men managed to link up with the 101st Airborne Division within 24 hours, but were then delayed further by a destroyed bridge over the Wilhelmine Canal, north of Eindhoven. Forced to build a prefabricated Bailey

"We have attempted our best, and we will **continue to do our best as long as possible**."

LAST MESSAGE FROM 1ST AIRBORNE DIVISION AT ARNHEM, SEPTEMBER 25, 1944

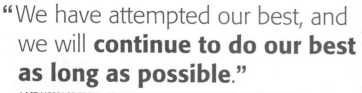

The end at Arnhem

With the failure of Operation Market Garden, thousands of British paratroops fell into German hands. Here, many of them are being marched away into captivity; morale remained high until the very end.

bridge, they fell nearly 36 hours behind schedule. The problems of XXX Corps were compounded by the fact that its flank protection had fallen some way behind, and its advance was restricted to a single road, with low-lying and

> **16,500** The number of Allied paratroops deployed on the first day of Operation "Market."
>
> **3,500** The number of Allied glider-borne troops that were deployed on the first day.

wet country making it difficult for vehicles to get through. The Germans took advantage of this and launched counterattacks on the flanks. Even so, a link-up with the 82nd Airborne was achieved on September 19 and, on the following day, British and Americans combined to capture the bridge over the Waal River at Nijmegen. However, at Arnhem the situation was beginning to get desperate. The two SS Panzer divisions were reacting strongly, and heavy fighting was taking place in the suburbs of the town.

Indeed, the Germans had recently carried out training in dealing with an airborne landing. The British hold on the northern end Arnhem bridge was now becoming ever more precarious. Bad weather also delayed the arrival of 1st Airborne Division's reserve, the Polish Parachute Brigade. When it did finally arrive, on September 21, it was dropped south of the Lower Rhine and could not get across the river to join up with the British paratroops. On the same day, the British at the northern end of the bridge were at last swamped after a prodigious four-day resistance.

An inevitable defeat

The German counter-attacks on XXX Corps continued and, twice, they managed to cut off the road running north to Nijmegen. This caused further delays, as did stiff German resistance south of Arnhem itself. There, the British paratroops were still holding out, but became ever shorter of ammunition, since most of the supplies being dropped were falling

Arnhem's final liberation

After three days of fighting, Canadian troops eventually liberated Arnhem on April 15, 1945. On arrival, soldiers found the inhabitants virtually starving after a grim winter.

Jump boots
Issued to US airborne troops, jump boots were designed to support the ankle, which could easily be twisted on landing.

into German hands. A further problem was that the radios they were using to contact the aircraft did not work. Horrocks's XXX Corps did finally reach the Lower Rhine and link up with the Poles but, by then, it was clear that the 1st Airborne Division was at its last gasp.

On 25 September those paratroops who were able, withdrew from Arnhem to the river and crossed that night. Only about one fifth of the division got back. Over 6,000 of them were captured. Field Marshal Montgomery's gamble had failed, and the liberation of the Dutch inhabitants of Arnhem had become a false dawn.

AFTER »

While Operation Market Garden was hugely imaginative, characterized by courage and self-sacrifice, especially at Arnhem, it had been overly ambitious.

MOVING FORWARD

The Allies were now left with a **deep salient** in Holland, which had to be held. It would, however, provide an excellent **jump-off position** for the operations to close up to the **northern part of the Rhine 298–99 »** the following February.

In the meantime, Eisenhower's **Broad Front strategy** continued to be employed, and there was some **bitter fighting**, especially in the Hürtgen Forest, southeast of the meeting point of the German, Dutch, and Belgian borders. Eventually, too, the **German forces were cleared** from the banks of the Scheldt River. This was then **swept for mines** and, by the end of November, the port of Antwerp was finally **open for business** once more.

BATTLE OF THE BULGE

Throughout this time, the Germans had been **secretly preparing** for what was to be their last **major counter-offensive**, aimed at restoring their **fortunes in the West 284–85 »**.

TECHNOLOGY

PARACHUTES

The modern parachute has been in use since the late 18th century. Not until World War I, however, was it used in war, both for baling out of stricken aircraft or balloons, and for dropping supplies. Early types were tethered but, in the early 1920s, the ripcord was introduced, enabling the wearer to deploy the parachute. The development of airborne forces began in the late 1920s in Italy and then Russia. It was the Germans who first used them during World War II, but the British and Americans soon followed suit.

Machine and submachine guns

The automatic weapons used by infantry in World War II ranged from basic but robust submachine guns, fired from the hip or shoulder, through light machine guns, carried by one man and mounted on a bipod for firing, to tripod-mounted general-purpose machine guns and larger caliber medium and heavy machine guns.

1 **Goryunov SG43 (USSR)**, introduced in 1943, a cheap but effective medium machine gun, mounted on wheels or a tripod. **2** **Ammunition belt (USSR)**, the type of feed used for the Goryunov, giving a rate of fire of 700 rounds per minute. **3** **PPSh-41 (USSR)**, a crude but highly effective submachine gun easy to mass-produce. Some six million were produced between 1941 and 1945. **4** **71-round drum (USSR)**, the drum magazine for the PPSh-41, which fired 7.62 x 25 mm Tokarev pistol rounds. **5** **Thompson (US)** submachine gun, famous as the "Tommy gun" of 1920s gangsters, widely used in the early stages of the war by Allied commandos and airborne troops, in the M1A1 box magazine version. **6** **Browning M2 HB (US)**, a recoil-operated belt-fed heavy machine gun, originally a World War I design; a heavy barrel (HB) version of the gun was

introduced in 1936. **7** **.50/12.7 mm M2 (US)**, a powerful cartridge designed for the M2 machine gun, effective against light armored vehicles and aircraft. **8** **Bren (Britain)**, the British Army's light machinen gun throughout World War II and the postwar period, firing the .303 rifle cartridge. **9** **MP40 (Germany)**, submachine gun with a pistol grip and folding stock, a cutting-edge weapon when introduced to arm German paratroopers in 1940. **10** **MG42 (Germany)**, the most effective general-purpose machine gun in the world when introduced in 1942. **11** **7.92 mm x 57 Mauser (Germany)**, the cartridge fired by the MG42—at an impressive rate of 1,200 rounds per minute. **12** **Type 96 (Japan)**, a light machine gun with a rate of fire of 550 rounds per minute. The cartridges had to be greased, so it often picked up dust or sand, causing the gun to jam frequently.

3 PPSH-41 (USSR)

4 71-ROUND DRUM (USSR)

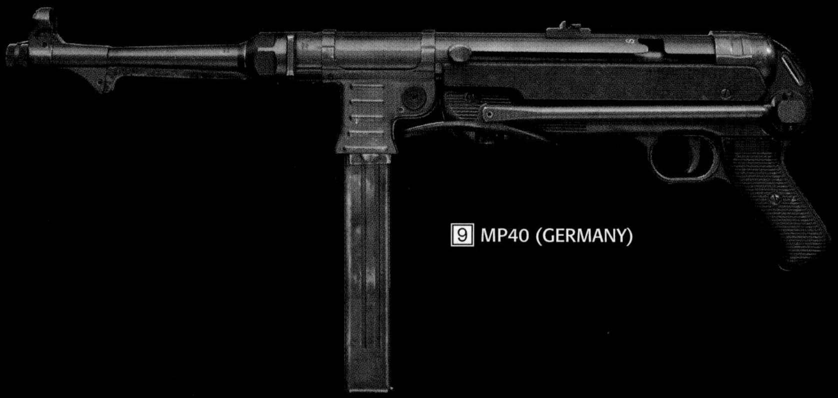

9 MP40 (GERMANY)

8 BREN (BRITAIN)

10 MG42 (GERMANY)

11 7.92 MM X 57 MAUSER (GERMANY)

2 AMMUNITION BELT (USSR)

5 THOMPSON (US)

7 .50/12.7 MM M2 (US)

6 BROWNING M2 HB (US)

12 TYPE 96 (JAPAN)

Battle of the Bulge

In the middle of December 1944, the Germans stunned the Western Allies by launching a major counter-offensive. Initially creating wide confusion, it was eventually contained and driven back, but not before the Germans had lost men and equipment that they could not afford to lose.

Numbed US prisoners
The Germans captured a considerable number of US troops, who were taken by surprise when the offensive began. In one case, at Malmédy, SS troops ruthlessly murdered some 80 US prisoners.

The plan for the offensive was finalized by mid-October 1944. Codenamed Watch on the Rhine, it was to be carried out by Field Marshal Walter Model's Army Group B, and would involve three armies. The newly formed Sixth Panzer Army, under Sepp Dietrich, and consisting of SS Panzer divisions and infantry, would carry out the main attack, while the Fifth Panzer Army, under Hasso von Manteuffel, would attack to the south. Infantry divisions of Erich Brandenburger's Seventh Army would then protect Manteuffel's right flank. The first objective of the operation was to gain crossings over the Meuse River and thereafter advance to Antwerp.

Not until later that month were Model and his superior as Commander-in-Chief West, Gerd von Rundstedt, let into the secret. They were aghast, considering the plan far too ambitious. Instead they proposed a more limited operation to trap the US forces around Aachen, but Hitler would have none of it. All Rundstedt and Model managed to gain was the postponement of the offensive until mid-December to allow them some precious time for preparation.

A promising start

The Eifel-Ardennes sector was held by Courtney Hodges's US First Army and was considered a quiet one. At the time of the attack it was held by two divisions recovering from heavy fighting in the Hürtgen Forest to the north and another that had only just arrived from the US. They had just one, weak, armored division to support them.

There were indicators that an attack might happen, but Allied intelligence dismissed them, believing that after the battering of the previous six months the Germans were no longer capable of an offensive. However, on December 16, after a short pre-dawn bombardment, the Germans did attack, thick fog adding to the immediate US confusion.

> " ... an operation of the **most extreme daring**"
>
> GENERAL ALFRED JODL, CHIEF OF OPERATIONS, ON HITLER'S COUNTER-OFFENSIVE

◀◀ BEFORE

The heavily wooded Ardennes region of southern Belgium had been the scene of the Panzer onrush at the beginning of Germany's May 1940 campaign in the West.

THE GERMANS PLAN A REPEAT OFFENSIVE
Hitler announced his thoughts at a conference in mid-September 1944. The main **Soviet summer offensive ◀◀ 270–71** had come to a halt on the Vistula River, providing a **breathing space**

HITLER PLANS HIS ATTACK

on the Eastern Front. If he could now seriously **disrupt the Western Allies**, it would halt their advance on Germany. He decided that **Antwerp** should be the ultimate objective, since it would split the British from the Americans. **Surprise was essential**. There was also a need to stockpile the **necessary materiel** and, because of the overwhelming **Allied air supremacy**, it would need **winter fog to cloak it**. Hence it would not take place until late November 1944.

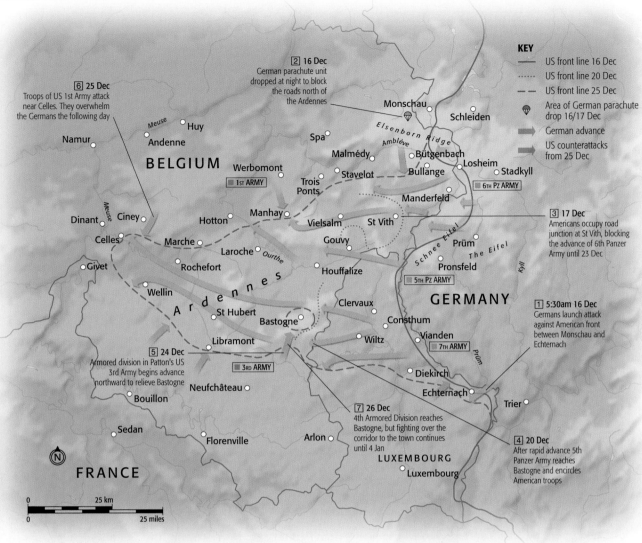

KEY

— US front line 16 Dec

······ US front line 20 Dec

– – – US front line 25 Dec

⬙ Area of German parachute drop 16/17 Dec

➡ German advance

➡ US counterattacks from 25 Dec

6 25 Dec
Troops of US 1st Army attack near Celles. They overwhelm the Germans the following day

2 16 Dec
German parachute unit dropped at night to block the roads north of the Ardennes

3 17 Dec
Americans occupy road junction at St Vith, blocking the advance of 6th Panzer Army until 23 Dec

1 5:30am 16 Dec
Germans launch attack against American front between Monschau and Echternach

4 20 Dec
After rapid advance 5th Panzer Army reaches Bastogne and encircles American troops

5 24 Dec
Armored division in Patton's US 3rd Army begins advance northward to relieve Bastogne

7 26 Dec
4th Armored Division reaches Bastogne, but fighting over the corridor to the town continues until 4 Jan

BELGIUM · GERMANY · FRANCE · LUXEMBOURG

1ST ARMY · 6TH PZ ARMY · 5TH PZ ARMY · 7TH ARMY · 3RD ARMY

Cold offensive
Hitler had chosen the winter months for his offensive with good reason: to make it difficult for the Allies to use their air power. However, fresh-fallen snow made traction difficult for the tracked vehicles of both sides.

AFTER »

The Allies regained the ground they had lost before the end of January and continued remorselessly to close up to the Rhine.

RENEWED THREAT FROM THE EAST
Worse for the Germans, they were now faced with **fresh crises in the East**. The Red Army began its **offensive across the Vistula River 298–99 »**, and the Hungarian oilfields around Lake Balaton, which were **vital to the German war effort**, had also fallen to the Soviets.

900 The number of German aircraft that took part in Operation Bodenplatte in 1945. They attacked 27 Allied airfields and destroyed 156 planes, but lost 300 of their own aircraft.

GERMAN DEFEAT APPROACHES
It was clear at the **beginning of 1945** that it would only be a **matter of time** before the Germans succumbed, and yet Hitler had **no thoughts of surrender**. Indeed, he increasingly believed that the **Western Allies** might finally **see sense and join him** in dealing with the true threat to Europe, **Soviet Communism**. He was, however, mistaken.

Matters were made worse by Germans in US uniforms infiltrating behind the lines. This even forced Eisenhower to become a virtual prisoner in his HQ at Versailles. Even so, in the north, only one of Dietrich's battle groups managed to make significant progress in the hilly wooded terrain. Manteuffel quickly broke through in the southern part of his sector and was now racing for the important communications center of Bastogne, near the Luxembourg border.

After three days, Dietrich's attack had virtually ground to a halt, partially owing to the skillful blowing up of bridges by US engineers, but also because his tanks were running out of fuel. Manteuffel continued to make progress, however. On the Allied side, Eisenhower gave Montgomery control of the northern half of the salient, while Bradley looked after the south. Quick to act, Montgomery deployed British troops to guard the Meuse crossings, while Bradley looked to Patton's Third Army,

30 THOUSAND Allied troops were killed or missing; 47,000 were wounded.

33 THOUSAND German troops were killed or missing; 34,000 were wounded.

Operation Watch on the Rhine
German troops advance, passing an abandoned US White half-track on the way. They frequently feasted on the US soldiers' rations and smoked the cigarettes of the soldiers they captured as they moved forward.

which had halted its advance eastward and was now turning north, to come to the rescue. Having reached Bastogne by this time, Manteuffel tried to seize it, but failed.

Allies gain the advantage
Leaving forces to invest Bastogne, Manteuffel continued his race westward. His spearheads had reached Dinant, just short of the Meuse, by the end of December 24, but this was as far as he was going to get. Patton's troops had now entered the arena and, on December 26, they relieved Bastogne, which had proved an obstinate thorn in the Germans' flesh. Manteuffel tried to drive Patton back, but could not. The weather had cleared by now, and the Allies were able to use the full might of their air power to help force the Germans back once and for all.

In sheer desperation, the Germans then launched a major air assault on January 1, 1945. The aim of the attack, codenamed Bodenplatte, was to destroy as many Allied aircraft as possible on the ground. It proved a disaster, with the Germans losing a large number of experienced pilots, gravely weakening their defenses over Germany itself.

The German advance
Germany's Fifth Panzer Army in the south enjoyed greater success than the Sixth Panzer Army in the north, but its increasing southern flank laid it wide open to General Patton's counter-stroke.

The Germans had also launched a subsidiary offensive further south, to the north of Strasbourg. However, while the Allies did surrender some ground, the Germans gained little else apart from more casualties, which they could now ill afford. As Rundstedt and Model had feared back in October, the Führer's Ardennes counter-offensive proved a costly gamble that failed.

TECHNOLOGY

SHERMAN TANK

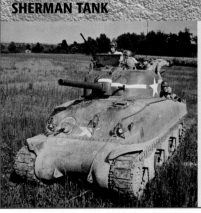

The American-built M4 Sherman was the most ubiquitous tank of the war, as far as the Western Allies were concerned. Entering service in 1942, it was used extensively by the British and Americans. With a crew of five, it mounted a 75 mm gun and three machine guns. Automotively it was very reliable and capable of a speed of 24 mph (38 kph). The one drawback of the M4 Sherman was a tendency to catch fire when hit, mainly because some ammunition was stowed in the turret.

US GENERAL Born 1885 Died 1945

George S. Patton

"An **army** is a team. It **lives, eats, sleeps, and fights as a team**."

GEORGE S. PATTON ADDRESSING HIS TROOPS BEFORE D-DAY, JUNE 1944

A brilliant tank commander, the controversial General George Patton played a key role in the North African and Sicilian campaigns, the invasion of France in 1944, and the advance into Germany during 1945. His strict discipline, self-sacrifice, and aggressive approach earned him the nickname "Old Blood and Guts"; these qualities also made him one of the few Allied generals who was both respected and feared by the Germans.

Patton came from a well-established military background that stretched back to the American Revolution. Graduating from West Point in 1909, he was commissioned as a cavalry officer—throughout his military life he played the part of the dashing cavalry commander. In 1916 his exploits hunting the Mexican revolutionary Pancho Villa in New Mexico became a big story in the American press.

North African command

After the humiliating American defeat at Kasserine Pass in February 1943, Patton took command of US II Corps and helped complete the defeat of the Axis forces in Tunisia.

From cavalry to armor

Patton was an early tank enthusiast and pioneer of armored warfare, recognizing that swift cavalry maneuvers could also be effected by tanks. In World War I, he commanded the newly formed US tank corps at the Battle of Saint Mihiel in September 1918 where he showed aggressive leadership and an innovative flair in his use of tanks.

During the inter-war years, Patton wrote articles on the use of tanks and petitioned Washington for funding

Blood and guts

Patton deliberately cultivated a tough guy image to motivate his men, but his highly polished helmet with its line of general's stars let them know exactly who was in charge.

to develop this powerful new weapon. Despite his enthusiasm, no money was made available. During this period he also met Dwight D. Eisenhower, under whom he would serve in World War II.

North Africa

When war broke out in 1939, Patton was commanding at Fort Meyer in Virginia. As German armies raced across Europe, Congress finally recognized the need for armored divisions and in April 1941 Patton was promoted to major-general and made commander of the 2nd Armored Division. Soon after Pearl Harbor, he took command of both the 1st and 2nd armored divisions and was put in charge of the Desert Training Center at Indio, California. Later in 1942 he worked with Eisenhower in planning Operation Torch, the series of Allied landings in North Africa.

In November 1942 Patton and his tanks landed on the Moroccan coast near Casablanca, but he saw no

Trademark revolver

Patton usually appeared in public carrying an ivory-handled revolver—on occasions he sported a pair. His favorite seems to have been this nickel-plated Colt .45 which he had owned sinced 1916.

significant action until March, when he was placed in command of the demoralized US II Corps. Determined to turn the corps into a tough fighting unit, Patton embarked on an intensive program of training and discipline, insisting that his men observed a strict uniform code, shaved every day, and wore a tie in battle. The men grumbled about the discipline, but Patton's measures paid off and by mid-May 1943, his forces played their part in forcing the Germans and Italians in Tunisia to

major role in a deception plan to mislead the German high command about the Allied invasion plans.

Across northern France

Patton's most spectacular achievements came as commander of the Third Army in the Allied breakout from Normandy and the drive to the German border. In August 1944 his army first moved southwest to secure Brittany then swept rapidly eastwards to the south of the main German forces resisting the Allied advance in Normandy. Seeing a chance to encircle the

Public relations

Patton peppered his speeches with colorful language. Even speaking to war correspondents, as here in France in 1944, he swore like a trooper. Critics called him foul-mouthed, but he always succeeded in inspiring his men.

> ## "You can't afford to be a **goddamned fool**, because, in battle, **fools** mean **dead men**."
>
> **PATTON IN A SPEECH TO HIS STAFF,** MARCH 1944

surrender. This campaign was Patton's first experience of working with the British general Bernard Montgomery. The two men would subsequently have a distinctly uncomfortable relationship marked by considerable rivalry.

Following his success in North Africa, Patton given command of the Seventh Army for the 1943 invasion of Sicily. His task was to protect the left flank of Montgomery's Eighth Army as it advanced to Messina, but in the event Patton rapidly took Palermo, then reached Messina before the British, but too late to stop the German withdrawal to mainland Italy.

It was a typically bold move but soon afterward Patton was in trouble. After a massacre of prisoners at Biscari, some of the men accused blamed Patton for instructing them to be ruthless. Further controversy erupted when news broke that Patton had slapped and abused two shell-shocked soldiers in military hospitals, accusing them of cowardice. This action nearly ended Patton's career. However, Eisenhower, who was then Supreme Commander in the Mediterranean, intervened on his behalf. Believing Patton too valuable to lose, he ordered an apology, which Patton made. He then sent him to Britain where he trained his men for the Normandy invasion and took a

Germans, General Omar Bradley ordered Patton to turn north to trap the German divisions around Argentan and Falaise. Patton rapidly got his tanks into position to do this, but, to his great annoyance, he was then ordered to halt. The same thing happened when

he advanced to within striking distance of Paris. Nevertheless, he was able to launch a series of rapid and spectacular armored thrusts to the east, taking Reims and Châlons, and not halting until he came up against strong German defenses at Nancy and Metz in November. During the German winter offensive in the Ardennes, Patton, on Eisenhower's instructions, moved his troops north with incredible speed to break through the German forces encircling Bastogne and help bring an end to the Battle of the Bulge.

By the end of January 1945, Patton's forces had reached the German frontier. In March his army crossed the Rhine, ahead of Montgomery, at Oppenheim. The Third Army then drove into the heart of Germany, ending the war in Czechoslovakia and Austria. The following June he was made a four-star general.

At the end of the war, Patton was made military governor of Bavaria, but his suggestion that former members of the Nazi Party could work for the administration was a step too far and he was relieved of his command. In December he was fatally injured in a car crash and buried in the same cemetery as soldiers who died at the Battle of the Bulge.

Bastogne 1945

Generals Bradley, Eisenhower, and Patton stand in the ruins of Bastogne, where Patton's swift advance from the south had relieved the encircled US forces.

TIMELINE

November 11 1885 George Smith Patton born on family ranch, San Gabriel, California.

1909 Graduated from West Point Military Academy as a cavalry officer.

1912 Represents US at the Stockholm Olympic Games; comes 5th in the modern pentathlon.

1913 Begins army career as cavalry lieutenant.

1916-17 Aide-de-camp to General John Pershing in Mexico and England.

1918 Commands tank corps in the Saint Mihiel and Meuse-Argonne offensives in the final campaigns of World War I.

July 1940 Promoted to tank brigade commander.

April 1941 Promoted to major-general.

January 1942 Put in command of 1st Armored Corps.

November 1942 As commander of Western Task Force, directs the amphibious landings near Casablanca during the Torch landings.

March 1943 Promoted to lieutenant-general and takes command of US II Corps.

April 1943 Commands Seventh US Army during the Sicilian campaign, taking Palermo and arriving in Messina before the British.

August 1943 Career nearly ends following his verbal and physical abuse of a battle-shocked American soldier in Sicily.

December 1943 Patton sent to England to command fictitious First US Army Group in southeast England as part of deception plan Fortitude South, launched to confuse German high command as to when and where the D-Day landings would take place.

August 1 1944 Patton's Third Army becomes operational in northern France, advancing first into Brittany, then east toward Paris.

August 19 1944 Patton's forces cross the Seine and continue to the Meuse.

December 13 1944 Captures Metz.

December 25/26 1945 Breaks through German encirclement at Bastogne, during the Battle of the Bulge.

March 22 1945 Third Army crosses the Rhine at Oppenheim.

April 1945 Promoted to four-star general.

May 1945 By the end of the war in Europe Patton and his troops have advanced across Germany to Austria and Czechoslovakia.

June 1945 Fêted as a war hero in Los Angeles.

September 1945 Serves as military governor of Bavaria but is relieved of position for suggesting members of the Nazi Party should be employed in administrative positions.

December 9 1945 Fatally injured in road accident during a game-shooting trip.

PATTON, THE HOMECOMING HERO, JUNE 1945

ENDGAME
1945

The final year of the war saw Germany overrun by the Allies. In the Pacific the conflict continued, culminating in the dropping of the atomic bomb on Japan, which brought the war to an end. In the postwar settlement the Allies split Germany into four zones of occupation.

ENDGAME

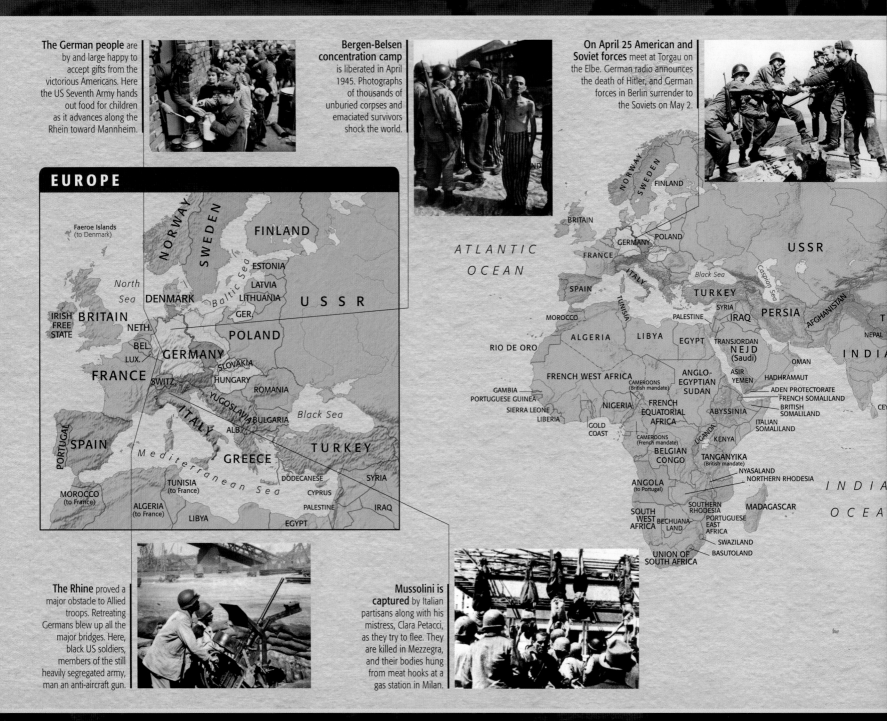

The German people are by and large happy to accept gifts from the victorious Americans. Here the US Seventh Army hands out food for children as it advances along the Rhein toward Mannheim.

Bergen-Belsen concentration camp is liberated in April 1945. Photographs of thousands of unburied corpses and emaciated survivors shock the world.

On April 25 American and Soviet forces meet at Torgau on the Elbe. German radio announces the death of Hitler, and German forces in Berlin surrender to the Soviets on May 2.

EUROPE

The Rhine proved a major obstacle to Allied troops. Retreating Germans blew up all the major bridges. Here, black US soldiers, members of the still heavily segregated army, man an anti-aircraft gun.

Mussolini is captured by Italian partisans along with his mistress, Clara Petacci, as they try to flee. They are killed in Mezzegra, and their bodies hung from meat hooks at a gas station in Milan.

The dawn of 1945 saw the Allies moving in for the kill in Europe, while ferocious fighting continued in the Pacific theater. Germany was firmly on the defensive now, its conquered territories overrun by an enemy that was advancing rapidly and in overwhelming force on every front. From the west and the south came the armies of Britain and America; from the east came the Red Army, in vengeful mood. And all the while, from above, bombs and incendiaries rained down on Germany, dropped by Allied forces intent on pounding Germany into submission. Infernal fires devoured Dresden, Leipzig, Chemnitz, and other cities.

Superficially, at least, the situation of Japan was more optimistic—though the Allied advance had acquired a grim inexorability now. Here, too, there was hellfire as men hacked and burned their way through the jungle thickets of the islands in desperate and ruthless

1945

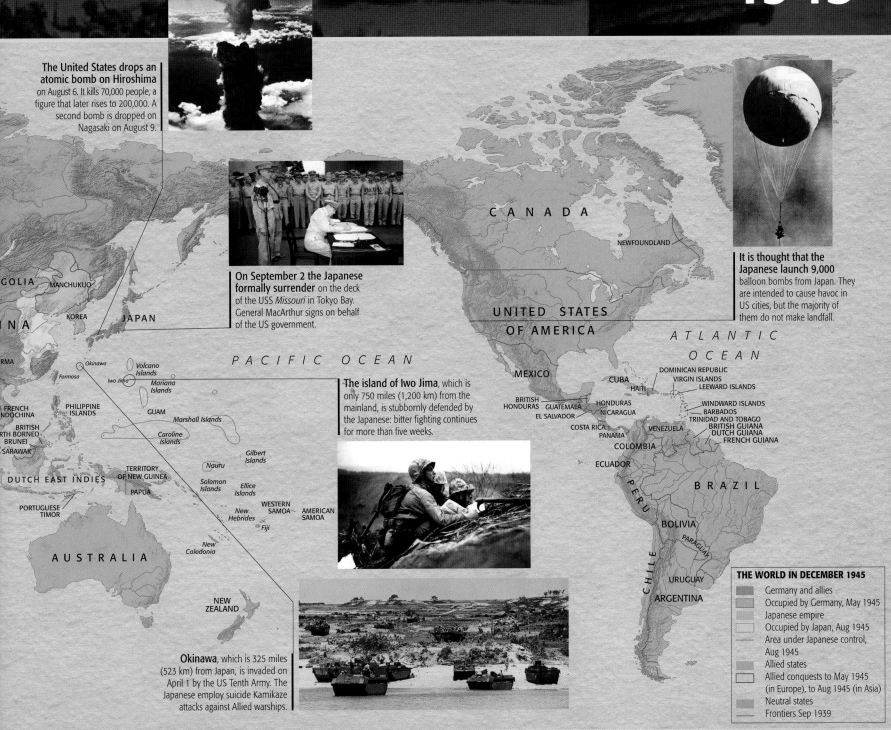

The United States drops an atomic bomb on Hiroshima on August 6. It kills 70,000 people, a figure that later rises to 200,000. A second bomb is dropped on Nagasaki on August 9.

On September 2 the Japanese formally surrender on the deck of the USS *Missouri* in Tokyo Bay. General MacArthur signs on behalf of the US government.

It is thought that the Japanese launch 9,000 balloon bombs from Japan. They are intended to cause havoc in US cities, but the majority of them do not make landfall.

The island of Iwo Jima, which is only 750 miles (1,200 km) from the mainland, is stubbornly defended by the Japanese: bitter fighting continues for more than five weeks.

Okinawa, which is 325 miles (523 km) from Japan, is invaded on April 1 by the US Tenth Army. The Japanese employ suicide Kamikaze attacks against Allied warships.

THE WORLD IN DECEMBER 1945
- Germany and allies
- Occupied by Germany, May 1945
- Japanese empire
- Occupied by Japan, Aug 1945
- Area under Japanese control, Aug 1945
- Allied states
- Allied conquests to May 1945 (in Europe), to Aug 1945 (in Asia)
- Neutral states
- Frontiers Sep 1939

close-quarter combat. Kamikaze pilots plunged their planes into US warships, immolating themselves in patriotic sacrifice, while their countrymen perished in their thousands in fearful firestorms in Japan's main cities. The greatest catastrophe of all was still in store, though: it came on August 6 when the first-ever atomic bomb (codenamed "Little Boy") was dropped on Hiroshima. A second (named "Fat Man") was dropped on Nagasaki three days later.

By that time, Hitler had killed himself, his country defeated. The Allies had come together in a palace at Potsdam to decide upon the postwar settlement. Germany had been carved up into four zones of occupation—American, British, French, and Soviet. Much of the east had been annexed altogether into Polish territory. But this too was now under Soviet domination, as were Czechoslovakia, Hungary, Romania, and Bulgaria; Stalin was now the master in the East.

ENDGAME 1945

Invasion of Germany ▪ Bombing of Dresden ▪ **Liberation of the concentration camps** ▪
Tokyo Firestorm ▪ Battle of Okinawa ▪ Deaths of Hitler and Mussolini ▪ **Battle for Berlin** ▪
VE Day ▪ **Bombing of Hiroshima and Nagasaki** ▪ **Japanese Surrender**

JANUARY	FEBRUARY	MARCH	APRIL	MAY	JUNE
		MARCH 7 US 9th Armored Division takes the undestroyed bridge at Remagen, establishing a bridgehead on the east bank of the Rhine. ≪ Soviet tanks on the Eastern Front	**APRIL 1** American landings on Okinawa. **APRIL 12** Death of President Roosevelt. He is succeeded by Vice-President Harry S. Truman.	**MAY 2** Soviets take Berlin after 12 days of fierce house-to-house fighting. ≫ "Raise the Banner of Victory in Berlin"	ВОДРУЗИМ НАД БЕРЛИНОМ ЗНАМЯ ПОБЕДЫ!
JANUARY 12 Soviets continue offensive in Poland. **JANUARY 12** Germans retreat as they accept failure of the winter offensive in the Ardennes.	**FEBRUARY 4** Stalin, Roosevelt, and Churchill meet at Yalta in Ukraine. They reach agreement on the occupation of Germany. ≫ Dead citizens of Dresden line the street	**MARCH 9/10** Massive US bombing raid on Tokyo. The ensuing firestorm destroys vast areas of the city, killing 100,000 people.	*Roosevelt Dead*		**JUNE 6** The Allies carve Germany up into four separate zones of occupation—Soviet, American, British, and French.
JANUARY 17 Soviet troops liberate the Polish city of Warsaw.		**MARCH 20** Gotthard Heinrici replaces Heinrich Himmler as Germany's commander on the Vistula Front. ≫ A Nazi eagle from the Reich Chancellery	≫ Americans reading of the death of Roosevelt **APRIL 15** British and Canadians liberate Bergen-Belsen concentration camp.	**MAY 7** The Germans unconditionally surrender to the Allies. **MAY 8** Europe celebrates VE (Victory in Europe) Day.	**JUNE 21** US forces complete the capture of the island of Okinawa.
JANUARY 22 The Burma Road, supply route to the Nationalist forces in southern China, is reopened by the Allies.		**MARCH 26** Last Japanese resistance on Iwo Jima is crushed. ≫ US troops battle the Japanese in Iwo Jima	**APRIL 28** Mussolini killed by Italian partisans. **APRIL 30** Hitler commits suicide in Berlin as Russians close in.	**MAY 23** President Karl Dönitz and his Flensburg Government captured and arrested by British forces.	≫ US flamethrower used in the Pacific
JANUARY 30 Soviet armies establish bridgehead on the Oder, just 40 miles (65 km) from Berlin.	**FEBRUARY 13/14** The Allied bombing of Dresden. **FEBRUARY 19** US landings on the island of Iwo Jima.			**MAY 29** Siege of Japan continues with Great Yokohama Air Raid. Over 30 percent of the city flattened—and up to 8,000 killed—in just over one hour.	**JUNE 26** Representatives of 50 countries meet in San Francisco to discuss the possibilities for peace and security in the post-War scene, sign the United Nations Charter.

"Today the guns are silent. A great tragedy has ended. A great victory has been won … We must go forward to preserve in peace what we won in war."

GENERAL DOUGLAS MACARTHUR, SUPREME ALLIED COMMANDER IN THE PACIFIC, SEPTEMBER 2, 1945

JULY	AUGUST	SEPTEMBER	OCTOBER	NOVEMBER	DECEMBER

JULY 16
"Trinity"—the first ever nuclear weapons technology test—is successfully carried out at Alamogordo, New Mexico, making possible the military deployment of the atomic bomb.

SEPTEMBER 2
Formal Japanese surrender aboard USS *Missouri*.

« Colonel Paul Tibbets waves from his B-29

NOVEMBER 13
De Gaulle becomes head of provisional French government.

⌄ Nazi war criminals at Nuremberg

DECEMBER 6
US government agrees $3.75 billion loan to help revive Britain's struggling postwar economy. This will finally be paid off in 2006.

AUGUST 6
The "nuclear age" begins—though the end of the World War II is brought forward—with the dropping of the atomic bomb on Hiroshima.

SEPTEMBER 27
MacArthur meets Hirohito. His appearance in regular uniform is seen as an insult to the Emperor—but secretly America supports Hirohito as a stabilizing influence.

14 DECEMBER
President Truman sends General George Marshall to attempt arbitration between Nationalists and Communists in the Chinese Civil War.

⌄ The "Fat Man" A-bomb dropped on Nagasaki

OCTOBER 9
Kijuri Shidehara becomes Prime Minister of Japan at the head of a constitutionalist government, committed to the pursuit of a peaceful future.

NOVEMBER 14
Start of Nuremberg Trials of major Nazi figures, including Hermann Goering and Grand Admiral Dönitz.

DECEMBER 16
Moscow Conference begins. US, Soviet and British representatives lead talks over post-War plans for Europe and the Far East, including occupations of Japan and Korea.

JULY 17
The victorious Allied leaders assemble outside Berlin for the Potsdam Conference.

AUGUST 8
The Soviet Union enters the war against Japan, starting with an invasion of Manchuria; in the days that follow it will attack the Japanese in China and Korea.

OCTOBER 15
The so-called "Peace Preservation Law"—actually designed to preserve the old imperial regime by suppressing political dissent—is formally repealed in Japan.

NOVEMBER 16
Japan Progressive Party founded: just one of a number of moderate political groupings beginning to emerge under the US occupation.

⌄ Polish and Russian children orphaned by the war

⌃ Attlee, Truman, and Stalin at the Potsdam Conference

⌃ Japan's formal surrender to the Allies

JULY 26
Attlee replaces Churchill as Britain's representative at Potsdam after Labour's landslide election victory.

AUGUST 9
The United States launches its second nuclear attack, this time upon Nagasaki. Six days later the Emperor Hirohito announces that his country is to surrender.

24 OCTOBER
Five permanent members of the Security Council (France, Republic of China, Soviet Union, United States, and Britain) ratify UN Charter bringing United Nations Organization officially into being.

Destruction of Germany's Cities

The advantage had swung the Allies' way: Germany was definitely on the defensive now. But this was no time for magnanimity or mercy. On the contrary, Britain and America unleashed a series of devastating air raids aimed at crippling military resistance and smashing civilian morale.

The sense that Germany was on the ropes only made its enemies more ruthless in their resolve. Far from relaxing, they redoubled their offensive efforts. Instead of scaling back their bombing raids, Britain and America increased them—in their scale, in their frequency, in their geographical spread, and in their intensity. In demonstration of their New Year's resolution, they mounted a major raid against Magdeburg on January 16: a third of the city was demolished, and 4,000 people were killed in the resulting firestorm. And this was not all. A follow-up raid the next night disrupted German rescue and salvage operations, compounding the city's chaos—especially as some devices were fitted with time-delays.

Magdeburg was hardly a major industrial city, but it had significance as a communications and transport center. It was psychologically important

Airborne overkill
US B-17 Flying Fortress bombers renew the attack on Dresden in April 1945. By now, the city beneath them had been pulverized.

too, located at the very heart of Germany. While the Allies clearly intended to smash the German war economy and morale—military and civilian—the bombing was also to make

clear the price of ongoing resistance to the German people. With airfields within easy flying range of the whole of Germany, all types of Allied aircraft buzzed far and wide in the weeks that followed. No town or city seemed to be safe from their attentions. Their small-scale attacks spread disproportionate consternation; terrified populations feared they were just the advance-guards of much more massive raids.

Those larger-scale raids were not long in coming: on February 21 more than 2,000 bombers flattened Nuremberg;

two nights later the target was Pforzheim. Only 360 British bombers made the long journey to this corner of southwestern Germany, but the firestorm they left behind killed 17,000 of the city's 79,000 inhabitants. On March 3 the USAAF mounted a raid on Berlin in broad daylight: 3,000 were killed and 100,000 left homeless in the German capital. There were attacks too on Dortmund, Würzburg, Potsdam, and other centers.

Absolute air superiority

The Allied aircraft had the freedom of Germany's skies: air defenses had been left badly weakened by shortages of arms, ammunition, and personnel, while most fighter planes had been grounded by fuel shortages. Those, that is, that had not already been sent to assist the increasingly frantic effort to defend the Eastern Front. The stricken cities may have been relatively insignificant in Germany's industrial infrastructure, but they had their part

BEFORE

From early in the war, the Allies had been mounting increasingly punishing bombing raids on the German people and industries.

A CONCERTED EFFORT
Strategic bombing had been part of the Allied plan from the very outset. Raids on the ports of Lübeck and Rostock in 1942 had outraged Hitler. He had responded with attacks on Exeter, Bath, Norwich, York, and Canterbury. These attacks on tourist centers became known as **"Baedeker Raids"** after a famous series of travel guides.

British efforts intensified under the leadership of "Bomber" Harris. May 1942 saw the first "thousand-bomber raid" against Cologne. In mid-1943 **a firestorm consumed the heart of Hamburg ‹‹ 214–15**. American **daylight raids ‹‹ 216–17** often suffered **heavy losses**, but then in early 1944 US long-range fighters destroyed much of the Luftwaffe's combat power. Germany was now **practically defenseless**.

ROTATING BINOCULARS USED BY GERMAN LOOKOUTS

Dresden in ruins
The Allied air raids of February 1945 reduced Dresden's once-celebrated cityscape to rubble. The angular, blackened structures that survived stood out, a suitably skeletal skyline for what was now a city of the dead.

to play in the country's defensive efforts. In the East, especially, where, irreversible as the advance of the Red Army now seemed, it was still being achieved at a horrific cost in casualties.

The Luftwaffe was still able to strike some useful blows, but these were usually accompanied by severe losses on the German side. On March 2, for example, the German fighter units lost 36 pilots in return for less than 10 American fighters and bombers shot down. Even units manned by elite pilots and using the new and superior Messerschmitt 262 jet fighter fared little better. There were so many Allied fighters and these often waited above the jets' airfields to attack them during landings and takeoffs when they were most vulnerable.

Dresden destroyed

This was the context in which, after what had been a remarkably quiet war, Dresden suddenly found itself in the front line. Until then famous mainly for its porcelain industry, this city of southeastern Germany had been spared the attentions of the bombers. But, with Russian forces nearing Germany's frontiers, the city gained importance.

So it was that on February 13–14 some 1,300 British and American bombers appeared in successive waves and started raining incendiaries and high explosives upon the German city.

From fire to fire
The thousands of casualties from February's bombing raids presented Dresden with a further crisis—that of disposing of the bodies. Here, the dead are lined up on a city street, ready for cremation.

It brought calamity upon calamity for the people of Dresden: those civilians who had fled the conflagration caused by the first wave of the British bomb attack and sought refuge along the banks of the Elbe River and in public parks were caught by the bombs of the second wave. A huge firestorm erupted, engulfing the city center and surrounding areas and spreading terror and destruction far beyond. Dresden, recalled one awestruck eyewitness, was "a single sea of flames." Beneath this terrible inferno, people crowded into cellars hoping to sit out the storm, but even in these hiding places they were hardly safe. Hour after hour, enormous blasts rocked the buildings and those inside were tossed about "like rag dolls," as one survivor remembered.

By the time the US had followed up with two further large-scale daylight bombing raids, almost 4,000 tons of ordnance had been dropped on the city. Perhaps between 25,000 and 100,000 people died in Dresden, making this one of the most controversial episodes of World War II.

> "We saw **terrible things**. Cremated adults shrunk to the size of small children …"
>
> LOTHAR METZER, DRESDEN, FEBRUARY 1945

AFTER

The air offensive of 1945 left Germany badly weakened. Morale among civilians was severely damaged and war production, particularly of fuel, completely crippled.

GERMANY'S DEATH THROES
Diehard Nazis insisted that the Allied air raids would only stiffen the resolve of the German people. Instead, as Hitler ranted his defiance, confidence in his authority quickly ebbed and the country subsided into **demoralized chaos**.

THE BREAKDOWN OF ORDER
Black marketeers enjoyed a boom and looters had a field day in the destruction and confusion. Emboldened, slave laborers slipped away from factories—adding to the difficulties in industry and the congestion on the roads, where tens of thousands of **refugees were already fleeing the Soviet advance 298–99 》**. And though the Gestapo treated the laborers with brutal severity—carrying out mass executions—its agents could not track them all down. **The raids had left Germany on its knees**, incapable of mounting the sort of coordinated defense that was going to be needed to see off **invasions from both west and east 304–05 》**.

The bombing of Dresden

On February 13, 1945, a total of 773 RAF Avro Lancasters bombed the German city of Dresden. Bombing was so intense that a firestorm engulfed the city. Estimated casualties range from 35,000 to 100,000 killed. Over the following two days, the USAAF sent more than 500 heavy bombers in further raids on the city. Even at the time, the bombing of Dresden caused enormous controversy.

"About 9:30pm the alarm was given. We children knew that sound and got up and dressed quickly, to hurry downstairs into our cellar which we used as an air raid shelter. My older sister and I carried my baby twin sisters, my mother carried a little suitcase and the bottles with milk for our babies ...

Some minutes later we heard a horrible noise—the bombers. There were nonstop explosions. Our cellar was filled with fire and smoke ... In great fear we struggled to leave this cellar. My mother and my older sister carried the big basket in which the twins were laid. With one hand I grasped my younger sister and with the other I grasped the coat of my mother.

We did not recognize our street any more. Fire, only fire wherever we looked ... On the streets there were burning vehicles and carts with refugees, people, horses, all of them screaming and shouting in fear of death. I saw hurt women, children, old people searching a way through ruins and flames.

We fled into another cellar overcrowded with injured and distraught men, women, and children shouting, crying, and praying ... then suddenly the second raid began. This shelter was hit too, and so we fled through cellar after cellar ... Explosion after explosion. It was beyond belief, worse than the blackest nightmare. So many people were horribly burnt and injured. It became more and more difficult to breathe ... all of us tried to leave this cellar with inconceivable panic. Dead and dying people were trampled upon ... The basket with our twins covered with wet cloths was snatched up out of my mother's hands and we were pushed upstairs by the people behind us. We saw the burning street, the falling ruins and the terrible firestorm ...

We saw terrible things: cremated adults shrunk to the size of small children, pieces of arms and legs ... whole families burnt to death, burning people ran to and fro ... many were calling and looking for their children and families, and fire everywhere ... and all the time the hot wind of the firestorm threw people back into the burning houses they were trying to escape from."

LOTHAR METZGER, AGED 9 WHEN DRESDEN WAS BOMBED

Devastation by fire
On February 13 two waves of Lancasters dropped 2,600 tons of high-explosive and incendiary bombs on Dresden, devastating approximately 12 sq miles (13 sq km) of the city in one night.

Holding the bridge
African-American GIs man an anti-aircraft gun near a bridge being built across the Rhine by engineers of the US Ninth Army in 1945. African-Americans in the US Army served in racially segregated units.

‹‹ BEFORE

Between December 1944 and March 1945, Germany's plight had been deepening by the day. Its enemies were now threatening the frontiers of the Nazi homeland.

EASTERN FRONT DISASTERS
The defeat at Kursk in the summer of 1943 finally dashed **Hitler's hopes for domination in the East ‹‹ 226–27**. With Operation Bagration, the Russians took complete control—though still sustaining **fearsome casualties ‹‹ 268–69**.

STRAW BOOTS WORN BY GERMAN SENTRIES

GERMANY THREATENED
The invasion of Italy in 1943 had gone some way toward meeting Joseph Stalin's demands for a **second front ‹‹ 210–11**. The Western Allies had already committed themselves with **the D-Day Landings of 1944 ‹‹ 258–59** and would soon be advancing east. Hitler's attempt to regain the initiative by the Ardennes offensive had been **repulsed by January 1945 ‹‹ 282–83**.

The Allies Invade the Reich

The outcome now seemed clear, but there was still a great deal to be done before the defeat of Germany was finally achieved. Some of the fiercest fighting of the war ensued as the Western Allies and the Soviets advanced inexorably upon a cornered enemy that was scrabbling frantically to survive.

By 1945 the Allied forces could at last smell victory. The Red Army was advancing rapidly from the East as German resistance crumbled. Almost the whole German province of East Prussia lay deep in the Soviet Union's territory by February. In all, six million Russian troops along the Eastern Front faced around two million Germans, as well as some 190,000 Axis allies. But in the vital central sector along the Vistula and Oder rivers, the Germans were still more decisively outnumbered and outgunned. And the Nazis knew only too well that they could expect no mercy from the Russians.

In the West the picture presented to German generals was hardly more cheering. Here, too, a formidable force was massing—1.5 million American, 400,000 British, and 100,000 Free French soldiers. Having thrown back

> **8 MILLION** The number of refugees fleeing through Germany ahead of the Russian advance; by February 1945, 50,000 reached Berlin each day.

the German attack in the Ardennes, Eisenhower's armies were pushing steadily toward the Rhine. For the Soviet forces, there was the heady sensation that the German wolf had at long last been cornered in its lair.

A savage spree of score-settling began. The anger that the Soviet troops felt toward the Germans was easy to understand, however, and Red Army reprisals were not just tolerated but encouraged by their Communist Party superiors. Terrible atrocities were committed: refugees were slaughtered and thousands of women raped. It was only the threat to discipline that finally made the Soviet commissars call a halt.

Carnage continues

The Red Army was still meeting fierce resistance. The East Prussian offensive alone claimed 584,000 Soviet casualties.

KEY MOMENT

THE WILHELM GUSTLOFF

At least 5,300 people died on January 30, 1945, when the passenger liner *Wilhelm Gustloff* was struck by three torpedoes from the Soviet submarine S-13 and sunk in the Baltic Sea. The ship had been evacuating German troops and civilians from Gdynia, near Danzig, and taking them to safety in Kiel, Germany. The ship went down in less than 45 minutes.

The instinct to push on to Berlin was strong, but the need for consolidation became clear. There were signs that German forces were regrouping in Pomerania. Meanwhile, fierce fighting was still raging in Hungary, despite the capture of Budapest in January.

Isolated and encircled

February had seen the Western Allies crossing Germany's frontier and advancing rapidly toward the Rhine—slowly at first but then too quickly for

Crossing the Rhine

Under the cover of artificial fog an amphibious DUKW (pronounced "Duck") sets off across the Rhine. Carrying troops of the US Seventh Army, it is part of Sixth Army Group involved in the advance into southern Germany.

Closing the ring

From January 1945 there were only defeats left for the German armed forces. Tough resistance continued everywhere along the Eastern Front but by March most German forces in the West were preparing for surrender.

any effective resistance to be mounted. Many German troops had been withdrawn to the Eastern Front; those who remained were concentrated in the Ruhr. An encircling movement was soon under way to trap them there. While Montgomery's British Second Army spearheaded the attack from the north, crossing the Rhine around Rees and Wesel, Omar Bradley's American 12th Army Group crossed the river at Remagen to the south. By April 3 an entire German army group had been trapped in the so-called Ruhr pocket.

Only heroism would help the German homeland now; an epic struggle on a legendary scale—the stuff of myth and dream, in other words. What else but extravagant fantasy could explain the

faith the Führer placed in the potential of the *Volkssturm* ("People's Storm") militia, which he had established in September 1944? All males between the ages of 16 and 60 had to join. They were to bring their own clothes, blanket, backpack, and cooking utensils. In other circumstances, perhaps, a stirring vision, but ordinary Germans had seen through their leader's promises by now; braced for defeat, they dismissed the last-stand rhetoric of the regime with sullen cynicism. But they still had to serve in the forces—rounded up at gunpoint by the Gestapo—and so the *Volkssturm* did indeed take to the field. Never properly equipped, armed, or trained, the Volkssturm still saw military action against some of the most seasoned, battle-hardened Allied troops. Over 175,000 of the *Volkssturm*'s soldiers were killed in all. The call-up continued, ever more frantic as the weeks went on, gathering up younger boys—and, eventually, even girls.

Front-line Frankfurt

A Nazi poster declares that the city of Frankfurt an der Oder—now in the front line—will be held by the heroic efforts of the German

KEY

— German front line Dec 15, 1944
-- German front line Mar 21, 1945
✺ Major bombing raid
➡ Allied advance
➡ German counterattack

LATVIA
Riga
■ ARMY GROUP NORTH (KURLAND)
■ 2ND BALTIC FRONT

5 Jan 22
Germans evacuate Memel

SWEDEN

LITHUANIA
Memel
■ 1ST BALTIC FRONT

DENMARK

16 Mar 30
Soviet forces capture Danzig
Gdynia
Königsberg
Danzig
■ ARMY GROUP CENTRE (NORTH)
■ 3RD BYELORUSSIAN FRONT

EAST PRUSSIA

North Sea
Baltic Sea

Kolberg

7 Feb 8
Canadians and British launch Operation Veritable

15 Mar 23–24
21st Army Group begins to cross the Rhine
Hamburg
■ ARMY GROUP VISTULA
Stettin
Torun
■ 2ND BYELORUSSIAN FRONT

2 Jan 13
Soviets begin advance into East Prussia

NETH.
Arnhem
Elbe
GERMANY
Berlin
Küstrin
Poznan
Warsaw
Vistula
4 Jan 17
Warsaw falls to Soviets

Amsterdam
Nijmegen
Rotterdam
Emmerich
Wesel
■ 1ST PARA ARMY
■ CANADIAN 1st ARMY
■ BRITISH 2nd ARMY

10 Mar 2
US troops reach the Rhine near Düsseldorf
Frankfurt an der Oder
Oder
POLAND
Lodz
■ 1ST BYELORUSSIAN FRONT

1 Jan 12, 1945
Soviets launch offensive in Poland

BEL.
Roermond
Brussels
Aachen
Düsseldorf
Cologne
Bonn
Remagen
■ 15TH ARMY
■ 5TH ARMY
■ US 9TH ARMY
Dresden ✺
Breslau
SILESIA
Baranow
■ 1ST UKRAINIAN FRONT

3 Jan 16
British launch Operation Blackcock to clear Roermond triangle
■ US 1ST ARMY
■ US 3RD ARMY
■ US 7TH ARMY
Coblenz
Frankfurt
LUX.
Oppenheim
Mannheim
Germersheim
12 Mar 7
US troops cross the Rhine at Remagen. By the 21st they have established a 19-km (12-mile) bridgehead
Prague
Cracow
Dniester
Carpathians

9 Feb 13/14
British and Americans bomb Dresden

14 Mar 22
Troops of Patton's 3rd Army cross the Rhine
Moselle
Strasbourg
Danube
■ 1ST ARMY
■ 19TH ARMY
Colmar
Rhine

11 Mar 5
Germans launch Spring Awakening offensive
Vienna

17 Mar 31
French cross the Rhine at Germersheim
■ FRENCH 1ST ARMY

6 Feb 5
Allies clear Colmar pocket
Basel
AUSTRIA
Lake Balaton
Budapest
■ 3RD UKRAINIAN FRONT
SLOVAKIA
■ 4TH UKRAINIAN FRONT
■ ARMY GROUP SOUTH
■ 2ND UKRAINIAN FRONT

8 Feb 13
Soviet forces take Budapest

13 Mar 15
Spring Awakening is halted by Soviet counterattacks

SWITZERLAND
ALPS
HUNGARY
Drava

FRANCE
Milan
Trieste
Zagreb
■ ARMY GROUP E
■ ARMY GROUP F
Venice
Belgrade
Po
ITALY
Genoa
Bologna
Ravenna
■ 10TH ARMY
■ 14TH ARMY
■ US 5TH ARMY
■ BRITISH 8TH ARMY
YUGOSLAVIA
Adriatic Sea

0   200 km
0   200 miles
Ⓝ

AFTER

The defeat of Germany was all but assured—though many more lives were yet to be lost before victory could be declared.

GERMAN PRISONERS

Along with **catastrophic casualties**, numerous German soldiers were taken prisoner in the last months of the war. Many were to spend months,

300 THOUSAND German troops were captured by the Allies in the "Ruhr Pocket."

2 MILLION Germans were taken in the Soviet advances of 1944–45.

even years, in captivity—sometimes in the **concentration camps** that their own country had created; of those in Soviet hands, thousands of soldiers **simply disappeared 334–35 ❯❯**.

RESIGNED TO DEFEAT

Despite **Hitler's desperate exhortations**, the enemy advance convinced the German people that the war was over. They ignored their leader's **demented defiance** and prepared to face the **consequences of defeat 338–39 ❯❯**.

Liberating the Nazi Death Camps

The opening-up of the Nazi concentration camps has come to seem a defining event of World War II; those who saw these dreadful sights would never be the same again. But life went on in the midst of death: Germany had still to be defeated and Hitler and his henchmen punished for their crimes.

In July 1944 Soviet troops had entered an abandoned installation at Majdanek in Poland and found evidence of Hitler's "Final Solution." Everywhere they looked there were bodies. The Germans had been well aware just how vile their deeds had been: they had started dismantling their gas chambers before being forced to flee by the Allied advance.

To try to hide what they had done and to prevent their inmates from falling into Allied hands, the Germans had

Disbelief
US troops and inmates at Buchenwald talk after the liberation of the camp on April 11, 1945. The inmates' expressions show that, after such a nightmare, they can hardly believe that relief has come at last.

BEFORE

The death camps had been a central part of Hitler's police state. Now they became a damning piece of evidence, revealing the full extent of Nazi evil.

RACIAL MISSION
From the beginning, Hitler had claimed to be **fighting for the cause of the Aryan race** and resisting the **"Jewish international world conspiracy" ‹‹ 26–27**. One of the main goals

NAZI EAGLE FROM A BELSEN TRAIN

of the Nazi regime was to **wipe out Europe's Jews** and other "undesirable elements" so that only a "superior" Aryan race remained.

Hitler's answer was the **concentration camp** and the first one was established within days of his coming to power. The early camps **treated their prisoners brutally** and it mattered little to the Nazis if they lived or died. But from 1941 **new camps whose sole aim was mass murder were established ‹‹ 176–77**.

evacuated camps lying in the invaders' way. Already weakened by months and years of abuse and malnutrition, inmates had been forced into gruelling journeys on foot—many thousands more would

> "Their **legs and arms were sticks** with **huge bulging joints,** and their loins were fouled by their own excrement."
>
> NEW YORK TIMES CORRESPONDENT, PERCY KNAUTH, ON BUCHENWALD'S INMATES, APRIL 1945.

not survive new brutalities on these horrendous "death marches." By 1945, however, the German war machine was imploding. There simply was not the time to cover up their horrific crimes effectively. At Auschwitz there were still more than 2,000 prisoners left to report what had happened. And with them a few remaining warehouses full of clothes, carpets, spectacles, artificial limbs, and more that imparted their own account of a crime beyond comprehension.

2,189 people were freed from Auschwitz.

836,255 women's coats were found there.

6 tons of human hair were found stored in bales in warehouses.

A vision of hell
In April 1945 soldiers of the US Third Army came upon Ohrdruf, part of the Buchenwald complex. Over a quarter of a million prisoners had passed through Buchenwald since it opened in 1937—not just Jews, but Roma, Communists, male homosexuals, the mentally and physically handicapped, and "asocials." Some 20,000 emaciated inmates were still there. "They looked no more than ghosts," one witness wrote. In the days that followed more death camps were freed, all telling the same tale of horror.

The British 11th Armored Division found 60,000 emaciated inmates at Bergen-Belsen, crammed into a camp

Punishment detail
Women guards are set to work piling the bodies of the dead into mass graves at Bergen-Belsen. Typhus was rife in the squalid conditions of the liberated camps, and thousands of "survivors" died.

designed to hold no more than about 2,000. No adequate attempt had been made to feed the prisoners, who had wasted away through sheer starvation—some resorted to cannibalism. Nor was there any sanitation to speak of. The floors of the inmates' huts had become latrines. In such conditions, typhus had taken hold and was spreading fast. One British officer wrote that the inmates of Belsen were "little more than living skeletons with haggard yellow faces." Many were on the edge of survival: in the next few weeks 500 people a day died. "There were men and women lying in heaps on both sides of the track," he recalled. "Others were walking slowly and aimlessly about—a vacant expression on their starved faces."

AFTER

For millions of victims, there was to be no "after," but their liberators gave what help they could. They also made efforts to bring their Nazi persecutors to justice.

PUNISHING THE GUILTY
Only much later would the *Shoah* (in Hebrew, "The Calamity") come into clear focus as a single historical event, **the Holocaust** (literally "sacrificial burning"). Yet it was already obvious that massive, **monstrous crimes had been committed**. They were to figure prominently in the case brought against the leading Nazis at the **Nuremberg Trials ›› 338–39**. Various

JOSEF KRAMER (LEFT), COMMANDANT OF BELSEN, BEFORE HIS EXECUTION IN 1945

concentration and extermination camp guards and commandants were also tried and **convicted for their crimes**. Many leading **Nazis escaped justice**, however, either fleeing to sympathetic countries like Argentina or simply through not being pursued vigorously enough by the Allies.

A NEW NATION
Ultimately, the Holocaust was far-reaching in its effects, giving new and crucial impetus to the **Zionist project**. Campaigners had been calling for a Jewish homeland in Palestine since the late 19th century, and the British had gone some way toward meeting that aspiration with the **Balfour Declaration of 1917**. Now change in the region was unstoppable: **the state of Israel was proclaimed in 1948 ›› 344–45**.

Discovery of Belsen

The British 11th Armoured Division entered the Bergen-Belsen concentration camp on April 15, 1945. Not knowing what to expect, they were met by horrific scenes—unburied corpses, mass graves, and nearly 40,000 "living skeletons," emaciated men, women, and children who were all starving to death. Typhus had broken out among the camp survivors, and there was no sanitation.

" … beyond the barrier was a swirling cloud of dust … And with the dust was a smell, sickly and thick, the smell of death and decay … I passed through the barrier and found myself in the world of nightmare. Dead bodies … lay strewn about the road and along the rutted track. On each side of the road were brown wooden huts. There were faces at the windows, the bony emaciated faces of starving women, too weak to come outside …

I have seen many terrible sights in the last five years, but nothing, nothing approaching the dreadful interior of this hut in Belsen … The dead and the dying lay close together. I picked my way over corpse after corpse … until I heard one voice that rose above the gentle undulating moaning. I found a girl. She was a living skeleton. Impossible to gauge her age because she had practically no hair left on her head and her face was only a yellow parchment sheet with two holes in it for eyes … beyond her … there were the convulsive movements of dying people too weak to raise themselves from the floor …

In the shade of some trees lay a great collection of bodies … There were perhaps 150, flung down on each other, all naked, all so thin their yellow skin glistened like rubber on their bones. Some of the poor starved creatures looked utterly unreal and inhuman …

… One woman, distraught to the point of madness, flung herself at a British soldier … She begged him to give her some milk for the tiny baby she held in her arms …. she put the baby in his arms and ran off crying … when the soldier opened the bundle of rags to look at the child he found it had been dead for days …

… Women stood naked at the side of the track, washing in cupfuls of water taken from the British Army water trucks. Others squatted while they searched themselves for lice … Sufferers from dysentery leaned against the huts straining helplessly, and all around was this awful drifting tide of exhausted people, neither caring nor watching … "

BBC REPORTER RICHARD DIMBLEBY, DESPATCH FROM BELSEN APRIL 17, 1945. A HEAVILY EDITED VERSION WAS BROADCAST ON APRIL 19, 1945.

Shocking images
To prevent the spread of typhus among survivors at Belsen, the British were forced to bury bodies in mass graves. Images such as these were relayed around the world, as proof of events at the concentration camps.

BEFORE ‹‹

The Russians had paused in their headlong drive to Berlin. The Western Allies too had taken time out to ensure that their flanks were covered.

SOVIET ADVANCES

By March **the Vistula–Oder Offensive had proved spectacularly successful**, bringing the Red Army within **striking distance of Berlin** ‹‹ **298–99**. Some had wanted to push on and take the German capital, but instead Stalin had instructed his armies to clear the Germans out of Pomerania on the flanks of the advance.

AUSTRIA FALLS

Further to the south, **Russian and American forces converged on Vienna**. Its fall to the Soviets, at the end of March sent a shockwave through the Reich. Since the *Anschluss*—greeted with **such enthusiasm in 1938** ‹‹ **42-43**—Austria had officially been a part of Germany.

ANSCHLUSS ACCLAIMED IN THE REICHSTAG

Meeting at the Elbe

Members of the US First Army meet Russian troops on the banks of the River Elbe at Torgau on April 25, 1945. Suspicion would soon set in between the Allies but, for the moment, after years of fighting, the mood was of shared relief and joy.

Final Offensives in Europe

German forces fought with the frenzy of cornered beasts, driven to acts of heroic resistance, if not by Nazi fanaticism or patriotic fervor then by desperation. But the certainty of victory did not make things any easier for the Allied invaders, who often had to battle for every yard of conquered ground.

With the Rhine behind them, the Western Allies were in a position to push on to Berlin. Field Marshal Montgomery urged an immediate dash for the Nazi capital. However, Allied Supreme Commander Eisenhower hesitated. Rumors were rife that the Nazi leadership was planning to retreat to the Bavarian uplands and the "Alpine Fortress" from which a rearguard action might be mounted. On Eisenhower's orders, then, the Seventh Army struck out southward through the Black Forest into Bavaria. Bradley led the First and Third Armies in a direct assault on central Germany south of the Ruhr, with Patton's Third Army then sent east toward Czechoslovakia.

Hard feelings

There was rivalry between the Allied nations—not to mention distrust among their commanders, the clash of egos continuing even under the thickest fire. Eisenhower had no wish to gratify Montgomery's desire for glory. Instead, Montgomery was directed to lead his Canadian and

Marching to the Brandenburg Gate

"Raise the Banner of Victory in Berlin!" urged this propaganda poster by Viktor Ivanov. By the beginning of May 1945, his countrymen were able to do just that.

British force across northern Germany to protect the Americans' flank—and to discourage the Russians from going into Denmark. For, if there was suspicion among the western Allies, the fear of Soviet intentions had never gone away entirely. This mistrust was returning with a vengeance now that the war was all but won.

The race for Berlin

The Russians had already spent several weeks consolidating their position in the East. By the beginning of April they were ready to renew their advance on Berlin. Infantry, tanks, and artillery were massed in an arc to the east of

the city: by April 14 there were 1.4 million men and many thousands of heavy weapons. Marshal Zhukov, commander of the First Byelorussian Front, launched his assault from the banks of the Oder on April 16. But, despite their overwhelming strength, progress was slow and painful—and extremely costly in casualties. Marshal Ivan Konev's First Ukrainian Front fared better—crossing the Neisse River, his armies thrust north and west to come toward the German capital from the south. Stirred up by Stalin, the rivalry between the Russian generals was just as fierce as that between their Western counterparts: both Zhukov and Konev were desperate to take Berlin.

This may have had an impact on their handling of the attack. Though Zhukov proceeded cautiously, Konev's advance was practically a charge. After breaking fierce resistance in the first few days, the way to Berlin opened up before him, and on April 19 and 20 his tanks covered 30 miles a day, making no attempt to secure the territory they were crossing. In his haste, Konev ended up tangling with the tanks of Lieutenant-General Vasily Chuikov, once the defender of Stalingrad, and now commander of 8th Guards Army, sent south by Zhukov into Berlin's suburbs.

The last stand

If Russian tactics were erratic, this was nothing to the total disarray now being seen throughout the German Army. General Heinrici had saved his army group only by beating a hasty retreat from the Oder. Even so, Busse and his Ninth Army had been encircled in the woodland south of the city; Wenck's

The Reichstag in flames
The battle for the Reichstag, Germany's parliament building, was ferociously intense. By the time the Russians captured it, on April 30, 200 of its 300 defenders had been killed.

Twelfth Army had been thrown back well beyond Berlin. Hitler hoped still that some hero would arise to rescue Germany in its hour of peril. He looked to his generals but they were paralyzed, powerless to act.

Not that the battle was by any means over. The Nazi high command was irrelevant but individual units fought for their lives. With nowhere to go, the Germans fell back into Berlin itself, defending it block by block as the enemy advanced. Groups holed up in public buildings and at key points in the city. On April 30 the red flag was finally flown from the Reichstag. But not until May 2 did Chuikov receive the final surrender of the city.

Friends ... for now
A week before, on April 25, a crucial encounter had taken place when US and Soviet troops had met at Torgau,

10 The percentage of an estimated 360,000 Soviet and Allied Polish troops killed in Germany that died in the Battle of Berlin. Losses were high because they were in such a hurry to beat the Western Allies to the city.

on the Elbe River. In its real, military significance, it was negligible, perhaps—no more than a parenthesis to the epic narrative unfolding nearby. But, as the propagandists on both sides grasped at once, it summed up that spirit of cooperation and comradeship between the Capitalist West and the Communist East, which had defeated the evil of Nazism and saved Europe.

The defeat of Nazi Germany
By the final weeks of the war the Red Army controlled Central and Eastern Europe. German forces still fought fiercely to hold back its advance, while all the time looking, if possible to surrender to the Anglo-Americans.

KEY
— German front line Apr 1
- - - German front line Apr 19
— Western Allied front line May 7
— Soviet front line May 7
➤ Allied advance
— Borders Sep 1939

AFTER

In the very moment of victory, Allied leaders were looking to prepare positions for the possible conflict to come.

TO THE VICTOR THE SPOILS
Allied leaders had agreed at Yalta that they would carve out **separate spheres of influence**. But their generals on the ground had a unique chance to define Europe's new frontiers and did their best to take as much territory as they could. **Soviet technicians went through eastern Germany like a whirlwind**, dismantling factories, plundering laboratories—and abducting scientists—and taking everything that might give them a technological or industrial edge.

A SHORT-LIVED PEACE
Within weeks after the meeting at the Elbe, the Americans and Russians were to be enemies themselves. Stalin would bring down an **"Iron Curtain" 340–41 »** across Europe. For 40 years, East and West would be locked into the **"Cold War" 348–49 »**.

Deaths of the Dictators

Mussolini and Hitler had transformed their countries, constructing political systems around the cults of their leadership.

FASCISM AND NAZISM
Both ideologies had claimed to bring order, national revival, and a new sense of purpose. But Fascism had drawn its deeper energy from

65 PERCENT of Italian voters supported Mussolini's Fascists in Italy's 1924 election.

43 PERCENT of voters supported Hitler in Germany's March 1933 election.

the desire for destruction; **Nazism had been a philosophy of death**. Mussolini's impressive electoral support had been **based on violence and intimidation ‹‹ 20–21**; Hitler's party had pledged racial purging and a **purifying war ‹‹ 26–27**. On these commitments, the dictators had delivered, dragging their countries, Europe, and much of the wider world into **a five-year nightmare**—only now approaching its end.

In the last days of the war, the crimes of great dictators at last caught up with them. Mussolini was captured and dealt summary justice by Italian partisans. Hitler took his own life, cheating his enemies of a precious prize, but forced to confront the final failure of his schemes.

Though the news had been bad for many months, and worsening by the day, Hitler had remained convinced of final victory. Germany, at bay, would find new reserves of resources and courage; new heroes who would bring salvation at the last. As the Western Allies streamed across the Rhine, he had comforted himself with the thought of the rude reception that awaited them once his forces had sorted out their difficulties on the Eastern Front. And even as the Soviet Army rampaged through Berlin, he harbored hopes of a counterattack.

Meanwhile, steadfastly staying at his post, Hitler remained holed up with his closest confidants in a bunker beneath the Reich Chancellery, the very center of the German state. In the last days, shells thumped down above them and the streets outside resounded with small-arms fire, but in the bunker an uncanny peace prevailed. It was broken at intervals by the news of this or that reversal or defection—most notably that of his trusted SS leader, Heinrich Himmler, who had been seeking secret negotiations with the Allies.

Exchanging vows
For the most part, though, Hitler was calm: at around 11:30pm on April 28 he sat down with his secretary, Traudl Junge, to dictate his will—and with it an extraordinary "Political Testament."

Hitler's bunker
Two Russian soldiers check the scene in the gardens of the Reich Chancellery in Berlin, where Hitler's remains were destroyed after his suicide. The jerrycans had contained gasoline, used to burn the Führer's body.

from arrest by the Germans, Mussolini had enjoyed a second career of sorts as the figurehead for a Nazi-dominated "Italian Social Republic."

Now, with Axis forces in Italy in retreat, Mussolini tried to flee to the safety of Switzerland. From there he hoped to fly to Spain, where he would be assured a warm welcome from his old friend and ally, General Franco. On April 27 he was caught near Lake Como by partisans and taken to Mezzegra, where his mistress, Clara Petacci—also captured—was brought to join him. On April 28 they were executed and their bodies hung up in public with those of other Fascist leaders in Milan the next day. Though news did reach Berlin of Mussolini's death, it is not

> **20** Percentage of Nazi Gauleiters that committed suicide in 1945; 10 percent of Army generals, 14 percent of Luftwaffe generals, and nearly 20 percent of admirals followed suit.

clear whether Hitler ever heard the circumstances. But he was all too well aware of the fate that awaited him if he should fall into his enemy's hands. By the early hours of

Dönitz takes charge
Grand Admiral Karl Dönitz presided over a short-lived German government after the Führer's death.

injection. It was all a loving mother could do, Magda wrote: "The world that will come after the Leader and National Socialism will not be worth living in, and therefore I have taken my children away. They are too dear to endure what is coming next."

Meanwhile, before fleeing for their lives, Hitler's attendants had taken the bodies of their leader and his wife outside. Dousing them in gasoline, they set them both on fire. It was a

An ignominious end
The bodies of Benito Mussolini, his mistress, Clara Petacci, and other members of Italy's Fascist leadership hang by their feet from meat hooks beneath the forecourt canopy of a gas station in Milan.

He was dying in a noble cause, Hitler insisted. A man of peace, he had led his nation in self-defense; the cause of the conflagration had been the Jews. Then, in the small hours of April 29, Hitler and his mistress, Eva Braun, exchanged marriage vows before a city official.

In Italy, meanwhile, things were looking no brighter for Mussolini. *Il Duce*'s authority had crumbled away to nothing many months before. On

April 30, Hitler had finally acknowledged to himself that his cause was lost. Far more than death, Hitler now feared public indignity and degradation.

Accordingly, having extracted promises from his minions waiting with him in the bunker beneath the Reich Chancellery that they would destroy his body, the Nazi leader made preparations for his suicide.

When his aides looked into his room a few minutes later, Hitler and his mistress were dead. Eva had taken poison; Hitler had shot himself. Before taking their own lives,

The eagle has fallen
Battle scarred, this Nazi emblem was found amidst the rubble of the Reich Chancellery.

crude cremation but a very effective one: when the charred bodies were later found and examined by the Russians, the remains could not be identified except by the Führer's dental records.

A lost cause
Despite its leader's death, Nazi Germany was fighting on—at least in theory. As Hitler had wished, Grand Admiral Karl Dönitz became Reich President on May 1. Dönitz's loyalty to his country was unquestioned, and his navy had not failed so obviously and spectacularly as the German Army and Air Force had in the latter part of the war.

The reality was that Dönitz saw his role as that of presiding over the Nazi surrender, trying to ensure the most advantageous terms for a nation that had only too clearly lost the war. Fierce resistance continued on the Eastern Front, but the aim of most German soldiers was now no longer to defeat their country's invaders but to find a way of breaking through toward the West. Their last hope was that, rather

> ## "Resist pitilessly the **world-poisoner of all peoples**, international Jewry."
> HITLER'S "POLITICAL TESTAMENT", APRIL 29, 1945

July 24, 1943, he had suffered the indignity of being dismissed by King Victor Emmanuel—for many years the dictator's pathetic puppet. Rescued

propaganda minister, Josef Goebbels, and his wife, Magda—penned up with their late leader in the bunker—had their six children killed by morphine

AFTER »

Excitement at Germany's defeat was tinged with grief and anger—and concern about the continuing conflict in the Pacific.

WAR CONTINUES IN THE EAST
If there was despair in Germany, there was jubilation in the rest of Europe and the US. But at the same time all were mindful that the war with Japan had not yet been won. **Not until June would the island of Okinawa be taken 312–13** », after some of the most frenzied fighting of the war. And only then could the screw finally be **tightened on Japan itself 314–15** ».

UNFINISHED BUSINESS
Amid the **euphoria over Germany's defeat**, moreover, there was an unsettling sense of incompleteness—a feeling that justice had been left undone. The invasions of Western Europe, the attacks on Britain—and still more the scorched-earth campaign in the East and the extermination camps: **so many Nazi outrages cried out for punishment**. One of the main priorities for the victorious powers was to be the establishment of **an international tribunal 338–39** » that would be able to administer justice for these crimes.

than falling into what they knew would be the unforgiving hands of the Russians, they might surrender to the Americans or British.

German troops in Italy and western Germany surrendered in the first days of May, and on May 7, Dönitz's representatives signed an unconditional overall surrender to the Allies at General Eisenhower's headquarters in Reims. The ceremony was repeated in Marshal Zhukov's Berlin headquarters the following day and "Victory in Europe" was proclaimed, sparking celebrations in all the Allied countries.

Happy crowds
London's Piccadilly Circus was the scene of rumbustious VE-Day celebrations, repeated in towns and cities across Britain, the Allied countries, and the United States. The mood in Berlin could hardly have been more different.

VE DAY

When Germany surrendered unconditionally to the Allies on May 7, 1945, at the American advance headquarter in Rheims, France, the war in Europe was officially over. The following day was designated VE (Victory in Europe) Day, and victory celebrations took place in Paris, London, and throughout Europe.

" This is it … This time this is Victory in Europe day … The Air Corps is really going to town and C-47 cargo planes, fighters, and even fortresses and other bombers are flying back and forth and buzzing the city. We're all dashing out on the balcony—it's a warm, warm day and the French windows are wide open. Everyone confesses to feeling a bit unable to concentrate … I actually knew yesterday morning … 'cause we'd seen the radio message from SHAEF [Supreme Headquarters Allied Expeditionary Force] … but it was confidential so we'd just go round grinning like cats that swallowed canaries … When we got off the metro by the Arc [de Triomphe], then we knew it for sure. People were milling around the Etoile, up and down the Champs Elysées, and they were shooting off fireworks while planes dropped flares. I was really excited then and I said I wasn't going to be in at any 12 o'clock … There was celebration up and down our street and up on the corner by the Arc people were singing and fireworks were still going on … As a matter of fact, they kept on all night. At three am, when Dorothy went on guard duty, she said it was still noisy and about 5 [am] I woke to hear a few 'yippees' up and down the street … "

AMERICAN BETTY M. OLSON, 29TH TRAFFIC REGULATIONS GROUP, STATIONED IN PARIS

" … American sailors and laughing girls formed a conga line down the middle of Piccadilly and cockneys linked arms in the Lambeth Walk. It was a day and night of no fixed plan and no organized merriment. Each group danced its own dance, sang its own song, and went its own way as the spirit moved … soldiers swung by one arm from lamp standards and laughing groups tore down hoardings … The young servicemen and women who swung arm in arm down the middle of every street, singing and swarming over the few cars rash enough to come out were simply happy … "

ENGLISH WRITER MOLLIE PAINTER-DOWNES'S DESCRIPTION OF VE DAY IN LONDON, FILED FOR "NEW YORKER" MAGAZINE

Victory celebration
Parisians and Allied soldiers make their way together down the Champs Elysées, Paris, on May 8, 1945, to celebrate Victory in Europe (VE) Day. Celebrations continued well into the night.

The Battle for Iwo Jima

BEFORE

Iwo Jima, a barren Pacific island a mere 8 sq miles (21 sq km) in area, was under the control of Japan until February 1945.

A SECONDARY TARGET
After the **American conquest** of the Marianas in the **summer of 1944** **‹‹ 238–39**, Okinawa was the next major objective. Iwo Jima was to be taken as a prelude to the Okinawa operation.

JAPANESE PREPARATIONS
US commanders **gravely underestimated** the difficulty of taking Iwo Jima. They believed the fighting would last only four days. But from the

> **23,000** The estimated number of Japanese Army and Navy troops on Iwo Jima who were killed in the fighting or who committed suicide. All the island's civilians had been evacuated.

summer of 1944, the Japanese had begun turning Iwo Jima into a **defensive stronghold**, intending to inflict maximum casualties on the US forces and **delay their progress** toward the mainland.

In February and March 1945, Iwo Jima—a volcanic Japanese island lying some 760 miles (1,220 km) southeast of Tokyo—became the most bitterly contested spot on the planet, as US Marines fought to evict resolute Japanese soldiers from a network of tunnels and bunkers hewn deep into the rock.

At 8:59am on February 19, 1945, US Marine landing craft began to unload men onto the black volcanic sand of Iwo Jima. As they spread out on the shore, there was at first an eerie lack of enemy resistance.

The men of Fourth and Fifth Marine Divisions might have been tempted to believe that the scale of the preparatory bombardment—two months of air attacks, three days of intensive shelling by US Navy warships, and a further barrage from offshore since 2:00am that morning—had succeeded in devastating the Japanese defenses. But this was far from the case. Japanese military engineers had burrowed into the volcanic terrain to create a network of underground passages that kept the defenders safe from bombs and shells.

Lieutenant-General Kuribayashi Tadamichi had decided to hold his men and guns hidden in long-prepared defensive positions, waiting for the best moment to open fire.

Attempting to move off the beaches, the US Marines were soon in difficulty. The assault forces, under the command of General Harry Schmidt, were aided by an array of ingenious amphibious vehicles, but many of these bogged down in the volcanic ash on the shoreline. Within a couple of hours the beaches were a clogged mass of men, vehicles, and equipment. When the Japanese artillery, mortars, and machine guns finally opened up, it was carnage. The Marines, advancing unsuspectingly toward well-concealed machine-gun posts, were mown down. The beaches

The landing beaches
US Marines of the Fifth Division begin the slow crawling advance inland from the shore of Iwo Jima on the first day of the battle. The terrain gave a narrow strip of cover at the water's edge but then became very exposed.

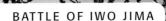

American rocketeers in action
Truck-mounted rocket launchers are used to pound the final Japanese positions in Bloody Gorge near the north end of the island on March 23. This was the last Japanese position to be captured.

became a chaotic mass of burning vehicles and equipment, the infantry seeking shelter in shallow foxholes.

After the landings
Yet, despite heavy casualties—some 2,500 men were killed or wounded on the day—30,000 Marines landed on Iwo Jima on February 19. By nightfall they had fought their way across the island to the west coast. Their next major objective was Mount Suribachi, the island's dominant volcanic feature, from which Japanese artillery—sited in positions protected by thick steel doors—fired down upon the Americans. The American fleet sitting off the island also came under attack from Japanese kamikaze pilots, who on February 21 sank the escort carrier USS *Bismarck Sea* and damaged several other ships, inflicting over 500 casualties. Mount

> " … on Iwo Jima, **uncommon valor** was a common virtue."

FLEET ADMIRAL CHESTER W. NIMITZ AFTER THE BATTLE OF IWO JIMA

Suribachi was taken by February 23, but fierce resistance went on in the north of the island.

Ongoing resistance
At this point Third Marine Division joined the battle, bringing the number of Marines engaged up to 70,000. The outnumbered Japanese fought on for another month. None expected to survive. The fighting was grim, close-quarters infantry warfare. The Marines had to take each Japanese strongpoint by assault, across desolate, bare terrain that offered no cover. The network of tunnels that the Japanese had dug meant that they were often able to reoccupy a position that had been cleared by the Marines at great cost, reappearing on the flanks or at the rear of an advance. Japanese defenses were so deeply embedded in the rock that one US officer noted: "The Japanese were not on Iwo Jima. They were in it."

The key weapons for clearing out underground positions were the flamethrower and the hand grenade.

US M2 flamethrower
US Marines used the manpack flamethrower. It had a range of 130 ft (40 m) and weighed a hefty 68 lb (31 kg).

Fixing a Japanese position
Even once a Japanese position had been located it was not always easy to identify its position exactly enough in the featureless terrain so that supporting US artillery could target it accurately.

However, the weaponry most feared by the Japanese were the "Zippo" tanks—eight modified Shermans that could project a jet of flaming liquid up to a distance of 490 ft (150 m).

Kuribayashi had ordered his men to avoid the costly "banzai" suicide charges that the Japanese had employed in earlier battles. But as the defenders were squeezed back into an ever smaller area, they increasingly gave up their tactics of holding out in fortified positions, instead emerging at night for desperate attacks on their enemy. The last of these, an attack on an American-held airfield on the night of March 25/26, may have been led by General Kuribayashi in person. After its failure, American commanders finally declared that the island of Iwo Jima was secured.

Only 216 Japanese soldiers are recorded as having surrendered during

US Marines suffered 23,573 casualties on Iwo Jima—5,885 of those killed. US Navy losses were 881 dead and 2,000 wounded.

JAPANESE SURVIVORS
A number of Japanese soldiers managed to **survive in tunnels and caves** after the battle ended, coming out at night to scavenge for food. The last two gave themselves up in 1949. The island remained under **US occupation** until 1968.

AN ISLAND AIRFIELD
The attack of Iwo Jima had been partly motivated by the desire to fly long-range **P-51 Mustang** fighter aircraft from the island to

US CARRIER AIRCRAFT ON THEIR WAY TO ATTACK THE TOKYO AREA ON JULY 9, 1945

escort B-29 bombers in daylight raids on Japan. This proved unnecessary when the USAAF resorted to **low-altitude night raids 314–15 »** that met with no significant Japanese resistance. The island's airfields did provide an **emergency landing strip** for American bombers.

the battle for Iwo Jima—mostly men too badly wounded to avoid capture. The rest fought courageously to the death, committed suicide, or simply went into hiding. Of the US Marines who fought on the island, one in three was either killed or wounded. The Medal of Honor, America's highest military decoration, was awarded to 27 of those who took part.

KEY MOMENT
VICTORY ON MT. SURIBACHI

The Marines captured the key strongpoint of Mount Suribachi on February 23, 1945. The first Stars and Stripes flag planted on the summit was too small to be seen by other troops on the island, and was replaced later in the day. This second flag-raising was captured by news photographer Joe Rosenthal in a photograph immediately recognized as a classic image of the Pacific campaign—and later used as the model for the Marine Corps War Memorial in Washington D.C., shown here. Of the six men who raised the flag, three died on Iwo Jima. The rest were brought home for public appearances to raise funds for the war effort.

Okinawa

American strategists decided to capture Okinawa as a forward base for the Allied invasion of Japan. The result was what some called "the cruelest battle" or, to the Japanese, the "wind of steel." The fight for Okinawa was awesome in its intensity, even for hardened veterans of the Pacific War.

The "Zero" was highly maneuverable, leading enemy fighters a dance in dogfights. Ultimately, it could not compete with the faster, more robust, and far more numerous Allied aircraft of 1943–45.

Radio aerial

Unlike previous Japanese naval fighters, the "Zero" had an enclosed cockpit. A complete radio set allowed not just communication but long-range direction-finding.

T-7178 aluminum body

Aileron

" My grave will be the sea around Okinawa ... I have **neither regret nor fear** ...**"**

KAMIKAZE PILOT, ENSIGN TERUO YAMAGUCHI, FROM A LETTER TO HIS FATHER, MARCH 1945

Low wing-loading gave the "Zero" a stalling speed of under 60 knots, making for extremely tight turns and enabling it to outmanoeuvre all Allied fighters for at least the first half of the war.

« BEFORE

The war in the Pacific was going the Allies' way—but painfully slowly and at excruciating cost. The Japanese were making them fight for every inch.

BOX AND SPOON USED BY AN ALLIED POW

SUICIDE ATTACKS

Victory seemed within reach for the Allies—the only question was whether they could pay the horrendous price the struggle was going to exact. That the Japanese were prepared to do anything to win was evident in their **introduction of the kamikaze suicide tactic** during the fighting for the Philippines in late 1944 **« 240–41**.

The largest island of the Ryukyu group, Okinawa was only 340 miles (550 km) from Kyushu, the southernmost of Japan's main islands. It would make an ideal base for a final assault on the Japanese home country —but the American forces were going to have to take it first.

To this end, they mounted what was to be the greatest amphibious assault of the Pacific War. General Simon Bolivar Buckner, Jr. led the attack with his Tenth Army—with over 100,000 US Army soldiers and 80,000 Marines. They were landed and backed up by a formidable fleet of 1,600 ships. No fewer than 40 US aircraft carriers were present to provide air support; planes came too from the British Pacific Fleet.

Impossible odds

The US faced a big but motley Japanese defending force: along with 70,000 Army troops, there were 9,000 Navy soldiers. Nearly 40,000 indigenous Okinawan islanders, mostly raw—and unwilling—recruits, were pressed into service. In addition, over 2,000 school

True to the death
Kamikaze pilots bow during ceremonies before setting off into action. "It is our glorious mission to die as shields of His Majesty. Cherry blossoms glisten as they open and fall," one pilot wrote.

students were conscripted: the boys as soldiers of the "Blood and Iron" Student Corps; the girls as nurses in the Himeyuri Student Corps. General Ushijima Mitsuru led the defense.

Japanese divisions

Left stranded, outnumbered, and outgunned, the Japanese were also hampered by tactical disputes among

Ushijima's staff. One group wanted an aggressive approach. A second faction favored a more cautious strategy: that they should dig in as deeply as they could on ground of their choosing and prepare to resist the Americans inch by inch. This was the strategy the Japanese followed. They would do little to defend most of the island but would fortify the south end and the Motobu peninsula further north.

That determination was one thing in which the Japanese were well equipped became clear once the battle began in earnest. On Easter Sunday— 1 April—the main US force began landing almost unopposed. The northern two thirds of the island was quickly captured, though it did take some days of heavy fighting before the Americans took entrenched positions on the Motobu peninsula.

But, if the fighting was fierce in the north, further to the south it was frenzied. The defenders were well dug-in and able to make use of a warren of natural caves to elude and ambush the disorientated US soldiers.

twice that number of Japanese are believed to have died. Many thousands of civilians were caught up among the casualties: hundreds, forced to fetch and carry for the defenders, were shot as combatants; others died in artillery bombardments or bombing raids; while others, in many cases, committed suicide. Japanese propaganda warned that, in the event of victory for the American "savages," Okinawan women and girls would be viciously raped and their menfolk murdered. To prevent this happening, thousands killed their children before killing themselves—often apparently forced to do so by Japanese troops.

Divine wind

Kamikaze suicide attacks had become a planned component of Japanese tactics since the Battle of Leyte Gulf in October 1944, but now they were developed to their full extent. The custom of *kamikaze* (the word means "divine wind") was rooted in the ancient Japanese Samurai tradition—the idealistic ardor of the young men who gave up their lives this way, recorded in their final letters, is very striking. But flying an explosives-laden plane or piloted bomb into an enemy ship to certain death was a brutal, ugly way to meet one's end.

Even Japan's largest remaining warship, the giant battleship *Yamato*, was to be used in a final suicide mission, Operation Ten-Go, leading a naval task force from Japan with only enough fuel aboard for a one-way trip. Its dispatch, however, was more dramatic gesture than serious intervention. Quickly—and inevitably—sighted, the ships had to run the gauntlet of relentless attacks from US submarines and carrier-borne aircraft. The *Yamato* was sunk after a two-hour blitz of bombs and torpedoes. Like most kamikaze attacks, its loss was ultimately pointless.

Not that these kamikaze attacks can have seemed that way to the comrades and families of the more than 4,000 US and Allied sailors killed. Over 400 Allied warships were sunk or damaged.

Despite these Japanese heroics, the Americans held on with tenacity; by the beginning of June it was clear that they were prevailing. Progress was cruelly slow and hideously costly in

Mitsubishi A6M Zero fighter
The "Zero" downed over 1,500 Allied aircraft in the course of the Pacific War. A top-secret aluminum alloy (T-7178) was used to build the body. Light construction was one of the secrets of its maneuverability.

Behind every boulder, it sometimes seemed, was a machine-gun nest or a booby-trap. The Americans pressed on, but they took terrible casualties. And, inevitably, inflicted them: an estimated 1,500 Americans were lost taking the strategic "Cactus Ridge" alone, but

OHKA PILOTED BOMB

The name Ohka meant "cherry blossom", which was an emblem of purity and hence of Japan itself, but there would be nothing light or delicate about the Ohka's flight. In effect a large bomb with wooden wings and rocket motors or a jet engine in the tail (depending on the type), it was to be carried into action by a "mother" aircraft before being released at a distance from the target.

The plane would then glide, guided by its pilot, until that target was within range, at which point the engine would be fired. At the speeds it reached then, the plane was virtually unstoppable. In practice, though, the Ohka was very vulnerable in the moments after launching, and difficult to aim when under power. Most of its pilots died in vain. The Americans called it "the Baka"—"idiot bomb."

The rocket's red glare
A US LCI(R) (Landing Craft, Infantry [Rocket]) releases a fusillade as it approaches Okinawa's shores. Rocket-armed landing craft could lay down a devastating concentrated weight of fire in a landing area.

casualties, yet the position of the Japanese was becoming more hopeless by the day. Tens of thousands had already been killed—many walled up in the caves they had been operating from. As they were thrown back, many committed suicide to avoid capture. For the first time in any of the Pacific War's campaigns, however, following a propaganda campaign promising fair treatment for those who yielded peacefully, hundreds were allowing themselves to be taken prisoner. On June 18 General Buckner was killed, caught by the blast from an enemy artillery round, but within four days his victory had been won.

110,000 Japanese troops were killed.

45,000 or more Okinawans died.

12,500 American sailors and soldiers fell.

Japanese surrender
Badly wounded, a Japanese naval lieutenant surrenders to US troops at Okinawa. Japanese soldiers were more ready to surrender after a broadcast by a captured comrade, assuring them of his own good treatment.

The loss of Okinawa deprived imperial Japan of its last important Pacific outpost. The question now was whether it could successfully mount its own self-defense.

ENDING JAPAN'S RESISTANCE
The **taking of Okinawa** and the other islands of the Ryukyu group left only clear blue water between the Allies and Japan. A concerted effort could now begin to **cut the country off**, both from its overseas forces and its essential supplies 314–15 ≫.

A SUICIDAL STRATEGY
To this day, **controversy continues on the island** over Japanese denials that their soldiers compelled Okinawans to kill themselves. A Japanese court case in 2007 found that the **army had indeed been culpable**.

ATOM BOMB DECISION
So heavy had US casualties been, so severe the accompanying **losses in aircraft, ships, tanks, and equipment**, that commanders viewed the forthcoming fight for Japan itself with mounting wariness. If the price paid was not to be unimaginably high (in Japanese as well as Allied lives), the final battle for the Japanese homeland

1,465 kamikaze attacks were made off Okinawa.

36 Allied ships were sunk, chiefly destroyers.

368 vessels were damaged, including carriers.

would have to be approached with extreme caution. Hence, perhaps, the resolution that, whatever doubts might remain, **the super-weapon under development would be deployed**. The ferocity of Japanese resistance at the Battle of Okinawa may well have helped bring about the detonation of the atomic bombs over **Hiroshima and Nagasaki 320–21 ≫**.

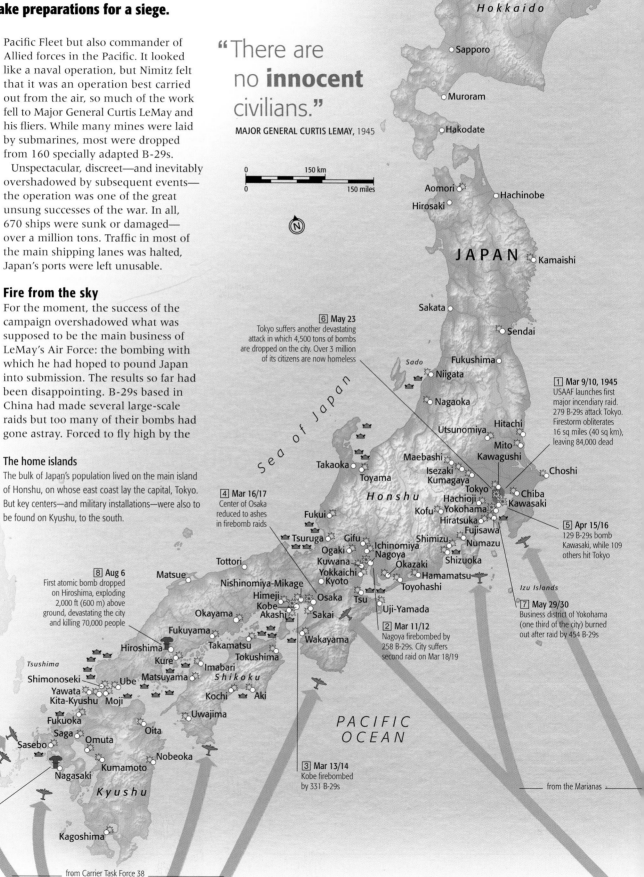

Japan under Siege

Iwo Jima and Okinawa had left the Americans under no illusions as to what it would cost to take Japan's "home islands" by storm. But Japan was not just protected by the sea—it was completely cut off by it. The Allies began to make preparations for a siege.

The codename did not beat about the bush: Operation Starvation was to bring Japan to its knees by cutting off all essential supplies from the outside world. Begun in March 1945, it was also intended to prevent the provisioning of Japan's fighting forces overseas. The operation was the brainchild of naval chief Admiral Chester Nimitz, who was not only commander-in-chief of America's

Pacific Fleet but also commander of Allied forces in the Pacific. It looked like a naval operation, but Nimitz felt that it was an operation best carried out from the air, so much of the work fell to Major General Curtis LeMay and his fliers. While many mines were laid by submarines, most were dropped from 160 specially adapted B-29s.

Unspectacular, discreet—and inevitably overshadowed by subsequent events—the operation was one of the great unsung successes of the war. In all, 670 ships were sunk or damaged— over a million tons. Traffic in most of the main shipping lanes was halted, Japan's ports were left unusable.

Fire from the sky

For the moment, the success of the campaign overshadowed what was supposed to be the main business of LeMay's Air Force: the bombing with which he had hoped to pound Japan into submission. The results so far had been disappointing. B-29s based in China had made several large-scale raids but too many of their bombs had gone astray. Forced to fly high by the

The home islands

The bulk of Japan's population lived on the main island of Honshu, on whose east coast lay the capital, Tokyo. But key centers—and military installations—were also to be found on Kyushu, to the south.

« **BEFORE**

Japan's Pacific possessions had been picked off by the Western Allies, who now had the perfect base for a final assault in Okinawa.

HEAVY GOING

Victory might be in sight, but Allied celebrations were muted. The war was being won, but it was not easy. The **British advance down Burma** « 248–49 had been a **bloody slog** under appalling conditions. The Americans had faced the sheer **determination** of the Japanese ever since starting their **central Pacific offensive** « 230–31 toward the end of 1943.

JAPANESE PRAYER FLAG

HOLY WAR

The Japanese would not just be **fighting for their lives** now but for a homeland they held sacred. The Allies could not expect them to yield an inch. Their objective had to be to **create so much disruption** on the home front that the resistance in the field **could not be sustained**. In the second half of 1944, therefore, a campaign of **sustained bombing** had begun.

KEY

- 🪖 Atomic air raids
- ✳ Big Six firebomb raids
- ✲ Firebomb raids
- ⚓ Areas mined by US aircraft
- ➡ Allied air attack routes

"There are no innocent civilians."

MAJOR GENERAL CURTIS LEMAY, 1945

0 — 150 km
0 — 150 miles

Map labels:

Hokkaido

Sapporo
Muroram
Hakodate

Aomori
Hachinobe
Hirosaki

J A P A N

Kamaishi

Sakata
Sendai

6 May 23
Tokyo suffers another devastating attack in which 4,500 tons of bombs are dropped on the city. Over 3 million of its citizens are now homeless

Sado

Fukushima
Niigata

Nagaoka

1 Mar 9/10, 1945
USAAF launches first major incendiary raid. 279 B-29s attack Tokyo. Firestorm obliterates 16 sq miles (40 sq km), leaving 84,000 dead

Utsunomiya
Hitachi
Mito
Kawaguchi

Maebashi
Isezaki
Kumagaya
Choshi

Takaoka
Toyama
Tokyo
Chiba

Sea of Japan

Honshu

Hachioji
Kofu
Yokohama
Kawasaki

4 Mar 16/17
Center of Osaka reduced to ashes in firebomb raids

Fukui
Hiratsuka
Fujisawa
Numazu

Tsuruga
Gifu
Shimizu
Ogaki
Ichinomiya
Nagoya
Shizuoka

Kuwana
Okazaki
Hamamatsu

Tottori
Yokkaichi
Kyoto
Toyohashi

Matsue

5 Apr 15/16
129 B-29s bomb Kawasaki, while 109 others hit Tokyo

Izu Islands

Nishinomiya-Mikage
Osaka
Tsu
Uji-Yamada

7 May 29/30
Business district of Yokohama (one third of the city) burned out after raid by 454 B-29s

Himeji
Kobe
Akashi
Sakai

8 Aug 6
First atomic bomb dropped on Hiroshima, exploding 2,000 ft (600 m) above ground, devastating the city and killing 70,000 people

Okayama
Wakayama

2 Mar 11/12
Nagoya firebombed by 258 B-29s. City suffers second raid on Mar 18/19

Fukuyama
Takamatsu
Tokushima

Hiroshima
Kure
Imabari
Shikoku

Tsushima

Shimonoseki
Ube
Matsuyama
Kochi
Aki

Yawata
Kita-Kyushu
Moji

Uwajima

East China Sea

Fukuoka
Saga
Oita

Sasebo
Omuta
Nobeoka

Kumamoto

3 Mar 13/14
Kobe firebombed by 331 B-29s

PACIFIC OCEAN

Nagasaki

Kyushu

from the Marianas ↗

9 Aug 9
Second atomic bomb explodes over Nagasaki, destroying over 40 percent of the city and killing around 50,000 people

Kagoshima

from Carrier Task Force 38

AFTER »

The last months of the Japan campaign were overshadowed by the events of August and the detonation of the first atomic bomb.

ETHICAL SHIFT
But the period was **more important** than is appreciated in shaping the outcome of the Pacific War. LeMay's logic—accepted by his masters— that **civilians could be killed** if this might help to save the lives of Allied servicemen, represented an important **ethical shift**. If there had ever been a taboo on the bombing of civilians, it had now been **explicitly lifted**, and the way was clear for the atomic bombs to be dropped on **Hiroshima and Nagasaki 320–23 »**.

50 The percentage of Tokyo's urban area that had been destroyed by fire by the war's end. Unexploded bombs were still found in Japan in 2008.

WHAT MIGHT HAVE BEEN
Operation Starvation had been so effective that, had it been **introduced earlier**, it has been argued, it might have **achieved Japan's defeat** all on its own. But the horrors of the Pacific War had been such that it is hard to imagine such a solution **satisfying Japan's enemies**. The country had first to be put to **sword and fire** and then brought low.

Working for the enemy
A captured Japanese officer helps direct US bombing attacks against his homeland. Captive troops also acted as translators, making sure the Japanese held their fire.

weather conditions and by the air defenses on the ground, they ended up scattering their payloads ineffectively. The massive air raids that had played so important a role in bringing Nazi Germany to devastation and defeat showed little promise of doing the same for imperial Japan.

But LeMay made a virtue of necessity, recognizing that if incendiaries were used instead of high-explosive bombs, there was less need to hit the target. This, he appreciated, had become a campaign against national morale, which meant it was a campaign against civilians. Japan's rugged interior was relatively inhospitable, most people were crowded into densely populated urban centers along the coasts. These were largely of timber construction: fire had always been a problem, so why not make it the main instrument of his attack?

The Tokyo firestorm
The first successful incendiary attack on Japanese-occupied Hankow, China, in December 1944, had been followed by a small-scale raid on suburban Tokyo in February 1945. Encouraged by the

Impotent gesture
A number of Japanese "balloon bombs" reached the United States, causing a stir, but very little damage.

results, LeMay planned a much larger attack for the night of March 9/10. Rather than ask his crews to aim for a particular factory or military installation, he designated a target area of over 12 sq miles (30 sq km). In all, 334 B-29s took part, a lead wave dropping napalm to illuminate the area, while the remainder followed up with M-69 magnesium cluster bombs and oil-based incendiaries. The entire area went up in flames, and much of the rest of eastern Tokyo besides. People found their skin seared, their clothes igniting on their backs in the scorching winds. "Hell could be no hotter," wrote French reporter Robert Guillain.

Rivers and canals offered no escape; people had to choose either to drown or cook their lungs in the super-heated air. Rescuers clearing up in the aftermath could not identify even the sex of the bodies they found in the Sumida River. "You couldn't even tell if the objects floating by were arms or legs or pieces of burned wood,"

recalled Dr. Kuboto Shigenori. As far as Curtis LeMay was concerned, his firestorm operation had been an unqualified triumph, and he was now determined to follow through with

334 B-29s took part in the Tokyo raid of March 9–10 1945.

90 THOUSAND civilians were killed in the raid.

40 THOUSAND civilians died as the firestorm spread.

further raids on Japan's home islands in the weeks to come. The sooner the Japanese woke up to the fact of their defeat, the fewer Allied lives would have to be lost fighting them.

Desperate measures
The reality appears to have been that the raid left the people of Japan too stunned to even comprehend what had happened. But there is no doubt that, between Operation Starvation and the incendiary campaign, their leaders' scope for effective action had been dramatically curtailed.

However, there had been signs that the Japanese high command had been clutching at straws since the end of 1944, when they had released the first of the "balloon bombs" from Honshu. These were gas balloons, armed with anti-personnel and incendiary devices. Over 9,000 of these weapons were launched, of which few reached their intended destination in the northwest of America. Beyond confirming to the Americans their view that they were fighting a foe of diabolical cunning, they had no impact on the course of the war.

Inspecting the damage
Emperor Hirohito visits the scene of devastation following the firestorm of March 1945, in Tokyo. Although it was easy to talk of resolve, it was much harder to maintain it.

US AIR FORCE CHIEF (1906–90)

CURTIS LEMAY

By the time America's war began, LeMay was already in command of the 305th Bomb Group. He led from the front, flying missions over Germany and North Africa before being sent to the Far East in 1944. Successful commands in China and the Pacific led to LeMay—now Major General— being given responsibility for air strategy against Japan itself. Here, he oversaw the switch from high-altitude precision bombing—used effectively in Germany but failing in Japan—to a strategy of low-altitude night-time area bombing.

BEFORE ≪

When Japan entered World War II, the country had already been at war for some years in Manchuria and China.

EMPIRE BUILDING
During the 1930s Japan, needing natural resources for industry, set out to create an empire in Asia and the Pacific. In 1931 Japan seized Manchuria and, in 1937, began a **war**

330 **The amount of rice in grams allocated to every member of the Japanese population from 1942. As a result, many people opted to purchase goods from the black market.**

against China ≪ 40–41. Japan entered the war in 1941 and, with victories in **Burma, Malaya, Singapore, the Dutch East Indies ≪ 158–59**, and **the Philippines ≪ 160–61**, had soon taken control of Southeast Asia.

Japanese society was highly organized at the time. Constant **propaganda** focused on the message that the individual was less important than the collective good.

TURNING POINT
With defeats at **Midway** and **Guadalcanal**, Allied victories in **the Philippines ≪ 240–41** and **Burma ≪ 248–49**, and the capture of **Iwo Jima** and **Okinawa**, by 1945 the country was expecting invasion.

EMPEROR OF JAPAN (1901–89)

MICHINOMIYA HIROHITO

Presented as a divine being, Hirohito was emperor of Japan from 1926 until his death. Although he was supreme ruler, he had little practical power: his function was effectively to legitimize decisions made by the Japanese government and military leaders. Privately he had been reluctant to go to war but did nothing openly to prevent it. By 1945, however, he had determined that the war should be brought to an end. Following the attacks on Hiroshima and Nagasaki, he urged the Japanese to accept the unacceptable, namely surrender.

Subjects of the Emperor

Life for the Japanese people on the home front was dreadful during the last few months of war. Allied bombing raids brought death and destruction to all the major cities. By summer 1945, Japan was facing defeat but military leaders and some elements within the government refused to surrender.

In 1941 Japan had not been prepared for a long war. Conflict with China had already stretched the country's resources and the nation relied heavily on supplies from outside; more than 20 percent of rice and over 70 percent of soybeans, for instance, were imported. Raw materials, such as oil, rubber, and bauxite, also had to be imported. The Japanese government introduced food rationing, but supplies were precarious. By 1944 the American naval blockade of Japan prevented food and raw materials from entering the country, while strategic bombing disrupted transport services and food supplies, causing severe hardship.

Starvation and bombing
By 1945 staple foods such as fish had disappeared and rice rations were miniscule; the daily ration was around one third of an average person's daily needs, and some of the population were on the edge of starvation. Average calorie consumption dropped sharply from a pre-war average of 2,265 to 1,900 in 1944, and 1,680 in 1945. People supplemented their diet with pumpkins and grasshoppers, and city dwellers left regularly on trips to the countryside hoping to exchange clothes and other items for fruit and vegetables. Despite government controls, prices of goods such as shoes soared to astronomical heights on the black

197,000 **The number of dead and missing Japanese civilians following the US bombing raid on Tokyo on the night of March 9/10, 1945.**

market. Malnutrition was widespread and the weight of newborn babies dropped alarmingly. With all available arable land already under cultivation, people grew meager crops on thin strips of land by rail lines.

Mass bombing added to the chaos and social breakdown. From March 1945 the US conducted a series of intensive bombing raids against Japanese cities. Thousands of B-29s—known to the Japanese as "B-San"—dropped massive

Schoolgirls at the lathe
Toward the end of the war, the labor shortage in Japan was so desperate that schoolgirls were recruited into factory work to help the war effort. Here, students from the Girls' National School are trained to use lathes.

Shipping losses
Japan went into the war with some six million tons of ocean-going metal-hulled ships, and added four million during the war. Their shipping losses, however, were dire. By August 1945 scarcely any were still operating.

bombloads on cities such as Osaka, Kobe, and Tokyo, killing thousands and making thousands more homeless. The government had made virtually no provision for air-raid shelters so families were forced to make their own, sometimes little more than a trench in the garden. City homes made of wood

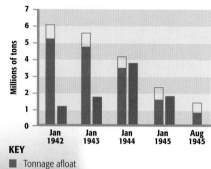

KEY
- ■ Tonnage afloat
- □ Tonnage laid up
- ■ Shipping lost during year

and paper offered little protection against incendiary bombs; in March 1945 Tokyo suffered dreadfully when a firestorm swept through the city. Industry too had collapsed by 1945.

There had been a growth in industry between 1942 and 1944 but the war effort was hampered by poor planning, rivalry between the army and navy, and lack of co-operation between government and big business. The government, under prime minister Tojo, established a munitions ministry, but with raw materials unable to enter the country, production declined. Absenteeism was also a problem as workers fled into the countryside to escape the bombing. In 1943, under the

2 THOUSAND tons of incendiary bombs were dropped on Tokyo.

8-10 MILLION civilians were evacuated from their homes.

950 THOUSAND Japanese civilians were killed in the war.

slogan "Men to the Front, Women to the Workplace," the government had started recruiting women; by 1945 women, Koreans, prisoners of war, old men, and children were being drafted in to help in factories, on the land, or in home defense.

Final stages

By spring 1945 it was clear Japan was facing certain defeat. Its navy was finished, its armies were scattered throughout Asia, and most major cities had been levelled to the ground. Despite the loss of Okinawa and overwhelming American military superiority, propaganda continued to urge the population to resist, and the government was deadlocked. Prime minister Suzuki (who took up office in April 1945) and other leaders were desperate to end

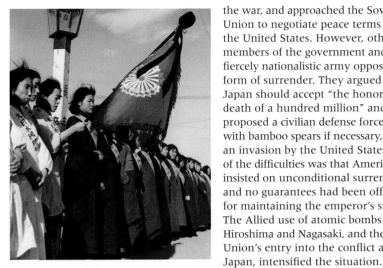

Honoring the dead
Citizens on the home front were expected to honor Japan's war dead. Women from the National Defense Association lined up to pay tribute to the casualties whose bodies were brought home by train.

the war, and approached the Soviet Union to negotiate peace terms with the United States. However, other members of the government and the fiercely nationalistic army opposed any form of surrender. They argued that Japan should accept "the honorable death of a hundred million" and proposed a civilian defense force, armed with bamboo spears if necessary, to repel an invasion by the United States. One of the difficulties was that America had insisted on unconditional surrender and no guarantees had been offered for maintaining the emperor's status. The Allied use of atomic bombs on Hiroshima and Nagasaki, and the Soviet Union's entry into the conflict against Japan, intensified the situation.

Finally, in August 1945, Emperor Hirohito, normally viewed as above politics, made a personal intervention and stated that for Japan's sake the war needed to end. On August 15 he broadcast the decision to the Japanese people. While for many Japanese the idea of surrender was anathema, for others the end of the war was a relief.

" The war situation has developed not … to Japan's advantage."
EMPEROR HIROHITO, ANNOUNCING JAPAN'S SURRENDER, AUGUST 15, 1945

AFTER »

When the war ended, Japan was ruined: more than 60 cities had been devastated and more than 40 percent of Japan's industry was destroyed.

SURRENDER
Japan **officially surrendered on 14 August 1945 324–25** », but many troops continued fighting. It was not until September that Japanese forces in Southeast Asia finally **conceded defeat**.

NAGASAKI AFTER THE ATOMIC BOMB

LIBERATING WOMEN
Some **2.5 million women** entered the work force between 1940 and 1945, although even as workers **Japanese women were regarded as second-class citizens.** However, in the postwar period under American occupation, women achieved a considerable degree of emancipation.

POSTWAR RECONSTRUCTION
Following the war, American occupying forces worked to **rebuild Japan's economy 342–43** » to serve as a **bulwark against Soviet aggression**.

Potsdam Conference

Germany had been defeated. Now it was time to divide up the spoils—and to decide upon the destiny of Japan. The negotiations conducted at Potsdam by the leaders of the victorious powers were to play an important part in shaping the postwar world.

None of the leaders was under any illusion about the likely difficulty of finding common ground when the conference got under way on July 17. This had been trying enough under the necessities of war. They already knew that, in the peace to come, they would each have different objectives and priorities; already, each was coming under different domestic pressures.

Power and preoccupation

Quite how compelling these might be was brought home to all when, halfway through the conference, on July 26, the news came in of Churchill's defeat in the General Election. He might be his nation's hero, but he was no longer to be their prime minister: his successor, the Labour leader Clement Attlee, immediately took his place at the conference negotiating table.

Feeding the hungry
Germany had been left devastated—and destitute—in defeat. One of the first tasks facing the Allies had been to set up soup kitchens, like this one in Mannheim.

it." Winston Churchill, he found "good but patchy … perhaps too ready to indulge in long dissertations, which were evidently not to President Truman's taste." Joseph Stalin, he wrote, "spoke quietly, shortly, in little staccato sentences." He was "often humorous, never offensive; direct and uncompromising … His eyes looked to me humorous, and often showed as mere slits, but he had a trick of looking up when he was thinking or speaking, to the ceiling to the right, and much of the time he would be pulling at a Russian cigarette." The Soviet leader had been portrayed in the Western propaganda of the pre-war period as a blood-soaked tyrant—and not without reason as spectacular

BEFORE

Victory in Europe was not surprising. Since America's entry into the war, and German defeats at Stalingrad, Kursk, and in Africa, it had been a question not of "if" but "when."

A NEW EUROPE
The Allied nations had long been making careful **plans for victory ‹‹ 202–03** but, while Stalin and the Western leaders had managed to put their **differences to one side** for the moment,

CAPTURED GERMAN STANDARDS

it seemed likely that they would **disrupt the postwar peace**. Germany had been divided into **de facto zones** after the war. Now the victorious Allies were going to try to put the beleaguered **country back together** as a preliminary to **reconstructing devastated Europe** as a whole.

"I can deal with **Stalin**. He is honest—but **smart as hell**."

HARRY S. TRUMAN, FROM AN ENTRY IN HIS DIARY, JULY 17, 1945

Stalin also had worries. His intelligence chiefs had already brought news of the Americans' new bomb: the developing situation was going to require the most careful handling. As for Truman, he had to manage his negotiations with Stalin as firmly as he could, securing the best possible outcome for the United States and its Western allies. At the same time, it was important not to let it be known exactly how strong a hand he thought he had, lest it become too clear, too soon, what the US was planning.

Personal relations

The leaders also differed greatly in their personal styles. The British Solicitor-General, Walter Monckton—a witness of the talks—recorded his impressions of the leaders taking part. Harry S. Truman was brief and to the point, he said: he "had come prepared on each subject with a short, firm, declaratory statement of US policy, and when he had said his little piece he did little in subsequent discussion except reaffirm

crimes had been documented against him even then. Westerners were so surprised to discover this monster was even halfway human that they allowed themselves to be charmed by this affable "Uncle Joe."

Clearing up the mess

In the course of their journey to the conference, the leaders had been given ample opportunity to see the shattered state that Germany was in. Major cities had lost up to 40 percent of their homes; displaced persons wandered about, and feral children lived in packs among the ruins. The country's industrial infrastructure had largely been destroyed and most of its people did not have enough to eat. While all agreed that Germany had to be punished, it nevertheless seemed important that reconstruction should be a priority.

> **Potsdam, situated southwest of Berlin, was famous in German history as a favorite spot of King Frederick the Great—the monarch who had built up Prussian militarism in the 18th century.**

The victors
Since the "Big Three" met at Yalta, Harry S. Truman (center) had followed Franklin D. Roosevelt into the presidency weeks before the conference, while British premier, Clement Attlee (left), replaced Winston Churchill halfway through. "Uncle Joe" was apparently a fixture.

Here too, though, perspectives differed: the German assault on the Soviet Union had left whole cities plundered and vast areas laid waste. The Russians were less eager to rebuild Germany than to take down any surviving factories they could find and ship them back east for reassembly in the USSR. It was an understandable reaction, Westerners admitted.

The dismantling of the Nazi state might have been considered uncontroversial, but here too important differences soon emerged. All agreed on the "Four Ds"—demilitarization, de-Nazification,

The immediate business of the Potsdam Conference concerned the reconstruction of Germany—and the defeat of Japan.

CONFLICTS OF INTEREST
The main protagonists were looking to the future, and seeking to **shape the postwar world** to their advantage. The longer negotiations went on, the clearer it became that the parties **could never agree**—even on the most **apparently uncontentious** issues. As the wrangling over Germany's **reconstruction** went on, the East and West administered their **respective zones** in their own way: **the resulting partition 340–41 »** was to last for 40 years.

A NEW REALITY
Despite **warm words at Potsdam**, the **chill between East and West** was palpable: the **Cold War 348–49 »** was already under way. The **Soviet Union** would now spend the **next half century** trying to overtake the Americans in the **"arms race."** This was to be half a century in which the world would be living **in constant fear** of a **nuclear war**.

THE TOP ALLIED GENERALS IN BERLIN

democratization, and decartelization— but there was no overall consensus on what these meant. If the Soviets' idea of "democratization" was at odds with those of the Western Allies, so was their interpretation of the word "decartelization." To Western capitalists it meant the breaking up of the big, state-supervised corporate cartels of the Nazi era and their opening up to free-market competition. To the Soviets, however, it meant an increase in state involvement through a program of wholesale nationalization.

The other war
Meanwhile, no one needed reminding that war still raged in the Far East, with Japan still defiant as the bombs rained down. Operation Starvation had placed a noose around Japan's neck which was steadily tightening. Some were now having second thoughts and had even put out secret feelers offering peace in return for retaining the monarchy. But

even if the Americans had been willing to agree to such a deal, it would have found no favor with the fanatics in government and the military, who were resolved that the country should go down fighting.

When they had first met at Potsdam, Stalin made a point of telling Truman that he would now pursue the war in the Far East. The president thanked him politely; America no longer anticipated needing help against Japan—nor did it want to be beholden to the Soviets. But Roosevelt had pressed the dictator to make a commitment months before at Yalta, when the outlook in the East had still been in doubt. Stalin was positively eager to undertake a campaign against Japan, which, at this stage in the war, could have only one outcome—that of bringing the Soviet Union an important territory, on the Pacific, at little cost.

> **31,000** The number of Soviet factories destroyed during the war. Stalin was anxious to begin rebuilding fast, and at Germany's expense.

A few days into the conference, on July 21, Truman received a telegram from the New Mexico desert confirming that a US atom bomb had successfully been tested. On July 24 he took Stalin to one side and told him the news. Stalin was not particularly impressed, much to the shock of the Western delegates, who assumed that he had failed to see the significance of the bomb. But he had been aware of its development for some time and had already taken steps to set up a similar program in the Soviet Union.

However, the arms race was a contest for the future. Right now, all sides agreed that there was a war waiting to be won. At the conference's conclusion, on August 2, the "Potsdam Declaration" was announced. Japan could choose, it said, between "unconditional surrender" or "prompt and utter destruction."

US PRESIDENT (1884–1972)
HARRY S. TRUMAN

A farmer's son from Missouri, Truman served as an artillery captain in WW1 and went into politics after it. He faced many economic problems in his first term, but fought a barnstorming campaign to come from behind and win reelection in 1948. His second term was grueling, and he decided not to run again in 1952.

Medals

The global conflict involved countless individual stories—not just of outstanding gallantry but of quieter courage, of dedicated service and self-sacrifice. All sides issued medals to acknowledge these contributions. Attitudes amongst the nations varied, as did the significance of the awards: only 180 received the British Victoria Cross, for example, whilst almost 15 million got the "War Medal" of the Soviet Union.

1 France and Germany Star, issued to all British Commonwealth personnel who served in France, Belgium, Luxembourg, the Netherlands, and Germany after D-Day. **2** Africa Star, given by Britain to Commonwealth troops for service not only in the North African Campaign, but also in East Africa—and even Malta and Syria. **3** Commemorative Medal of the Battle of Dunkirk, instituted by Britain in 1948 to honor those who took part in the Allied evacuation of 1940. **4** Burma Star, a British medal issued to all Commonwealth personnel serving in the Burma campaign. **5** Asiatic-Pacific Campaign Medal, a US medal, honored all who had served in the Pacific Theater. The first medal was issued to General Douglas MacArthur. **6** Purple Heart, awarded to all US personnel wounded or killed in action since April 1917, when the US entered World War I. The obverse of the medal depicts General George Washington. **7** Army Medal of Honor, the most prestigious decoration awarded by the US government, along with versions for the Navy and Air Force. The Medal of Honor was awarded 464 times during World War II. **8** Silver Star, an American medal awarded for special valor in the face of the enemy. **9** Iron Cross 2nd Class, a German award for bravery which had to be held before the Iron Cross 1st Class could be earned. **10** North African Medal, a German/Italian medal issued to commemorate cooperation in North Africa. When

Italy signed an armistice with the Allies, Hitler forbade his troops from wearing it. **11** War Merit Cross with swords, awarded by Germany for exceptional service in battle. A cross without swords was awarded to civilians aiding the war effort. **12** Croix de guerre, a French award for bravery in combat. Different degrees of the award are denoted by the various symbols attached to the ribbon. **13** German Cross Gold Class, an award for bravery of a higher rank than the Iron Cross 1st Class. Silver Class was a continuation of the War Merit Cross, being an award for exceptional service. **14** Order of the Red Banner, awarded for distinguished service in the Soviet military. The banner reads "Workers of the World, Unite!" **15** 7th Class, Order of the Rising Sun, decorated with three paulownia leaves. Membership of the order was bestowed for conspicuous service to the Japanese cause. **16** Medal for the Defense of Stalingrad, awarded by the USSR to more than 750,000 soldiers and civilians who took part in the Battle of Stalingrad, July–November 1942. **17** Medal for the Defense of Leningrad, given by the USSR to all those who helped defend the city; over one million were issued. **18** Order of the Red Star, which recognized "exceptional service" in the defense of the Soviet Union— though ultimately it had two million recipients. **19** Medal for the Victory Over Germany in the Great Patriotic War, 1941–45, given by the USSR to all who fought in the war.

7 ARMY MEDAL OF HONOR

6 PURPLE HEART (US)

5 ASIATIC-PACIFIC CAMPAIGN MEDAL (US)

1 FRANCE AND GERMANY STAR (BRITAIN)

2 AFRICA STAR (BRITAIN)

3 COMMEMORATIVE MEDAL OF THE BATTLE OF DUNKIRK (BRITAIN)

4 BURMA STAR (BRITAIN)

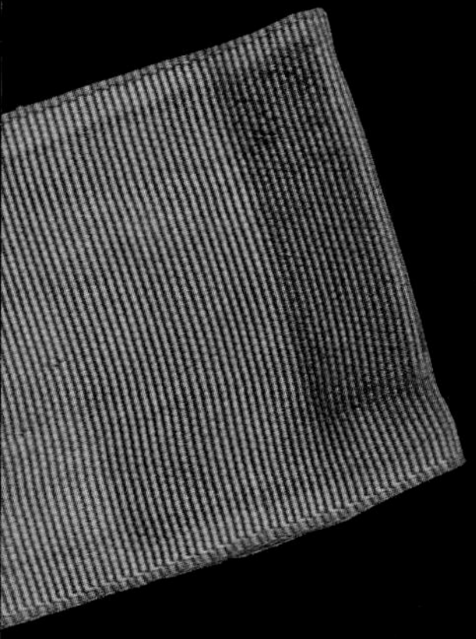

8 SILVER STAR (US)

9 IRON CROSS 2ND
CLASS (GERMANY)

10 NORTH AFRICAN MEDAL
(GERMANY/ITALY)

11 WAR MERIT CROSS
WITH SWORDS (GERMANY)

12 CROIX DE GUERRE (FRANCE)

13 GERMAN
CROSS, GOLD
CLASS (GERMANY)

14 ORDER OF THE
RED BANNER (USSR)

15 7TH CLASS, ORDER OF
THE RISING SUN (JAPAN)

17 MEDAL FOR THE DEFENSE
OF LENINGRAD (USSR)

16 MEDAL FOR
THE DEFENSE OF
STALINGRAD (USSR)

18 ORDER
OF THE RED
STAR (USSR)

19 MEDAL FOR THE VICTORY
OVER GERMANY IN THE GREAT
PATRIOTIC WAR, 1941–45 (USSR)

Hiroshima and Nagasaki

The dropping of "Little Boy" and "Fat Man" in August 1945 were unprecedented (and so far unrepeated) acts of atomic war. For the world, these historic events marked the beginning of the nuclear age— for Japan and its people, the impact was immediate and cataclysmic.

Major John E. Moynihan wrote "No white cross for Stevie" on the bulging body of "Little Boy" before it was loaded on board the B-29. His young son should surely now be spared the trauma of receiving news of his father's death: this most lethal of weapons, he hoped, would ultimately save lives. Then, in the early hours of August 6, the plane took off from the Pacific island airbase of Tinian. Only then did Colonel Paul Tibbets tell his crew just what sort of weapon it was that they were carrying in the bomb bay.

Two other aircraft joined them as they passed Iwo Jima: one with monitoring equipment to collect data on the blast, the other to take photographs. The two peeled away as the plane made its final approach to Hiroshima and climbed to a bombing height of 31,000 ft (9,500 m).

The bomb was released —and, for what seemed an eternity, nothing happened; "Little Boy" was set to detonate at an

Enola Gay
The pilot, Colonel Paul W. Tibbets, Jr., waves from the cockpit of his B-29. Below him, his mother's name, "Enola Gay," has been inscribed on the bomber's fuselage.

altitude of 1,850 ft (560 m). Then came a blinding flash, and the plane gave a violent judder as the shockwave hit it. A second wave followed. "The city was hidden by that awful cloud," Colonel Tibbets said, "boiling up, mushrooming, terrible, and incredibly tall." His tail gunner recalled: "A column of smoke is rising fast. It has a fiery red core. Fires are springing up everywhere."

Hiroshima devastated
Down below, the people of Hiroshima had been going about their normal lives. Defenders had spotted the planes, but assumed they were on reconnaissance.

The flash came first, and then a gigantic boom: "the sky split open over the city," said one survivor. Within a 1,100-yd (1-km) radius, human bodies literally melted in temperatures approaching 5,432°F (3,000°C). Further away a compression wave destroyed their internal organs. Survivors staggered in a daze, stripped of their clothes, their skin flayed by the force of the blast. No one knew to worry about the radiation that was to come.

Facing defeat
Whether defiant or simply dazed and in denial, Japan's rulers made no move to meet the demands of the Potsdam Declaration. But calamity on this sort of scale could not long be disregarded. Some 70,000 had died at Hiroshima (a figure that tripled when radiation took its toll in the years to come). Meanwhile, the incendiary raids continued, and the Soviets had entered the war with Japan.

This was the final straw. Until now, the Soviets had not been at war with Japan. However, in the early hours of August 9, the Red Army crossed into Manchuria in

« BEFORE

Scientists had for some years speculated on the possibility of harnessing the explosive power of nuclear fission for military use.

AMERICA LEADS THE WAY
A number of countries, including Germany, had carried out **preliminary research**. The US effort was stepped up with the building of a **top-secret** National Laboratory at Los Alamos, New Mexico, in 1943. Under the direction of physicist J. Robert Oppenheimer, a **team of scientists** worked frantically to build—and successfully test—an **atomic bomb** as part of the "Manhattan Project." The uranium-235 for the first **(Hiroshima)** bomb was enriched at Oak Ridge, Tennessee; plutonium was used for the second **(Nagasaki)** device.

THE MANHATTAN PROJECT

"Fat Man"
Weighing in at 10,200 lb (4,630 kg), the plutonium bomb dropped on Nagasaki was some 1,300 lb (600 kg) heavier than Hiroshima's "Little Boy."

TECHNOLOGY

B-29 SUPERFORTRESS

The B-29 was the workhorse of the Japan campaign, demonstrating its value in Operation Starvation and in the bombing of Japan's cities. A heavy bomber with four propellers, it was designed for high-altitude, daytime bombing raids. Flying at a height of 40,000 ft (12,000 m), it was out of reach of Japanese fighters, so in theory could ply back and forth at will. The reality was that weather seldom allowed sufficient visibility for effective high-altitude raids. The B-29 could carry a load of 9 tons (20,000 lb) and had a range of 3,750 miles (6,000 km). Later, as Japan's air defenses were degraded, LeMay increased its range by dispensing with the tail gunner and ordering a lower flying

altitude. The B-29's high-altitude capabilities came in useful for the attacks on Japan: "Little Boy" was dropped from 31,000 ft (9,500 m), and "Fat Man" from 29,000 ft (8,800 m).

Time stood still

This victim's watch stopped in the very instant of the blast at Hiroshima on the morning of August 6.

force. Defeat was now fast-approaching and guaranteed. "It is necessary," the emperor said as that day dawned, " to study and decide on the termination of the war."

In truth, there was little for the emperor to study and no scope for him to "decide" on anything—apart from the abject surrender the Allied nations had demanded. Just what "utter destruction" might feel like was brought home that afternoon, when the United States dropped a second atom bomb, this one on the southwestern port of Nagasaki.

Second time around

Major Charles W. Sweeney piloted another B-29, named *Bock's Car*. "Fat Man," significantly heavier than "Little Boy," had been armed with plutonium rather than uranium-235. It killed some 50,000 people (again, a figure that rose dramatically over the next few years).

Since the war was by now all but over, it has been mooted that this bomb was dropped either for scientific reasons—as a macabre true-life test—or for diplomatic ones—to send a warning message to the Soviet Union. And yet, three days after Hiroshima, there had been no hint of a Japanese surrender.

Even now, surrender was slow in coming, although the party around Emperor

Mushroom cloud

Now a macabre emblem of modernity, the smoke sent up by the blast over Nagasaki rose more than 60,000 ft (18,000 m) into the air.

Hirohito was now waking up to reality. But military fanatics were fighting on—and even staged an attempted coup. On August 14, Hirohito made a radio broadcast in which he called on the Japanese to lay down their arms. But his plea reached the people. who reacted first with disbelief, then broke down as what he said sank in. "Something huge had just cracked," wrote French reporter, Robert Guillain, "the proud dream of a greater Japan."

AFTER »

Japan had brutally built an empire, which it sought to defend to the death. Now, all it could do was submit to occupation.

JAPAN'S FATE

Japan had been saved from **"utter destruction,"** but not before months of **heavy bombardment** had taken its toll. The Allied occupiers now had to restore order. An **occupation government was established 304–05 »** under General Douglas MacArthur, which ruled for the next six years.

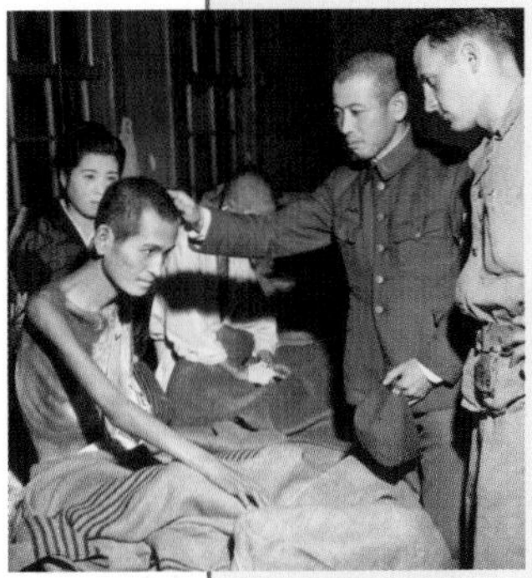

REBIRTH OF JAPAN

The **completeness** of Japan's defeat may have been key to the success of its eventual recovery, as it **reinvented itself**, first as a constitutional monarchy, then as an **industrializing nation**. Within one generation, an **economic rebirth 342–43 »** would make Japan one of the world's most important manufacturing nations.

VICTIMS OF THE NAGASAKI BLAST

Hiroshima

On the morning of Monday August 6, 1945 an American B-29 known as *Enola Gay*, flown by Colonel Paul W. Tibbets, dropped an atomic bomb on the Japanese city of Hiroshima. Most of the city was destroyed and more than 70,000 inhabitants were killed instantly from heat, bomb blast, and radiation. Thousands more died later from burns and radiation sickness. A second atomic bomb was dropped on the city of Nagasaki three days later, killing perhaps as many as 50,000 people and destroying nearly half the city.

"I had been on student mobilization working at a factory located about four kilometers to the east of here. At 8:15am, I saw a strong flash and felt intense heat ... the window panes in the factory blew up with a huge sound and women screamed in the workshop ... People who were near the windows were bathed in blood. I thought that a bomb [had] directly hit the factory ...

To the west, a mushroom cloud was forming over the city of Hiroshima. It was snow-white and rising fast up in the air ... While we were telling each other that something terrible had happened ... and discussing what we should do, crowds of people fleeing the city came in our direction ... We were speechless at the sight of this strange procession ... People looked like they were wearing rags, but what we thought to be rags was actually their peeling skin. As they walked on with wobbly steps, blood dripped from their wounds, deep and wide open, as if somebody scraped out parts of their flesh ...

We departed for the city to rescue survivors. Hiroshima had been turned into a hell. When I tried to help up a man lying on the ground, his burnt skin peeled and stuck to my hands. I found a man groaning under a fallen house, but I could not save him because of the approaching fire. Bodies burnt black, people lying dead on the ground like objects, in agony or already dead ... I spent several days in that hell trying to rescue people. In mid-September, I suddenly developed acute A-bomb disease and began suffering from high fever, bleeding and loss of hair ...**"**

NORI TOHEI, HIROSHIMA HIBAKUSHA (SURVIVOR)

Devastated city
The atomic bomb completely devastated Hiroshima.
Every building within 1 mile (1.6 km) of the impact
was destroyed and virtually every building or structure
within 3 miles (5 km) was damaged.

BEFORE

Japan had entered the war hoping to expand the empire it had been building through the 1930s, and consolidate the power it had achieved as head of the Greater East Asia Co-Prosperity Sphere **《 146–47**.

AN ABRUPT END
Now, after **four years of bloodshed**, the country had been forced into **unconditional surrender** by the dropping of the two **atomic bombs** on Hiroshima and Nagasaki **《 320–21**. The bombs had brought the war to a close with a jolting, **disorientating abruptness**.

A BOTTLE MELTED AT HIROSHIMA

HONOR AND DEATH
Japan had been **preparing itself for defeat**, but had fully expected to **go down fighting**. The narrative its forces had been fashioning—in Iwo Jima, in Okinawa, and, until now Japan itself—had been one of **patriotic loyalty to the death**. That narrative had found its most powerful expression in the suicidal courage of Operation Ten-Go and the **self-sacrificing** flights of the **kamikaze pilots 《 312–13**.

A FUTURE FOR JAPAN
The **people of Japan** were going to have to find a **new narrative to live by**. The only problem was that **no one knew** yet how the **postwar story** would be written.

Japan Surrenders

The Pacific War had been a race war, spectacular in its savagery, but it had ended in apocalyptic slaughter. There were real questions as to whether a genuine accommodation between winners and losers would be found; whether peace was going to be possible between them.

A hiatus followed Hirohito's surrender broadcast: most people shut the doors to their homes and sat listless. Those who had waited in vast crowds to hear the "imperial rescript" went on their separate ways without even speaking to one another, either weeping to themselves or simply stunned. Most of his subjects had never heard their emperor's voice before: to hear it now in such bitter circumstances heaped confusion upon confusion, shock upon shock. An eerie calm descended on the country: not only did the people have to adjust to a new mentality, but the Allies were still far away, and in no position to take charge. Days passed; nowhere was an occupying soldier to be seen, yet the idea of renewed resistance does not seem to have occurred. Those who had once felt most strongly that they should fight to the death were now impelled by that same patriotic spirit to accept their emperor's decision without question.

The struggle continues
The war was not yet over for Japanese forces fighting overseas. Communication was difficult at such distances, and many troops were completely cut off—if not by geographical barriers then by enemy armies. Not all Japanese officers were interested in heeding the order when it did come: the military had been some of the most fanatical in the imperial cause from the start and the most

America's Tianjin triumph
American troops liberate the city of Tianjin, in China, occupied by the Japanese since 1937. The Chinese had more tumults and travails to come. For the time being, however, they could rejoice in their freedom from the Japanese occupation.

MacArthur signs the surrender
The formal surrender was not signed until September 2, on board the battleship the USS *Missouri*. Japan's submission was unconditional, although the emperor's status as a sovereign was to be respected.

resistant to the idea of surrender at the end. On the front line, they had every motive to fight on. Even if they were ready to surrender, it was no easy matter to disengage from a struggle with enemies who were keen to fight on. Having invaded Manchuria as recently as August 9, the Soviet Union had no interest in ceasing hostilities they saw as bringing important territorial gains. On August 18, with the region secured, along with Sakhalin and the northern part of Korea, their forces attacked the strategically vital Kuril Islands.

The occupation begins
Douglas MacArthur, supreme Allied commander for the Pacific, arrived in Japan with his occupying army on August 28, with the formal signing of the "Instrument of Surrender" arranged for September 2, aboard the battleship USS *Missouri*. MacArthur received Japan's surrender on behalf of the Allies. It was offered by the defeated nation's foreign minister, Mamoru Shigemitsu.

Japan was no longer a sovereign state: its own administration was in the hands of an occupation government. This was mainly to comprise American military officers and civil servants, though there would be representatives from Britain, Australia, and New Zealand, too. The overseas empire was to be broken up: the US was to have authority in several strategic Pacific island groups as well as supervising the government of South Korea; the Soviet Union was to keep its conquests in Manchuria, North Korea, and the Kuril Islands; the Republic of China was to take Taiwan. A tribunal was to be established to try leading

military officers and statesmen for war crimes, as had been agreed between the victorious Allies in Europe.

In the meantime, MacArthur and his forces brought in food supplies. Whatever crimes had been committed, the Japanese could not simply be allowed to starve; with the agriculture and transport infrastructures in tatters, this was what was happening. The Americans prioritized the organization of effective distribution for supplies, although it was to be several years before hunger ceased to be a threat.

A constitutional monarchy
MacArthur was widely criticized in the West for his "kid-glove" treatment of a ruler who had by no means been an innocent bystander during his country's slide into aggressive nationalism. But even as he disarmed and dismantled the military, MacArthur lent discreet support to the imperial house. He hoped the emperor could be the figurehead of a new, democratic, peace-loving Japan.

AFTER

Surrender had come as a cataclysmic shock to the Japanese, and had undermined their very sense of who they were.

JAPAN'S REBIRTH
Paradoxically, though, this gave the Japanese an ideal opportunity for a fresh start; a **"clean slate"** on which they could begin again. So complete was **Japan's reinvention of itself 342–43 》**, that, within **decades of defeat**, it would become an **important economic power**. For the moment, however, things were **going to get worse** before they got better, as **radiation sickness** and **starvation** began to **take their toll 334–35 》**.

FAR EASTERN CONFRONTATION
China, happily **rid of its Japanese invaders**, was free to resume the **long-standing civil war** in which Mao Zedong's Communists were **ultimately to prevail 346–47 》**.

With the **new world superpowers**, America and the Soviet Union, already **locked in hostility** in Europe, **a second front** was now set to open in the **Cold War 348–49 》**.

> "We have resolved to **pave the way** for a grand peace for all the generations to come by **enduring the unendurable** and suffering the insufferable."
>
> EMPEROR HIROHITO, "IMPERIAL RESCRIPT ON SURRENDER", AUGUST 15, 1945

The surrender ceremony
All the pomp and circumstance in the world could not hide the extent of Japan's humiliation. The country had for years been pursuing the goal of imperial power: that it should have to bow the knee was unthinkable.

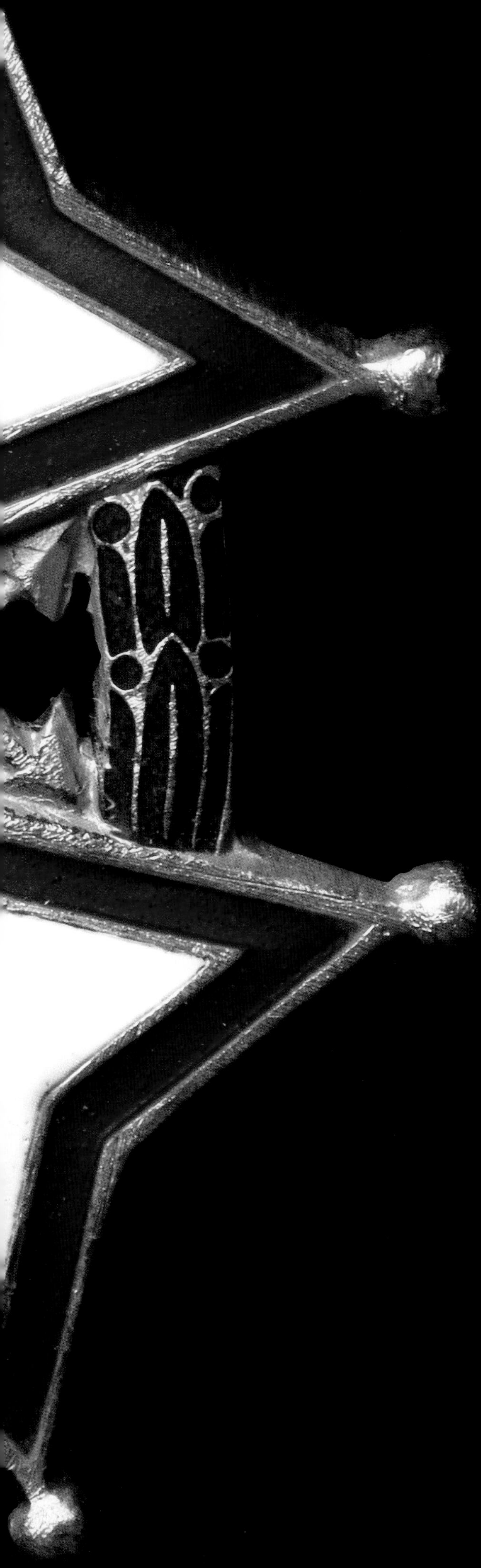

9
AFTERMATH
1946–1950

In the postwar world borders were redrawn. The USSR dominated the East, taking control of Central and Eastern Europe, while Germany remained in two halves for decades. The US, now the most powerful nation in the world, and the USSR, began a new war of ideologies.

AFTERMATH

In France reprisals against Nazi collaborators were violent but short-lived. At first some collaborators were executed without trial, while many women who had slept with Germans were branded by having their heads shaved.

Berlin was divided into American, Soviet, British, and French zones. In 1948 the Soviets attempted to blockade the Allied part of the city, but it was kept supplied by an airlift.

Israel was founded in May 1948 by the Jews of Palestine after the UN had proposed a plan for partition in 1947. This was opposed by neighboring Arab states, which promptly invaded.

Hermann Goering, the most prominent of the Nazi leaders to stand trial at Nuremberg, was sentenced to death for war crimes in October 1946, but committed suicide the night before he was due to hang.

Vienna, the capital of Austria, suffered the same fate as Berlin, being divided into sectors by the victorious Allies. Here, US troops march past a huge red star bearing the images of Lenin and Stalin.

India and Pakistan gained independence from Britain in 1947, an event celebrated by vast crowds in Delhi, the Indian capital.

In the postwar years national borders were crudely shifted and rearranged. Germany was split down the middle, while Poland, wiped from the map by the Molotov-Ribbentrop Pact of 1939, reappeared 100 miles (160 km) to the west at the end of the war. The other territories grabbed by Stalin before the German invasion of Russia in 1941 were absorbed into the USSR: Finnish Karelia, Lithuania, Latvia, Estonia, and Moldavia.

Japan's imperial possessions in Asia evaporated. So, for example, the puppet state of Manchukuo, which had been the Chinese province of Manchuria, reverted to Chinese rule and became the main bone of contention between Nationalists and Communists.

The European victors also let go of their overseas empires. Britain, France, and the Netherlands withdrew from Southeast Asia, and new independent nations came into being as they left. India won its

1946—1951

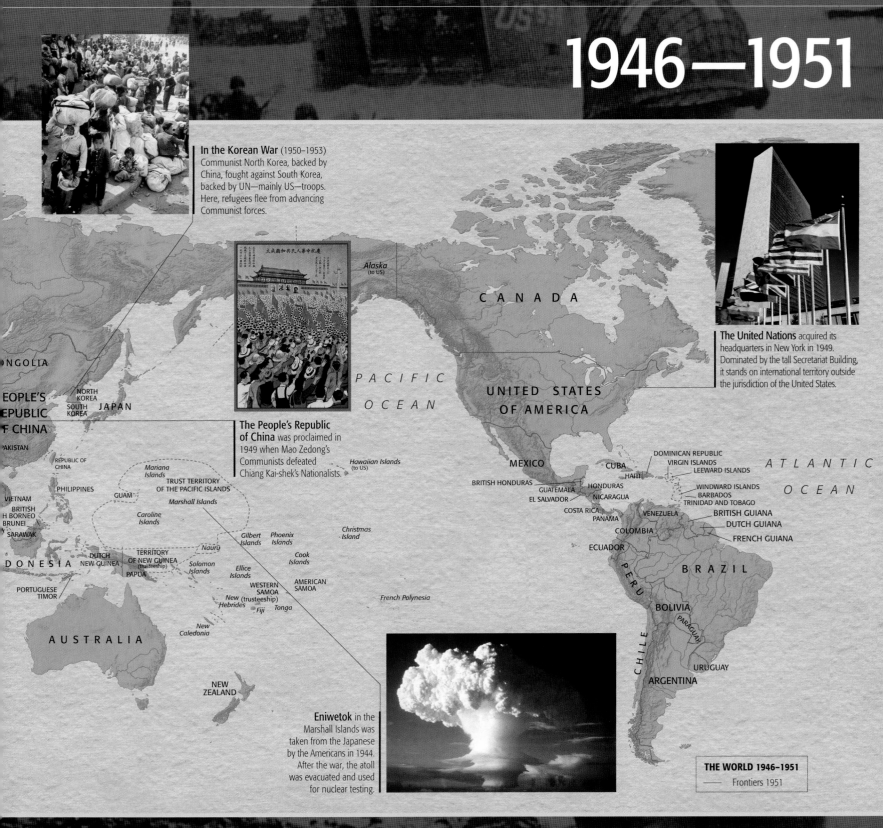

In the Korean War (1950–1953) Communist North Korea, backed by China, fought against South Korea, backed by UN—mainly US—troops. Here, refugees flee from advancing Communist forces.

The People's Republic of China was proclaimed in 1949 when Mao Zedong's Communists defeated Chiang Kai-shek's Nationalists.

The United Nations acquired its headquarters in New York in 1949. Dominated by the tall Secretariat Building, it stands on international territory outside the jurisdiction of the United States.

Eniwetok in the Marshall Islands was taken from the Japanese by the Americans in 1944. After the war, the atoll was evacuated and used for nuclear testing.

THE WORLD 1946–1951
—— Frontiers 1951

independence in 1947, and instantly became the largest democracy on Earth. The stricken Jews of the world achieved their long-held dream of a national home when in June 1948 the state of Israel was constituted in the Biblical land of Canaan.

Yet the main shift was not cartographical, but ideological. The new world order was dominated by two nations and two philosophies: liberal Western democracy under the leadership of America, and authoritarian state socialism championed by the USSR. The former camp included all the English-speaking nations of the world and the countries of Western Europe. The latter encompassed China (for a time), Stalin's Eastern European vassal states, and the revolutionary regimes that emerged from the wreckage of empire. Postwar history is the story of the long, dangerous tussle between two geopolitical giants—one in the East, the other in the West.

TIMELINE 1946—1951

The Nuremberg Trials ▪ **The Iron Curtain** ▪ **The United Nations** ▪ The Berlin Airlift ▪
Occupied Japan ▪ The Loss of Empires ▪ **The Two Germanies** ▪ Red China ▪ **The Cold**
War ▪ Nuclear Weapons ▪ **The Korean War** ▪ Remembering the War

1946

JANUARY 1
First meeting of UN General Assembly in London. 51 nations are represented.

MARCH 5
Churchill delivers "Iron Curtain" speech in Fulton, Missouri.

⌃ Churchill before making his speech at Fulton

JULY 1
US Army Constabulary, a special force for policing occupied Germany and Austria becomes operational.

⌃ Shoulder patch of the US Army Constabulary in Germany

JULY 4
US grants independence to the Philippines, but retains a large number of military bases in the country.

JANUARY–JUNE
In first half of the year thousands of illegal Jewish refugees reach Palestine. Later in the year British authorities expel new refugees and intern them in Cyprus.

⌃ Small ship full of Jewish refugees arriving at Haifa

NOVEMBER 20
Start of war in Vietnam between Viet Minh and the French colonial forces. It ends in 1954 with the division of the country into North and South Vietnam.

1947

1947
In the Chinese Civil War the Communists begin to gain the upper hand against the Nationalists.

⌄ Nationalist troops in China surrender to the PLA

MARCH 12
President Truman outlines the so-called "Truman Doctrine," a policy of providing aid to countries threatened by communist takeover. His immediate concern is to provide assistance to Greece and Turkey.

MAY 3
Japan establishes a constitutional democracy.

JUNE 5
US aid program for rebuilding Europe's shattered economies is announced by Secretary of State George Marshall. The Marshall Plan becomes an important part of America's fight against communism.

1948

JANUARY 30
Assassination of Gandhi, whose non-violent passive resistance to British rule had done so much to win independence for India.

FEBRUARY 25
Communist takeover in Czechoslovakia.

MAY 14
Proclamation of the state of Israel. The following day the armies of the country's Arab neighbors invade. Israel wins the ensuing war and 750,000 Palestinians flee their former homeland.

⌃ Mahatma Gandhi

NOVEMBER 2
Harry S. Truman elected to a second term as US president.

JULY 18
British seize the "Exodus," a ship of Jewish immigrants to Palestine. The 4,000 would-be immigrants are forced to return to displaced persons camps in Germany.

⌃ New West German currency introduced in 1948

JUNE 23
New currency introduced in West Berlin. Next day Soviets cut off all road and rail links to the western part of the city. The Western Allies respond by organizing massive airlift of fuel and food.

DECEMBER 23
Tojo Hideki, Japanese prime minister, is hanged for war crimes.

⌄ Berlin airlift

AUGUST 15
India gains independence. Partition of the former British dominion into India and Pakistan.

NOVEMBER 29
The UN General Assembly passes a resolution calling for the partition of Palestine between Arabs and Jews.

"The United States must regard the Soviet Union as **a rival, not a partner**. It must expect **no happy coexistence** of the **socialist** and **capitalist** worlds."

GEORGE F. KENNAN, FORMER US DEPUTY CHIEF OF MISSION IN MOSCOW, JULY 1947

1949

JANUARY 25
Foundation of Comecon (Council for Mutual Economic Assistance). The first members are the USSR, Bulgaria, Poland, Czechoslovakia, Hungary, and Romania.

≫ News of the Soviet atomic bomb in the Western press

TRUMAN SAYS RUSSIA SET OFF ATOM BLAST
ATOMIC BLAST IN RUSSIA
TRUMAN SAYS REDS HAVE EXPLODED ATOM!

APRIL 4
North Atlantic Treaty signed in Washington by the United States, Britain, France, Belgium, the Netherlands, Luxembourg, Portugal, Italy, Norway, Denmark, Canada, and Iceland.

≪ Mao Zedong

MAY
Stalin lifts the Berlin blockade.

MAY 23
Formation of the German Federal Republic (West Germany).

AUGUST 1
The Dutch agree to a cease-fire after four years of fighting to prevent Indonesia from gaining independence. In December they formally give up all their former colonies in Southeast Asia except Dutch New Guinea.

AUGUST 29
First test of an atomic bomb by the USSR adds a nuclear dimension to the Cold War.

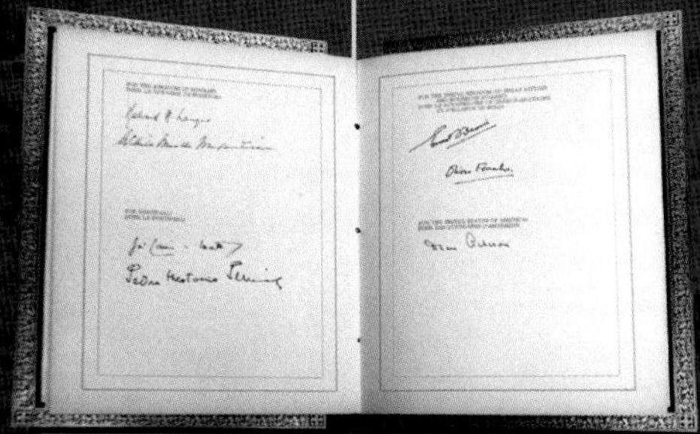

OCTOBER 1
Mao Zedong proclaims the People's Republic of China. The defeated Nationalist forces under Chiang Kai-Shek establish small rival state, the Republic of China, on the island of Taiwan.

OCTOBER 7
German Democratic Republic (East Germany) established in the Soviet sector of Germany.

1950

JANUARY 13 1950
Soviet representative at the UN protests at continued presence of Nationalist China on the Security Council rather than the new People's Republic of China.

FEBRUARY 1950
The People's Republic of China and the USSR sign the Treaty of Friendship, Alliance, and Mutual Assistance.

≫ Signatures to the North Atlantic Treaty

22 SEPTEMBER
UN forces enter Seoul, which they recapture after days of fierce house-to-house fighting.

JUNE 25 1950
North Korea invades South Korea. United Nations condemns this as an act of aggression and asks member states to go to the aid of the south.

≫ US troops in Korea

IL MANQUE
L'INDOCHINE A L'EMPIRE
français pensez-y!

⌃ French poster highlighting communist threat to Indochina

15 SEPTEMBER
Successful landing of UN forces, chiefly US Marines, at Inchon cuts supply lines to the North Korean forces to the south.

1951

JANUARY 4
In Korea, Chinese and North Korean forces retake Seoul.

JANUARY 16
The French, fighting to hold on to their colonies in Southeast Asia, defeat the Viet Minh outside Hanoi.

⌃ 38th Parallel, the border between North and South Korea

FEBRUARY 11
UN forces advance across the 38th Parallel, taking the fight into North Korea.

MARCH 18
UN forces retake the city of Seoul.

MAY 12
Americans test their first hydrogen bomb on Eniwetok Atoll in the Pacific.

JUNE 13
UN forces take Pyongyang, the North Korean capital.

JULY 10
Start of peace talks in Korean War, but fighting goes on for two more years, when a demilitarized zone is established along original frontier between the two states—the 38th parallel.

YOU ARE NOW CROSSING
38TH PARALLEL
CO B 728MP

SEPTEMBER 8
Treaty of Peace with Japan signed in San Francisco by 49 nations. USSR opposes terms of the treaty and does not sign it.

≫ President Truman at signing of the Japanese peace treaty

Counting the Cost

Millions died in the war, and for millions of survivors the ordeal continued after the guns stopped. A refugee crisis of unimaginable proportions developed in Europe as people carried far by the tides of conflict tried to return home, or else fell victim to waves of mass expulsion.

≪ BEFORE

By any measure, World War II was far and away the most costly and destructive conflict of all time.

THE PRICE OF WAR

The financial investment of the warring nations was huge. **The US spent about $341 billion on its war effort.** Russian historians have estimated that the war cost the Soviet Union as much as 30 percent of its national wealth. **Hitler poured $272 billion into his campaign for a Europe-wide Reich ≪ 220.**

LOST TREASURES

Thousands of important buildings and irreplaceable works of art were obliterated by bombs and shells. No price can be placed on what was lost: the baroque splendor of Dresden, Wren's London churches, the majestic palaces of Leningrad, and much more.

THE HUMAN COST

Modern estimates of the total death toll range from 55 million to **more than 70 million**.

Leaving the broken Reich
Displaced Persons (foreign forced laborers of the German Reich and areas occupied by the Germans) depart Munich in 1948 heading toward France.

The toll of the war was unequally spread. Poland lost 16 percent of its population; the US less than one third of one percent. Four times as many Allied citizens died as Axis ones; and almost two thirds of those killed in the war were non-combatants.

The 16 million non-combatant casualties of the war in China explain the huge preponderance of deaths on the Allied side, and the odd fact that more civilians died in the war than soldiers in battle. And these numbers are swollen by two separate but related aspects of Hitler's war. The first is the murderous policy of the Nazis toward the civilian population of the Soviet Union. More than 12 million Soviet citizens were killed in the course of the German invasion and retreat—in addition to the 10 million fighting men and women who perished.

The second factor in the high death rate among civilians was Hitler's policy of exterminating all Jews, wherever they fell into Nazi hands. Almost 8 million Jews lived in Europe before the rise of Hitler, and they represented a vibrant, rich, and ancient culture.

Returning home

In the immediate aftermath of the conflict, no one was counting the dead. It was as much as anyone could do just to bury them. In the spring of 1945, the living represented a far more pressing problem for the victorious Allied governments. During the last weeks of the war, the western areas of Germany were flooded with civilian refugees fleeing from the Red Army. After the surrender, these displaced people swelled the numbers of homeless Germans—the many thousands whose homes had been destroyed, or who had gone on the road to look for their missing relatives. In later months many German ex-POWs and soldiers returned home to find that their families were dead, or that their wives had made a new life with someone else in their absence. For many years after the end of the war, an army of these rootless *Heimkehrer* (homecomers) continued to drift from city to stricken city. An official estimate written in 1948 put their number close to 2 million.

A worse fate befell those Germans who lived outside the pre-war borders of Germany, or in the eastern lands that were ceded to other countries at the end of the war. The Allied policy toward these people was that they should be expelled from their homes, and resettled in one of the zones of occupation.

But redrawing national borders was no mere cartographic exercise. It entailed massive, and sometimes fatal, upheaval for millions of people and on some occasions, forced migrations were marked by vengeance. There were three million Germans in the Sudetenland, which reverted to Czechoslovakia at the end of the war. They were herded out of their homes at gunpoint or beaten across the border. When the borders of Poland were shifted westward, many Poles in the east of the country found

> ## "The **soldier must go home** … the refugee return to his country."
>
> WINSTON CHURCHILL, FROM HIS BOOK, "TRIUMPH AND TRAGEDY", 1954

110 MILLION The number of people who served in the armed forces of the fighting nations during World War II. 1.7 billion people participated in some way.

The defeated return home
Many German soldiers found themselves living on the bomb-torn streets—an army of uniformed tramps. They were among the lucky ones: they were at least free, and in their homeland.

In the decades following the war, some of the arbitrary injustices that took place were addressed by national governments.

AN ISRAELI FLAG IN JERUSALEM

REGRETS AND REDRESS

In 1952 West Germany agreed to pay more than 3 billion marks to the state of Israel as heir to victims of the Holocaust who had no surviving family. This money helped **the Israeli state 344 ››** to take root in its first, most fragile years. In 1995 Japan set up a fund to pay compensation to surviving **"comfort women,"** the mostly Korean and Chinese women forced into prostitution by the Japanese Army. Each victim received a letter from the Japanese prime minister: "... I extend anew my most sincere apologies and remorse to all the women who underwent immeasurable and painful experiences and suffered incurable physical and psychological wounds."

VICTIMS, NOT TRAITORS

During the **glasnost era** of the 1980s, the plight of Russians who fell into German hands was reassessed: they were now seen not as traitors, but as the **victims of two terror regimes.** For the majority of these unfortunate individuals, rehabilitation was long since posthumous.

---

themselves in what was now Soviet territory, and many Germans found themselves in what was now western Poland. All these people were then "repatriated," and cities changed their names and their character. Polish Lwow became the Soviet-Ukrainian city of Lvov; Breslau, emptied of its Germans, was repopulated with Poles and renamed Wroclaw.

Slave labor and gulags

Perhaps the most hapless and tragic group of survivors were the five million Soviet citizens who had been deported to Germany in the course of the war. Some had been virtually kidnapped by the advancing Germans and sent west as slave laborers; others were captured Russian soldiers who had volunteered to fight for the Wehrmacht rather than starve in a prisoner of war camp. Under the terms

Fractured streets
Berlin in 1946 was a city of rubble. Much of the spoil was dumped on the Brandenburg plain, where it formed an 262-ft (80-m) high artificial hill.

of the Yalta Agreement, Soviet citizens were to be repatriated, regardless of their own wishes. All of them were sent back to Russia, where they were uniformly treated as traitors and consigned to the gulag.

So the end of World War II was not the joyful day it should have been. It heaped unhappiness upon hardship and despair for many individuals, families, urban populations, and ethnic groups. The cost of the war comprises not just the the untold destruction and the many millions of war dead, but the trauma endured by the uncountable bereaved, the myriad individual futures blighted beyond repair. Even now the pain of it has not entirely gone away.

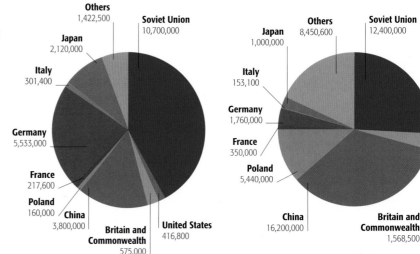

Military deaths during World War II
The Red Army bore the brunt of the war against Germany. As a result, the Soviet Union suffered by far the greatest number of military casualties.

Others 1,422,500
Soviet Union 10,700,000
Japan 2,120,000
Italy 301,400
Germany 5,533,000
France 217,600
Poland 160,000
China 3,800,000
Britain and Commonwealth 575,000
United States 416,800

Civilian deaths between 1937 and 1945
Chinese civilians suffered greatly at the hands of the Japanese during the 1937–45 Sino-Japanese War. The figures above include victims of the Holocaust.

Others 8,450,600
Soviet Union 12,400,000
Japan 1,000,000
Italy 153,100
Germany 1,760,000
France 350,000
Poland 5,440,000
China 16,200,000
Britain and Commonwealth 1,568,500

Postwar Refugees

When the war ended millions of dispossessed and homeless people were on the move in Europe. Made up of many different nationalities, they included concentration camp survivors, prisoners of war, and those transported as slave labor to Nazi-occupied territories. Camps and assembly centers were set up throughout Europe where displaced persons (DPs) were housed, fed, and eventually sent onward.

"You have to look through a block of ice to get the proper perspective on that first winter in Wildflecken ... 12,000 Poles frozen in with the eighteen UNRRA [United Nations Relief and Rehabilitation Administration] men and women assigned to care for them ... All life reduced to the stark simplicity of the supply line. Weekly boxcars of food and coal from Army depots in Würzburg [Germany] appeared automatically at our railroad station ... Every hour not given to crisis or sudden arrival was occupied with block visiting. We had some 2800 rooms in the camp in which the Poles were settling in for their winter in Slavic style. They nailed windows to stay shut ... bound babies like papooses ... and swung ever-burdened clotheslines ... The entire scale of the human condition could be seen in any single room ... It might be a bachelor's room bleak and bare ... Or ... a room where two or three families from the same village ... had managed to get together to create ... a semblance of the home they had left behind ... Most generally it would be a room into which the billeting committees had thrust heterogeneous families according to their size ... There were the rooms that always caught at one's heart, for they were partitioned off into family cubicles ...**"**

KATHRYN HULME, DEPUTY DIRECTOR, WILDLECKEN UNRRA DISPLACED PERSONS CAMP

"First we had the clothes which we wore there [Bergen-Belsen], which [were] full of disease and lice. We had to go through showers, then some powder ... They gave us different clothes ... and we were assigned so many people to a room ... People in Feldafing [camp] were from all over Europe. It wasn't only from Poland. We had Hungarian Jews, Rumanian Jews, Czech Jews, and also Greek Jews in this camp. Everyone just walking around and trying to mingle and find someone [relatives] ... we never did. But what the Americans also did is organize art schools. They brought in films. They ... organized our people, the survivors that were musicians and also traveling from other camps ... But the problem was, there was no future in being there. Where do we go from there?**"**

FELA WASCHAU, BERGEN-BELSEN SURVIVOR, DESCRIBING THE FELDAFING DISPLACED PERSONS CAMP, NEAR MUNICH, THE FIRST ALL-JEWISH DPS CAMP

Europe's displaced peoples
Between 1945 and 1947 UNRRA set up more than 700 DPs camps throughout Europe, where the homeless were given shelter, food, and medical treatment before being repatriated or sent on to make new lives elsewhere.

The **Fate** of the **Defeated**

The victors' armies occupied Germany and Japan, where they found a large proportion of the population homeless and hungry. Devastation was psychological as well as physical: the German and the Japanese sense of nationhood lay in ruins—like their shattered cities—and had to be rebuilt, brick by brick.

BEFORE

After the war the Allies divided Germany into four zones, each under the jurisdiction of one of the victorious nations: USSR, the US, Britain, and France. Japan was placed wholly under American control.

NEW REGIMES
The **Soviet zone** in eastern Germany, comprising the **territory occupied by Russian troops as they advanced ‹‹ 305**, was the largest of the four. It included all of the old state of **Prussia**, which was seen by the Russians as the **historic seat of German militarism**, and so the geographical source of Nazi aggression. Stalin was very glad to have this part of Germany under his sway. In the West the **US took control of southern Germany,** and **Britain administered the north**. French forces occupied a strip of territory bordering Switzerland and France itself. Japan, meanwhile, was occupied by American troops under **General Douglas MacArthur ‹‹ 244–45**, who for six years was in effect the **military ruler of the cowed Japanese people**. Little by little, both Germany and Japan were remade in the image of their occupiers.

In 1943 the Allies had agreed on a policy of unconditional surrender, knowing that their war aim was not merely to defeat the Axis militarily, but also to obliterate the political regimes and aggressive nationalist philosophies of Japan and Germany.

No one was sure how to achieve this. It was by no means clear that Germany would even be allowed to exist as an independent country ever again. Stalin's intention seems to have been to redivide the country into dozens of individually powerless statelets. France had a similar scheme: the Rhineland and Saarland would become satellites ruled from Paris, the industrial Ruhr would be an international zone, and the rest of Germany a jigsaw-like confederation rather than a sovereign state. The US vision, as expressed by the secretary of treasury, Henry Morgenthau, called for Germany to be stripped of all its modern industry and reduced to an almost medieval state of pastoralism. This plan was quietly dropped as the Cold War gained pace and Germany's industrial base became a valuable resource.

Facing starvation
Everyday reality for the German people—and also for the Japanese— was far removed from such geopolitical concerns. Much of the population in both countries was struggling merely to survive. Food shortages in Germany were acute, and many people who had survived both area bombing and the Allied invasion nowsuccumbed to malnutrition. The first and most frequent victims were children and babies.

In Japan hunger was just as endemic, and the black market universal. One Tokyo judge refused to buy food illegally, choosing to starve to death on his official rations.

US Army Constabulary badge
The force created to police occupied Germany and Austria (1946–52) wore this distinctive shoulder patch.

people more sympathetic to the values of the occupying powers and weaned them away from loyalty to the old regime. In Germany "denazification" was pursued rigorously by all four powers. Schools were banned from using Hitler-era textbooks on any subject: under the Nazis, even the teaching of math and chemistry was infected with racial ideology. Meanwhile, former members of the Nazi Party were removed from local government positions and banned from holding office. This policy was later abandoned because the administration could not function without the professional know-how of ex-Nazi bureaucrats.

Special knowledge was the salvation of the physicists and engineers who had developed the V-2 rocket. The advancing Americans mounted a special operation to net them before the Soviets. The biggest catch was Wernher von Braun, whose expertise

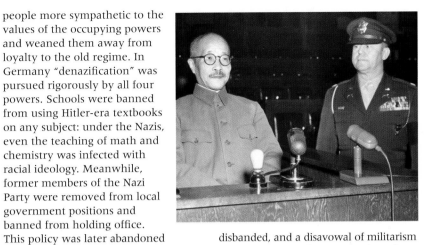

Tojo Hideki in the dock
Convicted of "crimes against peace," on the eve of his execution Tojo wrote: "From tomorrow, without offending anyone, I shall rest in peace beside the Amida Buddha."

disbanded, and a disavowal of militarism was written into the constitution of 1947. Article Nine stated that Japan would "forever renounce war as a sovereign right of the nation."

In 1946 Emperor Hirohito was made to concede publicly that he was not divine. He was fortunate not to be tried as a war criminal; MacArthur decided that to do so would cause such anger and consternation among the Japanese

the International Military Tribunal for the Far East—at which 28 military and political leaders stood trial. Sixteen former ministers, generals, and ambassadors were sentenced to life imprisonment; seven were sentenced to death. Chief among these was the wartime prime minister, Tojo Hideki. In 1945 he had attempted suicide to avoid capture by the Americans, but had succeeded only in wounding himself. In 1948 he was hanged alongside his foreign minister and war minister. It was his dubious distinction to be the only head of government to be executed for war crimes.

The Nuremberg trials
Of the 24 Nazi leaders originally indicted to stand trial for war crimes, 21 entered the dock on November 20, 1945. Seated on the far left of the front row is Hermann Goering and beside him Rudolf Hess.

In both countries the occupying forces provided emergency rations to the civilian population. Food aid served a political as well as a humanitarian purpose: it made the mass of ordinary

> "We aim to eliminate forever **its ability to function as a single state** in the center of Europe."
>
> JOSEPH STALIN'S PLAN FOR POSTWAR GERMANY, NOVEMBER 1943

was so valuable to the military that the Americans chose to overlook the fact that he had employed slave workers from concentration camps at his rocket-building facility. He and many of his team went on to enjoy long careers with the US Army and NASA.

In Japan, meanwhile, about 200,000 men who were deemed responsible for leading the war effort were removed by the Americans from their posts in government and business. The Japanese armed forces were completely

that the job of governing them would become impossible. But many leading figures in both regimes did face trial.

War crime tribunals

In Germany the tribunals of Nazi leaders at Nuremberg were not just a judicial undertaking. They were also a theatrical way of demonstrating to the German people the true nature of the regime they had lived under and enthusiastically supported. For many Germans, film evidence shown at the trials provided their first glimpse of

KEY MOMENT

THE PARTITION OF BERLIN

Berlin lay well inside the Soviet sector. But at Yalta Allied leaders had decided that the German capital, like Germany as a whole, should be divided into four administrative zones—Soviet, American, British, and French. This was meant to represent the collaborative efforts of the victorious powers in defeating Nazi Germany. In July 1945 the Russians allowed their three Western Allies to take possession of their portions of Berlin. But when relations between the USSR and the other Allies soured, the division of Berlin became a bone of contention—and later the very symbol of Cold War strife.

5,700 Japanese soldiers were indicted for war crimes.
475 were sentenced to death and executed.

the horror of the concentration camps. Twenty-four of Hitler's main henchmen were indicted at Nuremberg, and 12 were sentenced to death. Among them were Joachim von Ribbentrop, Hitler's foreign minister, and Hans Frank, governor-general of occupied Poland, who gloried in the sobriquet "slayer of Poles." Hermann Goering, the most senior of those convicted at Nuremberg, committed suicide on the eve of his planned execution. Japan also had its own Nuremberg—

AFTER ≫

The years of Allied occupation helped both Germany and Japan to rebuild their countries, and to create new and more democratic social institutions.

LIFE RESTORED
In the five years after the war, **life improved rapidly** for Germans in the western zones of occupation. **West Germany** (as it became) was **able to end food rationing before Britain**. The wreckage of the cities was cleared, mostly by female civilians who formed the majority of the manual labor force. By 1950 these "rubble women" (*Trümmerfrauen*) were thankfully extinct. In Japan women were the main beneficiaries of social reforms imposed by the Americans. For the first time, **Japanese women were granted legal equality with men** in matters of marriage, property, and inheritance.

ADOLF EICHMANN ON TRIAL IN ISRAEL, 1961

NAZIS PURSUED
The **prosecution of Nazi war criminals** did not end with Nuremberg. Well into the 1980s governments, and professional **Nazi-hunters** such as **Simon Wiesenthal**, continued to pry camp guards and SS killers out of their hiding places. The biggest catch was **Adolf Eichmann**, who oversaw **the extermination of 400,000 Hungarian Jews in 1944 ≪ 176–77**. In 1960 he was abducted from Argentina by Israeli agents, tried in Jerusalem, and sent to the gallows.

BEFORE

The question of the postwar division of Europe into spheres of influence was broached by Stalin and Churchill at a meeting between the two leaders in 1944.

DIVIDING UP THE BALKANS
At his **meeting with Stalin** in October 1944 **Churchill** scribbled the names of the **Balkan countries** on a scrap of paper together with some percentages: **Romania** should be 90 percent under Russian sway; **Greece**, conversely, was to be 90 percent Britain's; **Bulgaria**, 75 percent for Russia; **Yugoslavia** and **Hungary** 50:50. Stalin looked over Churchill's notes and marked the paper with a big check mark. Churchill thought better of it: "Might it not be thought rather cynical," he said, "if it seemed we had disposed of **these issues, so fateful to millions of people,** in such an offhand manner? Let us burn the paper." "No," Stalin replied. "You keep it." In the event, Churchill's scheme was not enacted. But a principle had been established:

111 MILLION
The total number of people in Eastern Europe who came under Communist rule by 1950 as a direct result of the war.

that all Europe was to be apportioned between the victors after the war. Stalin, of course, ultimately gained a much larger sphere of influence than Churchill had been prepared to concede in his impromptu calculations in 1944.

The Iron Curtain

The postwar political settlement created an ideological faultline across the center of Europe, and through the heart of Germany. To the east of this line, which came to be known as the "Iron Curtain," pro-Soviet Communist regimes were installed; to the west, broadly pro-American democracies prevailed.

The term "Iron Curtain" was coined by Winston Churchill in the week the war ended. He used it in a note sent to US president, Harry Truman, on May 12, 1945, in which he wrote of the Red Army that "an iron curtain is drawn down upon their front. We do not know what is going on behind."

Churchill's impression may have been accurate, but the joyful image of American troops greeting their Russian comrades-in-arms was still fresh in people's minds. Moreover, Truman still had the war with Japan to conclude: he was not ready to worry about Churchill's concerns over Europe. But the latter's pessimistic view of Stalin's intentions steadily hardened. The resonant phrase

he had used in his memo to Truman was still in his head when, in March 1946, he delivered a speech at Westminster College in Fulton, Missouri. In its most famous passage he said: "From Stettin in the Baltic to Trieste in the Adriatic, an iron curtain

The sealing of the border
In the 1950s there was one chink in the Iron Curtain between the Eastern Bloc and Western Europe; people were still allowed to pass between East and West Berlin. This ended in 1961 with the building of the Berlin Wall.

has descended across the Continent. Behind that line lie all the capitals of the ancient states of Central and Eastern Europe. Warsaw, Berlin, Prague, Vienna, Budapest, Belgrade, Bucharest, and Sofia, all these famous cities and the populations around them lie in what I must call the Soviet sphere, and all are subject in one form or another, not only to Soviet influence but to a very high and, in many cases, increasing measure of control from Moscow."

" … an **iron curtain** has descended across the Continent."

WINSTON CHURCHILL IN A SPEECH AT FULTON, MISSOURI, MARCH 1946

The Berlin airlift
West Berliners watch a plane flying in fuel and other essential supplies to their city. At the height of the airlift a supply plane was landing in Berlin every three minutes.

Moscow-backed governments soon gained control of almost all the nations of Central and Eastern Europe to which Churchill had alluded in his Fulton speech.

THE EASTERN BLOC
The European battle lines of the **Cold War 348–49 »** were well established by 1950. Stalinist Communist parties had seized power in Czechoslovakia, Poland, Hungary, Romania, and Bulgaria. In 1949 the Soviet sector of Germany also became a Communist state—the German Democratic Republic. Elsewhere, Yugoslavia remained Communist under Tito, but outside Moscow's sphere of influence, while Austria was spared the experience of Soviet socialism when the occupying powers withdrew in 1955.

Attempts were made to liberalize or even throw off the totalitarian yoke—notably in **Hungary in 1956** and **Czechoslovakia in**

THE FAILED HUNGARIAN REVOLUTION, 1956

1968—but such experiments were **violently suppressed by Soviet troops**. All of the Iron Curtain countries remained Soviet satellites until the collapse of the USSR and the dismantling of the Iron Curtain itself at the end of the 1980s.

KEY
- USSR
- Soviet dominated communist states by 1948
- Under Soviet occupation 1945–55
- Members of NATO in 1949
- Iron Curtain in 1948
- ⊗ Cities divided into zones of occupation

The division of postwar Europe
In 1949 many states to the west of the Iron Curtain joined the US to form NATO, a military alliance for their collective defense. The USSR and its satellites countered the NATO alliance in 1955 by forming the Warsaw Pact.

made territorial threats against Turkey and sponsored communist guerrillas in Greece, Truman adopted a much tougher stance. He announced that the US would act to support "free peoples who are resisting subjugation by armed minorities and outside pressures." He did not mention the Soviet Union by name, but it was clear that he was drawing a line in the sand, and that a year after Fulton he had come around to Churchill's view of Soviet expansion.

Berlin blockade
The first major test of the new "Truman Doctrine" came in 1948. In June the Allies introduced a reformed currency to the American, British, and French zones of occupation—and also to West Berlin, deep inside the Soviet sector. The Russians were outraged by what they saw as Western interference in Berlin where the Allies were, in their view, "merely guests." They responded by cutting off road and rail access from West Germany to West Berlin and by shutting down the city's electricity supply. Stalin had rung down the Iron Curtain with an ominous and resounding clang and West Berlin was, in effect, placed under siege.

It was now up to the Western powers to decide how to respond. One suggestion was to call Stalin's bluff by sending an armored column down the road from the Western sector to West

Berlin. This was rejected in favor of a less confrontational tactic: a humanitarian airlift. The British and Americans began to fly coal and other essential supplies into West Berlin. Stalin knew he could not shoot down American planes without risking all-out war, but reckoned that the Allies would not be able to supply Berlin in this way for long; sooner or later, they would have to relinquish the city to him. But he miscalculated: the airlift continued for 15 months. It might have gone on indefinitely, but in May 1949 Stalin backed down and lifted the blockade.

So the democratic powers had won their first serious confrontation with the USSR, and without a shot being fired. But in the meantime an icy chill had descended on East-West relations. The Iron Curtain was no longer just a physical frontier between states, it was now an ideological barrier between peoples, a dangerous and all but insuperable obstacle to lasting peace.

Once again, Churchill was correct in his analysis, but wrong in his timing. Most people in the United States and Europe were still hoping that the Allied victors could continue to cooperate in peace as they had done in war, and so build a better world order. Stalin was fondly referred to as "Uncle Joe" by many people in Britain, where he was seen as an object of affection and even admiration. President Truman, who had been on the podium in Fulton

when Churchill spoke, later said privately that the speech had caused him grave political embarrassment.

Accepting new realities
But Churchill was not alone in his gloomy prognosis. A week or two before his speech, a document known as the "Long Telegram" had begun to circulate in the US State Department. Written by a high-ranking official in the embassy in Moscow, it was an analysis of the USSR's attitude to the West. It described Soviet Communism as "a political force committed fanatically to the belief that with the US there can be no permanent modus vivendi, that it is desirable and necessary that … the international authority of our state be broken if Soviet power is to be secure."

The Long Telegram came to exert a profound influence on American foreign policy. In March 1947, as Stalin

105 The number of members of Britain's parliament who denounced the "iron curtain" speech as "inimical to the cause of world peace".

CHURCHILL'S "IRON CURTAIN" SPEECH, 1946

Many historians—Russian ones, in particular—see Churchill's famous "iron curtain" speech as the inaugural event of the Cold War. Stalin responded angrily to the speech, even comparing Churchill with the enemy they had just defeated: "Mr. Churchill and his friends bear a striking resemblance to Hitler and his friends. Mr. Churchill sets out to unleash war by proclaiming a race theory, that only nations speaking the English language are called upon to decide the destinies of the world."

Rebirth of Japan and West Germany

In the years after the war, a new Japan and a new Germany rose from the ashes of defeat. Japan became a constitutional monarchy; Germany—the western half, at least—became a model European democracy. With American help, both countries evolved into the most powerful economies in their respective regions.

All the Allies were in agreement that Germany should be made to compensate the countries against which it had waged war, and also that Germany should cover the costs of occupation. But there was little consensus as to how this should be achieved. At Yalta Stalin expressed his view that 20 billion dollars' worth of reparations should be extracted from Germany, and that half of this sum was due to the Soviet Union. Churchill was wary of such punitive reparations, and pointed out that just such a policy, imposed at the end of World War I, created the economic and political climate in which Hitler came to power.

Better marks
When the Deutschmark replaced the Reichsmark, West Germany was set on the path to economic recovery.

The Americans made the frugal suggestion that the German economy be put on its feet first, so that any reparations could come out of a balanced budget.

Stripping assets
In the event, each of the Allies implemented its reparations policy in its own way. The Russians were by far the harshest. Millions of tons of material and equipment were taken from Eastern Germany to the Soviet Union. The first wave of invading troops had freely looted the possessions of the German population: watches, jewelry, clothing, and suchlike. In their wake came battalions of the Red Army trained to seek out "trophies"—a term for artworks and museum exhibits, vehicles and machinery of all kinds, the contents of state archives, stockpiles of arms, raw materials, and food. Entire factories were swiftly and expertly dismantled and taken in pieces to Russia—just as in 1941, factories in Russia had been taken apart and moved east to Siberia to keep them out of German hands.

The Russians were not the only power engaged in asset-stripping. The French claimed for themselves the right to exploit the coal mines of the Saarland, in their zone of occupation, thereby strengthening the French economy at the expense of the German one. The British and Americans raised objections to the wholesale stripping of assets by the Russians, but they too were engaged in what they called the "demontage" of installations classified as "surplus," under a plan to reduce Germany's industrial output to a fraction of its levels before the outbreak of the war.

20 BILLION
The amount in US dollars decided on at the Potsdam Conference for Germany's war reparations, to be paid in machinery and plant to the Allies.

Breaking the war machines
In Japan General MacArthur was engaged in a very different form of deconstruction. Japan's war economy had been driven by the giant business conglomerates known as *zaibatsus*. The American instigated a program of "*zaibatsu*-busting," which involved forcing the holding companies to sell off their stocks to the general public, and breaking the *zaibatsus* down into their dozens or hundreds of constituent companies. Cartels and monopolies were outlawed, and trade unions encouraged.

All these measures—in both Germany and Japan—were carried out with the intention of making the defeated nations financially incapable of waging war. But by the end of 1947 it was becoming clear that the Allied policies were creating a politically dangerous

BEFORE

The occupying powers in Germany and Japan faced an economic conundrum, one that took several years of trial and error, and many disagreements, to resolve.

PROBLEMS OF RECONSTRUCTION
The Allies knew that the **shattered economies of the defeated nations had to be restored**, that the German and Japanese people had to be put back to work. But the occupying powers were eager to **prevent their former enemies from rebuilding industries** that might again serve as the engine of war. These problems were discussed at the Yalta Conference **« 295**, but no clear or unified policy was drawn up.

DIFFERENCES OF OPINION
In Japan, on matters of the reconstruction, there was **only one opinion that mattered: America's**—and, more specifically, General MacArthur's. However, in Germany each of the Allied powers took possession of its zone of the country with **different ideas about the nation's reconstruction**, and about how to best make Germany pay for its sins.

Honest toil
The rapid resurgence of Japan was due in part to the desire of people such as these silk workers to help rebuild the economy.

situation in both countries. In Germany the great mass of people was deeply impoverished, and the Americans were starting to be concerned that hunger and misery would make them receptive to Communist propaganda. The rising fear of Communism in the US also cast the *zaibatsu*-busting initiative in a different light: now it began to look like a distinctly un-American state-imposed socialism.

So there began a reversal in British and American policy toward their former enemies. In Japan the break-up of the *zaibatsu* giants was massively

AFTER »

Beginning in the 1960s, both Japan and West Germany went beyond the recovery of their economies and experienced a long-lasting economic boom.

JAPANESE ENTREPRENEURIALISM
In Japan this economic high-point was achieved partly by the **reconstitution of the zaibatsus** that the US had wanted to destroy. But American efforts at decentralization were not wasted: they created an economic space in which **small entrepreneurial concerns could flourish.** Among these were future household names, such as **Toyota, Honda, and Sony**.

SONY WALKMAN

GERMANY'S MIRACLE
The West German *Wirtschaftswunder* (economic miracle) of the 1960s was aided by the **destruction of wartime Germany's infrastructure**. Planners and administrators were handed a clean slate, a chance to build for a modern world, and they made the best possible use of the opportunity.

The people's car
The Volkswagen, originally designed as a cheap car for the model Nazi family, went back into production after the war. It came to be seen as a design classic and a triumph of German automotive engineering.

scaled down. In Germany, Britain and the US reduced the demontage program, and merged their two sectors into an economically unified "bizone." More than that, in 1948 the European Recovery Plan—better known as the Marshall Plan—was extended to the western zone of Germany. The US pumped about $3.5 billion into

Germany over the next few years, hoping to create a prosperous economy in which the people were well fed and gainfully employed, and therefore would be impervious to the attractions of Soviet socialism.

A crucial part of this plan was the reformation of the German currency: a new Deutschmark, minted in the US, replaced the almost worthless Reichsmark on June 20, 1948. On day one, everyone was allowed to exchange 40 old marks for 40 new ones (thereafter, the exchange rate was about 15 to one). On the same day, the

German authorities abolished price controls on manufactured goods and many foodstuffs. These measures were brutally deflationary—they wiped out any savings that private individuals had managed to scrape together—but they had the immediate effect of killing off

the black market, and liberating the official economy. More far-reachingly, they laid the foundations for a genuine, self-sustaining economic recovery.

Japan embraces democracy
Japan was rapidly changing too. MacArthur had said that he wanted Japan to become "the Switzerland of Asia," and the dreadful lessons of Hiroshima and Nagasaki perhaps speeded the adoption of a pacifistic world view. But the change in outlook went deeper than that—it amounted to a transformation of the national psyche. Japanese people embraced "democratization" with a growing enthusiasm that sometimes astonished their American overlords. There was also a widespread frenzy of national introspection and open-hearted discussion, the like of which was not to be seen again until the glasnost years in the Soviet Union. The US had expected to remain in Japan for decades—or maybe even as long as a century—but in accordance with the 1951 Treaty of San Francisco, the US withdrew from the country in 1952, and Japan regained its sovereignty.

> **"The Japanese people**, since the war, have undergone the **greatest reformation** in modern history"
>
> GENERAL DOUGLAS MACARTHUR'S FAREWELL ADDRESS TO CONGRESS, APRIL 19, 1951

◀◀ BEFORE

The final demise of Europe's vast overseas empires had its beginnings in the disastrous opening years of World War II.

VIETNAMESE REVOLUTIONARY HO CHI MINH

LOST PRESTIGE

In 1940 the **colonial peoples of the world were astonished by the rapid capitulation** of France ❮❮ **82–83**, and the undignified retreat of Britain ❮❮ **78–79**. Two years later the people of Malaya, Indochina, and Indonesia found that their **European overlords were powerless to halt the Japanese invasion** ❮❮ **158–59**.

FREEDOM FIGHTERS

It fell to **local guerrilla groups**—usually headed by Nationalists or Communists—to **resist the Japanese invasion forces** in Southeast Asia. Having fought to free their own countries, they were not about to **hand the land or the power back** to their former colonial masters.

INDIAN LEADER (1869–1948)
MAHATMA GANDHI

Gandhi earned the veneration of his people through his struggle for Indian independence and his commitment to non-violence. At the outbreak of World War II, Gandhi insisted that only a free India could support Britain effectively. Since no concession was immediately forthcoming, he led campaigns to obstruct the British war effort and was imprisoned for it. After the war, he hailed the decision to grant independence as "the noblest act of the British nation." He was assassinated by a Hindu fanatic a few months after his nation's liberation.

The **End** of Empires

One effect of the war was to weaken the hold of European nations on their colonies. In Asia and Africa liberation movements began to demand statehood and independence. Once the war was over, these demands became impossible to ignore and, surprisingly swiftly, the old imperial order crumbled away.

The slow dismantling of the European empires began long before World War II. Ever since the loss of its American colonies, British governments had inclined to the view that overseas possessions tend to go their own way once they reach political maturity. For the "white" dominions—Canada, Australia, New Zealand, and South Africa—that time had come after World War I. By 1939 they were to all intents and purposes entirely independent nations.

The British Empire struggles

But the volatile and destructive situation brought about by the war made global geopolitical change more likely and more rapid. In 1941 Roosevelt and Churchill signed the Atlantic Charter, which affirmed "the right of all peoples to choose the form of government under which they will live," and it had demanded that "sovereign rights be restored to those who have been forcibly deprived of them." That statement gave hope to Nationalists throughout the world, and Churchill quickly moved to quash those aspirations. "What we have, we keep," he said.

Yet by the end of the war it was clear that Britain was too exhausted, and its armed forces too thinly spread, to control or suppress national movements in its colonies. Moreover, the US— indisputably the most powerful nation in the world—was deeply attached to the idea that people had the right to choose their own government.

> **"I did not become His Majesty's prime minister in order to preside over the liquidation of the British Empire"**
>
> SPEECH BY WINSTON CHURCHILL, NOVEMBER 1942

Border crossing
Millions of desperate refugees crossed from Pakistan to Hindu India, and from India to Muslim Pakistan, after partition of the subcontinent in 1947. This mass two-way migration was the largest population transfer in history.

agree that the subcontinent would attain its freedom as two states: Muslim Pakistan and Hindu India. The hurriedly drawn borders meant that many found themselves in the wrong country. Millions fled across the new frontiers, harried along by people who had only recently been peaceable neighbors.

> In 1945 the British Commonwealth and Empire covered about 20 percent of the land surface of the globe, and embraced about a quarter of the world's population.

The creation of Israel
Violence attended the birth of another new nation the following year. The enormity of the Holocaust convinced the United Nations to grant a national home to the Jewish people within the British-administered "Palestinian Mandate." Jews had been emigrating there for decades—and more than 100,000 were smuggled in illegally during the war. Israel came into being in May 1948, but the Arab peoples of the region would not countenance a Jewish state in their midst. A coalition of Arab states attacked Israel as soon as its independence was declared. The war lasted into 1949, and ended in total victory for Israel. Bitterness did not end with the ceasefire: wars and constant strife between Jews and Arabs became the norm in the Middle East.

From colonialism to Communism
In other parts of the world, the struggle for self-determination turned into open war. Indonesia declared independence as soon as the war ended, but became engaged in a sporadic four-year conflict with Dutch forces. A similar scenario came to pass in Indochina, where

> In the 1960s the main center of European decolonization moved from Asia to Africa.

WINDS OF CHANGE
Algeria, France's main possession in North Africa, underwent a period of violent turmoil on its path to independence. But Britain's African empire was **dismantled remarkably quickly and peacefully**. The process began with the independence of Ghana (formerly the Gold Coast) in 1957, and can be said to have ended with Swaziland in 1968 (Rhodesia, a special case, took a little longer to achieve home rule). In Africa and elsewhere, **most of the nations that had once been ruled from London now joined the loose-knit Commonwealth**; the qualified term "British Commonwealth" was quietly dropped in the late 1940s.

FALL OF THE BERLIN WALL, NOVEMBER 1989

DISMANTLING THE USSR
The collapse of the Soviet Union in the late 1980s can be seen as the **final episode in the trend for decolonization**. All the nations of Eastern Europe perceived the end of Russian influence as a liberation. So did the "Soviet Socialist Republics" that became sovereign and independent states. At the end of the 20th century **the very idea of empire seemed to be dead and buried**.

Imperial France
"The Empire needs Indochina," proclaimed this French poster; but Indochina did not feel a need for France, and independence movements flourished after the war.

Roosevelt and, later, Truman were not willing to deny to smaller countries the prize that their own nation had won in 1776.

Partition of India
Political leaders in India had been outraged when the British viceroy declared war on Germany without consulting them. While the war was raging in Europe, they made a bargain with the desperate British government: Britain could freely make use of India's raw materials and fighting men, so long as self-rule was conceded after the war.

Independence was duly granted in 1947, but it came at a terrible price. Violence between the Muslim and Hindu communities led all sides to

Rearguard action
In 1954 French paratroopers were besieged by the revolutionary Communist and Nationalist forces of the Viet Minh at Dien Bien Phu. The Vietnamese defeated the colonial army, leading France to withdraw from the region altogether, and Vietnam gained its independence.

Communism takes its place," complained one US senator. Many of the nations that emerged from the rubble of the European empires looked to the Soviet Union for material help

"Our victory must bring with it the liberation of all peoples"

SUMNER WELLES, US UNDER-SECRETARY OF STATE, MAY 30, 1942

France became embroiled in a war against the Viet Minh, a coalition of Communist and Nationalist forces under Ho Chi Minh. The war ended in 1954 with a French withdrawal from the region, and with the division of Vietnam into two states: Communist North Vietnam, and an anti-Communist Republic of South Vietnam.

Situations like the one that developed in Vietnam presented a problem for the US. "When colonialism is ousted,

and political guidance. For their part, the US and the Soviet Union sought influence wherever they could, and in this way the process of decolonization became part of the Cold War. Some post-colonial nations managed to remain "non-aligned," but most gravitated toward one camp or the other. To some it looked like the old imperial powers had been replaced by two new ones—the American Empire and the Soviet Empire.

« **BEFORE**

The Nationalist government of China, under the leadership of Chiang Kai-shek, was at war with Mao's Communists for 10 years before war broke out with Japan in 1937.

A DISUNITED FRONT

When Japan attacked, Chiang Kai-shek was persuaded to join forces with Mao so that China would be in a stronger position to resist the invasion. But **the truce between Nationalists and Communists was fragile**, and often degenerated into armed conflict. Throughout the war years, both sides expended almost as much effort on trying to outmaneuver each other as they did on fighting against the Japanese.

THE COMMON ENEMY DEFEATED

The surrender of Japanese troops in China came abruptly, thanks to the US **A-bomb strikes against the cities of Hiroshima and Nagasaki** « **320**, and it took the two competing factions in China by surprise. Almost at once, the old quarrels between Nationalists and Communists, never wholly laid aside in the fight against a common enemy, were rekindled. **China had no time to celebrate** its part in the general victory; the country was already spiraling into a new war—this time with itself.

COMMUNIST LEADER (1893–1976)

MAO ZEDONG

Mao joined the Chinese Communist Party in 1921, the year it was founded. He was at first an orthodox Marxist-Leninist, but in the mid-1920s he began to formulate the un-Marxist idea that the peasant masses—rather than the urban proletariat—might form the vanguard of a socialist revolution. This adaptation of Marxist thinking to Chinese conditions was the core idea of Maoism. But it was no mere theory: through the years of struggle against the Nationalists and the Japanese, the rural population of China provided shelter and manpower to the Communist armies. It was the peasants who bore the brunt of China's wars, and they who carried Mao to power.

Red triumph

Communist fighters take Nationalist soldiers prisoner in July 1947. Many captured Nationalists joined the ranks of the People's Liberation Army (PLA), which helped Mao to victory in 1949.

Red China

The end of World War II did not spell peace for the Chinese people. Civil strife between Nationalist and Communist armies followed on seamlessly from the surrender of Japan. This internal conflict lasted five years, and led to the establishment of a new Communist state: the People's Republic of China.

China in August 1945 was a strangely divided country. The Kuomintang—the Nationalist government of Chiang Kai-shek—controlled all the southern parts of China, and most of the cities in the country. Communist guerrillas under Mao's leadership held large areas of the countryside in the northern provinces of Shanxi and Shandong. In garrisons throughout the country, Japanese troops waited for someone

in the north, and the Nationalists, in the south, were armed and poised for war. But a war in China was against the interests of the US president, Truman, who wanted a strong, united China that would act as a kind of policeman in the east Asian region. It was also important for the president that China should be pro-American, so the US government was supportive of Chiang Kai-shek. Truman tried to mediate between the two sides—while the US was supplying

The Nationalists had every reason to expect a swift victory. They enjoyed the recognition of all the major powers, including the Soviet Union, and they were still receiving aid from the US. They had the larger army, and a monopoly on air power and heavy

Springtime for Mao
After years of war, the People's Republic looked like a fresh beginning. "The flowers are opening and blooming at the new China," declared this 1949 poster.

> ## 5 BILLION The number of copies
> of Mao's *Red Book*, containing 427 of his quotations, which were published in China between 1964 and 1976.

artillery. However, the Communists were better organized and more committed to their cause. They soon reversed the early gains that had been made by the Nationalist forces and in doing so, the momentum of Mao's People's Liberation Army (PLA) became unstoppable: Beijing was won in January 1949, Nanking in April, and Shanghai the following May. The Nationalist armies were now in full retreat, and in the autumn they abandoned the mainland, retreating to Formosa (present-day Taiwan), taking the country's gold reserves with them.

In Beijing, on October 1, 1949, Mao proclaimed the establishment of the People's Republic of China, with him at its head.

> ## "An army that is **cherished** … by the people, and vice versa, is a nearly **invincible force**."
>
> A QUOTE FROM MAO'S "RED BOOK", FIRST PUBLISHED IN 1964

to come and take their surrender. At the beginning of August the Soviet Union had declared war against Japan, and Russian troops advanced across the border into the key industrial region of Manchuria, which had been under Japanese occupation since 1931. Here, under the disinterested gaze of the Japanese garrison, the Russians began to dismantle the modern factories and ship them back home.

No compromise

It was the Manchurian question that ignited the Chinese civil war. The region's industrial resources and reserves of raw materials were vital assets: no postwar reconstruction or modernization of China was possible without them. Communist forces moved quickly into Manchuria from their rural strongholds and then barred the routes into the region by destroying the railroads and blockading the ports. While the Nationalists were kept out, the Russians, who were already there, allowed vast stockpiles of Japanese weapons and material to fall into the hands of their fellow Communists.

So in 1945 the political situation throughout China was changing rapidly. By the end of the year the Communists, who were entrenched

Chiang with money and arms—by sending General George Marshall to China to try to convince the two sides to form a coalition government.

The people's war

Marshall spent over a year in China, but as no agreement could be reached the envoy eventually lost patience with the situation and left in January 1947. Civil war ensued.

Fast-track socialism

The Communists routinely sabotaged railroad lines during the Chinese civil war. Afterward, the same armies worked hard to repair the tracks, and so bind the country together.

AFTER »

The triumph of China's Communists over the Chiang Kai-shek's Nationalists came as a shock to the rest of the world.

THE ROAD TO KOREA

The US had grown used to having a pro-American government in the heart of Asia, so the "loss of China" was a bitter blow. **Marxist**

US TROOPS DISEMBARK IN KOREA

regimes were now in control of most of the Eurasian continent. The **US government refused to recognize the People's Republic**. The dubious Nationalist regime in Taiwan was treated as the legitimate government of China, and Chiang Kai-shek as its leader in exile. This stance was deeply offensive to Mao, and it shaped China's foreign policy for years to come. The new Chinese regime lived in constant **expectation of a US-backed re-invasion** of the mainland. In 1950, as the Korean war got under way, American generals flew to Taiwan to discuss just this possibility. **Mao responded by sending the PLA into North Korea**.

« BEFORE

The outcome of the war profoundly altered the geopolitical shape of the world, with the fall of established empires and the rise of two new global superpowers.

BEGINNING THE NUCLEAR AGE

The bombings of **Hiroshima and Nagasaki** **« 320–21** heralded the arrival of a weapon with unsurpassed destructive capabilities. Proliferation of such weapons created the terrifying possibilty that the next world war could destroy all humanity.

THE BOMBING OF NAGASAKI

TWO-POWER POLITICS

The US emerged from the war economically vibrant and **full of confidence**. The Soviet Union, for all its losses, had made **massive territorial gains** that extended its influence to the very heart of Europe **« 320–21**. Both countries had gained huge prestige around the world, and both wanted to use their eminence to **propagate their national world views**.

The Cold War

Relations between the US and the Soviet Union deteriorated rapidly after the war, and there were times when open conflict loomed. But instead the war turned "cold"—that is, it was waged by the bloodless means of subversion, diplomatic wrangling, arms stockpiling, propaganda, and espionage.

In the hopeful spring of 1945, many war-weary people around the world expected the collaboration between the victorious powers to be carried forward into an era of peace. A new worldwide organization—the United Nations—was inaugurated for that very purpose almost before the echoes of the guns had died away. The charter that the Soviet Union, the US, and other nations signed in June 1945 stated in its very first line that its purpose was "to maintain international peace and security, to take effective collective measures for the prevention and removal of threats to the peace, and for the suppression of acts of aggression …"

But the new and peaceful dawn did not materialize in the way that had been hoped. The old enmity between the Western powers and the Bolshevik state, which had been a feature of international politics since the Russian Revolution of 1917, swiftly reasserted itself once the common enemy had been crushed. Churchill was so alarmed by the huge numbers of Russian troops in the Soviet sector that in the first days of peace he even considered a plan—codenamed "Unthinkable"— to launch a preemptive strike against Russian forces in Europe. The chiefs-of-staff dismissed the idea as absurd.

Russian protectionism

The Russians, for their part, held the view that they had a perfect moral and political right to be in Eastern Europe, and that they had earned that right with the blood of millions of their own citizens. Twice in a generation, German invaders had come from the west. Russia wanted to have control of that dangerous corridor, to create a buffer zone between its own borders and any threat—German, or indeed American— that came from that direction. The Soviet occupation of Eastern Europe was not so much to do with spreading

Russian and US nuclear weapons

Nuclear weapons are now tens of times more powerful than those dropped on Japan. Although the US and Russia signed a non-proliferation pact in 1968, it has taken some time for the number of nuclear warheads to decrease.

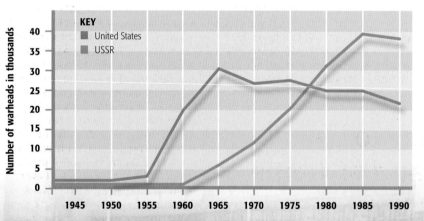

KEY
■ United States
■ USSR

Number of warheads in thousands

40 — 35 — 30 — 25 — 20 — 15 — 10 — 5 — 0

1945 1950 1955 1960 1965 1970 1975 1980 1985 1990

Weapons on show
During the Cold War, each anniversary of the October Revolution was marked by a military parade on Moscow's Red Square, displaying Soviet might to the world.

The Cold War had its seasons. Periodically there would be a thaw in relations, usually following a particularly chilly spell.

THE CUBAN MISSILE CRISIS

In 1962 the USSR secretly began to deploy nuclear warheads on Cuba, the new Communist state under Fidel Castro. The US intelligence services became aware of this and **President Kennedy** demanded that the nuclear warheads be removed. **Soviet premier, Nikita Khrushchev,** refused—and for a few days the threat of nuclear confrontation was real and imminent. But as in Berlin in 1948, **the Soviets backed down**. In

NIKITA KHRUSHCHEV SPEAKING AT THE UN

the 45 years between Hiroshima and the collapse of the USSR, this was the only occasion when nuclear weapons came close to being used.

END OF THE COLD WAR

The resolution of the Cuban missile crisis led to a period of warmer relations between East and West. But the political atmosphere froze again in the 1980s during President **Reagan's term**, when the US initiated the **Strategic Defense Initiative**, a plan to deploy satellites that could knock Soviet missiles out of the sky. The Soviet Union expressed amazement at America's readiness to begin the militarization of space, but the real problem was that **the USSR could no longer compete** technologically. It had already lost the arms race by the time the **Soviet Union fell apart in 1991**. With that cataclysmic event, the Cold War effectively came to an end.

Communism (as most Westerners believed throughout the Cold War) as with protecting Mother Russia.

So from a Russian viewpoint, it was iniquitous of the West to see their presence in Europe as a threat. As Stalin asked in 1946: "How can anyone who has not taken leave of his senses describe these peaceful aspirations of the Soviet Union as expansionist tendencies?" In practice, Stalin's peaceful aspirations meant imposing Stalinist dictatorships on all the countries of Eastern Europe.

Potential enemies such as anti-communists, priests, and intellectuals were ruthlessly purged, as they had been in Russia in the 1920s and 30s.

The nuclear arms race

In the course of the late 1940s and early 1950s, the confrontation between the US and Russia settled into a kind of stalemate—not so much a peace as an uneasy armed truce. The US and the nations of Western Europe formed a military alliance—the North Atlantic Treaty Organization—and the Soviet

Ready to respond

The B-52 Stratofortress was the archetypal Cold War aircraft. It was capable of carrying nuclear bombs, and in times of tension it patrolled close to Soviet airspace.

Union responded with the Warsaw Treaty (the "Warsaw Pact"), which melded the armed forces of the socialist bloc into a mutually supportive armed force. As the 1940s gave way to the 1950s, two vast international armies amassed on either side of the border between East and West Germany. Together they represented the largest concentration of troops in the world.

The Soviet Army was by far the larger of the two armies, but in the early days the US had the trump card of nuclear weapons. During the stand-off over Berlin in 1948, bombers capable of delivering nuclear weapons were moved from the US to bases in Britain, where they were within striking distance of Russian cities. In 1949 the USSR acquired its own bomb, and thereafter the two superpowers vied to outdo each other in the quantity and technical quality of their nuclear arsenals, and so gain the tactical advantage.

> # "Our enemies are to be found abroad and at home."
>
> BERNARD BARUCH, US FINANCIER AND POLITICAL ADVISER, APRIL 16, 1947

KEY MOMENT

THE RUSSIAN BOMB

For four years after the war, the US was the world's only nuclear power. However, during that time the Soviet Union made an immense effort to manufacture its own atomic bomb, and thereby put itself back on an equal tactical footing with the US. The first Soviet bomb, designated RDS-1, was made with uranium expropriated from the Nazi nuclear weapons program during the invasion of Germany in 1945. Its design relied a great deal on stolen plans that were obtained by Soviet agents in the US. The bomb was detonated in Kazakhstan on August 29, 1949; that great explosion was the starting pistol of the nuclear arms race.

NEW YORK HEADLINES REPORT THE SOVIET UNION'S FIRST TEST NUCLEAR EXPLOSION

The Holocaust remembered
Peter Eisenman's memorial aims to show that the ordered Nazi system grew out of control and lost touch with human reason.

<<
BEFORE

After the conclusion of World War I, the poppy became a symbol of remembrance for the war dead.

IN FLANDERS FIELDS
The idea of the poppy came from a **poem written by a Canadian officer** named John McCrae. From 1921, paper poppies were worn in the days leading up to November 11, the anniversary of the armistice at the end of the Great War. A tradition was born. After 1945, this annual act of commemoration was extended to remember the dead of the more recent war.

REMEMBRANCE POPPIES

The War Remembered

The years since the war have given rise to many monuments and statues, memoirs and novels, ceremonies and rituals, movies and documentaries. All such memorials are attempts to make sense of the cataclysm, to assign the war to its proper place in the story of the nations that took part.

Over the years, the events of the war were absorbed into the consciousness of the nations that took part, and in the process they were slowly transmuted into myth. That is not to say that the versions that people knew and believed were historically inaccurate; rather, the stories said something significant about how the nation saw itself. Dunkirk—a crushing defeat by any military measure—was seen as a lesson about how the British people could win out in the direst of situations by pulling together. The Battle of Britain became the story of "The Few," the small band of fighter pilots who took on the might of the Luftwaffe and won. This was a modern version of the ancient tale of the 300 Spartans who held back the Persian thousands at Thermopylae.

The propaganda of war
In Britain and the United States, action movies were the main channel through which the postwar generation formed its idea of what the war had meant. Dozens of war films had been made for propaganda purposes during the fighting; the hundreds more that were made for entertainment in the 1950s and 60s generally followed a similar patriotic line. Among them were blockbusters such as *The Great Escape*,

> "The morrow of **such a victory** is **a splendid moment** … in our great history."
>
> WINSTON CHURCHILL ADDRESSING PARLIAMENT, AUGUST 1945

The Guns of Navarone, The Longest Day, The Diry Dozen, and *Where Eagles Dare*—all of them parables with a simple moral: the Allied cause was just, and good ultimately triumphed over evil through both heroism and ingenuity.

In the Soviet Union, the war was viewed differently, and more somberly, as a colossal national sacrifice. It was taken as read that the Russian people had saved civilization by bearing the brunt of the Nazi attack. The official history of the war was propagated in school textbooks, on television, and through the lavish museums and war memorials in every major city. It emphasized the leading role of the socialist state in the war effort, and the primacy of the Communist Party in particular. Thus, the victory was presented as a validation of the Bolshevik regime that came to power in 1917. This interpretation of the meaning of the war contained the key implication, never openly stated, that the triumph over Nazism in the 1940s justified the untold terrors and torments that Stalin inflicted on the Soviet people in the 1930s.

In Germany a veil of shamed silence was at first drawn over the war. West Germany and Austria outlawed the display of Nazi imagery such as the swastika, and in the Federal Republic and Austria a special exception was made to the right of free speech in order to make it a crime to deny the Holocaust. The war was discussed in print, but usually in terms of bitterness and anguish. After the last of the German prisoners of war returned from the Soviet Union in the mid-1950s there was a flurry of German accounts of the Eastern Front, most of which went out of their way to stress the horror rather than the glory of the war. By the 1980s, it was possible for German storytellers to portray German fighting men sympathetically as the unwilling or at least conflicted participants in Hitler's scheme. The film *Das Boot*, which was a fictional account of a U-boat crew on patrol, was a kind of

Motherland calling
This stone statue commemorates those Russians who died at Stalingrad. It was erected on the summit of Mamayev Kurgan.

landmark in this respect. In 2004 Hitler himself was portrayed, if not with sympathy then at least as a human being rather than as a monster, in the acclaimed documentary drama *Der Untergang* (*Downfall*).

Graves of the dead

More permanent and poignant than all the books and films about the war are monuments raised to the dead in the places where they are buried. War cemeteries are to be found in almost every corner of the globe. Some of them take the form of a few gravestones in a corner of a churchyard; others comprise vast memorial complexes where hundreds lie together in mass graves. Many military cemeteries are located on the very battlefields where the soldiers actually fell, and this makes them particularly affecting. No one can fail to be moved by the serried

The war in Hollywood
The war films made by the Allies have always reveled in sacrifice and heroism; while the German war film is generally more apologetic, its heroes conflicted.

559 The number of cemeteries that have been created by the Commonwealth War Graves Commission to commemorate those who lost their lives fighting in World War II.

ranks of stone crosses on the bluff above Omaha Beach in Normandy, or by the windy peak of Mamayev Kurgan, which was the crucible of the battle for Stalingrad.

Nor could anyone emerge quite the same person from an afternoon in a place such as Dachau concentration camp in Germany. On the way visitors pass by a blank grey wall where an inscription written in Hebrew, French, English, German and Russian says: "Never Again."

More than 60 years have passed since the end of the Second World War. But we still live in its long shadow.

OLD SOLDIERS
The number of people in the world who can say that they bore arms in World War II is dwindling to zero. All over the world, veterans' associations are winding down because their members are too few or too frail. Within a generation there will be **no one left who has even childhood recollections** of such things as air raids, mass evacuation, the sight of the uniformed men passing through the streets … World War II is moving **beyond the horizon of living memory**, and into the realm of recorded history.

LOOKING BACK
But even when there is no one left who can remember the events of 1939 to 1945, the war will still loom large. Individuals and nations will continue to **mark the anniversaries** of battles and victories, because they feel that the rituals of remembrance are a debt owed to the wartime generation. And that is as it should be. "The tumult and the shouting dies, the captains and the kings depart," wrote Kipling prophetically in 1897. "Lord God of Hosts, be with us yet, lest we forget, lest we forget."

RUSSIAN WORLD WAR II VETERANS

A foreign field
Wherever they are in the world, war cemeteries have a sanctity and a significance all of their own. "When you go home," reads the memorial at one site. "Tell them of us and say, For your tomorrow, we gave our today."

Index

Page numbers in **bold** indicate main entries.

Acknowledgments

The publisher would like to thank the following for their kind permission to reproduce their photographs:

Key
a-above; b-below/bottom; c-center; f-far; l-left; r-right; t-top
IWM – Imperial War Museum
LMA – Lebrecht Music and Arts
MEPL – Mary Evans Picture Library
US NARA – US National Archives and Records Administration

2-3 LMA: Rue des Archives/Tal. **4 DK Images:** Jamie Marshall (tc). **Getty Images:** Heinrich Hoffmann/Time & Life Pictures (br). **5 Library Of Congress, Washington, D.C.:** (cl). **Shutterstock:** Stephen Mulcahey (tr). **6 Conseil Régional de Basse-Normandie / National Archives USA:** (tl) (tc). **Corbis: Bettmann (bl). Dreamstime.com:** J Klune (cr). **US Department of Defense:** Department of the Army. Office of the Deputy Chief of Staff for Operations. (br). **7 Corbis:** Hulton-Deutsch Collection (br). **iStockphoto.com:** ilbusca (c). **Shutterstock:** krechet (tr). **US NARA:** US Government (bl). **8-9 Getty Images:** Time & Life Pictures/US Coast Guard. **10-11 Getty Images:** Photographers Choice/Kevin Summers. **12 akg-images:** (bc). **The Art Archive:** Marc Charmet (tr). **Corbis:** Bettmann (tc). **Getty Images:** Hulton Archive (br); Popperfoto (bl). **LMA:** Rue des Archives/Tal (tl); Private Collection/Roger-Viollet, Paris (c). **13 The Bridgeman Art Library:** Private Collection (bl). **Corbis:** Bettmann (bc). **Getty Images:** Keystone (tl). **LMA :** Rue des Archives/Tal (cl). **MEPL:** (tr). **14 akg-images:** (tr). **Getty Images:** Roger Viollet Collection (bl); Three Lions (br). **LMA:** Rue des Archives/ Tal (tl). **MEPL:** (bc). **15 The Art Archive:** John Meek (c). **Getty Images:** Fox Photos (br); Hugo Jaeger/Timepix/Time & Life Pictures (bc). **IWM:** (bl). **LMA:** Interfoto/Hermann Historica Gmbh (tl). **TopFoto.co.uk:** Ullstein Bild (tr) (cl). **16 The Art Archive:** Marc Charmet (bl). **DK Images:** Collection of Jean-Pierre Verney (cl). **16-17 LMA:** Rue des Archives/ Tal (t). **17 Getty Images:** Roger Viollet Collection (br). **18 Getty Images:** General Photographic Agency. **19 The Bridgeman Art Library:** Private Collection/Roger-Viollet, Paris (tl). **Corbis:** Bettmann (tr). **Getty Images:** Hulton Archive (bc). **MEPL:** (cr). **www.historicalimagebank.com:** Don Troiani (cl). **20 akg-images:** (bl). **Getty Images:** Keystone (br). **Photolibrary:** De Agostini Picture Library (tr). **www.historicalimagebank.com:** Don Troiani (c). **21 Getty Images:** Three Lions (b). **LMA:** Interfoto/Hermann Historica Gmbh (t). **22 Alamy Images:** MEPL (cr); The London Art Archive/Visual Arts Library (l). **23 akg-images:** (ca) (bc) (cr). **Getty Images:** Keystone (tr). **24 The Art Archive:** John Meek (tr). **TopFoto.co.uk:** Ullstein Bild (b). **25 Corbis:** Bettmann (bc). **Getty Images:** Keystone (tr). **26 www.historicalimagebank.com:** Don Troiani (tr). **26-27 Getty Images:** Hugo Jaeger/Timepix/Time & Life Pictures (bc). **27 Corbis:** Bettmann (br). **28-29 Corbis:** Bettmann. **30 The Art Archive:** British Library (br). **Getty Images:** Topical Press Agency (t). **31 The Bridgeman Art Library:** Private Collection (bc). **Cody Images:** (tr). **32 Corbis:** Bettmann (bc). **32-33 LMA:** Rue des Archives/FIA (t). **33 Getty Images:** Popperfoto (br); Time & Life Pictures/Time Magazine (tr). **IWM:** (c). **34 akg-images:** (tr). **Getty Images:** Hulton Archive (bc). **35 Getty Images:** Popperfoto. **36 Corbis:** David J. & Janice L. Frent Collection (bc). **Getty Images:** Popperfoto (cl) (t). **37 Corbis:** Bettmann (br). **Library Of Congress, Washington, D.C.:** Albert M Bender (tc). **38 Corbis:** Bettmann (bl). **Getty Images:** General Photographic Agency (tl); Popperfoto (r). **39 AISA - Archivo Iconográfico S. A., Barcelona:** Library of Montserrat Abbey (tr). **akg-images:** Private Collection (bc). **LMA:** Interfoto/Hermann Historica Gmbh (tl). **40 MEPL:** (bc). **41 Corbis:** Bettmann (b). **TopFoto.co.uk:** Ullstein Bild (tc). **42 akg-images:** (bc). **Corbis:** Bettmann (tr). **43 akg-images:** Private Collection (bl). **Corbis:** Hulton-Deutsch Collection (br). **Getty Images:** Fox Photos (tc). **IWM:** (tr). **46 Corbis:** Hulton-Deutsch Collection (tr) (clb). **Getty Images:** Popperfoto (cb). **MEPL:** (tl). **TopFoto.co.uk:** Ullstein Bild (tc). **47 The Art Archive:** Dagli Orti (A) (c). **Corbis:** Bettmann (cb); Hulton-Deutsch Collection (tl). **Getty Images:** March Of Time/Time & Life Pictures (tr). **48 akg-images:** (bl) (br). **Corbis:** Bettmann (tc); Hulton-Deutsch Collection (tr). **Getty Images:** Keystone (bc). **TopFoto.co.uk:** Jewish Chronicle Archive/HIP (tl). **49 Corbis:** Bettmann/ Underwood & Underwood (tr); Hulton-Deutsch Collection (tl). **DK Images:** Eden Camp Museum, Yorkshire (cl); Ministry Of Defence, Pattern Room, Nottingham (br). **LMA :** Interfoto (cb). **TopFoto.co.uk:** Ullstein Bild (bl). **50 TopFoto.co.uk:** From the Jewish Chronicle Archive/HIP (cra). **50-51 Corbis:** Bettmann. **51 MEPL:** (cra). **52 DK Images:** IWM, Duxford (c); Royal Artillery Historical Trust (cb). **52-53 DK Images:** IWM, London (c). **54 Corbis:** Hulton-Deutsch Collection (r). **TopFoto.co.uk:** Ullstein Bild (cla). **55 The Bridgeman Art Library:** Private Collection/Peter Newark Military Pictures (br). **Corbis:** Hulton-Deutsch Collection (tr). **TopFoto.co.uk:** Ullstein Bild (bl). **56 akg-images:** (l). **Corbis:** Marcus Fþhrer/dpa (cr). **57 Getty Images:** Hulton Archive (tr); Keystone (tl). **MEPL:** (cb); Rue des Archives/Tallandier (bc). **58 Corbis:** Bettmann (cra). **LMA :** Interfoto (bl). **59 akg-images:** (bl). **The Art Archive:** Private Collection/Marc Charmet (tl). **60 Corbis:** Hulton-Deutsch Collection (ca). **IWM:** (bl). **60-61 DK Images:** Eden Camp Museum, Yorkshire. **61 Getty Images:** Hulton Archive (ca) (br). **62 akg-images:** RIA Novosti (br). **TopFoto.co.uk:** Ullstein Bild (bl). **63 Corbis:** Underwood & Underwood. **Getty Images:** Keystone (cra). **64 TopFoto.co.uk:** (t); AP (br). **65 DK Images:** Ministry of Defence Pattern Room, Nottingham (bl). **Getty Images:** Fox Photos (tc). **IWM:** (cra). **66 Corbis:** Bettmann (r); Hulton-Deutsch Collection (bl). **67 akg-images:** (tc). **Corbis:** Hulton-Deutsch Collection (bc). **DK Images:** IWM, London (c). **Getty Images:** Keystone (tr). **70 akg-images:** (tc). **Corbis:** Bettmann (tl) (br). **Getty Images:** Hulton Archive (tr); Popperfoto/Bob Thomas (bc). **LMA :** Rue des Archives/Tal (bl). **71 Corbis:** Bettmann (tl) (bc). **Getty Images:** Fox Photos (cra); Keystone (bl). **72 Corbis:** Bettmann (tr). **Getty Images:** Keystone/Horace Abrahams (bc); New York Times Co. (cr). **MEPL:** (tc). **TopFoto.co.uk:** (bl). **73 The Bridgeman Art Library:** Private Collection/Peter Newark Historical Pictures (tc). **Corbis:** Skyscan (tl). **Getty Images:** Keystone (cr) (br). **IWM:** (bl). **Mirrorpix:** (c). **74 Getty Images:** Hulton Archive (cra). **74-75 MEPL. 74-99 Library Of Congress, Washington, D.C.:** (t). **75 Getty Images:** Popperfoto (cb). **TopFoto.co.uk:** Ullstein Bild (crb). **76 Corbis:** Bettmann. **77 akg-images:** (ca). **LMA :** RA (cr). **TopFoto.co.uk:** Ullstein Bild (br). **78-79 Corbis:** Hulton-Deutsch Collection. **79 akg-images:** (cra). **80-81 LMA :** Rue des Archives. **82 Corbis:** Michael Nicholson (cr). **US NARA:** (b). **83 akg-images:** (tc). **DK Images:** IWM, London (cl) (cr). **LMA :** RA (b). **84 IWM:** (cl). **84-85 Getty Images:** Popperfoto. **85 Corbis:** Bettmann (tr). **Mirrorpix:** (b). **86 Getty Images:** Keystone/Horace Abrahams (r); Topical Press Agency/A. R. Coster (bl). **87 Alamy Images:** Pictorial Press Ltd (tl). **Getty Images:** Keystone (bc). **IWM. Science & Society Picture Library:** Science Museum (tr). **88 akg-images:** (tl). **DK Images:** IWM, London (tr). **89 The Bridgeman Art Library:** Private Collection/ Peter Newark Historical Pictures (cra). **Getty Images:** Fox Photos (crb). **Mirrorpix:** (l). **90-91 Corbis:** Bettmann. **92 Getty Images:** Fox Photos (br); Popperfoto (t). **IWM:** (bl). **93 TopFoto.co.uk:** Stapleton Historical Collection/HIP. **94 Birmingham Museum And Art Gallery:** (cr). **DK Images:** IWM, London (tr). **www.historicalimagebank.com:** Don Troiani (tl). **94-95 IWM:** (b). **95 akg-images:** (crb). **DK Images:** IWM, London (tl) (bc) (cra) (fcrb); Judith Miller / Huxtins (ftr). **IWM:** (fclb) (bl) (cla) (clb) (tc). **LMA:** RA (clb/coupon) (br). **96 Getty Images:** AFP (bl). **IWM:** (tl). **97 Getty Images:** Keystone. **98 Getty Images:** Bob Thomas/Popperfoto (cla). **98-99 Getty Images:** New York Times Co.. **99 IWM:** (tl). **102 akg-images:** (tl) (bl); Time & Life Pictures (tr). **Getty Images:** Time & Life Pictures/James Jarche (br). **MEPL:** (bc). **TopFoto.co.uk:** Ullstein Bild (tc). **103 Alamy Images:** INTERFOTO Pressebildagentur (bl). **The Art Archive:** Culver Pictures (tr). **Corbis:** Bettmann (cb). **US Department of Defense:** Department of the Army. Office of the Deputy Chief of Staff for Operations. (tl). **104 akg-images:** Ullstein Bild (br). **Corbis:** Bettmann (c). **DK Images:** IWM, London (tr). **Getty Images:** Heinrich Hoffmann/Time & Life Pictures (bl); Keystone (tl). **104-105 LMA :** Interfoto/ Sammlung Rauch (c). **105 akg-images:** Ullstein Bild (cl). **Getty Images:** Keystone (bl). **The Granger Collection, New York:** (bc). **TopFoto.co.uk:** Ullstein Bild (br). **US NARA:** (tr). **106 DK Images:** Jewish Historical Museum, Amsterdam (cb). **LMA :** RA (cla). **106-107 TopFoto.co.uk:** Ullstein Bild (t). **106-149 Shutterstock:** Stephen Mulcahey (t). **107 akg-images:** (br). **108-109 Corbis:** Bettmann. **110 LMA :** RA (cra). **110-111 LMA :** RA (b). **111 Corbis:** Bettmann (tl). **Getty Images:** Popperfoto (cra). **112 iStockphoto.com:** Duncan Walker (cl). **LMA :** Rue des Archives/Tal (r). **113 IWM:** Gunn (Sgt) (bc); Rue des Archives /Collection Gregoire (br). **LMA :** Rue des Archives/Tal (tl) (tr). **114 akg-images:** (tc). **The Art Archive:** National Archives Washington DC (fcl). **The Bridgeman Art Library:** Private Collection/DaTo Images (tl). **Corbis:** Swim Ink 2, LLC (cl). **Courtesy of The Museum of World War II, Natick, Massachusetts:** (cr). **Photolibrary:** De Agostini Picture Library (tc) (fcr). **114-115 Getty Images:** Laski Diffusion (bc). **115 akg-images:** (br). **The Art Archive:** Bundesarchiv Koblenz (fbr); IWM/Eileen Tweedy (tl); Eileen Tweedy (cl) (c). **DK Images:** IWM, London (bc). **Photolibrary:** De Agostini Picture Library (cr). **116 DK Images:** UK Crown (bl). **TopFoto.co.uk:** Ullstein Bild (c). **116-117 DK Images:** IWM, London. **117 Corbis:** Bettmann (br). **Getty Images:** Time & Life Pictures (cra). **Courtesy of the National Security Agency:** (bc). **Science & Society Picture Library:** Bletchley Park Trust (t). **118 IWM:** (cra). **TopFoto.co.uk:** (bl). **118-119 The Art Archive. 119 DK Images:** UK Crown (tc). **LMA:** Interfoto (crb). **120-121 MEPL:** Illustrated London News Ltd. **122 IWM:** Coote, R G G (Lt) (ca). **LMA :** Interfoto (clb). **122-123 akg-images:** Ullstein Bild. **123 akg-images:** Ullstein Bild (tr). **IWM:** (cr). **124 Getty Images:** Keystone (bc). **124-125 LMA :** Rue des Archives (c). **125 Getty Images:** Time & Life Pictures (tr). **126 Alamy Images:** Chris Howes/Wild Places Photography (tl). **IWM:** (c). **www.historicalimagebank.com:** Don Troiani (fcl) (cl). **127 IWM:** (br). **128 Getty Images:** Heinrich Hoffmann/Time & Life Pictures (l); Hulton Archive (tr). **MEPL:** Explorer Archives/Desmarteau (tc). **129 Corbis:** Bettmann (b). **MEPL:** (c). **www.historicalimagebank.com:** Don Troiani (cr). **130 TopFoto.co.uk:** Ullstein Bild (cla). **130-131 Getty Images:** Margaret Bourke-White/Time & Life Pictures. **132 LMA :** Leemage (cl). **132-133 akg-images. 133 The Art Archive:** (bc). **LMA :** Interfoto (cra). **134 Getty Images:** Keystone (bl). **LMA:** Interfoto (tr). **135 Getty Images:** Laski Diffusion (br). **136-137 akg-images. 138 akg-images:** Ullstein Bild (br). **Magnum Photos:** Soviet Group (bl). **www.historicalimagebank.com:** Don Troiani (tl). **139 Corbis:** Bettmann. **140 akg-images:** RIA Novosti (tr). **DK Images:** IWM, London (c). **TopFoto.co.uk:** (bl). **140-141 Getty Images:** Time & Life Pictures/Pictures Inc.. **141 TopFoto.co.uk:** Ullstein Bild (tl). **www.historicalimagebank.com:** Don Troiani (tr). **142 Getty Images:** Time & Life Pictures (tr). **TopFoto.co.uk:** (bl). **142-143 US NARA. 143 Getty Images:** Charles E. Steinheimer/Time & Life Pictures (tl). **144 Corbis:** Bettmann (bl); Oscar White (r). **145 The Art Archive:** Culver Pictures (tl). **The Bridgeman Art Library:** Private Collection/ Peter Newark American Pictures (c). **Getty Images:** Keystone (bc); Time & Life Pictures (br). **146 Hoover Institution:** (bl). **TopFoto.co.uk:** Ullstein Bild (bc). **147 Corbis:** Bettmann (br). **TopFoto.co.uk:** (tr); Roger-Viollet (l). **148 Getty Images:** Time & Life Pictures (bl). **148-149 US NARA:** (b). **149 akg-images:** (br). **Corbis:** Bettmann (tl). **US NARA:** (tr). **150-151 TopFoto.co.uk. 152-153 Alamy Images:** Tony Watson. **154 akg-images:** (tr). **Getty Images:** Scott Barbour (tl); Picture Post/Hulton Archive (cb); Popperfoto (crb). **LMA:** RA (clb). **155 The Art Archive:** National Archives Washington DC (tr) (c). **Corbis:** Bettmann (clb) (cb). **Getty Images:** Time & Life Pictures/US Navy (tl). **156 Corbis:** Bettmann (br). **DK Images:** IWM, London (crb). **Getty Images:** Keystone (bl); Time & Life Pictures (tc). **The Granger Collection, New York:** (tr). **IWM:** JE Russell (Lt) / Royal Navy official photographer (c). **157 The Art Archive:** (cla). **DK Images:** IWM, London (tc) (cr). **Getty Images:** Georgi Zelma/Hulton Archive (br). **IWM:** (tr). **TopFoto.co.uk:** (bl). **158 akg-images:** (tl). **Alamy Images:** INTERFOTO Pressebildagentur (b). **Getty Images:** Keystone (tr). **158-193 Conseil Régional de Basse-Normandie / National Archives USA:** (t). **160 Getty Images:** Time & Life Pictures. **161 akg-images:** Ullstein Bild (tc). **Corbis:** Bettmann (cr); Hulton-Deutsch Collection (br). **IWM:** Palmer (Lt) (bl). **162 Corbis:** Bettmann (cla) (bl). **Getty Images:** Time & Life Pictures/US Navy (cra). **162-163 DK Images:** IWM, London. **163 The Granger Collection, New York:** (tr). **164 The Art Archive:** National Archives Washington DC (cra). **164-165 MEPL:** (b). **165 Getty Images:** Frank Scherschel/Time Life Pictures (b). **166 Corbis:** Bettmann (cr). **Newspix Archive/Nationwide News:** News Ltd (bl). **166-167 DK Images:** IWM, London (t). **167 Newspix Archive/ Nationwide News:** News Ltd. **168 The Art Archive:** National Archives Washington DC (bc). **169 Corbis:** Bettmann (cl); Robert Sloan/Swim Ink 2, LLC (br). **170-171 Getty Images:** MPI. **172 The Art Archive:** Eileen Tweedy (cl). **DK Images:** H Keith Melton Collection (bl). **172-173 Getty Images:** Keystone. **173 DK Images:** H Keith Melton Collection (br); Ministry of Defence, Pattern Room, Nottingham (tl). **The Kobal Collection:** Central Office of Information (tc). **Rex Features:** (cr). **174 DK Images:** Courtesy of the late Charles Fraser-Smith (fbl); IWM, London (cl); H Keith Melton Collection (fcl) (bc) (fbr); RAF Museum, Hendon (cr). **175 DK Images:** IWM, London (cla) (cl) (fbl); H Keith Melton Collection (tl) (bl) (br) (clb) (cr) (tc) (tr). **176 akg-images:** RIA Novosti (tr). **Corbis:** Bettmann (cl). **176-177 Getty Images:** Scott Barbour. **177 akg-images:** Michael Teller (cr). **178-179 akg-images. 180 LMA** : RA (ca). **National Maritime Museum, London:** (cb). **180-181 IWM:** (t); JE Russell (Lt) / Royal Navy official photographer. **181 Corbis:** Bettmann (tr). **DK Images:** IWM, London (bc). **Shutterstock:** Marinko Tarlac (cb). **182 akg-images:** Ullstein Bild (ca). **182-183 Getty Images:** Popperfoto. **183 The Art Archive:** (cr). **DK Images:** IWM, London (cla). **TopFoto.co.uk:** Topham Picturepoint (tc). **184 TopFoto.co.uk:** (r). **185 Corbis:** Bettmann (tr) (bc). **DK Images:** IWM, London (tc). **Getty Images:** Hulton Archive (cra). **186 DK Images:** Royal Artillery Historical Trust (bc). **IWM:** (tc). **187 Corbis:** Bettmann (cl). **LMA :** (tr). **188 Getty Images:** Picture Post/Hulton Archive. **189 akg-images:** (ca) (br). **IWM:** (crb). **Shutterstock:** Marinko Tarlac (crb/background). **190 akg-images:** (t). **190-191 DK Images:** IWM, London. **191 Shutterstock:** Marinko Tarlac (tl). **TopFoto.co.uk:** RIA Novosti (tc). **192 akg-images:** (tr). **192-183 Getty Images:** Georgi Zelma/Hulton Archive. **193 Getty Images:** G. Lipskerov/Hulton Archive (ca). **Shutterstock:** Marinko Tarlac (tc). **194-195 The Art Archive. 196-197 Getty Images:** Laski Diffusion. **198 Getty Images:** Hulton Archive (tr) (bl) (br); Keystone (bc). **TopFoto.co.uk:** Keystone (tl); Ullstein Bild (tc). **199 Cody Images:** (tl). **Corbis:** Bettmann (tr) (b). **Getty Images:** Hulton Archive (c). **200 The Art Archive:** National Archives Washington DC (br). **aviation-images.com:** P Jarrett (tr). **Corbis:** Bettmann (c). **DK Images:** Royal Artillery Historical Trust (bc). **Getty Images:** G. Lipskerov/Slava Katamidze Collection (bl); Time & Life Pictures (tl). **201 Bovington Tank Museum:** Roland Groom (cra). **Getty Images:** Keystone (bl). **TopFoto.co.uk:** Ullstein Bild (tl). **US NARA:** (br). **202 Getty Images:** Hulton Archive (tl). **202-203 Alamy Images:** Fenris Oswin. **202-230 Conseil Régional de Basse-Normandie / National Archives USA. 203 Alamy Images:** Mediacolor's (cr). **IWM:** (tl). **Shutterstock:** Marinko Tarlac (tr). **US NARA:** (bc). **204 DK Images:** Explosion! The Museum of Naval Firepower (bc). **TopFoto.co.uk:** Ullstein Bild (clb). **205 DK Images:** Explosion! The Museum of Naval Firepower (cra) (br). **Getty Images:** Heinrich Hoffmann/Time & Life Pictures (crb). **IWM:** HW Tomlin (Lt) / Royal Navy official photographer (tc). **206-207 Getty Images:** Central Press. **208 DK Images:** IWM, London (c); Royal Signals Museum, Blandford Camp, Dorset (br). **IWM:** (cr). **209 DK Images:** IWM, London (tl) (br); H Keith Melton Collection (bl); Royal Signals Museum, Blandford Camp, Dorset (tr). **210 Getty Images:** Keystone (tc). **211 US NARA:** (tr). **212 IWM:** (t); Gladstone (Sgt) / No 2 Army Film & Photographic Unit (tc). **212-213 Getty Images:** Time & Life Pictures (b). **213 DK Images:** IWM, Duxford (cr). **Shutterstock:** Marinko Tarlac (crb). **TopFoto.co.uk:** Alinari (br). **214 aviation-images.com:** P Jarrett (ca). **Getty Images:** M. McNeill/Hulton Archive (bc). **214-215 Getty Images:** Hulton Archive. **215 Shutterstock:** Marinko Tarlac (tl). **TopFoto.co.uk:** Keystone (ca). **216 DK Images:** IWM, London (br). **217 DK Images:** IWM, London (br). **Getty Images:** Popperfoto (cl). **218-219 Getty Images:** Hulton Archive. **220 Corbis:** Bettmann (cla). **TopFoto.co.uk:** Ullstein Bild (tr). **221 akg-images:** (cl). **Getty Images:** Hulton Archive (r); Norman Smith/Hulton Archive (cr). **222 Getty Images:** AFP (tr). **222-223 LMA :** Colonel Jean Louis Mondage. **223 LMA :** Marcel Bernard/RA (br); RA (tl) (cra). **224 Corbis:** Hulton-Deutsch Collection (tc). **Getty Images:** Popperfoto (b). **225 The Airey Neave Trust :** (br). **IWM:** (tc). **226 TopFoto.co.uk:** Topham Picturepoint (cr). **226-227 TopFoto.co.uk:** Ullstein Bild (b). **227 akg-images:** Ullstein Bild (tl). **228 akg-images:** RIA Novosti (cra). **Getty Images:** Hulton Archive (l). **229 Corbis:** Bettmann (bl); The Dmitri Baltermants Collection (cra). **Getty Images:** Time & Life Pictures/British War Department/National Archives (cb). **TopFoto.co.uk:** RIA Novosti (tl). **230 Bovington Tank Museum:** Roland Groom (cr). **Corbis:** Bettmann (bc). **Shutterstock:** Marinko Tarlac (tr). **TopFoto.co.uk:** Topham/AP (cla). **230-231 US NARA. 231 Shutterstock:** Marinko Tarlac (clb). **TopFoto.co.uk:** Topham Picturepoint (bl). **232-233 Alamy Images:** Chris Howes/Wild Places Photography. **234 akg-images:** (tr); Ullstein Bild (tc). **Getty Images:** Keystone (bc) (br); Wall/MPI (tl). **LMA:** Rue des Archives (bl). **235 akg-images:** (b). **Getty Images:** Time & Life Pictures (tr). **TopFoto.co.uk:** Ullstein Bild (tl). **US NARA:** (c). **236 Conseil Régional de Basse-Normandie / National Archives USA:** (tr). **Corbis:** Bettmann (tl) (cr). **DK Images:** Royal Artillery Historical Trust (cb). **Getty Images:** Hulton Archive (ca); Popperfoto (bl). **237 akg-images:** (bl). **DK Images:** Musee de l'Air et de l'Espace / Le Bourget (tr). **IWM:** (cl). **LMA:** RA (cb); Rue des Archives (cr). **TopFoto.co.uk:** Roger-Viollet (tl). **238 akg-images:** (bl). **Getty Images:** Peter Stackpole/Time & Life Pictures (tc). **238-239 Getty Images:** Hulton Archive (t). **238-287 Dreamstime.com:** J Klune. **239 Getty Images:** J. R. Eyerman/Time & Life Pictures (br). **240 TopFoto.co.uk:** (tr). **240-241 US NARA. 241 LMA :** RA (tr). **242-243 Getty Images:** Popperfoto/Paul Popper. **244 Corbis:** Bettmann (r). **Getty Images:** MPI (bl); Time & Life Pictures (cla). **245 Getty Images:** Time & Life Pictures/C. F. Wheeler/ US Navy/National Archives (bc). **Courtesy of The Museum of World War II, Natick, Massachusetts:** (cra). **Naval Historical Foundation, Washington, D.C.. 246 TopFoto.co.uk:** Ullstein Bild (b). **US NARA:** (cl). **247 Corbis:** Bettmann (tl). **Getty Images:** William Vandivert/Time & Life Pictures (br). **TopFoto.co.uk:** Topham Picturepoint (bc). **248 Getty Images:** William Vandivert/Time & Life Pictures (bc). **249 Getty Images:** William Vandivert/Time & Life Pictures (cr). **TopFoto.co.uk:** Topham Picturepoint (cb). **250-251 Getty Images:** Keystone. **252 Getty Images:** Keystone (r); Popperfoto (cl). **Shutterstock:** Marinko Tarlac (clb). **US NARA:** (bc). **253 DK Images:** Royal Artillery Historical Trust (bc). **254 IWM:** (tr). **255 IWM:** (bl). **Shutterstock:** Marinko Tarlac (crb). **US NARA:** (cr). **256 Corbis:** Bettmann (r). **Eisenhower National Historic Site:** National Park Service, Museum Management Program, photograph by Carol M. Highsmith (cl). **US NARA:** (bl). **257 Alamy Images:** Michael Ventura (tc). **Cody Images:** (bc). **Corbis:** Bettmann (cr). **258 IWM:** Goodchild A (F/O) (cl). **258-259 TopFoto.co.uk:** Ullstein Bild. **259 DK Images:** Royal Artillery Historical Trust (crb). **US NARA:** (cra). **260-261 Getty Images:** Wall/MPI. **262 DK Images:** IWM, London (clb). **LMA:** (cla) (cra). **Shutterstock:** Marinko Tarlac (tr). **US NARA:** (br). **262-263 DK Images:** Royal Artillery Historical Trust (tl). **263 US NARA:** (crb). **264 DK Images:** IWM, London (bl) (cb); RAF Museum, Hendon (cr) (br). **264-265 DK Images:** IWM, London (tc). **265 DK Images:** IWM, London (bc); RAF Museum, Hendon (cl). **IWM:** (crb). **266 Getty Images:** Heinrich Hoffmann/Time & Life Pictures. **267 akg-images:** (br). **Getty Images:** AFP (bl). **TopFoto.co.uk:** Ullstein Bild (cra). **268 Getty Images:** Keystone (cra). **268-269 akg-images. 269 LMA :** Rue des Archives (br). **270 akg-images:** (cra). **270-271 akg-images:** (b). **271 DK Images:** Musee de l'Air et de l'Espace / Le Bourget (br). **TopFoto.co.uk:** Topham Picturepoint (cr). **272 TopFoto.co.uk:** Ullstein Bild. **273 DK Images:** IWM, London (cla). **Getty Images:** Popperfoto (bl). **Shutterstock:** Marinko Tarlac (cl). **Roland Smithies:** (c). **TopFoto.co.uk:** Roger-Viollet (cra); Ullstein Bild (bc). **274 DK Images:** IWM, London (crb). **Getty Images:** AFP (t). **275 Corbis:** Hulton-Deutsch Collection (tl). **IWM:** Tanner (Capt) (br). **www.historicalimagebank.com:** Don Troiani (tr). **276 Corbis:** Bettmann (b). **277 Corbis:** Bettmann (tl). **Getty Images:** Popperfoto (bc). **TopFoto.co.uk:** Art Media/HIP (cra). **278 akg-images:** (ca). **DK Images:** IWM, London (bc). **278-279 TopFoto.co.uk:** Topham Picturepoint. **279 DK Images:** IWM, London (c). **TopFoto.co.uk:** Roger-Viollet (bl). **280 DK Images:** IWM, London (cla). **IWM:** (ca). **LMA:** (clb). **280-281 TopFoto.co.uk:** AP. **281 Getty Images:** The Frank S. Errigo Archive/Hulton Archive (br). **IWM:** (tc). **Shutterstock:** Marinko Tarlac (crb). **283 DK Images:** Royal Artillery Historical Trust (cra). **284 Getty Images:** Heinrich Hoffmann/Time & Life Pictures (clb). **IWM:** (br). **TopFoto.co.uk:** (tr). **285 LMA:** (tr). **US Army:** (b). **286 akg-images:** (r). **Cody Images:** (l). **287 Corbis:** Bettmann (bc). **Getty Images:** Sonnee Gottlieb/Keystone (tr); Martha Holmes (br). **The Patton Museum:** (tl). **290 akg-images:** (tc). **Getty Images:** Hulton Archive (crb); Allan Jackson/Hulton Archive (tr). **LMA:** (clb). **TopFoto.co.uk:** Ullstein Bild (tl). **291 Getty Images:** J. R. Eyerman/Time & Life Pictures (bc). **LMA:** (cla). **US NARA:** (c). **US Army:** (tr) (tl). **292 akg-images:** (clb). **Corbis:** Bettmann (ca); The Dmitri Baltermants Collection (tl). **DK Images:** IWM, London (cb). **Getty Images:** Keystone (bc). **Courtesy of The Museum of World War II, Natick, Massachusetts:** (crb). **TopFoto.co.uk:** RIA Novosti (tr). **293 Alamy Images:** MEPL (cra). **Corbis:** Bettmann (cb). **Getty Images:** Keystone (br). **LMA:** Rue des Archives (clb). **US NARA:** (cla). **294 DK Images:** IWM, London (bl). **LMA:** (ca). **294-295 akg-images. 294-326 iStockphoto.com:** ilbusca. **295 akg-images:** (tc). **Getty Images:** Time & Life Pictures (cr). **296-297 Alamy Images:** INTERFOTO Pressebildagentur. **298 akg-images:** (br). **IWM:** (clb). **LMA:** (t). **Shutterstock:** Marinko Tarlac (crb). **299 akg-images:** (cra). **LMA:** (tc). **300 akg-images. 301 Getty Images:** Bentley Archive/Popperfoto (cr); George Rodger/ Time & Life Pictures (br). **302-303 Getty Images:** George Rodger/Time & Life Pictures. **304 Getty Images:** Allan Jackson/ Hulton Archive (bl). **Shutterstock:** Marinko Tarlac (crb). **TopFoto.co.uk:** RIA Novosti (ca). **US NARA:** (cl). **305 akg-images:** (tl). **306 Getty Images:** Hulton Archive (t). **TopFoto.co.uk:** Topham Picturepoint (br). **307 DK Images:** IWM, London (c). **TopFoto.co.uk:** Ullstein Bild (tc). **US NARA:** (br). **308-309 Corbis:** US Army/ Handout/CNP. **310 US NARA:** (cra). **310-311 US NARA. 311 DK Images:** Felix deWeldon (br). **Getty Images:** Keystone (tc). **LMA:** RA (cr). **Courtesy of The Museum of World War II, Natick, Massachusetts:** (c). **312 DK Images:** IWM, Duxford (clb). **Getty Images:** Keystone (br); MPI/Hulton Archive (cb). **312-313 Corbis:** Museum of Flight. **313 Corbis:** Hulton-Deutsch Collection (tc). **Royal Air Force Museum, Hendon:** (bl). **315 akg-images:** (bc). **Corbis:** Bettmann (br). **LMA:** RA (tc). **US Army:** (c). **316 Getty Images:** AFP (bl). **316-317 Getty Images:** Keystone. **317 akg-images:** (br). **Corbis:** Hulton-Deutsch Collection (tc). **318 TopFoto.co.uk:** Gurariya/RIA Novosti (bl). **318-319 LMA:** Rue des Archives. **319 Corbis:** Bettmann (cr). **Getty Images:** Eileen Darby/Time & Life Pictures (br). **320 DK Images:** Spink and Son Ltd, London (tr); IWM, London (cr). **321 DK Images:** IWM, Duxford (fbl); Spink and Son Ltd, London (br). **www.historicalimagebank.com:** Don Troiani (cl). **322 DK Images:** Bradbury Science Museum, Los Alamos (bc). **Getty Images:** Los Alamos National Laboratory/Time & Life Pictures (bl). **US NARA:** (ca). **322-323 Getty Images:** George Silk/Time & Life Pictures. **322-333 US NARA. 323 aviation-images.com:** Mark Wagner (tl). **Corbis:** Karen Kasmauski (cr). **Getty Images:** U.S. Marine Corps/ Hulton Archive (br). **Shutterstock:** Marinko Tarlac (tr). **324-325 Getty Images:** George Silk/Time & Life Pictures. **326 DK Images:** IWM, London (cla). **LMA:** RA (bl); Rue des Archives (tl). **327 Corbis:** Dave Davis/ Bettmann. **330 Corbis:** Bettmann (tl) (cb) (clb) (crb). **Getty Images:** Keystone (tc); David Silverman (tr). **331 Alamy Images:** Bill Bachmann (tr). **The Art Archive:** William Sewell (cla). **Corbis:** Bettmann (cb). **Getty Images:** Joseph Scherschel/Time & Life Pictures (tl). **332 akg-images:** (cr). **Alamy Images:** INTERFOTO Pressebildagentur (tr). **Cody Images:** (tc). **Getty Images:** Hulton Archive (tl) (bl); Time & Life Pictures (br). **www.historicalimagebank.com:** Don Troiani (cl). **333 akg-images:** (bc). **The Art Archive:** Musée des 2 Guerres Mondiales Paris/Gianni Dagli Orti (tc). **Corbis:** Roger Ressmeyer (bl). **Getty Images:** AFP (cr) (c); Keystone (cl); Time & Life Pictures (br). **334 akg-images:** (tc). **TopFoto.co.uk:** Ullstein Bild (bl). **334-351 Shutterstock:** krechet. **335 The Art Archive:** (tl). **Getty Images:** David Silverman (tr). **336-337 Getty Images:** Keystone. **338 www.historicalimagebank.com:** Don Troiani (br). **338-339 Alamy Images:** MEPL. **339 Corbis:** Bettmann (tc). **Getty Images:** Central Press (br); Keystone (bc). **340 akg-images:** Gert Schütz (ca). **340-341 Getty Images:** Walter Sanders/Life Magazine/Time & Life Pictures. **341 Getty Images:** Fox Photos (bc). **TopFoto.co.uk:** Ullstein Bild (cr). **342 akg-images:** (ca). **Corbis:** Horace Bristol (bc). **343 Alamy Images:** shinypix (cra). **Corbis:** Bettmann (tl). **344 Alamy Images:** INTERFOTO Pressebildagentur (bl). **Getty Images:** AFP (tl). **344-345 Corbis:** Bettmann (tc). **345 The Art Archive:** Musée des 2 Guerres Mondiales Paris/Gianni Dagli Orti (bl). **Getty Images:** AFP (fbl); Tom Stodda/Hulton Archive (cr). **346 Cody Images:** (r). **Corbis:** Bettmann (bl). **347 akg-images:** (br). **The Art Archive:** William Sewell (tr). **China Tourism Photo Library:** (bc). **348 Getty Images:** Hulton Archive (tl). **348-349 Corbis:** Bettmann (b). **349 Corbis:** Bettmann (tc). **Getty Images:** Ralph Crane/Time & Life Pictures (cr); Keystone (bc). **350 Alamy Images:** Avatra Images (t). **Getty Images:** Scott Barbour (bl). **351 Alamy Images:** Andrew Gransden (bl); Tommaso Sparnacci (br). **Corbis:** Reuters (crb). **The Kobal Collection:** Mirisch/United Artists (ca). **352-360 US Department of Defense**

Jacket images: Front and Back: **Corbis:** Hulton-Deutsch Collection **Getty Images:** Hulton Archive

All other images © Dorling Kindersley

For further information see: www.dkimages.com

Every effort has been made to gain permission from the relevant copyright holders to reproduce the extracts that appear in this book:

28 The Manchester Guardian correspondent E.A. Montague describing the opening of the Olympic Games. The Manchester Guardian 3 August 1936. Printed in *The Guardian Century Part Four 1930–1939*.
81 *The Evacuation at Dunkirk, 1940*. Eyewitness to History, www.eyewitnesstohistory.com (2008).
120 *Iron Coffins: A U-Boat Commander's War 1939–1945*, Herbert A. Werner. Reprinted by permission of Henry Holt and Company, LLC.
137 *Leningrad Under Siege: First-Hand Accounts of the Ordeal*, Pen & Sword Books Ltd, 2007.
150 *Attack At Pearl Harbor, 1941 – the Japanese View* Eyewitness to History, www.eyewitnesstohistory.com (2001).
290 *Bombing of Dresden* Permission granted by www.timewitnesses.org
309 *A WAC's War: reminiscences, 1965*, Betty M. Olson, Minnesota Historical Society
309 *London Celebrates VE Day, 1945*. Eyewitness to History, www.eyewitnesstohistory.com (2007)
336 Fela Waschau testimony is used with the permissionof the U.S. Holocaust Memorial Museum, Washington, DC.

DK would like to thank the following people for their assistance on the book:

The Wardrobe: The Rifles (Berkshire and Wiltshire) Museum and staff
The Army Medical Services Museum and staff

Helen Peters for the index; Manisha Thakkar for editorial assistance; Roland Smithies, Martin Copeland, Karen VanRoss, Jenny Baskaya for picture research assistance and Richard Horsford for design assistance